PRINCIPLES OF
TORT LAW

Fourth Edition

Cavendish
Publishing
Limited

London • Sydney

PRINCIPLES OF

TORT LAW

Fourth Edition

Vivienne Harpwood, LLB, Barrister
Reader in Law, Cardiff Law School

Cavendish
Publishing
Limited

London • Sydney

Fourth edition first published in Great Britain 2000 by Cavendish Publishing Limited, The Glass House, Wharton Street, London WC1X 9PX, United Kingdom.
Telephone: +44 (0)20 7278 8000   Facsimile: +44 (0)20 7278 8080
Email: info@cavendishpublishing.com
Website: http://www.cavendishpublishing.com

First edition   1993
Second edition   1996
Third edition   1997
Fourth edition   2000

British Library Cataloguing in Publication data

Harpwood, Vivienne
Tort law – 4th ed (Principles of law series)
1 Torts – England 2 Torts – Wales
I Title II Principles of tort law
346.4'2'03

ISBN   1 85941 467 2

Printed and bound in Great Britain

PREFACE

Tort is a broad church and many hymns, ancient and modern, can be heard within it. It is an ideal subject for undergraduate study because it shows how the law develops and responds to changing social and economic conditions. The origins of tort can be traced to the early years of the last millenium, and it has survived to enter this millenium while still undergoing a process of evolution. Jurisprudentially, it is intriguing because it demonstrates the shifting boundaries of judicial creativity. All the traditional subject matter of tort is analysed here in detail but particular emphasis is placed on exploration of complex and contentious areas and topics which students find perplexing.

This fourth edition updates the material in the previous edition in the light of recent developments in this fast moving area of law. There is discussion of numerous cases decided at appellate level, including those concerning duty of care, liability for psychiatric injury, breach of duty, quantum and occupiers' liability, as well as other mainstream areas of tort studied on undergraduate and professional courses. The impact of the Human Rights Act 1998 on the law of tort is discussed. The substantive law is set in the context of the Civil Procedure Rules 1998, changes in the availability of legal aid and other institutional and social changes. The book is carefully structured and has been updated with the student very much in mind.

This book is the product of many years of lecturing and tutoring tort and would not have been possible without the stimulus and encouragement of colleagues and students too numerous to mention.

Vivienne Harpwood
September 2000

CONTENTS

8 CAUSATION AND REMOTENESS OF DAMAGE 149

13   TRESPASS TO THE PERSON   287

TABLE OF CASES

B

C

D

E

F

G

H

I

M

R

S

T

U

V

W

X

Y

Z

TABLE OF STATUTES

TABLE OF STATUTORY INSTRUMENTS

TABLE OF EU LEGISLATION

CHAPTER 1

AN OVERVIEW OF THE LAW OF TORT

The aim of this chapter is to consider the definition, objectives and scope of the law of tort, and to take an overview of the subject.

1.1   What is tort?

The word 'tort' is derived from the Latin *tortus,* meaning 'twisted'. It came to mean 'wrong', and it is still so used in French: '*J'ai tort*'; 'I am wrong.' In English, the word 'tort' has a purely technical legal meaning – a legal wrong for which the law provides a remedy.

Academics have attempted to define the law of tort, but a glance at all the leading textbooks on the subject will quickly reveal that it is extremely difficult to arrive at a satisfactory, all-embracing definition. Each writer has a different formulation, and each states that the definition is unsatisfactory.

To use Professor Winfield's definition as a starting point, we can explore the difficulties involved:

> Tortious liability arises from the breach of a duty primarily fixed by law; this duty is towards persons generally and its breach is redressable by an action for unliquidated damages.

In order to understand this definition, it is necessary to distinguish tort from other branches of the law, and in so doing to discover how the aims of tort differ from the aims of other areas of law such as contract law or criminal law. The main emphasis here will be on the distinction between tort and contract, as these two subjects are closely related. Criminal law will be dealt with separately, below.

1.2   Tort and contract

The scope and objectives of tort as compared with contract are often discussed in the context of duties fixed by law and people to whom the duties are owed.

1.2.1   Duties fixed by law

Many liabilities in tort arise by virtue of the law alone and are not fixed by the parties. The law, for example, imposes a duty in tort not to libel people and not to trespass on their land. The details of these duties are fixed by the law itself, and not by the parties. By contrast, the law of contract is based notionally on agreements, the terms of which are fixed by the parties.

However, in modern law, it is unrealistic to suppose that contract and tort are so very different from each other. Terms of contracts are now imposed upon the parties by numerous statutes, quite independently of any 'agreement', and indeed, the notion of true agreement has long been discredited in many contractual situations, since few individual consumers have real bargaining power. Moreover, it is possible for the parties in tort to arrive at agreement to vary the tortious duties which the law imposes. The Contracts (Rights of Third Parties) Act 1999 will allow third parties to enforce contractual terms directly in certain circumstances.

1.2.2 Duties to whom? The relationship between the parties

As duties in tort are fixed by law, the parties to an action usually have no contact before the tort is committed. The pedestrian who is injured by a negligent motorist will probably never have met the defendant until the accident which gives rise to the legal action. Of contract, it is often said that the parties will, through negotiation or by the very act of contracting, have had some contact and be fully aware of their legal duties before any breach of contract occurs.

This is too simplistic a view. Contracting parties often have little or no contact, and many of the terms of the contract may be implied by the operation of various statutes. In tort, the parties may well know one another before the tort is committed, as for example the doctor who negligently injures a patient who has been receiving a course of treatment, or the neighbour who allows fumes to pour over adjoining property, causing a nuisance. The distinction between the branches of law is again blurred.

The notion of relationship or proximity between the parties has been given much greater prominence in tort in recent cases than ever before. This draws the two branches of the law even closer.

The relationship between the parties is the basis for distinguishing between tort and contract when dealing with the notion of remoteness of damage. Here the courts consider the question: 'for how much of the damage suffered in a case should the defendant be held responsible?'. The rules of contract require a closer relationship than the rules of tort in dealing with this issue.

1.2.3 Redressable by an action for unliquidated damages

The remedy for breach of duty in tort is usually an action for damages, though equitable remedies are also available in appropriate cases. The *main aim of tort* is said to be compensation for harm suffered as a result of the breach of a duty fixed by law. Tort seems to place greater emphasis on wrongs of commission rather than wrongs of omission. A less obvious aim of tort is to deter behaviour which is likely to cause harm.

The *main aim of contract* on the other hand is to support and enforce contractual promises, and to deter breaches of contract. Contract then has no difficulty compensating for wrongs of omission. The doctrine of consideration, based on mutual promises, is all important in the law of contract, and failure by omission to keep the terms of a promise is a breach of contract which the law will seek to amend.

The distinction in practice is less clear, as many fact situations could give rise to an action in both contract (if there is a contract in existence) and tort. Numerous examples of this are to be found in cases of professional negligence, for example, where the parties may also have a contractual relationship (doctors, surveyors, architects, etc). In such cases, it again becomes necessary to decide whether to sue in contract or in tort. However, it often makes little difference to the outcome which branch of the law is chosen (see *Johnstone v Bloomsbury AHA* (1991)).

Circumstances may arise in which it is necessary for a claimant to decide whether to base an action on tort or contract, or at least to plead both. The considerations which may be relevant are that there may be more generous limitation periods (time limits) within which to bring an action in tort rather than in contract; the need to prove fault is not always present in contract, whereas it is frequently necessary to do so in tort, and the range of remedies and amount of damages which are available in tort may be greater than in contract. The courts now take the view that where professionals owe duties to their clients in both tort and contract, the claimant has a free choice as to which remedy to pursue. The extent of this concurrent liability was confirmed by the House of Lords in *Henderson v Merrett Syndicates Ltd* (1994). In that case, it was held that the duty of care which was owed in tort to Lloyd's 'names' by their managing agents was not precluded by the existence of a contract between the same parties. In a later case in which the choice between contract and tort was relevant, *Holt and Another v Payne Skillington (A Firm) and Another* (1996), the Court of Appeal held that where a duty of care in tort arose between the parties to a contract, wider obligations could be imposed by the duty in tort than those which arise under the contract. In the earlier case of *Tai Hing Cotton Mill Ltd v Lui Chong Hing Bank Ltd* (1986), the Privy Council had held that, in commercial situations, if a contract exists between the parties, the proper action lies in contract rather than in tort. In *Holt v Payne Skillington*, however, the arguments raised in the *Tai Hing Cotton* case were rejected by the Court of Appeal. The defendants contended that if, as here, there is a contract in existence, the duties of the parties in contract and tort are to be defined according to the express and implied terms of the contract, and would, if necessary, be limited by those terms. Accordingly, it was argued, there could be no expansion of liability by means of a duty of care in tort. However, the Court of Appeal accepted the claimant's arguments that a consideration of the facts of each individual case would determine whether a duty of care in tort existed which was wider than any duties imposed by contractual terms. Such a tortious duty, if it arose, was imposed by the general law and would not arise out of the common intention of the parties to any contract. The matter was also discussed in *Spring v Guardian Assurance* (1995) in connection with the existence of a possible implied term in contracts of employment requiring employers to exercise care in writing references. Further examples of cases which highlight the advantages of one action over another will be encountered throughout this book.

In recent years, the distinction between tort and contract has been blurred by new departures, and the differing aims of the two areas of law have become less clear. The development of the doctrine of promissory estoppel in contract suggests that contract may be moving closer to tort. When conditions allow that doctrine to apply, it may be possible to side-step the doctrine of consideration.

Developments in tort in the 1980s, in particular, the case of *Junior Books Ltd v Veitchi Co Ltd* (1983), now discredited and confined to its own particular facts, gave rise to the view that the tort of negligence was being used in what should have been a contractual situation. This will be considered in detail later.

Since the rise of the tort of negligence, the law of tort places great emphasis on the need to prove fault. The aim here is to compensate for wrongs suffered through the fault of another person. Damages will usually only be awarded in tort if the claimant can establish fault. The system requires that someone be blamed for the injury sustained.

Contract on the other hand has been less concerned with fault as a basis of liability, and it is often unnecessary to prove fault in order to be compensated for a breach of contract. All that is necessary to prove is that the act which caused the loss was committed. This is known as strict liability, and is a feature of much of the law relating to sale of goods.

However, there are established areas of strict liability in tort, such as libel and trespass.

One important distinction between contract and tort which has been emphasised in recent cases (for example, *Murphy v Brentwood DC* (1990)) is that, in the case of compensation for defective products, tort is concerned only with unsafe products, but contract will provide compensation for shoddy products too.

1.2.4 Unliquidated damages

The aim of tort damages is to restore the claimant, in so far as money can do so, to his or her pre-accident position, and this purpose underlies the assessment of damages. Tort compensates both for tangible losses and for factors which are enormously difficult to quantify, such as loss of amenity and pain and suffering, nervous shock, and other intangible losses. Tort damages are therefore said to be 'unliquidated'. The claimant is not claiming a fixed amount of compensation.

The aim of the award of damages in contract is to place the claimant in the position he or she would have been in if the contract had been performed. Contract is less willing to contemplate awarding damages for such nebulous factors as injury to feelings. The damages are described as 'liquidated'. The claimant has assessed exactly how much the breach of contract has cost and claims that fixed amount.

However, recent years have seen a willingness on the part of the courts to award damages for 'disappointment' in contract in some unusual cases, indicating that contract is willing to recognise and compensate certain intangible losses (*Jarvis v Swans Tours* (1972)).

Tort will not only provide a remedy in the form of money compensation but will, like contract, grant an equitable remedy in appropriate circumstances. For example, an injunction may be awarded to prevent repeated acts of trespass. Numerous equitable remedies are provided by the law of contract but these are often difficult to obtain, as it is necessary to prove that money would not be the real answer to the claimant's problem. In tort, the situation which calls for an injunction will usually be very clear cut and there will be fewer obstacles in the way of obtaining the remedy than in contract.

The textbooks provide a detailed analysis of these matters, and it will be evident that the distinction between contract and tort is blurred. The two subjects were classified as separate topics by the early textbook writers when law began to be treated as a suitable subject for academic study. It is not surprising that some writers call for a different approach to these common law subjects by sweeping aside the dichotomy, and dealing with the 'common law of obligations' as a whole. This approach would do away with some of the problems of definition.

1.3   Tort and criminal law

The same fact situation, for example, a road accident, may give rise both to criminal prosecutions and to tort actions. Tort, as part of civil law, is concerned with actions by private individuals against other individuals or legal persons. Criminal law is concerned with prosecutions brought on behalf of the state for breaches of duties imposed upon individuals for the protection of society. Criminal prosecutions are dealt with by criminal courts, and the standard of proof is more stringent than in civil cases. The consequences of a finding of criminal guilt are regarded as more serious for the individual concerned than are the consequences of civil liability.

Both areas of law are concerned with the breach of duties imposed by law, but the criminal law has different priorities. It is concerned with the protection of society by deterring wrongful behaviour. It is also concerned with the punishment of criminals. These concerns may also be found in tort, but are secondary to the main objective of compensation. A motorist who is speeding is far more likely to be worried about being caught by the police than being sued by a person whom he happens to injure if he is negligent. Nevertheless, tort does have some deterrent value. For example, motorists who have been negligent have to pay higher insurance premiums.

To complicate matters, criminal law does make provision for compensating victims in some cases, by compensation orders or through the Criminal Injuries Compensation Board, but this is not the main objective of the criminal law.

Similarities and differences may be found between tort and criminal law, and, at the very least, Winfield's definition should have made clear that tort is a branch of civil law to be distinguished from criminal law.

There are some instances in which people have brought civil claims in an effort to encourage prosecutions in criminal law. For example, the family of a woman who was killed by her former boyfriend succeeded in having him branded as a killer in a successful civil claim for assault and battery heard in the High Court in 1998 (*Francisco v Diedrich*). The Crown Prosecution Service had decided not to prosecute.

1.4 Other definitions of tort

We have considered some aspects of one writer's definition of tort. Further analysis deeper into the subject should reveal more similarities and differences between tort and contract law, tort and criminal law, and tort and other areas of law such as quasi-contract. The simple fact is that the boundaries of the subject are not clearly definable.

1.5 Insurance and the law of tort

Underpinning the modern tort system is the system of insurance which provides payment of compensation in most tort cases. Indeed, it is usually not worth the trouble and expense of suing in tort unless the defendant is insured (or is very wealthy). It is possible to insure against liability in tort in relation to many different activities. For example, motorists are compelled by statute to insure against liability for injuries to third parties and passengers (see Road Traffic Act 1988), manufacturers insure against harm caused by their products, and occupiers and employers take out insurance policies to cover the cost of accidents. Insurance is also important in relation to sporting and educational activities, and clubs and schools are covered by insurance policies. Many large public bodies carry insurance but some act as their own insurers, taking upon themselves the risk of paying damages if they are found liable. To some extent, insurance can influence the way in which people behave. Thus, motorists are aware that their insurance premiums will be higher if they are found negligent and may be encouraged to take fewer risks. However, some motorists have to pay higher premiums because they fall into a high-risk category. Figures published in 1999 by the Office for National Statistics indicate that young men under the age of 25 years are three times more likely to die in a road accident than women of the same age group, and are much more likely to be involved in accidents than older motorists. To allow for this, young men pay higher premiums than other motorists.

In the field of health care, the Clinical Negligence Scheme for Trusts, which provides insurance cover for medical negligence claims against NHS Trusts, offers lower premiums to Trusts which can demonstrate that they have sound risk management procedures. However, such incentives do not always have the desired effect and, in health care in the US, the practice of defensive medicine is regarded as counter-productive to the provision of good services. Defensive medicine is practised when doctors undertake procedures such as X-rays in order to avoid being sued rather than for clinical reasons.

There is, of course, a counter-argument concerning insurance – that people who are aware that they are insured are likely to be less careful because they can be confident that their insurance company will compensate any victims of their wrongful activity. Insurance can also create problems of waste because it is impossible to predict when liability will arise and people may over-insure. It has also been claimed that in some cases insurance motivates the law of tort. For example, in road accident cases, a judge may be more willing to find in favour of the claimant because he knows that there will be a source of compensation available to support him through insurance. He may find the defendant legally to blame though morally he should not be responsible (see *Nettleship v Weston* (1972)). Nevertheless, insurance is a useful way of spreading the cost of compensating people who suffer injury as a result of negligence. Insurance allows people to recover damages for negligent driving from close relatives, so easing the burden of caring within families.

1.6 An overview of the law of tort

In order to understand tort, it is necessary to withdraw for a moment from the problems of definition and take an overview of the subject to consider the nature of the duties which are imposed and the interests which are protected by this branch of the civil law.

Tort has been used for many centuries to protect personal interests in property. Some of the earliest actions known to English law are those concerned with protecting interests in land. These include the torts of nuisance and trespass to land.

Tort has also been concerned with protecting people from intentional interference through actions for assault and battery and false imprisonment; and the reputation, through the torts of libel, slander, malicious prosecution and injurious falsehood. Purely financial interests, economic and trading interests have more recently been brought within the province of tort, and their scope is still unclear, but personal property has been protected by tort for hundreds of years.

The long history of the law of tort has been somewhat haphazard, and it is an area of law which is still developing. Since only 1932, when negligence was first officially recognised by the House of Lords as a separate tort, has negligence been of central importance. However, the vast majority of tort actions today are for negligence, and negligence has proved the most appropriate action in modern living conditions, especially since the development of the motor car.

The continued development of tort can be seen in the tort of breach of confidence which some authorities claim is not a tort at all, contending that it belongs to equity. The Court of Appeal has recently referred to the equitable origins of this action in *R v Department of Health ex p Source Informatics* (2000). The issue under consideration concerned the passing of anonymised patient information by pharmacists, for a fee, to the appellants ('Source'), a UK subsidiary of a US company. Source then sold the information to pharmaceutical companies in order to enable them to market their products more successfully.

Source sought a declaration to the effect that there was no breach of confidence involved in passing on anonymous information about patients. The Court of Appeal proceeded on the basis that the information was properly anonymised and that the anonymity of patients could be guaranteed. The unanimous view of the Court of Appeal was that participation by doctors and pharmacists in the scheme proposed by Source would not expose them to any serious risk of successful breach of confidence proceedings by a patient. The Court of Appeal considered the classic statement of the prerequisites of a successful claim for breach of confidence by Lord Greene in *Saltman Engineering Co Ltd v Campbell Engineering Co Ltd* (1963) and the legal basis of the doctrine of confidentiality was considered. Whilst recognising that the action for breach of confidence lies in the law of tort, the Court of Appeal also reviewed the cases which had been decided on equitable principles. It seemed that the one consistent theme to emerge from the authorities was that the confidant was under a duty of good faith to the confider, and 'the touchstone by which to judge the scope of his duty and whether or not it had been fulfilled was his own conscience, no more and no less'. The test to be applied here was whether a reasonable pharmacist's conscience would be troubled by the proposed use of patient's prescriptions – would a pharmacist think that, by entering Source's scheme, he would be breaking his customers' confidence by making unconscientious use of the information they provide? The conclusion of the court was that, in a case involving personal confidences, the confidence was not breached where the identity of the confider was protected. As this was the case here, the pharmacists' consciences ought not to have been troubled.

Thus, the reasoning of the Court of Appeal appears to merge the tort of breach of confidence with principles of equity, which lie at the heart of the development of the law in this area.

Occasionally, it is possible to observe the dynamic nature of tort in the development of little-used, rather obscure torts in modern conditions. For example, in *Three Rivers DC and Others v Bank of England* (*No 3*) (1998), the unusual tort of 'misfeasance in public office' was revived in an attempt to provide remedies for those who suffered losses in the BCCI incident. The Court of Appeal held that, in order to succeed in a claim for this tort, it had to be proved that there had been a deliberate and dishonest abuse of power. The official concerned must have known that the claimant would suffer loss as a result, or must have been reckless or indifferent as to that result. The House of Lords dismissed the appeal in this case, ruling that a public officer would be liable for the tort of misfeasance in public office if he or she acted knowingly or with reckless disregard to the likelihood of causing injury to either the claimant or a person who was a member of the class to which the claimant belonged.

In *Docker v Chief Constable of West Midlands Police* (2000), the House of Lords held that the police are not immune from action by former defendants alleging conspiracy to injure and misfeasance in public office.

Not every wrongful act is actionable as a tort. There are some activities which cause harm but are not treated as torts. The case of *Bradford Corpn v Pickles* (1985) is an example of this. Here, the defendant had prevented underground streams flowing through his land onto the claimant's land, to force them to buy his land at a much inflated price. The House of Lords held that the defendant could not be liable because every landowner has a right to take water from his own property even if it means that neighbouring properties are deprived of water altogether. This is an illustration of a principle known as *damnum sine injuria* (a wrong without a legal remedy).

The opposite side of the same principle, *injuria sine damno,* is present in cases where no damage is suffered but a tort action is available because the interest to be protected is regarded as being of vital importance. The tort of trespass to land is an example of this. To obtain an injunction to prevent further acts of trespass, it is enough to prove that the defendant has walked onto the claimant's land, and there is no need for any damage to have been caused.

1.7   Case law

Although there are some statutory developments, tort is essentially a common law subject, developed by the judges, often in response to changes in social and economic conditions. It is important to appreciate that many of the decisions have been influenced by judicial policy founded on pragmatic considerations and notions of social justice, such as loss distribution, based on the extended use of insurance.

Many of the decisions appear to conflict and judges may seem to be doing one thing but saying another. It may appear that the judge has decided what the outcome of a case is to be, and found reasons to support that decision later. As will be seen, it is usually only in the great landmark cases like *Donoghue v Stevenson* (1932) that the policy behind the decisions is discussed openly and in depth by the judges. All these factors may cause confusion in the early days of the study of tort. The best book to read on these matters is PS Atiyah (Cane, P (ed), *Accidents, Compensation and the Law,* 1999). It is only towards the end of the study of the law of tort that it will be possible to form a complete picture of the subject. It is worth returning to this first chapter at the end of the entire book, to put the subject into perspective. Some of the points missed at this very early stage will be more intelligible and some of the first glimmers of understanding will be clarified.

1.8   Other systems of compensation

Tort is not the only means whereby a person who suffers as a result of a wrongful act may receive compensation. Indeed, tort is the least efficient system of compensation. Other sources include the social security system, the industrial injuries scheme, the criminal injuries compensation system, charitable gifts, and first party insurance.

1.9   Torts of strict liability

Although the vast majority of tort actions are for negligence, there are some torts in which it is not necessary to prove fault. All that needs be proved is that the defendant committed the act complained of, and that the damage was the result of that act. These are termed torts of 'strict liability'.

However, the term 'strict liability' covers a wide variety of circumstances and does not itself withstand strict scrutiny, as it is so indeterminate. It is therefore an easy label to attach, but remains conceptually awkward. To some extent, strict liability appears to occupy a continuum with complete absence of concern for any mental element on the part of the defendant at the one end, to the other end where the rules are sufficiently relaxed to allow some consideration of voluntariness, as in the tort of trespass.

Some strict liability is of very ancient origin, whereas other examples, such as the instances of strict liability, introduced by the Consumer Protection Act 1987, are fairly recent. However, all have in common the fact that the society in which they originated demanded particular protection for potential claimants in the circumstances, and the emphasis tends to be on the type of activity rather than the defendant's conduct in carrying it out. There may be no obvious reason for such emphasis, and some authorities suggest that strict liability is merely a form of loss distribution (see Atiyah, PS, *Accidents, Compensation and the Law*, Cane, P (ed), 1999, Chapter 4). Another argument is that, because many of the torts of strict liability are concerned with particularly hazardous activities, the defendant bears some initial blame for being prepared to impose hazards on others, and it would offend justice and morality to impose the requirement of proving fault in such circumstances. However, instances of strict liability are often haphazard, and it seems strange that driving, arguably one of the most hazardous activities in modern life, does not attract strict liability. Many of the instances in which strict liability has been imposed are the response by judges to the particular circumstances of the cases before them, as in *Rylands v Fletcher* (1868), or by Parliament to the demands of pressure groups, as in the Consumer Protection Act 1987 and the Vaccine Damage Payments Act 1979.

The conclusion must be that there is no general underlying rationale, but a series of *ad hoc* adjustments prompted more by pragmatism than principle.

Strict liability is imposed to varying degrees in the following circumstances:

- liability for dangerous wild animals;

- liability for livestock straying onto neighbouring land;

- liability for defective products under the Consumer Protection Act 1987;

- liability under the rule in *Rylands v Fletcher*;

- liability for breach of statutory duty, if the statute in question imposes strict liability. This will be a matter of statutory interpretation in each case;

- liability for defamation;

- liability for man made objects causing damage on the highway.

In almost all of these torts, strict liability is subject to exceptions and defences. Indeed, in some instances, there are so many avenues of escape from strict liability that the term hardly seems appropriate to describe the particular tort (see sections on the Consumer Protection Act 1987, Chapter 15, and *Rylands v Fletcher*), Chapter 11. Moreover, absolute liability, which does not admit of any defence at all, is almost never to be found outside the criminal law.

On the other hand, in the law of negligence, there are certain circumstances where in effect there is strict liability, as in the case of learner drivers (*Nettleship v Weston* (1971)), the egg-shell skull cases in remoteness of damage, and in many of the cases in which the defendant was insured, in which judges have mysteriously found in favour of the claimant.

This further supports the view that tort suffers from internal contradictions and inconsistencies derived in part from haphazard decisions and judicial policy making, and that therefore, the search for some grand design giving coherence to different areas of tort is misguided and naive.

Details of the torts of strict liability will be covered in course of this book.

1.10 The Human Rights Act 1998

For several years, UK judges have been hearing arguments about the European Convention on Human Rights, and it taking into account when considering issues in tort, with a view to promoting consistency between the common law and the Convention. This position has been formalised by the coming into force of the Human Rights Act 1998 in October 2000. This Act provides that, wherever possible, UK legislation must be interpreted in such a way as to be compatible with the European Convention on Human Rights. Although the Human Rights Act 1998 has no effect on the continued validity of a statute or statutory instrument, the higher courts have the power to issue declarations of incompatibility, if satisfied that any legislation is incompatible with the Convention. This is intended to alert Parliament to the need to change the law, but it does not have any effect on the position of the parties to the litigation that led to the declaration. It is up to Parliament to decide how to respond and there are fast track procedures to amend incompatible legislation, if it is decided that this is necessary.

Certain statutes are likely to come under scrutiny – for example, the Police and Criminal Evidence Act 1984, breaches of which can, in certain circumstances, give rise to civil claims for damages for assault, battery and false imprisonment. The Human Rights Act 1998 makes it unlawful for public authorities (including courts and tribunals) to act in a way which is incompatible with a Convention right. If the alleged tortfeasor is a private individual rather than a public authority, Art 6 of the Convention might assist a claimant, who is a 'victim' as defined by the Act. It provides that everyone is entitled to a fair trial in the determination of his or her civil rights and obligations. If there is no existing tort remedy equivalent to a Convention right, the judges are required, by Art 6, to develop one.

The bulk of the law of tort has been developed by judges, through their decisions in the cases. The effect of the 1998 Act is that, when hearing tort cases, the judges are required to ensure that tort law (and indeed, all of the common law) is not incompatible with Convention rights. There is already a well established place within the law of tort for considering many of the matters that are contained within Convention rights. For example, the tort of trespass to the person has for many years protected individuals from inhuman and degrading treatment and torture. The Convention, in Art 3, protects the same rights. In future claims for assault and battery, the courts will be required to take into account Art 3 and the jurisprudence of the European Court of Human Rights (ECHR) on the subject. It will, therefore, be unusual for a person to base a claim solely on an infringement of a Convention right, as there are already tort actions which can be used; arguments based on the infringement of Convention rights will simply be added to the contentions of claimants. However, in the case of claims involving less highly developed torts, such as those concerning alleged infringements of privacy, it is possible that cases will be brought based purely on the Convention.

1.10.1 An example

An example of a case which might involve human rights arguments is that of Ian Brady, who failed in his claim that the prison authorities were acting unlawfully in force-feeding him. Brady is now considering seeking relief in the ECHR. Article 3 of the European Convention provides that there is a right not to be subjected to torture or inhuman or degrading treatment. This must be balanced against the right to life in Art 2 of the Convention. Brady claimed that the force-feeding to which he was subjected was painful because no local anaesthetic was used when the naso-gastric tube was inserted. He also considered that it was degrading. However, case law in the ECHR suggests that the treatment must be cruel in the extreme before it can amount to torture, and it is unlikely that Brady's treatment meets that description. It appears that Brady would have a tenuous case if he did seek a ruling from the ECHR (see 13.8.6).

1.10.2 The future of human rights and tort law

It is much too soon to do more than speculate about the effect of the Human Rights Act 1998 on the law of tort. The Convention rights that are likely to prominent as far as tort is concerned are: the prohibition of inhuman or degrading treatment or punishment (Art 3): the right to liberty and security (Art 5); the right to a fair trial (Art 6); the right to respect for privacy, family life, home and correspondence (Art 8); the right to freedom of expression (Art 10); and the right to freedom of assembly and association (Art 11). Some of these have already been scrutinised by the courts and such cases are discussed in the relevant sections of this book. Whatever happens, students of tort law will need to be familiar with the large body of case law that has already been developed by the ECHR.

1.11 A summary of the objectives of tort

The objectives of the law of tort can be summarised as follows:

* Compensation

    The most obvious objective of tort is to provide a channel for compensating victims of injury and loss. Tort is the means whereby issues of liability can be decided and compensation assessed and awarded.

- Protection of interests

  The law of tort protects a person's interests in land and other property, in his or her reputation, and in his or her bodily integrity. Various torts have been developed for these purposes. For example, the tort of nuisance protects a person's use or enjoyment of land, the tort of defamation protects his or her reputation, and the tort of negligence protects the breaches of more general duties owed to that person.

- Deterrence

  It has been suggested that the rules of tort have a deterrent effect, encouraging people to take fewer risks and to conduct their activities more carefully, mindful of their possible effects on other people and their property. This effect is reflected in the greater awareness of the need for risk management by manufacturers, employers, health providers and others which is encouraged by insurance companies. The deterrent effect of tort is less obvious in relation to motoring though the incentives to be more careful are present in the insurance premium rating system.

- Retribution

  An element of retribution may be present in the tort system. People who have been harmed are sometimes anxious to have a day in court in order to see the perpetrator of their suffering squirming under cross-examination. This is probably a more important factor in libel actions and intentional torts than in personal injury claims which are paid for by insurance companies. In any event, most cases are settled out of court and the only satisfaction to the claimant lies in the knowledge that the defendant will have been caused considerable inconvenience and expense. The claimant also risks financial loss if the case is decided against him or her and this is a factor to be weighed in the balance when retribution is sought.

- Vindication

  Tort provides the means whereby a person who regards him or herself as innocent in a dispute can be vindicated by being declared publicly to be 'in the right' by a court. However, again, it must be noted that many cases never actually come before a court and the opportunity for satisfaction does not arise.

- Loss distribution

  Tort is frequently recognised, rather simplistically, as a vehicle for distributing losses suffered as a result of wrongful activities. In this context loss means the cost of compensating for harm suffered. This means re-distribution of the cost from the claimant who has been injured to the defendant, or in most cases the defendant's insurance company. Ultimately, everyone paying insurance or buying goods at a higher price to cover insurance payments will bear the cost. The process is not easily undertaken and it involves considerable administrative expense which is reflected in the cost of the tort system itself. There are also hidden problems attached to the system, such as psychological difficulties for claimants in using lawyers and courts, and practical difficulties such as the funding of claims which may mean that many who deserve compensation never receive it. It has been suggested that there are other less expensive and more efficient means than tort for dealing with such loss distribution.

- Punishment of wrongful conduct

  Although this is one of the main functions of criminal law, it may also play a small part in the law of tort, as there is a certain symbolic moral value in requiring the wrongdoer to pay the victim. However, this aspect has become less valuable with the introduction of insurance.

1.11.1 An illustration of the operation of the tort system

The issues raised by the road traffic accident described below illustrate some facets of the objectives of tort and its relationship with other systems of compensation.

1.11.2 The scenario

A, a man aged 27, had consumed five pints of beer in a public house one Sunday lunchtime. He left for home on foot in the early afternoon when road and weather conditions were good. His route took him across a busy main road close to the centre of a city, but as this was a Sunday he decided to take a chance and cross the road some distance from the traffic lights and adjoining pedestrian crossing. He looked to the right and noticed that the lights were red and that there were two cars just approaching the traffic lights. Then he looked to the left and began to cross the road. As he reached the centre of first carriageway, he realised that the cars were now approaching at speed and that he might not be able to reach the central reservation. He dithered for a moment and the next thing he knew he was hit by the car driven by B. A was taken to hospital and detained there for 10 weeks suffering from multiple injuries. After leaving hospital, A slowly recovered, but still suffers from mild post-traumatic stress disorder and has pain in his legs which were operated on immediately after the accident. A will always walk with a slight limp and he may develop arthritis at some distant future date as a result of the accident. He also has numerous scars on his face and arms, and will require cosmetic dental treatment to replace damaged teeth. He is paying for private dental treatment and hopes to recover the cost of this from B. However, the estimated speed of the car which hit A was 45 mph and he is lucky to have survived at all. A has at last managed to find another job as a lorry driver earning a comparable salary to that which he had before the accident. B was convicted by magistrates of driving without due care and attention and was fined £150 and given nine penalty points.

A is now seeking compensation from B by means of a tort action. He is still angry about having been injured by B and would like to see B suffer by being brought before a civil court because he believes that B 'got off much too lightly' in the magistrates' court. A is also hoping to receive a large sum by way of compensation for the pain he has suffered.

A will need to consider how he can pay for legal advice and representation. He has received a large sum in State benefits during the recovery period and before he could find a new job. He is surprised to learn that this will be deducted from any award of damages which he will receive. He is also surprised to discover that because he has made such a good recovery he will not receive a particularly high award, especially as he has found a job. In addition, A is amazed that he is likely to be found at least 25% contributorily negligent because he told the doctor who admitted him to hospital that he had drunk about five pints of beer just before the accident. This is recorded on his medical notes, though A has no recollection of having told the doctor this. Witnesses have stated that they thought he took a chance in trying to cross the road when he did.

In the event, the case never reaches court. A is told that a sum of £10,000 has been paid into court by lawyers acting for B's insurance company. He is advised to accept this, because if the judge makes a lower award he will have to pay the costs of the other side from the date of paying in. His barrister is concerned that there may be a finding of a high percentage of contributory negligence (up to 40%). The case is finally settled three years after the accident for £12,000. The legal costs involved which include solicitors' fees, the advice of a barrister, including a case conference and expert medical examinations and reports, total £5,000.

B is now having to pay very much higher motor insurance premiums and is worried about losing his licence if he is prosecuted for another driving offence in the near future. A does not know about this.

1.11.3 Are the objectives of tort met in this case?

If one considers whether all the objectives of tort have been met in this situation, it is apparent almost immediately that they have not. To take the picture from A's perspective: the tort system has protected A's interests through the negligence action. However, A does not feel that he has had his revenge. He has not had the opportunity of seeing B squirming under cross-examination, and he does not even know about B's fears for his driving licence, a criminal law matter in any event. He has had the support of the NHS and State benefits during the most crucial period of his hospitalisation and recovery, but feels that he has had to wait much too long to obtain his tort damages.

He is disappointed that he will only receive part of the compensation which he thought he deserved because the case is to be settled out of court, and he had never even heard about contributory negligence before this happened to him. He feels that he will go on suffering for a long time because of the injuries which he received. However, he is more fortunate than many pedestrians who are injured. At least he could afford to pursue his claim through his conditional fee agreement. Those without such financial support frequently give up as soon as they discover the cost of litigation.

As far as B is concerned, tort has had some deterrent effect because he will now probably drive more carefully, at least for a while, to avoid having to go on paying higher insurance premiums, as these will gradually be reduced if he has no more accidents. He has probably had some sleepless nights worrying about what will happen, but he is reassured that the insurance company will pay any compensation. He has been more concerned about the criminal prosecution, as he wanted to avoid publicity because he was a married man and was in the car with a girlfriend on the day of the accident. He is also worried about committing another driving offence and losing his licence, and he will consciously drive more carefully. To that extent, he has been more concerned about criminal law matters than about tort.

From the point of view of society as a whole, tort has ensured that A is compensated. The insurance system has to some extent been driven by tort, and B's original insurance cover which provided the compensation was compulsory under the Road Traffic Act 1988 (usually regarded as a criminal law statute). Compulsory insurance for motorists means that all motorists help to pay compensation to people who are injured like A. This has achieved a form of loss distribution. The general deterrent effect of contributory negligence is minimal. A had never even heard of the rule and there are many road users who have not. The law has allowed recovery of the costs of A's financial support from B's insurance company, but the NHS and the state benefit system have proved quicker and more efficient than the tort system in providing medical care and money to A at the very time he needed it.

This commonplace accident raises doubts about some of the claims which are made for tort and lead us to question seriously how far the present system really fulfils its objectives. It is clear that the State has provided better and more efficient support for A at the most crucial time and a lower cost than tort. This has been a simple case in which there was sufficient evidence that B was at fault because there are witness statements and a police report as well as a criminal conviction. Also, A's injuries, although unpleasant, will have no serious lasting effect on him. However, there are many cases which are far more complex and where the issuing of proceedings is a real gamble. For example, suppose no one had witnessed the accident and A had no recollection of what happened. It might be difficult to prove that B was actually at fault, especially if he states that A had run out unexpectedly into his path. There could be complex issues concerning causation of the injuries, and the issue of quantum is often much more complicated than in this case. Suppose A has no legal aid and cannot find a solicitor willing to act for him on a conditional fee (no win, no fee) basis. It would be very likely that A would bring no legal action at all in such circumstances and the legal system would have failed him.

We will return to this scenario when considering the criticisms of tort in Chapter 20 at the end of the book.

AN OVERVIEW OF THE LAW OF TORT

Problems of definition

Tort is difficult to define. Problems of definition are best dealt with by comparing the scope and objectives of tort with those of other law subjects such as contract and criminal law.

Even the attempt to achieve a comparison is a rather naive over-simplification of the position in modern law, when tort and contract have been drawn together at various times and pulled apart by the vagaries of judicial policy. The classification is a matter of convenience for academic writers, but is often self-defeating and masks the underlying purposes of the law.

Protection of interests

Tort protects a variety of different interests and imposes corresponding duties on people in general. Not every damaging act will be legally actionable, and even people who have undoubtedly suffered wrongs which have been committed maliciously may be without a remedy in certain circumstances (*Bradford Corporation v Pickles* (1895)).

Most of the law of tort in practice is concerned with the tort of negligence and, in particular, from the point of view of a practising solicitor, with motor accidents and work accidents.

Insurance and tort

The relationship between tort and insurance is complex. Insurance provides a means of distributing losses.

Strict liability

There are some torts which are described as torts of 'strict liability'. This label is misleading. The term covers a wide spectrum of the law of tort and the 'strictness' varies in degree, though there is no absolute liability.

Note the circumstances in which varying forms of strict liability apply:

- dangerous wild animals;

- livestock straying onto adjoining land;

- defective products – the Consumer Protection Act 1987;
- *Rylands v Fletcher* (1868);
- some breaches of statutory duty;
- defamation;
- man made objects falling onto highways;
- false imprisonment.

Other systems of compensation

Tort should not be considered in isolation. The full picture of compensation for injury can only be understood in the light of other sources of financial support which are available to people who suffer injury.

Human rights and tort

The Human Rights Act 1998 may prove important in the future development of the law of tort. The important Convention rights in relation to tort are to be found in Arts 3, 5, 6, 8 and 11 of the European Convention on Human Rights.

Objectives of tort

These can be summarised as follows:

- compensation;
- deterrence;
- vindication;
- loss distribution;
- punishment.

Conclusion

Tort is difficult to define. It suffers throughout from many internal inconsistencies as a result of haphazard decisions and judicial policy. It must be concluded that the search for a grand design which gives the law of tort internal coherence is naive and is likely to prove inconclusive.

CHAPTER 2

INTRODUCTION TO THE TORT OF NEGLIGENCE

In legal practice today, of all the tort actions, it is negligence which has pride of place. By far the most tort claims are brought in negligence and, even if other torts such as breach of statutory duty or nuisance are involved in a particular case, negligence is frequently pleaded as well. This has not always been the case. Negligence is a relatively recent action to emerge in its own right in the long history of tort. This chapter will introduce the tort of negligence by tracing the rise of fault as a basis of liability and analysing the case of *Donoghue v Stevenson* (1932). The chapter concludes by setting out the criteria which need to be satisfied in order to establish a successful claim in negligence.

2.1   Fault

Although much emphasis is placed on the notion of fault in the modern law of tort, this is a comparatively recent development.

Legal historians have different theories about the significance of fault in early law. However, it is clear that the need to prove fault in order to establish liability in tort became increasingly important towards the end of the 19th century. As social attitudes changed following the reforms pioneered by Chadwick and others, the volume of social legislation designed to improve the lives of employees, tenants and citizens generally naturally increased. Ascribing responsibility became easier with the advancement of science, as did greater competence in determining causation, which made it easier from a pragmatic point of view to establish fault. There was a trend away from selfish individualism towards greater social and civic responsibility. This trend eventually manifested itself in legal decisions, culminating in the case of *Donoghue v Stevenson* in 1932, although there had been a large number of specific actions based on fault before this case. Allowing for a degree of cultural lag, the common law will inevitably follow some years behind enlightened social attitudes. Indeed, the majority decision in that case came as a surprise to some experts in 1932 because of the dearth of favourable precedents, and it involved a degree of ingenuity on the part of the judges, especially Lord Atkin. This case could be regarded as a bringing together of the previous causes of action and the creation of a new one relating to product liability.

2.2 *Donoghue v Stevenson* and the modern tort of negligence

In *Donoghue v Stevenson* (1932), the appellant brought an action against the manufacturer of ginger beer bought for her by a friend at Minchella's cafe in Paisley. She drank some of the ginger beer and when the rest was poured into her glass she noticed the remains of what appeared to be a decomposed snail floating out of the opaque bottle into her tumbler. The appellant suffered gastro-enteritis and nervous shock as a result of having drunk some of the ginger beer, and the nauseating sight of the foreign body in her drink.

The case proceeded to the House of Lords on the preliminary point as to whether an action existed for the tort of negligence irrespective of the fact there was no contract between the appellant and the manufacturer of the ginger beer. The basis of the case was that the manufacturer owed a duty to the consumer to take care that there was no harmful substance in his product, that he had breached this duty and that she had been injured as a result.

The House of Lords reviewed the few relevant existing precedents and by a majority of three to two decided in favour of the appellant, so establishing the existence of negligence as a separate tort in its own right for the first time by an authoritative court. The two most significant speeches are those of Lord Atkin, expressing the majority view, in favour of the appellant, and of Lord Buckmaster, who was in the minority.

2.2.1 The policy arguments

Lord Buckmaster expressed fears that if the case were to be decided in favour of the appellant it was difficult to see how trade could be carried on. This economic consideration undoubtedly weighed heavily on the minds of the minority judges. However, social justice considerations involving the need to compensate consumers who are injured through the negligent acts of manufacturers, won the day. The majority, described later by Devlin as 'bold spirits' as against the 'timorous souls' in the minority, were prepared to take a creative leap and to generalise from slight pre-existing authority.

Lord Atkin, to calm the fears of the minority that a flood of actions might follow this case, emphasised the need for 'proximity' between the parties:

> Acts or omissions which any moral code would censure cannot in a practical world be treated so as to give a right to every person injured by them to demand relief. In this way, rules of law arise which limit the range of complainants and the extent of their remedy.

He went on to attempt to limit the scope of future actions by formulating his famous 'neighbour principle'. It was only when this principle applied, he argued, that a duty of care can be established and the basis of a negligence action will be in place:

> The rule that you are to love your neighbour becomes, in law, you must not injure your neighbour; and the lawyer's question 'who is my neighbour?' receives a restricted reply. You must take reasonable care to avoid acts or omissions which you can reasonably foresee would be likely to injure your neighbour. Who then in law is my neighbour? The answer seems to be – persons so closely and directly affected by my act that I ought reasonably to have them in contemplation as being so affected when directing my mind to the acts or omissions which are called in question.

Ironically, this very limitation was used later, as will be seen, as a device to extend the scope of the tort of negligence beyond the manufacturer/consumer situation into a wide range of fact situations affecting many spheres of life.

In principle, the appellant could proceed with her action. It did not matter that there was no contract between the appellant and the manufacturer. However, the manufacturer died before she was able to proceed with her action and the case was settled out of court for £100. The facts relied upon by the appellant were never proved, and to this day no one knows with certainty that the foreign body in the drink was a snail, nor that it was this which caused the illness. It could, for example, have been contaminated ice-cream or something the appellant ate for supper the previous day which made her ill.

Trade was still carried on despite the fears of the minority, and the cost of consumer products increased because manufacturers, fearing legal actions, began to insure their products on a systematic basis, so spreading the cost of compensating consumers who are injured throughout the consumer population as a whole. Manufacturers improved their mechanisms for quality control to the benefit of the whole of society. In fact, with the passage of time, the common law, through the operation of the doctrine of *res ipsa loquitur* (the situation speaks for itself), made it difficult for manufacturers to escape liability for foreign bodies in foodstuffs, and this has been confirmed by statute in the Consumer Protection Act 1987.

2.2.2   The significance of the decision

At least five important points emerge from *Donoghue v Stevenson:*

- negligence is a separate tort in its own right;

- an action for negligence can exist whether or not there is a contract between the parties;

- an action for negligence will succeed if the claimant can prove: a duty of care is owed by the defendant to the claimant; a breach of that duty by the defendant; resulting damage which is not too remote;

- in order to establish the existence of a duty of care the 'neighbour principle', based on reasonable foresight, must be applied. This is a minimum requirement and would not justify liability in all cases;

- a manufacturer of drinks owes a duty of care to the consumer not to cause injury by negligently allowing foreign bodies to contaminate those products.

Note: *Donoghue v Stevenson* only provides a remedy to consumers in the case of products which are likely to cause injury to health. It does not offer a remedy for shoddy or unmerchantable goods. That is the province of contract.

Since 1932, the law concerning duty of care has moved on. The modern approach was established in 1990 in *Caparo Industries v Dickman* (see below, 3.2).

2.3 Establishing liability for negligence

It is difficult to define negligence in simple terms. As Lord Atkin explained in *Donoghue v Stevenson* (1932):

> To seek a complete logical definition of the general principle is probably to go beyond the function of the judge, for the more general the definition the more likely it is to omit essentials or to introduce non-essentials.

Many years later, Lord Roskill explained the position in the following terms in *Caparo Industries v Dickman* (1990) when he said:

> There is no simple formula or touchstone to which recourse can be had in order to provide in every case a ready answer to the question whether, given certain facts, the law will or will not impose liability for negligence or, in cases where such liability can be shown to exist, determine the extent of that liability.

2.3.1 What must be proved: duty; breach; damage

Despite the difficulties, lawyers need to have a conceptual framework within which to decide whether there is the basis of a claim or the possibility of a good defence, and it is now well established that, in order to succeed in an action for negligence, the claimant must prove each of three elements: first, that a legal duty of care is owed to him or her by the defendant; secondly, a breach of that duty; thirdly, a causative link between the breach of duty and the injury or loss. Linked to the element of causation, the claimant must establish that the damage which was suffered is not regarded in law as too remote. If the claimant is successful in proving each of these elements, the value of the claim (*quantum*) must be assessed. It is this framework which is set out here under three general headings: (1) duty of care; (2) breach of duty; and (3) damage.

Each of these elements requires detailed consideration, and there are numerous authorities to be examined under each of the three headings, as the tort of negligence has been developed for the most part through the cases. The rest of this chapter and the five chapters which follow will be devoted the task of explaining the three elements of the negligence action.

2.3.2 Duty of care

The first matter to be proved is that the defendant owed a duty of care to the claimant. Unless it is possible to establish this in the particular circumstances of the case, there will be no point in considering whether a particular act or omission which has resulted in harm was negligent. The tests for deciding whether or not a legal duty of care is owed will be discussed at length later in this chapter and in the following two chapters. As will be seen, the existence of a duty of care depends upon foresight, proximity and other complex factors.

It should be noted that in the vast majority of negligence cases there is no dispute about the existence of a duty of care. Most negligence cases in practice are fought on the issues of breach of duty and causation. Nevertheless, the impression given in many of the textbooks is that disputes frequently arise about whether or not a duty of care exists. One reason for this is that the cases which do arise tend to involve important issues of legal principle in areas of human activity in which the law is developing or is unclear. These cases often reach the House of Lords and Court of Appeal and are therefore given much prominence in the Law Reports and in the media. On the other hand, the very many cases concerning breach of duty turn on their own special facts. Most are now decided at county court level and never appear in the Law Reports, the more so now that the financial limits of county court claims have been increased. Still more of such claims are settled out of court or at the door of the court. The same is true of many cases involving causation. Thus, it appears to students new to the study of tort that there are as many, if not more, claims involving disputes about the existence of a duty of care than about the other elements of negligence. This false picture places undue emphasis on the duty of care element of negligence. For this reason, some tort courses in universities begin the study of negligence by examining breach of duty and causation and only cover duty of care at a later stage.

2.3.3 Breach of duty

The second matter to be considered is whether the defendant was in breach of the duty of care. This element lies at the very heart of the negligence action. It involves consideration of whether the act or omission of which the claimant complained amounts in law to a negligent act. As will emerge from the detailed chapter on this subject (Chapter 7), what is in issue is whether the defendant met the standard of care required by law when undertaking the particular activity. This element of the negligence action therefore involves proof of fault in legal terms on the part of the defendant, and in law fault means acting unreasonably in the particular circumstances. This often happens when the risk of harm arising from an activity outweighs the cost or inconvenience of taking precautions to avoid it. Like duty of care this involves considerations of foreseeability.

Different standards of care apply in different situations. For example, experts are expected to exercise a higher standard of care than lay people, and all depends on the circumstances of each case, as will be seen from the detailed study of the cases in Chapter 7.

Courts and lawyers are concerned with the very basic factual details of exactly what happened in each individual case and, when the particulars of the claim are drafted by lawyers acting for the claimant, they must refer in detail to what acts or omissions are the subject of the claim. In a road traffic claim arising out of an accident in which a pedestrian was knocked down by a car at traffic lights, the particulars of claim might contain the following allegations of negligence on the part of the driver of the car.

(1) Failing to observe that the lights had changed to red.

(2) Failing to stop at a red traffic signal.

(3) Travelling at excessive speed.

(4) Failing to keep a proper lookout.

(5) Failing to observe that the claimant was on the pedestrian crossing with the traffic lights in his favour.

(6) Failing to observe that the claimant was in the process of crossing the road.

(7) Failing to take sufficient notice of ice on the road

And so on, depending on the circumstances.

The defence filed on behalf of the motorist would seek to answer these allegations and would probably allege contributory negligence on the part of the claimant.

Some of the factual matters involved in such a claim would be agreed on the basis of admissions by the defendant, and possibly an admission of a small amount of contributory negligence on the part of the claimant. The dispute can then be narrowed down to one or two points. For example, it may be that there is a dispute about whether the lights actually were red when the motorist proceeded. Much will depend upon witness statements and whether or not the police successfully prosecuted the motorist for related criminal offences.

Thus, in legal practice, there is much emphasis on factual matters in relation to breach of duty, but this is not the picture presented by many of the textbooks which of course need to analyse the legal rules rather than concern themselves with facts. Students should not forget this when grappling with the question of breach of duty.

2.3.4 Causation and remoteness of damage

The third question is whether the breach of duty complained of was the cause of the damage suffered. Once a duty of care and a negligent act or omission have been proved, this third element of negligence must be dealt with. The burden of proof is on the claimant to establish that the negligent act caused, or substantially contributed to, the damage or injury which he or she suffered. Once again, facts are important. Take, for example, a case in which it is claimed that a claimant who had a vasectomy operation was not warned by the surgeon that there is a small risk that the operation might reverse itself naturally so that a man may become fertile again at some future time. This did in fact happen, and the man's wife has become pregnant. In order to succeed in his claim for negligence, the claimant would need to establish the doctor owed him a duty of care; that there was a breach of duty in failing to warn him of the small risk of reversal; and that the failure to warn caused the pregnancy. It is this last element which involves proving causation, and causation could well be disputed by the defendant even if he admitted failure to warn (which is unlikely). The defence might argue successfully that the claimant would have had the operation anyway, even if he had been warned. There may even be an argument that the wife had become pregnant by another man. The burden would be on the claimant to show on a balance of probabilities (that is, at least a 51% likelihood) that the baby was his own, that he would not have had the operation if he had known of the risk, or that he would have insisted on regular fertility checks to ensure that there had been no natural reversal. There would be expert evidence from doctors on these matters.

The law will not provide compensation for damage which it regards as too remote from the accident itself. This, as will be seen, is a question of law rather than fact. It is the law which places a limit on recovery, and the legal principles involved will be discussed at length in a later chapter (Chapter 8). The rules state that the defendant will not be liable for damage which is too far removed from the negligent act or omission because the defendant could not have foreseen the particular kind of damage which occurred. The concept of foresight which is considered in relation to duty of care and breach of duty also arises at this stage in the negligence action. It is not always clear whether the courts are considering foresight in relation to duty of care, or foresight in relation to remoteness of damage (Chapter 8). These difficulties will be explored in the chapter covering remoteness of damage. Once it is established that there is foreseeability of the type of harm, the extent of the loss suffered by the claimant does not need to be considered. The defendant must take his claimant as he finds him. For example, if a pedestrian is knocked down by a motorist, it is foreseeable that he will suffer personal injuries. The defendant will therefore be liable if the claimant had a minor bruise or if he had a pre-existing heart weakness which meant that he suffered a heart attack because of the shock of the accident and died as a result.

Assessment of the damages is often closely related to issues of causation. For example, if the claimant states that he has suffered a back injury through being required to lift heavy objects at work without proper supervision, medical experts will be asked to give evidence about the injury which he has sustained. The orthopaedic surgeon instructed to give evidence for the claimant will usually write a report which supports the claimant's case. He may, for example, state that the injury will mean that the claimant can no longer work because of the pain and disability which he sustained. He may well state that the claimant's back was in sound condition before the accident and that he could have expected to work for another 15 years until retirement age. However, the claimant will also be examined by an orthopaedic surgeon acting for the defendant. This report might state that the claimant already had problems with his back, though these had not started to cause any pain before the accident. His opinion might be that the claimant would only have had another five years of work left to him before the latent back problem began to develop to cause a disabling condition. There is a dispute here about how much of the injury was caused by the work accident and how much arose naturally. The answer will affect the award of damages. Many such disputes about medical matters arise in personal injuries cases, and the parties often reach a compromise and settle the case out of court. Such factual matters do of course affect quantum of damage (how much compensation the claimant will receive).

INTRODUCTION TO THE TORT OF NEGLIGENCE

Few torts require proof of malice or even positive intention. Exceptions include intentional torts to the person and misfeasance in public office.

Donoghue v Stevenson

Fault has dominated tort in modern law.

Donoghue v Stevenson (1932) laid the foundations of the law of negligence. Five aspects of the *ratio* include:

- negligence is a separate tort;
- the absence of privity of contract is irrelevant in tort;
- to establish negligence, the claimant must prove: a duty of care is owed by the defendant to the claimant; breach of that duty by the defendant; and damage as a result of the breach, which is not too remote;
- the neighbour principle as a test for the existence of a duty of care must be applied;
- manufacturers owe a duty of care to consumers in respect of the goods which they provide to ensure that they do not threaten health or safety.

Read the case, paying attention to the weight which the judges attached to various arguments of policy considerations of social justice and loss distribution which were regarded as particularly important.

Note: the *Donogue v Stevenson* principle did not apply to defects in the quality of goods. That is the province of the law of contract.

The three elements which must be proved in order to succeed in negligence are:

- duty of care;
- breach of duty;
- damage – causation and remoteness.

CHAPTER 3

DUTY OF CARE – GENERAL PRINCIPLES

3.1   Duty of care

The first consideration in any negligence action is whether the claimant was owed a duty of care by the defendant.

Despite the fact that it may appear from the discussion later in this book that there are circumstances when a duty of care has been limited or excluded by the courts, there are very many situations in modern life when a duty of care is owed. The legal basis for the existence of such duties is discussed in the next chapter, but some examples of 'duty situations' are described below.

These instances are based on established lines of precedent, but that does not mean that it may not be possible for a court to distinguish the cases and find that no duty is owed in certain circumstances, as described in Chapter 5. Thus, in general, motorists and other road users owe a duty of care to one another in relation to physical injuries. Doctors and other health care professionals owe a duty of care to patients. Parents owe a duty of care to their children, as do teachers who are temporarily in *loco parentis* (acting in the place of parents). Manufacturers owe a duty of care to consumers of their products. Employers owe various duties of care at common law to their employees.

3.2   The test for determining the existence of a duty of care

The modern approach to deciding whether a duty of care exists involves applying one or more of three tests based on: (a) foresight; (b) proximity; (c) considerations of justice and reasonableness in imposing the duty (*Caparo v Dickman* (1990)).

3.2.1   Foresight

In *Donoghue v Stevenson* (1932), the notion of foresight of the claimant as a member of a group who is likely to suffer harm as a result of the defendant's acts or omissions is notionally of importance as a deciding factor for liability. However, although it is possible to find cases in which it is argued purely on the question of foresight that a duty of care exists, it is too simplistic to suggest that foresight or 'reasonable contemplation of harm' alone is the test for the existence of a duty of care. It should be regarded as simply one aspect to be weighed in the balance. Many of the cases cannot be explained by reference only to foresight. Indeed, in *Marc V Rich & Co v British Marine Co Ltd* (1996), the House of Lords took the view that, whatever the nature of the harm, the court should consider foresight, proximity and whether in all the circumstances it is fair, just and reasonable to impose a duty of care.

It is still possible to find decisions today which are arrived at by using the simple test of reasonable foresight. For example, in *Topp v London Country Bus (South West) Ltd* (1993), the claimant was unsuccessful because he was unable to establish that the defendant ought reasonably to have foreseen that a joy-rider would have stolen the bus which his employee left unattended in a layby. His wife was killed through the negligence of the unidentified joy-rider when he collided with her and knocked her off her bicycle.

In *Margereson v JW Roberts Ltd, Hancock v Same* (1996) (a case which was also concerned with causation), it was held that the owner of an asbestos factory should reasonably have foreseen that children who played near the factory might develop pulmonary injury through dust contamination.

However, there were, and still are, a number of 'grey areas' in which the extent of liability and the scope of the duty of care are less clear (see Chapters 4, 5 and 6).

3.2.2 Proximity

Closely related to foresight is the notion of 'proximity'. This concept was considered in *Donoghue v Stevenson* itself and was mentioned in the early cases on negligence. In some cases, proximity has become a more important consideration than foresight as a device for controlling the existence and scope of duty of care in personal injury cases. However, foresight will often be sufficient. In *Yuen Kun Yeu v AG of Hong Kong* (1978), Lord Keith referred to proximity as a synonym for foreseeability on the one hand, and on the other as referring to the whole concept of the relationship between the claimant and the defendant as described in *Donoghue v Stevenson* by Lord Atkin. Proximity plays an important part in the reasoning in many of the cases concerning the extent of liability for economic loss caused by negligent misstatement, as will be seen in Chapter 5. It has also been regarded as important in relation to the scope of duty of care in omissions rather than positive acts. In the Canadian case of *Canadian National Railway v Norsk Pacific Steamship Co* (1992), the majority judges in the Canadian Supreme Court went on to reject a general test of proximity as a test for liability applicable throughout the law of negligence. In effect, the concept is but one of the factors which may apply in the process of judicial reasoning, whereby judges are enabled to arrive at the decisions which they believe to be just in individual cases.

Proximity has proved very important in determining whether a duty of care exists in nervous shock cases (see Chapter 4). Time will tell whether the operation of the Human Rights Act 1998 will lead to the development of more duties in tort (see 1.10).

3.2.3 What is fair, just and reasonable

It appears, from a number of decisions in the 1980s that the test for the existence of a duty of care is now approached in three stages.

The approach recommended in *Caparo Industries plc v Dickman* (1990) and other cases is to deal with the question of duty of care in three stages. The first is to consider whether the consequences of the defendant's act were reasonably foreseeable (which can create confusion with the test for remoteness of damage); the second is to ask whether there is a relationship of proximity between the parties; and third is to consider whether in all the circumstances it would be fair, just and reasonable that the law should impose a duty of a given scope upon one party for the benefit of the other.

There are many examples of recent cases in which the courts draw upon the so-called 'incremental' approach, rejecting the two-stage test in *Anns v Merton BC* (1978). One such example is *Ephraim v Newham LBC* (1993), where the Court of Appeal used the 'fair, just and reasonable' criterion to reject the claim of a tenant who had relied upon the advice of the defendants in obtaining accommodation and who, acting upon that advice, obtained accommodation in a house which lacked proper fire escapes. She was seriously injured in a fire. The local authority had a mere power, not a duty under the Housing Act 1985, to require the necessary works to be carried out by the landlord, and it was held that there was no duty of care in negligence.

The three-stage approach was used in *Ancell v McDermott* (1993); *Punjab National Bank v de Bonville* (1992); *Marc Rich v Bishop Rock Marine* (1995); *Aiken v Stewart Wrightson* (1995); *Jones v Wright* (1994); *Spring v Guardian Assurance* (1995); and in *Kent v Griffiths and London Ambulance Service* (2000); *Barrett v Enfield BC* (1999), amongst many other cases discussed in this book.

The question immediately arises as to whether the three-stage test is very different from the two-stage test. It is certainly more complicated and has the disadvantage of appearing to be more restrictive, inhibiting the development of the law.

Considerations of 'what is fair, just and reasonable' are in reality co-extensive with policy arguments, but such considerations should now only become relevant after the questions of foresight and proximity have been settled. This was also the case under the earlier two-stage test (see 3.8). What now appears to be happening in some cases is that some judges are dealing with policy, in a covert fashion, without openly discussing the issues, by merely finding that there is insufficient *proximity* between the parties if they desire the development of the law to be restricted. This is apparent in, for example, some of the law relating to psychiatric injury.

However, it is impossible to generalise and there are cases in which there is open discussion of policy (see *British Telecommunications plc v James Thomson & Sons (Engineers) Ltd* (1998); *Palmer v Tees HA* (1999)).

Attempts to re-formulate the criteria mask the inevitable problem of patrolling the boundaries of liability and attempting to adapt the law to changing circumstances.

For the judges, a restrictive approach has the advantage of acknowledging their traditional constitutional role as learned interpreters of the law rather than law makers. Yet, as Lord Reid has said in acknowledging that judges can and do make law:

> Those with a taste for fairy tales seem to have thought that, in some Aladdin's cave, there is hidden the common law in all its splendour and that on a judge's appointment there descends on him knowledge of the magic words Open Sesame ... But we do not believe in fairy tales any more.

The next two chapters will examine in detail the development of the scope of duty of care in negligence in relation to nervous shock and economic loss. Chapter 4 will outline instances in which the courts have held that no duty of care exists. In many of the cases which will be considered in these chapters, judicial policy has played an important part.

3.3 The operation of judicial policy in negligence

Judges have used the concept of 'duty of care' as a device for implementing policy considerations of various kinds. It will also become apparent that judicial policy is important in connection with breach of duty, causation and remoteness of damage, and that it operates in other areas of tort. However, for our purposes, policy can be dealt with here in relation to duty.

3.4 Definition of 'policy'

Winfield defined policy in the following way:

> The use of the word 'policy' indicates no more than that the court must decide not simply whether there is or is not a duty, but whether there should or should not be one, taking into account both the established framework of the law and also the implications that a decision one way or the other may have for operation of the law in our society.

What Winfield meant was that judges can and do 'make up' the law as they go along in response to changing social conditions. Although this is an over-simplification of Winfield's statement, one only has to examine a number of lines of cases in tort which deal with the scope of the duty principle to observe that many of the decisions have less to do with the logical application of pre-existing legal rules than with matters of social or economic pragmatism.

3.5 Factors influencing judicial policy

The factors which influence judges may include the following considerations (the list is not exhaustive):

- Loss allocation. Which party can best afford to bear the loss? Which party is insured (the deepest pocket principle)? This is often behind decisions in road accident cases, for example, *Nettleship v Weston* (1971).

- The 'floodgates' argument. This involves the fear that a flood of claims may follow a particular decision, and is found in a number of 'grey areas' of negligence, such as nervous shock.

- Whether the imposition of a duty would create inconsistencies with other areas of the law.

- Moral considerations.

- Practical considerations such as forward-planning for manufacturers.

- The notion that professional people like doctors and barristers need to be protected from the threat of negligence actions which could inhibit their professional skills and judgment (*Saif Ali v Sydney Mitchell & Co* (1980), now overruled by *Hall v Simons and Others* (2000)). In *Hatcher v Black* (1954), Denning MR expressed the view that medical negligence was like a 'dagger at the doctor's back'.

- The respective constitutional roles of Parliament and the judiciary. Judges are not happy about becoming involved in making new law. 'The policy issue where to draw the line is not justiciable': *per* Lord Scarman in *McLoughlin v O'Brian* (1983).

- Judicial reluctance to create new common law duties where none previously existed.

- The idea that there should be no duty owed to members of an 'indeterminate class' of potential claimants.

It is still possible to find a straightforward discussion of the policy issues which arise in novel situations, despite the many twists and turns which have taken place during the 1980s and 1990s in the attitudes of the judges to whether policy is a matter for open deliberation. For example, in *Goodwill v British Pregnancy Advisory Service* (1996), the claimant was suing for an unwanted pregnancy. She claimed that her partner had not been properly advised as to the possibility of his vasectomy operation not being successful. This operation had been performed some four years previously before the couple had met and formed a relationship, and the claimant's partner had later been advised that he was sterile and need use no other form of contraception. It was held by the Court of Appeal that the claim should be struck out because the claimant was a member of a class of persons which was indeterminately large and she was not therefore foreseeable. The claimant and defendant were not in a sufficient or special relationship such as gave rise to a duty of care and there were no policy reasons why they should treat such a tenuous relationship as giving rise to a duty, though a duty would have been owed at the time of the operation and subsequently advice given to the man's then sexual partner.

- Whether imposing a duty would encourage people to take more care. For example, in *Smoldon v Whitworth and Nolan* (1997), it was held that the referee of a colts rugby match owed a duty of care to the claimant, a player injured when a scrummage collapsed. The Court of Appeal stressed that the case was confined to its own special facts involving colts rugby as it was played in 1991 before the rules changed and was of the view that it was just and reasonable to impose a duty as it was proven beyond doubt that it was a well known risk of the game that collapse of a scrum could cause very serious neck injuries. It was not necessary to establish a high level of probability of the *type* of injury involved. The claimant was found not to be *volens*. There had been no previous case in any jurisdiction in which a referee had been held liable to a player, but comments on the decision by members of the rugby fraternity have indicated that in future, despite the judge's cautious confining of the decision to its facts, referees will need to be extra careful. The first defendant, another player, was held not to have been negligent. A spokesman for Rugby League is quoted in *The Times* as saying: 'This decision has ramifications for all sport in the UK, however humble.' This decision was confirmed on appeal ((1997) PIQR 133).

3.5.1   Legal reasoning

The reasons which judges give for their decisions can be analysed into a number of different categories of reasoning. Legal philosophers have identified the following categories:

- **Goal and rightness reasons**

  Summers has identified, among other reasons, 'goal reasons' and 'rightness reasons'.

  'Goal reasons' are forward looking, to achieve some social or economic aim, such as compensating consumers. *'Rightness reasons'* appeal to justice or fairness regardless of the consequences.

- **Principle and policy**

  Dworkin has produced a celebrated dichotomy, 'principle' and 'policy', which is discussed in some of the cases (for example, *McLoughlin v O'Brian* (1983)).

What analysts like Summers and Dworkin are doing is exploring the deep structure of legal reasoning and attributing certain sorts of justification to certain judges who may in fact say very little by way of explanation for their decisions. This is in part because judges are under considerable pressure not to be seen to be making law, which is the function of the legislature.

If the judges in later cases had wished to restrict development of the law of negligence, they could have treated *Donoghue v Stevenson* as a departure which should be confined to its own particular facts or, at the very most, have treated it as applying only to consumer cases involving foreign bodies in foodstuffs. However, what has materialised is a massive expansion of the law of negligence. In effect, what the notion of 'duty of care' does is define the interests which are protected by the tort of negligence. As we shall see, these interests are by now many and varied, which is why some experts take the view that negligence is 'taking over' the law of tort and usurping the territory of some of the other torts.

3.5.2 Role of the 'duty' principle in developing the law as a policy device

What began to happen after 1932 was that judges interpreted the *ratio decidendi* of *Donoghue v Stevenson* by stating it in abstract terms focussing on 'the neighbour principle'. Whenever a novel fact situation presented itself, the judge would ask whether a duty of care was owed in *that* situation. If the judge thought it appropriate to compensate the claimant in a particular case, it was a fairly straightforward matter of deciding that a duty of care was owed by the defendant to that claimant, and the rest followed, provided of course that breach and consequent damage could also be established.

This 'backward reasoning', often thinly disguised, and based on notions of judicial policy, is an important feature of tort, and much turned upon the decisions which followed quickly upon *Donoghue v Stevenson*. Manufacturers of many different kinds of products began to seek advice from their lawyers and insurers as to whether the newly developing law would apply to their goods.

Within a matter of a few years, it was decided that a duty of care was owed by manufacturers of clothing to their consumers. In the case of *Grant v Australian Knitting Mills* (1936), the claimant suffered dermatitis caused by a chemical used in the manufacture of woolly underpants made by the defendant. It was held that a duty of care was owed to him, and the defendants were liable even though the illness he suffered was extremely rare (one complaint in 5,000,000).

3.6   Latent policy decisions

It is possible to identify a number of negligence decisions which were clearly policy driven but where the judges do not admit to this. Instead, they cling to precedent or use the concept of reasonable foresight and the neighbour principle to their own ends as policy devices, so remaining within the confines of the traditional role of the judge, which is to interpret and apply the existing rules of law. In this category belong a number of cases in which the decision expressed by the judge or judges was that on application of the neighbour principle, no duty of care was owed because the claimant was not reasonably foreseeable by the defendant.

One example of this is the case of *King v Phillips* (1952). A mother who suffered nervous shock when she saw her child in a situation of great danger and presumed him to have been injured, was unable to succeed in her action for nervous shock caused by the negligence of a taxi driver who reversed into her son's bicycle. The reason given by the Court of Appeal for denying the mother a remedy was that she was too far away from the scene of the accident, and therefore outside the scope of reasonable foresight. No one would seriously believe that a motorist could not reasonably foresee the possibility of psychiatric harm to the mother of the child in such circumstances, even if she was some distance from the scene of the accident. Probably, the real reason for the decision was fear of 'floodgates' opening to permit a large number of similar claims.

3.7   Explicit policy decisions

Judges do sometimes discuss at length the policy issues involved in particular cases. This is both interesting and helpful to lawyers who have to advise their clients in other similar situations. It enables them to predict with greater certainty the trends in judicial thinking, and represents a major departure from the hypocrisy which surrounds many of the earlier decisions.

The important explicit policy decisions made by the House of Lords and Court of Appeal are often described as 'landmark' cases; the first of these is *Donoghue v Stevenson* itself. The House of Lords discussed at length in that case the social and economic consequences of the possible outcomes. The majority of judges were satisfied with the control on future development of the law which Lord Atkin imposed in the concept of 'duty of care' and the 'neighbour principle'. The neighbour principle was confirmed by the House of Lords in *Hedley Byrne & Co v Heller & Partners Ltd* (1964) as a flexible test which could be applied in any fact situation. In *Dorset Yacht v Home Office* (1970), the neighbour principle as a basis for the duty of care was treated as a statement of principle to be applied in all cases unless some reason for its exclusion could be justified. Many of the cases which establish that no duty of care is owed in particular circumstances, involved explicit exposition of the policy reasons for denying the claimant a remedy.

The 1970s was an important decade for those who favoured open recognition of the 'legislative function' of the courts (see *Symonds* (1971) 24 MLR 395).

3.8   The development of a two-stage test and open discussion of policy

Although the two-stage test outlined here has now been superceded by the present three-stage test, it is important to consider the two-stage test in the development of the modern law.

In *Anns v Merton BC* (1978), Lord Wilberforce made a statement which established the famous 'two-stage' test which was to be cited and relied upon in many of the most important policy decisions which were responsible for the expansion of the law of negligence in relation to nervous shock and in economic loss in the 1980s. His words were:

> Through the trilogy of cases, *Donoghue v Stevenson, Hedley Byrne v Heller* and *Home Office v Dorset Yacht Company Ltd*, the position has now been reached that in order to establish that a duty of care arises in a particular situation, it is not necessary to bring the facts of that situation within those of previous situations when a duty of care has been held to exist. Rather, the question has to be approached in two stages. First, one has to ask whether, as between the alleged wrongdoer and the person who has suffered the damage, there is a sufficient relationship of proximity or neighbourhood such that, in the reasonable contemplation of the former, carelessness on his part may be likely to cause damage to the latter, in which case a *prima facie* duty of care arises. Secondly, if the first question is answered affirmatively, it is necessary to consider whether there are any considerations which ought to negative or to reduce or limit the scope of the duty or the class of persons to whom it is owed, or the damage to which a breach of it may give rise.

This statement had a liberating effect on the law. Stage one was the simple application of the neighbour test, based on proximity, treating the *Donoghue v Stevenson* principle as a principle of general application. Stage two was the crucial policy stage at which the court could legitimately discuss any reasons of public, social, economic or other policy reasons for denying a remedy.

In direct contrast to the decision in *King v Phillips* (1952) (see 3.6 above) is that in *McLoughlin v O'Brian* (1983), another nervous shock case, in which the House of Lords was no longer constrained to try to bring the facts of the case within those of previous decisions in which a duty of care for nervous shock had been held to exist. Instead, relying on the two-stage test, their Lordships went on to weigh the policy issues in the fullest possible discussion.

3.9 The retreat

3.9.1 Criticisms of the two-stage test

In a number of oft-quoted statements criticising the two-stage test, various attempts were made to halt the expansion in the law which it had made possible. While it is clear that Lord Wilberforce's approach should not have been treated 'as if it were a statutory definition' (*per* Lord Reid in *Dorset Yacht*), it did provide a useful and honest statement of the reality of the progress of the law. The wisdom of the more liberal approach was doubted by Lord Keith in *Governors of the Peabody Donation Fund v Sir Lindsay Parkinson & Co Ltd* (1985) in which he said:

> A relationship of proximity in Lord Atkin's sense must exist before any duty of care can arise, but the *scope* of the duty must depend on all the circumstances of the case ... In determining whether or not a duty to take care of particular scope was incumbent upon a defendant, it is material to take into account considerations of whether it is just and reasonable that it should be so.

The introduction of a 'just and reasonable test' in all the circumstances of each case has been seized upon by some of the writers as suggesting a significantly different approach to that of Lord Wilberforce in *Anns v Merton BC*, but it is not easy to establish any real distinction between assessing what is just and reasonable in all the circumstances and taking into account the policy considerations which ought to negative or reduce or limit the scope of the duty.

In *Curran v Northern Ireland Co-ownership Housing Association* (1987), Lord Bridge cautioned against the use of a principle 'of general application from which a duty of care may always be derived unless there are clear countervailing considerations to exclude it'.

In *Leigh and Sullivan Ltd v Aliakmon Shipping Company Ltd* (1985), a case which later went on to the House of Lords, Lord Oliver expressed the view that the two-stage test should not be regarded:

> ... as establishing some revolutionary test of the duty of care, the logical application of which is going to enable the court in every case to say whether or not a duty of care exists. Nor, as it seems to me, can it properly be treated either as establishing some new approach to what the policy of the law should be or as conferring upon the court a free hand to determine for itself in each case what limits are to be set.

Lord Oliver was set against the idea of each court developing its own policies without reference to settled authorities. Lord Brandon favoured a return to the application of pre-existing authorities in order to establish the existence of a duty of care. This is consistent with the attitude of caution which judges have traditionally taken towards open acknowledgment of policy issues.

In *Yuen Kun Yeu v AG of Hong Kong* (1988), Lord Keith inveighed further against Lord Wilberforce's approach:

> The two-stage test formulated by Lord Wilberforce for determining the existence of a duty of care has been elevated to a degree of importance greater than it merits and greater perhaps than its author intended.

He took the view that the second stage should only be applied in exceptional circumstances, presumably of the kind discussed in *Rondel v Worsley* (1969), which are regarded as true 'public policy' matters, when, in the 'public interest', there should be no liability. The same approach was adopted in *Hill v Chief Constable of West Yorkshire* (1988).

In *Rowling v Takaro Properties Ltd* (1988), Lord Keith again expressed fears about the application of the two-stage test as a general principle on the grounds that to attach too much importance to policy matters might detract from the real issues in a case, so that important and relevant considerations might be overlooked.

In *Caparo Industries plc v Dickman* (1990), Lord Roskill favoured a return to the traditional categorisation of duty of care, rejecting the notion of a more general approach.

In *Murphy v Brentwood* (1990), Lord Keith recommended an 'incremental' approach by reference to decided authorities rather than the more general approach of Lord Wilberforce which permits considerations of vague policy matters, which cannot apply in all cases. Indeed, *Murphy* marked the end of any possibility of adoption of the two-stage test for the future.

3.10 The incremental approach – the three-stage test

As was explained at the start of this chapter (3.2), the courts now favour what has been described as 'an incremental approach' where reasoning by analogy with reference only to existing cases should prevent sudden 'massive extensions' of the duty of care (see *Council of the Shire of Sutherland v Hayman* (1985), an Australian High Court decision approved by the House of Lords in *Murphy*). While permitting themselves the luxury of discussing policy issues only in difficult cases, and for the most part hiding the real issues behind what appears to be a logical application of the authorities, the courts have returned to an approach which is rather more rigid that the two-stage test. This three-stage test is explained above, 3.2.3.

DUTY OF CARE – GENERAL PRINCIPLES

The criteria for determining the existence of a duty of care are:

- foresight;

- proximity;

- is it fair, just and reasonable to impose a duty?

The law has been shaped by judges in accordance with prevalent notions of 'policy', whereby the court decides not merely whether there is or is not a duty in any given situation but whether there should or should not be one, taking into account the existing legal rules and the social implications.

Factors influencing policy

Some of the factors which influence the outcome of cases and the development of the law are:

- loss allocation;

- the floodgates argument, fear of a rush of claims;

- moral considerations;

- practical considerations;

- public policy considerations, such as professional work loads and responsibility;

- constitutional arguments;

- reluctance to create new restrictions on the behaviour of individuals;

- the idea that the claimant is a member of an 'indeterminate class';

- whether imposing a duty would encourage others to take care (*Smoldon v Whitworth* (1996)).

Policy decisions

Policy decisions have been of two kinds: latent and explicit.

Latent policy decisions are those in which the judges do not acknowledge the true reason for the decision (for example, *King v Phillips* (1952)). *Explicit policy* decisions are those in which the judges are prepared to discuss and analyse the reasons for deciding for and against a particular outcome (for example, *Donoghue v Stevenson* (1932); *Hedley Byrne v Heller* (1964); *Home Office v Dorset Yacht Company* (1970)).

Note that, in many of the cases in which it has been held that no duty of care is owed, the policy considerations have been openly weighed by the judges and clearly established.

The two-stage test

The two-stage test was introduced by Lord Wilberforce in *Anns v Merton* (1978) to establish whether a duty of care exists:

- stage one: proximity and foresight;

- stage two: consideration of the policy reasons which might lead to a restriction of the scope of the duty of care.

The influence of this liberating approach led to a major expansion of the law of negligence in the 1980s (see *McLoughlin v O'Brian* (1983); *Junior Books v Veitchi* (1981)).

The retreat from the two-stage test

Keith, Bridge and Oliver LJJ led an attack on the *Anns* approach. Criticism of the two-stage test was based on the fact that it had been treated as though it were a statutory definition. The real reason for the criticism was probably that it permitted so much flexibility that the law was in danger of expanding too rapidly.

The following cases contain critical statements and are illustrations of the retreat from the two-stage test:

The *Peabody* case (1985);

Curran v Northern Ireland Co-ownership Housing Association (1987);

The *Aliakmon* (1985);

Yuen Kun Yeu v AG of Hong Kong (1988);

Rowling v Takaro Properties (1988);

Caparo v Dickman (1990).

Murphy v Brentwood DC (1990) finally ended the reign of *Anns* by openly condemning the two-stage test and recommending an incremental approach.

The three-stage test

The new approach should be 'incremental' and should involve a three-stage test (*Caparo v Dickman* (1990)):

- reasonable foresight;

- proximity;

- was the imposition of a duty 'fair, just and reasonable' in all the circumstances?

This approach was used in:

Ephraim v Newham LBC (1993);

Punjab National Bank v de Bonville (1992);

Ancell v McDermott (1993);

Jones v Wright (1994);

Spring v Guardian Assurance (1995);

Palmer v Tees HA (1999);

Kent v Griffiths and London Ambulance Service (2000).

CHAPTER 4

DUTY OF CARE – PSYCHIATRIC INJURY

The object of this chapter is to examine the cases concerning psychiatric injury, or nervous shock, as it was called in the earlier cases, and to trace the development of the scope of duty of care within that context. This will help towards an understanding of the role of policy in the tort of negligence, and the extent of judicial law-making in this narrow area of the subject.

'Nervous shock' cases form an area of law which illustrates well the operation of judicial policy. By close examination of the cases, it is possible to trace the changing attitudes of lawyers, doctors and of society in general over a period of about 100 years, to psychiatric injury. From the same cases, it is also possible to elicit changing judicial attitudes to the scope of duty of care and to the whole issue of policy decisions.

Psychiatric injury, like pure economic loss, is sometimes described as a 'grey area' of negligence because judicial attitudes are constantly developing and new formulations of the scope of the duty of care are regularly produced. This means that the law is rather unclear at times and the cases are frequently difficult to reconcile.

4.1 What is 'nervous shock'?

Before proceeding with the cases, it is necessary to define 'nervous shock' which is the rather quaint term still used by lawyers for various kinds of psychiatric injury. Physical symptoms may accompany the mental distress which the claimant suffers. For example, a pregnant woman who suffers nervous shock may miscarry (though some doctors now doubt that this can happen), and a person with a certain heart condition may suffer a heart attack. Although these kinds of physical symptoms may have facilitated claims in the early days when judges were more sceptical about claims for psychiatric harm, it is not now necessary for the claimant to prove that physical symptoms were suffered in order to succeed in a claim.

However, there must be evidence that the claimant has suffered a serious psychiatric condition which is more than mere temporary grief or fright. Medical evidence is very important in claims for nervous shock, and psychiatrists now know much more about the condition than they did when the first claims were brought. As scientific knowledge has increased, judges have become increasingly willing to recognise that the condition described by lawyers as 'nervous shock' exists.

With the development of the railway network in the 19th century, an increasing number of claims arose out of railway accidents, and one writer, Grichsen, D (*Nervous Shock and Other Obscure Injuries of the Nervous System in the Clinical and Medico-Legal Aspect*, 1882), identified nervous shock injuries as part of a clinical pattern following railway accidents. He concluded that many accidents resulted in 'severe and prolonged' nervous shock, 'weariness', 'cramps', 'twitching' and other symptoms. Charles Dickens described symptoms of weakness and faintness following a railway accident in which he was involved as a passenger.

People who suffered no physical injuries but who sustained psychological harm might not have considered legal action until medical science identified and documented the condition, and it was not until 1888 that the first case reached the courts.

One of the reasons why judges were initially reluctant to recognise that a duty of care could be owed in relation to psychiatric injury, was that its very existence as a medical condition was doubted by them. They feared that the illness could be faked more easily than physical conditions, and at times even seemed to mistrust psychiatrists, because so much conflicting psychiatric evidence was presented in the nervous shock cases. They also feared that once claims for nervous shock began to succeed, the 'floodgates' would be opened to allow a rush of claims. In a famous article in 1953 ('The shock cases and area of risk' (1953) 16 MLR 14), Professor Goodhart explained this reluctance in the following terms:

> The principle of the wedge is that you should not act justly now for fear of raising expectations that you may act still more justly in the future – expectations which you are afraid that you will not have the courage to satisfy.

However, once it became clear that psychiatrists were prepared to give consistent support to the existence of psychiatric illness arising from mental trauma, the number of successful claims increased.

4.1.1 Recognised symptoms of psychiatric injury

As well as producing the physical symptoms discussed above, nervous shock manifests itself in a number of ways.

In recent years, a form of psychiatric injury known as 'post-traumatic stress disorder' (PTSD) has been identified, and this forms the basis of many claims which are brought as a result of mass accidents and disasters. PTSD is a serious long term medical condition which can be distinguished from temporary feelings of shock which most people experience immediately after witnessing an accident.

There are two main systems of classification of psychiatric illnesses currently in use in the UK. These are the Diagnostic and Statistical Manual of

Mental Disorders of the American Psychiatric Association which first recognised PTSD in 1980, and the Glossary of Mental Disorders in the International Classification of Diseases, which recognised the condition in 1987 for the first time.

The definition of PTSD provided by the first of these is that the condition must be traceable to a traumatic event which is outside the normal range of human experience. Examples would include serious threats to the individual's own safety, or to that of his or her close relatives, or even seeing a complete stranger who has been severely injured or killed. A variety of symptoms may be experienced by the sufferer. These include nightmares about the traumatic event, or 're-living' the experience. Other common symptoms include irritability, lack of interest in everyday life, aggression, poor concentration, lack of emotional response, and avoidance of anything which might prompt a reminder of the traumatic event, and unreasonable or 'pathological' grief.

Some individuals may be particularly prone to the condition, and this led judges in some of the earlier cases to produce the extraordinary and contradictory view that only people of 'normal fortitude' could succeed in a claim for nervous shock. It later emerged that what was intended here was that a claimant who was abnormally sensitive would only succeed in an action for nervous shock if a so called 'normal' person would also have suffered nervous shock of some kind in the same circumstances. Neurotic individuals and people with alcohol or drug abuse problems seem to be particularly vulnerable. In the Zeebrugge arbitration, there was concern expressed about the variety of terms used to describe the claimants' psychiatric conditions: 'Many of the victims suffered from PTSD, of course some victims suffered from other psychiatric illnesses, for example, depression.'

In addition to PTSD, courts have awarded damages for nervous shock when the symptoms were described rather vaguely to include 'depression' (*Chadwick v British Railways Board* (1967)) and 'personality change' (*McLoughlin v O'Brian* (1982)).

By the time *McLoughlin v O'Brian* was decided in 1982, the legal profession had accepted the condition described as 'nervous shock', and had arrived at an understanding of it, expressed by Lord Wilberforce in that case, in the following terms:

> Although we continue to use the hallowed expression 'nervous shock', English law, and common understanding have moved some distance, since recognition was given to this symptom as a basis for liability. Whatever is known about the mind-body relationship (and the area of ignorance seems to expand with that of knowledge), it is now accepted by medical science that recognisable and severe physical damage to the human body and system may be caused by the impact, through the senses, of external events on the mind. There may thus be produced

what is as identifiable an illness as any that may be caused by direct physical impact.

It should also be noted that there is no difficulty in making an award if the claimant was the subject of sexual abuse and suffered PTSD as a consequence (*Re GB, RB and RP* (1996)). Awards have also been made to people suffering from psychiatric disorders caused by the fear that they might develop an illness sometime in the future. For example, six people who are suffering from psychological problems caused by the fear that they may one day contract Creuzfeldt-Jakob Disease (CJD) as a result of treatment with human growth hormone which may have been contaminated, have now been awarded a total of £500,000. None of these patients has yet shown signs of contracting the disease, but Morland J has ruled that they are suffering rational fears which no amount of counselling or therapy can obliterate (*Group B Claimants v Medical Research Council and Another* (1998)).

4.2   Development of the law

The topic is best approached chronologically so that the development of the law can be traced logically over the years. It must be borne in mind that there is no problem about awarding damages for nervous shock if the claimant also suffers physical injuries in the same accident. Difficulties only arise if there is psychiatric injury without any form of bodily injury.

The first attempt to claim damages for nervous shock was in *Victorian Rly Comrs v Coultas* (1888). Little medical evidence was available in those days to assist the court in arriving at its decision, and the Privy Council refused the claim, expressing the fear that a flood of claims would follow if this succeeded. It was thought that 'a wide field of imaginary claims' would be opened.

The first successful nervous shock case was *Dulieu v White* (1901). The court was prepared to recognise and compensate the claim of a publican's wife who suffered a severe fright when a horse-drawn van crashed through the window of the bar where she was working, cleaning glasses. She was pregnant at the time and the child was born prematurely soon after the accident. The recovery of damages was limited by the judge, Kennedy J, to the particular facts here which involved real and immediate fear of injury to the claimant herself. He formulated a limitation on the scope of liability for nervous shock which became known as the 'Kennedy limitation':

> There is, I am inclined to think, one limitation. Shock, when it operates through the mind, must be a shock which arises from a reasonable fear of immediate personal injury to oneself.

This limitation was used in later cases to restrict the scope of liability for nervous shock. However, the principle was not applied consistently in all cases which followed, and eventually it fell into disuse after higher courts had extended the scope of liability.

4.2.1   Fear for relatives and friends

Soon, courts began to award damages to people who had feared for the safety of close relatives. In *Hambrook v Stokes* (1925), the court was prepared to award damages for nervous shock when a mother, who had been made to fear greatly for the safety of her children at the sight of a lorry careering out of control towards them, suffered nervous shock, had a miscarriage and died. The court took the view that it would be unfair and indeed 'absurd' to deny a remedy when a mother feared for the safety of her children in circumstances where had she feared for her own safety the claim would have succeeded. She had witnessed the experience through her own unaided senses – a theme which was later developed by Lord Wilberforce in *McLoughlin v O'Brian* and refined in *Alcock v Chief Constable of South Yorkshire* (1991), as will be seen.

As the notion of nervous shock became more acceptable to lawyers, articles began to appear in legal literature which explained the medical aspects of the condition, and more actions were brought before the courts. New limitations began to be suggested by judges, ostensibly based on the notions of foresight and proximity formulated by Lord Atkin in *Donoghue v Stevenson*, though in reality the true reasons for the decisions were issues of policy.

4.2.2   The impact theory

Whereas shock had initially been treated as a form of physical injury, probably because the early cases had involved miscarriages as the physical manifestation of shock, a new view began to emerge, which was that there had to be foreseeability of some impact occurring to the claimant. This was known as the 'impact theory', and it meant that damages would only be awarded if the claimant was within the foreseeable area of impact, or geographically close enough to the scene of the accident.

4.2.3   The 'area of shock' theory

Still more recently another theory emerged, which was that, even if a claimant is outside the foreseeable area of impact, damages may still be recoverable as long as the claimant was within the foreseeable area of shock. The remnants of this approach are still in existence today, but in some of the older cases it is difficult to discern which approach is favoured.

In *Bourhill v Young* (1943), the claimant, an Edinburgh fish wife, had just alighted from a tram when she heard the impact from a serious accident 50 yards away on the other side of the road and outside her line of vision. She later walked over to the scene and suffered nervous shock as a result of what she saw. She gave birth to a still-born child very soon afterwards, but her claim for nervous shock failed. Three judges in the House of Lords held that she was outside the area of impact, and that as she was a total stranger to the motorcyclist involved in the accident she was outside the area of foresight of shock. Their Lordships accepted that the test was that of foresight of shock. It was also decided that as a pregnant woman she was not 'normal' in terms of what she could endure by way of shock, and she was not entitled to succeed in her claim.

In *Brice v Brown* (1984), the difficult subject of people of 'normal fortitude' was again considered, though in the context of remoteness of damage. A woman and her daughter were involved in a minor car accident, and the girl of nine suffered slight physical injuries. The mother, who was very neurotic, suffered serious nervous shock. The court decided that the mother's claim should succeed. The test which was applied was that if a person of ordinary phlegm would have suffered nervous shock in these circumstances, the claimant should succeed, and could then recover compensation for the full extent of her illness. If not, she could recover nothing at all.

In *Page v Smith* (1996), further light was thrown on the notion of 'normal fortitude' (see 4.6.1 below).

In the strange case of *Owens v Liverpool Corpn* (1933), relatives in a funeral procession succeeded in their actions for nervous shock when they saw the hearse collide with a corporation vehicle and the coffin fell out on the impact. The only emotions which the relatives could have experienced were those of enhanced grief and horror. The relative in the coffin was already dead, so there could have been no claim based on fear for the safety of that person.

The courts continued to extend the scope of liability for nervous shock. In *Dooley v Cammel Laird & Co Ltd* (1951), a crane driver recovered damages when he witnessed an accident involving a workmate.

In *Kralj v McGrath* (1986), a woman who suffered nervous shock when she saw the dreadful condition of her child who was the victim of a negligent delivery by a doctor succeeded in her action for nervous shock.

4.2.4   Rescuers

In *Chadwick v British Railways Board*, a passer-by who assisted the official rescue teams at the scene of a serious rail disaster had suffered nervous shock and eventually committed suicide. He did not know any of the victims personally, but he witnessed horrific sights. The case represents an extension of liability for nervous shock which applies only to rescuers who come upon an accident and assist in rescuing in the immediate aftermath. This is an example of the special consideration which the law affords to rescuers.

A professional rescuer, or indeed any rescuer who is present while an accident is still in the process of happening, will qualify in his or her own right as a primary victim of an accident, and will recover damages for nervous shock even though he or she suffers no physical injury during the rescue. In November 1992, a fireman who had been involved in the rescue of the victims of the fire at King's Cross Underground Station, was awarded £147,683 damages for nervous shock. While the defendants admitted liability and a number of other actions by firemen for nervous shock were settled out of court, the dispute in this case was about the amount of the award. (The highest previous award to a fireman for PTSD had been £13,000.) The claimant in this particular action, a Mr Hale, had suffered nightmares about dead people or skeletons, severe depression which had almost led to the breakdown of his marriage, and had only been able to manage a desk job since returning to work. He was unlikely to be able to continue working. The judge concluded: 'He will continue to suffer from a deep-rooted depression which is unlikely to abate, and affects his whole outlook on life' (*Hale v London Underground* (1992)).

In *Wigg v British Railways Board* (1986), the defendants were liable when a guard had been negligent in starting a train before a passenger had boarded properly. The driver, who had stopped the train as soon as possible, went to the passenger's assistance but he was already dead. The driver, with 20 years' experience, suffered nervous shock even though this sort of accident was described as 'an occupational hazard' and the claimant had experienced two previous incidents in which people had died on the railway line in 1979 and 1980.

Despite the special consideration which the law has afforded to rescuers, there is now evidence of a more restrictive approach (see below, 4.6.1).

4.3　Expansion of liability

In all the early successful claims, the claimants who experienced fears for the safety of loved ones or colleagues (or, in the rescue cases, rescue victims) had witnessed the scene of the accident through their own senses. In *McLoughlin v O'Brian* (1981), however, the courts were prepared to extend liability to a situation in which the claimant only saw her family after they had been removed from the scene of the event to a hospital casualty department. The claimant was the mother of four children. She was not present when her family were involved in a tragic road accident, liability for which was admitted by the defendant. She was at home at the time, about two miles away from the scene of the crash. By the time she had been informed of the accident, and called to the casualty department of the hospital, about an hour had elapsed, but the members of her family were still in various states of shock and had not been cleaned up after the accident. One of her children had died, her husband was severely shocked and suffered bruising, and the other two children were badly injured. The claimant suffered a serious psychiatric illness as a result of the events and of what she had seen. The House of Lords held that the mother was owed a duty of care by the defendants. Extending the previous ambit of the duty of care, they unanimously agreed that although she had not been present at the scene, she had come upon the accident in its immediate aftermath.

Lord Wilberforce and Lord Edmund-Davies considered that it was open to the court to decide the issue upon grounds of policy, relying on Lord Wilberforce's two-stage test in *Anns v Merton* (1978). The relevant policy issues which might have operated to negative the claim were discussed at length, and were all rejected. Lord Wilberforce stated that close family ties would mean that there was a sufficiently close relationship between the parties to satisfy a claim, but unrelated bystanders would be too remote. Any relationships falling between these two ends of the spectrum would need to be dealt with case by case on their own facts. Claimants would need to be present in the immediate aftermath of a tragedy in order to succeed in a claim, but information received from a third party would not be sufficient to constitute the 'immediate aftermath'.

Lord Bridge and Lord Scarman considered that this particular claimant could succeed on the foresight test alone, and that a test of 'reasonable foresight' was sufficient to decide liability in cases of nervous shock.

Even if fear of the opening of the floodgates was a relevant consideration, it was unlikely to be a problem in cases such as this, which are extremely unusual.

4.3.1 Cases involving the 'immediate aftermath'

In *Jaensch v Coffey* (1984), a woman, who saw her husband in hospital in a serious condition after he had been injured, succeeded in her claim for nervous shock.

In the later case of *Attia v British Gas* (1987), which was decided on application of the reasonable foresight test alone, it was decided that a claimant, who had returned home to witness the sight of her house burning down, could obtain damages for nervous shock caused by the defendants' negligence in installing central heating.

In two High Court cases (*Hevican v Ruane* (1991), which did not go to appeal, and *Ravenscroft v Rederiaktieblaget* (1991), which was reversed on appeal (1992)), after the *Alcock* case (see below, 4.4.1), both claimants succeeded in their claims for nervous shock.

In the first of these cases, a father who was at home when he was told of his son's accident, and in a police station when he learned that he had died, but later saw his body at a hospital, suffered severe long term depression. Although he did not arrive at the hospital in the 'immediate aftermath' of the death, his claim was allowed.

In the second case, a mother was called to a hospital after her son had been killed in a crushing accident at work. She never saw the body, and later she suffered a prolonged grief reaction. She, like the father in the *Hevican* case, was found to be a person of normal fortitude, and, once again, although she was not present in the 'immediate aftermath' of the accident, her claim was initially allowed, but could not stand on appeal after the decision in *Alcock*.

In both cases, the judges accepted that as a medical fact the presence of a person at the scene or in the immediate aftermath makes no difference to the likelihood of a psychiatric illness developing.

Both judges based their decisions on the 'reasonable foresight' test. It must surely be reasonably foreseeable that a parent who merely hears about the death or serious injury suffered by a child may suffer nervous shock even without actually witnessing the event at first hand.

It is likely that *Attia* and these two cases represent the furthest limit of the expanded duty of care in relation to nervous shock, and the correctness of both decisions is now in serious doubt since the *Alcock* case which followed them.

4.4   Contraction of liability for nervous shock

The policy reasons considered as relevant but rejected by the two judges who considered them in the House of Lords in *McLoughlin*, are familiar arguments against extending the scope of duty of care in relation to nervous shock. However, the fears are often over-stated. Psychiatric illnesses are not easy to simulate now that there have been considerable advances in medical science and knowledge of the symptoms of these conditions. It is unlikely that there will be large numbers of claims by people who were not present at the scene of accidents. Awards of damages for nervous shock have remained relatively low, with the exception of the award to a fireman in the King's Cross fire, a rescue case, discussed above (*Hale v London Underground* (1992)), where the claimant was forced to give up work because of a psychiatric illness

Indeed, in the *Ravenscroft* case, expert evidence was adduced to the effect that only a very small percentage of the population will suffer from an extreme grief reaction. The argument that judges cannot and should not change the law is somewhat naive, and in any event this kind of case is best left to piecemeal judicial development. The Law Commission has criticised the contraction of liability for psychiatric injury. It recommends extending the categories of people able to claim (see 4.7).

4.4.1   Restrictions on the scope of the duty

When the House of Lords gave further detailed consideration to the scope of liability for nervous shock in *Alcock v Chief Constable of South Yorkshire* (1991), certain restrictions were introduced, and some of the unanswered questions in *McLoughlin v O'Brian* were clarified.

In *Alcock*, the House of Lords considered 10 claims for nervous shock by relatives of the victims of the Hillsborough football stadium disaster. The police had admitted negligence in allowing too many people into the stadium, as a result of which 95 people had died and 400 needed to be treated in hospital. The tragedy had been broadcast on television as it was happening.

The claims involved clarification of a number of points which included the following:

- could people other than parents, children and spouses claim for nervous shock?;

- how far did the 'immediate aftermath' extend?;

- could people who witnessed on television events as they happened to their loved-ones succeed in claims for nervous shock?

In rejecting all 10 claims, the House of Lords held that the three relevant factors in considering whether a duty of care exists in a particular claim for nervous shock are:

- the proximity of the claimant in time and space to the scene of the accident;

- the relationship between the accident victim and the sufferer;

- the means by which the shock has been caused;

The mere fact that nervous shock was foreseeable could not in itself give rise to a duty of care. Lord Wilberforce, in the spirit of the two-stage test in *Anns*, had expressed this view in *McLoughlin v O'Brian*, taking the line that policy required claims to be limited by the courts for fear of a flood of claims, and it was this view which the House of Lords chose to follow in *Alcock*:

- the claimant can prove a close tie with the victim, witnessed the events on television, and in breach of the broadcasting rules, saw close up shots of a loved-one. The action would lie against the broadcasting company (a secondary victim);

- the claimant can prove a close tie with the victim, and witnessed a cataclysmic event on television (a secondary victim). (This category is less clear than the previous one.)

4.4.2 Proximity

The concept of proximity is of particular importance in claims for psychiatric injury. It has led to the idea of 'primary' and 'secondary' victims (see. 4.6.1).

In *Alcock*, not one of the claimants had actually witnessed the events happening to a loved one at very close quarters. Those who were present at the ground were too far from the scene to observe the faces of the victims. One claimant who had identified his brother eight hours later in the mortuary fell outside the 'immediate aftermath', and those who had seen the events on television would not have seen details of faces of individuals because broadcasting rules had been observed.

There is continued emphasis on the need for a secondary victim to be present at the scene of the accident or to arrive in the immediate aftermath. In *Tranmore v TE Scudder Ltd* (1998), a father who arrived at the place where his son had been killed two hours earlier, when the building in which he had been working collapsed, did not succeed in his claim for damages for psychiatric injury. He was beyond the 'immediate aftermath' of the accident. The Court of Appeal referred to the Law Commission Report No 249, *Liability for Psychiatric Illness* (see below, 4.6), in which the Commission had recommended the creation of a new statutory duty of care in cases where the claimant had a close tie of love and affection with an accident victim. Although such a change in the law, if accepted by Parliament, would abolish the 'immediate aftermath' restriction, under the existing law the claimant could not bring himself within the 'immediate aftermath' and the claim failed for lack of proximity.

4.4.3 The close tie of love and affection

None of the claimants in *Alcock* who might otherwise have qualified, including brothers and brothers-in-law, had proved a close tie of love and affection with the victim, but that did not mean that in future cases it would not be possible to admit to the class of possible claimants for nervous shock people who are not spouses, parents or children of the victims. This represents the opportunity to expand the class of people who can claim for nervous shock. Rescuers and other people directly involved in the events might be included. However, in future, it would be wise to plead a close tie of love and affection when a claim is initiated. Those claimants who had lost a son and a fiancé, would probably have succeeded on the closeness of their relationships with the victims, but were too far away from the events to succeed.

4.4.4 The means by which the shock was sustained

As to the means by which the shock was caused, those people who actually witness events at close quarters are within the scope of the duty of care. The events must be witnessed through the claimant's own sight or hearing either as they happen or in the immediate aftermath, which must be very soon after the events. Eight hours was too long in *Alcock*. Their Lordships did not absolutely rule out the possibility of claims based on observation of the events on simultaneous television. If, for example, the broadcasting rules were broken and details of faces of individuals were shown, there might be a claim available against the broadcasting company, as a *novus actus interveniens*. There might also be some circumstances when a claim would be available against the person responsible for tragedy itself, for example, cases like that involving the destruction of the US space shuttle.

4.5   The immediate effects of *Alcock*

After *Alcock*, it seems that a duty of care in relation to nervous shock was owed in the following cases:

- The claimant was present at the scene and also suffered physical injury – that is, he or she was a primary victim (see *Page v Smith* (1996), below, 4.6.1).

- The claimant was present at the scene and his or her own safety was threatened – that is, he or she was a primary victim (*Chief Constable of West Yorkshire v Schofield* (1999)).

- The claimant can prove a close tie with the victim, and witnessed the events at close quarters – even though the claimant, was a secondary victim.

- The claimant can prove a close tie with the victim and saw him or her very soon (probably not more than two hours) after the accident happened – even though the claimant was a secondary victim.

  In *Taylor v Somerset HA* (1993), a widow whose husband died as a result of a heart attack and who within an hour viewed his body in an attempt to settle her disbelief, failed in her claim for nervous shock. It was held that she did not fall within the 'immediate aftermath' principle because her visit to the mortuary was not for identification purposes, and her husband's body bore no signs of violent injury. This decision is a clear attempt to follow the restrictive trend in nervous shock cases.

- If the claimant was a rescuer or a member of the professional rescue services, he or she will be a primary or secondary victim depending on circumstances. In *Piggott v London Underground* (1995), four firemen at the Kings Cross fire were awarded damages for PTSD. It is clear from recent decisions that there is no automatic finding that a rescuer is a primary victim, and that to be a rescuer a person must actually participate in the rescue activity. A rescuer must actually be present at the scene or in its immediate aftermath and should not automatically be regarded as primary victim. (See *White v Chief Constable of South Yorkshire*, below, 4.6.2.)

  In *Duncan v British Coal* (1996), the claimant worked at a colliery in Yorkshire. He was 275 metres away from the scene of an accident in which one of his fellow workers was crushed to death. He arrived at the scene of the accident and gave him mouth-to-mouth resuscitation, but it was too late to save the victim. There was no sign of blood or injury on the body, but the claimant developed a serious psychiatric illness as a result of what he had seen. His claim was based on the fact that he was a rescuer, that he was himself within the area of risk and was a primary victim, and that he had witnessed the immediate aftermath of the accident. He failed on each of these points, and was unable to prove that he was in a special relationship with the victim as required by *Alcock*.

So, in *McFarlane v EE Caledonia* (1994), a bystander who was helping to receive casualties from the Piper Alpha oil-rig disaster did not succeed in his claim. A mere off duty bystander who is owed no duty under the master-servant relationship and who does not participate in the rescue cannot succeed. However, he may do so if he is linked by ties of love and affection to a primary victim of the disaster which he witnesses. Following this restriction, in the later case of *Robertson and Rough v Forth Road Bridge* (1995), the claim failed when the claimants witnessed a friend and workmate being killed. In this case, three workmates had been working together in a gale repairing the Forth Bridge. They found a large metal sheet and put it on a pick-up truck. One of them sat on the piece of metal. The first claimant drove the truck and the second claimant drove behind in another vehicle. A sudden violent gust of wind blew the man sitting on the sheet of metal over the side of the bridge and he was killed. Both claimants failed on their actions. They were not rescuers; they did not have sufficient ties of affection with the deceased; and they were not primary victims because they were not active participants in what had occurred. They fell into the category of bystanders.

4.5.1 Pre-accident terror

The case of *Hicks v Chief Constable of South Yorkshire Police* (1992) prevents claims for 'pre-accident' terror, which have been successful in America. The claims in respect of the terror suffered immediately before the deaths of two girls in the Hillsborough disaster, and for pain and suffering experienced as they died, were rejected by the House of Lords in this case, partly on the grounds that the time involved, minutes instead of hours or days, was too short. There have been numerous cases in which pain and suffering between the accident and the death could be compensated, but the timescale involved in these was much longer than in *Hicks*. If there is to be a successful claim for nervous shock, evidence of psychiatric injury must be presented to the court and this is not possible when the person concerned dies almost immediately.

4.6 Developments since *Alcock*

Since *Alcock*, the courts have consistently taken a restrictive approach to finding a duty of care in relation to psychiatric injury, despite a report by the

Law Commission which recommended removing many of the restrictions on liability (*Liability for Psychiatric Illness*, Law Com No 249 (1998)).

4.6.1 Primary and secondary victims

In *Page v Smith* (1996), a distinction was drawn in the House of Lords between primary and secondary victims. A primary victim is person who is a 'participant' in an accident, described by Lord Oliver as someone involved in an accident who suffers from what he sees or hears. Such a person is usually well within the range of foreseeability. A secondary victim is someone who is not a direct participant but who merely witnesses an accident or arrives in the aftermath of an accident. In his Lordship's view, such a person is almost always outside the range of foreseeable physical injury and it follows that there are more limited circumstances in which a secondary victim can succeed in an action for psychiatric injury. It is secondary victims who are required to satisfy the additional criterion set out in *Alcock* which requires proof of a special emotional tie with a person injured in the accident.

In *Chief Constable of West Yorkshire v Schofield* (1998), the Court of Appeal had little difficulty in finding that the trial judge had been correct in deciding in favour of a claimant who was a primary victim. A woman police sergeant had suffered post traumatic stress disorder after a fellow officer had unexpectedly fired three rounds of ammunition in a room which the officers were searching for firearms. Indeed, as Hutchison LJ pointed out, this was not a case in which the question of possible injury to others in a traumatic event was relevant. The woman police officer was herself present and was a primary victim. As that trial judge had found that the other officer had been negligent and should have foreseen that the claimant might suffer physical or psychiatric injury, there was sufficient proximity to give rise to liability.

In *Cullin and Others v London Fire and Civil Defence Authority* (1999), the Court of Appeal held that the issue as to whether the claimants were primary or secondary victims was a mixed question of fact and law.

In *Hunter v British Coal Corpn and Another* (1998), the Court of Appeal held by a majority of 2:1 that a workman who was not present at the scene of an accident in which a colleague had died was not entitled to recover damages for depressive illness suffered as a result. The claimant was about 30 m away from the scene of the accident in which a fire hydrant had burst in a mine, and he blamed himself for the accident. The Court of Appeal identified this situation as being outside the conventional cases of post-traumatic stress disorder. As Lord Justice Brook explained:

> It was not a case in which the claimant was involved as a rescuer. Nor did he ever see the deceased's body or the scene of the accident until after it was cleared up. There was nothing particularly out of the ordinary about the shock to his nervous system which he suffered when he was told, 15 minutes later, that his workmate had died.

This case was seen to be a case of 'survivor's guilt', for which the law is reluctant to provide compensation. A comparable situation arose in the Australian case of *Rowe v McCartney* (1976), and there, too, the court refused to make an award on the basis that the guilt suffered by the survivor was not a foreseeable consequence of the accident. The claimant was distinguishable from those who succeeded in their claims in *Young v Charles Church (Southern) Ltd* (1997); *Dooley v Cammel Laird* (1951); and *Galt v British Railways Board* (1983), which also involved employment accidents, in which the injuries suffered were a direct consequence of the breaches of duty which had occurred.

However, it appears that rescuers who are employees of the defendant may be able to succeed in claims for psychiatric injury on the basis that their employers have failed to provide adequate counselling to enable them to make a recovery after they have witnessed a traumatic event. This argument is being pursued by two policewomen who suffered psychiatric injury after attending the Dunblane massacre.

4.6.2 Rescuers – a new approach

Rescuers are in a less favoured position since the distinction between primary and secondary victims has been clearly enunciated. In *Page v Smith* (1996), where the claimant was actually involved in a car accident and, as such, could be classified as a primary victim, he suffered no physical injuries as a result of the impact, but was held by a majority of 3:2 by the House of Lords to be able to claim damages for psychiatric injury. The House of Lords emphasised the fact that certain control mechanisms are necessary to limit the number of claims for psychiatric injury where the claimant is a secondary victim, but that these mechanisms have no part to play in cases where the claimant is a primary victim. Thus, for example, the need to establish that it must have been foreseeable to the defendant that the psychiatric injury would have been suffered by a person of normal fortitude is not relevant in the case of primary victims. In the present case, the claimant had experienced an exacerbation of the condition known as ME (myalgic encephalomyelitis) and suffered a relapse in this condition as a result of a minor road accident.

When the appeal in the *Frost* case was heard in the House of Lords under the name of *White v Chief Constable of South Yorkshire* (1999), the opportunity was taken to explore, yet again, the boundaries of liability for psychiatric injury. The respondents had been present at the Hillsborough football stadium disaster in 1989, and were serving officers in the South Yorkshire Police Force. The tragedy had been caused by the negligence of a senior officer in the force. All of the respondents were claiming damages for psychiatric injury, contending that their role as both rescuers and employees of the police force put them in the position of primary victims, according to the classification in *Alcock*. The legal positions of both rescuers and employees in relation to claims for psychiatric injury were examined in depth.

The majority in House of Lords took the view that, although all of the appellants were more than mere bystanders, as they were on duty and assisted in the aftermath of the tragedy, to recognise their claims for psychiatric injury would expand substantially the boundaries of liability. By a majority of 4:1, it was decided that to allow employees, by virtue of their employment positions, to claim damages for psychiatric injury as 'primary' victims of injuries caused by their employer to third parties would not be 'fair, just or reasonable'. It was pointed out that the law denied redress to other groups who had suffered psychiatric harm as a result of the Hillsborough and who were even more deserving of compensation, and it would not be fair to single out police officers for special treatment.

By a majority of 3:2, it was decided that it would not be right to allow rescuers a position of special privilege if they had not been exposed to personal danger of physical harm in the course of the accident occurring. There were two reasons why rescuers should not be given special treatment by the law – first, there was a problem in defining who was a rescuer and who was simply a bystander; and, secondly, it would offend notions of distributive justice to allow rescuers particular privileges.

The law which had developed since *Alcock* was reviewed and the control mechanisms established in that case were carefully considered by the House of Lords. Relevant policy considerations were outlined, which were broadly similar to those discussed in *McLoughlin v O'Brian* (1983). These included:

- the difficulty of distinguishing between acute grief and psychiatric injury;

- the unconscious effects of bringing claims which could interfere with the process of recovery and rehabilitation;

- the likely increase in claims, which would be the result of allowing the law in this area to expand;

- the fact that the burden of liability on defendants could be disproportionate to the tortious act.

The House of Lords acknowledged that, since the *Alcock* case, the search for coherent principle in this area of law had been abandoned, and that what was necessary now was to approach each case in a practical way, in order to achieve fairness for each individual. The appeal was allowed and the officers were denied remedies.

An earlier example of this practical approach can be found in *Young v Charles Church* (1997), in which the claimant's claim for psychiatric injury failed at first instance in negligence and breach of statutory duty. He was found to have been only a secondary victim. He was employed on a building site and was erecting scaffolding with two workmates. He handed a long scaffolding pole to one of the other men and turned away to pick up another pole. As he was doing this, he heard a loud bang and a hissing sound when his workmate touched an overhead electric cable with the pole. The claimant realised immediately that his workmate had been killed and saw the ground onto which he had fallen bursting into flames. He ran for help to an office 600 yards away. When he returned to the scene of the accident, an ambulance had already arrived. As a result of what he had seen and heard, the claimant suffered a psychiatric illness. However, the Court of Appeal held that he could recover for breach of statutory duty under reg 44(2) of the Construction (General Provisions) Regulations, which were held to give protection to employees from the kinds of injuries which can be foreseen as likely to be caused by dangerous electrical equipment. These injuries included nervous shock.

4.6.3   The role of foresight

Foresight formed the basis of the decision in *Gibblett v P and NE Murray Ltd* (1999). There, it was decided by the Court of Appeal that the claimant would have been able to recover damages for a psychiatric condition which made her incapable of having sexual relations and children of her own, if physical injury in the road accident was foreseeable. In this case, the reasoning in *Page v Smith* (1995) was followed by the court. The claimant was a front seat passenger in a car which was stationary at a roundabout when the defendant's vehicle drove into the rear. The impact was relatively minor and liability was not in dispute. She suffered a mild to moderate whiplash injury, and any organic disability suffered was minimal. Over the next few years, however, the claimant had complained of seriously disabling symptoms which had no organic or clinical basis and which could only be explained on a psychiatric level. She claimed damages for psychiatric injury, including the exacerbation of pre-existing neurosis and somatisation disorder, or 'total body pain', as she put it. The trial judge awarded £12,500 general damages for pain, suffering and loss of amenity.

On appeal, the claimant argued that the trial judge did not find a causal link between the accident and the psychiatric disorder and did not recognise the injuries sufficiently in the award of damages. She also submitted that the trial judge erred in rejecting her claim for damages for her temporary inability to continue sexual relations or to have a family. The Court of Appeal took the view that it was clear from the size of the award that the judge had recognised some psychiatric overlay which was attributable to the accident and which resulted in more pain than normal. He had, however, held that the defendant was not liable for damage of a kind which a reasonable person would not have foreseen, even though the scale of such damage may have far exceeded what could have been foreseen. The Court of Appeal ruled that the judge had erred in finding that the claimant's inability to have a family, as a result of her psychiatric illness, was, as a matter of law, too remote a consequence of a minor car accident. Personal injury was reasonably foreseeable and the form that it took was immaterial (*Page v Smith* (1996)).

The test of causation in the instant case was:

> Did the accident, on the balance of probabilities, cause or materially contribute to, or materially increase the risk of the development or prolongation of the symptoms of, the psychiatric illness?

If the claimant passed this test, she would be entitled to damages for the consequences, which were a natural result of the more acute condition. It was open to the judge, however, to find that, on the facts, the accident did not cause the break-up in the claimant's relationship and her failure to have a family. There were grounds to conclude that these would have happened in any event. Since the judge clearly found against her on the issue of causation, his error on the issue of forseeability made no difference to the outcome of the appeal.

4.6.4 Employees

Although there is now a line of cases developing in which employees are claiming damages for psychiatric injury on the basis that employers have a duty to provide counselling to those of their employees who have been affected by accidents or other traumatic situations, the law on this matter is still not clear. It appears that the person concerned need not even be an employee for a duty to provide counselling to arise. In *Leach v Chief Constable of Gloucestershire* (1999), the Court of Appeal found that a voluntary worker who had acted as an 'appropriate adult' during police interviews with Fred West was not owed a duty of care by the police. It was held that there was nothing in Code C of the Police and Criminal Evidence Act 1984 which imposed a duty of care on the police in relation to voluntary workers, even though the claimant in this case had been locked in a cell on numerous occasions, alone with Fred West, who admitted in her presence to having committed many horrifying acts of depravity and murder. Her claim for damages, based on her contention that the police owed her a duty of care to protect her from physical or psychological harm in her capacity as an 'appropriate adult', was struck out. However, the case was allowed to proceed to trial on the issue of failure to provide counselling services.

4.6.5 Sudden shock or slow appreciation

It has emerged that there will only be liability if shock was sudden rather than the gradual appreciation by a secondary victim of a horrifying event, as in *Sion v Hampstead HA* (1994), in which the claimant's psychiatric illness was the result of a continuous process of attending intensive care and realising that medical negligence could have caused the victim's injuries. Peter Gibson LJ said:

A psychiatric illness caused not by a sudden shock but by an accumulation of more gradual assaults on the nervous system over a period of time is not enough.

In the case of primary victims, the slow appreciation over a long period of time of the possibility of having been infected by a frightening illness is sufficient. In the CJD litigation, *Andrews and Others v Secretary of State for Health* (1998), Morland J decided that a claimant could recover compensation, whether he or she was a person of normal phlegm and ordinary fortitude or one with a vulnerable personality, as long as he or she could prove that his or her psychiatric illness was caused by his or her becoming aware of the risk that he or she might already be infected with CJD, and that he or she suffered a genuine psychiatric illness. In a further CJD case, *Schedule 2 Claimants v Medical Research Council and Secretary of State for Health* (1998), Morland J held that, in the CJD cases, there was no reason why foreseeability of shock and psychiatric injury should be limited to an period of time contemporaneous with, or almost contemporaneous with, the negligent event. If the psychiatric injury was foreseeable, it should be untrammelled by spatial, physical or temporal limits.

The policy issues which emerged from the *Alcock* case were restated in *Sion v Hampstead HA* (1994) by Staughton LJ:

> It is ... recognised almost universally that the common law ought to impose some limit on the circumstances in which a person can recover damages for the negligence of another. The common law has to choose a frontier between those whose claims succeed and those who fail. Even the resources of insurance companies are finite, although some jurists are slow to accept that. For the present, the frontier for one type of claim is authoritatively and conclusively fixed by the House of Lords (in the *Alcock* case).

4.6.6   A summary of developments since *Alcock*

Since the *Alcock* case, most of the litigation involving psychiatric injury has turned on two matters: (1) the nature of the illness suffered, that is, whether the symptoms amount to a serious psychiatric illness; and (2) causation. These developments are discussed in detail in the light of the new law.

* The nature of the psychiatric illness

  It has always been the case that no one will succeed in a claim for nervous shock unless the trauma which is suffered leads to a serious illness (see 4.1). Mere shock or temporary grief will not be enough. As Lord Bridge said in *Alcock*:

  > The first hurdle which a claimant must surmount is to establish that he is suffering not merely grief, distress or any other normal emotion but a positive psychiatric illness.

Thus, in *Reilly v Merseyside RHA* (1994), there was no liability on the part of the defendants when a husband and wife were trapped in a lift on a visit to a hospital to see their new grandson. Both suffered claustrophobia, and the husband, who had angina, thought he would choke, later had difficulty walking up to the ward and suffered chest pains and insomnia for a while afterwards. The wife, who already suffered from claustrophobia, was very distressed by the event and had difficulty breathing until they were released from the lift. She also had problems with insomnia afterwards. Although the defendants admitted that they had not maintained the lift properly, the Court of Appeal held that the unpleasant feelings which were suffered by the claimants amounted to no more than ordinary human emotions, and they had not established an identifiable psychiatric illness.

By contrast, in *Tredget v Bexley HA* (1995), a couple who had experienced great distress as a result of the frightening circumstances surrounding the death of their newly delivered baby, were able to prove serious psychiatric illness and were awarded damages.

There are some primary victims who develop symptoms of psychiatric injury over a long period of time. A claim may well fail for limitations reasons if the claimant does not begin proceedings until after a long period of time has elapsed (*Crocker v British Coal Corpn* (1995)), which involved a claim brought by a victim of the 1966 Aberfan disaster. Similar problems can also arise in the cases of individuals who have suffered physical or sexual abuse as children.

A distinction has been drawn between PTSD which is regarded as an actionable psychiatric condition, and pathological grief disorder, which is not always linked causally to a traumatic event. In *Calscione v Dixon* (1993), the claimant was the mother of a 20 year old who had died of injuries which he had sustained in an accident on his motorbike. The defendant admitted negligent driving, but denied liability for *all* the alleged psychiatric illness suffered by the claimant. The nature of the claimant's psychiatric conditions was explored in an effort to decide what was recoverable, and the case turned ultimately on causation. Part of the claim failed because she could not prove a direct causal connection between her symptoms and the accident. The Court of Appeal held that she had suffered some PTSD, but her more serious symptoms were attributable to events which had occurred after her son's death, including an inquest and a private prosecution which she had brought against the defendant. It was held that the trial judge had been correct to separate PTSD and pathological grief disorder.

In *Vernon v Bosely* (1996), however, the Court of Appeal was of the view that damages are recoverable for nervous shock which is partly attributable to pathological consequences of grief and bereavement. In this case, the claimant had witnessed his children drowning in a car negligently driven into a river by their nanny. The defendants accepted that he fell within the categories of people entitled to claim according to the *Alcock* case. However, they contended that he did not suffer from PTSD as opposed to pathological grief disorder which he would have suffered even if he had not been present at the scene and witnessed the events in person. The claimant had a somewhat 'egg-shell' personality and had not made a success of his life. He had bought a failing business which was doomed to flounder for economic reasons, but after the accident his failure to cope with everyday matters meant that the business failed more quickly and his marriage broke up. The Court of Appeal found that damages were recoverable for nervous shock notwithstanding that the illness might also have been considered to be a pathological consequence of the grief and bereavement. It was not necessary therefore to research the various minute permutations of psychiatric medicine to discover which part of the damage was attributable to the traumatic event and which to bereavement.

- Causation and remoteness of damage

  It may be difficult to prove causation if many years have elapsed since the event which caused the psychiatric trauma. Even if the limitation rules (see 20.10) are satisfied, the claimant has the task of proving on a balance of probabilities that the event caused the psychiatric illness which developed later. A study by the Institute of Psychiatry concludes that children who witness disasters are more likely to suffer from depression and to harbour suicidal thoughts as adults than their peers. Of course, anyone who is actually present and part of a disaster as it happens (a 'primary victim') would not have as much difficulty establishing causation as a person who despite falling within the *Alcock* limitations was not actually part of the event. It was reported in March 1996 that a seaman who had been assisting in the recovery of bodies after the Zeebrugge ferry disaster and who was suffering from PTSD, some nine years after the tragic event was seeking leave of the court to sue his employers because the claim was outside the limitation period. He had not brought the action before because he had not realised that he was suffering from a recognised medical condition and had not sought medical advice. In the intervening years, he had suffered many flashbacks of the traumatic events and taken to drink. His marriage had broken up and he was no longer able to work because of his illness.

  If the claimant is a primary victim, and already has a pre-disposition towards psychiatric problems, this is no reason for a court to deny a remedy. In these 'egg-shell personality' cases, the claimant will succeed if it can be proved that some kind of psychiatric injury was foreseeable, but the exact form of illness suffered by the claimant need not be foreseen. In *Page v Smith* (1996), the claimant had a history of myalgic encephalomyelitis (ME) and had been unable to sustain satisfactory long term employment for many years, though he had been recovering quite well from a bout of the illness immediately before the accident. After a frightening, though relatively minor, car accident, his medical condition deteriorated and the ME was exacerbated. The condition became chronic and he would never be able to work again. The House of Lords applied the thin skull rule. It was held that if a driver was negligent and caused an accident, he would be liable for nervous shock to a primary victim of the accident (that is, someone actually involved in the accident which he had caused) if personal injury, whether physical or psychiatric, of some kind was foreseeable. It was irrelevant that the defendant could not reasonably have foreseen that the claimant had an egg-shell personality (a pre-existing tendency towards psychiatric problems). Lord Browne-Wilkinson said:

> Any driver of a car should reasonably foresee that if he drives carelessly he will be liable to cause injury. In the present case, the defendant could not foresee the exact type of psychiatric damage ... The claimant had an egg-shell personality, but that is of no significance ... Once a duty is established, the defendant must take the claimant as he finds him.

Lord Lloyd, while agreeing with this view, thought, on the basis of reasoning in the earlier cases such as *Bourhill v Young* (1943) (see 4.2.3 above), that there would only be liability to secondary victims (that is, people not actually involved in the accident) if psychiatric injury would have been foreseeable in a person of normal fortitude in the circumstances.

The principles of remoteness of damage and the 'egg-shell' concept are explained in Chapter 7. These matters are usually considered after it has been established that a duty of care exists and that there has been a breach of that duty. For the sake of completeness, they are being dealt with here in the main body of the discussion on nervous shock. Refresh your memory on these nervous shock cases when you read the chapter dealing with causation and remoteness of damage.

If the claimant suffers psychiatric illness as a result of some cause other than a sudden traumatic event (for example, work stress), there may also be liability at common law, providing damage of that type was foreseeable and the claimant is a primary victim.

There is still considerable interest in the way in which the law in this area is developing and the Law Commission produced an extensive review and report on the subject in 1998.

4.7   The Law Commission Report

Law Commission Report No 249, *Liability for Psychiatric Illness*, which was based on wide ranging consultation, recommended legislation to remove what the Commission concluded were unwarranted restrictions on liability for negligently inflicted psychiatric illness. The main recommendation was that restrictions based on the physical and temporal proximity of the claimant to the accident and on the means by which the claimant came to learn of the accident should be removed. The Report also recommended that two other restrictions should also be removed – the requirement that the illness must be caused by a shock, and the requirement that the illness must not be the result of death, injury or danger to the defendant him or herself. However, the Law Commission recommended that the restriction based on a tie of love an affection between the accident victim should remain.

The Law Commission produced a draft Bill to deal with the recommended changes in the law. In *Hunter v British Coal Corpn* (1998), Brook LJ, in the Court of Appeal, referred to the Law Commission's recommendations and concluded that, as the matter was so 'policy charged', it would not be the proper function of the courts to 'don a legislative mantle in this controversial field again', though, if that were to be done, it would be a matter for the House of Lords and not the Court of Appeal.

Although the House of Lords has subsequently considered the question of psychiatric injury in *White v Chief Constable of South Yorkshire* (1999) (see above, 4.6.2), the opportunity was not taken to remove the restrictions placed on the liability in *Alcock v Chief Constable of South Yorkshire* (1991). It seems that it is now for Parliament to find time in its busy legislative programme to deal with the issues in the Law Commission Report, if it is considered necessary to change the law on liability for negligently inflicted psychiatric illness.

4.8 The future of psychiatric injury claims – a developing area of law

The case of *W v Essex CC and Another* (2000) gives some indication that the House of Lords is now prepared to contemplate extending the scope of the duty of care in special circumstances and that the law in this area is still developing. It is useful to consider this case in detail. The claimants were appointed specialist adolescent foster carers by the defendant council and they had explained, when they were approved by the council, that they were unwilling to accept any child who was known to be, or was suspected of being, a sexual abuser. However, despite that stipulation, the council placed with them 15 year old boy, G, who had admitted to and had been cautioned by the police for an indecent assault on his own sister and who was being investigated for an alleged rape. The claimants were not told that this was the case, even though these facts were recorded on the council's files and were known to the social worker concerned. Serious acts of sexual abuse against the claimants' children (who were also claiming against the council) were alleged to have been committed between 7 April and 7 May 1993, after the boy had arrived at the foster home. It was alleged that, because of the abuse, both parents and children suffered injury. The parents' claim was for psychiatric injury.

The council and the social worker who placed the boy applied to strike out the claims and, at first instance, the court struck out all the claims made by the parents, but refused to strike out the claims by the children. In 1998, the Court of Appeal upheld the judge's order in respect of the children's claim in negligence and unanimously upheld the order in respect of the parents' claim in negligence. By the time of the hearing, the defendants accepted that the claim by the children should proceed. The parents before the House of Lords argued that the claim for their own injury should also proceed to trial. They contended that the defendants were negligent in placing a known sexual abuser in their home when they knew of G's history and of the parents' anxiety not to have a sex abuser in their home with four young children. When they discovered the serious acts of sexual abuse on their children, including anal and vaginal penetration and oral sex, the claimants suffered psychiatric illness and damage, including severe depression and post-traumatic stress disorder.

Lord Slynn explained that the power to strike cases out before they come to a full trial is one which must be exercised cautiously, but that it would not be necessary to prove at this stage that the parents' claim would definitely succeed if the case came to trial. He referred to *X (Minors) v Bedfordshire CC* (1995), where the question was whether a duty of care arose in child abuse cases, as well as special educational needs cases.

In *W v Essex CC and Another* (2000), Lord Slynn ruled that there was an arguable case. The parents had made it clear that they were anxious not to put their children at risk by having a known sex abuser in their home. The council and the social worker knew this and also knew that the boy concerned had already committed acts of sex abuse. The risk was obvious and the abuse actually happened.

The defendants had submitted that, where it is accepted that damages may lie for psychiatric injury, the law recognises a distinction between 'primary victims' and 'secondary victims'. The former are those who were involved in the event causing the psychiatric injury, 'mediately or immediately as participants' (*Alcock v Chief Constable of South Yorkshire* (1991)). They also argued that only if the parents were within the range of foreseeable physical injury were they primary victims, and, if such physical injury had been foreseeable, then a claim might lie for psychiatric injury, even if it was not itself foreseeable (*Page v Smith* (1996)). The defence contended that the parents were not 'participants' in this sense in the injury to their children, nor was it foreseeable that, if G was placed with the family, the parents would suffer physical injury. On that basis, the parents were only secondary victims; thus, the risk of psychiatric injury to them must be foreseeable in persons of normal fortitude in order for them to be compensated for psychiatric injury . In addition, there must be a sufficiently proximate relationship with the person causing physical harm to that other. Here, the parents had the necessary ties of love for their children, but the defence argued strongly that they were neither near enough in time or space to the acts of abuse, nor did they have direct visual or oral perception of the incident or its aftermath. The parents only knew about the incidents after they had happened.

The defendants also rejected any suggestion that the parents could claim to be entitled to damages on the ground that they felt that they had participated in, contributed to or laid the foundation for the commission of the acts of abuse on their children by arranging for G to be brought into their home.

Lord Slynn pointed out that there have been important developments in the law concerning liability for psychiatric injury which indicate beyond doubt that it can constitute a head of damage.

In his Lordship's opinion, it was important in the present case to bear in mind all of the policy factors, together with the limitations recognised in *Alcock*. However, Lord Slynn said that it is right to recall that, in *McLoughlin v O'Brien* (1983), Lord Scarman recognised the need for flexibility in dealing with new situations not clearly covered by existing case law, and that, in *Page v Smith* (1996), Lord Lloyd said that, once it is accepted that a defendant could foresee that his or her conduct would expose the claimant to personal injury, 'there is no justification for regarding physical and psychiatric injury as different "kinds of damage"'.

In the present case, the House of Lords considered that it was impossible to say that the psychiatric injury claimed was outside the range of psychiatric injury which the law recognises as deserving of compensation. It certainly amounted, on the face of it, to more than 'acute grief'. The parents' previously happy marriage had broken up, and both had suffered reactive depression and could no longer act as foster parents. Their sex lives had been ruined. The effect on the family had, allegedly, been devastating.

However, this was only the beginning of the claim. The question of whether the parents were primary of secondary victims was not absolutely clear, and the issue of the categorisation of those claiming to be included as primary or secondary victims is not finally closed. It is, in Lord Slynn's view, a concept still to be developed in different factual situations. If the psychiatric injury suffered by the parents flows from a feeling that they brought the abuser and the abused together, or that they have a feeling of responsibility that they did not detect earlier what was happening, that does not necessarily prevent them from being primary victims. Indeed, in *Alcock* (1991), Lord Oliver said:

> The fact that the defendant's negligent conduct has foreseeably put the claimant in the position of being an unwilling participant in the event establishes of itself a sufficiently proximate relationship between them and the principal question is whether, in the circumstances, injury of that type to that claimant was or was not reasonably foreseeable.

Whilst there has to be some temporal and spatial limitation on the persons who can claim to be secondary victims, the concept of 'the immediate aftermath' of the incident has to be assessed in the particular factual situation. It might well be that, if the matter were investigated in depth, a judge would think that the temporal and spatial limitations were not satisfied. On the other hand, he might find that the flexibility to which Lord Scarman referred indicated that they were. *W v Essex CC and Another* (2000) was far from being a clear cut case, and it did not justify being struck out. The House of Lords unanimously dismissed the appeal.

It is important to recognise, as Lord Slynn observed, that the law concerning psychiatric injury is still a developing area of law, in which the courts must proceed incrementally (*Caparo Industries plc v Dickman* (1990)).

W v Essex CC and Another is a case which suggests that there is considerable scope for clarifying and even developing the law. There are several matters in relation to psychiatric injury which require clarification, and this claim highlights some of them. They include: the exact scope of the category of 'primary victims'; the extent of the limitations as to time and space placed on claims of secondary victims; whether it is possible to include in the category of those entitled to succeed, individuals who believe that they have failed in their responsibility to primary victims; and the justification for distinguishing between foresight of physical and psychiatric injury. The trial of this case on its facts is awaited with interest.

4.8.1 'Bullying' claims

Recent developments suggest that employees who suffer psychiatric injury as a result of being bullied at work may be awarded damages in civil claims against their employers. In order to succeed it would be necessary to prove that the employer knew of the employee's tendency to psychiatric illness and took no steps to help (*Walker v Northumberland County Council* (1994)). There are several cases pending involving teachers who claim that they have been bullied by colleagues. It has also been suggested that head teachers who take no steps to deal with bullying of students by other pupils may face claims (*The Times*, 9 August 2000). (See 14.2.5).

DUTY OF CARE – PSYCHIATRIC INJURY

Development of the law

The development of the duty of care in relation to 'nervous shock' or psychiatric injury is an illustration of the approach of the judges to one of the 'grey areas' of liability for negligence.

Note the medical definition and the way in which the law has developed with better understanding of the problems of psychiatric injury by the medical profession.

Originally, there was no duty in relation to nervous shock (*Victorian Railway Comrs v Coultas* (1888)).

The duty was first recognised, subject to the limitation that the claimant was required to experience fear for his or her own safety in *Dulieu v White* (1901).

Duty was expanded to encompass fear for other people and includes:

- Relatives: *Hambrook v Stokes* (1925);

- Dead relatives: *Owens v Liverpool Corpn* (1933);

- Workmates: *Dooley v Cammel Laird* (1951). But see *Hunter v British Coal* (1998).

- Rescuers: *Chadwick v British Railways Board* (1968); *Wigg v British Railways Board* (1986); *Hale v London Underground* (1992); *Frost v Chief Constable South Yorkshire* (1996); but see *White v Chief Constable of South Yorkshire* (1999).

- Property damage: *Attia v British Gas* (1987).

Judicial reservations about psychiatric injury

Reservations about claims for nervous shock continued to exist. Reasons for these were discussed in detail in *McLoughlin v O'Brian* (1981), an explicit policy decision, but before that reservations were not openly considered by the judges, so a number of rationalisations were made:

- The claimant was not a person of normal fortitude: *Bourhill v Young* (1943); *Brice v Brown* (1984);

- The claimant was outside the geographical area of foresight: *Bourhill v Young* (1943);

- The claimant was unforeseeable: *King v Phillips* (1952);

- The claimant did not come upon the immediate aftermath of the accident: *McLoughlin v O'Brian* (1981); *Alcock v Chief Constable of South Yorkshire* (1991);

- There was no proof that nervous shock was actually suffered: *Hicks v Chief Constable of South Yorkshire* (1992).

Expansion of liability for psychiatric injury

The two-stage test of Lord Wilberforce was applied in *McLoughlin v O'Brian* (1991). There was proximity based on foresight, and there were no policy reasons in this case for restricting the scope of the duty of care.

The claimant does not need to be present at the scene, provided he or she sees the victims in the immediate aftermath of the accident (in this case, one hour later). Possible reasons for the judges' reservations about awarding damages for psychiatric injury are:

- fear that claims may be faked;

- fear of a flood of claims;

- fear of injustice to defendants and their insurers if large awards of damages are to be payable;

- Parliament, not the courts, should decide major issues which are likely to expand the law and create new areas of liability.

Contraction of liability for psychiatric injury

In *Alcock v Chief Constable of South Yorkshire* (1991), claims for nervous shock by relatives and friends of victims of the Hillsborough Stadium disaster failed. The limits of the scope of the duty of care in relation to nervous shock were spelled out.

In determining whether a duty of care is owed for psychiatric injury, the concept of 'proximity' now has a very prominent role.

Future successful claims

In future, in order to succeed in a claim for nervous shock, the claimant must prove one or more of the following:

- presence at the scene and part of the accident with or without suffering physical injury himself: *Page v Smith* (1996);

- a close tie of love and affection with the victim and presence at the scene or in the immediate aftermath (not more than two hours);

- he was a member of the rescue services – but note developments in recent cases;

- a close tie and close-up shots of the victim on TV (action against the broadcasting company);

- *possibly*, a close tie and sight of a catastrophic event involving the victim on TV.

Recent claims have turned on the nature of psychiatric illness, causation and remoteness of damage and the concepts of primary and secondary victims.

There must be a sudden shock not a gradual awareness:

- *Reilly v Merseyside HA* (1994): no psychiatric illness;

- *Tredget v Bexley HA* (1995): psychiatric illness suffered;

  But see *Group B Plaintiffs v MRC* (1998).

- Causation problems: *Page v Smith* (1995); *Vernon v Bosely* (1996); *Calscione v Dixon* (1993);

- Primary and secondary victims: *Page v Smith* (1996); *Frost v Chief Constable of South Yorkshire*; *Duncan v British Coal* (1996); *White v Chief Constable of South Yorkshire* (1999).

The Law Commission's recommendations

Law Commission Report No 249 recommended legislation to remove 'unwarranted restrictions' on liability for psychiatric injury.

The Report recommended that restrictions based on proximity in time and space between secondary victims and primary victims be removed. However, it recommended that the restriction requiring a tie of love and affection between secondary victims and accident victims should remain.

The future

Cases will continue to be considered on their own special facts within the framework established by *Alcock v Chief Constable of South Yorkshire* (1991). There may still be scope for developing the law (*W v Essex CC and Another* (2000)).

NERVOUS SHOCK CASES

Name	Relationship with victim	Present at scene	Immediate aftermath	Present at other times	Damages awarded
Victorian Rly Comrs v Coultas (1888)	Self	Yes			No
Dulieu v White (1901)	Self	Yes			Yes
Hambrook v Stokes (1925)	Mother of children in danger	No		Just before accident	Yes
Owens v Liverpool Corpn (1933)	Corpse	Yes			Yes
Bourhill v Young (1943)	None		Yes		No
Chadwick v BRB (1968)	Rescuer		Yes	Out of sight but within earshot	Yes
Hale v London Underground (1992)	Rescuer	Yes	Yes		Yes
Wigg v BR (1986)	Rescuer	Yes			Yes
Dooley v Cammel Laird (1951)	Workmate	Yes			Yes
McLoughlin v O'Brian (1982)	Husband and children	No	Yes		Yes
Jaensch v Coffey (1984)	Wife		Yes		Yes
Kralj v McGrath (1986)	Mother of damaged baby	Yes			Yes
Alcock v Chief Constable of South Yorkshire Police (1991)	Fiancé	No		Several hours later	No
	Brothers in law, etc		No		No
	Brother			8 hours later	No
Taylor v Somerset AHA (1993)	Wife	No	No	Within 1 hour	No

Summary: Duty of Care – Psychiatric Injury

Name	Relationship with victim	Present at scene	Immediate aftermath	Present at other times	Damages awarded
Palmer v Tees HA (1998)	Mother	No	No	After 3 days	No
Chief Constable of West Yorkshire v Schofield (1993)	None	Yes	N/A	N/A	Yes
Reilly v Merseyside RHA (1994)	Self	Yes	N/A	N/A	No
Tredget v Bexley HA (1995)	Self	Yes	N/A	N/A	Yes
Vernon v Bosely (1996)	Father	Yes	N/A	N/A	Yes
Page v Smith (1996)	Self (primary victim)	Yes	N/A	N/A	Yes
Sion v Hampstead HA (1994)	Parents	Yes	Yes	N/A	No
Piggott v London Underground (1995)	Rescuers	Yes	Yes	N/A	Yes
Robertson v Forth Road Bridge (1994)	Workmate (secondary victim)	Yes	N/A	N/A	No
McFarlane v EE Caledonia (1994)	Bystander helping rescue (secondary victim)	Yes	N/A	N/A	No
Frost v Chief Constable of South Yorkshire (1996)	One rescuer who was a primary victims	Yes	Yes	No	Yes
White v Chief Constable of South Yorkshire (1999)	Rescuers who were secondary victims	No	Yes	No	No
Duncan v British Coal (1996)	Workmate (secondary victim)	No	Yes	No	No
Young v Charles Church (1996)	Workmate (secondary victim)	Yes, as bystander	Yes	No	Yes. Br of stat duty
Hunter v British Coal (1998)	Workmate	Close by, not present	Yes	Just before accident	No

Name	Relationship with victim	Present at scene	Immediate aftermath	Present at other times	Damages awarded
Leach v CC Gloucestershire (1999)	Appropriate adult	Present during police interview	N/A	No	Case proceeding to trial
Gibblett PC v Murray (1999)	Self	Yes	Yes	N/A	Yes, but not for nervous shock
Group B Plaintiffs v MRC (1998)	Self	Yes	N/A	N/A	Yes

CHAPTER 5

DUTY OF CARE – ECONOMIC LOSS

The second 'grey' area in which the scope of duty of care in negligence has been difficult to define with certainty is that relating to economic loss. The object of this chapter is to explore the limits of liability in this area.

The law of contract has no difficulty in compensating economic losses. Tort, although it has been prepared to compensate the victims of fraudulently occasioned losses, through the tort of deceit, has had considerable problems about compensating financial losses caused by negligence. The judges have been concerned about the opening of the floodgates to a proliferation of claims. There is a fear that the consequences of financial loss might spread too rapidly and be experienced too widely. There are other policy reasons why there has been reluctance to create too wide an ambit of liability for economic loss. These include the notion that economic losses are less likely to be foreseeable than physical losses, and the idea that people should expect to lose money if they 'gamble' with it in the hope of making a substantial gain, an argument regularly produced in relation to the legal actions by Lloyd's 'names'. Some people also believe that economic loss is less deserving of compensation than personal injuries. This has meant that the development of the law has been dependent upon various trends in social policy and judicial attitudes, and some of the cases are difficult to reconcile in consequence. The law is often illogical and decisions appear to have been made on an arbitrary *ad hoc* basis.

5.1   Economic loss caused by careless statements

The clearest picture of emerging liability for economic loss in tort lies in the field of negligent misstatement.

5.1.1   Statements made by the defendant

In *Candler v Crane, Christmas & Co* (1951), the Court of Appeal held that no duty of care arose in tort in relation to careless advice given by accountants in preparing a company's accounts which they knew would be relied upon by third parties (the claimants). Denning LJ, in a famous dissenting judgment, argued that the defendants did owe a duty of care to their employer or client 'and any third person to whom they themselves show the accounts so as to induce them to invest money or take some other action upon them'.

This view was later proved correct when the House of Lords were prepared to extend the ambit of the duty of care in this area in the landmark case of *Hedley Byrne v Heller & Partners Ltd* (1964). The appellants in that case were advertising agents who were worried about the financial status of one of their clients, E Ltd. The appellants' bankers asked E's bankers, who became the respondents in this case, about the financial position of E Ltd. The letter sent in reply by the respondents said that E was 'a respectably constituted company, considered good for its ordinary business engagements. Your figures are larger than we are accustomed to see'. Acting in reliance on this statement the appellants lost a substantial sum of money when E Ltd went into liquidation. The respondents were protected by a disclaimer with which they had prefaced their statement, but the House of Lords held that if it had not been for the disclaimer, a duty of care would have been owed to the appellants in the circumstances. The House of Lords gave some indication of the circumstances when such a duty of care will arise. These are discussed below.

5.1.2   The special relationship

There must be reasonable reliance within a 'special relationship between the parties'. The exact meaning of the special relationship was not fully explained in *Hedley Byrne,* and this left scope for the judges in later cases to use the notion of 'special relationship' as a device for the development of judicial policy. From the later decisions, it emerged that, at first, the special relationship was treated in rather narrow terms, as a relationship in which the person giving the advice was in the business, or represented that he was in the business, of giving advice of the particular kind that was sought.

Later, in a dissenting judgment in *Mutual Life Assurance Co v Evatt* (1971), it was suggested that the special relationship could include any business or professional relationship. This view was approved at first instance in *Esso Petroleum Co Ltd v Mardon* (1976), but on appeal the case was decided in contract rather than tort, so the position remained unclear. However, it was clarified in *Howard Marine and Dredging Co Ltd v Ogden & Sons Ltd* (1978), and it can now be stated with confidence that in any business or professional relationship there is potential for the special relationship to exist.

Social relationships are still excluded, however, unless the circumstances make it clear that carefully considered advice was being sought. In *Chaudhry v Prabhakar* (1988), the claimant asked a friend to help her to find a second hand car. She specifically explained that she did not want to buy a car which had been involved in an accident. The defendant found her a car which he recommended that she should buy but, in the event, it was discovered that the car had been involved in a serious accident, and was unroadworthy. The defendant was liable even though he was not a qualified mechanic, but the Court of Appeal made it clear that this was an unusual case which turned upon its own special facts, and did not establish a general rule of liability in all such cases.

5.1.3 Reliance

There must be reliance by one party upon the advice of the other. In *Lambert v West Devon BC* (1997), a local authority was liable when the claimant had relied on their advice that he could begin building even though planning permission had not yet been approved. If the statement which was made did not influence the claimant's judgment, then it cannot be the basis of a negligence action.

Therefore, in *Jones v Wright* (1994), the claimant's claim was struck out as disclosing no cause of action when they could not establish that they had relied on an audit carried out by the defendants. The claimants were investors whose money was held on trust by a company which had been audited by the defendants. They alleged that the auditors should have discovered that there had been misuse of trust monies. It was decided that the mere fact that there was a relationship of trust between the investors and the company did not place a duty of care on the auditors of the company, and not only had there never been an assumption of a duty to the investors, neither had there been any reliance on them. If the 'just and reasonable' test was applied, there could be no finding that a duty of care was owed.

In *Goodwill v British Pregnancy Advisory Service* (1996), the Court of Appeal held that, in order to succeed in a claim for financial loss occasioned by negligence, the claimant has to prove that the defendant knew or ought to have known that the advice was likely to be acted upon without independent inquiry by the claimant.

5.1.4 Reliance must be reasonable

The claimant's reliance on the defendant's statements must be reasonable in all the circumstances. Like the notion of 'special relationship', that of 'reasonable reliance' has been seized upon and used by the judges as a device for implementing policy. The person relied upon must have known, or have been in such a position as to be reasonably expected to have known, that the other party was relying on the statement, and the reliance must have been reasonable. In *Caparo Industries v Dickman* (1990), Lord Oliver stated that the person giving the advice must have known by inference that the statement would be received by the claimant or class of persons to which the claimant belonged, and acted upon without further independent advice being sought.

In *Yianni v Edwin Evans* (1982), a prospective purchaser relied upon advice given by a surveyor to the building society from which he was seeking a mortgage. The building society had required payment of a fee by the prospective purchaser in the usual way, so that it could instruct the surveyor to value the property to ensure that it was worth the amount which they were prepared to lend. The building society even informed the purchaser in writing that he should instruct his own independent surveyor, but he did not do this. Evidence was produced to the effect that only 15% of private house purchasers have a separate independent survey before purchase, and the court concluded that it was reasonable for the purchaser to rely on the building society survey if the building society was happy to do so. It transpired that the surveyor was negligent and that considerable expenditure was required to remedy a major defect in the property. The defendant surveyor was liable. A duty of care existed, as the test of reasonably foreseeable reliance was satisfied.

In *Harris v Wyre Forest DC* (1989), a survey had been carried out by a local authority surveyor before the purchase of a property, for which the local authority was providing a mortgage. The purchaser was not permitted to see the survey, but presumed that it must have been favourable because the mortgage went ahead. It was decided that it was foreseeable that the purchaser would rely on the survey, even though there was a clause excluding liability for negligence in the surveying process. The insertion of an exclusion clause was not reasonable under the Unfair Contract Terms Act 1977, and the defendant local authority was liable to the claimant in negligence.

In *Smith v Eric S Bush* (1990), which the House of Lords heard at the same time as *Harris v Wyre*, it was held that because the surveyor knew that the purchaser was relying on his survey, a duty of care was owed. Lord Griffiths said:

> It should only be in cases where the advisor knows that there is a high degree of probability that some other identifiable person (than the immediate recipient of the advice) will act upon the advice that a duty of care should be imposed.

This was the case here and, moreover, the size of the purchase price was relatively small when compared with the cost to the purchaser of commissioning an independent survey. This approach favours private purchasers rather than large commercial concerns, and this same approach has been adopted in later cases, particularly where a commercial firm is involved in the same kind of business as that about which advice is sought.

5.1.5 Discharging the duty

A case in which a surveyor did succeed in escaping liability was *Eley v Chasemore* (1989). The surveyor in this case had undertaken a full structural survey but had not advised the claimant about necessary underpinning. However, he had advised the claimant to insure against 'ground-heave, settlement and landslip'. It was held that he did owe a duty of care but that he had discharged it by advising on insurance.

5.1.6   A 'case by case' approach

There have been a large number of cases involving accountants in recent years, perhaps as a result of the so called 'boom years' of the property and financial markets in the 1980s. The most significant of these is probably *Caparo Industries plc v Dickman* (1990). This case provided the House of Lords with an opportunity to restate the principles involved in the notions of 'special relationship' and 'reasonable reliance'. It concerned a public company whose accounts the appellants had audited as required by the Companies Act 1985. The respondents, who already owned shares in the company, purchased more shares and made a successful takeover bid for the company. When the appellants suffered a considerable loss as a result of the takeover, they complained that the accounts had been negligently prepared by the respondents. The case turned upon the question as to whether the appellants owed a duty of care to the respondents. The House of Lords decided that a limited duty of care is owed to shareholders by a company's auditors. No duty was owed to individual members of the company in relation to decisions as to whether to purchase further shares. The duty only existed in relation to the control that shareholders are required to have over the affairs of the company, for which they need details of its accounts. Therefore, there was no liability for the loss incurred by the appellants in this case. No duty of care was owed to them in that respect. The principle applies to existing shareholders, prospective shareholders and institutional lenders who suffer financial losses as a result of inaccurate statements in negligently prepared accounts. The House of Lords treated as crucial the purpose for which the statement was made. Unlike the statement in *Smith v Bush* (1990), the statement in *Caparo* was unconnected with the purpose for which it was relied upon.

5.1.7   Summary of *Caparo v Dickman*

The House of Lords favoured a 'case by case' approach to the question of duty of care, based on directly relevant existing authorities, and rejected a general test of liability based on reasonable foresight in these kinds of cases.

A summary of Lord Oliver's explanation of the current state of the law is that a relationship is required before the duty of care can exist and:

* the advice must be required for a purpose, either specified in detail or described in general terms;

* the purpose must be made known, either actually or inferentially, to the advisor at the time the advice is given;

* the advisor must know, either actually or inferentially, that the advice will be communicated to the advisee, either as a specific individual or as a

member of an ascertainable class in order that it should be used by the advisee for the known purpose;

- it must be known, either actually or inferentially, that the advice will probably be acted upon for that purpose without independent advice or inquiry;

- the advice must be so acted upon to the detriment of the advisee.

His Lordship concludes:

> That is not to suggest that these conditions are either conclusive or exclusive, but merely that the actual decision in the case does not warrant any broader propositions.

The law is unlikely to expand now that this much narrower approach is clearly favoured by the House of Lords. The new approach is the result of a change in policy, and is the reaction to the expansion in the law which was made possible after the liberating effect of Lord Wilberforce's two-stage test in *Anns v Merton BC* in 1978. The underlying fear is of the opening of the floodgates to a rush of claims, or liability 'in an indeterminate amount for an indeterminate time to an indeterminate class' as it was expressed in *Ultramares Corpn v Touche* (1931) by Cardozo LJ.

In future, companies will need to make their own independent inquiries and will not be able to rely on annual accounts to help them to arrive at their decisions on the financial viability of other concerns which they intend to take over.

5.1.8 Further developments

It was inevitable that further cases on this subject would be heard by the courts, because the *Caparo* decision allows the courts to decide what is fair and reasonable in the circumstances of each case. Many advisors might therefore consider it worth fighting cases, particularly as large sums of money are often involved. Consistency will be difficult to achieve in the future.

In 1991, the Court of Appeal heard the case of *James McNaughton Papers Group Ltd v Hicks Anderson & Co*. Neill LJ, who gave the leading judgment, indicated that there are six important considerations in determining whether a duty of care exists in these cases:

- the purpose for which the statement was made;

- the purpose for which the statement was communicated;

- the relationship between the advisor, the recipient of the advice and any third parties;

- the size of the class to which the recipient of the advice belongs;

- the knowledge and experience of the advisee;

- whether the advisee was reasonable to rely on the advice.

It was held that a duty of care was not owed in this case by auditors who had prepared draft accounts for use in negotiations for the takeover of another paper company, MK Papers. The accounts were prepared at the request of MK Papers who initiated the takeover talks. At a subsequent meeting, the defendants admitted that MK Papers were just about breaking even, but later it transpired that they were faring very much worse than that, and that the accounts had been misleading. It was not reasonable for the claimants, who were experienced business people, to rely solely on the draft accounts which had been prepared for MK Papers. They should have taken independent financial advice.

In *Morgan Crucible plc v Hill Samuel Bank Ltd* (1991), the directors and financial advisors of a company (the takeover of which was being considered), made certain statements about the accuracy of financial records and forecasts as required by the City Code. They intended a specific bidder to rely upon these statements. The bidder did so rely, and later alleged that financial loss had been incurred as a result. As the original statement of claim had been drafted before the *Caparo* case, it was based on reasonable foreseeability. Following *Caparo*, it was necessary to amend the statement of claim to the narrower basis of one previously identified bidder. The Court of Appeal held that it was at least arguable that this case was distinguishable from *Caparo* presumably because the identifiable bidder had emerged before specific statements were made about the financial status of the company. Leave was therefore given to amend the statement of claim.

It remains to be seen how far the courts are prepared to continue with this line of cases, given that there is in existence the Fifth European Directive on Harmonisation of Company Law, which states that a duty of care is owed by a company's auditors to third parties in relation to negligent acts which cause financial loss.

Paradoxically, despite the apparent trend *away* from expansion of the ambit of the duty of care relating to pure economic loss, cases decided by the House of Lords since *Caparo v Dickman* (1990) appear to have marked an extension of liability in this area. The case of *Henderson v Merrett Syndicates Ltd* (1994) is very significant and important reading on this subject, as it indicates the view which the House of Lords is taking on the development of the law in this area. As in *White v Jones* (1995) and *Spring v Guardian Assurance* (1994) (see 5.1.9 below), the scope of liability for economic loss was extended in this case. In the *Henderson* case, which arose out of the losses suffered by Lloyds' names, the House of Lords held that Lloyds' underwriting agents owed a duty of care to their names (both to direct and indirect names). The underwriters argued that the position should be governed by the terms of the contracts between the parties and not by the law of tort which favoured the claimants because of the more advantageous limitation periods in tort. In the course of arriving at the decision, the nature of the contract/tort relationship was explored, and the advantages of using one branch of the law rather than the other were considered to be more than merely academic, as very real practical advantages for claimants were offered by tort in this case. Lord Goff brought the case within the *Hedley Byrne* principle and pointed out that this was a classic example of the relationship within which *Hedley Byrne* should apply. One of the main factors of importance in imposing liability in this case was the 'assumption of responsibility' by the defendants. The agents claim to have special skills to give advice as to the risks which are to be underwritten, and assume responsibility for that advice. The names in their turn place reliance on the advice which they receive. In reviewing the *Hedley Byrne* principle, Lord Goff restated the law and recognised that the scope of *Hedley Byrne* extends beyond negligent misstatement, though probably only in non-professional relationships. The decision is underpinned by important policy implications. The problems at Lloyds have generated a large amount of litigation and not everyone believes that the names deserve the protection of the law, given that they were richer than average, and were hoping to become wealthier through what was essentially a gamble with their money. Against that background is the cavalier way in which the names were treated by the underwriters, many of whom were able to make considerable financial gains through their inside knowledge. The principles established in this case were applied by the High Court in *Aiken v Steward Wrightson Members Agency Ltd* (1995), another case arising out of the Lloyds' crisis, and in *NM Rothschild and Sons Ltd v Berensons and Others* (1995).

The important issue of assumption of responsibility which was raised in *Jones v Wright* (1992) and the *Henderson* case prevented the claimants claiming damages in *McCullagh v Lane Fox and Partners Ltd* (1995). The action was brought by the purchasers of a house against an estate agent acting for the seller of the property. Although the purchasers had relied on the negligent statement and had suffered financial loss as a result, they were not entitled to accept that the agent had assumed responsibility for the statement, especially as there was a disclaimer in the sale particulars on which the agent was entitled to rely as, in the circumstances, the Unfair Contract Terms Act 1977 would not prevent him from so doing.

In 1995, the House of Lords again considered some of these issues in *Marc Rich & Co v Bishop Rock Marine* (1995). The case involved the nature of the duty of care which may arise in the surveying of a ship. The House of Lords applied the three-stage test from *Caparo v Dickman* (1990), and commented that it is now settled law that there must be foreseeability and proximity and the elements of justice and fairness must be satisfied in all negligence cases. More significantly, it was stated that with regard to these elements there is no distinction between direct physical damage and indirect physical damage or economic loss. However, in this case, it was held not to be fair, just and reasonable to impose a duty, and this is a good example of the use of the test in *Caparo v Dickman* (1990) as a means of restricting the scope of liability for practical or policy reasons.

The other House of Lords case in which the scope of liability for economic loss was extended was *Spring v Guardian Assurance* (1994) in which it was held by a majority of four to one that an employer owes a duty of care to employees and ex-employees not to cause economic loss by writing careless references. The relationship is one of sufficient proximity, and it is fair, just and reasonable to impose a duty because of the reliance which the employee places on the employer. Here, the claimant's employer had supplied a reference for him which incorrectly stated that he was a man of little integrity and had been involved in selling unsuitable insurance policies to clients. As a result, the employee failed to obtain another job after he had been dismissed by the defendants. As he was unable to prove malice, there would have been a successful defence to libel on the basis of qualified privilege (see Chapter 18). The case was sent back to the Court of Appeal on the causation issues involved but the House of Lords' decision raises a number of important points. For the purposes of this discussion, there are two main issues which deserve particular attention.

- Lord Goff again followed the line that this case fell within the limits of the *Hedley Byrne* case, and considered that the rule was not limited to situations in which advice or information is provided, but that it also extends to other services. This could herald a more sensible approach than the artificial distinction which had previously been drawn between negligent words and negligent acts causing pure economic loss. On this point, Lord Lowry agreed.

- Policy matters and the two-stage test in *Anns v Merton* (1978) (which had been discredited in later cases) were discussed. Lord Keith thought that this case fell within the two-stage test, though it is strange that this test should have been referred to at all as it had been cast aside as inappropriate in so many recent cases (see Chapter 3). However, the majority view was that the case should be decided in the light of the 'just and reasonable' test approved in cases since *Murphy v Brentwood* (1991). There was much discussion of the present state of the employment market and the need for extra vigilance on the part of employers when writing references, though it was considered to be unlikely that an employer would owe a duty of care to the prospective employer receiving the reference.

In the Scottish case of *McFarlane v Tayside Health Board* (1999), the House of Lords took the view that the cost of bringing up a child born after an unsuccessful sterilisation operation was an economic loss. Lord Slynn treated the claim as one which fell into the broad category of economic loss. As such, he thought that it should be handled with caution in the light of the reluctance of the courts to create liability for pure economic loss in the absence of closer links between the act and the damage than were foreseeably provided. His Lordship concluded that it would not be fair, just and reasonable to impose a duty on the doctor or his employer in the circumstances of this case (*Caparo Industries v Dickman* (1990)).

This approach was confirmed in *Rand v East Dorset HA* (2000), where it was admitted that the defendant's negligence had resulted in the wrongful birth of a disabled child. In January 1988, doctors wrongfully failed to inform Mr and Mrs R of the results of a scan which disclosed the likelihood that Mrs R would give birth to a Down's Syndrome baby. It was accepted by the defence that this negligent omission had deprived Mr and Mrs R of the opportunity to terminate the pregnancy and that, if they been given the results, Mrs R would have had an abortion. The parents brought a claim for damages to cover the financial consequences flowing from that negligence. The judge accepted that the claimants could bring a claim based upon the extended principle of *Hedley Byrne* (1963) for the financial consequences flowing from the admitted negligence of the defendant, limited to the consequences of the child's disability. The claim for the cost of maintenance and the cost of care for the child was a claim for pure economic loss, as was the claim for loss of profits of the residential care home that the claimants ran (see Chapter 19).

5.1.9   Statements made by a third party

There are some cases which do not fit neatly into the requirement of reliance within a special relationship. For example, *White v Jones* (1995) rests on principles which make it difficult to reconcile with *Hedley Byrne*. It concerns a will which was made by the father of a family who deliberately cut his daughters out of his will after a quarrel but later became reconciled with them. He instructed his solicitors to change the will in order to give them £9,000 each as previously intended. However, the solicitors did nothing for a month, and the father again told them to amend the will, but they still did nothing and one month later the father died. The daughters succeeded in their action for economic loss against the solicitors in an appeal to the House of Lords, despite the fact that the daughters could not demonstrate that they had relied directly on the solicitors. The decision is rather surprising in the light of the previously restricted interpretation of *Hedley Byrne* in the recent past, though the case of *Ross v Caunters* (1980), in which the facts were similar had also been decided in favour of disappointed beneficiaries. In *White v Jones* (1995), there was sufficient proximity to form the basis of a duty of care.

In *Gibbons v Nelsons* (2000), it was held that a solicitor's duty of care to an intended beneficiary of whom he was unaware was limited. The duty was only owed if the solicitor knew about both the benefit that the testator wanted to confer and the person or class of persons upon whom the benefit was intended to be conferred. Similarly, in *Worby v Rosser* (1999), it was held by the Court of Appeal that a solicitor who is preparing a will is not under any duty of care to inquire whether the testator has capacity to make a will, nor must he or she ascertain whether or not the testator was being unduly influenced.

In *Gorham v British Telecommunications plc* (2000), the Court of Appeal held that, if an insurer owed a duty of care to a customer when advising about pensions and life assurance, it also owed a duty to the customer's dependents, as intended beneficiaries.

It can be concluded that, as far as these rather specialised cases are concerned, there is not necessarily any need to establish 'reliance' within the special relationship.

In *White v Jones* (1995), Lord Goff argued that the usual reason for not allowing recovery for pure economic loss, that of fear of unlimited liability, did not apply here because the loss to the daughters was limited both in amount and in the number of potential claimants.

In *Ministry of Housing and Local Government v Sharp* (1971), a clerk in the land registry had negligently omitted to notice a planning charge and issued a clear certificate. This meant that the Ministry lost compensation to which it would have been entitled when the land was developed. The Court of Appeal held that the employers of the clerk were vicariously liable. The claimant was reasonably foreseeable. This was an extension of *Hedley Byrne* outside the traditional special relationship as the reliance was made by the purchaser in this case, yet a third party, the Ministry, was able to claim because that purchaser's reliance on the statement had resulted in a loss to them.

These cases were distinguished in *Clark v Bruce Lance & Co* (1988). In this case, there was much less proximity between the parties and it is easy to see why the Court of Appeal were not prepared to extend the scope of liability.

The question of whether a duty to third parties existed was further considered in *Possfund Custodian Trustee Ltd v Diamond and Others* (1996). In this case, the issue was whether those responsible for a company's prospectus owed a duty of care to subsequent purchasers of shares. The action was not struck out as there were arguments which could be made relating to proximity and reliance, and the issue as to whom the prospectus was aimed.

It is difficult to reconcile these cases with the *Hedley Byrne* requirements. They can perhaps be explained by the fact that the relationship between the claimants and the defendants is very close, and that only one person could possibly have suffered a loss. The possibility of indeterminate liability to a large number of different potential claimants does not therefore arise. See, also, *Ross v Caunters* (1980) where a lawyer failed to make a valid will for a client who wanted to benefit the claimant.

A more recent case in which these issues were considered by the House of Lords is *Williams v Natural Life Health Foods Ltd* (1998). The second defendant in this case had established a company to franchise various health foods and to run a shop of his own. The claimants, who wanted to obtain a franchise, contacted the company for information. They received a brochure and prospectus, which indicated that the second defendant was experienced and highly successful; relying on this, they proceeded to obtain a franchise. The claimants claimed damages, from both the company and the second defendant, for pure economic loss suffered after their shop failed to make a profit. As the company had gone into liquidation, the proceedings were eventually brought only against the second defendant.

The House of Lords held that the action must fail, on the basis that there was no special relationship between the claimant and the second defendants. At no stage in the negotiations at the pre-contract stage had the claimants had any contact with the second defendant, and there were no personal dealings of a direct or indirect nature between them which could have indicated that the second defendant has assumed any responsibility for the claimants' affairs. They had relied on statements made by the company, but there was no evidence that they had ever relied on the second defendants to take steps to safeguard their position as franchisers. Lord Steyn did, however, state that there is a 'gap-filling' function of the law of tort, and that this arises especially in cases in which the law of contract proves wanting because the rules of privity of contract prevent justice from being done.

5.2   Economic loss caused by negligent acts

Economic loss caused by negligent acts is often difficult to understand because in many of the cases there is an artificial distinction drawn between acts and statements which result in economic loss.

In an article which examines the development and current state of the law in this area in detail, Markesinis and Deakin identify as one of the doctrinal weaknesses of the common law the fact that the courts have attempted to create artificial distinctions between the various kinds of damage in these cases ('The random element of their Lordships' infallible judgment: an economic and comparative analysis of the tort of negligence from *Anns* to *Murphy*' (1992) 55 MLR 619).

Furthermore, the judicial gyrating had led to the almost ridiculous situation that architects and engineers who give negligent advice leading to the construction of shoddy buildings may be liable to the buildings' owners, 'but the builders, whose negligence produces the same result, will not'.

The reason why a distinction developed is perhaps best explained by returning to the decision in *Hedley Byrne*, and examining the way in which the House of Lords in that case attempted to justify their extension of liability. It appeared that, while the judges in that case were prepared to expand the scope of liability for negligent statements causing economic loss, they were reluctant to widen it further to cover negligent words causing economic loss. The reason given was that 'words are more volatile than deeds'.

In later cases involving losses caused by acts, the courts were able to use this view to perpetuate the policy of restricting a rapid expansion of the law.

5.2.1 'Pure' economic loss distinguished from other types of economic loss

A further distinction was made between 'pure economic loss' and economic loss which is consequent upon physical damage to property.

This distinction is illustrated in *Spartan Steel and Alloys v Martin & Co (Contractors) Ltd* (1973). The claimant operated a stainless steel factory on a small industrial estate, and the defendant's employees negligently cut off the electricity supply to the factory by damaging a cable when they were digging up the road. The claimants claimed damages for the 'melt' which was currently in the machinery, for physical damage to the machinery itself, and for the loss of profit on four further melts which could not be carried out until the machinery was operational again. The Court of Appeal allowed the claim for the damage to the melt in the machines, and for loss of profit on that. However, they did not allow the claim for loss of profit on the four further melts. The further loss was undoubtedly foreseeable, but as Lord Denning conceded, 'the question, at bottom, was one of policy'. The line of liability had to been drawn somewhere, and it was a matter of pragmatism that the line was drawn where it was. Lord Denning explained that such losses were better borne by the entire community than by the defendants. Considerations such as the fear of a proliferation of claims also played a part in the decision.

In *Weller v Foot and Mouth Disease Research Institute* (1966), the claimants were auctioneers who were unable to carry on their business because of a serious outbreak of foot and mouth disease in cattle in the area. This had been caused by the escape of a virus from the defendant's research establishment. Farmers were obliged to slaughter cattle with the disease and auctions were forced to close to control its spread. The claimants were denied a remedy. Their loss was too remote from the original act of negligence which had caused financial losses directly to the farmers but only indirectly to the auctioneers.

5.2.2 Expansion of liability

It is very clear that in the above cases the cause of the loss was an act and that the damage was economic loss. However, in other cases, the distinction is less obvious.

In *Dutton v Bognor Regis UDC* (1972), the Court of Appeal held that the local authority was liable when the owner of a building suffered financial loss as a result of defective foundations having to be repaired. The foundations were defective because of a negligent inspection carried out by the defendant's building inspector. It is difficult to distinguish between a negligent act of inspection, and a negligent statement which is made that the foundations of a building are adequate, and comply with regulations. It is also difficult to distinguish between damage to property (that is, the building) and financial loss which is consequent upon having to repair the damage to the building. The claim was successful because there was a threat of injury to health from the damaged property. If the defect had only meant that the property was defective, or of poor quality, but not dangerous to health or safety, the claim would have failed. *Donoghue v Stevenson* only established liability for injury to health or safety, not for damage to the quality of a manufactured or fabricated product alone. If the ginger beer in that case had merely been a poor colour, or unpleasant to taste, there would have been no duty of care owed. What made the difference, and gave rise to liability in tort, rather than in contract, was the fact there was injury to the claimant's health.

One possible explanation for the over-complicated approach in *Dutton* is that the facts did not fall squarely within the *Hedley Byrne* line of cases, nor within the *Donoghue v Stevenson* principle, unless there is an act causing potential injury to health. If injury to health is merely threatened, the loss, it can be argued, is a purely financial one. Fearing a further expansion of the *Hedley Byrne* cases, the court produced a cautious formulation of the facts of *Dutton* to achieve that desired result without apparently opening the floodgates.

However, this formulation was in itself confusing because it focussed too closely on injury to health.

A confusing line of cases followed, beginning with *Anns v Merton BC* (1978), in which the House of Lords approved *Dutton*. In this case, the council negligently failed to inspect the foundations of a block of flats. It transpired that the foundations were too shallow and some years later when many of the flats had changed hands it became apparent that there was a serious defect in their construction. The claimant claimed that the damage to the properties threatened health and safety. The claim succeeded. This was an explicit policy decision in which the whole issue of the desirability of arriving at decisions on grounds of policy was openly discussed, and in which Lord Wilberforce formulated his famous two-stage test which paved the way for an expansion of liability.

It is interesting to observe the way in which the trend towards expansion continued for some years, and was later discredited when it appeared to the judges that they had moved too far in the direction of an indeterminate liability for pure economic loss caused by negligent acts. This is arguably the nature of the loss in *Anns*, where there was a threat to health and safety rather than actual injury. In *Donoghue v Stevenson*, by contrast, there was alleged injury to health.

The expansion continued in *Batty v Metropolitan Property Realisations* (1978). In this case, an action was brought by the owner of a house which had been built near an embankment on land which was unstable and subject to landslips. The house was one of several built in a small close, and part of the garden slipped away. The house itself was unsaleable. The builders were liable for negligence in that they had not anticipated these problems even though the house itself was still standing. The evidence suggested that the house would become dangerous at some time in the future. This case introduces a wider liability than *Anns v Merton* because the court was prepared to award damages for possible future threats to health and safety, and at the time of the hearing the only loss was an economic loss, coupled with anxiety.

In *Dennis v Charnwood BC* (1982), it is possible to see the timescale involved in some of these cases, a factor which compounds the difficulties in making an award for economic loss. The facts were as follows:

1955	A house was built on an old sand pit. The local authority advised that a concrete raft was necessary to support the foundations.
1966	Small cracks began to appear in the walls. The builder inspected these, reassured the owners, and filled in the cracks.
1976	Very large cracks appeared in the walls.
1977	It was clear that the concrete raft was inadequate.
1982	The Court of Appeal held that the local authority were liable in negligence for the defects to the property which were likely to cause danger during the normal lifespan of the building.

Once again, it is difficult to see how the liability of the local authority was based on acts rather than advice.

5.2.3 The 'high-water' mark

In *Junior Books v Veitchi Co Ltd* (1983), the House of Lords stretched the scope of the duty of care in negligence to its limit and, with some reservations, found that a duty of care existed in relation to a defect in quality of a product even though there was no threatened danger to health or safety. The defendants were flooring specialists and were nominated as subcontractors by the claimants who had employed the main contractors. The defendant subcontractors had allegedly been negligent in the laying of a factory floor, with the result that the floor was defective but not dangerous. The defect was therefore only one of quality. Under normal circumstances, tort would not compensate such defects, the usual remedy being an action for breach of contract. In this case, there was no action available against the main contractors, and the only hope of a remedy was in tort. It was held, on a preliminary point that there was a duty of care owed in the particular circumstances of this case. On its facts, it was difficult to envisage a situation closer to contract than this. The claimants had themselves specified which particular subcontractor should carry out the work. The defendants should therefore have known that the claimants would be relying upon their skill and experience. There was close proximity between the parties and there could be no fears of opening the floodgates to numerous actions arising out of this claim as the claimants were foreseeable as an individual enterprise.

The judges acknowledged that there were a number of policy decisions in this area, including *Spartan Steel v Martin* (1973), and Lord Wilberforce's two-stage test in *Anns* was discussed.

Lord Brandon dissented, fearing that tort was about to usurp the province of contract, and provide compensation for defects in the quality of manufactured and fabricated products.

The case was much criticised by academics in that it appeared to be an attempt to lay the foundations for a general duty of care relating to pure economic loss caused by negligent acts, where there was no danger to health or safety involved, and the courts began to draw back from the position in *Junior Books* as soon as opportunities presented themselves.

5.2.4 Contraction of liability

Following the decisions in which the scope of liability was extended, there were a number of cases in which it became apparent that the judges were having reservations about the rapid expansion of liability. As in *Junior Books v Veitchi Co Ltd* (1983), the facts are somewhat complicated in these cases by a structure of contracts and of subcontracts. However, this is often perceived as the reason for restricting further expansion of the scope of the duty principle.

In *Muirhead v Industrial Tank Specialities Ltd* (1985), the Court of Appeal distinguished *Junior Books*. The claimants in this case were wholesale fish-merchants who hit upon the idea of buying lobsters when they were cheap, storing them in tanks, and selling them some months later when lobsters were scarce and the prices were higher. They bought a tank for the purpose of storage from the first defendants along with seven pumps which the first defendants had obtained from the second defendants. The motors on the pumps had been manufactured in France and, because they were defective, they regularly cut out, with the result that the lobsters could not be stored and the claimants lost money. The claimants obtained judgment against the first defendants in contract, but they went into liquidation, so they sued the second defendants in tort. Their claim failed on the grounds that they could not rely on *Junior Books*. That case must, it was held, be restricted to its own very particular facts. There must be both real reliance by the claimant (such as nomination of a particular product, supplier or subcontractor) and close proximity between the parties before a duty of care will be held to exist in cases where there is a negligent act causing a defect in the quality of a product.

5.2.5 The courts recognise the artificial distinctions made in previous cases

In *D and F Estates v Church Commissioners* (1988), a firm of builders employed subcontractors to carry out plastering work in a block of flats. The subcontractors were negligent, and the plaster began to fall off the walls some time after the flats had been let to various tenants. One of the occupants of the flats sued the builders (the main contractors) for negligence, alleging that they should have known that the plastering work was sub-standard. The sum claimed was the cost of replacing the defective plaster. In rejecting the claimant's claim, the House of Lords cast doubt on the decisions in the *Dutton* and *Anns* cases, on the grounds that economic loss was not recoverable in tort by a remote claimant if a defect is discovered before any actual damage involving danger to health or safety is done. In the words of Lord Bridge:

> If the defect is discovered before any damage is done, the loss sustained by the owner of the structure who has to repair or demolish it to avoid a potential source of danger to third parties would seem to be purely economic.

At last, the artificial distinction between damage to property and economic loss was openly recognised and rejected. The distinction has been further discredited in later cases (see *Marc Rich & Co v Bishop Rock Marine* (1995)).

In *Simaan General Contracting Co v Pilkington Glass (No 2)* (1988), the defendant had supplied goods to a subcontractor engaged by the main contractor, and the main contractor, the claimant in this case, suffered a loss as a result. There was no liability in negligence here, as Bingham J said:

> There is no general rule that claims in negligence may succeed on proof of foreseeable economic loss caused by the defendant even where no damage to property and no proprietary or possessory interests are shown.

A number of other decisions limited the ambit of *Anns* by restricting the liability of local authorities.

In the *Governors of the Peabody Donation Fund v Sir Lindsay Parkinson* (1984), it was held that a local authority, which is exercising its supervisory powers under a statute, does not owe a duty of care to the owner of a building who employs architects or engineers for professional advice.

A greater burden is now placed on professional advisors than on local authorities, as was confirmed in *Investors in Industry Commercial Properties Ltd v South Bedfordshire DC* (1986) and, indeed, in the *Murphy* case which is discussed below. This can only operate to the detriment of the building owner, because local authorities have perpetual succession and do not disappear or go into liquidation in the same way as commercial enterprises.

5.2.6 The new limits on liability

The death-knell of *Junior Books* was finally sounded in *Murphy v Brentwood DC* (1990). In 1970, the claimant bought a house which had just been built by a construction company, using a concrete raft to secure the foundations. The local authority had received plans and calculations for the foundations and had referred them to a firm of consulting engineers to be checked prior to approval being granted. On the recommendation of the consulting engineers, the local authority approved the plans under the building regulations. By 1981, it became apparent that the foundations were inadequate and, in 1986, the claimant sold the house for £35,000 less than it would have been worth without defective foundations. The claimant relied upon the fact that there was imminent danger to the health and safety of his family because gas and soil pipes had broken during settlement of the building. The House of Lords held that there was no liability on the part of the defendants. A dangerous defect which had manifested itself before it had actually caused physical injury, was pure economic loss. The true loss consisted of expenditure of money required to repair the building. This so called 'dangerous' defect was a defect in quality, and it was not the province of tort to provide a remedy for such defects. As the Lord Chancellor explained:

> In these circumstances, I have reached the clear conclusion that the proper exercise of the judicial function requires this House now to depart from *Anns* in so far as it affirmed a private law duty of care to avoid damage to property which causes present or imminent danger to the health and safety of owners, or occupiers, resting on local authorities in relation to their functions of supervising compliance with building bylaws or regulations, that *Dutton* should be overruled, and that all decisions subsequent to *Anns* which purported to follow it should be overruled.

The House of Lords made it clear that damage to another part of the same building or structure, caused, for example, by inadequate foundations, does not constitute 'damage to other property', and will not be actionable.

The House of Lords took the opportunity to state that the two-stage test of Lord Wilberforce in *Anns* was not to be regarded as universally applicable.

Murphy was followed in *Department of the Environment v Thomas Bates & Son Ltd* (1990), in which the claimants failed to obtain damages for the cost of repairing a building which had been constructed of low-strength concrete, but was not dangerous.

Ironically, despite the fact that builders may now escape liability in negligence when there is no injury to health as a result of negligent construction work, there is still the possibility of an action in nuisance if adjoining land is threatened and of highway nuisance for which liability may be strict if there is a threat to people using the highway. (See Markesinis, B and Deakin, S, 'The random element of their Lordships' infallible judgment: an economic and comparative analysis of the tort of negligence from *Anns* to *Murphy*' (1992) 55 MLR 619.)

5.2.7 Summary

Looking back over the 1990s, it is possible to observe a period of expansion in the law relating to nervous shock and economic loss. However, the serious reservations which many academic lawyers and some senior judges expressed, particularly about economic loss, eventually gave way to a more restrictive approach and, as the decade passed, the scope of the duty of care relating to economic loss has in almost all its various aspects become narrower. Recent cases concerning nervous shock also indicate a more restrictive attitude. The trend towards a policy of expansion is unlikely to return in the foreseeable future.

The implications of this retreat have clear ramifications for business practice, for insurance, for individuals, and for lawyers, and it is interesting to note that a rather more relaxed and expansive attitude may be creeping back into the decisions since 1993, following cases such as *Spring v Guardian Assurance* (1994) and *Henderson v Merretts Syndicate* (1994). While these cases may turn on particular policy issues, the fact that the House of Lords has been prepared to expand the boundaries of liability for economic loss in these instances is certainly worthy of note, as many other cases are likely to turn on these decisions. The scope of the duty of care in relation to economic loss has caused much difficulty and for many of the same reasons as that relating to nervous shock. Policy considerations such as fear of too rapid an expansion of liability have been behind many of the decisions.

DUTY OF CARE – ECONOMIC LOSS

Careless statements causing economic loss

Hedley Byrne v Heller (1964) was the first case to establish that a duty of care could exist in respect of careless statements. Limitations were placed on the scope of the duty:

- It was necessary to prove that the advice was given and received within a special relationship.

  This notion was later expanded to include any business or professional context (*Howard Marine v Ogden* (1987)), but not social occasions unless the circumstances made it clear that carefully considered advice was being sought (*Chaudhry v Prabhaker* (1988); *Goodwill v BPAS* (1996)).

- The claimant had to demonstrate reliance on the statement.

  Note, especially, the house purchase cases:

  Yianni v Edwin Evans (1982);

  Harris v Wyre Forest DC (1989);

  Smith v Bush (1990).

- Wrongful birth cases:

  McFarlane v Tayside Health Board (1999);

  Rand v E Dorset HA (2000).

Reliance on a statement by third party which causes loss to the claimant

'Special relationship' and 'reliance' were re-stated in *Caparo v Dickman* (1990) by the House of Lords. Note Lord Oliver's explanation of the five particular circumstances when the duty will now apply:

- the advice must be required for a purpose, either specified in detail or described in general terms;

- the purpose must be made known, either actually or inferentially, to the advisor at the time the advice is given;

- the advisor must know, either actually or inferentially, that the advice will be communicated to the advisee, either as a specific individual or as a member of an ascertainable class in order that it should be used by the advisee for the known purpose;

- it must be known, either actually or inferentially, that the advice will probably be acted upon for that purpose without independent advice or inquiry;

- the advice must be so acted upon to the detriment of the advisee;

- the defendant must have assumed responsibility to the claimant (*Jones v Wright* (1994)).

Further expansion of the law seemed unlikely (*James McNaughton Papers Group v Hicks Anderson & Co* (1991); *Morgan Crucible v Hill Samuel* (1991); *MHLG v Sharp* (1971); *Clark v Bruce Lance* (1988)). But note new developments (*Jones v Wright* (1994); *Spring v Guardian Assurance* (1994); *Williams v Natural Life Health Foods* (1998)).

Economic loss caused by negligent acts

The distinction between losses caused by 'words' and those caused by 'acts' has never been clear. The reason for attempts to distinguish between the two was probably that the courts were trying to restrict the ambit of liability for economic losses. See:

Spartan Steel v Martin (1972);

Weller v Foot & Mouth Disease Research Institute (1966);

Pritchard v Cobden (1988).

The distinction is now less important (*Marc Rich v Bishop Rock Marine* (1995)).

Expansion of liability

The following cases are important examples from the liberal years in which the courts were prepared to extend the scope of liability (*Dutton v Bognor Regis UDC* (1972); *Anns v Merton BC* (1978); *Batty v Metropolitan Property Realisations* (1978); *Dennis v Charnwood* (1982)).

The 'high-water' mark occurred in *Junior Books v Veitchi* (1983) in which it was held that there could be liability for damage which did not give rise to a threat to health or safety.

Contraction of liability

Much disquiet was expressed about the decision in *Junior Books*, and, in the following cases, the courts retreated from the position which had been reached in that case by restricting it to its special facts and refusing a remedy in tort for defects in quality alone (*Muirhead v Industrial Tank* (1985) (real reliance and close proximity were both required); *D and F Estates v Church Comrs* (1988); *Simaan General Contractors v Pilkington Glass* (1988); *Investors in Industry v S Bedfordshire DC* (1986)).

In *Murphy v Brentwood DC* (1990), the House of Lords departed from *Anns* – the artificial distinction between damage to property and economic loss was discounted; the two-stage test was discredited; there is no liability in tort for a defect in quality.

In *Department of the Environment v Thomas Bates & Son Ltd* (1990), *Murphy* was followed and the retreat was complete. However, there is still a duty of care owed by builders to later purchasers, and if there is privity of contract there may still be liability in contract for defects in the quality of a building.

See, also, the Defective Premises Act 1972, below, Chapter 11.

Note the special line of cases beginning with *White v Jones* (1995), and the recent case of *Gorham v British Telecommunications plc* (2000).

CHAPTER 6

SITUATIONS IN WHICH
NO DUTY OF CARE IS OWED

6.1 The 'no duty' cases

It has now been established that, in a number of situations, no duty of care is owed. Most of these decisions rest on policy considerations, and some grey areas remain.

6.1.1 Lawyers

Until July 2000, a barrister (and any advocate, since the intervention of the courts with the Legal Services Act 1990) did not owe a duty of care to a client in connection with any representation in court or anything preparatory thereto.

This was decided by a unanimous House of Lords in *Rondel v Worsley* (1969). Although the exact scope of the immunity from action was unclear after it was extended in *Saif Ali v Mitchell & Co* (1980), the rationale behind it was stated by the House of Lords to be based on public policy which, it was thought, demanded that barristers should not continually be looking over their shoulders in fear of negligence actions.

The question of advocates' immunity came before the Court of Appeal again in 1998 in *Arthur Hall & Co v Simons; Barrett v Woolf Seddon Cockbone v Atkinson, Dacre and Slack; Harris v Scholfield, Roberts and Hill* (1998), where it was held that the immunity of advocates from negligence suits was justified by reference to public policy considerations. The Court of Appeal was clearly aware that the European Court of Human Rights (ECHR) might be called upon to rule as to the compatibility of *Rondel v Worsely* (1968) with the European Convention on Human Rights, but treated that case as binding for these appeals. However, pending reconsideration of *Rondel* and *Saif Ali* by the House of Lords, it was held that the *ratios* of those cases were binding on the lower courts. The court took the view that any extension of the basic forensic immunity beyond the limit recognised in those cases must be scrutinised carefully.

This policy is being challenged before the ECHR by Mohammed Yusuf Patel, whose claim was rejected by the House of Lords in 1998.

However, the House of Lords have now ruled that the immunity of barristers and solicitors from claims arising out of the negligent conduct of cases has ended. The decision was unanimous in relation to civil cases, but three of the seven Law Lords dissented in relation to criminal cases. Thus, advocates may now be sued for negligence in relation to their performance in court or matters closely related to it (*The Times*, 21 July 2000).

6.1.2 Legal proceedings

Judges, witnesses and parties to legal proceedings do not owe a duty of care in relation to those proceedings on grounds of public policy (*Sirros v Moore* (1975)).

6.1.3 Other causes of action

No duty of care is owed in circumstances when its imposition would supplant other causes of action, such as a public law action.

6.1.4 Other sources of compensation

No duty would be owed in circumstances where a remedy might be available under another compensation system, as in *Jones v Department of Employment* (1989), when the social security system might have provided a remedy.

6.1.5 Claimant is a member of an indeterminately large class of persons

No duty of care will arise if the claimant belongs to a class of people which is too large to allow any relationship to exist with the defendant. In *Goodwill v British Pregnancy Advisory Service* (1996), no duty was owed by the defendants to the claimant when they gave negligent advice to a man having a vasectomy, who became the claimant's sexual partner some time later.

In medical cases, the courts have been unwilling to extend liability beyond the immediate doctor/patient relationship. This is probably based on a fear that the floodgates will open to a large amount of litigation if a duty of care were to be found in relation to relatives and others who are not immediately proximate to the doctor and patient concerned. Recent cases include an unsuccessful action by relatives of a child who died because of a negligent diagnosis and who claimed that there was a duty on the part of the doctors not to conceal the truth of what had happened (*Powell v Boldaz* (1997)).

In *John Munroe (Acrylics) Ltd v London Fire and Civil Defence Authority and Others* (1997), it was held that no duty of care was owed by a fire brigade to respond to a call for assistance. Nor, simply by responding to an emergency call, did the fire brigade put itself into a position of assuming responsibility to people likely to be hurt in a fire. Contrast this with *Kent v Griffiths and London Ambulance Service* (2000), in which it was held that the claimant was identifiable as an individual (see below, 6.4.2).

6.1.6 Wrongful life

There is no duty of care in relation to wrongful life. In *McKay v Essex AHA* (1982), a child had been born with severe disabilities because her mother had suffered from rubella in the early stages of pregnancy. The defendants had been careless in their testing and treatment of the mother. The child, through her mother, claimed damages for negligence on the grounds that she should never have been born at all. She claimed that her mother should have been advised to have the pregnancy terminated. The claimant was denied a remedy because the court decided that no duty of care existed in such circumstances. To hold otherwise, it was decided, would be against public policy.

6.1.7 The police

Although the police owe a duty of care to prisoners in their care (*Clarke v Chief Constable of Northamptonshire Police* (1999)), they owe no duty of care to the public in general to prevent them becoming the victims of crime.

Hill v Chief Constable of West Yorkshire (1988) established that the mother of the last victim of Peter Sutcliffe, known as the 'Yorkshire Ripper', could not succeed in an action against the police for negligence because no duty of care was owed to individual members of the public by the police. It could well have been that the police had not been sufficiently diligent in their investigation of the crime and that the mass killer should have been apprehended sooner, so avoiding the death of Jacqueline Hill. However, it was against public policy, and also very impractical, to hold that the police owed a duty of care. There could be no general duty of care in respect of the possible crimes which could be committed by a person whose identity was unknown to the police at the time, and there was no proximity in relation to this particular victim over and above any other potential victim. The only circumstances where a duty is owed by the police to the public would seem to be when they have a suspect in custody and negligently allow that person to harm someone, either by that person escaping or while in custody.

Osman v Ferguson (1993) demonstrates the reluctance of the UK courts to find the police liable. In that case, the Court of Appeal refused to allow a negligence action to proceed in circumstances where the police had chosen not to act on warnings that a teacher, who was infatuated with a pupil, was suffering from a psychiatric disorder and was likely to commit serious offences. In the event, the teacher killed the boy's father and seriously injured the son. The Court of Appeal recognised that there was 'an arguable case' based on the very close proximity between the police, the family and the teacher, whom they had interviewed about the acts of vandalism which he had previously committed at the boy's home. However, there was immunity from action for negligence in cases involving the investigation and detection of crime. Lord Justice McCowan said:

> The House of Lords' decision on public policy immunity in the *Hill* case dooms this action to failure. It is a plain and obvious case falling squarely within the House of Lords' decision.

The relevant policy issues seemed to be the 'time, trouble and expense' which would be involved in defending such cases and the possibility of a flood of claims, coupled with the re-opening of cases without reasonable cause.

There can be no doubt on the facts that there was proximity between the parties and, for that reason, a *prima facie* duty of care arose. This would mean that the case does not fall squarely within the decision in *Hill v Chief Constable of West Yorkshire* (1988), in which there was insufficient proximity to give rise to the initial duty of care.

The special position of the police was confirmed in *Ancell v McDermott and Another* (1993), in which it was held that the police are under no duty of care to road users in general to protect and warn them of particular road hazards which are within their knowledge, but which the police have not created. In this case, the police had become aware of an incident in which diesel fuel was spilled onto the road, but, although they reported the matter to the local highways department, they did not attempt to warn approaching vehicles. A car skidded on the spilled fuel and one person was killed and several were injured. The Court of Appeal invoked the 'incremental approach' to negligence and considered what was just and reasonable in the circumstances, rejecting the notion that there could be a single general test for the duty of care which can be applied to every situation. In the circumstances of this particular case, it would be unfair to impose a duty of care on the police. Lord Beldam said:

> A duty of care would impose upon a police force potential liability of almost unlimited scope. Not only would the class of persons to whom the duty was owed be extensive, but the activities of police officers which might give rise to the existence of such a duty would be widespread.

It is interesting to note that, in using these criteria, Lord Beldam uses the very words of Lord Wilberforce in *Anns v Merton BC* (1978) when establishing the two-stage test which the Court of Appeal in this case rejected (see Chapter 3).

In *Alexandrou v Oxford* (1993), it was held at first instance that the police did owe a duty of care to the claimant because they had been alerted by a burglar alarm which was sited on the claimant's shop premises and, when activated, signalled the police station. The police had been in breach of their duty when they had failed to check the premises properly after they had been alerted to the possible presence of an intruder. On the specific facts of this case, it is possible to distinguish it from cases which fall within the *Hill* principle, because there was an assumption of responsibility by the police for the safety of the premises when they had agreed to the direct line between the burglar alarm and the police station. Yet, on appeal, it was held that this case fell within the *Hill* principle and, indeed, that it was indistinguishable from *Hill*. Explaining the relationship which arose as a result of the direct line to the police station, Glidewell LJ said:

> If as a result ... the police came under a duty of care to the claimant, it must follow that they would be under a similar duty to any person who informs them, whether by a 999 call or in some other way, that a burglary ... is being or is about to be committed. It follows, then, that ... there was no special relationship between the claimant and the police.

The reasoning in this case is difficult to understand in terms of proximity because common sense suggests that there is a very obvious distinction between the general relationship which the police have with the public at large (as in *Hill*) and the very much closer proximity which exists between police officers at a particular station and an individual who has chosen, and indeed paid, to have a direct line from his or her burglar alarm to that police station. It is much easier to rationalise the outcome which the judges required in this case in more general terms of public policy, on the grounds that it would not be fair, just and reasonable to impose a duty of care in the circumstances of the case. However, the only fair and just reason for denying the existence of a duty in this situation must be some preconception that there is a need to protect the police from litigation. There are several justifications for such a view. It was suggested in *Hill v Chief Constable of West Yorkshire* (1988) that fear of litigation might lead to 'defensive policing', which would add to the cost and time spent by the police in dealing with investigations, with no obvious public benefit. A second justification lies in the proposition that no individual should be burdened with the duty to protect others from the acts of third parties, though there are recognised exceptions to this, as in *Dorset Yacht Co v Home Office* (1970).

The third justification can be found in the wider public policy context of policing generally, where there is a well established principle of public law that the courts will not interfere with police discretion except in the most extreme circumstances. This is especially important at higher levels of policing when the cases indicate that enormous discretion is vested in a chief constable in relation to how he or she decides upon policing priorities for his or her area, although, of course, police officers of even the lowest ranks are sometimes required to exercise discretion at street level. Chief constables regularly make important decisions as to what particular crimes they intend to target within their budgets. In one area, motoring offences may be a priority; in another, catching burglars or drug dealers or controlling prostitution may be the focus of attention; in yet another, inner city policing or controlling demonstrators may be the main target of funds, and so on, but, providing the chief constable is acting within the law and does not abdicate responsibility for law enforcement, the courts will not question his or her priorities (the *Blackburn* cases (1968; 1973)). This attitude was reflected in Lord Scarman's report on the Brixton riots, which concludes:

The exercise of discretion lies at the heart of policing ... Successful policing depends on the exercise of discretion in how the law is enforced. The good reputation of the police as a force depends upon the skill and judgment which policemen display in the particular circumstances of the cases and incidents which they are required to handle.

Despite the general public policy rule that there is no duty of care owed by the police to the public as a whole, each case should be decided on its own particular facts, and it is possible to find cases in which the police *have* been held to owe a duty of care.

In *Swinney v Chief Constable of Northumbria Police (No 2)* (1999), it was held that, when an informant gave information to the police in confidence in the course of an investigation, the police owed a duty of care to take such steps as were reasonable to avoid disclosing information unnecessarily to the general public. However, the judge found that, in the circumstances of this particular case, the police had not been in breach of that duty. In the course of arriving at this decision, Jackson J explained that the claimants were not merely members of the general public, but had a special relationship with the police, which gave rise to proximity. The public policy considerations were more evenly balanced in this case than in *Hill v Chief Constable of West Yorkshire* (1989), *Alexandrou v Oxford* (1993) and *Ancell v McDermott* (1993). The policy arguments involved were discussed fully, as was the ruling of the ECHR in *Osman v UK* (1999)), in the course of the judgment.

A related problem was raised in *Elguzouli-Daf v Comr of Police of the Metropolis and Another* (1995), *McBreaty v Ministry of Defence and Others* (1994). The claimant in the first case had been detained and charged by the police with handling explosives after a bomb had been planted at a Royal Marine barracks, but he continued to maintain that he was innocent and that traces of explosive substances on his hands were the result of innocent contamination. After 85 days in custody, the Crown Prosecution Service (CPS) offered no evidence against him at committal proceedings because they could not exclude the possibility of innocent contamination. He brought an action for negligence against the CPS on the grounds that the prosecution should have been discontinued earlier and he should have been discharged from custody sooner, as the flaw in the evidence had been apparent from the start. The claimant in the second case had been charged with rape and, after he had been in custody for 22 days, the CPS abandoned the prosecution because forensic examination had revealed that semen on a swab taken from the victim could not have been his. He claimed that the CPS had been negligent in not obtaining, processing and communicating the negative results of the forensic tests sooner. The Court of Appeal upheld the decision at first instance that both actions should be struck out. The policy issues were considered by the court, and on balance it was decided that the welfare of the community as a whole outweighed the interests of individualised justice, so precluding the existence of a duty of care by the CPS to individuals aggrieved by CPS activities. The fear that a defensive approach by the CPS might inhibit the discharge of its central function of prosecuting crime was an important factor in the decision. Accordingly, it would not be fair, just and reasonable to impose a duty of care on the CPS in relation to people who might be prosecuted by them. In arriving at this view, the Court of Appeal considered the earlier case of *Welsh v Chief Constable of Merseyside* (1993), in which the CPS had been found negligent in not informing the magistrates' court that the Crown Court had already taken the accused's previous offences into account, as a result of which he was re-arrested and detained further. It was decided that the *Welsh* case was distinguishable from the two cases before the Court of Appeal because, in that case, there had been a clear assumption of responsibility by the CPS to keep the magistrates' court informed of the fact that the claimant's previous offences had already been taken into consideration by the Crown Court. The judge had repeatedly emphasised that this was of particular importance. It follows that there may still be some cases in which the CPS may owe a duty of care to those people whom it prosecutes, providing a sufficient relationship of proximity can be established through the special assumption of particular responsibility for the accused.

It seems that the assumption of responsibility is an important factor in determining the existence of a duty of care in cases involving the police and the CPS. In *Kirkham v Chief Constable of Greater Manchester* (1990), it was decided that the police had been negligent in not informing the prison service that a prisoner whom they were placing in their care was a suicide risk. The decision was based on the fact that the police, in taking the man into custody, had assumed responsibility for him. The same principle applies, as will be seen in relation to the assumption or imposition of responsibilities, in the rescue cases.

Once the police have custody of a prisoner, they have responsibility for the care of that individual and owe him or her a duty of care. In *Reeves v Comr of Police for the Metropolis* (1999), the House of Lords held that, where the police owed a duty to prisoner to ensure that he did not commit suicide, they were not entitled to rely on defences of *volenti* or *novus actus interveniens* (see Chapter 20) if a breach of their duty did in fact result in the suicide of the prisoner. However, the amount of damages awarded would be reduced where the prisoner was of sound mind, in order to take account of contributory negligence.

6.1.8 The human rights arguments

The European Convention on Human Rights (ECHR) has considered the policy adopted by the UK courts in the police cases in *Osman v UK* (1999). The Court ruled, by 17 votes to three, that, although there had been no violation in the *Osman* case of Arts 2 and 8 of the Convention (the right to life and the right to private life respectively), the exclusionary rule established by the House of

Lords in *Hill v Chief Constable of West Yorkshire* (1988), based on public policy, which operates as a watertight defence for the police in civil claims, amounts to a disproportionate restriction on the rights of individuals.

As all UK courts will be obliged to take the European Convention into account in their deliberations once the Human Rights Act 1998 becomes operational in October 2000, this decision could well have an important impact on future cases which involve the duty of care owed by public services.

6.2 Claimant caused his or her own misfortune

No duty of care is owed when it can be shown that the claimant caused his or her own misfortune. In *Governors of the Peabody Donation Fund v Sir Lindsay Parkinson* (1985), it was decided that the claimants were not owed a duty of care because they should have taken independent advice from a qualified expert to ensure that building regulations were followed.

6.3 Rescue cases

There is no duty to rescue a person in danger. This rule is an extension of the principle that there is no liability in negligence for a mere omission, or failure to act. In theory, it is possible to watch a child drowning in a puddle without attracting legal liability. However, if a person undertakes to carry out a specific duty towards an individual, a duty of care is owed to that person and, in some instances, the law imposes such a duty even if the person upon whom the duty is placed does not wish to take it on. Thus, parents are expected by law to care for their children, and parents would have a duty of care in relation to their children who are in danger and require rescuing.

Similarly, people employed to undertake rescues, such as ambulance drivers and firemen (*Salmon v Seafarer Restaurants Ltd* (1983)), or other caring duties have a duty of care to potential victims. This duty may be described in the employment contracts of members of the rescue services.

However, in *Digital Equipment and Others v Hampshire CC* (1997), the Court of Appeal held that merely by attending and fighting a fire, a fire brigade was not under a duty of care to owners of the premises on which the fire was burning. The fire brigade would only be liable if it had negligently created a further danger causing extra damage (unless it could be shown that the particular damage would have occurred in any event). Stuart Smith LJ explained that a fire brigade did not enter into a relationship of sufficient proximity with the occupier or owner of the premises to give rise to a duty of care merely by attending to fight a fire.

A doctor owes a duty of care to his or her own patients. If a doctor fails to treat a patient, that could be an act of negligence (*Barnett v Chelsea and Kensington HMC* (1969)). A GP owes a duty of care to all patients on the practice list and could be found negligent for failing to treat them. Yet, if the same doctor drove past an accident whilst off duty and did not intervene to help the injured, there would probably be no negligence. A doctor's duty does not extend to the whole world. 'Good Samaritan' acts may be avoided by doctors, as, once embarked upon, they could attract liability if the doctor is careless in the treatment given. A rescuer owes a duty to those rescued to carry out the operation using reasonable care. There are some exceptions to these rules. For example, midwives owe a duty of care by statute to attend any woman in labour and rules of maritime law require the operators of fishing vessels in the North Sea to go to the aid of other vessels in distress. Even if a person has been responsible for the safety of another, that duty may cease. In *Griffiths v Brown* (1998), it was held that a taxi driver owed no duty of care to a passenger who was clearly drunk, once he had set him down close to his destination.

It remains to be seen whether the Human Rights Act 1998 will lead to the development of a duty to rescue in UK law. Such a duty does exist in Australia (*Lowns v Woods* (1996)).

6.4 Duties owed by other public authorities

The question of whether a duty of care is owed by various public authorities is frequently brought before the courts. There have been several cases concerning the duties owed by local authorities, health authorities and others to children and adults with special needs and to children and others in their care.

6.4.1 Health authorities and local authorities

In *Palmer v Tees HA and Hartlepool and East Durham NHS Trust* (1999), the Court of Appeal ruled unanimously that a health authority was not liable for the death of a child, Rosie Palmer, who was murdered by a psychiatric outpatient. This decision was not unexpected, in view of the restrictive approach taken in the past in cases of this kind, the most celebrated being that of *Hill v Chief Constable of West Yorkshire* (1988).

The Court of Appeal decided the *Palmer* case on the basis that there was insufficient proximity to impose a duty of care in negligence on a health authority in relation to a child who was sexually abused and murdered by an outpatient. Nor was a duty owed to the child's mother in respect of psychiatric injury suffered on learning of her daughter's injuries and death.

The defendants and their predecessors had been responsible for administering and managing the NHS Trust where a patient, Shaun Armstrong, had received treatment, and for providing psychiatric care and care in the community.

Shaun Armstrong had, on 30 June 1994, abducted, sexually abused and murdered four year old Rosie Palmer. He was diagnosed as suffering from personality disorder and psychopathic disorder, and had attempted suicide five times. In June 1993, while in hospital, he had told his carers that a child would be murdered when he was discharged from hospital. It was argued on the claimant's behalf that the defendants had failed to recognise a real, substantial and foreseeable risk that Shaun Armstrong would commit serious offences against children, causing injury or death, and that they had failed to take steps to treat him and/or detain him in order to reduce that risk.

The Court of Appeal agreed that the three-stage test for a duty of care established by the House of Lords in *Caparo Industries plc v Dickman* (1990) should be applied here. On that basis, it was not sufficient to say that the mother's mental anguish and psychiatric injury were foreseeable. A link based on proximity was necessary. The situation here was distinguishable from that in *Dorset Yacht Co v Home Office* (1970), where borstal boys readily and repeatedly escaped and interfered with yachts in the immediate course of their escape. That was foreseeable, as was the risk of damage to yachts, and, most importantly, the potential victims in the *Dorset Yacht* case were identifiable.

The crucial authority on the matter was considered to be *Hill v Chief Constable of West Yorkshire* (1988). The facts in that case differed from those in the present case, but *Hill* had established that the vital point was that there must be some relationship between the defendant and the victim, and the victim must have been identifiable as an individual. An important question was what measures the defendants could have put in place to avoid the specific danger to the child. In this case, the victim and her mother were not identifiable as particular individuals who might suffer damage. This meant that there was insufficient proximity between the victims and the defendants, who could not have known and warned them about the danger, even if it had been realised. Accordingly, the Court of Appeal ruled that the judge had correctly held that there was no proximity as between the respondents and the murdered child. It was inevitable that the action would fail. The appeal was dismissed.

For policy reasons, the courts have been reluctant to establish that a duty of care exists in claims of this kind. The dominant reason given in the cases is the fear of a flood of claims, but the families of victims of crimes committed by psychiatric patients have been pressing for an extension of liability. Pressure groups such as the Zito Trust are anxious for members of the public to be provided with better protection, even at the expense of the liberty of psychiatric patients. They draw attention to cases such as that of Lin and

Megan Russell, a mother and daughter who were murdered by Michael Stone in a country lane in Kent. It was open to the Court of Appeal in the *Palmer* case to find that, in general terms, on the application of *Caparo v Dickman*, it would be 'fair, just and reasonable' to impose a duty of care in cases of this kind, and, although the opportunity was not taken, it is still open to the House of Lords to bring about a change in the law. When the Human Rights Act 1998 comes into force, the judges may look with fresh eyes on what is meant by 'fair, just and reasonable' in the context of duty of care in cases of this kind.

M v Newham BC (1994) concerned the cases of M, joined with others, involving five children aged between three and 11 years. They claimed that the local authority had not acted sufficiently expeditiously to remove them from a dangerous situation, even though fears had been expressed on regular occasions for their safety by relatives, teachers and the police. In M's case, the local authority had incorrectly arrived at the conclusion that M had been abused by a man cohabiting with her mother. The Court of Appeal held that, in each of the cases, no duty of care in negligence was owed and, although the Children Act 1989 does place duties on local authorities in relation to children in their areas, it does not give rise to civil liability. Moreover, to impose a duty of care on local authorities, doctors or health authorities in these circumstances would not be just and reasonable (see Chapter 3). The actions were struck out.

However, in *E v Dorset CC* (1994), the Court of Appeal took the view that, at least at common law, it is arguable that a duty of care is owed by the employees of local authorities, including teachers and educational psychologists, to ensure that children with special needs do not suffer when they are not provided with special facilities. In *Dowling v Surrey CC and Another* (1994), it was held that a local authority owed a duty of care to children who are left by their parents in the care of childminders whom they approve and register. The county council officers were aware that there was a significant risk to any young child left in the care of a particular registered childminder, and they were in breach of their duty when they did not warn the parents of the risk and a child was injured.

In *Reed v Doncaster MBC* (1995), it was decided that the defendant council did not owe a duty of care to a tenant in respect of goods and furniture left temporarily in an inadequately secured council house after the tenant had been re-housed, following several incidents of racial harassment. There were no special circumstances in existence in this case by which the council had control over the third parties who caused the damage, and they could not be held responsible. This decision is not surprising in the light of the reluctance of the courts to expand the scope of the duty of care in negligence in recent years and the obvious financial problems which the existence of a duty in this kind of situation would cause local authorities.

In *Clunis v Camden and Islington HA* (1997), the Court of Appeal held that there is no common law duty which exists alongside the statutory duty on a health authority to provide aftercare services under s 117 of the Mental Health Act 1983. The claimant, who suffered from schizophrenia, had been convicted of manslaughter after he had killed a complete stranger in an unprovoked attack. His action against the defendant health authority was based on the contention that there had been a breach of a common law duty owed to him to treat him with reasonable care and skill while he was at large in the community.

In *Gower v Bromley LBC* (1999), the Court of Appeal held that the staff at a special school for disabled pupils owed them a duty of care to educate them in accordance with their needs. The local authority could be vicariously liable if teaching staff failed in this duty. The claimant was 16 years old and was suffering from the degenerative disease known as Duchenne muscular dystrophy. This illness affects speech and movement, but not intellectual capacity. However, he had been educated between the ages of nine and 12 at a school where he alleged that the staff were professionally incompetent and where he had not been provided with the necessary electronic equipment which would have enabled him to learn and to communicate and socialise effectively. Although his parents had removed him from this school at the age of 12, he had failed educationally and had suffered psychological and emotional damage. He alleged that he had suffered damage as a result of the failure of staff to make appropriate educational provision for him at the correct standard to meet his specific requirements.

In *Barrett v London Borough of Enfield* (1999), it was held that a claim by a person who alleged that he had not been properly cared for while in local authority care under the Children Act 1989 should not be struck out, and that the claimant should have the right to fight the case in court. This was a landmark case, and it is expected that many claims will be brought by people who believe that they were mistreated in local authority care. The appellant had been taken into care but had never been placed for adoption. He alleged that this failure on the part of the local authority had caused him to suffer psychiatric illness and difficulties with alcohol. He had been moved six times to different homes and he claimed that the local authority had failed to safeguard his welfare.

The appeal concerned the preliminary point as to whether the issue was justiciable in the light of earlier rulings in which it had been held that local authorities do not owe a duty of care to children in certain circumstances. The House of Lords distinguished this case from *X (Minors) v Bedfordshire CC* (1995), which concerned the decision whether or not to take the initial step of taking a child into care, whereas *Barrett* concerned events which had occurred when the child had already been taken into care. Explaining that it would be proper to proceed with the decision on an 'incremental' basis, as required by *Caparo v Dickman* (1990), Lord Slynn explained that each case should be considered in the context of its own facts and of the particular statutory framework which was applicable, in order to decide whether the matter was justiciable. In this particular case, the allegations were directed at the way in which the local authority had exercised its powers, and it was arguable that, as far as some of the allegations were concerned, a duty of care had been owed by the local authority, and that had been broken. However, the case also involved the question of the exercise of discretion as to whether to place the child for adoption, which the trial court might find not to be justiciable at all.

The interests of the child could not be properly protected if there was no jurisdiction to consider whether a duty of care existed, and it by no means followed that, if the court were to decide that a child could not sue his or her parents for negligent decisions made by them in relation to upbringing, there could necessarily be no duty imposed on a local authority. The House of Lords considered that the question of whether it would be just and reasonable to impose a duty of care on the local authority should not be decided in the abstract for all acts or omissions of local authorities, but each case should be considered on its own facts.

Although the issues in the *Barrett* case were not clear cut, and the claimant might experience difficulties in his claim, he was entitled to have the allegations investigated. He was not a member of an indeterminate class, but was identifiable as an individual already in the care of the local authority, and one who had been placed there by the operation of statute. Thus, it would not constitute a new category of negligence to hold that the defendants owed him a duty of care. As this was a difficult and developing area of law, it would be wrong to decide issues on the basis of hypothetical facts without considering the details of individual cases. *Osman v UK* (1999) was mentioned as an example of a case which involved Art 6 of the European Convention on Human Rights and the question of whether a public body (in that case, the police) could owe a duty of care in negligence. English law had been criticised by the ECHR, which considered that, in the light of that decision, it would be difficult to foretell what would be the result if the case were struck out by the House of Lords.

This area of law is exceptionally difficult because of the complexity of the issues involved, and because the law gives a discretion to public bodies such as local authorities. Many of the cases concern omissions on the part of those bodies, rather than positive acts of negligence. Several House of Lords decisions (see *Anns v Merton BC* (1978)) have established that, if a discretion is imposed on a local authority, there could only be liability if it were exercised so carelessly and unreasonably that there had been no exercise of the discretion imposed by Parliament; then, the body concerned could not be said to have exercised the discretion at all and would have acted outside the statutory power given to it by Parliament. If the exercise of the discretion involved policy making about matters such as allocation of resources, it would be extremely difficult to establish that a local authority had acted beyond the power given to it by Parliament.

The questions to be determined are: first, whether the alleged negligence in the exercise of the discretion granted by statute involved policy considerations – if so, the matter would be non-justiciable; and, secondly, whether the acts which formed the basis of the cause of action fell within the scope of the statutory discretion – if they did not, the question as to whether it would be fair, just and reasonable to impose a duty of care should be considered by the court. What the House of Lords concluded in *Barrett*, which concerned the *way* in which a discretion is exercised, is that it is a matter for the judge at the trial to decide whether the case gives rise to policy issues such as the balancing of competing interests and, if so, then at that stage the case can be struck out as non-justiciable, but it should at least go ahead for the matter to be decided at full trial, and not simply struck out on the basis of generalisations drawn from other cases and hypothetical facts.

Another important decision in this area of law is *W v Essex CC* (2000), concerning the extent of the duty of care owed by local authorities for psychiatric injury (see Chapter 4).

6.4.2 Duty of the ambulance service

Basic principles of tort were relied upon in the arguments presented in the recent case of *Kent v Griffiths, Roberts and London Ambulance Service* (1998) concerning the duty of care owed by an ambulance service. Despite the cases in which it has been held that there is no general duty of care owed by public services, such as the police and fire brigade, the claimant in this case relied on the contention that, once she had been named and her condition and address were known to the ambulance service, and had relied on the service to take her to hospital and to provide any treatment required en route, a duty of care to her as an individual would arise.

The full trial of this case on liability was held later in the High Court and resulted in an appeal to the Court of Appeal. In *Kent v Griffiths, Roberts and London Ambulance Service (No 2)* (2000), the appeal concerned the question of whether the ambulance service owed a duty of care to a particular patient in the circumstances of the present case, and whether there had been a breach of that duty.

(It had previously been decided in an earlier appeal by a differently constituted Court of Appeal, on the preliminary matter as to whether the claim should be struck out as disclosing no justiciable cause of action, that there was indeed an arguable case.)

The facts of *Kent* are as follows. The 26 year old claimant, who was married with one child, was pregnant for the second time. She suffered from asthma and, on 16 February 1991, she was very wheezy, so she telephoned her doctor, who arrived at the house at around 4pm. At 4.25 pm, she telephoned the third defendant, using the 999 service. She gave her name, age and address, and an indication of her medical condition, and requested that an ambulance be sent to the claimant's home at once as a matter of urgency, to take the her to Queen Mary's Hospital. The person who received that telephone call agreed to direct an ambulance to the house, the distance from the ambulance station to the claimant's home being about seven miles. The nationally recommended maximum standard time from the receipt of a call to arrival of an ambulance at the scene was 14 minutes.

At 4.38 pm, the claimant's husband telephoned the ambulance service, and he was told that they were well on their way. At 4.54 pm, the doctor telephoned the ambulance service again, and was told that 'the ambulance is on its way to you, it should be a couple of minutes'. In fact, the ambulance did not arrive until some 38 minutes after the first call, and the first defendant then travelled with the claimant in the ambulance on the journey to the hospital, which took about six minutes. They arrived at around 5.15 pm. During the journey to the hospital, the claimant was given oxygen intermittently, but, before the journey was over, she suffered a respiratory arrest, resulting in serious memory impairment, a personality change and a miscarriage.

Turner J had ruled that the ambulance service was in breach of its duty of care to the claimant. He stated:

> I should have found it offensive to and inconsistent with concepts of common humanity if, in circumstances such as the present, where there had been an unreasonable and unexplained delay in providing the services which the ambulance service was in a position to meet, and had accepted that it would supply an ambulance, the law could not in its turn provide a remedy.

It was accepted by the defence that two of the requirements for the existence of a duty of care, as stated in *Caparo v Dickman* (1990), were present here. These were foresight and the requirement that it should be fair, just and reasonable for a duty to exist. However, the defendants contended that the necessary relationship of proximity between the parties, also laid down as a requirement in that case, was not present. The Court of Appeal rejected this argument, holding that the ambulance service is more aptly compared with a hospital or health service than with other emergency or voluntary services. The ambulance service was held to be at least under a public law duty as part of its statutory function. It was wholly inappropriate to regard its officers as volunteers, as the defence had suggested. The judge at first instance had been correct in holding that the ambulance service owed a duty of care to the claimant and had, in all the circumstances of the case, been in breach of that duty.

The Court of Appeal held that, in certain circumstances, an ambulance service could be liable to a patient if an emergency 999 call has been accepted and the ambulance fails, for no good reason, to arrive within a reasonable time. However, it was held that there is no general duty owed to the public by the ambulance service to respond to a telephone call for help. It is crucial that a 999 call must have been accepted and that the patient was relying on the timely arrival of an ambulance. Lord Woolf remarked that the case might well have been differently decided if the question of resources had been raised, as the courts are reluctant to be drawn into arguments about resources.

It is common practice for the person, usually a doctor, who calls for the ambulance to state not only the name and address of the patient, but also to give some details about the condition of the patient, indicating the urgency of the situation. It does seem fair, just and reasonable in those circumstances that a duty of care should be found to exist once the call has been expected and is relied upon. The patient is not a member of an indeterminate class and is likely to suffer physical harm rather than pure economic loss or mere property loss. The need for an ambulance to attend is dependent upon the supply of sufficient information for the ambulance service to enable it to recognise the urgency of the situation and the address or location of the patient. It will still be possible, in future cases, to defend a claim based on non-attendance or late attendance, if it can be proved that weather or traffic conditions prevented the ambulance reaching the patient either in time or at all. This matter would be considered under the general heading of breach of duty. However, the court rejected the argument that there might not be a duty of care if there were a conflict of priorities at the scene of an accident. Lord Woolf considered that the issue of breach of duty might be sufficient to provide a defence in an appropriate situation.

In *R v Comr of Customs and Excise ex p F and I Services Ltd* (2000), the judge remarked that the scope of duties owed by public authorities in the exercise of their statutory functions is a developing area of law, and it could not be stated with any certainty that the Commissioner did not owe a duty of care in this case.

A distinction was drawn between the exercise of a discretion and the performance of a duty in *R v Newham London BC ex p Anthony Lumley* (2000). This was an application for judicial review of the failure by the council to exercise its discretion in securing accommodation for the applicant pending the outcome of a review of the council's decision that the applicant was not in priority need of housing as a homeless person. The applicant had made a formal application as a homeless person for accommodation. His solicitors had set out the circumstances of his homelessness and explained that the applicant was at risk to himself and was 'vulnerable' as a result of mental illness within the meaning of s 188(3) of the Housing Act 1996. The council's advisor found that the applicant was in priority need and he was provided with temporary accommodation pending the council's final decision on his application, but that application was later refused and the applicant was told that he had to leave his temporary accommodation within a few days. The council failed to respond to a request to house the applicant pending a review of the decision, and the applicant's solicitors submitted that the council had a public law duty to behave reasonably. They argued that five days' notice for a man who had health problems, no income except welfare benefits and no capital was not long enough to enable him to arrange accommodation for himself, so that the notice period was unreasonable.

The trial judge granted the applicant permission to apply for judicial review and the council agreed to accommodate him pending the hearing. It was held that, until the council had received the solicitors' request for a review, there had been no decision which the council was required by law to make pursuant to s 188(3) of the 1996 Act. However, it was the council's duty to be proactive in making its inquiries into the claim that the applicant suffered from mental illness. They had had sent a questionnaire to his GP, who responded in a way which tended to support the claim. They sent the response to a medical assessment officer, who was not a psychiatrist, but that person had made no inquiries of his own and did not see the applicant before completing a form with boxes to tick, indicating that the applicant was not considered to be vulnerable on medical grounds. No reasons had been given by the medical assessment officer for his findings.

Accordingly, it was held that the council's original decision was seriously flawed. It had failed in its duty to pursue proactively inquiries of its own into the applicant's medical condition after information from his GP that the applicant suffered from severe depressive reaction. Moreover, it had not given the applicant an opportunity to respond to the findings of its medical assessment officer. These matters had not been taken into account in the decision to terminate the temporary accommodation. It was unjust that any judgment had been made on the medical evidence in the file because the council had not carried out its duties properly. Justice demanded that temporary accommodation should be continued for a vulnerable, homeless applicant until a lawful decision on his application had been made. The application was allowed.

6.5   Conclusion

In many of the cases discussed in this section, the single common factor has been that the courts have referred to *Caparo v Dickman* (1990) and the three-stage test. From this, we must conclude that many of the decisions turn on issues of policy and considerations of whether it would be 'fair, just and reasonable' to impose a duty. For that reason, it is difficult to predict the outcome of decisions and this is an interesting area of law in which there are sure to be important developments. In particular, the courts have indicated, in the more recent cases concerning liability of public authorities, that human rights considerations could well mean that the extent of liability will increase (see 1.10).

SITUATIONS IN WHICH
NO DUTY OF CARE IS OWED

'No duty' situations

Consider what particular policy issues were important in each of the following 'no duty' cases. It has been held in a number of cases that no duty of care is owed.

- Legal proceedings

  People who rely on lawyers to bring or defend legal actions on their behalf until July 2000 had no redress against them in negligence, because the House of Lords had established that no duty of care is owed in relation to legal proceeding (*Rondel v Worsley* (1969); *Saif Ali v Mitchell* (1980)). However, in *Hall v Simons and Others* (2000), the House of Lords changed the law, and a duty is now owed by advocates.

- Judges, witnesses, etc

  The law protects judges and witnesses from negligence actions on grounds of public policy (*Sirros v Moore* (1975)).

- Where another compensation system provides a remedy

  If the claimant could obtain compensation by using another system, such as the Criminal Injuries Compensation Board, there may be a 'no duty' situation in negligence (*Hill v Chief Constable of West Yorkshire* (1988)).

- Wrongful life

  It has been held to be against public policy to claim that one should never have been born at all (*McKay v Essex AHA* (1982)).

- Where the claimant is a member of an indeterminately large class of people

  (*Goodwill v British Pregnancy Advisory Service* (1996); *Monroe v London Fire and Civil Defence Authority* (1991)). But, see *Kent v London Ambulance Service* (2000); *Palmer v Tees HA* (1999).

- Police cases

  There appears to be a movement on the part of judges to protect the police from negligence actions in certain cases by holding that no duty of care is owed (*Hill v Chief Constable of West Yorkshire* (1988); *Ancell v McDermott* (1993); *Osman v Ferguson* (1994); *Osman v UK* (1999)). But, see *Clark v CC Northamptonshire Police* (1999); *Swinney v CC Northumberland (No 2)* (1999); *Reeves v Comr of Police of the Metropolis* (1999).

- Claimant caused his or her own misfortune

  If it can be shown that the claimant was him or herself responsible for the misfortune which befell him or her, no duty of care in negligence exists in some cases (*Governors of the Peabody Donation Fund v Parkinson* (1984)).

- No duty to rescue

  There is no duty in law to carry out a rescue, though certain people who undertake responsibility to care for others, or who are required by law to do so (for example, parents) do owe a duty of care to their charges (*Barnett v Chelsea and Kensington AHA* (1969); *Salmon v Seafarer Restaurants* (1983); *Hale v London Underground* (1992)).

  Note the generous approach taken by the courts in the past towards rescuers, as there is no legal duty to carry out a rescue in many instances, but many people consider that there may be a moral responsibility. Should the courts also be as generous to members of the professional rescue services who are contractually bound to carry out rescues?

- Local authorities and other public bodies

  Clunis v Camden and Islington HA (1997); *Digital Equipment v Hampshire CC* (1997); *Barrett v Enfield BC* (1999); *W v Essex CC* (2000); *R v Newham ex p Lumley* (2000); *Gower v Bromley* (1999).

  Note the fact that, in many of these cases, the courts refer to the three stage test in *Caparo v Dickinson* (1990) when reaching decisions. Note, also, the likely impact of the Human Rights Act 1998 on this area of law.

- Ambulance service

  Kent v London Ambulance Service (2000).

CHAPTER 7

BREACH OF DUTY – THE STANDARD OF CARE

The second consideration for the claimant is to establish that there has been a breach of duty on the part of the defendant. This lies at the heart of the negligence action and represents what negligence in essence really means – fault on the part of the defendant. Fault in law is unreasonable behaviour in a particular situation.

Two matters are involved in deciding whether there has been a breach of duty. The first centres on the question, 'how ought a person in the position of the defendant have acted in the circumstances?'. This is a question of law, which sets the standard of care that the defendant was required to meet. The second question concerns the factual matter as to whether or not the defendant met that standard.

7.1   The 'reasonable man' test

The traditional formula which the courts employ is to ask whether the defendant has observed the requisite standard of care in all the circumstances. The standard of care of 'the reasonable man' is what is usually expected. Failure to act as a reasonable man would have acted is an indication of negligence.

In practice, the position is that the 'reasonable man' formula is, like the concept of duty of care, a control device which the judges use to arrive at decisions which they consider to be fair or appropriate in the circumstances. A number of policy questions may be involved. For example:

- who can best bear the loss in the particular case?;

- was the defendant insured?;

- what implications will the particular case have for future cases?;

- what standard of safety can potential claimants expect?;

- what is fair and just on the particular facts?;

- what are the implications of a particular decision for society as a whole?

Thus, the 'reasonable man' formula is, in reality, like the notion of duty of care, a device which allows the judges to arrive at decisions on grounds of policy or expediency. There are now no juries in negligence cases. Whereas at one time, before the use of juries in these cases was discontinued, it was arguable that the jury could decide whether, as average, reasonable people, they thought the defendant had met the required standard, such argument is no longer possible, as it is the judge alone who must decide.

However, as far as possible, the standard is objective and the judge formulates the position in terms not of what the particular person ought to have done in the circumstances, but what a reasonable person should have done in those circumstances.

Bearing this in mind, it is still necessary to consider the various interpretations of the expression 'reasonable man'.

Here are some of the better known formulations:

- *Per* Alderson B in *Blythe v Birmingham Waterworks* (1865):

  Negligence is the omission to do something which a reasonable man, guided upon those considerations which ordinarily regulate human affairs, would do, or doing something which a prudent and reasonable man would not do.

- *Per* Greer LJ in *Hall v Brooklands Auto-Racing Club* (1933):

  The person concerned is sometimes described as the 'man on the street', or the 'man on the Clapham Omnibus', or as I recently read in an American author the 'man who takes the magazines at home and in the evening pushes the lawnmower in his shirt sleeves'.

- *Per* Lord Macmillan in *Glasgow Corpn v Muir* (1943):

  The standard of foresight of the reasonable man eliminates the personal equation and is independent of the idiosyncrasies of the particular person whose conduct is in question.

- AP Herbert in his *Uncommon Law* (1977), Eyre Methuen:

  The reasonable man is never a woman.

- CK Allen in *Law in the Making*, 7th edn, 1964, Clarendon:

  Nobody is deceived by the fiction that the judge is stating not what he himself thinks, but what an average reasonable man might think.

7.2 The cases

The cases reveal the judges' approach to the problem of deciding whether, in a particular case, the standard of care has been met by the defendant. A number of general propositions can be elicited from the cases.

The legal standard of care applicable in a variety different fact situations is now settled law. What is regarded as 'reasonable' behaviour varies according to the circumstances of each case, and the standard of care usually relates to the activity being carried out by the defendant, rather than to his or her personal characteristics. It should be noted that negligence may occur in the omission to take some action or other, as well as in the taking of some positive negligent action. However, the House of Lords has warned against relying too heavily on previous cases to decide what behaviour can be regarded as meeting, or failing to meet, the appropriate standard of care.

7.2.1 Reasonable assessment of risk

It is reasonable to assess the risks involved in a particular situation, and to consider whether precautions are necessary, bearing in mind the magnitude and likelihood of harm.

If the defendant had an opportunity to reflect, he or she is expected to carry out a basic assessment of risks. The reasonable person is expected to consider the likely consequences of particular actions and weigh them against the precautions which are necessary to avoid injury. A defendant who can show that sensible consideration has been given to the implications of particular activities is less likely to be found negligent than one who has not. Risk management of this kind is commonplace in industry. However, in many everyday activities, such as driving, incidents can arise that demand 'spur of the moment' decision making; in such circumstances, risk assessment and management are clearly irrelevant.

It would be unreasonable not to weigh up the risks involved and to balance them against the difficulties, inconvenience or expense of taking steps to avoid them.

In *Bolton v Stone* (1951), a cricket ball was hit right out of a cricket ground and onto a road where the claimant was standing 100 yards away from the batsman. The ball cleared a 17 foot high fence which was 78 yards from the batsman. During the trial, evidence was produced that the ball had only been hit out of the ground about six times in the previous 30 years. It was held by the House of Lords that the defendants had not acted unreasonably in failing to guard against the remote risk involved.

Lord Reid said:

> Reasonable men do in fact take into account the degree of risk, and do not act upon a bare possibility as they would if the risk were more substantial.

In *Hilder v Associated Portland Cement Manufacturers Ltd* (1961), a case involving similar facts to those in *Bolton v Stone* (1951), it was held that there had been negligence when a football was kicked from an open piece of land with a low boundary wall, onto a highway, and the claimant, who was riding on the adjacent road on his motorcycle, was killed when he was hit by the ball.

In *Haley v London Electricity Board* (1965), it was held that the likelihood of a blind person walking along a busy pavement, and falling into a hole dug there by the defendants, should have been anticipated and guarded against by them. A large number of blind people live in London, and it is statistically likely that eventually a blind person will walk on a city street and perhaps fall into an unguarded hole.

Obviously, the greater the potential harm, the more important it is to take sensible precautions against it, and the less reasonable it is to ignore the need to take such precautions.

In *Paris v Stepney BC* (1951), the defendants were held to have been unreasonable in failing to supply safety goggles to a one-eyed workman. The consequence of their lack of care was the total blindness brought upon the workman when a chip of metal flew into his one good eye.

The care taken by the defendant should be commensurate with the risk, and there may be some situations in which the reasonable person need take no precautions at all, because no one is expected to guard against remote events or outrageously improbable events.

7.2.2 Unforeseeable risk cannot be anticipated

The defendant may have a defence based on current knowledge at the time of the incident. The standard of knowledge required of a defendant is that which was available at the time that the alleged negligence occurred. The defendant is judged only in the light of knowledge available at the time of the alleged negligent act.

A reasonable person is not expected to anticipate unknown risks. Unforeseeable risks cannot be anticipated and failing to guard against them will not be negligence.

This is sometimes known as the 'state of the art defence'. It is best illustrated by the case of *Roe v Minister of Health* (1954). The claimant was one of two patients who suffered pain and permanent paralysis from the waist down, after being injected with a spinal anaesthetic called nupercaine. The nupercaine had been stored in glass ampoules which had in turn been placed in phenol solution, a disinfectant. Evidence was produced at the trial to the effect that minute invisible cracks had formed in the glass ampoules, which had allowed some of the nupercaine to be contaminated by phenol solution which had seeped through the cracks. Although this evidence has since been doubted, it was accepted at the trial, and on the grounds that such a phenomenon had not previously been discovered, and could not therefore be guarded against, the defendants escaped liability for negligence.

However, once it is suspected that there may be a risk of harm, it is necessary to reappraise the situation. In *N v UK Medical Research Council; sub nom Creutzfeldt Jakob Disease Litigation* (1996), it was held that there had been a negligent failure to carry out a full reappraisal of the use of Human Growth Hormone (HGH) once it was suspected that it could cause Creutzfeldt-Jakob Disease (CJD). HGH had been used as part of a clinical trial programme to treat children from 1959. By 1977, it was suspected that children who had received the treatment had contracted CJD.

7.2.3   The utility of the conduct

The reasonable person assesses the utility of the conduct which is being carried out. For example, risky measures might be necessary in order to save lives.

In *Watt v Hertfordshire CC* (1954), a woman had been trapped under a car, and the claimant was a fireman, and a member of the rescue team. He was injured by a heavy piece of equipment, which in the emergency circumstances, had not been safely secured on the lorry on which it was being transported. His action for negligence failed on the grounds that the risk of the equipment causing injury in transit was not so great as to prevent the efforts to save the woman's life.

Driving at excessive speed, while not normally acceptable, is perhaps justified, in exceptional circumstances, as in the case of emergency services racing to assist an injured person. However, the case law suggests there is no special case for exempting employees of the emergency services if they cause injury to other road users when responding to emergency calls. In *Ward v London CC* (1938), a fire engine driver was held to have been negligent when he drove across a light-controlled crossing when he should have stopped. In *Griffin v Mersey Regional Ambulance* (1998), a motorist collided with an ambulance which was proceeding across a junction against a red traffic light, and the ambulance driver was held to have been negligent, but there was a 60% reduction in the damages to take account of contributory negligence.

7.2.4   The expense of taking precautions

It would not be negligent to fail to take a precaution which is prohibitively expensive in the light of a risk which is not very great.

In *Latimer v AEC* (1953), the owners of a factory which had been flooded did all that was possible to cover slippery areas with sawdust. The alternative would have been to close the factory. When the claimant slipped on the floor and was injured, he sued for negligence, basing his claim on the fact that his employers should have closed the factory. This extreme measure was held to have been unnecessary, and the claim failed.

In *Smith v Littlewoods Ltd* (1987), vandals set fire to a cinema that had been left empty and derelict. The fire spread to adjoining buildings, causing property damage, but no one was injured. The defendants had tried to take precautions to prevent vandals entering the property, but they were unaware of their presence there and had no reason to believe that adjoining landowners considered that there was any threat from them. The monetary loss in this case was substantial, but the likelihood of the events occurring which caused the damage was low. The House of Lords held that there was no breach of duty here.

In *Withers v Perry Chain Co Ltd* (1961), employers of a man who was very prone to dermatitis were not liable when they found no alternative work for him that did not involve contact with chemicals. They had no such work available, and there was nothing they could have done to avoid his injury, short of dismissing the claimant. In *Overseas Tankship (UK) Ltd v Miller Steamship Co Pty Ltd, The Wagon Mound (No 2)* (1967), the Privy Council took the view that a reasonable man may ignore a very small risk if there is a valid reason for doing so, but he should not ignore a small risk if the elimination of that risk is a simple and cheap matter.

It has occasionally been successfully argued that limited resources made it impossible for defendants to take precautions necessary to prevent harm. These arguments did not succeed in *Selfe v Ilford and District HMC* (1970). The claimant was admitted to a hospital ward after a suicide attempt and was put on the ground floor along with three other patients, all of whom were known suicide risks. The claimant climbed through an unlocked window and jumped out, in another suicide attempt, and sustained serious injuries. The judge chose not to accept arguments on behalf of the defence that scarce resources prevented proper staffing. Despite this decision, there have been others in which mentally ill patients who have attempted suicide have brought unsuccessful claims. For example, in *Thorne v Northern Group HMC* (1964), a depressed patient was sent home from a general hospital, and soon afterwards committed suicide at home. It was held that there had been no negligence on the part of the staff at the hospital, as this was not a patient who should have been kept under constant supervision.

In *Knight v Home Office* (1990), it was held that the higher standard of care to be expected in hospitals did not apply to remand prisons. Pill J said:

> To take an extreme example, if the evidence was that no funds were available to provide any medical facilities in a large prison, there would be a failure to achieve the standard of care appropriate for prisoners. In a different context, lack of funds would not excuse a public body which operated its vehicles on the public roads without any system of maintenance for the vehicles, if an accident occurred because of lack of maintenance.

Despite cases of this kind, the courts are reluctant to enter into a formal cost-benefit analysis, and the decisions are often based on a 'gut reaction' by judges, taking into account factors such as the social utility of particular conduct as well as the cost of safety measures.

7.2.5 Lack of special skills

Ordinary people who do not possess special skills are not expected to exercise the same standard of care as skilled people.

For example, in *Phillips v Whiteley Ltd* (1938), a jeweller who pierced the claimant's ears, was not expected to take the same hygiene measures as a surgeon performing an operation. The claimant contracted a serious blood disorder after having her ears pierced by the defendant jeweller. He had performed the procedure in a white-washed room, and dipped the instruments in disinfectant, passed them through a flame, and placed them under running water. It was held that he had taken reasonable steps in the circumstances.

In *Wells v Cooper* (1958), an amateur handyman had fixed a door handle. It came off in the claimant's hand and he fell backwards and was injured. His negligence action failed because the defendant had shown the same degree of skill as a reasonably competent carpenter in undertaking the work.

7.2.6 Contributory negligence and the standard of care

If a case concerns the question of contributory negligence, the approach taken by the courts may be more subjective, and the judges tend to consider what behaviour would have been reasonable for the *particular* claimant, in the circumstances. For example, children can be treated more leniently than adults when the courts are deciding whether they have taken sufficient care for their own safety.

7.2.7 Children

Children are not expected to be as careful as adults.

Although there are few English cases on this point, there is authority from other common law countries which suggests that children are not expected to exercise as high a standard of care as adults. In *McHale v Watson* (1966) it was held that the standard is that of the reasonable child of the defendant's age.

In *Mullin v Richards* (1988), the Court of Appeal held that a 15 year old schoolgirl was not negligent when, while she and a school friend of the same age were 'fencing' with plastic rulers, the friend was injured in the eye. Games of that kind were not prohibited by the school and were played quite frequently. Hutchinson LJ followed approach taken in *McHale v Watson* (1966), saying:

> The question ... whether an ordinarily prudent and reasonable 15 year old schoolgirl in the defendant's situation would have realised as much.

There are parallels which may be drawn from other areas of English law. For example, in occupiers' liability, where the standard of care is very similar to that in the ordinary law of negligence, the Occupiers' Liability Act 1957 states that 'an occupier must expect children to be less careful than adults' (s 2(3)(a)).

In contributory negligence, where again similar standards apply, it has been held that the appropriate standard of care is that of a child of the age of the claimant (*Gough v Thorne* (1966)). The Pearson Commission endorsed this in 1978, taking the view that no child under the age of 13 years should be found contributorily negligent. However, unusually in *Armstrong v Cottrell* (1993) it was held that a 12 year old was one third to blame for her injuries, the judge being of the opinion that 12 year olds should know the Highway Code. It appears that the courts deal with each case on its facts. Thus, in *Morales v Eccleston* (1991), an 11 year old boy who ran out into the road after his football was found to be 75% contributory negligent.

While occupiers' liability and contributory negligence provide useful guidance, it should be borne in mind that the approach tends to be more subjective in both these instances than in ordinary negligence, with the courts looking at the situation from the standpoint of the child.

The law does expect young children to be supervised, and, if they are not adequately supervised, the adults responsible for them may be sued for negligence. In *Fowles v Bedfordshire CC* (1995), a local authority was held to be negligent in allowing young people to do gymnastics at a youth centre without supervision. Local authorities and teachers take the place of parents as regards children in their charge, and must exercise the standard of care of the reasonably prudent parent. In *Jenney v North Lincolnshire CC* (1998), the Court of Appeal held that a local authority had been negligent, because they had failed to demonstrate that there was a non-negligent explanation for the presence of a schoolchild on a major road during school hours (see 7.2.9).

7.2.8   The sick and disabled

People who are ill or disabled are not expected to exercise as high a standard of care as other people in the same situation, but, on the same basis as children, would probably be judged according to the standard of people suffering from the particular disability.

7.2.9   Carers and organisers

People who care for others and are responsible for them must take steps to see that they are reasonably safe. The standard of care is higher for carers of very vulnerable people, such as young children and the sick and disabled, than it is for others who are able to take some responsibility for themselves.

In *Morrell v Owen and Others* (1993), it was held that the duty of care owed to disabled athletes by coaches and organisers is greater, and the standard of care required is higher, than that owed to able-bodied athletes. The claimant in this case was a paraplegic amateur archer who was injured by a stray discus suffering brain damage as a result. The judge took the view that a blow from a misthrow was entirely foreseeable and that the BLASA coaches and organisers should have taken more comprehensive safety precautions.

In some instances, carers have been held to be guilty of the crime of manslaughter when they failed to discharge their duty to people in their care. Such a finding would almost automatically result in the settlement of any civil claim against them. In the prosecution of the managing director of an activity centre responsible for a canoeing disaster at Lyme Bay in which several young people were killed, both he and his company OLL Ltd were found guilty of manslaughter. It was held that there was gross negligence on the part of the managing director, and this factor led to the finding of corporate manslaughter.

In *Barrett v Ministry of Defence* (1995), the defendants were liable for failing to take proper care of an airman who died when he inhaled his own vomit after a long drinking session. The same principle can be extended to professional people, who are responsible to their clients because professional people have knowledge or skills which are denied to others.

In *Jebson v Ministry of Defence* (2000), the Court of Appeal held that an adult should normally be aware of dangers created by his actions, and could not rely on others to exercise care on his behalf when he is drunk. However, if a duty of care was implied in respect of a person likely to be drunk, that duty could not later be avoided.

In *Metropolitan Police Comr v Reeves (Joint Administratrix of The Estate of Martin Lynch (Deceased))* (1999), duty police officers had been informed by a doctor that a prisoner, Mr Lynch, was a suicide risk. They could have taken relatively simple precautions which would have prevented the prisoner committing suicide, and were held to have been negligent in failing to do so.

People with the power or duty to control others must take reasonable steps to prevent them from causing harm by their acts or omissions. Accordingly, parents and others who take charge of children may be primarily liable if their children are out of control and other people suffer foreseeable damage as a result.

In *Watson v British Boxing Board Of Control* (1999), the organisers of a boxing match were negligent when they failed to provide proper ringside medical facilities. The claimant suffered serious brain damage during a boxing match as a result of a blow to the head. As the Board had failed to provide both proper equipment and trained medical specialists, it was in breach of its duty to the claimant. The claimant was not *volenti* (that is, he had not consented to the injury).

In *Bacon v White and Others* (1998), a diving instructor was in breach of his duty of care to a novice diver who died while scuba diving. Although there had been a breach of the rules of the governing body of the sport, this did not necessarily define the standard of care in this case, but, nevertheless, the proper standard of care had not been met because the claimant was a novice and was owed a higher standard of care than in the case of skilled participants in this particularly hazardous sport. Similarly, referees owe a duty of care to players, especially if they are young and new to the game (*Smolden v Whitworth and Nolan* (1997)).

7.2.10 Drivers

It would appear that all drivers are expected to exercise the same high standard of care. In *Roberts v Ramsbottom* (1980), the defendant driver, an elderly man, suffered a stroke and became mentally and physically incapable of driving safely. He was held to have been negligent when he caused accidents. By contrast, in *Mansfield v Weetabix* (1997), the Court of Appeal ruled that, if the loss of control occurs when the driver is unaware that he or she is suffering from a medical condition, whether the onset is gradual or sudden, the driver should not be found to be negligent.

Statistics show that most negligence claims involve road traffic accidents. The basic principles of negligence apply equally to virtually all road users, and the standard of care is that of the reasonable road user. In very exceptional cases, however, there are some variations in this standard in the case of particular classes of individual. Reasonable drivers are not entitled to assume that other road users will exercise care, and they will be liable for foreseeable injury caused by their negligence. The Highway Code gives guidance on sensible driving, and the reasonable person is expected to be familiar with its contents. However, it is not safe to assume that there is negligence every time a person fails to observe the Highway Code. Failure to observe the Highway Code does not in itself give rise to liability on the part of the defendant, but this may be relied upon to establish liability in a civil case. If the defendant has committed a traffic offence, there may also be a finding of negligence, and, if the defendant has been convicted of a driving offence arising out the facts of the case where there is a negligence claim, that claim will usually be settled out of court in the claimant's favour. Section 11 of the Civil Evidence Act 1968 allows evidence of a person's criminal convictions to be used in civil proceedings, and the burden of proof will be reversed.

Car owners are expected to take reasonable steps to maintain their vehicles in good order. They should obtain MOT certificates when necessary, but a valid MOT certificate will not of itself absolve a defendant from liability for an accident caused by a defective vehicle.

The position of drivers has probably been influenced by the requirement of compulsory liability insurance. As Atiyah points out (see Atiyah, PS, *Accidents, Compensation and The Law*, 1999, Cane, P (ed)):

> The tendency to objectivise the standard of care, and to ignore the personal characteristics of the defendant, which has gathered force during the past fifty years or so, may have been influenced by insurance considerations. Since the defendant is not going to pay the damages personally, judges may be (consciously or unconsciously) more concerned with the hardship to the

claimant ... and may therefore be more willing to find a defendant negligent even though he has done nothing morally culpable.

In *Nettleship v Weston* (1971), a very inexperienced learner driver crashed and injured her instructor. Her instructor had knowingly put himself in a relationship with an underskilled person. She was, however, held by the Court of Appeal to have been negligent. Although she was only learning to drive, she should have exercised the same standard of care as a reasonably competent experienced driver, although she was told by Lord Denning that she should not regard herself as morally blameworthy.

7.2.11 Experts, professionals and people with special skills

Experts are expected to demonstrate the same high standard of care as other experts in the same field.

An expert is required to exercise the same standard of care as a reasonably competent person trained in that particular trade or profession. This applies to people of all professions, but the cases demonstrate that members of the professions may be able to escape liability by relying on the *Bolam* principle, established in a medical negligence case.

In *Bolam v Friern HMC* (1957), the test was stated thus, *per* McNair J:

> A doctor is not guilty of negligence if he has acted in accordance with a practice accepted as proper by a responsible body of medical men skilled in that particular art. Putting it another way round, a doctor is not negligent if he is acting in accordance with such a practice, merely because there is a body of opinion that takes a contrary view.

A doctor is not expected to exercise the highest expert skill, so a GP would only be required to meet the same standards as other competent GPs, rather than those of consultants. Even within this framework, different standards have been held to apply in certain circumstances. For example, in *Knight v Home Office* (1990), it was held that a prison doctor could not be expected to exercise the same standard of care as a doctor working in an NHS hospital. In that case, a prisoner had committed suicide, and the judge recognised that the resources available for care and supervision of prisoners who might commit suicide was a resource allocation matter for Parliament.

However, in *Brooks v Home Office* (1999), it was held, distinguishing *Knight v Home Office* (1990), that a woman prisoner who is being held on remand can expect the same standard of obstetric care as would be available to her outside prison, subject to the constraints of having to be transported and having her freedom restricted. However, the claimant's case failed because she could not prove that the breach of duty caused the damage complained of.

In the *Bolam* case itself, there were two schools of thought about the treatment of patients who receive ECT. One recommended that relaxant drugs should be used, and the other that they should not because of the risk of fractures. The claimant, who had not been warned of the risk, had been given the relaxant drugs, and had not been restrained to prevent injury, suffered fractures as a result. On the basis of the test formulated by the judge, the action failed.

Although the statement was only a direction to the jury in a High Court case, it has been adopted by the House of Lords with approval in later cases and is regularly re-stated in medical negligence cases.

In effect, it means that provided the doctor concerned was able to produce expert witnesses prepared to testify that they would consider the course of action taken by the defendant to be in keeping with a responsible body of medical practice, he or she could escape liability. Professional people are well organised, and have every incentive to protect one another from negligence claims, except in cases of blatant negligence, in which case the action is likely to be settled out of court. The result is that claimants are at a disadvantage. Indeed, the Pearson Commission in 1978 commented that only 30–40% of medical negligence claims are successful, as opposed to 60–80% of negligence claims generally.

The justification for the *Bolam* rule was stated by Lord Scarman in *Maynard v West Midlands RHA* (1985):

> Differences of opinion exist, and continue to exist, in the medical as in other professions. There is seldom any one answer exclusive of all others to problems of professional judgment. A court may prefer one body of opinion to the other; but that is no basis for a conclusion of negligence.

7.2.12 Some criticisms of *Bolam*

A number of criticisms of the *Bolam* principle have been expressed. They can be summarised as follows:

- the rule is unfair to claimants and too protective of the professions;

- the rule allows the professions to set their own standards, when professional standards should be reviewable by the courts;

- the *Bolam* test is a state of the art descriptive test, based on what is actually done, whereas in negligence generally the test is a normative test, based on what should be done (see Montrose, 'Is negligence an ethical or sociological concept?' (1958) 21 MLR 259);

- the *Bolam* test in medical cases allows treatments which are only marginally acceptable to meet an acceptable standard of care. In the *Bolam* case itself, the treatment which injured the claimant was even in those days almost obsolete, and was known to carry a high risk of fractures. Articles had appeared to that effect in the medical press for many years;

- while requiring the defendant to conform to a 'responsible' body of opinion the cases never actually define what is 'responsible'. How many doctors would be required to form a 'responsible body'?;
- the rule is yet another example of the professions protecting one another: see *Hatcher v Black* (1954) in which Lord Denning described the negligence action as a 'dagger at the doctor's back'.

7.2.13 Challenges to *Bolam*: the *Bolitho* test

Some of the arguments which were raised against *Bolam* in the older cases were resurrected in a new series of cases which have been hailed as challenging the *Bolam* test. The cases turn on two basic points: whether judges can choose between two bodies of medical opinion, and the concept of what constitutes 'a responsible body of medical opinion'.

Can the judge make a choice between two bodies of medical opinion? The indications from more recent cases at High Court and Court of Appeal levels are that although judges cannot question medical opinion if it is responsible, they may sometimes *initially* decide whether a particular body of opinion *is* responsible. Thus far, a judge is able to make a choice between two bodies of opinion. In *Newell v Goldburg* (1995), Mantell J held that, by 1985, doctors who did not warn vasectomy patients that there was a risk of natural restoration of the severed vas, and therefore a risk of pregnancy, 'could not be considered to be acting reasonably or responsibly'. In *Lybert v Warrington HA* (1996), it was held by the Court of Appeal that a warning given by a gynaecologist about the possible failure of a sterilisation operation, was inadequate despite the fact that it was in accordance with standard practice of gynaecologists at the time.

Deviation from standard practice? Although the courts have never produced a satisfactory definition of 'responsible', the term is frequently interchangeable with 'respectable' or 'reputable', but since judges treat medical experts with great respect, it would only be in the most extreme circumstances that medical opinion or practice which deviates from what is usually regarded as standard practice would be considered to be anything but respectable or reputable.

The matter has now been clarified by the House of Lords ruling in *Bolitho v City and Hackney Health Authority* (1997). Although the new test is simply a modification of the *Bolam* test, it provides the opportunity for a new approach to expert evidence in relation to the standard of care.

In 1984, a two year old boy, Patrick Bolitho, was admitted to hospital, suffering from croup. His treatment was under the care of Dr Horn, the senior paediatric registrar, and Dr Rodger, the senior house officer in paediatrics. Patrick was quickly discharged from hospital, but was soon re-admitted with further breathing problems, so arrangements were made for him to be nursed on a one to one basis. The next morning, Patrick seemed much better, but in the afternoon the nurse was very concerned, because he was wheezing badly and had turned white. She bleeped Dr Horn, who promised to come and check him as soon as possible, but when the nurse returned to him Patrick was much better, so it was decided that Dr Horn did not need to come. A second episode occurred and the nurse again became very worried and telephoned Dr Horn, who was in clinic. She told the nurse that she had asked Dr Rodger to see Patrick, but the batteries in her bleep were flat and she did not receive the message from Dr Horn. Meanwhile, Patrick's condition again improved and he was chatty and active. About half an hour later, the nurse became concerned yet again and telephoned the doctors. The emergency buzzer meant that Patrick was experiencing severe breathing difficulties, and a cardiac arrest team was called, but Patrick's respiratory system had become completely blocked and it was about 10 minutes before his heart and breathing functions were restored. As a result of this episode, Patrick suffered severe brain damage and died some considerable time later. His mother continued proceedings as administratrix of his estate.

The defendants admitted that Dr Horn was in breach of her duty of care, as she should have attended Patrick or should have ensured that a deputy did so. The case turned on causation, and the court had to consider what Dr Horn would have done if she had attended Patrick when called to do so and whether this would have made any difference to the outcome. It was agreed that, if Dr Horn had intubated the little boy before the serious episode (to provide an airway), he would not have suffered the cardiac arrest. The trial judge ruled that, if Dr Horn would have intubated the patient had she seen him, the action should succeed, but if she would not have intubated him, the claimant could only succeed if it could be established that such failure was contrary to accepted medical practice. This last issue involved the application of the *Bolam* test to *causation* in the event of a negligent omission. On the facts, the trial judge found that Dr Horn would not have intubated had she gone to check on Patrick.

The second question concerned the correct test to be applied to determine causation when there is a negligent omission. The House of Lords found that the trial judge had been correct to ask what course of action would have been followed by a reasonably competent medical practitioner. The experts for the defence unanimously stated that intubation would not have been appropriate. The claimant's experts assumed that Patrick had suffered a gradual decline into respiratory failure in the two hours before the final catastrophic event. The defence experts were of the opinion that there had been a sudden blockage of the respiratory system on each of the occasions and that Patrick's condition was not that of a child passing through stages of gradual progressive hypoxia.

The trial judge had ruled that there were two opposing bodies of medical opinion here, each representing responsible views of distinguished and truthful medical experts. Relying on *Maynard v West Midlands RHA* (1984), he said that he was in no position to choose which of these opinions he preferred.

He therefore decided that it had not been proved that the breach of duty by Dr Horn caused the damage. The House of Lords agreed with the majority in the Court of Appeal in accepting that the trial judge had taken the correct approach. Lord Browne-Wilkinson, delivering the judgment of the House, explained the law:

> The two questions which he had to decide on causation were: (1) what would Dr Horn have done, or authorised to be done, if she had attended Patrick? And (2) if she would not have intubated, would that have been negligent? The *Bolam* test has no relevance to the first of those questions but is central to the second.

In *Bolitho*, counsel for the appellant had argued before the Court of Appeal and House of Lords that the judge had been wrong to treat the *Bolam* test as requiring him to accept the views of an expert which were not based on logic. Counsel for the appellant argued that it was for the court, and not for doctors, to decide the standard of care in professional negligence cases. What is important about *Bolitho* is that the House of Lords accepted this argument to some extent. Their Lordships concluded that the court is not always bound to find that a doctor can escape liability for negligence by providing evidence from experts that his opinion and actions were in accordance with accepted medical practice. Lord Browne-Wilkinson continued:

> The use of these adjectives – responsible, reasonable and respectable – all show that the court has to be satisfied that the exponents of the body of medical opinion relied upon can demonstrate that such opinion has a logical basis. In particular, in cases involving, as they so often do, the weighing of risks against benefits, the judge, before accepting a body of opinion as being responsible, reasonable or respectable, will need to be satisfied that, in forming their view, the experts have directed their minds to the question of comparative risks and benefits and have reached a defensible conclusion on the matter.

Two highly persuasive cases supported this view. In *Hucks v Cole* (1993), the Court of Appeal found that a doctor had been negligent in not treating with penicillin a patient who was suffering from a condition which could lead to puerperal fever – a potentially fatal illness. Despite expert evidence that there were some doctors who would not have given the patient penicillin, the court believed that it was correct to select which expert view was 'correct', and chose that of the experts for the appellant. In the second case, *Edward Wong Finance Co Ltd v Johnson Stokes and Master* (1984), the Privy Council held that, even though the defendants had acted in accordance with an almost universal practice, they had still been negligent because that practice was not reasonable or responsible. Lord Browne-Wilkinson went on to explain that, in the vast majority of cases, the fact that distinguished experts are of a particular opinion will normally mean that the opinion is reasonable, and that only in rare cases will it be possible to demonstrate that the professional opinion does not 'withstand logical analysis'.

In the *Bolitho* case, the House of Lords unanimously decided that the case was not one in which the court could choose between the two expert views. Evidence given for the defence by the expert, Dr Dinwoody, could not have been dismissed as unreasonable or illogical, as intubation is far from being risk free, especially in a young child. The appeal therefore failed.

The decision in this case is significant because it has implications for all other types of professional negligence actions. Although the view that there may be a departure from *Bolam* is cautious, the case does allow the court to choose between two bodies of opinion in appropriate circumstances. However, this will only be possible if the judge is unable, as a matter of 'logic', to accept one of the professional opinions. These cases are likely to be rare, but, unfortunately, the House of Lords did not provide clear guidance on this. However, it seems that risk management by professional people will be regarded as important in future cases. It is already important in many industries and professions, such as heavy industry and even the healthcare professions.

Although the *Bolitho* case suggests that there will be more opportunities for claimants to succeed in professional negligence claims, it is unlikely to make a great deal of difference, though it may lead to more cases being settled before trial.

Bolam / *Bolitho* applies only to matters of professional opinion and not when the judge is taking expert advice on matters of fact. In *Penney and Others v East Kent HA* (1999), the Court of Appeal ruled that, where the judge was required to make findings of fact which were the subject of conflicting expert evidence, *Bolam*, as modified by *Bolitho*, had no application at this early stage in the enquiry, which is concerned with establishing the truth of factual evidence.

Under reforms introduced in the National Health Service by the Health Act 1999, health bodies will be required to implement guidance designed to improve standards of quality of care on a uniform basis. Clinical guidelines will be written by the Royal Colleges under the auspices of the National Institute for Clinical Excellence, and will be distributed throughout the NHS. It is possible that the courts will use these guidelines to determine the appropriate standard of care in clinical negligence cases. It will be difficult for doctors who deviate from these official guidelines to defend claims for negligence, unless there are specific reasons which justify such a departure from recognised good practice.

The new standards will ensure that the same high quality standards of care and treatment for conditions such as diabetes and coronary heart disease are available throughout the country in all primary care, local hospitals and specialist centres.

The decision in *Thomson v James and Others* (1996) is an indication of the importance of guidelines in professional practice. In that case, a GP had failed to observe the government advice when advising the parents of child about the vaccine for measles, mumps and rubella. In the event, the child who was not given the vaccination, on the advice of the GP, later contracted measles, and following complications, meningitis. She is permanently brain damaged as a result. The doctor was found at first instance to have been negligent.

However, on appeal, the case failed on the question of causation and the Court of Appeal did not discuss the effect of the guidelines on the standard of care. One might expect a return to the approach in *Hunter v Hanley* and the need to satisfy the test laid down in that case. The view of the court in *Hunter v Hanley* (1955) a Scottish case which preceded the *Bolam* case by two years was that:

> ... there is a heavy onus on the pursuer (claimant) to establish three facts, and without all three his case will fail. First, it must be proved that there is a usual and normal practice; secondly, it must be proved that the defender has not adopted that practice; and, thirdly, (and this is of crucial importance) it must be established that the course the doctor adopted is one which no professional man of ordinary skill would have taken if he had been acting with ordinary care.

7.2.14 Acceptable professional standards

A skilled or professional person is not required to have expert skill or competence in the particular field: 'It is sufficient if he exercises the ordinary skill of an ordinary competent man exercising that particular art', *per* McNair J, again in *Bolam*.

Experts are not expected to keep abreast of every new development or to have knowledge of all new ideas and practices. In *Crawford v Charing Cross Hospital* (1983), the claimant suffered brachial palsy because of the position of his arm during a blood transfusion while he was having surgery. He claimed that the anaesthetist should have been aware of the risk because an article on the subject had been published in the *Lancet* six months previously. It was held that there had been no negligence. The reasonable doctor cannot be expected to keep up to date with the entire literature all the time.

The latest General Medical Council advice on this matter is that a doctor must keep up to date with new developments, not only in medicine, but also in those aspects of law which are relevant to their practice. Arrangements for doctors to attend professional development courses should help to ensure that they do so. However, it is accepted that it may take some time for research findings to be made known to all doctors in a particular field.

In these days of much improved communications and emphasis on fast dissemination of professional information on electronic databases, it would be much more difficult to argue that keeping up to date is not to be expected. Changes brought about by the Health Act 1999 will ensure that the latest authoritative guidance be given to all doctors (see below, 7.2.13).

Failure to warn a patient of the risks involved in a particular medical procedure may amount to negligence. Much will depend upon whether the doctor concerned, who made the decision whether or not to give information to the patient, followed the practice of a responsible body of medical opinion, on application of the *Bolam* test. It is for the doctor to assess the risks involved and the capacity of the patient to understand the relevant information. This paternalistic approach is characteristic of the attitude of the English courts to the doctor-patient relationship. Much is left to the professional judgment of the doctor, and the autonomy of the patient takes second place. This is not so in other jurisdictions where a doctrine of 'informed consent' operates to allow the patient access to full and frank information about treatments and prognoses.

In *Sidaway v Governors of Bethlem Royal and Maudsley Hospitals* (1985), a patient suffered pain and partial paralysis in her arm after an operation to remove pressure on a nerve root. The operation was performed with all care and skill possible, but it carried a small risk (less than 1%) that the patient would suffer paralysis, and the patient alleged that she had not been informed of this risk. The House of Lords held that in cases involving risks, exactly how much information must be given depends upon the *Bolam* principle. A doctor's duty of care will be discharged if he or she conforms with the practice of a responsible body of medical opinion in deciding how much to tell a patient. Lord Bridge thought that if the risk was as high as 10% a patient should be informed of it. In the case of Mrs Sidaway, where the risk was only about 1%, expert witnesses from the branch of the medical profession concerned, gave evidence that they would not normally inform a patient of so small a risk.

The question of how much information a patient is entitled to receive in order to provide valid consent to treatment has been considered again by the Court of Appeal in *Pearce v United Bristol Healthcare NHS Trust* (1999). Mrs Pearce was pregnant with her sixth child. The expected date of delivery of the baby was 13 November 1991, and, on 27 November, she saw her consultant, an employee of the defendants, and asked if labour could be induced or the baby delivered by elective caesarean section, as she was anxious because the baby was so overdue. The consultant examined Mrs Pearce, explained the risks of an induced labour and advised her to have a normal delivery. Mrs Pearce accepted the consultant's advice. She was admitted to hospital on 4 December and the baby was delivered stillborn.

Mrs Pearce and her husband brought an action, arguing that they should have been told that there was an increased risk of still birth if the delivery was delayed longer than the 27 November, and that, if she had been made aware of the risk, she would have opted for an elective caesarean section as soon as possible.

The Court of Appeal dismissed the appeal. It was held that, when deciding how much information to provide to a patient, a doctor must take into account all the relevant circumstances, including the patient's ability to understand the information and his or her physical and emotional state.

This view was based upon an analysis of *Sidaway* (1985) and *Bolitho* (1997). The Court of Appeal took the view that it is the legal duty of the doctor to advise the patient about any 'significant risks' which may affect the judgment of a reasonable patient in making a decision about treatment. In the case of Mrs Pearce, there was a very small increased risk of still birth if the delivery was delayed after 27 November. This risk was in the order of one or two in 1,000, and the medical experts indicated that, in their view, this was not a significant risk. As Mrs Pearce had been in a distressed state at the time that she received the advice, this was not a case in which it would be proper for the court to interfere with the opinion of the doctor who treated the patient. The Court of Appeal took the view that, even if she had been advised of the risk, Mrs Pearce, on the evidence, would have opted to have a normal delivery.

Although the outcome of this case is not surprising, given the very low risk of still birth, there are certain aspects of the Court of Appeal's ruling which are worth noting, as there is an indication of a new approach to the question of information provision prior to obtaining consent to treatment. First, it seems that that *Bolitho* test is likely to be of relevance in consent cases, despite the fact that Lord Browne-Wilkinson expressly excluded information and consent from the discussion in *Bolitho*. Secondly, Lord Woolf indicated that it is for the court, and not for doctors, to decide on the appropriate standard as to what should be disclosed to a patient about a particular treatment. He stated:

> If there is a significant risk which would affect the judgment of a reasonable patient, then, in the normal course, it is the responsibility of a doctor to inform the patient of that risk if the information is needed so that the patient can determine for him or herself as to what course he or she should adopt.

This suggests an approach similar to that taken in the Australian case of *Rogers v Whittaker* (1992), in which the Australian High Court ruled in favour of doctors disclosing all material risks which the reasonable patient might regard as significant, taking into account the particular patient. The patient in that case had asked several times for details of the risks and complications of her treatment, and had not been told that she had a one in 14,000 chance of becoming blind.

In *Carver v Hammersmith and Queen Charlotte's Special HA* (2000), the court stated that, before consent is provided by a competent adult, the patient is entitled to receive some explanation of the treatment to be provided. How much detail should be given by the doctor depends on the circumstances of the particular case, but the courts appear to be moving towards insisting that doctors give fuller consideration to the autonomy of the patient as stated in

Pearce v United Bristol Healthcare Trust (1999). In *Carver*, the defendant health authority was found liable in negligence for the failure of its doctor to explain that the 'Bart's test' for Down's Syndrome was not a diagnostic test, unlike amniocentesis, but was only a screening test which could not detect one in three Down's Syndrome foetuses.

See, further, the cases in Chapter 20 on consent as a defence.

7.2.15 Trainee experts

Those who are learning skills are required to exercise the same standard of care as people who have already acquired such skills.

The case of *Nettleship v Weston* (1971) demonstrates that people who are learning a skill must exercise the same high standard of care as those who are already proficient in that skill.

Trainee solicitors, accountants, nurses, cooks, doctors and others should all take heed of this principle. The case of *Wilsher v Essex AHA* (1988) confirmed this some 15 years later. Junior doctors are required to adhere to the same standard of care as those who are more senior. If there is a problem with which a junior person cannot deal, then the standard of care will be met if that person seeks advice from someone more senior. In *Wilsher*, a doctor working in a special care baby unit negligently misread the oxygen levels in a baby's blood, with the result that the baby became blind. The concept of 'team negligence' was introduced, and it was held that everyone working in the unit was expected to exercise the same professional standard, and to look to a more senior person for advice if necessary. In fact, the case was sent back to the High Court for the issues of causation to be decided, but potentially there had been negligence here.

7.2.16 Clinical negligence

Clinical negligence cases fall into a special category which has been given priority treatment by the Lord Chancellor's Department and the Department of Health because of growing concern about the increase in claims in recent years.

A report of the Audit Commission in April 2000 suggests that much of the government's promised cash-injection into the NHS will be wiped out by defending clinical negligence claims and the cost of paying damages. The report states that thousands of patients die or are seriously injured every year as a result of medical errors, and that one in every 14 patients suffers an adverse event such as a diagnostic error. In the year 2000, there is an estimated 36% increase in the cost of outstanding clinical negligence claims. The increase in claims is possibly the result of people being better informed and more litigious than in previous years. In the NHS, the Patients' Charter encourages patients to complain and raises their awareness of the possibility of errors, and some patients pursue claims after exhausting the avenues offered by NHS Complaints System. As treatments become more complex and sophisticated, there is greater potential for mistakes and equipment failure.

It is not only the number of claims that has increased. Since the decision in *Wells v Wells* (1998), the amount paid in damages is now higher, especially in cases involving accident victims who require a substantial amount of future care. The decision in *Heil v Rankin* (2000) (see Chapter 19) inevitably means that awards of general damages will increase, and there have been many claims awaiting settlement on the basis of the outcome of that litigation.

7.2.17 Professional negligence claims generally

It is not only the medical profession which is being targeted by claimants. In *Adams v Rhymacy District Council* (2000), the Court of Appeal held that the *Bolam* test applies to all those who exercise a particular skill, regardless of whether the particular defendant possesses the relevant qualification. Claims for negligence against the professions in general have risen rapidly in recent years, and solicitors have seen a sharp increase in the contributions which they pay to the Solicitors Indemnity Fund, which provides compulsory insurance cover for the profession.

One reason for the rise in the number of claims against solicitors (and other professional people, such as valuers) is thought to be the rapid rise and fall in the property market at the end of the 1980s (see, for example, *Bristol & West Building Society v Fancy and Jackson* (1997) and *Platform Homes v Oyston Shipways Ltd* (1999)). In *Merivale Moore plc v Strutt and Parker* (1999), it was held that advice given in unqualified terms by surveyors and valuers to their clients, who relied upon that advice, justified a finding of negligence. The advice should have carried a warning of the risks involved in the purchase of the property in question.

Another reason why the number of claims against solicitors has risen is the recent extension to the *Hedley Byrne* principle, which allows claims by people other than clients (see *White v Jones* (1995), above, 5.1.9).

The use of conditional fee agreements could mean that it will be possible for more claimants who would not have qualified for legal aid to bring claims in respect of negligent work by professional people such as accountants, solicitors, surveyors and valuers. Although professional people carry indemnity insurance, the steady rise in claims is a growing cause for concern.

In *Hyde v JD Williams & Co* (2000), the Court of Appeal ruled that, if a profession has different schools of thought, a professional person must be judged against the lowest acceptable standard.

7.3   Proof of negligence and *res ipsa loquitur*

In most cases, the claimant has the task of amassing the evidence and proving the case alleged against the defendant, on a balance of probabilities. This is often a very difficult and, in some cases, an impossible task, and the case is dropped.

However, in some circumstances, the courts are prepared to draw an inference that there has been negligence and it will then be for the defendant to demonstrate that there has been no negligence in the circumstances. This situation is described as *res ipsa loquitur* (translated as 'the situation speaks for itself'). Clearly, this situation will make matters much easier for the claimant. Note that the use of Latin phrases such as *res ipsa loquitur* are frowned upon by the courts since the Civil Procedure Rules 1998 – see *Fryer v Pearson* (2000).

Although it was at one time described as a 'legal doctrine', *res ipsa loquitur* has recently been recognised by Lord Megaw as:

> ... no more than a common sense approach, not limited by technical rules, to the assessment of the effect of evidence in certain circumstances.

If the facts of a particular case are suitable, in that the criteria set out in *Scott v London and St Katherine's Docks* (1865) apply, the case will be appropriate for the operation of *res ipsa loquitur*.

The criteria are as follows:

- the accident must be one which cannot easily be explained. Its cause must be unknown;

- the incident would not have happened had it not been for lack of proper care;

- the defendant must have been in control of the situation.

In the *Scott* case itself, some bags of flour fell out of the upper window of a warehouse injuring the claimant. The Court of Appeal, directing a new trial, set out the criteria for *res ipsa loquitur* to apply. The trial judge had found in favour of the defendant because there was no evidence that he had been negligent, even though the circumstances suggested that there must have been negligence of some kind.

7.3.1   Unknown cause

If the circumstances of an accident are known, it is for the claimant to prove negligence. However, the claimant is at a great disadvantage if the cause is unknown and *res ipsa loquitur* places responsibility for providing an explanation upon the defendant. If no-one really knows what happened, the defendant is best placed to provide an explanation, particularly if he or she was in control and had some knowledge denied to the claimant.

In *Widdowson v Newgate Meat Corp* (1997), the claimant, who had a serious mental disorder, had been walking along a dual carriageway when he was struck by a van which was being driven by an employee of the defendants. In a statement to the police, the driver of the van had said that he had been driving at about 60 mph at the time with his headlights on full beam, and that he had been aware that the van had hit something, though he had not known what it was. The trial judge had ruled that, as the claimant did not give evidence, he could not decide who was at fault, and he was not prepared to allow *res ipsa loquitur* to apply. However, the Court of Appeal held that, although it was not common for judges to allow the use of *res ipsa loquitur* in road traffic accidents, in this case it could be justified.

7.3.2 Lack of proper care

Cases which illustrate the lack of proper care speak for themselves. For example, it was held in *Chapronière v Mason* (1905), that a stone in a Bath bun could only have been there through some carelessness in its manufacture. In *Cassidy v Minister of Health* (1951), it was held that when a patient entered hospital for a minor operation on two stiff fingers, but left hospital with four stiff fingers, there must have been negligence at some point on the part of the doctors.

7.3.3 Control by the defendant

If the defendant has control of the situation, and the claimant had little or no knowledge of events, it is logical that the defendant should be made to provide an explanation, and that *res ipsa loquitur* will apply.

However, it should be noted that the burden of proof is on the claimant to show that any cause of the accident outside the control of the defendant was unlikely (*Lloyd v West Midlands Gas Board* (1971)).

7.4 *Res ipsa loquitur* and medical cases

There are some people who would argue that *res ipsa loquitur* should almost always apply to cases where there is an allegation of medical negligence since, in many cases, the three criteria above will be satisfied, and, in medical cases, the claimant greatly needs assistance, as it is often difficult to obtain evidence from the medical team who are accused of negligence. However, the courts have been reluctant to allow its application in medical cases (with one or two exceptions, for example, a dentist breaking a patient's jaw). Lord Denning, in *Hucks v Cole* (1968), said that it should only apply against a doctor in extreme cases, and the Pearson Report in 1978 rejected its general application in medical cases for fear of an escalation of claims and a rise in doctors' insurance premiums, as has occurred in America, where *res ipsa loquitur* frequently operates to the disadvantage of doctors.

Res ipsa loquitur was frequently applied in cases involving foreign bodies in foodstuffs. However, since the Consumer Protection Act 1987, its use in these cases has become unnecessary.

7.5 Effects of *res ipsa loquitur*

It has been argued that *res ipsa loquitur* has the effect of reversing the burden of proof and effectively creating strict liability in cases when it applies, because it is almost always impossible for the defendant to provide an explanation as to what exactly happened. In *Ward v Tesco Stores* (1976), for example, the claimant slipped on some spilled yoghurt on the floor in Tesco's. Although the store claimed to have operated an efficient scheme of patrolling the store to look for spillages, they could not explain how long the yoghurt had been on the floor, and could produce no other evidence. They had little chance of successfully defending the claim. (But compare this with *Fryer v Pearson* (2000) (see above, 7.3), in which it was held that the mere fact a bottle had fallen at a supermarket checkout was insufficient to raise the inference of negligence.)

This view has now been discredited to some extent, and has been overtaken by the view that *res ipsa loquitur* does not go as far as was originally believed, but that it simply raises an inference that there may have been negligence on the part of the defendant, and gives the defence the task of explaining what happened.

The true effect of the application of *res ipsa loquitur* was explained in *Ratcliffe v Plymouth and Torbay HA* (1988) by Hobhouse LJ, when he said:

> *Res ipsa loquitur* is not a principle of law; it does not relate to or raise any presumption. It is merely a guide to help to identify when a *prima facie* case is being made out. When expert or factual evidence has been called on both sides at a trial, its usefulness will normally have long since been exhausted.

In practice, the application of the maxim usually eases the claimant's difficulties in proving negligence and places the defendant in the position of having to rebut the inference that he or she has been negligent. One advantage of this is that there may be an early settlement of the case.

7.6 The Consumer Protection Act 1987

In some circumstances, the need to prove fault (breach of duty) has been abolished by the Consumer Protection Act 1987. This is discussed in Chapter 15.

BREACH OF DUTY – THE STANDARD OF CARE

The reasonable man test

The test for breach of duty is 'the reasonable man' test. In effect, this test is a device which allows judges to control the outcome of cases, but notionally at least, the standard of care is objective.

Over the years, judges have formulated several different versions of 'the reasonable man' test.

Points to note from the cases include:

- The reasonable man assesses the risks and balances them against the practicality of taking precautions (*Bolton v Stone* (1951)).

- The reasonable man is not expected to guard against unknown risks (*Roe v Minister of Health* (1963)).

- The reasonable man considers the utility of the conduct needed to avoid a risk (*Watt v Hertfordshire CC* (1954)).

- The reasonable man can take into account the cost of taking precautions (*Latimer v AEC* (1953)).

- The reasonable man is not expected to exercise the same standard of care as an expert when carrying out skilled work (*Phillips v Whiteley* (1938)).

- Children are probably expected to be less careful than adults.

- Sick and disabled people are not expected to be as careful as people who are well and able-bodied, taking into account the particular disability.

- Drivers are all expected to exercise the same standard of care. This applies to learner drivers as well as experienced drivers (*Nettleship v Weston* (1971)).

- All experts, even those who are still training, are expected to exercise the same high standard of care as people with equivalent expertise.

- Experts have been able to escape liability for negligence by pointing to established practice. Note the many criticisms of the rule in *Bolam v Friern Hospital* (1957).

  Medical cases to illustrate this proposition include the following: *Whitehouse v Jordan* (1981); *Wilsher v Essex AHA* (1988); *Sidaway v Governors of Bethlem Royal Hospital* (1985). But note the effects of official guidelines (*Thompson v James* (1996)).

  The Australian case of *Rogers v Whitaker* (1992) demonstrates that there may be room for a new approach to the question of negligence in relation to treatment. See, also, *Pearce v United Bristol HC NHS Trust* (1999); *Bennett v NHS Litigation Authority* (1999).

Challenges to *Bolam*

Lybert v Warrington HA (1995); *De Freitas v O'Brien* (1995); *Bolitho v Hackney* (1992); *Hucks v Cole* (1968); *Talia Kushnir v Camden and Islington HA* (1996).

Modification of *Bolam*

Bolitho v City and Hackney HA (1997).

The reversal of the burden of proof: *res ipsa loquitur*

The situation described as *res ipsa loquitur* (translated as 'the situation speaks for itself') was recognised in *Scott v London and St Katherine's Docks* (1865) and the courts are prepared to draw an inference that there has been negligence and it will then be for the defendant to demonstrate that there has been no negligence in the circumstances. The three pre-requisites are:

- the cause of the accident must be unknown and unascertainable;

- the accident would not have happened if the defendant had exercised all reasonable care;

- the defendant must have had control of the situation.

These points are illustrated by *Chaproniere v Mason* (1905) and *Cassidy v Minister of Health* (1951); *Widdowson v Newgate Meat Corpn* (1997).

Is strict liability the answer?

The Consumer Protection Act 1987 purports to create numerous strict liability situations but is subject to many exceptions.

The proposed EC Directive on Services will, when implemented, bring services into line with goods as in the Consumer Protection Act 1987.

Vaccine Damage Payments Act 1979 creates strict liability for vaccine damage.

CHAPTER 8

CAUSATION AND REMOTENESS OF DAMAGE

8.1 The relationship between causation and remoteness of damage

In strict theory, causation (called 'cause in fact') and remoteness (called 'cause in law') must be dealt with as two separate requirements in each case. Causation is a matter of fact and requires the claimant to prove that the negligent act caused the damage complained of. The rules concerning remoteness of damage are a matter of law and broadly require the claimant to establish that the damage was of a kind which was reasonably foreseeable. It is concerned with setting a limit on the extent of the harm for which the defendant should be held liable. However, it is not always a clear cut issue to establish where causation ends and remoteness begins, nor is it always a simple matter to separate some aspects of remoteness from issues which arise in relation to duty of care. Both causation and remoteness of damage frequently turn on issues of policy. Both are relevant throughout the law of tort and are dealt with in connection with negligence for the sake of completeness.

8.2 Causation

The claimant will not succeed unless it can be demonstrated that the negligent act of the defendant caused or materially contributed to the damage complained of. This matter is a question of fact.

The task of establishing a causal connection between the act of the defendant and the damage suffered by the claimant is not always simple. Often, there may be a complex set of conditions present, or even two concurrent sets of circumstances, and it can be difficult to untangle the web of circumstances to pin-point liability.

8.2.1 A typical examination problem

To take a road accident for example: A's car has faulty brakes because of a poor repair done by a B, a junior mechanic who should have been supervised. A is driving late at night along a slippery wet road, which has been poorly maintained by the local highway authority. He has chest pains and feels dizzy. C, a child, runs into the road, whilst a teacher, on duty as the children leave school, attends to a sick child. A sees C, but just as he is about to apply the brakes, he has a heart attack, and loses consciousness. The brakes would have failed in any case, but a deep rut in the road causes the car to swerve into the child, killing him. A is also killed. He had visited his doctor the day before complaining of chest pains, but the doctor had negligently failed to diagnose a serious heart condition. Who is responsible for the two deaths?

It need not be necessary to establish a single cause of the damage, and indeed there are often concurrent causes, in which case responsibility may be apportioned. In such cases, the various defendants, their lawyers and insurers, often argue as to the proportion of liability each should bear, and frequently a case which might have been settled out of court at an early stage if there had only been one defendant, will be taken to trial or settled at the door of the court because the defendants are fighting one another.

Potential defendants in the above case would be A's estate, the local highway authority, the local education authority, the garage, the child's estate, and the doctor. Not all of these would be worth suing, but insured defendants, and local authorities who are their own insurers, certainly would.

Traditionally, the courts have applied various metaphors to assist in establishing cause. Judges speak of 'chains of causation', 'conduit pipes', and so on. Various tests are applied by the courts. For example, the following questions may be asked:

- has the chain of causation been broken?;

- would the harm to the claimant have occurred 'but for' the defendant's negligence, or would the harm have been suffered anyway?;

- was there a *novus actus interveniens* (a new intervening act)?

A close study of some of the cases in this area will assist (or confuse) you. Bear in mind that causation is important throughout the law of tort, even when there is strict liability. It is merely for the sake of convenience that it is dealt with here, and in most of the textbooks, in the context of negligence.

8.2.2 The 'but for' test

When the damage would have happened anyway, even without the defendant's negligence, there will be no liability on the part of the defendant. This 'but for' test is often applied first, and is rather a simplistic approach. It is not very helpful in multi-factorial situations, such as our road accident problem. There are some relatively simple situations when it can work well.

In *Robinson v Post Office* (1974), a patient who was to be given an anti-tetanus vaccination was not tested properly for an allergic reaction before the vaccination was administered, and he did develop an allergy. However, as the result of the test would not have been discovered in time, and as the vaccination was necessary almost at once, it was decided that the failure of the doctor to test for the allergy did not in fact cause the damage.

In *Barnett v Chelsea and Kensington Hospital Management Committee* (1969), a night watchman was taken to hospital vomiting and suffering from severe stomach pains, but the casualty doctor on duty sent him away to see his own GP. He died soon afterwards of arsenic poisoning, and it was discovered that an unknown person had put arsenic in the tea of the the watchmen on duty on a particular site. There was no dispute about the fact that the doctor had been negligent. What was in issue here was whether that negligent act had caused the man's death. It was held that it had not. The man would have died anyway. Much of the evidence turned upon the question of whether he would have survived if he had been given an antidote as soon as possible after arriving at the hospital, and it was proved that he would not. The defendants were not liable.

8.2.3 *Novus actus interveniens*

It may sometimes be possible to establish that a *novus actus interveniens*, or intervening act has caused the damage and that the original defendant is not liable. Such an event is said to 'break the chain of causation'. This is most likely to be the case when the two possible causes are separate in time. However, as has been observed elsewhere in the law of tort, judges often use the concepts which they have created as a means of arriving at the decisions which they consider to be the most desirable in the circumstances.

An example of this might be found in the case of *Wright v Lodge* (1993). The first defendant's car had broken down late at night in very thick fog and she was held to have been negligent in leaving it on the carriageway. The second defendant was a lorry driver who was travelling too fast, collided with the abandoned car and slewed across the road crashing into several cars. It was held that she could not be held liable for the injuries caused to the drivers of the cars which were damaged by the lorry, because the second driver was not merely negligent but reckless and this factor broke the chain of causation.

As Fleming says, the various metaphors used in establishing causation are (Fleming, JG, *An Introduction to the Law of Torts*, 1977):

> ... only a screen behind which the judges have all too often in the past retreated to avoid the irksome task of articulating their real motivation.

An intervening act will not break the chain of causation if it can be established that the intervening actor was not fully responsible for his or her actions, perhaps because he or she has been put into a dilemma by the original actor.

8.2.4 The 'dilemma' principle

For example, in *Sayers v Harlow BC* (1958), the defendant claimed that the claimant's own act was the entire cause of her misfortune. She had been locked in a public lavatory belonging to the defendants because of a faulty door lock and, faced with the prospect of remaining in the lavatory all night, she decided to try to climb out. She did this by attempting to stand on a toilet roll holder, which spun around and threw her onto the floor. As a result of the fall, she suffered injuries, and sued the council for compensation. It was held that since she had been put into a dilemma by the council, her actions were not unreasonable, and she was not fully responsible for the damage suffered, but she was contributorily negligent, and the damages were reduced accordingly. The chain of causation set up by the defendants had not been broken.

In *Wieland v Cyril Lord Carpets* (1969), the claimant had been injured and was forced to wear a surgical collar. This restricted her neck movements, and she could not look down through her bifocal glasses. She fell down a flight of stairs as a result, and sued the defendants for negligence. The original defendants were liable for all the injuries because they should have foreseen that the claimant's life would be restricted by the original injury. She was not unreasonable in attempting to carry on her life as normal.

By contrast, the case of *McKew v Holland and Hannan and Cubbitts (Scotland) Ltd* (1969) was decided in favour of the defendants, who had negligently injured the claimant's leg. As a result, the leg was likely to give way at any time. Without asking for help, he attempted to climb a flight of stairs, and the injured leg gave way, causing him further injuries. It was held by the House of Lords that the act of climbing the stairs constituted a *novus actus interveniens* which broke the chain of causation. The risk taken by the claimant was unreasonable. The defendants could not be liable for every foreseeable consequence of their actions.

This decision is difficult to accept, given that under basic principles of remoteness of damage (to be discussed later in this chapter), the defendant must take the victim as he finds him. It follows that where the defendant actually creates a foreseeable risk it should be all the more likely that he would be liable for the consequences of the risk which he himself created.

8.2.5　The claimant was not responsible for his own acts

In *Kirkham v Chief Constable of Greater Manchester* (1990), the police were held liable for the suicide of a person whom they had transferred to Risley Remand Centre, without informing the authorities there that he was a high suicide risk. His act of committing suicide was not a *novus actus interveniens*, even though to many people suicide is an unreasonable act. The balance of his mind was disturbed, and he was incapable of making a rational decision. The police knew this, so the chain of causation remained intact.

In *Pigney v Pointers Transport Services* (1957), the defendants were liable for the suicide of a man who had committed suicide after sustaining head injuries as a result of their negligence. His suicide was not a *novus actus interveniens*.

8.2.6   The foreseeability of the intervening act

In *Lamb v Camden LBC* (1981), the claimant owned a house in London which had been damaged when the defendants negligently caused serious subsidence to the property by fracturing a water main. Later, squatters moved into the house and caused considerable damage. Rather surprisingly, since the evidence indicated that the house was in an area in which squatters regularly operated, the Court of Appeal held that the acts of the squatters were not foreseeable by the Council and therefore amounted to a *novus actus interveniens*.

If the intervening act is foreseeable, it is unlikely that the chain of causation will be broken. The degree of likelihood of harm occurring is also an important consideration. This is illustrated by the very early case of *Scott v Shepherd* (1773), in which the defendant threw a lighted squib into a market house. It was picked up by the person on whose stall it had landed, and thrown onto another stall. Again, the owner of that stall threw it onto another where it exploded and caused the claimant to lose an eye. The person who had thrown the squib originally was liable. There is a clear example of an unbroken chain of causation here.

In the case of *Smith v Littlewoods Organisation Ltd* (1987), the problem of the likelihood of harm was dealt with by reference to the question of duty of care rather than causation or remoteness of damage. In that case, Littlewoods had failed to protect a derelict cinema which they owned from vandals who caused a fire which spread to adjoining properties. It was held that the occupiers had insufficient knowledge of the presence of trespassers and did not owe a duty of care to spend large amounts of money attempting to keep them out.

8.2.7   Omissions

Special difficulties can arise when the negligent conduct takes the form of an omission rather than a positive act. The court must then consider what would have happened if the defendant had opted to act instead of omitting to do so. This problem was considered in the case of *Bolitho v City and Hackney Health Authority* (1997), the facts of which are set out in Chapter 7, where the issue of causation is explained in detail. That case has been followed in *Brock v Frenchay Healthcare Trust* (1999), where it was alleged that the defendants were negligent in their care of the claimant. When he was 16 years old, he had fallen off his bicycle. He had not been wearing a crash helmet at the time. He was taken to hospital. No fracture was detected in an X-ray of his skull, and the claimant was discharged.

At about 3 am the following morning, it was apparent that he was very seriously ill, and he was taken to hospital by ambulance. His Glasgow coma scale was recorded as 3 (the lowest level on the scale) and the neurosurgical team was called to carry out an emergency operation. He was ready for the drug, Mannitol, to be given at 4.15 am. This could have helped to relieve the pressure on his brain, but the anaesthetist did not administer the drug until the surgeon arrived 15 minutes later. The claimant was irreversibly brain damaged. The trial judge accepted that there was no negligence on the part of the doctor for failing to identify a skull fracture on the X-ray when the claimant had first been admitted to casualty, and that there was no negligence in respect his discharge from casualty.

The crucial issue was whether the omission to give Mannitol earlier had made any difference to the claimant's condition. Both parties accepted that the decision of the House of Lords in *Bolitho v City and Hackney Health Authority* (1997) was directly relevant in determining causation in this case.

The Court of Appeal found that the judgment of the trial judge had contained a remarkably clear analysis of both the facts and the evidence in this case, and at no time was it decided that the claimant would have gained any benefit from an earlier administration of Mannitol. Accordingly, the appeal was dismissed and leave to appeal to the House of Lords was refused.

8.2.8 Several causes

Where there are several possible causes, the 'but for test' does not provide a simple solution. The causes may occur in succession or they may be concurrent. If the causes occur successively, the second act may create the same damage as the first or it may create more damage. For example, in *Performance Cars v Abrahams* (1962), a Rolls Royce car had been damaged in a collision caused by the first defendant's negligence but, at a later date, the second defendant crashed with the Rolls Royce. It was held that the second defendant was not liable for the respray, as that was already necessary as a result of the damage caused by the first defendant.

In *Baker v Willoughby* (1970), the claimant suffered an injury to his ankle in an accident, as a result of which he could only undertake light work. He was employed as a watchman when he was shot in the same leg during a robbery while he was at work. The leg had to be amputated. The House of Lords, refusing to apply the 'but for' test, held that the first defendant was only liable to compensate the claimant for the first injury, and not for the amputation. If it had been possible to sue the robbers they would have been liable for the amputation of an imperfect leg, and would not have had to pay as much compensation as would have been payable for a perfect leg. This seems to be a fair and realistic approach, since, as Lord Reid pointed out, compensation is payable for the losses which arise from an injury, such as loss of amenity and earning power, and not for the injury itself. The second injury had not taken these losses away, and it was unfair for the defendants to argue that he should receive no compensation because he was worse off than they had made him in the first accident.

In *Jobling v Associated Diaries* (1982), the claimant had suffered an injury to his back at work which reduced his earning capacity by 50%. It was discovered, between the date of the accident and the date of the trial that the defendant had developed a serious back condition which was entirely unrelated to the injury. This is a situation which is common in cases of back injury and the arguments centred on the fact that the vicissitudes of life must be taken into consideration. He became completely unable to work. The House of Lords held that the compensation for loss of earnings should be available only to a cut off point of the date when he was finally unable to work. The decision was probably based on policy, the relevant issue being fear of over-compensating certain claimants who might have other sources of compensation available to them. This case is distinguishable from *Baker v Willoughby* (1970) because the second event was a natural one, rather than one which had been caused by a deliberate act, but it is not easy to see how the two cases are compatible.

The position now seems to be that, if the second event was caused by negligence or a deliberate act, *Baker v Willoughby* (1970) will apply, but, if the second event is attributable to a natural cause, *Jobling* will apply.

Consider the following situation: A injures B's arm through negligent driving. B needs an immediate blood transfusion and surgery to save the arm, but B is a Jehovah's witness, and refuses the blood transfusion. B dies. Is A liable for B's death?

8.3   Problems in proving causation

Causation is a question of fact which it is necessary for the claimant to prove. In civil cases, a proposition must be proved 'on a balance of probabilities'. This is sometimes extremely difficult, especially where it is possible for the defendant to argue that there are a number of other causative factors besides the one relied upon by the claimant. For example, if a child is born with cerebral palsy and the parents sue the doctor who delivered the baby for negligence, the defence might argue that there are a number of possible causes of cerebral palsy. It could be the result of natural causes such as inherited disease, or of some event which occurred in the womb through no one's fault, perhaps through placental deficiency which was undetectable by ultrasound scan at the crucial stage in pregnancy.

Some of the cases in this area appear to be contradictory, and there are many difficulties involved in them which make the outcomes seem unfair to the claimants in some instances.

In *Bonnington Castings v Wardlaw* (1956), the claimant suffered pneumoconiosis after years of working in a dusty industry. The claimant claimed that his employers did not provide proper washing facilities or extraction fans for the safety of their employees. There were two main dust sources in his work place. One was the pneumatic hammers for which the employers were not liable for any breach of duty. The other was the swing grinders for which the employers had failed to provide extraction fans. The claimant could not establish which type of dust he had inhaled most. However, the House of Lords held that because the dust from the swing grinders was at least a contributory cause of the illness, the claimant should succeed for the full amount of his claim. All that was necessary was that he should establish on a balance of probabilities that the dust from the swing grinders was a definite contributory factor in the illness. The House of Lords agreed to this even though it was impossible on the facts to make a realistic assessment of the proportion of dust inhaled from either source. This case clearly operated in the claimant's favour.

A different approach was taken in *Hotson v East Berkshire HA* (1987). The claimant was a 13 year old school boy who had injured his knee when he fell from a rope. An X ray had been taken of the knee by the hospital and no injury was apparent, so no further exploratory examination was made. The boy continued to suffer pain and five days later he returned to the hospital and a hip injury was diagnosed and treated. However, the boy developed a condition known as avascular necrosis, which is caused when the blood supply to an injury site is restricted. This results in pain and deformity and eventually in most cases in osteoarthritis. Although the boy may have suffered the condition in any case as a result of the injury, there was a 25% chance that if it had been properly treated immediately, he would have made a full recovery. It was held at first instance that the claimant should receive 25% of the full award available for the injury, so that he would be compensated for a 25% lost opportunity of recovering. The House of Lords held that he should receive nothing. He had not been able to establish that, on a balance of probabilities, the defendant's negligence had caused his injury, as there was a 75% chance that he would have developed the avascular necrosis even if they had not been negligent in their original treatment. If he had so succeeded, he would have had an award of the full amount of the compensation available. To win on causation, the claimant must therefore establish that there is at least a 51% chance that the negligent act caused the damage in question. This 'all or nothing' approach is logically consistent with the rule that in a civil action it is necessary to prove the case on a balance of probabilities.

The *Hotson* principle that proof of causation should be based on a balance of probabilities (the 51% rule) seems to be eminently logical, but it can mean that some claimants are denied any remedy at all even though it is reasonably likely that the negligent act of the defendant caused the loss. The rules of causation based on *Hotson* are effectively a means of limiting the number of successful claims and operate ultimately to the benefit of defendants' insurers. However, there is some evidence that courts do not slavishly follow the *Hotson* line. In *Stovold v Barlows* (1995), for example, the claimant claimed that he had lost the sale of his house through the defendant's negligence. The court decided that if it had not been for the defendant's negligence there was a 50% chance that the sale would have gone ahead. The Court of Appeal, following the line taken by itself rather than the House of Lords in *Hotson*, halved the claimant's award on that basis. In *Allied Maples Group v Simmons and Simmons* (1995), the Court of Appeal held that the claimant has to prove that he had a real or substantial chance as opposed to a speculative chance. If he can do this, the evaluation of that chance is to be treated as part of the quantum of damages. See, also, *Platform Home Loans v Oyston Shipways Ltd* (1999) (below, 20.1.7).

In *Wilsher v Essex AHA* (1988) (see Chapter 7), the House of Lords decided that, on the medical evidence, there were six possible causes of retrolental fibroplasia, and that excess oxygen was just one of these. The burden of proving causation is on the claimant, and that burden had not been discharged in this case. The case was sent back for retrial on the issue of causation. The trial judge had taken the view, which the House of Lords rejected, that the burden of proof had shifted onto the defendants once the claimant had established that the illness could have been caused by the negligent act of the defendants in administering an excess of oxygen to the baby.

8.4 Contributory negligence and causation

Causation is relevant in deciding whether the claimant has contributed to the damage suffered by not taking sufficient care for his or her own safety.

In the seat-belt cases, for example, the percentage of the contribution made by the claimant to the damage suffered is assessed in order to establish how much should be deducted from the compensation available to account for the claimant's own contributory conduct. This is a question of fact which must be considered in each case.

There may be an act of the claimant which operates as a *novus actus interveniens* and so absolves the defendant from all liability. If this is the case, the claimant is denied a remedy by operation of the maxim *volenti non fit injuria* because he or she has consented to run the risk of harm. (This is dealt with in Chapter 20.) This argument was relied upon but rejected by the courts in *Sayers v Harlow BC* (1958) and *Gough v Thorne* (1966), discussed above.

On the other hand, the claimant's own carelessness, while not amounting to a *novus actus interveniens*, may well amount to contributory negligence. This was the case in *Sayers v Harlow BC* (1958) where the claimant's damages were reduced in proportion to her own contributory act, but not in *Gough v Thorne* (1966), where the Court of Appeal decided that the 13 year old had not been contributorily negligent, and there was no reduction from the award.

8.4.1   The importance of causation in legal practice

There is a good deal of impressive academic literature devoted to discussion of the problems of causation (see Hart, HLA and Honoré, T, *Causation in the Law*, 2nd edn, 1985).

Although many pages of the standard English textbooks are devoted to the difficulties which arise in establishing causation, in practice, as with duty of care, the problem seldom arises. *Hotson* and *Wilsher* were very exceptional cases, but they do illustrate that causation may be a problem in cases where there is complex medical or scientific knowledge.

8.5   Remoteness of damage

It is not sufficient merely for the claimant to establish a causal connection between the act of the defendant and the damage which the claimant suffers. It is also necessary to establish that the damage was not too remote. This is a matter of law, and legal rules have been formulated to determine the question of remoteness of damage which have been established in answer to the question: 'For how much of the damage is the defendant liable?'

8.5.1   Direct consequences

Originally, the defendant was liable for all the damage which was the direct consequence of the wrongful act whether or not the extent or type of harm was foreseeable.

In *Re Polemis and Furness, Withy & Co* (1921), a stevedore negligently dropped a plank of wood from a great height into the hold of a ship. Benzine had leaked into the hold, and the movement of the plank caused vapours to ignite. Eventually, the whole ship was destroyed. It was held that the stevedore firm was liable for the destruction of the ship, because that was a direct consequence of their employee's negligent act. It did not matter that total destruction of the vessel was not a foreseeable consequence of the act. The test for remoteness of damage was the direct consequences test.

8.5.2   Was the direct consequences rule fair?

This rule may seem rather hard on defendants. The negligent stevedore could probably have foreseen that a workman in the hold would have been injured, or that damage might have been caused to the fabric of the ship, but his employers were made to pay for such an unforeseeable consequence as a fire. In cases involving large business enterprises, the rule is probably not too difficult to understand. Insurance companies pay the damages if the defendant is properly insured and the case will usually be settled out of court.

If the defendant is a private individual who does not carry insurance, it would not be worth the expense of bringing a legal action. In one sense, the fairness or otherwise of the rule does not matter, as long as the law is able to fix liability.

It seems eminently fair that if someone has to suffer a loss as a result of a wrongful act, it should be the perpetrator of the act, the defendant, who should do so, rather than the claimant who has done nothing wrong. The more so if the defendant is insured and can bear the loss.

However, the rule in *Re Polemis* was much criticised as being unfair and out of step with modern notions of morality. It seemed to operate in a punitive fashion once liability for the negligent act had been established, and it failed to distinguish between 'small' acts of negligence and gross negligence. As Viscount Simonds said in *The Wagon Mound (No 1)* (1961), which made some headway in changing the rule, though not as much as is apparent at first sight:

> It does not seem consonant with current ideas of justice or morality, that for an act of negligence, however slight or venial, which results in some trivial foreseeable damage, the actor should be liable for all the consequences, however unforeseeable and however grave, so long as they can be said to be direct.

The judges seemed to be bent on changing the law, and a new rule was formulated by the Privy Council in the *Wagon Mound (No 1)* (1961), a case on appeal from Australia. This rule was soon adopted by the House of Lords in *Hughes v Lord Advocate* (1963). The new formula complicates matters considerably and, as will be seen, also produces some apparently unjust results.

The Wagon Mound (No 1) concerned an accident which occurred when a ship was loading oil in Sydney harbour. Some of the oil leaked onto the water, where it floated and mixed with flotsam and debris already in the water. Eventually, it was ignited by sparks from welding operations on the other side of the harbour. The ensuing fire caused enormous damage. It was held that since the particular type of oil did not easily ignite, the type of harm which occurred was not foreseeable by the officers in charge of the ship though property damage of some kind, through oil pollution, was foreseeable. *Re Polemis* was strongly criticised. The new test for remoteness of damage in tort was to be: 'Was the way in which the accident happened (the type of harm) reasonably foreseeable?' If so, the defendant will be liable for the full extent of the damage, no matter how unforeseeable that was.

The cases below demonstrate the difficulties involved.

8.5.3 What damage must be foreseeable?

In *Hughes v Lord Advocate* (1963), two boys decided to climb down into a manhole which the Post Office employees had negligently left open in the street, though they covered it with a striped canvas tent, and surrounded it with paraffin lamps. As part of the prank, the boys took one of the paraffin lamps into the manhole to explore. The lamp was dropped into the manhole and there was an explosion which caused one of the boys severe burns. Although the evidence suggested that an explosion was unforeseeable, a fire certainly could have been foreseen, and the House of Lords held that damage caused by fire was in this case indistinguishable from damage caused by an explosion and subsequent fire. The exact details of how the accident occurred did not need to be foreseen, as long as the damage was broadly of a type which was foreseeable.

The explosion was a variant of what was foreseeable and the precise circumstances did not need to be foreseeable. By contrast, in *Doughty v Turner Manufacturing Co* (1964), the circumstances of the accident were wholly unforeseeable.

In *Doughty v Turner Manufacturing Co Ltd* (1964), the claimants were injured in a work accident, but recovered nothing because the way in which the accident happened was unforeseeable. At a time when it was believed that asbestos was a safe and inert substance, several workmen were injured when an asbestos lid slipped into a vat of boiling sulphuric acid. There was an unforeseeable explosion resulting in a serious fire in which the men were burned. The Court of Appeal held that although splash injury was foreseeable, an explosion and fire were not, so the employers were not liable for any of the damage. This case is also an illustration of the principle that there is no breach of duty if the circumstances of an accident could not have been known at the time, in the light of existing scientific knowledge (see *Roe v Minister of Health* (1954)).

Some of the earlier cases suggested that it should be possible to foresee the category of damage which results from the negligent act, such as economic loss, damage to property, or personal injury. However, this approach does not seem to have been adopted consistently by the courts. It seems that what must usually be foreseeable is *the way in which the accident happens* as well as the category of harm. For example, personal injury caused by burning. In *Tremain v Pike* (1969), a farm labourer contracted a disease, leptospirosis, from handling material on which rats had urinated. He failed in the action which he brought against his employer because, while a rat bite was foreseeable, the court held that the method by which this disease was contracted, was not. The decision has attracted a good deal of criticism, partly because the evidence which was accepted about the unusual nature of the disease which the claimant suffered was doubtful, and partly because the judge took too narrow a view of the scope of the test for remoteness of damage.

In *Crossley v Rawlinson* (1981), the claimant was hurrying to extinguish a fire in a motor vehicle. He had a fire extinguisher in his hands, and when he tripped in a hole in the road, he could not break his fall with a free hand and was injured. The defendants were not liable for his injury as this was not a foreseeable consequence of their negligence. The way in which the injury had occurred was not foreseeable.

In *Bradford v Robinson Rentals* (1967), the claimant was requested by his employers to travel for several hundred miles in a van with no heater in extremely bitter weather. He suffered frostbite and succeeded in his action against his employer because the damage which he suffered was held to have been of a kind which was reasonably foreseeable.

In *Margereson v JW Roberts Ltd, Hancock v Same* (1996), the Court of Appeal upheld the High Court finding in favour of the claimants who had developed mesothelioma many years after they had inhaled asbestos dust when they played as children near an asbestos factory operated by the defendants. The defendants admitted that they had not taken adequate steps to control the dangerous emissions of asbestos dust from the factory. The Court of Appeal took the view that the defendants should have been aware of the dangers of asbestos dust even before 1925 when the first claimant was born. The only legal issue concerned the duty of care owed to the claimants, and it was decided that the defendants would be liable only if the evidence demonstrated that they should reasonably have foreseen that there was some risk of injury to the lungs, not necessarily the specific injury which was eventually suffered by the claimants. It was not possible to draw any distinction between the position of the claimants and that of employees who worked within the factory.

Difficulties may arise if damages are claimed for further losses which are incurred after the initial loss or damage is suffered, as in cases such as *McKew v Holland* (1969) and *Lamb v Camden BC* (1981) which have been discussed under the general umbrella of causation, but which illustrate that causation and remoteness are inextricably intertwined. The question arises as to whether these problems properly belong to the causation stage of the case or to the remoteness stage.

In *Jolley v London Borough of Sutton* (2000), the Court of Appeal allowed an appeal by the council against a finding of liability under s 2 of the Occupiers' Liability Act 1957. Although the appellants had been negligent in allowing a boat to remain on land, knowing that the vessel was in a dangerous condition and was an allurement to children, the accident which occurred was of a different type to anything that the council could have foreseen. What had happened was this: the 14 year old claimant and a friend had decided to repair the boat, and for six weeks they had worked on it at evenings and weekends. They had raised the boat off the ground using a car jack and some pieces of wood, and the boat fell on the claimant while he was underneath it, causing him to suffer severe injuries to his spine. He was a paraplegic by the time of the trial and was confined to a wheelchair. The Court of Appeal decided that, while it was difficult for the council to anticipate exactly what children would do when they were playing, what the boys had been doing in this case was very different from normal play and the circumstances of the accident were unforeseeable.

The House of Lords disagreed and found in favour of the claimant, ruling that occupiers should not underestimate the power of children to do self-mischief.

There are several cases in which the damage was of an unusual type, but was nevertheless recoverable. These include *Jones v Jones* (1985) in which it was held that divorce was a foreseeable consequence of the defendant's negligence, though this was not followed in *Pritchard v Cobden* (1988) and *Meah v McCreamer* (1986). It was decided that the claimant could obtain compensation for having suffered a personality change which resulted in a term of imprisonment for rape, though the remoteness issue concerning Meah's clear intention to rape was not argued in this case.

Some writers support the view that, if the damage in question is property damage, the approach of the courts is narrower than in cases of personal injuries or economic loss.

8.5.4 Confusion between the duty and remoteness levels

One factor which has caused some confusion is the use of foresight as a test to establish liability when considering both whether there is a duty of care owed and also whether the damage is too remote. This has been a particular problem in some nervous shock cases (see *Bourhill v Young* (1943)).

8.5.5 The thin skull rule

Once it is established that the type of harm is foreseeable, it is not necessary to prove that the defendant could forsee the extent of the likely damage. This situation is brought about by the existence of a rule which also occurs in criminal law, which is that a defendant must 'take the victim as he finds him'. This is also known as the 'thin skull rule', taking its name from a medical condition which means that people who suffer from it incur serious injury and often death, from what to other people would only be a minor bump on the head. The rule is best illustrated by the cases themselves, but is based on the principle that there needs to be a pre-existing susceptibility in the claimant which will result in a high award for damages in some cases.

In *Smith v Leech Brain & Co* (1962), the claimant's husband was splashed on the lip at work with molten metal. He suffered, as was foreseeable, a splash injury, a minor burn. However, it transpired that the particular body cells which were damaged were in a pre-cancerous condition at the time, and he developed cancer and died of the disease. The defendants were liable for the man's death. Even though the only foreseeable injury was a splash injury causing a burn, the man was a 'thin skull' individual, and developed an unforeseeable and much more serious condition than that which a normal person would have suffered in the circumstances (compare *Doughty v Turner* (see 8.5.3 above)).

In recent years, it has been established that there will be liability for nervous shock even if the claimant has an 'egg-shell personality' which predisposes the development of psychiatric illness (*Page v Smith* (1995) – see Chapter 3). The same principle applies to psychiatric illness caused by work stress providing there is foresight of the type of harm (*Walker v Northumberland* (1994)).

Although there is no direct authority on the point, there is a definite view that the thin skull rule would apply to property damage as well as to personal injury. As to economic loss, the authority is the *Liesbosch Dredger v SS Edison* (1933). The defendants negligently caused the claimant's dredger to sink, and the claimants were forced to hire another vessel at an inflated rate in order to fulfil contractual obligations. They claimed that they were too poor to buy another dredger, and for that reason had been forced into the hire contract. It was held by the House of Lords that the claimants could not claim for the additional expense which they had incurred under the hire contract. That was the result of their own impecuniosity, and was not foreseeable by the defendants.

However, doubts have been expressed about the rule in the *Liesbosch Dredger* case. Soon after the case, there was an indication that some judges did not approve of the rule and, more recently, in *Dodd v Canterbury CC* (1980), Lord Donaldson expressed the opinion that the rule might need to be reviewed by the House of Lords. In that case, the Court of Appeal was prepared to distinguish the situation from that which arose in the *Liesbosch Dredger* case. Building operations being carried out by the defendants caused damage to the claimant's property and the defendants denied liability until shortly before the trial was due to take place. The claimants did not carry out the necessary repairs to the damage during this time because if they lost the case they feared that they would not be able to pay for them. By the time of admission of liability the cost of carrying out the repairs had risen, but the claimant was allowed by the Court of Appeal the full cost of the repairs. The reasons for the distinction are somewhat dubious. One was that the claimant had reasons other than lack of funds (that is, the doubtful outcome of the trial) for delaying the repairs. The other was that the claimant in the *Dodd* case was not poor in the true *Liesbosch Dredger* sense because he did have funds, but did not want to risk losing them. Surely both of these factors could apply in almost any case, and it might be possible to make these distinctions in many future instances. In *Jarvis v Richards* (1980), the *Liesbosch Dredger* case was again distinguished, this time because it was decided that the defendant could have foreseen the claimant's impecuniosity. In *Mattocks v Mann* (1993), the claimant's car was damaged by the negligence of the defendant and he took it off the road to be repaired and hired a cheaper car. However, from time to time, the claimant would run out of money because he was unemployed, and would send back the hire car and use public transport. The Court of Appeal did not deny the claimant the cost of recovering for the car hire. He had acted reasonably and with commercial prudence and should not be penalised.

It seems that, in today's climate, the *Liesbosch Dredger* rule is barely relevant and it remains to be seen what approach the House of Lords would take if called upon to review it.

8.5.6 Policy issues in remoteness

There is clearly a strong element of policy involved in the law on remoteness of damage. Reasoning based on the scope of the duty is sometimes presented in cases on remoteness as it was in relation to duty of care in *Caparo v Dickman* (1990). In *Banque Bruxelles Lambert SA v Eagle Star Insurance* (1997), the House of Lords held that a valuer of property was not liable for all the direct consequences of his negligent conduct; he was liable only for those that fell within the scope of the duty of care he owed to the person relying on the information he had supplied. Here, a valuer had been negligent in overvaluing a property, on the security of which a lender had advanced money to a borrower. The property market had fallen in value and the lender suffered losses, but the House of Lords held that the valuer would not be liable for that part of the lender's loss which was the result of the fall in value of the property market. Lord Hoffman, who gave the leading speech, distinguished between the breach of a duty to provide information and the breach of a duty to provide advice. He took the view that, if the scope of the duty is merely to provide information, upon which another person can make a decision as to how to proceed, the defendant will not be liable for unforeseeable losses. However, if the duty is to provide advice, the defendant is liable for all the losses flowing from negligent advice. Losses which can be attributed to the fall in the property market could not be said to be caused by the defendant's negligence because they did not fall within the scope of the duty. The actual loss was quantified as the difference between the negligence valuation which had been given and the amount of a non-negligent valuation that should have been given at the time.

8.5.7 Applying the rules: an example

In reality, there is little practical difference between the test in *Re Polemis* and that in the *Wagon Mound*. In most cases, consequences which are reasonably foreseeable are also the direct consequences of the defendant's act. It is only in very extreme cases that this is not so. The thin skull test ensures that, except in the case of economic loss, even unforeseeable consequences attract liability once it is established that the type of accident is reasonably foreseeable. It may be of interest to note that this makes it very difficult for examiners to set problem questions in this area because, by its very nature, an unforeseeable type of damage is difficult to dream up. As a result, the problems which are set are often extremely bizarre. There follows a possible examination question which required a good deal of imagination and ingenuity to draft.

Jerry bought a tin of canned herring from a supermarket. He opened the tin and noticed that the fish was an odd colour. Deciding not to risk eating it himself, he gave it to his cat, Tom, for tea. Tom ate the fish and immediately had an epileptic fit, in the course of which he bit the milkman who had called to be paid. The milkman, a haemophiliac, bled to death, and the cat was seriously ill for several weeks. Tom was a specially trained cat and was due to appear in a film the next day. Jerry could not afford to buy another trained cat and, in order to meet his contractual obligations, he hired another cat at a much inflated price.

Discuss the issues of causation and remoteness of damage which arise in this situation.

8.6 Justification for the remoteness rules

The restrictions which are placed on the scope of liability by the remoteness rules can be justified, in that they do succeed in preventing indeterminate liability to an indefinite number of people. A theme which runs throughout policy discussions in tort is that it is necessary to place a limit on the amount of damage which is recoverable. However, it is questionable as to whether justice is served by the rules of remoteness in their present form. Some may consider that the just approach is that taken in *Re Polemis*, as enunciated by Viscount Simonds (see above, 8.5.2), while others might argue that it would be more just for innocent victims of negligent conduct to be better served by the remoteness rules.

CAUSATION AND REMOTENESS OF DAMAGE

Causation

The claimant must prove that the damage complained of is the result of the defendant's breach of duty. This is a question of fact. There must be an unbroken chain of causation. An event which breaks the chain of causation is known as a *novus actus interveniens*.

Proof is on a balance of probabilities (*Hotson v East Berkshire AHA* (1987)). But see the more recent approach in *Stovold v Barlows* (1995).

Various different approached have been formulated, with the 'but for' test as the usual starting point:

Robinson v Post Office (1974);

Barnett v Chelsea and Kensington HMC (1969);

Sayers v Harlow BC (1958);

Wieland v Cyril Lord Carpets (1969);

McKew v Holland (1969).

Note the difficulties for defendants who are in some way involved in creating the risk (*Kirkham v Chief Constable of Greater Manchester* (1990)).

Note Fleming's assessment that the various tests are merely a mask behind which the judges can avoid articulating their real motivation.

Great difficulties exist in considering causation in situations where there are several concurrent causes as, from a purely practical point of view, it is not possible to separate causative events. The following cases are virtually impossible to reconcile and are best explained as 'policy decisions':

Baker v Willoughby (1970);

Jobling v Associated Dairies (1982);

Bonnington Castings v Wardlaw (1956);

Wilsher v Essex Area AHA (1988).

Causation in cases of omission

Bolitho v City and Hackney Health Authority (1997);

Brock v Frenchay Healthcare Trust (1999).

Causation in contributory negligence

The court must consider whether the claimant's lack of care for his or her own safety contributed to his or her injuries. See the seat-belt cases:

Froom v Butcher (1976);

Condon v Condon (1974).

Remoteness of damage

The question to be asked in relation to remoteness of damage is 'For *how much* of the damage is the defendant liable?'. The judges have determined the limits of what damage is to be compensated by laying down the rules for determining remoteness of damage.

The two possible approaches are:

- The directness test (*Re Polemis* (1921))

    This test provides that the defendant is liable for all the direct consequences of the negligent act.

- The foreseeable consequences test (*The Wagon Mound (No 1)* (1961))

    This test provides that the defendant is liable for all damage of a type which is reasonably foreseeable. The way in which the accident happens must be foreseeable.

In reality, there is little difference between the two tests as, in most situations, the way in which the accident happens is foreseeable. In only the most unusual circumstances will the claimant be denied a remedy by the *Wagon Mound* test. Morally, it could be argued that, if there is any loss caused by the defendant, he or she should bear it, and not the innocent claimant and, from this perspective, the directness test is fairer.

What damage must be foreseeable?

The type of damage and the way in which the accident happens must be foreseeable, though some writers maintain that if the damage is property damage, the courts take a narrower approach:

Hughes v Lord Advocate (1963);

Tremain v Pike (1969);

Crossley v Rawlinson (1981);

Margereson v WJ Roberts (1996);

Jolley v London Borough of Sutton (2000).

The thin skull test

The extent of the damage need not be foreseeable:

Smith v Leech Brain (1962).

Property damage/economic loss

Liesbosch Dredger Case (1933);

Dodd v Canterbury CC (1980);

Matlocks v Mann (1993).

Policy and the negligent valuation cases

Bank Bruxelles Lambert SA v Eagle Star Insurance Co Ltd (1997).

CHAPTER 9

BREACH OF STATUTORY DUTY

It is sometimes possible to bring an action in tort for breach of a duty imposed by statute. The action is known as an action for 'breach of statutory duty'. Although this is an important area of tort in English law, especially in relation to employers' liability, other jurisdictions, notably the USA and Canada, have criticised English law and have tended to assimilate breach of statutory duty into the general law of negligence.

The first question which arises is whether an action in tort will lie for the breach of duty created in a statute which does not specifically contemplate a tort action. An essential element in this tort is the interpretation of the statute in question and, for this purpose, the basic principles of statutory interpretation apply. This in itself creates a problem because there are few fixed 'rules' as such in the interpretation of statutes, and it is not easy to predict which 'rule' or canon of construction an individual judge will follow, unless precedent already exists on the interpretation of the particular words of the statute.

In general, it appears that the statutory provisions which give rise to tortious liability for breach of statutory duty are relatively few but, once it is established that an action in tort could arise, there may be advantages to the claimant, because the burden of proof is reversed and, in some cases, liability will be strict.

The statutes with which we are concerned are usually criminal in nature and are often aimed at preventing accidents and injuries by imposing controls upon certain types of conduct. In particular, industrial safety legislation is frequently used as a basis for an action for breach of statutory duty, and this area of tort finds a natural place for discussion along with employers' liability. Indeed, with the implementation of EC Directives imposing more stringent duties on employers, breach of statutory duty has become a very significant cause of action for employees injured at work.

Although the criminal law framework was designed to deter employers from exposing their workers to unnecessary risks, there have been many criticisms of the reluctance to prosecute employers for breaches of the law, and of the low levels of fines imposed by the courts when there are successful prosecutions (see, for example, the comments and guidance of the Court of Appeal in *R v Howe and Son (Engineers) Ltd* (1999)). This is a matter which the Law Commission has considered and reforms have been recommended (*Accidents at Work*, Law Com 51/17).

9.1 What must be proved?

The action for breach of statutory duty is complex and involves proving a number of propositions. The claimant must prove:

- the statute was intended to create civil liability. The court may here consider the general context of the statute and the precise nature of the statutory provision;

- the statutory duty was owed to the individual claimant;

- the statute imposed the duty on the defendant;

- the defendant was in breach of the duty;

- the damage was of a type contemplated by the Act.

9.1.1 The statute was intended to create civil liability

The claimant must first establish that the statute relied upon imposed a duty upon the defendant which gives rise to civil liability, even though the statute in question does not mention the possibility of compensation in civil actions. It might seem an impossible task, given the predominantly literal approach favoured by the English courts to statutory interpretation, to prove that the intention of Parliament was to support civil liability in a statute which is essentially criminal or quasi-criminal in nature, and indeed it is difficult to establish initially that a cause of action for breach of statutory duty arises.

The courts take various factors into account when deciding upon the intention of Parliament in relation to a particular statute. This is often a matter of guesswork and the consideration of policy issues, and there is a good deal of inconsistency in the cases. It will be interesting to observe whether there will be a change of approach since *Pepper v Hart* (1992) which permits courts to look at *Hansard* in order to discover the intention of Parliament.

Some statutes explicitly state whether they give rise to civil as well as criminal liability (for example, the Health and Safety at Work, etc, Act 1974 and the Management of Health and Safety at Work Regulations 1992). Others specifically exclude liability for breach of statutory duty, for example, the Guard Dogs Act 1975. Most are silent on the matter.

- **What was the general context of the statute?**

  The courts consider the general context of the statute and the nature of the statutory duty in question. In *Cutler v Wandsworth Stadium Ltd* (1949), Lord Simonds said:

  The only rule which in all circumstances is valid is that the answer must depend on a consideration of the whole Act and the circumstances, including the pre-existing law, in which it was enacted.

In practice, the courts have tended to rely on certain presumptions that they have developed. It should be noted that many cases concern the interpretation of subordinate legislation, where the approach is similar to that taken in cases concerning the interpretation of statutes generally.

If the act was intended primarily for the general benefit of the community, rather than for the particular benefit of individuals or a class of individuals, it will not usually give rise to a right of action for the benefit of individuals in tort (*Lonrho v Shell Petroleum* (1982)).

While there are no hard and fast rules, it appears that, if the Act in question was intended to give guidance on matters of welfare, such as the provision of facilities for the general public benefit, it will not give rise to a cause of action to individuals for beach of statutory duty. If, however, the Act is concerned with the welfare of an identifiable group of individuals, such as homeless persons, an action for breach of statutory duty may arise (*Thornton v Kirklees BC* (1979) (since overruled)).

In *O'Rourke v Mayor and Aldermen of the London Borough of Camden* (1998), the claimant had just been released from prison and had nowhere to live. He applied for accommodation to the defendant council, on the basis that he was homeless and in 'priority need' because of his vulnerability. The council investigated his application and carried out the inquiries specified in s 62 of the Housing Act 1985. He was housed in temporary accommodation for a time, then evicted by the defendants. He sought damages for breach of the statutory duty under s 63(1) of the Housing Act 1985, which states:

If the local housing authority have reason to believe that an applicant may be homeless and have a priority need, they shall secure that accommodation is made available for his occupation pending a decision as a result of their enquiries under s 62.

The House of Lords rejected his claim for breach of statutory duty, ruling that the *Kirklees* case, which had been cited by the council, had been wrongly decided. Lord Hoffman found several factors to support the view that Parliament did not intend to confer private rights of action here. He pointed out that many functions of the housing authority contained elements of discretion, and expressed the view that it would be strange if errors of judgement in broad areas of discretion incurred liability to compensate private individuals.

Both negligence and breach of statutory duty need to considered in cases of this kind, and the cases also concern negligence arising out the careless exercise of a discretion provided by a statute. The leading case of *Caparo v Dickman* (1990) is used to determine the issue of whether a duty exists, and both negligence and breach of statutory duty are relevant to the duty problem. Although many of the cases are decided in negligence, the law of negligence is still developing in ways which might assist people who have been aggrieved by the incompetent exercise of statutory functions. Thus, in *Barrett v London Borough of Enfield* (1999), the House of Lords held that a claim by a person who alleged that he had not been properly cared for in local authority care under the Children Act 1989 should not be struck out (see 6.4).

In the employment context, it seems that safety provisions (for example, those in the Mines and Quarries Act 1954) are more likely to give rise to civil liability than those concerned with health and welfare of employees. The general duties in ss 1–9 of the Health and Safety at Work Act 1974 specifically do not give rise to civil actions, but, by s 47 of the same Act, the Regulations made under the Act do give rise to civil liability unless they state otherwise.

The Health and Safety at Work Act 1974 is the product of comprehensive reform of the previous law relating to the health and safety of the workplace following recommendations by the Robens Commission. The general duties in ss 1–9 are concerned with securing the health, safety and welfare of all employees and visitors to all work environments. They create duties 'so far as is reasonably practicable' to ensure healthy and safe places of work, safe plant and machinery and safe use of substances used in the workplace. Uniquely, employees as well as employers are involved in the safety process. In addition, the Act makes provision for Regulations to be formulated which are specific to particular industries, processes and work environments, and which in turn give rise to specific duties. Many of the Regulations must conform with EC standards.

The Act and Regulations made under it are concerned with enforcing safety standards and with preventing health and safety problems rather than with providing compensation to employees who become sick or injured, and for that reason its general sections specifically exclude civil actions.

If the statute concerned creates a duty but does not mention a penalty for its breach, it is usual for a court to find that a cause of action for breach of statutory duty in tort exists (*Cutler v Wandsworth Stadium Ltd* (1949)).

If the statute under scrutiny provides a penalty or a remedy of some kind, it is unusual for it to be held to give rise to an action for breach of statutory duty (*Cutler v Wandsworth Stadium Ltd*), unless it is clear that the statute intended to provide an enforceable right to a particular individual or class of people, but it is impossible to state general rules and it is possible to find cases which contradict these propositions.

- **What was the precise nature of the statutory provisions?**

It seems that the more precise the wording of the statute the more likely it is that the breach of duty will give rise to civil liability. In *Monk v Warby* (1935), it was held that if a person who is not insured to drive a car uses the vehicle with the permission of the owner and negligently injures a third party, the person who is injured can sue the *owner* of the vehicle for breach of his clearly defined duty under s 143 of the Road Traffic Act 1988 (a duty not to allow an uninsured person to drive the vehicle).

In *Groves v Wimborne (Lord)* (1898), it was held that a manufacturer was liable to an employee who was injured when the defendant was in breach of a precise statutory duty to fence certain dangerous machinery.

However, more general and vague statutory provisions are less likely to give rise to an action for beach of statutory duty. For example, duties to see that machinery is 'properly maintained' do not usually give rise to a civil action.

9.1.2   The statutory duty was owed to the individual claimant

Unless the claimant is able to establish that the duty which was created by the statute was intended to be owed to him as an individual or as a member of a class of individuals, there will be no action available (see above).

It can be an advantage to a claimant, whatever the nature of the statute under consideration, if it can be proved that he or she is a member of an ascertainable class of people for whom the legislation was enacted. Where the statute was passed for the protection or benefit of an particular class of people, rather than the public at large, there is a presumption that an action for breach of statutory duty will be available to the individual member of the class who has suffered injury. There is scope for the exercise of judicial discretion at this point. Even if the claimant does fall into such a class, the courts might be unwilling to find that a right to a civil claim exists if the nature of the obligation was not such that, if broken, it would be likely to give rise to personal injury, injury to property or economic loss. Thus, in *Pickering v Liverpool Daily Post* (1991), the House of Lords held that a patient at a psychiatric hospital had no right to a civil action for breach of privacy when information about his application to a mental health tribunal had been issued contrary to regulations. The statute could not be used to provide a cause of action where no such action previously existed at common law.

It is difficult to state with certainty that the presumption relating to membership of a class will be applied in every case. There have been some cases in which no claim for breach of statutory duty has been available, even though a statute was clearly passed for the protection of a particular class, as in *X (Minors) v Bedfordshire CC* (1995). This case suggests that, if the statute involves difficult policy issues and there is an element of discretion involved in the performance of the duty, there must be no doubt in the wording of the Act that Parliament intended it to give rise to civil liability. However, that particular decision was based on policy issues and has been questioned before the European Commission.

This will be a matter of interpretation in each case. However, the scope is very wide and the potential for civil actions is great. For example, in *Garden Cottage Foods v Milk Marketing Board* (1984), it was held that an action for breach of statutory duty could arise out of breach of an article of the EC Treaty. For that reason, the courts approach this problem with caution.

In *Knapp v Railway Executive* (1949), a railway worker was injured when a gate at a level crossing swung back and hit him. It was held that there was no liability for breach of statutory duty because the statute in question which required the defendant to keep gates of level-crossings in the correct position at all times, was held to be intended for the protection of road users crossing the lines, not of railway employees.

In *Atkinson v Croydon Corpn* (1938), it was held that the defendants were liable for breach of statutory duty to the father of a girl who had contracted typhoid because of the breach of their statutory duty to provide a pure supply of water. He was able to claim for expenses which he had incurred in the treatment of his daughter's illness, and his action arose from his being a rate-payer and one of the class of people to whom the duty was owed. The daughter who was not a rate-payer had no action for breach of statutory duty.

In *Hewett v Alf Brown's Transport* (1992), the claimant, the wife of a lorry driver, suffered lead poisoning, as a result of exposure to lead when cleaning her husbands overalls. The Control of Lead at Work Regulations and code of practice imposed duties upon employers to protect their employees from the dangers of exposure to lead. The Court of Appeal held that this did not apply to the claimant, and she was without a remedy.

These principles were referred to by the Court of Appeal in *Clunis v Camden and Islington HA* (1997), in which it was held that there was no indication in s 117 of the Mental Health Act 1983 that Parliament intended to confer a right on private individuals to bring an action for breach of statutory duty in respect of that section (see Chapter 6).

9.1.3 The statutory duty was imposed on the particular defendant

The precise words of the Act must be interpreted in order to establish whether the particular defendant has a duty under it. Only if the statute imposes a duty on the defendant can a civil action be maintained against him.

9.1.4 The defendant was in breach of the statutory duty

Here, the standard of care imposed by the statute is of vital importance. In some cases, the claimant will be assisted by the fact that there will be strict liability for breach of the statutory duty, depending on the construction of the Act in question.

Unfortunately, there is a good deal of inconsistency in the application of the law in these cases, and there is a suspicion that policy plays an important part in the decisions. Lord Denning has said that 'You might as well toss a coin in order to decide the cases'.

However, it may be possible to elicit some principles from the cases. For example, if the provision uses the words 'must' or 'shall' in relation to a particular duty, it is likely that the duty will be absolute and liability strict. In *John Summers & Sons v Frost* (1955), it was held not to be defence to an employer to demonstrate that it was impracticable to fence machinery, because the relevant statute, s 14(1) of the Factories Act 1961, provided that any part of the machinery *must* be securely fenced. However, in other actions for breach of statutory duty arising out of the same section, it has been held that it did not apply to materials in the machine.

The House of Lords, in *Nimmo v Alexander Cowan and Sons* (1968), held that that the term 'reasonably practicable', as used in s 19 of the Factories Act 1961, required the employer to demonstrate that he or she had taken such precautions as were reasonably practicable. It seems that, if the word 'practicable' appears without the qualification of 'reasonably', the standard to be applied falls midway between that in negligence and strict liability.

Statutes creating criminal law penalties are construed strictly. For example, in *Chipchase v British Titan Products Co Ltd* (1956), the claimant was denied a remedy for breach of statutory duty. Regulations in the particular industry specified that a platform placed at a height of more than 6 ft 6 in from the ground should be at least 34 in wide. The platform from which the claimant fell was only 9 in wide, but it stood only 6 ft above the ground. It was held that the claim for breach of statutory duty could not succeed.

If the statutory provision uses, as is very common, the words 'in so far as is reasonably practicable', the duty is not absolute, and the standard of care probably lies somewhere between the standard of reasonable care in negligence and that of strict liability. In *Edwards v National Coal Board* (1949), Asquith LJ described the duty as a balance between the sacrifice which is necessary to avoid a risk and the magnitude of the risk involved.

The Health and Safety at Work, etc, Act 1974 and regulations made under it have the aim of preventing accidents, but lawyers have found that the industrial safety legislation has been used very successfully as a starting point for civil liability when employees are injured in accidents. There have been many successful claims by injured employees, many of whom receive financial support from trade unions. The regulations made under the Health and Safety at Work, etc, Act 1974 should be studied carefully in order to determine their scope. Many specifically state that they do give rise to civil liability in the event of a breach. For example, five of what have become known as the 'Six-pack' Regulations state that breaches do create civil liability.

The liability of employers can sometimes extend far beyond their usual premises. In *Fraser v Winchester HA* (1999), a claim for damages arose out of a situation which had come about when the claimant was assisting as a support worker on a holiday for disabled young people. She was usually employed by the defendant as a resident support worker at a home for disabled young people. The residents took an annual holiday and the claimant agreed go camping with one resident, as she had been his sole carer. A camping gas cylinder which the claimant had been inserting into a camping stove exploded and she was badly injured. She was given no instructions about the use of the camping stove, nor about changing the gas cylinders. The claimant brought proceedings against the health authority, claiming damages for negligence and for breach of statutory duty under the Provision and Use of Work Equipment Regulations 1992. The defendant argued, on the principle in *Ratcliff v McConnell* (1999), that there was no breach of any duty, as the risk was so obvious that no warning, nor any training or instruction, was necessary.

The Court of Appeal held that considerable responsibility had been placed on the claimant, but she had been provided with inadequate and hazardous equipment and training. In these circumstances, the defendant was in breach of its duty towards her. As there was an obvious risk, the claimant had been one third contributorily negligent.

Courts frequently lean against the imposition of strict liability unless the statute specifically states that strict liability will apply. This is a general presumption of statutory interpretation (*Sweet v Parsley* (1965)) and applies equally to breach of statutory duty when the court is considering the nature of the statutory duty in question. In *Brown v National Coal Board* (1962), it was held that the words to 'take such steps as may be necessary for the keeping of the road or working place secure' did not create a strict liability situation. The manager responsible had exercised reasonable care and skill in all the circumstances and was not liable.

The burden of proving that the measures taken by the employer were within the notion of what was practicable or reasonably practicable is on the defendant and, in this respect and because in some cases liability is strict, the claimant is at an advantage in comparison with the claimant in ordinary negligence actions.

Should the claimant allege that the exercise of statutory powers is careless it must be demonstrated that there would have been a duty of care at common law in the same circumstances. If the exercise of a discretion is in question and the decisions complained of fall within the ambit of the statutory discretion, they cannot be the subject of a common law action. If, however, the decision falls outside the discretion because it is so unreasonable, there is not necessarily any reason to exclude all common law liability. Lord Browne-Wilkinson said:

There must come a stage when the discretion is exercised so carelessly or unreasonably that there has been no real exercise of the discretion which Parliament conferred.

However, the courts cannot adjudicate on policy matters where social values or resource allocation are concerned. The statement of the law concludes:

If the decision falls outside the statutory discretion, it can (but not necessarily will) give rise to common law liability. However, if the factors relevant to the exercise of discretion include matters of policy, the court cannot adjudicate on such policy matters and therefore cannot reach the conclusion that the decision was outside the ambit of the statutory discretion. Therefore, a common law duty of care in relation to the taking of decisions involving policy matters cannot exist.

In *Stovin v Wise* (1996), the House of Lords held that a statutory power given to a public body could not create a duty of care where no previous duty had existed. Whether any such duty existed to a private person depended on the construction of the statute.

9.1.5 The damage must be of a type which the statute contemplated

The nature of the remedy given in the statute is a consideration in determining whether the statute gives rise to civil liability. It seems that, if no remedy is provided by the statute, and this is coupled by an intention to benefit a particular class of people, it is interpreted as indicating that Parliament intended the statute to create civil liability. The reason for this may be that, without a civil remedy, there would be no other way for the statute to provide the intended benefit. However, where the statute creates its own framework of procedures for decision making and enforcement, it is unlikely to give rise to separate civil liability.

In *Lonrho Ltd v Shell Petroleum Co Ltd* (1981), Lord Diplock said that the rule is this: if a statute provides for a *criminal* sanction, it will not give rise to *civil* liability. There are two exceptions to this rule. The first is where the duty is imposed on the defendant for the protection or benefit of a particular class of individuals, and the second is where the statute creates a public right and the claimant suffers some damage over and above that suffered by the public. However, even in this, there is no consistency.

There will only be an action for breach of statutory duty if damage which was suffered was within the contemplation of the objects of the statute. In *Gorris v Scott* (1874), there was no action for breach of statutory duty because the claimant suffered the loss of his sheep from the deck of a vessel when they were swept overboard. The statute in question was concerned with the loss of livestock through the spread of disease. This point is concerned with the question of remoteness of damage. In *Young v Charles Church* (1997), the Court of Appeal held that nervous shock was among the kinds of injury contemplated by the Construction (General Provisions) Regulations 1993.

9.1.6 The injury must have been caused by the defendant's breach of statutory duty

The claimant will not succeed unless it can be proved that the breach of statutory duty caused the injury of which he or she complains. Again, the scope of the duty of care depends upon the construction of the statute, and no single standard of care exists. The rules for establishing causation applicable in common law negligence also apply to breach of statutory duty. In *Stringer v Bedfordshire CC* (1999), which involved a claim for breach of statutory duty arising out of a breach of s 41 of the Highways Act 1980, the judge held that, although there were defects on the highway, these did not cause the accident, in which an inexperienced driver lost control of her car.

9.1.7 Breaches of European legislation

Some emerging issues arise as a result of the relationship between UK law and European law concerning private law remedies in the UK law of tort, and in the European context. Many recently introduced regulations have their origins in European Community (EC) Directives. A large number of these have now been implemented in the UK. In *Garden Cottage Foods v Milk Marketing Board*, (1984), the House of Lords concluded that it might, in certain circumstances, be possible for a breach of statutory duty claim to arise when there had been a breach of an obligation arising under EC legislation which is 'directly effective'. However, in *Bourgoin SA v Ministry of Agriculture, Fisheries and Food* (1986), the Court of Appeal turned down a claim for breach of the duty arising under Art 30 (now Art 28) of the EC Treaty, concluding that judicial review would be a more appropriate remedy. There are more recent decisions of the European Court of Justice which suggest that, if a State fails to implement a directive, there may be an obligation to compensate private persons for any damage suffered as a result.

9.2 Defences

If the statutory duty is not absolute, there will be a defence, as there is for breach of the employer's common law duty, if a safety precaution is not provided but the claimant would not, on a balance of probabilities, have made use of it even if it had been available. This is a matter of causation (*McWilliams v Sir William Arrol & Co Ltd* (1962)). This should not be confused with the defence of *volenti* (see Chapter 20).

Volenti non fit injuria is not normally available, for reasons of public policy, in an action by an employee against his or her employer for breach of statutory duty (*ICI v Shatwell* (1965)).

However, a defence will be available if the claimant's own wrongful act puts the employer in breach of statutory duty. In *Ginty v Belmont Building Supplies Ltd* (1959), the claimant was working on a roof and chose not to use special crawling boards as a safety measure. This was a breach of the relevant statutory regulations. It was held that the employer was not vicariously liable to the employee for his own wrongful act. This defence will not apply, however, if the employee is injured through the wrongful act of another employee.

9.2.1 Contributory negligence

The defence of contributory negligence will be available in appropriate cases in an action for breach of statutory duty (*Caswell v Powell Duffryn Collieries Ltd* (1940)), and it is possible for an employee who is 100% contributorily negligent to be denied any compensation (*Jayes v IMC (Kynoch) Ltd* (1985)).

In *Rushton v Turner Asbestos* (1960), the Court of Appeal held that an employee who was ordered into a dark, cramped area to carry out a task was only one-third contributorily negligent when his error resulted in an injury to himself. In *Marlton v British Steel* (1999), an employee who was burned was one-third contributorily negligent when he worked too close to hot coke ovens without wearing fire resistant clothing, even though the employer had failed to provide protective clothing.

9.2.2 Delegation

Although in some cases the defence of delegation has been raised, it is not normally successful. This defence involves alleging that the person on whom the duty was imposed had delegated that duty to another person, such as an independent contractor. The defence appears to have fallen into disuse in recent years, but it may become more important with the implementation of the comprehensive duties imposed by the regulations made under the Health and Safety at Work, etc, Act 1974.

BREACH OF STATUTORY DUTY

What must be proved?

To succeed in an action for breach of statutory duty, the claimant must establish that the statute which created the duty also supports civil liability. Much will depend on the interpretation of the statute in question, and the rules of statutory interpretation should be borne in mind when considering the scope of this tort. Many of the cases are difficult to reconcile and much depends on policy.

The statute was intended to create civil liability

In order to decide whether the statute was intended to create civil liability, the court may look at:

- **The general context of the Act**

  Statutes intended to operate for the general benefit of the community will not usually create a civil liability:

  Lonrho v Shell (1982);

  Thornton v Kirklees BC (1979);

  Cutler v Wandsworth Stadium (1949);

  Clunis v Camden and Islington HA (1997);

  O'Rourke v London Borough of Camden (1998).

- **The precise nature of the statutory provision**

  If the wording of the statute is very precise, it is more likely to give rise to a tort action:

  Monk v Warby (1935);

  Groves v Wimborne (1898).

The statutory duty was owed to the particular claimant

The claimant must be able to prove that the duty was owed to him or her as an individual. People outside the statutory relationship will not succeed:

Garden Cottage Foods v Milk Marketing Board (1948);

Knapp v Railway Executive (1949);

Atkinson v Croydon Corpn (1938);

Pickering v Liverpool Daily Post (1991);

Hewett v Alf Brown's Transport (1992);

Clunis v Camden and Islington HA (1997).

The statute imposed the duty on the defendant

The precise words of an Act must be interpreted in order to establish whether the particular defendant has a duty under it. Only if the statute imposes a duty on the defendant can a civil action be maintained against him.

The defendant was in breach of the duty

Where the defendant was in breach of the duty, liability may be strict, and all depends upon the wording of an Act and its interpretation. This element can give the claimant an advantage which is not afforded by ordinary negligence:

Brown v NCB (1962);

John Summers v Frost (1955);

Nimmo v Alexander Cowan (1968).

Note the reversal of the burden of proof and the consequent advantage to the claimant.

The damage was of a type which was contemplated by the Act

There will only be an action for breach of statutory duty if damage which was suffered was within the contemplation of the objects of the statute:

Gorris v Scott (1874);

Young v Charles Church (1997).

The injury was caused by the defendant's breach of the duty

If the statutory duty is not absolute, there will be a defence, as there is for breach of the employer's common law duty, if a safety precaution is not provided but the claimant would not, on a balance of probabilities, have made use of it even if it had been available. Note the possible use of European Regulations.

Defences

There are some defences available for breach of statutory duty, but these must be read in the light of the particular statute. They include:

- The duty was not absolute and claimant would not have made use of safety equipment even if it was provided. This is part of the issue of causation: *McWilliams v Sir William Arrol*.

- *Volenti* (not usually available in employment cases).

- Contributory negligence: *Caswell v Powell Duffryn Collieries* (1940); *Jayes v IMC (Kynoch) Ltd* (1985).

- Delegation.

CHAPTER 10

OCCUPIERS' LIABILITY

10.1 Introduction

It is accepted that 27% of reported accidents occur in the home (Pearson Report, vol 2, para 16), yet, although reliable statistics on the matter are difficult to obtain, it appears that few claims arise out of domestic accidents (see Harris, D, *Compensation and Support for Illness and Injury*, 1989). A number of reasons have been suggested for this. It could well be that people are unaware of the possibility of making a claim in such circumstances, or that they are reluctant to sue relatives and friends (most claims for accidents on property are brought against companies by members of the public).

Another possible reason for the relatively small number of claims is that while property owners are required by mortgage lenders to insure their buildings under the terms of most mortgages, occupiers' liability is covered by house contents insurance which is not compulsory, and many house owners choose to skimp on this. A lawyer is unlikely to advise a client to sue the average uninsured householder.

Occupiers' liability is a field in which until relatively recently there was only a limited duty owed in law to others, but which has been extensively overhauled by statute and common law developments to include the imposition of liability akin to that in negligence in numerous situations (Atiyah, P, *Accidents, Compensation and the Law*, Cane, P (ed), 1999.

In modern law, the liability of occupiers for people who are injured on their premises is governed by the Occupiers' Liability Acts of 1957 and 1984. Before 1957, the common law applied, and liability depended upon the type of entrant; for example the highest standard of care was that owed to people entering the land as contractors. The next highest standard of care was owed to people who had some mutual business interests with the occupier and who were called invitees, and so on. Trespassers however, were owed only a minimal duty and in most cases no positive duty of care at all. The position at common law was complex and confusing and for that reason the law was simplified by the Occupiers' Liability Act 1957.

10.1.1 Application of common law

Before embarking upon a detailed study of the statutes themselves, it is still necessary to consider where any of the previous common law still applies. For example:

- It is important to establish whether a person who was once a trespasser has become a licensee or lawful visitor and is therefore owed a duty of care under the Occupiers' Liability Act 1957. There is a considerable amount of common law on this subject and this will be discussed in detail later, but the Act itself is silent on the matter.

- 'Premises' are not defined by statute, and the common law definitions still apply.

- The Act is silent on the position of users of public and private rights of way, and the common law still applies here.

The House of Lords recently tackled a difficult matter concerning the legal position of users of rights of way in *McGeown v Northern Ireland Housing Executive* (1994). The claimant lived on a housing estate belonging to the Northern Ireland Housing Executive, and her house was in a terrace on one side of a small cul-de-sac. She was injured on a footpath which belonged to the defendants, and which began as an informal footpath between the terraces but which had become a public right of way. Her injury was caused by tripping on a hole which had developed through lack of repair to the footpath (non-feasance). Her action was for negligence and/or breach of statutory duty. Lord Keith in the leading judgment confirmed the old rule in *Gautret v Egerton* (1867) that the owner of land over which a right of way passes owes no duty towards members of the public in relation to non-feasance (doing no repairs). He thought that this rule was justified by the fact that an impossible burden would be placed on landowners if they had not only to submit to letting people walk over their land, but also to keep the rights of way in a good condition. His view was that a person exercising a right of way does so not by permission but in the exercise of a right, and therefore falls outside the definition of a 'visitor' under the Occupiers' Liability Act 1957. If the path had not become a public right of way, the defendants would have owed the claimant a duty of care and would have been liable for her injuries. The question here was whether the previous licence to cross the land had been merged into the public right of way and been extinguished as a result, or whether it still had an independent existence of its own. He took the view that the establishment of a public right of way ruled out the element of permission, so no duty of care was owed. Lord Browne-Wilkinson, while agreeing that *Gautret v Egerton* was good law, thought it best to leave open the question as to whether people using public rights of way could still have visitor status, bearing in mind the fact that some landowners encourage people to cross their land and use facilities which they provide, so allowing them to continue as invitees under the old law.

The claimant was not entitled to any compensation.

In this confusing situation, the claimant appears to have fewer rights than casual visitors. The Occupiers' Liability Act 1957, on its wording, suggests that people in the claimant's position might be entitled to more generous treatment, as s 2(6) states:

> ... that for the purposes of the section persons who enter premises for any purpose in the exercise of a right conferred by law are to be treated as permitted by the occupier to be there for that purpose, whether they have permission or not, thereby falling within the category of persons to whom the common duty of care is owed.

This wording seems to include those using public or private rights of way, but judges have decided that the old law survives and such people are not 'visitors'. This was the decision in *Greenhalgh v British Railways Board* (1969) in which Lord Denning held that the operative words were 'For the purposes of this section', that is, for the purposes of s 2 of the Occupiers' Liability Act 1957, which defines only the extent of the occupier's duty to visitors rather than extending the categories of people who can be defined as visitors.

The Law Commission has considered these anomalies in the past but so far nothing has been done to clarify the situation.

However, the Countryside and Rights of Way Bill 2000, which was introduced into Parliament in March 2000, sets out to remedy this situation in cl 13. (The Bill is outlined at the end of this chapter at 10.12.) Clause 13 places entrants who go onto land under the new rights of access in a similar position to highway users.

- It seems that the ordinary law of negligence applies in situations where injury is caused through something other than the state of the premises. For example, if a person is injured on someone's property because a tractor is driven negligently the ordinary law of negligence will probably apply (see below).

   In the case of *Ogwo v Taylor* (1987), Lord Justice Brown stated that a fireman who had been injured while fighting a fire on premises was covered by the ordinary law of negligence because the injury was not caused by a defect in the state of the premises.

   Compare this case with the sort of situation that routinely arises under the Occupiers' Liability Act 1957, such as that in *Taylor v Bath and North East Somerset DC* (1999). There, the claimant recovered damages after falling on the slippery surface of tiles at the side of a swimming pool. This is one of many cases involving accidents in swimming pools. By contrast, in *Ingram v Davison-Lungley* (2000), the owner/occupier of a private swimming pool was not in breach of the common duty of care under s 2 of the 1957 Act when a visitor fell and injured herself on the swimming pool steps. She been trying to climb down into the water in an unusual way.

- Common law still applies in assessing the legal status of 'regular trespassers', when considering whether they have become licensees.

However, the law is still not absolutely clear on this subject and some of the writers take the view that it is possible that the Occupiers' Liability Act 1957 might apply even when injury is caused by something other than the state of the premises because sub-s 1 of the Act states that the Act applies 'in respect of dangers due to the state of the premises or to things done or omitted to be done on them'. Nevertheless, it is widely accepted that 'vehicles' fall within the definition of 'premises' and, as there is virtually no litigation involving accidents caused by negligent handling of vehicles under the Occupiers' Liability Act 1957, and a definite preference for the ordinary law of negligence in such circumstances, it is likely that the Act does not usually encompass dangerous activities which do not arise out of the state of the premises. In practice, it is of little importance which action applies, unless the defendant is covered by insurance for one form of liability rather than the other, and unless there is a definite distinction between the rules for determining breach of duty. It is likely that the approach in occupiers' liability could be more sympathetic to claimants, however, in that it requires the occupier to have consideration for the position of the particular visitor.

10.2 Liability under the Occupiers' Liability Act 1957

The duty of occupiers to their lawful visitors is clearly set out in s 2(1) of the Occupiers' Liability Act 1957 which states:

> An occupier of premises owes the same duty, the common duty of care to all his visitors except insofar as he is free to and does extend, restrict, modify or exclude his duty to any visitor or visitors by agreement or otherwise.

In order to understand the scope of the duty and the operation of the law, it is necessary to break down this section into its various elements.

10.2.1 What is meant by the word 'occupier'?

As the Occupiers' Liability Act 1957 is silent on the meaning of 'occupier', the common law applies. Originally, the test to identify who an occupier is, was that of control. Basically, the person who had control over the premises was the occupier. But, in the case of *Wheat v E Lacon & Co Ltd* (1966), it was held that there could be more than one occupier of the premises at a time. In that case, the defendant owned a pub which was managed by an employee. The employee and his wife had rooms on the first floor of the pub as their private house but they had no interest in the premises. It was provided under an agreement with the defendants that there should not even be a tenancy between them. The wife was given permission to take in paying guests in part of the first floor, the only access from which was by means of an outside staircase at the rear of the premises. The hand rail of the staircase ended above the third step of the staircase which was unlit. When the claimant and her husband were guests at the pub one night, the claimant's husband fell downstairs and died from his injuries. It was held that both the employees and the defendant (the owner of the pub) were occupiers.

In *Revill v Newbury* (1996), it was held that the person who rents an allotment is the occupier for the purposes of the Occupiers' Liability Act 1984.

In *Harris v Birkenhead Corporation* (1976), it was held by the Court of Appeal that a person could be an occupier even if he was not actually present on the premises to be in control. In fact, in this case, a local authority had the legal control of premises because they had issued a compulsory purchase order on the house, and notice of entry. They were the occupiers even though they had not actually taken possession of the premises.

As in other areas of law, the determining factor in cases such as these could well be the question of which potential defendant carries liability insurance.

10.2.2 What is meant by the word 'premises'?

There is no definition of the word 'premises' in the Occupiers' Liability Act 1957. Once again, it is necessary to turn to the common law for guidance. Clearly, 'premises' will include houses, buildings, land and so on, but it is likely also that ships in dry dock (*London Graving Dock v Horton* (1951); *Hartwell v Grayson* (1947)), vehicles, lifts (*Haseldine v Daw & Son Ltd* (1941)) and aircraft (*Fosbroke-Hobbes v Airwork Ltd* (1937)) will also be considered premises for the purposes of the Act as they were at common law. In *Wheeler v Copas* (1981), it was held that a ladder could be regarded as premises, and claims for the disaster at Bradford City football stadium were founded in occupiers' liability rather than the ordinary law of negligence, so structures like stadiums for spectators are 'premises'.

10.2.3 What is 'the common duty of care'?

The word 'common' is used to demonstrate that the new duty under the Act is common to all types of 'visitor', that is, most categories of *lawful* visitor, as trespassers were still not owed a duty under this Occupiers' Liability Act 1957. 'Visitors' does not include users of public or private rights of way (*McGeown v N Ireland Housing Executive* (1994) (above). The common duty of care is defined in s 2(2) of the Occupiers' Liability Act 1957 as:

> ... the duty to take such care as in all the circumstances of the case is reasonable to see that the visitor will be reasonably safe in using the premises for the purpose for which he is invited or permitted by the occupier to be there.

It should be noted that it is the visitor who must be made safe and not necessarily the premises. This could mean that dangerous parts of the premises can be fenced off and need not themselves be repaired so long as the visitors are safeguarded while on the premises.

The point is that duty is only owed to the visitors while they are undertaking the purpose for which they are permitted or invited to be on the premises. If the visitor decides to do something which he is *not* permitted to do, then the duty of care under the Occupiers' Liability Act 1957 would not be owed. For example, tradesmen are permitted to visit premises in order to deliver goods but if the postman decided to take a trip around the garden and climb the apple tree, then the 1957 common duty of care would not be owed to him. He would, in those circumstances, be a trespasser and the duty owed would be that imposed on the occupier under the Occupiers' Liability Act 1984.

In *Glenie v Slack and Others* (1998), the owner and occupier of an unsafe track built for motorcycle side-car races was held to have been in breach of the duty of care in negligence and of his duty under s 2 of the Occupiers' Liability Act 1957. The track and the fencing were held to have been inadequate and inherently unsafe. The passenger in the side car was killed and the claimant was very seriously injured when a motorcycle combination crashed. There was a finding of 50% contributory negligence.

10.3 Children

One important aspect of the Occupiers' Liability Act 1957 is that it gives examples of the operation of the duty of care. Section 2(3)(a) of the Occupiers' Liability Act 1957 provides that an occupier must be prepared for children to be less careful than adults. This is an important point in that it demonstrates what is meant by the duty to see that the *visitor* will be safe. Thus, the duty is a subjective rather than an objective duty, judged from the point of view of the visitor.

10.3.1 The allurement principle

It is in this context that it is necessary to consider the cases in which courts have found occupiers liable to children who have been attracted by 'traps' onto certain parts of premises and injured there.

For example, in *Glasgow Corpn v Taylor* (1922), a seven year old child was playing in a public park when he noticed some attractive poisonous berries on a bush. The bush was not fenced off and the child picked the berries and ate them. He died later as a result. It was held that the occupiers were liable because the berries constituted a 'trap' or 'allurement' to the child.

In *Jolley v London Borough of Sutton* (2000), it was held that an abandoned boat in a dangerous condition constituted an allurement to two boys (see Chapter 8).

An allurement will not necessarily make a child trespasser a lawful visitor. So, for example, in *Liddle v Yorkshire (North Riding) CC* (1944), it was held that the defendants were not liable when a child who was a trespasser was playing on a high bank of soil close to a wall. He jumped off the bank of soil trying to show his friends how bees flew and he was injured. It was clear in this case that the child was a trespasser as he had been warned off by the defendant on previous occasions. The pile of soil could not therefore make him a lawful visitor.

It used to be the case that the courts were prepared to assume that in the case of very young children the responsibility was that of their parents to ensure that they were safe.

In *Phipps v Rochester Corpn* (1955), a child aged only five was walking across the defendant's land when he fell into a trench. The child was a licensee because he played there often with other children and the defendant had done nothing to warn the children away. However, it was held that, even though as a licensee he was a lawful visitor, the occupiers of the land were not liable, because the parents should have been taking care of the child.

This reasoning was also followed in *Simkiss v Rhondda BC* (1983). In that case, a seven year old girl fell off a slope opposite the flats where she lived. Her father had allowed her to picnic there because he considered that the slope was not dangerous. As the children sat on a blanket, they were able to slide down the slope, and this was how the accident happened. Nevertheless, the local authority were not liable, according to the reasoning of the Court of Appeal. Since the child's father did not consider the area dangerous, it could not be argued that the defendants should consider it dangerous.

Despite these two cases, there are many cases in which the courts have been particularly lenient towards child trespassers and it is very unusual nowadays for a court to find that there is no liability on the part of an occupier towards children on the grounds that their parents should have been taking care of them. Nevertheless, as a general principle, children should normally be supervised.

10.3.2 Duties to contractors

The second example in the Occupiers' Liability Act 1957 of the operation of the common duty of care is that given in s 2(1)(b), in which it is said that an occupier may expect that a person in the exercise of his calling will appreciate and guard against any special risks ordinarily incidental to it, so far as the occupier leaves him free to do so.

10.3.3 Risks ordinarily incidental to particular occupations

In the case of *Roles v Nathan* (1963), the Court of Appeal considered the scope of s 2(3)(b) of the Occupiers' Liability Act 1957 in relation to the death of two chimney sweeps. The men had died after inhaling carbon monoxide fumes while they were cleaning the flue of a boiler through a hole in the chimney. The occupier had warned them not to continue with their work while the boiler was alight because of the danger from the fumes and indeed had removed them bodily from the danger area on two occasions. It was held that the occupier was not liable because he had in fact discharged his duty of care under the Occupiers' Liability Act 1957 by warning them of the particular risks. Lord Denning also stated that the risks involved were ordinarily incidental to a chimney sweep's trade and, therefore, the men should have been aware of them and taken steps to guard against them. He went on to explain that if the deaths had been caused by something unrelated to the business of being chimney sweeps, for example, if the stairs leading to the cellar had collapsed, then the occupier would have been liable. So, for example, a window cleaner who falls off a dangerous ledge while cleaning windows could not complain to the occupier. But, if the same window cleaner had been injured while walking through the house to get to a window sill, then that would be a breach of the common duty of care.

However, in the case of *Salmon v Seafarer Restaurants Ltd* (1983), a fireman was badly injured while fighting a fire at a fish and chip shop. It was held that the occupier was in breach of the common duty of care even though fighting fires was something which the fireman was obviously employed to do. The fireman had exercised the ordinary skills of firemen.

In *Ogwo v Taylor* (1987), a fireman was injured by steam when fighting a fire in an attic. Again, it was held that the occupier was liable. However, it was pointed out in this case that the occupier would not have been liable had the fireman taken some unnecessary risk which could break the chain of causation. The claimant won the case, however, in negligence. The House of Lords took the view that there would only have been liability under the Occupiers' Liability Act 1957 if, for example, there had been failure to warn of a hazard.

10.4 Discharge of the duty of care

There are a number of ways in which the occupier may discharge the duty of care. He could, for example, personally guide his visitors around his property to avoid all dangerous obstacles. However, it is much more common practice for occupiers to place notices on property warning of particular dangers.

Section 2(4)(a) states:

> Where damage is caused to a visitor by danger of which he has been warned by the occupier, the warning is not to be treated without more as absolving the occupier from liability unless, in all the circumstances, it was enough to enable the visitor to be reasonably safe.

This is a matter for the judge to decide on the basis of the evidence presented to the court. For example, in *Zucchi v Waitrose* (2000), the Court of Appeal held that there was no breach of duty under s 2 of the 1957 Act, as Waitrose had properly considered its duty of care to all of its visitors. It was not liable when a customer was hit on the leg by a two litre bottle of mineral water, as it had carried out regular assessments of the risks of goods falling, as this bottle did, from the conveyors at the checkouts in its stores.

Each case will, of course, turn on its own facts. In some circumstances, a warning notice will be perfectly adequate but in others it will not. For these purposes, the law is concerned with the particular visitor and the effect of a notice upon the individual in question. The test is subjective. For example, if the visitor is a child who has not learned to read, or somebody who cannot understand English, or a person who is blind, a warning notice will not be adequate. This should be compared with the rules in the law of contract relating to notice of exclusion clauses where the test is objective, and it is sufficient merely that there is notice at the time of contracting. So far as occupiers' liability is concerned, the Occupiers' Liability Act 1957 specifically states that a warning notice is not enough unless in all the circumstances it was enough to enable the visitor to be reasonably safe. In some cases, *res ipsa lequitur* may apply (see Chapter 7).

In *Fryer v Pearson* (2000), house owners were found not liable for an accident involving a visitor kneeling on a needle in the carpet. It was not established that they knew that it was there or had allowed it to remain there. This was not a suitable case for the operation of *res ipsa loquitur*. The Court of Appeal took the view that the position of a householder was different from the case of a customer slipping on the floor of a shop, as in *Ward v Tesco Stores Ltd* (1976). Here, it was simply not possible to infer from the evidence that the respondents had caused or permitted the needle to remain in the carpet.

10.4.1 Examples of warning notices

It is important at this point to distinguish between warning notices which are genuine attempts by the occupier to discharge the duty of care and make visitors safe, and exclusion clauses which are attempts by the occupier to escape liability and avoid the common duty of care. A warning notice can mean that the occupier will not be liable because he has done sufficient to discharge the duty. An exclusion clause will not operate in many circumstances because of the Unfair Contract Terms Act 1977 (see **Chapter 9**).

In the case of a dangerous staircase, a warning notice might read:

Take care – these stairs are dangerous. Under no circumstances should members of the public attempt to use them.

An exclusion clause might read:

> Under no circumstances will the occupier of these premises be liable for injury to people using these stairs.

The situation is confused because many notices are a mixture of warning and exclusion. For example:

> These stairs are very dangerous, please take care. Under no circumstances will the occupier be liable for injury to people who use them.

If a danger is obvious, even a warning notice may add no further information to assist a visitor in taking care, and the occupier is entitled to assume that visitors will take care when danger is apparent for all to see. In *Staples v West Dorset DC* (1995), the Court of Appeal ruled that the council had no additional duty to warn visitors of obvious danger caused by wet algae on a high wall on the Cobb at Lyme Regis (where *The French Lieutenant's Woman* was set and filmed). Visitors should be able to evaluate the danger involved.

There are some cases in which the courts have taken the view that warning notices would be of no use because they would be ignored or are beyond the scope of an occupier's duty. In *Whyte v Redland Aggregates Ltd* (1997), the Court of Appeal held that an occupier's duty did not extend to erecting 'no swimming' signs at disused gravel pits.

10.5 Exclusion of liability

How far is the occupier free to extend, restrict, modify or exclude his duty to any visitors? The situation is now governed by the Unfair Contract Terms Act 1977.

10.5.1 Business occupiers

The Unfair Contract Terms Act 1977 applies to business premises which are defined in s 1(3). 'Business' includes professions, government and local authority activities. Thus, hospitals and schools would be regarded as businesses for the purposes of the Unfair Contract Terms Act 1977 in the same way as shops, stately homes and so on.

By s 2(1) of the Unfair Contract Terms Act 1977, any attempt to exclude liability for death or personal injuries caused by negligence, including breach of the common duty of care under the Occupiers' Liability Act 1957 will be void.

Any attempt to exclude liability for property damage will be subject to the reasonableness test.

Occupiers cannot therefore on business premises exclude liability for death, or personal injury caused by their negligence arising out of the state of the premises, and if they do try to exclude liability for property damage this will only be possible if such exclusion is, in the view of the court, reasonable in all the circumstances of the case.

10.5.2 Private occupiers

It should be noted that, since the Unfair Contract Terms Act 1977 only applies to business premises, private occupiers will still be able to exclude liability even for death and personal injury. It is therefore still necessary to consider the state of the law before the Unfair Contract Terms Act 1977 was passed.

In the case of *Ashdown v Samuel Williams & Sons Ltd* (1957), notices had been placed on the defendant's land which excluded liability for negligence, and the Court of Appeal held that when the claimant entered the land, her entry was subject to the conditions in the notice and therefore she was merely a conditional licensee. Sufficient steps had been taken to bring her attention to the conditions. The defendants were therefore not liable for her injury.

In *White v Blackmore* (1972), the claimant's husband was killed in a field when a car in a race became entangled with safety ropes. A notice at the entrance had stated that the organisers would not be liable for any accidents causing damage or injury. The Court of Appeal held that this notice was effective.

In the same way, it is still open to non-business occupiers to exclude liability by means of notices. There are some grey areas where it is not easy to determine the status of the occupier. For example, although schools and hospitals are regarded as business premises, suppose a hospital decided to allow employees to use the swimming pool outside working hours. At this point, would the premises be business premises? Or, suppose a school registered as a charity had a gymnasium which it allowed parents to use during the evenings, would the premises for these purposes be business premises?

10.5.3 The Occupiers' Liability Act 1984 concession to business occupiers

One problem which arose after the Unfair Contract Terms Act 1977 was passed was that certain occupiers, for example, farmers, were restricting entry to their land to hikers and hill walkers who had previously enjoyed recreational activities on the land. Section 2 of the Occupiers' Liability Act 1984 therefore amends the Unfair Contract Terms Act 1977 by providing that liability may be excluded towards people who enter business premises for the purpose of recreation or education unless access to the premises falls within the main business purpose of the occupier.

Thus, it may now conceivably be possible for a charity which allows the swimming pool to be used by people purely for recreation, to exclude liability for death or personal injury.

Note, also, the effects of the Countryside and Rights of Way Bill 2000, which is outlined at the end of this chapter.

10.5.4 Exclusions of liability to contractors

Section 3(1) provides that where an occupier is bound by contract to allow strangers to the contract to enter the premises, the duty owed to the stranger cannot be restricted or excluded by the contract.

10.5.5 Liability of occupiers for damage and injury caused by independent contractors

Section 2(4)(b) of the Occupiers' Liability Act 1957 states:

> Where damage is caused to a visitor by a danger due to the faulty execution of any work of construction, maintenance or repair by an independent contractor employed by the occupier, the occupier is not to be treated without more as answerable to the danger if in all the circumstances he acted reasonably in entrusting the work to an independent contractor and had taken such steps (if any) as he reasonably ought in order to satisfy himself that the contractor was competent and that the work had been properly done.

It should be noted that this section should only be applied to faulty execution of construction, maintenance or repair work. In the case of any other type of work then, the occupier will be liable under the old common law rules.

However, provided the work does fall within the section, occupiers can escape liability for damage caused by their contractors provided they have taken reasonable steps to ensure that the contractor was competent. Obviously, it is not easy for ordinary people who know nothing about technical work to be sure that they are employing competent people, but a simple check perhaps with local trades associations or local authorities may clarify the position.

The occupier must also take steps to check the work has been done properly. Once again, if the work is particularly technical, an ordinary person would not be expected to know of defects. The only cases on this are rather old but the case of *Haseldine v Daw* (1941) does illustrate the point. The occupiers employed what appeared to be a competent firm of lift engineers to maintain the lift on their premises. The claimant was killed when the lift suddenly fell from the top to the bottom of the lift shaft. The occupiers were not liable because they had appointed apparently competent engineers to do the work. They could not be expected to check whether the work had been done in a satisfactory way as it was too technical.

There are some circumstances where independent contractors have control over premises in such a way as to make them occupiers of the premises for purposes of the Occupiers' Liability Acts 1957 and 1984. In such circumstances, the duty owed would be the common duty of care under s 2 of the Occupiers' Liability Act 1957 or the duty imposed in relation to trespassers under the Occupiers' Liability Act 1984.

If, however, the contractor is not an occupier then liability will be in the ordinary law of negligence.

10.6 Defences available under the Occupiers' Liability Act 1957

The general tort defences apply to occupiers' liability. The defences of *volenti* and contributory negligence are considered here.

10.6.1 *Volenti*

The defence of *volenti non fit injuria* applies by s 2(5). Occupiers do not owe a duty to visitors in respect of risks willingly accepted by them.

Some illustrations are as follows:

- *Simms v Leigh Rugby Football Club Ltd* (1960)

  The claimant was a professional rugby player. It was held that he had accepted the risk of playing on a rugby ground that complied with bye-laws of the Rugby League.

- *Bunker v Charles Brand & Sons Ltd* (1969)

  It was held in this case that mere knowledge of danger was insufficient for the defence of *volenti* to operate unless that knowledge was enough to enable the visitor to be reasonably safe for the purpose for which he wanted to use the premises. Again, it is important to distinguish between warning notices and exclusion clauses.

Duties to third parties who enter the premises under a contract cannot be excluded by the terms of that contract (s 3(1) of the Occupiers' Liability Act 1957).

10.6.2 Contributory negligence

Damages may be apportioned in the usual way under the Law Reform (Contributory Negligence) Act 1945 if the visitor suffers damage through lack of care on his own part.

10.7 Liability for persons other than 'visitors'

In occupiers' liability law, 'visitors' for most practical purposes means 'lawful visitors', that is, all visitors other than trespassers, though there are certain relatively obscure further categories of non-visitors (see above, 10.2.3).

Most people who fall into the category of 'persons other than visitors' are in fact 'trespassers' under the Occupiers' Liability Act 1984, though the term 'trespasser' is never used in the legislation.

Initially, at common law, there was no positive duty to trespassers. There was a limited and negative duty not to disregard trespassers in a reckless fashion and a duty not to set man-traps or to put anything on land with the deliberate intention of harming trespassers (*Illott v Wilks; Bird v Holbreck* (1828)), although it was possible to take deterrent measures to keep people out (*Clayton v Deane* (1817) – broken glass on top of a wall). However, that was as far as common law duty extended.

On the surface, it was simple: an occupier owed a duty to visitors and no duty at all to trespassers The early common law was extremely harsh in this respect and it led to a number of devices being developed by the courts in order to do what judges saw as justice in particular cases. So, for example, if it was at all possible to find on the facts that the trespasser had become a lawful visitor through repeated acts of trespass which were not objected to by the occupier, the court would do so. Once it had been established that a trespasser had, through this process, become a lawful visitor (or licensee) then a duty of care was owed both at common law and later under the Occupiers' Liability Act 1957.

10.7.1 Trespassers defined

A trespasser may be defined as a person whose presence on land is unknown to the occupier or, if known, is objected to by the occupier in some practical way. Each case turns on its own facts. Thus, in many instances, it was possible for the courts to find that people who had been repeatedly trespassing on land had become lawful visitors, though there was no fixed period of time or number of occasions on which the trespass had to occur in order to establish a lawful presence on land.

Note, also, the effects of the Countryside and Rights of Way Bill 2000, which is outlined at the end of this chapter.

10.7.2 The harsh common law cases

The early case of *Robert Addie & Sons (Collieries) Ltd v Dumbreck* (1929) illustrates the harsh nature of the rule that occupiers owed no liability to trespassers. In that case, children frequently played on machinery belonging to the colliery but were regularly warned away by servants of the occupier. On one occasion, a child was seriously injured when playing on the property, and it was held that the occupier owed no duty of care since the child was a trespasser. This decision reflects the prevailing social attitudes that land was sacred and the trespassers deserved no protection since they were behaving in a manner which could be described as morally wrong.

Following this decision of the House of Lords, the only way in which a court could come to the assistance of a child trespasser was to find either that the occupier had recklessly disregarded him (*Excelsior Wire Rope Co v Callan* (1930); *Mourton v Poulter* (1930)) or that the child had, through repeated acts of unchallenged trespass, become a lawful visitor. In fact, there are many cases in which the courts were able to find in favour of the child by stretching the rules.

10.7.3 A change of policy

However, in the case of *British Railways Board v Herrington* (1972), it was impossible for the court to find that the child in question had become a licensee. He had been injured on an electrified line belonging to British Rail, and was one of several children who had repeatedly climbed through a hole in a fence to play on the railway line and had frequently been warned away by servants of British Rail.

By this time, it was possible for the House of Lords to effect a change in the law, as the case occurred after the Lord Chancellor's Practice Statement in 1966 which permitted the House of Lords to depart from a previous decision in circumstances when it appeared 'right to do so'. In the press release which accompanied the Lord Chancellor's practice statement, he made it clear that it would be possible to depart from a previous decision if social conditions and attitudes had changed during the years which had intervened since the earlier case. It is for this reason that the House of Lords was prepared to depart from the decision in *Robert Addie v Dumbreck* (1929) in order to find in favour of the child. Their Lordships established a new, but limited, duty of care owed by occupiers to child trespassers. This duty became known as the duty of 'common humanity'. In effect, this meant that where an occupier has the knowledge, skill and resources to avoid an accident he or she should take steps as a humane person to do so.

In the *Herrington* case, it would have been a fairly simple matter for British Rail to have repaired the hole in the fence, which was in a dilapidated condition, to stop people getting onto the railway line. Had this been done, the occupier would have taken the steps which were reasonable in the circumstances, and the child would probably not have been injured.

10.7.4 The duty of common humanity

In considering the 'duty of common humanity', the courts were able to take into account the occupier's wealth, skill and ability, and the financial resources available to him to take steps to prevent an accident. As the test is subjective, it is more akin to some of the nuisance cases (for example, *Leakey v National Trust* (1980)), than the cases on breach of duty in negligence.

A review of all the cases which were decided after *Herrington* will demonstrate that in each case the defendant occupier was a large public concern. Presumably, individuals would not have been worth suing as considerable resources, both financial and in terms of person-power, would be needed to keep trespassers out of premises. We do not, however, know how many cases were settled out of court, and whether any of these were actions against private individuals as opposed to public corporations.

In only one of the cases was it held that the occupier was not liable to the child trespasser. That case was *Penny v Northampton BC* (1974), in which a child was injured when he threw an aerosol can onto a fire which was burning on a rubbish tip which covered an extremely large site of about 50 acres, belonging to the Corporation. It was decided that it would be too costly and impractical for the council to fence in the rubbish tip and the court did not look in depth at the financial resources available to the council on that particular occasion.

The occupier was liable to the child trespasser in each of the following cases, though there are different approaches taken as to the test for liability. In some the approach is subjective, that is, 'what should the particular occupier, with his own particular special knowledge, skill and resources have done to prevent the accident?'. In others, the test is closer to an objective approach, that is, 'what should the reasonable occupier, with the knowledge that the defendant ought to have inferred from the circumstances, have done to prevent an accident?'.

Some illustrations are as follows:

- *Southern Portland Cement Ltd v Cooper* (1974)

  A 13 year old was injured playing on a large pile of waste cement which had been allowed to accumulate close to an overhead wire on the defendant's premises. The council took the view that since the danger had been created by the positive activity of the occupier the test for liability should be objective rather than subjective.

- *Pannett v McGuinness* (1972)

  A five year old child was playing on a building site where advertising hoardings were being burned. He had been warned away several times with other children with whom he was playing. It was held that the occupier was liable as his employees knew of the presence of children and steps could have been taken to prevent the accident to the child.

- *Harris v Birkenhead Corp* (1975)

  The defendants had attempted to board up empty properties which were the favoured haunt of vandals, particularly children. However, on one occasion, a child entered a building through a smashed door, went up to the top floor and fell out of a window, suffering severe brain injury. The defendants were liable to the child trespasser, and in this case the test applied to establish liability was closer to an objective test, that is, a reasonable man with the knowledge which that particular occupier possessed, should have appreciated that a trespasser could come onto the premises, and therefore should have realised that it would be inhumane not to give a warning of the danger.

Cases decided after *Herrington* and before the Occupiers' Liability Act 1984 came into force in which occupiers were held liable to trespassers all concerned children. However, after the Law Commission Report (Law Com No 75, Cmnd 6428 (1976)) in which it was recommended that the kind of protection afforded by *Herrington* ought to be extended to adults, the Occupiers' Liability Act 1984 was passed.

10.8 Liability under the Occupiers' Liability Act 1984

The Occupiers' Liability Act 1984 is concerned with the duty of an occupier to persons 'other than his visitors'.

Technically, the Occupiers' Liability Act 1984 covers three categories of entrants though, for most practical purposes, the most important is trespassers.

10.8.1 Persons exercising a statutory right of way

People who enter land exercising rights conferred by an access agreement or order under s 60 of the National Parks and Access to the Countryside Act 1949, are entrants.

10.8.2 Persons exercising a private right of way

Persons exercising a private right of way form a category of entrants which appears to have slipped through the net of both sets of legislation, leaving the law in a somewhat confused state though, in the view of some authors, the purpose of the occupiers' liability legislation was to restrict the categories of visitors to two, rather than to create duties where none had previously existed.

It had been decided in the case of *Holden v White* (1982) by the Court of Appeal that people using a private right of way were not visitors, for the purposes of the Occupiers' Liability Act 1957, of the occupier of the servient tenement, and therefore no duty of care had been owed to them. While it is clear that the Law Commission intended that people using a private right of way should be covered by the Occupiers' Liability Act 1984, there may still be some circumstances in which the Act does not apply to such people. If the owner of the servient land is not an occupier, the Act does not apply. Common law would then need to be relied upon, in which case there would be no liability for omissions, that is, non-feasance.

The position of people using public rights of way is governed by s 1(7) of the Occupiers' Liability Act 1984, which states that the Act does not apply to people using the highway. This means again that the liability of the occupier of a highway would be governed by the common law which states that he will only be liable for negligent misfeasance, that is, positive acts and not for omissions (that is, non-feasance). Therefore failure to repair public rights of way will not incur any liability (*Gautret v Egerton* (1867)). In *McGeown v Northern Ireland Housing Executive* (1994), the House of Lords confirmed the rule in *Greenhalgh v British Railways Board* (1969) that the law which imposes minimal duties on occupiers survives the statute and that users of public rights of way are not 'visitors'. This is discussed above, 10.2.3. However, under s 1 of the Highways (Miscellaneous Provisions) Act 1961, highway authorities are liable both for negligent misfeasance and for non-feasance. This is now enacted in s 58 of the Highways Act 1980. This is further confirmed by the Countryside and Rights of Way Bill 2000, cl 13 of which places certain classes of entrants in the same position as highway users.

10.8.3 Trespassers, both children and adults

The Occupiers' Liability Act 1984 replaces the rules of common law to determine whether a duty is owed by an occupier:

> ... to persons other than visitors, in respect of injury on the premises by reason of any danger due to the state of the premises or things done or omitted to be done on them.

The scope of this duty is limited to personal injury, as property damage is not covered. This reflects in part the attitude of many people that trespassers are still not worthy of full protection in law.

Section 1(3) deals with the circumstances in which the occupier owes this new duty. The duty is owed if:

(a) he is aware of the danger or has reasonable grounds to believe it exists;

(b) he knows or has reasonable grounds to believe that the other person is in the vicinity of the danger concerned, or that he may come into the vicinity of the danger (in either case whether the other has lawful authority for being in that vicinity or not); and

(c)   the risk is one against which in all the circumstances of the case he may reasonably be expected to offer the other some protection.

The law does not impose an impossible burden on occupiers, even in situations where they know that trespassers are likely to be present. For example, in *Bailey v Asplin* (2000), the Court of Appeal ruled that an occupier was not liable to a child who was injured when a wall fell on him. The occupier had inspected the wall and had not found any signs of a defect, and this had been sufficient to discharge the duty of care to trespassers.

The scope of s 1(3) of the Occupiers' Liability Act 1984 was examined in *Revill v Newbury* (1996). In that case, a trespasser had entered an allotment and attempted to break into a shed. The defendant, who rented the allotment, was sleeping in his shed when he heard the intruder and fired a shotgun through a hole in the door, injuring the intruder quite seriously. The Court of Appeal decided that the trespasser was entitled to compensation for his injuries, and in so deciding Neill LJ stated that s 1 of the Occupiers' Liability Act 1984 was concerned only with the safety of premises and dangers arising out of the state of the premises. Therefore, the fact that the defendant was the occupier was irrelevant. Section 1 was helpful insofar as it defined the scope of the duty owed at common law to an intruder on premises who was caught there at night. The issue of liability had to be decided here on the same basis as the criteria under s 1(4) which defines the standard of care as involving the duty to take such care as in all the circumstances of the case is reasonable to see that the intruder does not suffer injury on the premises by reason of the danger in question. He considered that there was no justification for the application of a two-stage decision by which the court should first decide whether there had been a breach of duty and then whether despite that breach the claimant should be denied a remedy because he was engaged in criminal activities. To establish whether there was liability at common law, the question was that which should be asked under s 1(3)(b) if the statute had applied, that is, whether the defendant had reasonable grounds to believe that the claimant was in the vicinity of the danger. The force which the defendant had used to deter the trespasser was out of all proportion to the force used by the claimant to enter the property so the defence of self-defence could not apply here. Nor would the defence of *volenti non fit injuria* be appropriate as the claimant had not consented to run the risk of being shot. The defence of *ex turpi causa* also failed for reasons discussed in Chapter 11.

Section 1(5) provides that the duty may be discharged by taking such steps as are reasonable in all the circumstances of the case to warn of the danger concerned, or to discourage persons from incurring the risk. This section contemplates the posting of notices on land to warn of danger but once again as under the Occupiers' Liability Act 1957, it is likely that the effect of such notices on the visitor in each case will be considered by the court, and notices may not be enough of themselves to warn of danger. It could well be that adults are more likely to be found to have accepted the risk of injury and to be *volenti*, a defence provided for by s 1(6) if a notice is posted on the property.

In *Ratcliffe v McConnell* (1998), it was held that a student who trespassed in a college swimming pool at night had willingly accepted the risk, under s 1(6), of injury. The swimming pool was enclosed by high walls and the entrance was through changing rooms, which were kept locked at night and when the pool was not in use. At the entrance to the pool was a notice with the word 'WARNING' printed in red, which prohibited taking glasses or bottles into the pool area and contained a statement giving the times when the pool was locked and entrance prohibited as between 10 pm and 6.30 am. The shallow end and deep end of the pool were also clearly marked. There was a security light which was activated by movement, but this gave little light. On the morning in question, the claimant, who said he had drunk four pints of beer, and two friends, went to the pool at 2 am. The claimant climbed over the gate and took a running dive into shallow water. He hit his head and, as a result of his injuries, became tetraplegic, with no hope of recovery.

The Court of Appeal found that the claimant was aware of the dangers of diving into shallow water and had known that the pool was closed for the winter and contained less water than usual. The court unanimously ruled that the defendants had done all that could reasonably have been expected of them in the circumstances, and that the claimant had consented to run the risk of injury under s 1(6) of the Occupiers' Liability Act 1984.

The case is very instructive and is well worth reading, because Stuart Smith LJ examines the history and development of the law concerning duties of occupiers to trespassers, concluding that the nature and extent of what it is reasonable to expect of the occupier will vary very much depending on numerous factors, such as the age and mental capacity of the trespasser, the character of the danger and the resources of the occupier.

In *Jolley v Sutton LBC* (2000), the House of Lords ruled that occupiers should not underestimate the power of children to harm themselves. This same principle would apply to both lawful visitors and trespassers.

10.9   The nature of the statutory duty

The duty under the Occupiers' Liability Act 1984 is a duty to take such care as is reasonable in all the circumstances, to prevent injury to the non-visitor. This is intended to be an objective standard of care, and what should be done by the occupier will be dependent upon the particular facts of the situation prevailing in each case.

The greater the danger the more important it is for an occupier to take precautions to warn trespassers to keep away from it. In *Westwood v The Post Office* (1973), it was held in the case of an adult trespasser that a notice on a door stating 'only authorised attendant is permitted to enter' was enough to inform the average intelligent person that there was danger and that people should keep out.

In some circumstances, the white lie 'beware of the bull' is a very effective deterrent to prospective trespassers.

It is not only warning notices with which the Occupiers' Liability Act 1984 is concerned. Any appropriate measures may be taken to discourage people from taking risks. However, in the case of children, even fencing off dangerous areas may not be enough since it is well known that children enjoy the challenge of climbing over fences which are designed to keep them out.

10.10 Excluding liability under the Occupiers' Liability Act 1984

A particular problem in relation to exclusions of liability has arisen since the Occupiers' Liability Act 1984 was passed. This Act does not refer at all to the question of whether occupiers can exclude liability under the Act, that is to trespassers. However, the Occupiers' Liability Act 1957 does permit occupiers to restrict, modify or exclude their common duty of care.

The Unfair Contract Terms Act 1977 probably did not apply to exclusions of liability to trespassers, to whom at that time only a limited duty of common humanity was owed, and it is clear that the Act cannot apply to the new duty to trespassers created by the Occupiers' Liability Act 1984 which will be discussed later. It is arguable that since the duty owed to trespassers is and was the absolute minimum which the law permits, occupiers should not be allowed to exclude that particular duty (Mesher, J, 'Occupiers, trepassers and the Unfair Contracts Terms Act 1977' [1979] Conv 58). It is certainly arguable that it would be against public policy for lawful visitors to be in a worse position than trespassers as regards exclusions of liability upon non-business premises. As Parliament did not choose to do so, it is now up to the courts to develop the law in this area and to clarify this difficult and confusing point.

10.11 Liability of people other than occupiers for dangerous premises

It is well established that not only will occupiers be liable for dangers arising out of the state of premises, but other classes of people such as independent contractors, landlords and builders may also be held responsible for accidents which arise out of the state of premises for which they are regarded as having responsibility.

10.11.1   Independent contractors

If an independent contractor has control over premises, he will probably be treated as an occupier and will owe the respective duties of an occupier under the Occupiers' Liability Acts 1957 and 1984. If, however, a contractor is not an occupier then it is likely that the ordinary law of negligence applies (*AC Billings & Sons Ltd v Riden* (1958)).

10.11.2   Landlords

If a landlord retains control through the granting of a licence to occupied premises, then he may himself be an occupier and owe the requisite duties under the Occupiers' Liability Acts 1957 and 1984. Even if the landlord grants a tenancy, he may be treated as an occupier if he has retained control over parts of the building which are used in common, for example, in a block of flats where the landlord retains control of stairways and corridors.

When the landlords lets premises then, he no longer has control over them and a different set of rules applies. The law in this area is very complex because the Defective Premises Act 1972 is regarded as a confusing statute and quite independently of that, the law has been developed by judges sometimes contradicting provisions of the Act. In addition, the Defective Premises Act 1972 and the common law have developed to create duties where none previously existed.

In the early cases, the courts treated landlord and tenant situations as basic contract situations, and therefore the approach was that of *caveat emptor* (let the tenant beware).

In *Cavalier v Pope* (1906), the wife of a tenant sued a landlord when she was injured falling through the kitchen floor which was defective because of the landlord's negligent failure to maintain the premises (that is, non-feasance or omission). The House of Lords held that there could be no action in negligence against the landlord for harm suffered as a result of danger on the premises. Any duty which did exist would be towards the husband who was the tenant, and would not extend any further.

In 1932, the case of *Bottomley v Banister* extended this immunity to vendors of premises. Later cases extended the immunity even to situations in which the landlord had actually created the danger (misfeasance) before letting or selling the premises. There was a series of decisions in later years in which the judges attempted to restrict the scope of these earlier cases by abolishing immunity which had previously existed in relation to dangers which had been created after the premises were let or sold. However, these cases did not affect the landlords' and vendors' immunity in respect of negligent non-feasance, that is omissions. The Defective Premises Act 1972 was passed in a climate when it was believed that tenants were treated harshly, both by landlords and the law, and therefore the Act was intended to introduce extensive changes to the liability of landlords for defects in their premises.

Section 4 of that Act provides that:

(1)   where premises are let under a tenancy but which puts on the landlord an obligation to the tenant for the maintenance or repair of the premises, the landlord owes to all persons who might reasonably be expected to be affected by defects in the state of the premises a duty to take such care as is reasonable in all the circumstances to see that they are reasonably safe from personal injury or from damage to their property caused by a relevant defect.

The duty is owed if the landlord knows of (whether as the result of being notified by the tenant or otherwise), or if he ought in all the circumstances to have known of, the relevant defect. Relevant defects are comprehensively defined in s 4(3) as defects:

... in the state of the premises existing at or after the material time and arising from or continuing because of an act or omission by the landlord which constituted or would, if he had had notice of the defect, have constituted a failure by him to carry out his obligation to the tenant for the maintenance or repair of the premises.

These provisions apply to landlords who have powers to enter and repair the premises (express or implied) and to landlords who are under an obligation to repair, but no duty is owed in respect of defects which arise out of the failure by the tenant to carry out express obligations under the tenancy agreement (s 4(4)).

Landlords' obligations to repair may be found in the tenancy agreement itself, either expressly or by implication, or may be imposed by statute.

One important statutory obligation is that in the Landlord and Tenant Act 1985 which requires the lessor of a dwellinghouse for a term of less than seven years to keep the structure and exterior of the premises and installations for the supply of water, gas, electricity, sanitation, space heating or water heating in good repair.

The duties under s 4 of the Defective Premises Act 1972 cannot be excluded or restricted by any term of any agreement.

Duties are not only owed to the tenant, but to any person who might reasonably be expected to be affected by a defect in the premises, for example the wife or husband of a tenant or people using a highway adjoining the premises, people on adjoining land and visitors to the premises.

The obligations under the Landlord and Tenant Act 1985 have been further extended by the Housing Act 1988 to cover the situation where the disrepair is not in the premises itself, as in the basement of a building or where it affects the common parts of a building such as the roof.

10.11.3 Builders

At common law, there was an anomalous rule that if a builder owned the premises but had sold or let them he would not be liable in tort for any dangers he had created (*Bottomley v Banister* (1932)). However, if the builder did not own the premises, the ordinary law of negligence applied if people were injured as a result of work which was done negligently on the premises.

Section 3 of the Defective Premises Act 1972 is aimed at removing this anomaly. It provides that where work of construction, repair, maintenance or demolition or any other work is done on or in relation to premises any duty of care owed because of the doing of the work, to persons who might reasonably be expected to be affected by defects in the state of the premises created by the doing of the work, shall not be abated by the subsequent disposal of the premises by the person who owes the duty.

10.11.4 Developments at common law

In 1972, judges removed the immunity of builders who were vendors and builders who were lessors in the case of *Dutton v Bognor Regis UDC* (1972). This decision was later approved by the House of Lords in *Anns v Merton BC* (1978). Although on certain other points these two cases have now been overruled by the House of Lords' decision in *Murphy v Brentwood DC* (1990), there is clear authority that the ordinary law of negligence as stated in *Dutton v Bognor Regis* and *Anns v Merton* still applies to builders. In the words of Lord Keith:

> In the case of a building, it is right to accept that a careless builder is liable on the principle of *Donoghue v Stevenson* where a latent defect results in physical injury to anyone ... or to the property of any person.

However, this only covers damage in the form of personal injury or damage to property but not damage to the building itself, which is treated as an economic loss and therefore not recoverable. If the claimant wishes to claim for damage to the building itself, there may be an action for breach of statutory duty for breach of building regulations under s 38 of the Building Act 1984, or there may be an action against the builder under s 1 of the Defective Premises Act 1972. Indeed, since *Murphy*, unless there is a contract between the parties, the owner of property which suffers a mere defect in quality, as opposed to a defect which gives rise to danger, will find the most appropriate remedy to be an action under the Defective Premises Act 1972 if, bearing in mind its various drawbacks, such an action is available. This is somewhat ironic, as at the time the Act came into force, and in the years immediately following, the common law remedies before *Murphy* considerably eclipsed the Defective Premises Act 1972.

Section 1 applies only to people taking on work in connection with the provision of a dwelling and covers building of dwellings and also conversion and enlargement. The duty in s 1 is owed to the person who requests or orders the dwelling to be built, enlarged, extended, etc, and to every person who acquires an interest whether legal or equitable in the dwelling. The duty is to see that the work which he takes on is done in a 'workmanlike' or, as the case may be, 'professional' manner with proper materials and so that as regards that work the dwelling will be fit for habitation when completed.

10.11.5   Limitations to s 1

Section 1 does, however, have a number of limitations.

First, there is a defence which provides that a person who takes on any such work for the other person on terms that he or she is to carry it out in accordance with instructions given by, or on behalf of that other, shall to the extent to which he does it properly, in accordance with those instructions, be treated for the purposes of this section as discharging the duty imposed on him by sub-s 1, except where he owes a duty to that other to warn him of any defect in the instructions and fails to discharge that duty.

The *second* limitation is that s 1 applies only to dwellings.

The *third* limitation is that s 2 of the Defective Premises Act 1972 excludes dwellings covered by 'approved schemes'. This, in practice, means that virtually all new houses are excluded from the operation of s 2 because most new houses are covered by the NHBC scheme. This means that s 1 is probably confined to extensions and conversions. This scheme, the full title of which is the National Housebuilders Certification Scheme, provides that builders agree that they will obtain insurance cover for the dwelling at the same time guaranteeing the house is properly constructed. The insurance will cover any unfulfilled judgment or award against a builder.

The *fourth* limitation is that it is unclear whether s 1 applies to professional people other than builders who take on work for or in connection with the provision of a dwelling. This means that the positions of architects and surveyors have not yet been clarified. In the case of *Sparham-Souter v Town and Country Developments (Essex) Ltd* (1976), the point was left undecided. However, as the words 'professional manner' are used in the Defective Premises Act 1972, it is likely that it was intended to extend to professional people such as architects, surveyors, engineers, and so on, as well as builders.

The *fifth* limitation is that it is unclear whether the Defective Premises Act 1972 covers pure economic loss. There has been some difficulty in the cases in distinguishing pure economic loss from damage to the building itself. For example, if a crack appears in a wall, is that an economic loss created by the extent of putting the building back into a safe condition? Or, if the building is no threat to safety or health, is the loss a pure economic loss or is it damage to the building itself which according to *Donoghue v Stevenson* would not be recoverable in negligence? (See Chapter 5 on Economic Loss.)

Since the common law did not allow recovery of pure economic loss in these circumstances, it was expected that the Defective Premises Act 1972 would provide a remedy for such a loss but this is not clear from the Act itself. If economic loss is not covered, then the Act goes no further than the common law in providing a remedy.

The *sixth* and perhaps the most serious limitation on s 1 is that the limitation period for the purpose of litigation is six years from the date when the building was completed. This is far worse then the common law position in negligence which provides that time runs for the purposes of limitation from the date of the damage which may of course occur long after the building has been completed (with the possibility of an extension under the Latent Damage Act 1986).

The limitation period under the Defective Premises Act 1972 is not even capable of providing as much protection as the limitation period under the NHBC scheme as, under that, there is provision for insurance cover from 10 years from the date the work is completed.

All these problems must be borne in mind by lawyers advising clients how to approach the problem of defects in construction work. However, the Court of Appeal has held that s 1 applies to active negligence, that is misfeasance, and also to omissions, that is non-feasance (*Andrews v Schooling* (1991)) where there is a failure to carry out necessary remedial work on a building.

The correct approach to any problem concerning liability of builders, architects, vendors and so on, is firstly to establish when to sue and whether the action would best lie at common law or under the Defective Premises Act 1972.

It should be borne in mind that, in some cases, the common law of nuisance provides a remedy, for example, where there is strict liability to structures which adjoin a highway under the rules in *Wringe v Cohen* (see 11.7.2) or under *Cambridge Water Co v Eastern Counties Leather plc* (1992).

Moreover, there may be an action under the rule in *Rylands v Fletcher* (1868). Here again, liability is strict and it is a much simpler matter for the claimant to base an action in *Rylands v Fletcher* than under the more complex rules of common law or the Defective Premises Act 1972 in which it is necessary to prove fault.

Bearing in mind that, at present, liability in negligence is in the process of being curtailed by the courts, whereas liability in nuisance and indeed strict liability may be expanded, it seems sensible first of all to consider the question of strict liability before proceeding to look at the common law of negligence under the Defective Premises Act 1972.

10.12 The Countryside and Rights of Way Bill 2000

The Countryside and Rights of Way Bill, introduced into the House of Commons on 3 March 2000, contains measures intended to improve public access to the open countryside and registered common land, while also recognising the interests of land owners. It will have some impact on the law relating to occupiers' liability and the law of trespass. The Bill amends the law relating to rights of way and nature conservation. Part 1 of the Bill is intended to give people greater freedom to explore the countryside. It provides a new statutory right of access for open-air recreation to mountain, moor, heath, down and registered common land (the 'right to roam') situated at at least 600 m above sea level. The Bill also includes a power to extend this right to coastal land by order and allows landowners voluntarily to dedicate any land to public access in perpetuity.

However, there are to be restrictions on the new right. For example, the Bill includes provisions for landowners to exclude or restrict access for any reason for up to 28 days a year without seeking permission. Landowners will be able to seek further exclusions or restrictions on access if they need to do so for land management reasons. The Countryside Agency and the National Park Authorities will have the power to approve applications and exclusions and restrictions on grounds of nature and heritage conservation, fire prevention and to avoid danger to the public.

Clause 1 provides a statutory right of entry to certain land situated at 600m or more above sea level. Clause 2 gives people a right of entry onto access land (defined in cl 1) for the purposes of open-air recreation, provided that they do not break any of the restrictions set out in Sched 2. Under sub-s 3, the right does not apply where entry is prohibited in or under any other public legislation. Clause 3 allows the Secretary of State to extend the statutory right of access to all or any part of the foreshore and land adjacent to the foreshore.

Schedule 2 imposes restrictions on behaviour which is not compatible with the quiet exercise of the right of access. Restricted activities include the use of any vehicle (including bicycles), craft (on water) and horse riding. This also includes restrictions for the control of dogs, including a requirement for dogs to be kept on leads during certain periods and in the vicinity of livestock. People who break any of these restrictions will lose their right of access for the remainder of the day and may be treated as trespassers by the owner of that land. The law of trespass is thus made somewhat more complicated by the Bill.

For the purposes of occupiers' liability, cl 12 provides that the right of access does not *increase* the liability of a person interested in the land in respect of the state of the land or things done on it. Clause 13 amends the Occupiers' Liability Act 1957 so as to reduce the liability of occupiers of land towards people who exercise the right of access, to the same level that would be owed to trespassers. It also provides, by amending the Occupiers' Liability Act 1984, that occupiers will owe no duty to people exercising the right of access, nor to trespassers, in respect of natural features of the landscape on land accessible under the new right of access.

Clause 14 creates an offence of displaying a notice containing false or misleading information on or near access land which is likely to deter the exercise of the statutory right.

OCCUPIERS' LIABILITY

The law relating to the liability of occupiers of premises is now mainly statutory, but it is still necessary to consider the common law rules in certain instances upon which the statutes are silent.

Occupiers' Liability Act 1957

The definition of 'occupier' depends on common law. Various tests include the 'control' test, which is based on responsibility for the premises (*Wheat v Lacon* (1966); *Harris v Birkenhead Corporation* (1976); *Revill v Newbury* (1996)).

The definition of premises includes lifts, ladders, vehicles, ships, aircraft, houses, land, allotments.

Occupiers owe the 'common duty of care' to all lawful visitors. This includes the duty to ensure that the visitor will be reasonably safe for the purposes for which he or she is permitted to be on the premises (s 2).

Occupiers should assume that children will be less careful than adults. Note the cases on traps and allurements (*Glasgow Corpn v Taylor* (1922); *Jolley v London Borough of Sutton* (2000)). It is not safe to assume that parents will be looking after any children on the property, but much depends on the circumstances (*Phipps v Rochester Corpn* (1955); *Simkiss v Rhondda BC* (1983)).

Occupiers are entitled to assume that contractors will appreciate and guard against any risks which are ordinarily incidental to their employment (*Roles v Nathan* (1963); *Ogwo v Taylor* (1987)).

Exclusion of liability

The common duty of care may be discharged in a variety of ways, including the use of notices to warn of dangers, but the occupier must beware of falling foul of the Unfair Contract Terms Act 1977 which outlaws certain types of exclusion clause on business premises. Note the wide definition of 'business'. However, under a concession in the Occupiers' Liability Act 1984, business occupiers are now entitled to exclude liability to visitors who do not enter the property as part of the occupiers' main business purpose. Private occupiers can exclude liability as under the common law (*Ashdown v Samuel Williams* (1957)).

Exclusion of liability to trespassers is a difficult area which needs clarification by statute. The matter was not dealt with in the Occupiers' Liability Act 1984 as would have been expected.

Liability of occupiers for the torts of independent contractors on their premises

The occupier will not be liable for the torts of independent contractors on the premises providing he or she was reasonable in employing the contractor, and had taken reasonable steps to check the work (*Haseldine v Daw* (1941)).

Defences of *volenti* and contributory negligence apply, subject to the provisions of the Unfair Contract and Terms Act 1977.

Liability to persons other than visitors

For the most part people 'other than visitors' are trespassers, but note the other categories of persons who may be included in the term, for example, users of public and private rights of way (*McGeown v Northern Ireland Housing Executive* (1996)).

Liability to trespassers has expanded during the course of the 20th century. Note the progression of cases from *Addie v Dumbreck* (1929) to *Herrington v British Railways Board* (1972) and the judicial circumlocutions to avoid the position whereby an occupier could escape liability even in the early days. Cases since 1972 all involved large companies or public bodies:

Southern Portland Cement v Cooper (1974);

Pannett v McGuiness (1972);

Harris v Birkenhead Corp (1975);

Penny v Northampton BC (1975).

The Occupiers' Liability Act 1984 now applies to all trespassers, imposing a limited duty of care on occupiers to take reasonable steps to offer protection to trespassers from dangers which should be known to exist on the property. Note the details of s 1(3).

A trespasser may consent to run a risk of injury: *Ratcliffe v McConnell* (1999).

Liability of people other than occupiers

Independent contractors may be liable in their own right.

The liability of landlords depends for the most part on the terms of the Defective Premises Act 1972, and cannot be restricted or excluded.

Details of liability of builders is contained in the Defective Premises Act 1972 which imposes wide ranging duties but is subject to numerous drawbacks, such as the defence of working under instructions; the fact that the Defective Premises Act 1972 only applies to dwellings; the position of architects, etc, is unclear; the question of recovery for pure economic loss under the Act is unclear; the limitation period is only six years from completion of the work.

Builders may also be liable at common law in negligence, nuisance, *Rylands v Fletcher* and contract.

Note the effect of the Countryside and Rights of Way Bill 2000.

CHAPTER 11

TORTS RELATING TO LAND

11.1 Introduction

Some of the earliest actions known to English law were concerned with the protection of interests in land. The strict rules governing the old categories of claims concerning land and other interests, and indeed the actions themselves, were abolished in the 19th century during a period of reform and rationalisation of the legal system and its procedures, but the ancient forms of action still influence the way in which the law of tort is classified, and continue to have a bearing on the elements of the torts themselves. The introduction of negligence as a separate tort in 1932 has complicated matters by providing an alternative and, in some instances, some would argue, a more useful remedy to people who complain of interference with property rights.

Although many pages of tort textbooks are devoted to nuisance, trespass, the rule in *Rylands v Fletcher* (1868), and other actions which involve land, in practice, these torts only rarely require consideration, as the vast majority of actions are for negligence. Nevertheless, as academic topics, the torts relating to land cannot be ignored, not least because these torts provide a very fertile area for examiners when setting problem type questions, the solutions to which often involve untangling the various threads of the torts from a complex fact situation. This demands the ability to distinguish clearly between each of the various actions. The chart at the end of this section (see p 272) may help students to do this. The following summary of the torts relating to land outlines their main elements in a structured form to provide a sound basis for learning and understanding the topics, and relates these torts to the tort of negligence.

11.2   Trespass to land

Trespass to land was one of the earliest actions to emerge in the common law. Although it is important primarily as a civil action, there are forms of statutory trespass which are crimes under various by-laws and other legislation such as the Criminal Law Act 1977. The Public Order Act 1986 created criminal offences in connection with the mass trespass of vehicles on land, following Margaret Thatcher's vow to quell the disruption caused by the 'peace convoy' which consisted of several hundred vehicles and caravans parking on farmland in the West of England in mid-summer during the early 1980s. Further forms of criminal trespass were created by the Criminal Justice and Public Order Act 1994.

11.2.1   Outline definition

The tort of trespass to land consists of 'directly entering upon land, or remaining upon land, or placing or projecting any object upon land in the possession of the claimant, in each case without lawful justification'. The tort is actionable *per se*, without the need to prove damage.

11.2.2   Direct interference

The element of directness is what distinguishes trespass from nuisance. Nuisance applies where invasion or entry on property is indirect. This may consist of entering upon the land, however slight that entry may be (for example, leaning on a wall, as in *Gregory v Piper* (1829)), or by walking across a field, or by throwing objects onto the land, or refusing to leave when permission to be there has been withdrawn. Indirect interference would consist, for example, of allowing smoke to drift onto neighbouring land or tree roots or branches to encroach onto neighbouring property.

11.2.3   Entering upon land

To amount to trespass, entry can be above or below the surface of the ground or into the airspace above the land.

Land is defined in s 205 of the Law of Property Act 1925 to include: 'Land of any tenure, mines and minerals, corporeal and incorporeal hereditaments.'

It includes any buildings and fixtures attached to the land as well as the land itself, the airspace above and the ground beneath to the centre of the earth. The latin maxim *cuius est solum eius est usque ad coelum at ad inferos* is often used to describe the possession of land in this context. Roughly translated, this means 'whoever possesses the land also possesses the sky above it to the highest heavens and the earth beneath it to the greatest depths'. This maxim cannot be regarded as decisive in modern times when mineral exploitation and air travel and satellites are common place. Even 100 years ago, it was described as 'fanciful' by Bowen LJ in *Wandsworth Board of Works v United Telephone Co Ltd* (1884), and it has virtually no significance today.

11.2.4 Trespass to the airspace

The defendant committed trespass by allowing an advertising hoarding to project eight inches into the claimant's property at ground level and just above ground level in *Kelsen v Imperial Tobacco Co Ltd* (1957). However, it was held that trespass to the airspace is not committed unless it is at a height that interferes with the claimant's ordinary use of the property. In *Bernstein v Skyviews and General Ltd* (1978), the defendant flew over the property of Lord Bernstein and took aerial photographs. It was held that trespass was not committed because a landowner's rights only extend to a reasonable height above the property, not to a height of several hundred feet above the land. The judge, Griffiths J, could not find a case to support the claimant's argument that his property should be protected to an unlimited height from trespass. He took the view that the latin maxim could not be applied literally because it would lead to the absurdity that every time a satellite passed over any land the tort of trespass would be committed.

Although this approach is laudable from a practical point of view, it is merely one of a number of first instance decisions on this point and does not take account of the Civil Aviation Act 1982 nor the international agreements concerning satellites.

However, in *Anchor Brewhouse Developments Ltd and Others v Berkley House (Docklands Developments)* (1987), the claimant obtained interlocutory injunctions to prevent the boom of a crane swinging across his land. This was necessary even when the crane was not in use to prevent it being blown over in high winds. Scott LJ distinguished between missiles, bullets, satellites which fly over land, and cranes and other structures which project onto it. In the latter case, he regarded the matter as inappropriate for balancing competing rights, and treated the claimant's interest in land as of paramount importance. It is clear from this decision that invasion of air space emanating from *land* will always be a trespass, and over-flights will only be a trespass within an unreasonable height over property.

In *Woolerton v Costain* (1970), counsel for the defendants conceded that the boom of a crane swinging 50 feet above the claimant's land amounted to a trespass.

In the light of the conflicting first instance decisions, what is needed is a ruling on this point by the Court of Appeal or the House of Lords in order to clarify the law.

Section 76(1) of the Civil Aviation Act 1982 provides that no action shall lie in nuisance or trespass:

> By reason only of the flight of an aircraft over any property at a height above the
> ground which ... is reasonable.

The same Act provides that compensation shall be payable without proof of
fault, for damage or injury caused by anything falling from a civil aircraft.

11.2.5   Trespass to the ground beneath the surface

Trespasses to the subsoil, of the type caused by mining operations in *Bulli Coal
Mining Co v Osborne* (1899), have been limited by the Nationalisation Acts
under which mineral rights beneath land in the UK were vested in the Crown.

11.2.6   Trespass by entry onto the land itself

Any entry onto the land amounts to a trespass and, often, the remedy which is
sought is an injunction to deter repeated acts of trespass. Even leaning a
ladder against a wall can amount to trespass (*Westripp v Baldock* (1938)). Many
disputes arise about the exact location of boundaries and there have been
cases which have lasted many years involving claims for trespass relating to
very small areas of land.

11.2.7   Trespass by remaining on land

Every day that a trespass continues gives rise to a new cause of action.

If a person who entered land under a licence has that permission
withdrawn, there will be an obligation to leave the property (by the most
obvious convenient route) but, should that person refuse to leave the land or
to remove objects from it when asked to do so, the tort of trespass will be
committed from the moment of that refusal.

If the person who entered the land did so by lawful authority, and he or
she abuses that authority, he or she will be treated as having been a trespasser
from the moment he or she entered the property (*The Six Carpenters Case*
(1610)). This is known as trespass *ab initio*, and does not apply if the defendant
entered with the permission of the occupier rather than by authority of the
law. It would apply in situations when police or customs officers enter
property for a specific purpose authorised by law, but then proceed to search
for something unconnected with that purpose. In *Jeffrey v Black* (1978), the
claimant was arrested for stealing a sandwich from a pub, and he successfully
sued for trespass to land when the police called in the drug squad to search
his flat for illegal drugs. The law only permits the police to conduct a search in
such cases in connection with the crime for which a suspect has been arrested.
Any other type of search amounts to a trespass.

Trespass *ab initio* was criticised by Lord Denning in *Jones v Chic Fashions
(Llanelli) Ltd* (1968) but, despite such criticism, it can provide an important

source of compensation for the abuse of power by officials with the same objective as an award of exemplary damages which may also be made in such cases.

11.2.8   Trespass by placing things on land

A common form of trespass is the dumping of rubbish, but the cases also involve parking of vehicles, and allowing objects to project onto adjoining land. The occupier may take reasonable steps to remove such objects.

In *Arthur v Anker* (1996), it was held that a motorist who had trespassed by parking his car on private property was taken to have consented to wheel-clamping because he had read a notice warning that wheel-clamping would be carried out. The fee charged for release of the vehicle was reasonable, the vehicle was released without delay and there were means by which the motorist could offer payment of the fee. No tort or crime had been committed by the clampers. The remedy of distress damage *feasant* was not available to the defendants, however. There was no evidence that they had suffered any damage. In *Jones and Another v Stones* (1999) (see below, 11.2.11), placing flowerpots and an oil tank on a boundary wall amounted to trespass.

11.2.9   Trespass to the highway

As the highway may only be used for passing and repassing, blocking a highway or remaining stationary on it for longer than is reasonable will amount to trespass (*Randall v Tarrant* (1955)). It will also be trespass to interfere unlawfully with the rights of the person who owns the subsoil beneath a highway (*Harrison v Duke of Rutland* (1893)). Similar acts could also amount to public nuisance. However, in the criminal case of *DPP v Jones and Another* (1999), it was held that a non-obstructive peaceful assembly on the verge of a road at Stonehenge was a peaceful, non-criminal use of a highway.

11.2.10   In the possession of the claimant

Trespass is a tort which evolved to protect a person's possession of land, and as such the claimant must be the occupier of the land. This means that, in some circumstances, the fee simple owner can be sued by a tenant or other person in occupation of the land. Any person in *de facto* possession can sue anyone who does not have an immediate right to recover possession of the property. In *Manchester Airport plc v Dutton* (1999), the Court of Appeal upheld the right of a licensee to claim possession against a trespasser, even though that licensee might not be in actual possession at the time of the trespass.

11.2.11 Without lawful justification (defences)

There are certain circumstances when the law regards trespass as justifiable, and these form defences to an action for trespass to land. They are as follows:

- **Statutory rights of entry**

  Defences to trespass are provided by numerous statutes which give rights of entry to various people. For example, the Police and Criminal Evidence Act 1984, the Public Order Act 1986 and the prevention of terrorism legislation are among the many statutes which allow the police to enter property for specified purposes, including arrest and search. Other public servants, including social workers, Inland Revenue and immigration and customs officials and officers of bodies such as the electricity boards can enter property for different purposes specified by statute, but if the purpose for which entry was permitted is exceeded, the tort of trespass is committed.

  The Access to Neighbouring Land Act 1992 permits entry onto neighbouring land by court order in circumstances when a landowner refuses a neighbour entry onto land in order to carry out repairs. The order will only be available if the applicant can show that the work is necessary for the preservation of his or her property and that it cannot be carried out satisfactorily without entry onto the neighbour's land. The works involved must not include the development or improvement of land, and the court has power to attach numerous conditions to the entry order. The Access to Neighbouring Land Act 1992 might be regarded as a statutory extension to the defence of necessity. The Party Wall, etc, Act 1996 allows a similar right of entry to demolish, build or repair party walls between properties (see above, **11.12.4**).

  The Countryside and Rights of Way Bill 2000 provides a right to roam across certain areas of land (see Chapter 10).

- **Common law rights of entry**

  At common law, people are permitted to enter land in the possession of some other person in certain circumstances, for example, to abate a nuisance (see below).

  There are several instances of everyday acts of trespass by abuse of rights of entry which are virtually ignored in modern times. For example, there is a common law right to use the foreshore, which belongs to the Crown, for the sole purpose of passing and repassing on foot or with boats. It is an abuse of such a right to sit or lie to sunbathe on the foreshore or to bathe in the sea.

- **Necessity**

  There is a defence if the act of trespass was necessary provided there was no negligence on the defendant's part. However, the defence probably only applies when there is a threat to life or property.

In *Rigby v Chief Constable of Northamptonshire* (1985), the defendant successfully pleaded necessity when he caused a fire by firing CS gas into a shop owned by the claimant, in an attempt to eject a dangerous psychopath.

In *Esso Petroleum Co Ltd v Southport Corpn* (1956), a case which caused some difficulty in distinguishing between trespass and nuisance, the defence of necessity succeeded when a ship's captain was forced to discharge oil, which later polluted the shore, in order to save his ship which had run aground.

For the defence of necessity to apply, it is not sufficient for the defendant to argue that his or her actions were necessary to draw public attention to what he or she believed to be a genuine danger to the public at large. In *Monsanto plc v Tilly and Others* (1999), the defendants were campaigners against genetically modified crops. They had entered onto the land of the claimant as trespassers and had damaged crops as part of a publicity programme. The Court of Appeal concluded that the real purpose of the campaign was to give the defendants the opportunity to publicise their views in court, and that their defence of necessity was not a genuine defence at all. It was only in exceptional circumstances that necessity would apply as a defence to trespass. Mummery LJ explained that, even in an emergency situation, the defence of necessity could not be justified unless there were very exceptional circumstances, if there is in existence (as there was in this case, in the Department of The Environment) a public authority responsible for looking after the relevant public interests.

- **Licence or consent of the claimant**

  Permission by claimants forms licences of various kinds to enter and use property. Such licences may be express or implied and are granted for specific purposes. For example, tradesmen have an implied gratuitous licence to enter property to deliver their goods. People attending cinema or concert performances have an implied licence to enter premises and attend such performances. Lodgers have a licence to stay in the rooms which they hire, and so on. Many licences can be revoked at the will of the licensor, and each will depend upon the circumstances under which the licence was granted. If it was granted under a contract, it would be necessary to study the terms of the contract in order to discover how the licence may be revoked. There are some authorities to the effect that a contractual licence can be revoked at will, even if it means that the licensor could be sued for breach of contract (*Wood v Leadbitter* (1845)) and others which suggest that if an equitable remedy would be available to prevent the breach of contract, that the licence is irrevocable for that very reason (*Winter Garden Theatre (London) Ltd v Millenium Productions Ltd* (1948)). A licence coupled with an interest, in property, for example, can never be revoked.

Repeated acts of trespass which are not objected to can give the trespasser an implied licence to use property. This makes such a person a lawful visitor for the purposes of the Occupiers' Liability Act 1957, and the resulting duty of care owed to such people is greater than that which is owed to trespassers under the Occupiers' Liability Act 1984.

If the purpose for which the licence was granted is exceeded, the tort of trespass is committed. For example, the tradesman who leaves the path to the door and wanders around the garden is a trespasser, and the theatre-goer or party guest who is disruptive is also a trespasser. Reasonable force may be used to ensure that such people leave the property if they refuse to do so when so requested (*Collins v Renison* (1754)). People who break restrictions imposed on behaviour by the Countryside and Rights of Way Bill 2000 become trespassers.

If a claimant delays before bringing a claim for trespass, this will not necessarily mean that a licence has been granted for the trespass to be committed, nor that the claimant has acquiesced and is estopped from bringing a claim. Much depends on the type of act which constitutes the trespass and on the length of time involved. In *Jones and Another v Stones* (1999), the Court of Appeal held that mere delay in complaining about relatively minor acts of trespass was not sufficient to establish estoppel by acquiescence within the tests laid down in the leading case of *Wilmott v Barber* (1880). The criteria established in that case for what amounts to acquiescence indicated that it would also be necessary for the claimant to prove that the defendant had encouraged or allowed the acts of trespass, that the trespasser had acted upon that encouragement to his or her detriment and that it would be unconscionable to allow the claimant to assert his or her legal rights.

- **Reasonable defence of people or of the property itself**

  A person in possession of land has a defence to a claim for trespass to the person if he or she can prove that he or she acted in good faith in the course of defending his or her property or people on the property, including him or herself. However, any force used must not be disproportionate to the force used by the intruder. If the defendant uses excessive force, he or she may have a claim brought against him or her by the trespasser. In some cases, prosecutions are brought against landowners who overstep the mark. In *Revill v Newbury* (1996), the defendant was prosecuted and was acquitted of malicious wounding when a trespasser on his allotment was hit in the arm and chest by more than 50 pellets. However, the civil claim brought against the burglar succeeded and resulted in the payment of more than £4,000 damages. See, also, *Cross v Kirby* (2000) (see Chapter 20), in which the defence was pleaded alongside that of illegality in a claim by a hunt saboteur against a landowner who tried to remove him from his property.

In April 2000, Tony Martin, a landowner, was convicted of murder after he killed an intruder with an illegal shotgun.

- **Adverse possession**

  After 12 years' adverse possession, the right to recover land is lost.

11.2.12 Trespass is actionable *per se*

There is no need to prove damage in order to succeed in an action for trespass. All that is necessary to prove is that the alleged act was committed. Even the most trivial acts of trespass are actionable, and this principle is an illustration of the importance attached by the law from the earliest times to protection of the possession of property.

11.3 Remedies for trespass

A number of remedies exist once trespass has been proved. Some of these are, like the tort of trespass itself, of very ancient origin, and are little known and seldom used.

11.3.1 Damages

As the most trivial acts of trespass can be actionable, the physical damage to the land may be very slight. In such cases the damages awarded will only be nominal. If there is substantial damage to the property, then an appropriate award of compensation can be made. In suitable cases, an injunction may be awarded in addition to damages.

11.3.2 Injunctions

In many instances, what the claimant requires is an injunction to prevent further acts of trespass. In cases in which the physical damage is only very small, this is usually the remedy which is sought, and which is likely to be obtained except in the most exceptional circumstances. For example, when people persist in trespassing by walking over land, or by parking on private property the landowner needs to be able to keep them out in future, and this is best achieved by means of an injunction. Often, the mere threat of legal action is enough, hence, the common, but legally inaccurate, notice 'Trespassers will be prosecuted'. Often, a more effective deterrent is that favoured by some householders of putting up a notice which reads 'Beware of the dog'.

11.3.3 An action for recovery of the land

If the claimant has been deprived of lawful possession of the land by the defendant, it may be possible to obtain from the court an order to enable him or her to recover the property. The claimant must show that he or she has better title to the property than the defendant.

11.3.4 Re-entry and defence of property

The person entitled to possession of the land may re-enter and use reasonable force to remove the trespasser, his or her property or to prevent the acts of trespass (*Hemmings v Stoke Poges Golf Club* (1920)). If a disproportionate amount of force is used, this will amount to trespass to the person, and the trespasser could bring a successful action for assault, battery or false imprisonment. In *Harrison v Duke of Rutland* (1893), the claimant, in an attempt to interrupt the claimant's grouse shooting, stood on the highway, and waved his umbrella and handkerchief. He was held down and restrained by the Duke's servants, and sued for trespass to the person. His action failed. It was held they were merely taking lawful steps to prevent a trespass.

The law may provide protection to trespassers even when they are engaged in criminal activities. In *Revill v Newbury* (1996), the defendant, aged 76, was sleeping in his shed on an allotment when he was disturbed at 2 am by a trespasser who was trying to break in. He fired his shotgun through a small aperture in the shed door and shot the claimant in the arm and chest at a range of five feet. The claimant was later prosecuted for the offences which he had committed that night and pleaded guilty to the criminal charges, but the defendant was acquitted on charges of wounding. However, the intruder claimed damages in tort for assault and battery, breach of the duty owed to trespassers under the Occupiers' Liability Act 1984, and negligence. The defendant put forward defences of *ex turpi causa* (illegality), accident, self-defence and contributory negligence. The judge at first instance had rejected the defences of *ex turpi causa*, accident and self-defence, though he did make a finding of contributory negligence and awarded damages of £4,033 to the claimant trespasser. The Court of Appeal confirmed that a claimant in a personal injuries case is not debarred from recovering damages even is he or she is a trespasser embarking upon a criminal act, if the force used against him or her is disproportionate to the force which he or she is using. The defence of self-defence cannot apply if the person under attack used greater force than a reasonable man would have used in the circumstances. The defences of *ex turpi causa* (see Chapter 20) and accident were also rejected. This case is discussed more fully in connection with the Occupiers' Liability Act 1984.

By contrast, in a criminal prosecution in 1995, the owner of a vineyard was acquitted of deliberately wounding two burglars whom he shot when he startled them in the course of stealing on his property on which £12,000 worth of wine was stored. The injuries which he inflicted were found to have been accidental. He had fired at a door and into the air when he heard the intruders and panicked, but had shot both of them. No civil action has been brought by either of the burglars, one of whom was quoted as saying, 'We knew what we were doing that night. We were on his property stealing his stuff. He should not have been prosecuted'.

It is now common practice for people to employ firms of wheel-clampers to remove vehicles parked on private property. This kind of self-help is permitted provided the fine imposed for recovery of the vehicles is not excessive.

If a person uses or threatens violence to re-enter the land, he risks prosecution under s 6 of the Criminal Law Act 1977, unless he or she is a displaced residential occupier.

11.3.5 An action for *mesne* profits

An action for *mesne* profits is available to people who have suffered financial losses through being deprived of possession of their land. Such losses include the deterioration of the property and the cost of recovering it.

11.3.6 Distress damage *feasant*

If goods or animals are left unattended on land, the occupier may retain these until any damage done by them has been paid for. Actual damage to the property, for example, broken windows, must be suffered, and this remedy is an alternative to bringing an action, which means that no action may be initiated while the object is still in the possession of the occupier.

11.4   Nuisance

Nuisance may be classified into various categories. The most common division is into statutory nuisance, public nuisance and private nuisance, and although there are distinct differences between all three categories, it is sometimes still possible for the same fact situation to give rise to all three actions. For the sake of clarity, it is essential to preserve the distinctions by dealing with each category separately.

11.5   Statutory nuisance

A number of nuisance actions have been created by statute, often on an *ad hoc* basis, and usually in response to pressing social need. For example, the work of Edwin Chadwick and others resulted in the great public health legislation of the 19th century which was responsible for the control of infectious diseases and a radical improvement in living conditions. This legislation, which included the Public Health Acts of 1845 and 1875, created many statutory nuisances. More recently, these statutes have also included legislation to improve the environment, such as the Clean Air Act 1956 and the Control of Pollution Act 1974. These nuisances are quasi-criminal in nature, and are enforced by officers of local authorities, whose usual policy is to prevent nuisance by serving abatement notices, and who only prosecute in the magistrates' courts as a last resort. The advantage of this system to private individuals is that they can complain to the appropriate local authority department about whatever nuisance is troubling them, such as noise or noxious fumes, and if the situation is covered by one of the relevant Acts, it can be dealt with without the expense and inconvenience of bringing an individual civil action, and also, in some instances, without the acrimony which such a civil action can create between neighbours. A solicitor consulted by a client who complains of what could be a statutory nuisance will usually explore this avenue before advising the client to resort to the trouble and expense of a civil action.

11.6 Public nuisance

Public nuisance is primarily a crime, prosecuted by the Attorney General. As a tort, it bears little relationship with private nuisance and, to some extent, is a misnomer, perhaps being best described as a 'conceptual dustbin' into which a number of disparate and unconnected acts of interference with peoples' interests have been dumped. It is only available when the claimant has suffered damage over and above other members of the public.

11.6.1 Outline definition

Public nuisance has been defined as an act 'which materially affects the reasonable comfort and convenience of life of a class of Her Majesty's subjects': *per* Romer LJ in *AG v PYA Quarries* (1957).

In *AG v PYA Quarries*, dust and vibrations caused by the operation of a quarry amounted to a public nuisance, although the defendants tried to argue that too few people were affected by their acts for them to amount to anything more than a private nuisance, if that.

It is useful to examine each element of this definition.

11.6.2 Materiality

In many of the other cases on nuisance, the relevant question was the degree of interference which the activity caused. The acts complained of must have been such as to cause real disturbance, but this is a question of fact in each case.

Some examples of acts amounting to public nuisance are: organising a pop festival, which caused noise and a large amount of traffic (*AG of Ontario v Orange* (1971)); blocking a canal (*Rose v Miles* (1815)); queuing on a highway, so causing an obstruction (*Lyons v Gulliver* (1914)); picketing on a highway (*Thomas v NUM* (1985)); interference with navigation rights in the River Thames (*Tate and Lyle Industries v GLC* (1983)). In *R v Johnson (Anthony Thomas)* (1996), the Court of Appeal held that making obscene telephone calls to numerous women on many occasions constituted a public nuisance. The conduct materially affected the reasonable comfort and convenience of a class of people.

11.6.3 Reasonable comfort and convenience

The requirement of reasonable comfort and convenience is thought to be the common factor between public and private nuisance, which have little else in common. In both torts, the claimant must establish that the interference with comfort and convenience is substantial enough to amount to a nuisance and is beyond what would reasonably be expected. To succeed in a tort action for public nuisance, however, the claimant must prove that he or she has suffered special or extra damage over and above that suffered by other members of the community. The criminal law is adequate to prevent repetitions of the harm, but the object of the civil law is to compensate, and tort is limited to those cases in which extra harm has been suffered. For example, if, as has happened in recent years, large numbers of 'new age travellers' were to congregate on farmland, the whole neighbourhood may complain of the crime of public nuisance, and the farmer whose land had been camped upon could sue for trespass, but people whose livelihoods had been affected by close proximity to loud noise, which had for example interfered with breeding animals, could sue in tort for public and possibly private nuisance. One important distinction between public and private nuisance here is that, for acts to amount to private nuisance, there must be continuity or repetition of the acts over a period of time, whereas, in public nuisance, there appears to be no such requirement, and a single act is probably enough to amount to the tort.

The requirement of interference with comfort covers noise and other disturbances, but there is no need, as there is in private nuisance, to prove injury to health or even substantial interference in order to succeed in an action for public nuisance. Interference with convenience could include the obstruction of entrances to land and highway-obstruction. It is unusual for the inconvenience caused by delay to the claimant to amount to sufficient inconvenience to be a public nuisance.

11.6.4 A class of Her Majesty's subjects

There must be sufficiently large numbers of people affected by the defendant's behaviour before an action for public nuisance can be sustained. Essentially, the tort is concerned with protecting the interests of the public, and individuals can only be protected by the tort as part of the wider community. The Court of Appeal in *AG v PYA Quarries* did not define how many people constitute a 'class', but Lord Denning indicated that there would be an action for public nuisance if the disturbance was so widespread that it would be unreasonable to expect only one individual to try to prevent it. The question is more one of the effect upon the community than one of the numbers involved. In *AG v Hastings Corpn* noise from occasional stock-car racing did not amount to public nuisance because the area was sparsely populated and too few people were affected on too few occasions in the year.

11.7 Highway nuisance

Nuisances which affect the highway are covered by the tort of public nuisance, but an individual would only succeed in a tort action if there was special damage suffered as a result of the obstruction of the highway. This type of nuisance has been used in the public order situation as a criminal offence for many years to control demonstrations and picketing and has now been superseded to some extent by statutes such as the Highways Act 1980 and the Public Order Act 1986. However, there are still some civil actions brought for highway nuisance which fall into two broad categories: obstruction of and interference with highways, and objects falling, or likely to fall, onto highways.

11.7.1 Unreasonable use and obstruction of the highway

Strictly speaking, the highway may be used only for passing and repassing. Any other use of the highway, such as standing or sitting on the road or placing objects upon it could constitute a public nuisance if the conduct involved is unreasonable. Highway nuisance was defined by Lord Simmonds in *Jacobs v London CC* (1950) as:

> Any wrongful act or omission upon or near a highway, whereby the public are prevented from freely, safely, and conveniently passing along the highway.

Examples of highway nuisance include: queues for theatres (*Lyons v Gulliver* (1914)); putting up a stand to watch the King's funeral procession (*Campbell v Paddington Corpn* (1911)); unreasonable use of the highway during the night by heavy lorries (*Halsey v Esso Petroleum* (1961)); unreasonable parking of an unlit vehicle on a highway at night (*Ware v Garston Haulage* (1944)); constantly slicing golf balls onto a highway, one of which caused a taxi-driver to lose an eye (*Castle v Saint Augustine's Links* (1922)).

As in private nuisance, there must be unreasonable use of the highway for the tort to be committed. Anything which constitutes unreasonable use, even of a minor nature and particularly if it is solely for the defendant's convenience will be a public nuisance, as in *Farrell v John Mowlem & Co Ltd* (1954), in which the claimant was injured tripping over a pipeline laid across a pavement.

In *Goodes v East Sussex CC* (2000), the appellant had suffered very serious injuries in a motor vehicle accident when his vehicle skidded on ice and left the road. It was agreed between the parties that, on the day in question, a lorry had salted the roads, including the relevant one, but in a sequence different from that which was expected. There was no allegation of a want of care on the claimant's part. The House of Lords held that the duty under s 41(1) of the Highways Act 1980 does not encompass a duty for Highway Authorities to prevent the formation and accumulation of ice and snow on a highway. Nor is there a duty under that section to remove ice and snow after it has accumulated. Their Lordships reviewed the law on highway nuisance, and concluded that if Highway Authorities were to be subject to a duty to prevent or remove the accumulation of ice and snow, that was a matter for Parliament.

11.7.2 Threats to the highway from adjoining premises

The rule in *Wringe v Cohen* (1940) sets a standard equivalent to strict liability for man made structures which cause a danger to highways from adjoining premises. In that case, the Court of Appeal held that the person responsible for repairing premises which adjoin a highway is liable for dangers created by those premises if he or she knew or *ought to have known* of the danger. Liability is not absolute. The exceptions to this are when the danger was caused by a trespasser, or was the result of some natural process causing a latent defect of which the occupier was unaware. Indeed, some writers, including Winfield, take the view that the cases fall into two clear categories, those involving man-made structures, when liability is strict, and those involving natural projections such as trees, when liability depends upon proof of negligence. In *Caminer v Northern and London Investment Trust Ltd* (1951), the landowner was not liable when a tree with diseased roots fell across a highway, as it was not possible to detect that the tree was in danger of falling. In *British Road Services v Slater* (1964), a landowner was not liable when a branch of a tree growing on his land but overhanging the highway knocked a large package off a high vehicle, damaging the claimant's lorry which was travelling behind. The defendants were found not liable because the breach could not be regarded as a foreseeable source of danger.

However, in *Chapman v London Borough of Barking and Dagenham* (1998), the Court of Appeal upheld the decision of the trial judge, who had found the defendants liable for injuries caused by a tree branch. The branch had broken off in high winds, crushing the claimant in the cab of his van. Following *Noble v Harrison* (1926), it was held that there would be liability in nuisance if a landowner neglects to remedy a natural defect on his or her land within a reasonable time.

Occupiers of premises which adjoin the highway are responsible for their maintenance and would also bear responsibility for any damage caused by their disrepair if this amounted to a danger to the highway or persons using it. In *Tarry v Ashton* (1876) an adjoining land occupier was liable to a passer-by who was injured by a lamp which fell from the premises. Although the occupier attempted to escape liability on the grounds that he had employed an independent contractor to keep the premises in repair, it was decided that the duty to maintain premises so close to a highway could not be delegated. This is one of the exceptions to the rule that an employer is not liable for the torts of an independent contractor.

Under s 41 of the Highways Act 1980, highway authorities are responsible for maintaining the highways, but under s 58(1) can escape liability if it can be demonstrated that reasonable care had been taken to ensure that the particular part of the highway concerned in a legal action was not dangerous for traffic. Section 58(2) provides that in deciding on the question of reasonable care regard must be had to the nature of the highway and the appropriate standard of maintenance. There is an unresolved problem as to whether, as the majority of judges held in the Court of Appeal decision of *Griffiths v Liverpool Corporation* (1974), liability is almost absolute, except for the s 58 defence, or whether negligence should be proved, as the wording of the Act suggests.

It should be noted that, for most accidents on a highway, the usual action is negligence and it is somewhat anomalous that highway nuisance has been singled out for special treatment at a time when proof of fault is the normal expectation.

11.7.3 Defences to public nuisance

The general defences in tort apply to public nuisance (see Chapter 20) but, in addition, the defence of statutory authority has proved useful. For example, in *Allen v Gulf Oil* (1981), it was held that where Parliament has expressly or impliedly authorised the construction of works, in this case the installation of an oil refinery, that authorisation carries with it the right to do all that is necessary for the authorised purpose, without the fear of an action for nuisance being brought.

A further analogous defence based on planning permission was successfully pleaded in the first instance decision of *Gillingham BC v Medway (Chatham) Dock Co* (1992). In this case, Buckley J held that as planning law operates through delegated powers within a statutory framework approved by Parliament, the character of a neighbourhood can be changed by planning permission to such an extent that what would previously have been a public nuisance may not be so after the change of use. Here, the council had given the defendants permission to operate a commercial port on the site of the old naval dockyard at Chatham. This had generated heavy commercial traffic by day and night, which passed through what had previously been a quiet residential area. The council, despite their previous assurance to the defendants that they would have unrestricted access to the dock area, brought this action on behalf of the residents seeking a declaration that heavy traffic through the area at night was a public nuisance, and seeking an injunction to restrain the traffic. It was held that there was no public nuisance here in the light of the changed use of the area under properly considered planning regulations.

However, *Wheeler v Saunders* demonstrates that planning decisions do not necessarily give developers immunity from a nuisance action, even if the development is the inevitable consequence of that planning consent.

The defence of act of a stranger has also proved useful (see *Wringe v Cohen* (1940), 11.7.2 above).

Prescription, which is a good defence to private nuisance does not apply to public nuisance.

11.8 Remedies for public nuisance

The basic remedies of damages and injunctions are sought by claimants in public nuisance cases. Often, a remedy provided to one claimant can be of benefit to a whole community.

11.8.1 Damages

If the claimant has suffered personal injuries or financial loss, this would have to be pleaded as particular damage over and above that suffered by the general public, and damages will be awarded accordingly. However, only compensatory damages will be payable. In *Gibbons v South West Water Services Ltd* (1992), the Court of Appeal held that exemplary damages would not be awarded to claimants who had suffered illness as a result of drinking water which had been contaminated by a grossly excessive dose of aluminium which had accidentally been introduced into the water supply at a treatment works. The defendants had acted in a high handed manner and had sent a misleading letter which stated that the water was safe to drink. Even before the rule in *Rookes v Barnard* (1964), and *Cassell v Broome* (1972), which laid down the limits for the awarding of exemplary damages, it had never been contemplated by the House of Lords that exemplary damages could be awarded for public nuisance, and it was not for the courts to consider such an award now, given the much restricted use of exemplary damages. Even if it had been possible to apply *Rookes v Barnard* to this case, the court could not award exemplary damages, as the defendants were not exercising executive power derived from government, nor was their behaviour calculated to make a profit by committing the tort, as was required by that case.

11.8.2 Injunctions

Often, the claimant will be seeking an injunction to restrain further repetition of acts of public nuisance. As an equitable remedy, this is discretionary, and could be refused in some circumstances. In *Gillingham BC v Medway (Chatham) Dock Co* (1992), Buckley J held that, even if there had been a public nuisance committed, he would have exercised his discretion and refused an injunction because the claimant had assured the defendant when granting planning permission for change of use, that access to the area would be unrestricted.

11.9 The distinction between public and private nuisance

The torts of public and private nuisance are distinct and separate and have evolved independently of one another though there are some conceptual overlaps.

Public nuisance	Private nuisance
• Protects land and other interests	• Essentially protects land
• Primarily a crime	• Only a tort
• Claimant must prove special damage over and above that of public	• Claimant must prove damage
• Single act can be enough	• Single state of affairs is necessary
• No defence of prescription	• Prescription is a defence
• Exemplary damages are not available	• Exemplary damages may be available
• Strict liability for some forms of highway nuisance	• Fault must usually be proved, some exceptions

11.10 Private nuisance

Private nuisance complements the tort of trespass, and offers options for action to a claimant who is unlikely to succeed in an action for trespass.

Traditionally, this tort has protected against physical interference of an indirect nature with crops, land and the use or enjoyment of land. Although it is a very ancient tort, the law of nuisance is continuing to develop and the judges appear to be in the process of creating a new branch of nuisance to protect individuals, including tenants, from harassment. In *Khorasandjian v Bush* (1993), the Court of Appeal held that the courts have power to grant injunctions to restrain defendants from pestering claimants by making nuisance telephone calls.

11.10.1 Outline definition

A working definition of private nuisance is as follows:

> Private nuisance consists of continuous, unlawful and indirect interference with the use or enjoyment of land, or of some right over or in connection with it. Proof of damage is usually necessary.

Each element of this definition will be discussed and clarified, and a useful approach to dealing with problem-type questions on the topic is to memorise the definition and to work through it systematically, applying it to the facts of the problem.

11.10.2 Continuous interference

Actions for private nuisance arise when there has been continuous interference over a period of time with the claimant's use or enjoyment of land. In *Delaware Mansions Ltd v Westminster CC* (1999), the Court of Appeal held that a local authority had a duty to abate a nuisance caused by tree roots undermining the foundations of a block of flats. That duty was not nullified simply because the damage had occurred before the freehold interest was obtained. There was a continuous nuisance in this case which could have been remedied at very little cost if immediate action had been taken. There is no set period of time over which the events must occur to amount to a private nuisance. Much depends upon the neighbourhood and the other surrounding circumstances. Temporary interferences do not usually amount to actionable nuisances. However, a temporary, but very substantial state of affairs may amount to a nuisance, as in *De Keyser's Royal Hotel Ltd v Spicer Bros Ltd* (1914), in which noisy pile driving at night during temporary building works was held to be a private nuisance.

A single act giving rise to a complaint will not normally constitute private nuisance, though it could be a public nuisance. However, there are one or two instances of cases in which what appears to be a single act has been held to amount to a private nuisance. On closer examination, however, it will be observed that these apparently isolated acts were the culminating event in a state of affairs which has prevailed for some time. In *SCM v Whittall & Son Ltd*

(1970), Thesiger J explained that a single escape of materials from the defendant's land may constitute a private nuisance, if the same event had occurred before as a result of activities on the land as it had in *British Celanese v Hunt (Capacitators) Ltd* (1969). In that case, the foil had blown from the defendant's land where it was stored and had damaged an electricity substation, causing the electricity to a small industrial estate to be cut off. The same problem had occurred once a few years previously and had arisen because of the way in which the material was stored on the defendant's property. The judge had no difficulty in finding that what had occurred was a private nuisance.

However, the case of *Crown River Cruises Ltd v Kimbolton Fireworks Ltd and Another* (1996) is difficult to reconcile with these cases. Here, a barge moored on the Thames close to the Battle of Britain fireworks display in 1990, and a passenger vessel moored to it, had been set alight after a firework display of about 20 minutes which had been held close by. Potentially inflammable material had fallen for 15 or 20 minutes onto the barge, and several hours later the passenger vessel caught alight and was very badly damaged. The time involved was so short that it could hardly have amounted to 'continuous interference', and the case is best explained by reference to the authorities on fire and liability for its spread which rest on principles not directly applicable to the ordinary law of private nuisance (see 11.14 below).

Temporary building works may amount to nuisance, but builders will not be liable if they can show that they have used all reasonable care and skill to avoid disturbance or annoyance. However, if there is more than mere inconvenience, and if what is done amounts to physical damage to the claimant's land, damages may be recoverable (*Clift and Another v Welsh Office* (1998)).

11.10.3 Unlawful interference

The unlawfulness of the defendant's conduct is to be found in the element of unreasonableness which the claimant must prove. Reasonable activities on the defendant's land do not amount to nuisance. It is only when they become unreasonable in character because of the way in which they interfere with the claimant's use or enjoyment of neighbouring property that they are unlawful and may be actionable. The factors which courts take into account in assessing the reasonableness or otherwise of the defendant's use of land are as follows:

- **The defendant's conduct in the light of all the circumstances**

    In reality, what the courts are considering here is the question of fault, but the approach is more flexible than that taken in negligence actions.

    In relation to nuisance arising from naturally occurring hazards, the courts have adopted a subjective approach to the reasonableness or otherwise of the defendant's conduct, based, among other matters, on his or her financial circumstances. This distinguishes nuisance from negligence, where the approach is ostensibly objective. An example of the way in which the courts dealt with the question of reasonableness is to be found in *Leakey v National Trust* (1980). The National Trust owned land upon which was located a large mound of earth which was being gradually eroded by natural processes, and was sliding onto the claimant's property. It was held by the Court of Appeal that natural encroachments of this kind could amount to nuisances in some circumstances, and that landowners had a duty to do all that was reasonable in the circumstances to prevent encroachments onto adjoining property, but that in these cases, the relevant circumstances included the ability of landowners, both physically and financially, to take steps to prevent the danger, and also the neighbours' ability to protect themselves from the danger. Megaw LJ said:

> The criteria of reasonableness include, in respect of a duty of this nature, the fact of what the particular man, not the average man, can be expected to do, having regard, amongst other things, where a serious expenditure of money is required to eliminate or reduce the danger, to his means.

The same approach can be found in *Solloway v Hampshire CC* (1981), in which a claim by householders whose property had been damaged by encroaching tree roots which were the responsibility of the Local Authority, was defeated because the Authority lacked the resources to undertake checking and remedial work to all buildings in their area which might be affected by encroaching tree roots. As Sir David Cairns explained:

> If it could be said to be a reasonably foreseeable risk, I am satisfied that it was a risk such that the cost and inconvenience of taking steps to remove or reduce it would be quite out of proportion to the risk.

- **The locality**

Whether the defendant's activities amount to a nuisance will depend upon the area in which they are carried out. It was explained in *Sturges v Bridgman* (1879) that: 'What would be a nuisance in Belgravia Square would not necessarily be so in Bermondsey.'

An area like Bermondsey which was full of tanneries using excreta in the tanning process, and which was accustomed to the noise and pollution of heavy industry is less likely to provide fertile ground for successful private nuisance claims than a quiet residential suburb, but this does not mean that people living in industrial areas will never be able to succeed in nuisance actions, as much will depend upon the extent and degree of the activities of the defendant in the light of what is customary in the particular area, and there will be limits as to what people are able to tolerate even in commercial or industrial localities.

It has been argued that this rule as to the locality of the nuisance only applies to cases in which a claimant complains of interference with use or enjoyment of land, and that, if the activities cause physical harm to the land itself, the character of the neighbourhood is not a relevant consideration. This view is based on the old case of *St Helen's Smelting Co v Tipping* (1865), in which the claimant complained of damage to trees as a result of fumes from copper smelting by the defendants. He succeeded in his claim despite the fact that he lived in a manufacturing area. The House of Lords drew a rather forced distinction between nuisances which caused damage to the land and to crops, and those which merely affected the use or enjoyment of the land, stating that the character of the neighbourhood is only of relevance in the case of the latter.

However, despite this case, there have been instances much more recently in which damages have been awarded for private nuisance when the only complaint in private nuisance has been one connected with the use or enjoyment of the land, and the locality has been highly industrialised. In such cases, other factors which are of relevance in assessing the lawfulness of the defendant's conduct have carried greater weight, and this is illustrative of the fact that locality is only one of several factors which the judges weigh in the balance.

Nevertheless, in *Blackburn v ARC Ltd* (1998), it was held that permission to fill in a quarry was granted for only a temporary period, and this should not mean that nuisances were inevitable. The smells and noise generated by the work amounted to a nuisance because they were held to be more than those which must be tolerated in modern living conditions. The position was revised in *Murdoch v Glacier Metal Co Ltd* (1998), in which the Court of Appeal confirmed the principle that noise must be judged in the context of the character of the locality. The character of a locality can change over the years.

- **Sensitivity of the claimant**

  It is consistent with the notion of 'give and take' which pervades the law of nuisance that abnormally sensitive claimants are unlikely to succeed in their claims for private nuisance, since their perceptions of the defendant's conduct are not the criteria by which the activities are to be judged. The standard of tolerance is that of the 'normal' neighbour.

  The leading case is *Robinson v Kilvert* (1889), in which the claimant's claim was for damage to abnormally sensitive paper stored in a cellar which was affected by heat from adjoining premises. The claim failed because ordinary paper would have been unaffected by the temperature.

  However, if the ordinary use of land would have been affected by the defendant's activities, the claim will succeed. In *McKinnon Industries v Walker* (1951), a crop of delicate orchids was damaged by fumes from the neighbouring premises, and although the plants were unusually delicate the claimant succeeded in a nuisance action because ordinary flowers would have suffered a similar fate.

Similar principles operate in relation to personal discomfort. In *Gaunt v Finney* (1827), Lord Selbourne LC explained the situation in this way:

> A nervous or anxious or prepossessed listener hears sounds which would otherwise have passed unnoticed, and magnifies and exaggerates into some new significance originating within himself sounds which at other times would have been passively heard and disregarded.

The maxim *sic utere tuo ut alienum non laedas* has been said to apply in cases of nuisance, and it means, in rough translation, 'you should use your own land in such a way as not to harm other people'. Although this notion has been described as 'mere verbiage', it still has some influence on the way in which nuisance cases are decided, and the principle of sensitivity is an example of this. The courts do not regard use of land as unreasonable merely because an unduly sensitive neighbour objects to such use.

In order to overcome the subjective approach to the problem, technical standards are sometimes referred to, but these are not conclusive. For example, in *Murdoch v Glacier Metal Co* (1998), the Court of Appeal ruled that the World Health Organisation guidelines on the standard of nighttime noise which is likely to disturb sleep was not conclusive. Neither would the fact that there was evidence that sleep was disturbed necessarily mean that there was a nuisance.

- **The utility of the defendant's conduct**

In nuisance cases, judges are concerned with balancing the conflicting interests of neighbouring landowners and householders, and will be less inclined to consider that an activity amounts to a nuisance if it is useful for the community as a whole taking into account all the surrounding circumstances, such as locality and the duration of the activities. Although it has been stated on several occasions that 'public benefit' is no defence to nuisance, if an activity is beneficial to the community as a whole, the judge will sometimes be prepared to find that the defendant has not behaved unreasonably. In *Miller v Jackson* (1977), the Court of Appeal held that the playing of cricket on a particular ground had been for many years a benefit to the whole community, but that since the construction of houses close to the cricket ground, it had become a nuisance because the interference with the use and enjoyment of the adjoining properties was substantial. (Note Denning MR's famous dissenting judgment in this case.) On the other hand, there are several cases in which activities are of benefit to the community, and because of their temporary nature they have been found not to be a nuisance. Among such activities is building work, provided it is carried out at reasonable times of the day, as in *Harrison v Southwark and Vauxhall Water Co* (1891).

We must conclude from the various cases that 'public benefit', while not a defence in itself is one of a number of relevant factors, and the courts do not simply dismiss out of hand arguments based upon it.

- **Malice**

  Malicious behaviour on the part of the defendant will certainly contribute to the impression that his or her conduct has not been reasonable, and may therefore amount to a nuisance. It is not necessary to establish malice in order to succeed in a nuisance action, but, if it is possible to prove that the defendant's activities were motivated by malice, the claimant has a good chance of succeeding.

  In *Christie v Davey* (1893), the claimant had for several years been giving music lessons and holding musical evenings in his semi-detached house. The defendant, irritated by the noise, banged the party walls, shouted, blew whistles and beat tin trays with the malicious intention of annoying his neighbour and spoiling the music lessons. An injunction was granted to restrain the defendant's behaviour.

  In *Hollywood Silver Fox Farm v Emmett* (1936), the defendant was liable in nuisance when he deliberately fired guns close to the boundary with his neighbour's land where silver foxes were kept, so interfering with their breeding habits, as they are nervous animals and likely to eat their young if frightened. It appears that here the court was prepared to accept that what might otherwise have been a lawful act on the defendant's own land had become a nuisance because of the malice involved, although other factors, such as the frequency of the shots may also have been relevant.

  There is a line of cases concerning the right to abstract water from one's land which do not appear to be easy to reconcile with the cases on malice in nuisance. These cases include *Bradford Corporation v Pickles* (1895), in which the House of Lords held that even where the claimant was deliberately diverting water from his neighbour's property with the intention of forcing them to buy his land at an inflated price, he was committing no legal wrong because no one has a right to uninterrupted supplies of water which percolates through from adjoining property. Here, dubious and even malicious motives alone could not create a cause of action where none had previously existed (*damnum sine injuria*).

  More recently, this case has been approved and applied several times, for example, *Langbrook Properties v Surrey CC* (1969) and *Stephens v Anglia Water Authority* (1988), and it seems that these cases do not directly contradict the nuisance cases which deal with malice as they are distinguishable on the ground that cases concerning percolating water stand as a category on their own, being based upon ancient rules relating to water rights which can be separated from the general law of nuisance.

- **The state of the defendant's land**

  It is no longer the case, as it appears to have been at common law, that the defendant is able to leave the processes of nature to do their worst on his or her land without the fear of a nuisance action from neighbours. The law was changed in *Goldman v Hargrave* (1967), a Privy Council decision. This case is rather confusing as it appears to equate nuisance and negligence, and much of the terminology used in it by the judges is the language of negligence. An occupier of land in Australia did not take steps to extinguish a burning tree which had been struck by lightning, even though it was foreseeable that a wind, common in that area, could fan the flames and cause danger to adjoining land. He was liable for nuisance when the fire damaged neighbouring property. This was adopted into English law by the Court of Appeal in *Leakey v National Trust* (1980), in which it was held that an occupier must take such steps as are reasonable to prevent or minimise dangers to adjoining property from natural hazards on his land, in this case the risk of landslides caused by the processes of nature.

  In *Holbeck Hall Hotel Ltd v Scarborough BC* (2000), the Court of Appeal held that the owner of land which formed the lower part of a cliff owed a 'measured' duty to prevent higher land being damaged by lack of support caused by erosion. This duty would only arise, however, if the owner of the lower land knew, or ought to have known, that there was some patent defect on his or her own land which gave rise to the danger, and it was reasonably foreseeable that the defect would damage the higher land if nothing was done to remedy the situation. The Court of Appeal emphasised that there would be no duty to remedy the fault if the defect was latent or hidden and could only be discovered by further investigation. In this respect, the law has moved forward since the decision in *Leakey*. Much of the reasoning in the case was based on considerations that are usually taken into account in negligence cases, and the three-stage test in *Caparo v Dickman* (1990) was referred to.

  In *Bradburn v Lindsay* (1983), it was held that the owner of one semi-detached house was liable in nuisance to the adjoining house owner for the spread of dry rot, a naturally occurring fungus which damages the fabric of buildings and which he should have attempted to eradicate.

  The subjective test for reasonableness, based on the defendant's financial ability to remedy the nuisance, has, so far, been confined to naturally occurring nuisances, and although it is an unusual approach, it has been approved by the Court of Appeal on at least two occasions, and with the weight of this authority behind it, there is no reason why the principle could not be extended by the courts to all claims for nuisance, if it were to prove useful as a device for imposing or negating liability in the particular case. This is yet another example of the operation of policy, and is an important instance of judicial reasoning in which the courts have, unusually, been prepared to enter into an explicit cost-benefit analysis in reaching a decision as to liability. A similar analysis was to be found in the pre-1984 cases on liability for injury to trespassers, which began with *British Railways Board v Herrington* (1972), in which the House of Lords was prepared to impose the responsibility for preventing an accident upon an occupier if he had 'the knowledge, skill and resources to do so'.

11.10.4 Indirect interference

The requirement that the interference with the claimant's use or enjoyment of land be indirect, distinguishes nuisance from trespass, which covers only direct entry onto land, and negligence, which encompasses both direct and indirect acts.

Indirect interference includes the following: allowing smoke and fumes to drift onto the neighbouring land (*St Helen's Smelting Co v Tipping* (1865)); allowing unpleasant stenches to invade adjoining land (*Bliss v Hall* (1838)); smells and fumes from candle-making (*Bone v Searle* (1975)); smells from manure; disturbing neighbours' sleep by noise and vibrations (*Halsey v Esso Petroleum* (1961)); allowing tree roots to suck moisture from adjoining soil, so causing subsidence (*Solloway v Hampshire CC* (1981)); quarry blasting (*Harris v James* (1876)); pollution of rivers with factory effluent (*Pride of Derby Angling Assn v British Celanese* (1953)).

11.10.5 Interference with the use or enjoyment of land or some right over or in connection with it

The tort of private nuisance is concerned primarily with land, and provided the damage complained of is physical damage to the land itself, including buildings, fixtures, crops, rights of way and anything else which falls within the definition of land in s 205 of the Law of Property Act 1925, there is no doubt that such damage will be covered by private nuisance. In the case of interference with servitudes, that is, rights of way and other easements, profits *á prendre*, rights of support, riparian rights and so on, liability is strict in many cases, and there is no need to prove damage. This, however, is an exception to the general rule in nuisance.

In *Crown River Cruises Ltd v Kimbolton Fireworks Ltd and Another* (1996), it was held in a first instance decision that damage to a floating barge on the Thames permanently attached to a mooring on the river bed of which the claimants had exclusive possession under a licence, was actionable in private nuisance. There were two vessels involved, a 'dumb' barge which acted as a mooring for other barges and vessels, and a passenger barge which was attached to it. The barge which was itself also used as mooring was for the better use and enjoyment of the claimant's mooring right, and thus gave rise to the possibility of an action for private nuisance. There was also a finding of negligence against the defendants who had not themselves taken any steps to inspect the contents of the barge for inflammable material, but had relied on the diligence of the second defendants. The fire on board the passenger vessel was caused by the negligent failure of the second defendants to attend to flammable material which had fallen on to the barge.

There has been some doubt as to whether other types of damage will be protected by private nuisance. 'Enjoyment' of land is a somewhat nebulous concept, but it is protected by the tort as long as the court is satisfied that the interference is substantial after balancing all the various interests involved, including those of the defendant. Much depends on the degree of interference. Interference with purely recreational activities, such as watching television, has been held not to be actionable in private nuisance (*Bridlington Relay v Yorkshire Electricity Board* (1965)). Where the interference was carried out by electrical means, doubt has been expressed as to whether this type of case would be decided in the same way today, when television serves educational and other purposes besides mere recreation. (See the Canadian case of *Nor-Video Services Ltd v Ontario Hydro* (1978).)

However, in *Hunter and Another v Canary Wharf Ltd; Hunter and Another v London Docklands Development Corpn* (1997), the House of Lords held that interference with television reception by a tall building with stainless steel cladding could not amount to an actionable public or private nuisance. This view was reached by analogy with a well established line of cases, some of them very old, in which the same conclusion was reached in relation to the presence or erection of a building in the line of vision, on the basis that this was not interference with use or enjoyment of land.

In the first action, the claimant, with many others, was seeking damages in nuisance for years of interference with television reception caused by Canary Wharf Tower which is 250 metres high and 50 metres square. In the second action, the claimants were suing the London Docklands Development Council in negligence for deposits of dust on their properties caused by the building of the Limehouse Link Road. The issues raised in both cases were heard together as preliminary issues.

If injury to health, such as headaches caused by noise, is complained of, then, providing the claimant is not unusually sensitive, there will be a remedy in private nuisance.

One serious limitation which the English courts had imposed on claims for personal injuries in nuisance is that only a person who has a proprietary interest in the land affected by the nuisance will succeed in a claim. In *Maloney v Laskey* (1907), the claimant failed in her claim for personal injuries caused by a lavatory cistern falling on her head because of vibrations from machinery on adjoining property. She was merely the wife of the tenant, and had no proprietary interest herself in the land. The view of the Court of Appeal was:

> No principle of law can be formulated to the effect that a person who has no proprietary interest in property, no right of occupation in the proper sense of the term can maintain an action of nuisance arising in an adjoining house.

It is logical that this rule should have applied to private nuisance in the light of its history, and it is of little significance now that the negligence action has been highly developed and would cover such situations.

However, in *Hunter v Canary Wharf* (1996), the Court of Appeal held that in the light of the trend towards giving additional legal protection to occupiers, the relevant criterion is 'occupation of property as a home'. Pill LJ, who gave the leading judgment, said:

> It is no longer tenable to limit the sufficiency of that link by reference to proprietary or possessory interests in land. I regard satisfying the test of occupation of property as a home as providing a sufficient link with the property to enable the occupier to sue in private nuisance.

This trend has been observed in other jurisdictions (in Canada in *Devon Lumber v McNeill* (1988) and New Zealand in *Howard Electric v Mooney* (1974)), and in England in *Khorasandjian v Bush* (1993), in which it had been held by the Court of Appeal that the wife of the owner of the matrimonial home had the right to an injunction to prevent harassing telephone calls to the property. In this last case, Dillon LJ had justified the decision as follows: 'The court has at times to consider earlier decisions in the light of changed social conditions.'

He continued:

> If the wife of the owner is entitled to sue in respect of harassing phone calls, then I do not see why that should not also apply to a child living at home with her parents.

This approach was to be welcomed, though it remained to be seen how far it would extend the scope of actionable nuisance to relatives, carers and casual lodgers. It seems strange that the Court of Appeal was prepared to move with the times in this respect but was not minded to regard the interference with television reception affecting some 30,000 people as capable of amounting to an actionable nuisance in modern law. This ambivalence has been described by one writer as an example of the 'great British compromise' (Burnet, D, *Housing Law*, 2nd edn, 1999).

The House of Lords ((1997) *The Times*, 15 April) has reversed the decision of the Court of Appeal in *Hunter v Canary Wharf* (1997). After carefully reviewing the law of nuisance in detail, their Lordships concluded that landowners are entitled to build on their land as they wish, provided planning requirements are met. Accordingly, they will not be liable in nuisance for erecting large buildings which interfere with the television reception of other people living in the vicinity. However, their Lordships did not rule out the fact that on occasion interferance with television reception might be protected by the law of nuisance in appropriate circumstances, but the mere fact that a building was in the way, as in this case, was not enough.

On the separate point concerning the right to sue in nuisance, it was decided by a majority (Lord Cooke dissenting), that an action in private nuisance can only be brought by a person with a proprietary interest in the land affected, so no action is available in nuisance to other people sharing the same house who do not have a proprietary interest in the land. This decision is a restatement of the long established law of nuisance and the House of Lords has not taken the opportunity to extend the law which had been offered by the Court of Appeal in this case and in the earlier case of *Khorasandjian v Bush* (1993). One reason for that is the fact that the position is to some extent covered by the statutory recognition of the tort of harassment in the Protection from Harrassment Act 1997 which deals with the problems of nuisance telephone calls which arose in that case. In *Khorasandjian v Bush*, the Court of Appeal had been prepared to extend the right to sue in nuisance to people who, in the words of Pill LJ, have a 'substantial link' with the land, such as the use of the land as a home. The House of Lords considered that it would be too difficult to decide who should be included in that category, and that, in any event, such an extension of the right of action would transform nuisance from a tort to land into a tort to the person which was not an acceptable way for the law to develop. The tort of negligence was the correct action in such cases. Lord Hoffman considered whether there was any policy reason why the old rule should be abandoned and stated:

> Once nuisance has escaped being a tort against land, there seems no logic in compromise limitations, such as that proposed by the Court of Appeal, requiring the claimant to have been residing on land as a home ... There is a good deal in this case and in other writings about the need for the law to adapt to modern social conditions. But the development of the common law should be rational and coherent. It should not distort principles and create anomalies merely as an expedient to fill a gap.

Lord Lloyd took a similar approach, expressing the view that 'it is one thing to modernise the law by ridding it of unnecessary technicalities, it is another thing to bring about fundamental change in the nature and scope of a cause of action'.

The House of Lords' decision in *Hunter v Canary Wharf* (1997) is of great importance and should be read carefully. It reviews all the major decisions on the points in issue and reasserts the common law principles, concluding that it remains necessary to maintain a distinction between nuisance and negligence and ending much of the academic speculation on the subject.

11.10.6 Who can sue in private nuisance?

Private nuisance protects anyone who has the use or enjoyment of the land affected. Anyone who owns rights over or in connection with that land may also bring an action for nuisance.

The Court of Appeal held, in *Pemberton v Southwark LBC* (2000), that even a tolerated trespasser may sue for nuisance, if he or she has sufficient interest in the land affected by the nuisance. However, in *Delaware Mansions Ltd v Westminster CC* (1998), it was held that a management company which was owned by tenants who had purchased the freehold of a block of flats had insufficient interest in the property to establish a right to sue in private nuisance. Their individual claims in negligence also failed and, as the right to sue had not been assigned to the management company, there could be no claim by the company in negligence. The formation and running of a management company of this type is the usual way in which tenants proceed in organising the maintenance of blocks of flats after purchasing the freehold, and this case is important because it indicates that those who are involved in advising the tenants must be aware of the pitfalls of the situation.

Concerns about the indeterminacy which afflicts nuisance and negligence actions may also arise from the case of *Hunter and Others v Canary Wharf Ltd; Hunter and Others v London Docklands Development Corpn* (1996). The second action in this case was for negligence resulting in annoyance, discomfort and damage to property caused by deposits of dust when a new road was being constructed. The Court of Appeal, taking the view that dust is an inevitable consequence of modern life, and that a reasonable amount of cleaning is to be expected of householders, nevertheless held that, if the dust was excessive and could be shown to have caused physical damage to the property rendering a diminution in its value, there could be a claim for damages in negligence to cover the cost of cleaning and repair. Pill LJ said:

> In my opinion, the deposit of dust is capable of giving rise to an action in negligence. Whether it does depends on proof of physical damage and that depends on evidence and the circumstances.

Such an approach is more consistent with the law of nuisance.

Habinteg Housing Association v James (1994) is a case which illustrates that a claimant who has suffered considerable damage may be unable to claim any compensation if the facts of the case mean that there is no action available in English law, despite the fact that, at first sight, it would appear that there might be an action for nuisance or negligence. In such circumstances, the conclusion must be that the law of tort, even in conjunction with the patchwork provided by related public law, is inadequate to meet the demands of individual justice. The case concerned the tenant of a flat owned by a housing association. Under a standard form agreement signed in 1986, there were covenants by which the landlord agreed to maintain and keep in good repair the structure and exterior of the premises. There was no specific mention in the tenancy agreement of responsibility for vermin control. The tenant soon discovered that the flat was infested with cockroaches and that, with the tenants and people on the same estate, her food, carpets and furniture were contaminated and damaged. The infestation was eventually cured after five years when the local authority, acting under powers conferred on them by the Public Health Act 1936, served notice on the landlords requiring them to put an end to the problem. The infestation was eradicated, by means of disinfestation of the whole block, by means of public health law which is aimed at preventing further damage. However, the tenant sought tort damages for £10,000 to cover past loss and inconvenience. The Court of Appeal held that as there was no evidence that the infestation had started in and spread from the landlord's flat as a result of breach of the repairing covenants, there could be no action for nuisance. Nor could there be an action for negligence, though it was conceded that this might be possible in certain circumstances on the collapse of a nuisance action. However, it was impossible to construct a duty of care in this situation because both physically and legally the block disinfestation only became possible once the abatement notice had been served on the landlords by the local authority.

The Law Commission (Law Commission Report No 238, 1996) has recently considered the problems raised by this particular case and other gaps in the law relating to the responsibility of landlords for the condition of property in both the private and public sectors, and its main recommendation is the updating of the implied covenant for fitness for human habitation in s 8 of the Landlord and Tenant Act 1985.

11.10.7 Proof of damage is usually necessary

Yet another factor which distinguishes nuisance from its companion trespass, is that, in order to succeed in nuisance, the claimant must prove that damage has been suffered. Private nuisance is not actionable *per se*, with the exception of interferences with servitudes, discussed above.

11.10.8 The relationship between private nuisance and negligence

The claim has been made that negligence is gradually encroaching upon some of the other torts, especially private nuisance, and that one day negligence will take over from nuisance. Glanville Williams (*Foundations of the Law of Tort*, 1976) explains the trend in this way:

> Why should we not say that people are under a duty of care not to allow a noxious escape of such a nature that the claimant cannot reasonably be expected to tolerate it? It follows that nuisance is a branch of the law of negligence. It merely adds to the list of duties of care.

There are a number of confusing judicial statements on the subject and, in some instances, judges use the terminology associated with negligence in nuisance cases. For example, in *Leakey v National Trust*, Lord Megaw said:

> The considerations with which the law is familiar must all be taken into account in deciding whether there has been a breach of duty, and if so what the breach is.

In *Bolton v Stone* (1951), counsel admitted that the case could not be one of nuisance as there was no negligence involved and, in *Hurst v Hampshire CC* (1997), it was that foreseeability is a prerequisite for nuisance.

More recently, the three-stage test for duty of care in negligence was used in *Holbeck Hall Hotel Ltd v Scarborough BC* (2000), a nuisance case in which the two torts clearly merged.

Further problems are created by the fact the courts appear to distinguish between the two torts without giving reasons for the distinction, and without explanation of how the distinction is to be made.

It is true that the same fact situation may give rise to actions in both private nuisance and negligence, and that fault of some kind must be proved in order to succeed in both, except in nuisance cases involving interference with servitudes.

It is in relation to the concept of 'reasonableness' which is referred to in determining liability in both nuisance and negligence that the problems arise.

The notion of reasonableness frequently involves foresight of harm, and this issue gave rise to crucial considerations in *Cambridge Water Co Ltd v Eastern Counties Leather plc* (1994). The claimant used a borehole to extract groundwater for domestic use and consumption, and it emerged that the water in this borehole had become polluted by spillages of solvents over many years at the defendant's tannery. The claimant's claim in negligence, nuisance and *Rylands v Fletcher* failed. The House of Lords decided that there had been reasonable use of the land on the basis of 'give and take' and, therefore, the nuisance action must fail. Lord Goff explained the position in the following words:

> If the user is reasonable, the defendant will not be liable for consequent harm to his neighbour's enjoyment of his land; but, if the user is not reasonable, the defendant will be liable, even though he may have exercised reasonable care and skill to avoid it ... But, it by no means follows that the defendant should be held liable for damage of a type which he could not reasonably foresee; and the development of the law of negligence in the past 60 years points strongly towards a requirement that such foreseeability should be a requirement of liability for damages in the law of nuisance. For if a claimant is in ordinary circumstances only able to claim damages in respect of personal injuries where he can prove such foreseeability on the part of the defendant, it is difficult to see why ... he should be in a stronger position to claim damages for interference with the enjoyment of his land where the defendant is unable to foresee such damage.

This in effect means that there is a similar 'state of the art' defence in nuisance to that which exists in negligence cases such as *Roe v Minister of Health* (see 7.2.2 above) and in product liability under the Consumer Protection Act 1987. The law thus provides no incentive to those developing new techniques in manufacturing to ensure that their products and methods are safe to use or environmentally friendly. However, it is arguable that the test of substantive liability is still reasonable user, and a foresight of the kind of damage is merely the application of remoteness to nuisance. While it would be unfair to impose strict liability retrospectively through nuisance or the rule in *Rylands v Fletcher* for the mistakes of the past when there is no such strict liability in the ordinary law of negligence or the law of product liability, this does mean that the relationship between the various torts is now closer than ever despite the fact that there were precedents in existence before the *Cambridge Water Company* case which ruled that liability in relation to ground water pollution was strict (*Ballard v Tomlinson* (1885)). In view of the serious threat which manufacturing industry still presents to the environment through recently publicised phenomena, such as acid rain and the hole in the ozone layer, the arguments in favour of strict liability for situations such as that arising in the *Cambridge Water* case are strong.

However, the notion of fault in negligence involves different considerations to that in private nuisance, although the reasonableness of the defendant's behaviour is assessed in both torts. As we have seen, nuisance allows explicit consideration of the claimant's economic position in some cases, whereas in negligence, cost-benefit analysis is shunned, at least openly. The relevant factors for determining fault in nuisance include the nature of the locality and other factors which would not usually be relevant in negligence, but that is merely because of the importance of land in the equation. In both torts, it is possible for the judges to arrive at decisions on grounds of policy, using the the reasonableness test to justify such decisions.

Lord Reid summed up the situation in *The Wagon Mound* (1967), when he said:

> It is quite true that negligence is not an essential element in nuisance. Nuisance is a term used to cover a wide variety of tortious acts, and in many negligence in the narrow sense is not essential ... Although negligence in the narrow sense may not be necessary, fault of some kind is almost always necessary, and generally involves foreseeability.

In effect, the standard of care in nuisance is more variable than that in negligence, and nuisance appears, despite its ancient origins, to be capable of flexible development in the light of social trends. As Shaw LJ points out in *Leakey v National Trust* (1980):

> Seen in the light of Megaw LJ's analysis and exposition of the long line of cases, the judgment in *Goldman v Hargrave* may represent the climax of a movement in

the law of England expanding that part of the law which relates to liability for nuisance.

Quite apart from the obvious historical difference, there are further important distinctions between nuisance and negligence, particularly in relation to who can sue and to what type of damage may be recoverable, and also to the remedies which may be required, and despite the claims that have been for negligence, the two torts remain conceptually distinct from one another.

11.10.9 Who can be sued for private nuisance?

Any person who creates the nuisance can be sued, whether or not that person is the occupier of the land at the time of the action. However, it is most usual for the occupier to be sued, and the occupier may also be vicariously liable for the nuisances of servants and independent contractors if the duty concerned is non-delegable. Occupiers who adopt and continue to allow nuisances on their land may also be liable, even if such nuisances are created by predecessors in title, trespassers or third parties (*Sedleigh Denfield v O'Callaghan* (1940)).

A single individual or enterprise may be identified and sued for nuisance in cases where the accumulation of several activities causes interference with adjoining property. It is not a valid defence for the individual who has been singled out to attempt to prove that the contributory acts of others are responsible for the nuisance, even though the activities of each one, taken alone would not amount to a nuisance. In *Pride of Derby and Derbyshire Angling Association v British Celanese Ltd* (1953), fishing in a river was ruined by pollution from several factories, but the defendants could not escape liability by pleading that they were not the only polluters.

A landlord may be liable for nuisances emanating from land in certain exceptional circumstances, for example if the landlord had knowledge of the nuisance before letting, or where the landlord reserved the right to enter and repair the premises.

In *Hussain and Another v Lancaster CC* (1998), the Court of Appeal held that a local authority could not be liable in nuisance or negligence for failing to take the necessary steps to prevent council tenants and members of their households or families from committing acts amounting to criminal harassment of owners of property nearby. The acts involved in this case were committed by several identifiable people and included the shouting of threats, racial abuse and various forms of intimidation. The Court of Appeal reviewed the cases concerning responsibilities of landlords and local authorities in nuisance for the acts of their tenants and rejected arguments advanced by counsel for the claimants that local authorities are responsible for common parts of their land such as avenues and walkways, and that this responsibility creates the necessary links between the tenants properties and the land of the claimants. It was held that the harassment did not, as the judge at first instance had found, emanate from common parts of the estate. Arguments based on negligence also failed, on the basis that it would not be fair, just or reasonable to hold the council liable in the circumstances (see *X v Bedfordshire CC* (1995)).

By contrast, local authorities have been held liable in nuisance for the repeated acts of travellers whom officials knew were on council property as licensees. In *Lippiatt and Another v South Gloucestershire CC* (1999), the Court of Appeal distinguished the *Hussain* case on the grounds that the conduct of the people who created the nuisance in *Hussain* was not linked to, nor did it emanate from, the houses in which they were tenants. As indentifiable individuals, each of the offenders could have been personally liable in public nuisance. In the present case, however, the travellers were permitted by the council to congregate in a particular, relatively small area of land, and they used this as a base for committing the criminal acts in question. The council could, therefore, be regarded as responsible for the nuisance because of the continuing presence of the travellers on council land, from which they committed acts of trespass on the claimants' properties.

In the case of licensees, the preconditions for a landowner's liability are, in the words of Mummery LJ, as follows:

> The claimant's use and enjoyment of his rights in his land was interfered with by the continuing presence on the defendant's land, of persons whose actual or apprehended activities included, to the knowledge of the defendant, harmful acts repeatedly committed by them on the claimant's land from their base on land occupied (that is, owned) by the defendant.

It seems that landlords are not responsible for the nuisances of tenants in the absence of authorisation, express or implied (*Smith v Scott* (1973)). This lighter burden on landlords presumably reflects the fact that they have parted with possession of the property and have less control over what happens on it than a licensor has over licensees such as travellers.

The law on landlords' liability for nuisance is still developing. For example, in *Southwark LBC v Mills* (1998), the Court of Appeal held that a landlord cannot be compelled to carry out soundproofing of flats to prevent one set of tenants from annoying others. Mantell LJ, faced with conflicting lines of authority on the point, was reluctant to construe a covenant of quiet enjoyment in a lease 'as encompassing a promise to alter or improve' the premises. The House of Lords (2000) confirmed that the covenant for quiet enjoyment could not be used to demand repairs or improvements.

11.11 Defences to private nuisance

The general tort defences apply to nuisance. These include consent, *volenti non fit injuria*, contributory negligence, Act of God, act of a stranger and, possibly, inevitable accident (see Chapter 20).

In addition, there are other defences which are of particular importance in private nuisance.

11.11.1 Prescription

If the nuisance has been continued for 20 years without interruption, the defendant will escape liability by pleading a prescriptive right to commit the nuisance.

The 20 years is counted from the time that the claimant becomes aware of the nuisance for the first time, even if the nuisance had been continued for many years before the claimant moved into the neighbourhood. The leading case is *Sturges v Bridgman* (1879), in which the defendant had operated a confectionery manufacturing business for more than 20 years when the claimant, a doctor, built a new set of consulting rooms in his garden immediately adjacent to the building which housed sweet-making machinery. The claimant then complained of nuisance from the noisy machinery and brought a successful legal action against the defendant. The court decided on the facts that there was no nuisance until the consulting rooms were built, and that the 20 years began to run from that date, so the defence of prescription was not available.

In *Miller v Jackson* (1977), the argument favoured by Lord Denning that the claimants who had bought property near a place where they knew that cricket had been played for many years had no right to complain of the nuisance it caused, was rejected by the majority of the Court of Appeal, as it is not a defence to argue that the claimant 'came to the nuisance'.

11.11.2 Statutory authority

There will be a defence to private nuisance if it can be shown that the activities complained of by the claimant were authorised expressly or impliedly by a statute. As Lord Dunedin explained in *Corporation of Manchester v Farnworth* (1930):

> When Parliament has authorised a certain thing to be made or done in a certain place, there can be no action for nuisance caused by the making or doing of that thing if the nuisance is the inevitable result ... The onus of proving that the result is inevitable is on those who wish to escape liability for nuisance.

In *Allen v Gulf Oil Refining Ltd* (1981), it was held that the defence of statutory authority operated to the benefit of the oil refinery which was causing great inconvenience and annoyance to local residents who complained of unpleasant odours, noxious fumes, vibrations, heavy traffic and loud noise in their previously quiet rural setting.

In *Hunter v Canary Wharf* (1996), the Court of Appeal took the view that, in establishing fast track planning permission procedures by statutory instrument under the Local Government Planning and Land Act 1980, Parliament had not granted immunity to a nuisance action by means of a defence of statutory authority in relation to a particular structure built as a result of the procedure. In *Wheeler v Saunders* (1995), it was held that, unlike Parliament, planning authorities have no power to authorise a nuisance except insofar as they have statutory authority to allow a change in the character of a particular neighbourhood and the nuisance was the inevitable result of authorised use. In this case, there was no change in the character of the neighbourhood, but only a small change of use allowing the building of pig units which did not amount to a strategic planning decision. The defence of statutory authority did not apply in an action for nuisance arising out of the foul smells which emanated from the pig units.

The character of different localities will change over the years as they are developed, and the way in which this happens depends on the judgment of the planning authorities to whom Parliament has delegated the delicate task of balancing the interests of the community with those of the individuals. This point was made in *Gillingham BC v Medway (Chatham) Dock Co Ltd* (1992), where the local authority was bringing an action in public nuisance against the defendant company, to whom they themselves had granted planning permission.

11.12 Remedies for private nuisance

There are a number of remedies for private nuisance. Some are self-help remedies for which the aggrieved party need not trouble the courts.

11.12.1 Damages

Compensation will be paid if it can be proved that damage to land, personal injuries or substantial inconvenience have been caused. The amount payable will be calculated according to the basic principles for assessing damages in tort.

11.12.2 Injunction

A very common remedy for nuisance is the award of an injunction, and this will be almost automatic in many cases, though the court does have a discretion to award damages in lieu of an injunction. An injunction will be refused if the interference with the claimant's land is trivial (*Shelfer v City of London Electric Lighting Co* (1895)), as the courts do not wish to collude in allowing defendants to 'buy off' the rights of claimants (*Kennaway v Thompson* (1981)). However, an injunction was refused in *Miller v Jackson* (1977), and damages were paid instead, which would have been small consolation to the claimants who were in real physical danger in their gardens from stray cricket balls.

The prerequisite for damages being awarded in lieu of an injunction is that it would be oppressive for the defendant if an injunction were to be granted. In *Gafford v Graham* (1998), the basis for the award of damages was the sum which the claimant might reasonably have demanded for relaxing the relevant restrictions in perpetuity. The claimant in that case was refused an injunction because he had stood by and watched while the defendant had built a structure and had made no complaint at the time.

11.12.3   Abatement of the nuisance

This ancient self-help remedy involves the claimant in taking steps to prevent the nuisance by entering the defendant's property and removing the source of the nuisance. Anything belonging to the defendant must be left on his property, even tree branches which have spread from adjoining land should, strictly, be returned. A person entering land in the process of abating a nuisance will have a defence to trespass.

The claimant must normally give notice of the abatement, but need not do so in an emergency or if the nuisance can be abated without entering the defendant's land.

Even this remedy can give rise to problems as the landowner who feels aggrieved by damage to boundary trees or hedges may seek an injunction and damages against the neighbour attempting to abate the nuisance. This is what happened in the much-publicised case of a dispute between neighbours over a 22 ft high hedge (*Stanton v Jones* (1995)).

In *Burton v Winters* (1993), there had been a long-standing boundary dispute between the parties, which arose out of the fact that a garage had been built along the boundary line by the defendant's predecessors in title. The wall did encroach onto the claimant's property by four and a half inches, and technically this amounted to a trespass, but the judge refused an injunction because the encroachment was minimal, but he ordered the payment of damages because of the diminution in value of the claimant's property. There continued a campaign of harassment by the claimant which meant that the garage was damaged and eventually the defendants obtained an injunction to prevent the claimant interfering further with their property. Despite this the criminal damage and harassment continued and the claimant was sentenced to two years' imprisonment for contempt of court. The claimant continued to argue for the right to abate the nuisance and self-help to remedy the trespass and the Court of Appeal held that these remedies were no longer available to her, expressing the view that the common law remedies should be limited in scope because they can lead to further problems in disputes between neighbours.

11.12.4 The Party Wall, etc, Act 1996

This Act allows landowners to demolish, build or repair walls between their own and adjoining properties. 'Party Structure Notices' must be served on adjoining landowners before the work is carried out and, if the owner of the neighbouring land objects, the dispute can be settled by a surveyor, who has the power to apportion the cost of the work. The Act allows disputes to be settled without going to court.

11.13 The rule in *Rylands v Fletcher*

The mid-19th century saw the emergence of a new form of strict liability in the rule in *Rylands v Fletcher* (1868), at a time when fault was beginning to dominate liability in tort.

Although Blackburn J and the House of Lords, in expounding the rule, claimed merely to be stating a long standing principle of the common law, most writers now agree that in fact new law was being made. A number of attempts have been made to explain the policy reasons which lay behind the formulation of this new law, the most popularly accepted view being that the judges, who were drawn from the landed gentry, resented the newly emerging wealth of the industrial developers, and wished to burden them with strict liability for polluting adjoining land. In fact, despite its claim to be a rule of strict liability, the rule in *Rylands v Fletcher* has many attributes of fault liability today. As will be seen, the concept of reasonableness, akin to that in nuisance, has crept into the law through the notion of 'non-natural user', and the rule has not been developed in English law to provide protection against all hazardous activities, and Scots law has rejected the rule altogether. In Australia the rule in *Rylands v Fletcher* has been abandoned altogether in favour of referring everything to 'proximity'.

11.13.1 Facts of the case

In *Rylands v Fletcher* (1868), the defendants employed independent contractors to construct a reservoir on their land. When digging the reservoir, the contractors found mine workings on the land, and failed to seal these properly before completing their work and filling the reservoir with water. As a result, water flooded through the mine shafts into the claimant's mines on the adjoining property. The defendants could not be held liable in nuisance because the flood was caused by a single act rather than a continuous state of affairs, nor could they be liable for trespass because the entry onto the land was indirect. There was no evidence of negligence on the part of the landowner and at that time negligence had not developed as an independent tort. Ultimately, the judge stated a new principle of liability to cover this situation.

11.13.2   The rule

Per Blackburn J:

> The person who, for his own purposes, brings onto his land and collects and keeps there something likely to do mischief if it escapes must keep it in at his peril and if he does not do so, he is *prima facie* liable for all the damage which is the natural consequence of its escape.

To this the House of Lords added the additional requirement that there must be non-natural user (that is, use) of the land for the rule to apply.

11.13.3   The person who brings onto his land

The law distinguishes between things which grow or occur naturally on the land, and those which are accumulated there artificially by the defendant. Thus, rocks (*Pontadawe RDC v Moore Gwyn* (1929)), thistles (*Giles v Walker* (1890)) and naturally collecting water do not fall within the rule. However, vegetation deliberately planted, water collected in bulk or in artificial configurations (*Rickards v Lothian* (1913)), and rocks or minerals, such as colliery waste which are dug up and left on land by the defendant, do fall within the rule.

In *AG v Corke* (1933), it was held that gypsies are 'things likely to do mischief if they escape'.

11.13.4   For his own purposes

It seems that the rule will only apply if the landowner brings something inherently dangerous onto his land for his own purposes, rather than for those of another person, such as a tenant (*Rainham Chemical Works v Belvedere Fish Guano Co* (1921)).

11.13.5   Non-natural user

The above examples explain why the House of Lords clarified the rule by stating that the use of the land must be non-natural. However, the concept of non-natural user has proved a useful policy device in later cases, by which the ambit of the rule has been restricted. For example, in *Read v Lyons* (1947), it was argued that running a munitions factory in wartime is natural use of land. Lord Porter said:

> All the circumstances of the time and place must be taken into consideration, so that what might be regarded as dangerous or non-natural may vary according to those circumstances.

Much will depend upon the prevailing social and economic climate. In *Musgrove v Pandelis* (1919), it was held that it was non-natural use to keep a car with petrol in its tank in a garage. There is little doubt that a similar case would be decided differently today.

In *Mason v Levy Auto Parts Ltd* (1967), the defendants were liable under the rule in *Rylands v Fletcher* when flammable material stored on their land ignited and fire spread to neighbouring property. The storage of the materials amounted to non-natural use of the land. The issue of non-natural user was also considered in the *Cambridge Water* case in which the question of spillages of industrial effluent which affect ground water could not be regarded as 'non-natural' since chemical spillages were regarded as normal in the particular industry at the time.

11.13.6   Something likely to do mischief

The substances which are collected must be inherently dangerous but this is open to interpretation by the courts and has been subsumed into the 'non-natural user' rule.

11.13.7   Escape

There will be no liability in *Rylands v Fletcher* (1868) unless there is an escape of the dangerous materials from the defendant's land. In *Read v Lyons Ltd* (1947), the House of Lords clarified the requirement of escape. The claimant was working in a munitions factory during the Second World War when she was injured by an explosion. There did not appear to have been negligence on the part of the employers, and as the explosion had occurred on their own premises, there was no escape from their property. The result was that the claimant was without a remedy. This case has been criticised for restricting the development of strict liability for dangerous activities (see Fleming, *Textbook on Torts*) at a time when it could be argued that developing industry was creating yet more hazardous uses of land. Indeed, in the USA, the rule of strict liability has been so extended.

11.13.8   Who can sue under *Rylands v Fletcher* and for what damage

There is some authority to the effect that, in order to sue in *Rylands v Fletcher* (1868), the claimant must have an interest in land in the area which is affected, but there are also many cases in which the opposite view has been expressed. If the purpose of the rule is to control and compensate for ultra-hazardous activity, then logically there is no need for the claimant to have any interest in land. If however, the rule is merely an extension of nuisance, then some interest in land would be expected as a basis of a claim.

In *Rigby v Chief Constable of Northamptonshire* (1985), the view was expressed that if there is an escape from the defendant's control on the highway onto the claimant's land the rule in *Rylands v Fletcher* can apply. This was approved in *Crown River Cruises Ltd v Kimbolton Fireworks Ltd and Another* (1996), where the judge was of the opinion that there were strong arguments to extend the same principle to accumulations in or on a vessel in a navigable river.

11.13.9   Is *prima facie* answerable for all the damage which is the natural consequence of the escape

The owner of land close to the escape can recover damages for physical harm to the land itself and to other property (in *Halsey v Esso* (1961), the owner of a car recovered compensation for damage to its paintwork when it was parked on a public road). An adjoining landowner can also recover for personal injury. In *Hale v Jennings* (1938), the claimant was injured when a chair-o-plane escaped from the defendant's fairground machine onto his property. The judge had no difficulty in awarding him damages for personal injury. In *Read v Lyons* (1947), however, a much more cautious approach was taken to the question of recovery for personal injuries, but with no definite conclusion.

It is uncertain whether damages for economic loss are recoverable under the rule in *Rylands v Fletcher* (1868). In *Weller v Foot and Mouth Disease Research Institute* (1966), it was held that an action for pure economic loss could not be sustained in *Rylands v Fletcher* because auctioneers who lost money through the escape of a virus from the research establishment had no interest in the land affected.

In the *Cambridge Water* case, the conclusion of the House of Lords in relation to *Rylands v Fletcher* was that the damage must be of a kind which is a foreseeable consequence of the escape.

The question of whether a person who is not an occupier of land close to the escape can obtain damages for personal injuries is even more open to doubt and is still unresolved.

Damage which is too remote will not be recoverable, but the test for remoteness in *Rylands v Fletcher* has never been clearly stated, and there are those who argue that *The Wagon Mound* test should not apply as it would be unduly restrictive.

11.13.10   Defences

A number of well established defences to the rule in *Rylands v Fletcher* (1868) mean that liability is not absolute, although it is strict.

- **Act of a stranger**

  If a trespasser or other person acting independently, and over whom the defendant had no control, causes the escape, the defendant will not be liable. The intervention must be unforeseeable for the defence to apply, and this aspect has been criticised, as it has the capacity to remove the tort from the realms of strict liability almost into the province of negligence.

Examples are:

Perry v Kenricks Transport Ltd (1956): a child threw a lighted match into the empty petrol tank of an old motor coach parked on the defendant's land. The petrol cap had been removed by some unknown person. As their actions were unforeseeable, the defendant escaped liability, and much of the language used in the course of the case was that of negligence.

Rickards v Lothian (1912): the defendant was not liable when an unknown person blocked a basin on his property and caused a flood which damaged a flat below.

In India, it has been held that *whenever* there is an escape of something dangerous stored on premises, such as chlorine gas, the occupier will nevertheless be strictly liable in *Rylands v Fletcher*. This would be the case regardless of who caused the accident and whether or not it was foreseeable. In *Mehta v Union of India* (1987), the Supreme Court held:

> If an enterprise is engaged in a hazardous or inherently dangerous activity and harm results to anyone on account of such activity, the enterprise is strictly and absolutely liable to compensate all those affected by the accident.

- **Default of the claimant**

  If the escape is wholly the fault of the claimant there will be no liability (*Eastern and SA Telegraph Co Ltd v Cape Town Tramways Co Ltd* (1902)).

  If the claimant's acts were merely contributory, damages will be reduced for contributory negligence.

- **Statutory authority**

  It may be the case that a statute exists which obliges a person or body to carry out a particular activity. If so, the defence of statutory authority may apply, but all hangs upon the construction of the statute. Often, statutes which authorise hazardous activities impose strict liability for accidents which may occur as a result of such activities, for example, the Nuclear Installations Act 1965.

- **Act of God**

  An Act of God is an event which 'no human foresight can provide against, and of which human prudence is not bound to recognise the possibility' (*per* Lord Westbury in *Tennent v Earl of Glasgow* (1864)). In *Nichols v Marsland* (1876), the defendant was not liable in *Rylands v Fletcher* (1868) when exceptionally heavy rain caused artificial lakes, bridges and waterways to be flooded and damage adjoining land. In *AG v Cory Bros* (1921), however, it was held that exceptionally heavy rain in the Rhondda valley in Wales (where the Aberfan disaster occurred in 1967), was not an Act of God.

- **Consent**

  If the claimant has consented to the accumulation of the dangerous things, there will be a defence to *Rylands v Fletcher* (1868), particularly if the activity is for the benefit of the claimant (*Peters v Prince of Wales Theatre Ltd* (1943)).

11.13.11 What will become of the rule in *Rylands v Fletcher*?

It is clear that the scope of strict liability for hazardous activities has been restricted over the years, and the courts in the UK have never taken the opportunity to extend the rule in *Rylands v Fletcher* (1868) even in an age of environmentally conscious pressure groups.

As recently as 1996, there is evidence that judges are very reluctant to extend the scope of this tort. In *Crown River Cruises Ltd v Kimbolton Fireworks and Another* (1996), Potter J considered and rejected the opportunity of extending the rule in *Rylands v Fletcher* to the escape of accumulations of dangerous material on a barge to a vessel moored alongside it. His reason was based on the trends detectable in current judicial and academic opinion.

However, in *Cambridge Water Co Ltd v Eastern Counties Leather* (1994), Lord Goff expressed the view that the storage of dangerous chemicals on land is a 'classic case of non-natural user', and this could have important implications for the future though, in that particular case, there was no imposition of strict liability for 'historic' pollution, that is damage done at a time when it was not realised that the storage of the chemicals was dangerous. The House of Lords rejected the idea of extending *Rylands v Fletcher* into a tort for hazardous activities as has been done in the United States and India.

In 1970, the Law Commission produced its Report on *Civil Liability for Dangerous Things and Activities* and recommended rationalising and extending the rule in *Rylands v Fletcher* where activities are 'abnormally dangerous'.

In 1978, the Pearson Commission recommended that there should be a statutory scheme for compensating personal injuries caused by certain dangerous activities. The controllers of unusually hazardous activities could be required to take out insurance cover, and the activities which would fall into the special categories could be identified by an advisory committee, and legislated for by statutory instrument. The defences available would be more limited than at present.

None of the recommended changes has been implemented and it is extremely unusual for an action under the rule in *Rylands v Fletcher* to reach the courts today. A recent example is *E Hobbs (Farms) Ltd v The Baxenden Chemical Co Ltd* (1992) (see below, 11.14.1).

11.14 Liability for fire

The law relating to damage caused by fire and its spread is confused. Most fire damage today is compensated by insurance, and it is only very occasionally that liability at common law or by statute requires consideration.

11.14.1 Common law

The law has been concerned about liability for the spread of fire since mediaeval times and, in very early common law, the usual remedy was by means of a special action on the case for allowing the escape of the fire. However, none of the writers is clear as to the exact basis of liability for fire or its spread, or as to whether liability was strict or required proof of fault.

Three possible actions are available at common law:

- **Rylands v Fletcher**

  If the fire was deliberately started, in the sense of being accumulated on the defendant's land, there could be liability under the rule in *Rylands v Fletcher* (1868). However, it appears from the case of *Mason v Levy Autoparts Ltd* (1967) that the approach of the courts is to consider the reasonableness of the defendant's conduct in keeping things on the land in the process of non-natural use, which are likely to ignite and the fire spread to the claimant's land. This appears to be closer to negligence than strict liability, and is in keeping with the views expressed in cases such as *H and N Emanuel Ltd v GLC* (1971), in which Denning MR said that an occupier would not be liable for the escape of fire which was not caused by negligence. In *E Hobbs (Farms) Ltd v The Baxenden Chemical Co Ltd* (1992), in which a fire started in some debris below a work bench and spread to an adjoining building, it was held that there was liability under the rule in *Rylands v Fletcher*.

- **Nuisance**

  In the case of *Goldman v Hargrave* (1967), the Privy Council held that an occupier may be liable for the spread of a fire which began naturally, through lightning or even deliberately through the act of a stranger, if he failed to take steps to prevent its foreseeable spread to adjoining land.

- **Negligence**

  If a person is injured (*Ogwo v Taylor* (1987)), or suffers property damage (*Attia v British Gas* (1987)) in a fire, there will be the possibility of an action for negligence, or under the Occupiers' Liability Act 1957.

  If the activity which causes the fire is ultra-hazardous, an employer will be liable for the acts of his independent contractors (*Balfour v Barty-King* (1957), *Spicer v Smee* (1946)).

In *Crown River Cruises Ltd v Kimbolton Fireworks and Another* (1996), it was held that there was liability in nuisance and negligence for the spread of fire after debris from a firework display had landed on a barge on the River Thames and ignited and spread after some hours to a vessel moored to it.

11.14.2 Statute

In addition to the common law remedies, there is a statute which despite its name covers the whole country.

The Prevention of Fires (Metropolis) Act 1774 provides that no one shall be liable for the spread of a fire which begins 'accidentally'. However, this Act has been interpreted very restrictively. In *Filliter v Phippard* (1847), it was held that the Act did not apply to fires which were started negligently, or which started intentionally but which spread accidentally. The word 'accidentally' in the Act was held to refer to fires which started by mere chance or whose exact cause was not known. In *Collingwood v Home and Colonial Stores* (1936), fire broke out on the defendant's premises as a result of defective wiring. It was not possible to prove negligence and the defendants escaped liability.

The Railway Fires Acts 1905 and 1923 provide for payment of a small amount of statutory compensation for damage to land caused by sparks from railway engines (hardly applicable in these days of diesel power).

The rule in modern law appears to be that there is no statutory liability for the spread of fire unless there is negligence. However, the rule in *Rylands v Fletcher* (1868) could apply, creating strict liability at common law, but this has been so manipulated over the years that it is very close to liability requiring proof of fault.

11.15 Distinguishing between the various torts to land

It is often difficult, when faced with a fact situation which is particularly complex, to establish which of the torts relating to land apply, and to distinguish between them. Sometimes, several actions will arise out of the same series of events. In *Halsey v Esso* (1961), for example, residents in a previously quiet area complained of noise made by lorries entering and leaving an oil refinery by day and night, of smuts from the refinery damaging washing on their clothes lines, of fumes affecting the paintwork on their cars parked on a public highway, and of nauseating smells which affected their enjoyment of their property. Their claims succeeded as follows: loss of sleep and smells – private nuisance; damage to cars on the highway – public nuisance and *Rylands v Fletcher*.

The Summary attempts to identify the main points of distinction between the more important torts discussed in this section. However, it must be remembered that a chart of this kind is, by its very nature, a rough and ready exercise, and is unable to deal with several of the finer points of distinction which are dealt with in the text. Nevertheless, it should provide a useful rough guide and working model in tackling the basics of the subject. Note that the tort of negligence is included because an action for negligence may be available as an alternative to the other torts in certain cases.

TORTS RELATING TO LAND

Trespass to land

Definition:

> Directly entering upon land or remaining upon land, or placing or projecting anything upon land in the possession of the claimant without lawful justification. Trespass is actionable *per se*.

Elements

The entry must be direct, and may be above or below the ground or into the airspace above the ground. This distinguishes trespass from the tort of nuisance.

Much depends on the height and extent of the infringement and the court must take all the circumstances into account. The following cases demonstrate the meaning of infringement (*Kelsen v Imperial Tobacco Co* (1957); *Bernstein v Skyviews* (1978); *Anchor Brewhouse v Berkley House* (1987); *Woolerton v Costain* (1970)). For practical reasons, aircraft must be allowed to cross the airspace of landowners below. Parliament has legislated for this. The most recent Act is the Civil Aviation Act 1982.

Tunnelling beneath land can be trespass since tunnelling can weaken the foundations of buildings. It is usually carried out to extract minerals (*Bulli Coal Mining Co v Osborn* (1899)). See, also, the Nationalisation Act 1948 (mining rights are vested in the Crown).

The merest entry is sufficient (leaning a ladder on a wall) and is regarded as an infringement of property rights (*Westripp v Baldock* (1938)).

Most cases involve people, including officials like police officers, entering property (*Jeffrey v Black* (1982); *Jones v Chic Fashions* (1968); *Randall v Tarrant* (1955)).

The person in possession sues because the tort of trespass protects possession rather than ownership.

Defences and rights of entry

There are many defences to the tort of trespass.

Numerous officials including police officers, Inland Revenue officials, and officers of certain bodies have rights of entry by statute, for example, Police and Criminal Evidence Act 1984, Public Order Act 1986.

Self-defence can operate to excuse the defendant if he or she uses reasonable force to protect his or her property. Ancient common law rights might exist to enter other people's land, for example to abate a nuisance.

The defence of necessity applies as long as the defendant was not negligent (*Rigby v Chief Constable of Northants* (1985); *Esso v Southport Corporation* (1956)) or if there are very special circumstances (*Monsanto v Tilly* (1999)).

Only reasonable force may be used in defence of property (*Revill v Newbury* (1995)).

There are many forms of licence or permission to enter and use land (*Wood v Leadbitter* (1845); *Winter Garden Theatre v Millenium Productions* (1948)). However, a delay in bringing a claim will not necessarily amount to a licence (*Jones v Stones* (1999)).

Remedies

Remedies for trespass include: injunction, action for recovery of land, re-entry, action for mesne profits, distress damage feasant and damages.

Public nuisance

The definition of public nuisance *per* Romer LJ in *AG v PYA Quarries* (1957):

> An act which materially affects the reasonable comfort and convenience of life of a class of her Majesty's subjects.

Note the slight connection between public and private nuisance.

Elements

There must be more than mere intermittent interference, that is, 'materially affects' (*AG Ontario v Orange* (1971)). The frequency and degree of interference are considered by the court (*Rose v Miles* (1815); *Lyons v Gulliver* (1914); *Thomas v NUM* (1985); *Tate and Lyle v GLC* (1983)).

The effect of the nuisance upon the community is taken into account. A single act of interference is probably enough (compare private nuisance).

Whether a sufficiently large section of the community to constitute a 'class' is affected depends on numbers of people involved (*AG v Hastings Corpn* (1950)).

The claimant must prove damage over and above that suffered by the rest of the public.

Highway nuisances are included as 'public nuisances', for example, *Halsey v Esso* (1961).

There is strict liability for man made encroachments onto the highway (*Wringe v Cohen* (1940)), but proof of fault is required in the case of natural encroachments (*Caminer v N and L Investment Trust* (1951)).

Note the relationship with the Highways Act 1980 and other legislation affecting the highway which supersedes the common law (*Goodes v East Sussex County Council* (2000)).

Defences

Defences to public nuisance include the usual common law tort defences but many statutes can create the right to commit public nuisance, for example, *Allen v Gulf Oil* (1981). Act of a stranger is also a successful defence.

Private nuisance

Definition of private nuisance:

> Continuous unlawful interference with the use or enjoyment of land, or of some right over or in connection with it. Proof of damage is essential.

Elements

A state of affairs which gives rise to the nuisance must be proved. This must usually have been continuing over a fairly long period of time, but one or two cases can be found when the nuisance existed for a relatively short time, for example, *De Keyser's Royal Hotel v Spicer* (1914); *Clift v Welsh Office* (1998); *Blackburn v ARC Ltd* (1999).

A single act may be enough to constitute a nuisance if it can be shown to have been the culminating event in a series of events, for example, *British Celanese v Hunt* (1969).

Note the requirement of unreasonable use of land which has been used as a control device by the judges. Factors considered are:

- the conduct of the defendant in all the circumstances. Note the subjective approach here as compared with the tort of negligence: *Leakey v National Trust* (1980); *Gillingham v Medway Docks* (1992); *Clift v Welsh Office* (1998);

- the locality: *Sturges v Bridgman* (1879); *Murdoch v Glacier Metal Ltd* (1998);

- the sensitivity of the claimant: *Robinson v Kilvert* (1889); *McKinnon Industries v Walker* (1951); *Gaunt v Finney* (1827); *Murdoch v Glacier Metals Ltd* (1998);

- the utility of the defendant's conduct: *Miller v Jackson* (1977);

- malice: *Christie v Davey* (1893); *Hollywood Silver Fox Farm v Emmett* (1936);

- the state of the defendant's land: *Bradburn v Lindsay* (1983); *Leakey v National Trust* (1980); *Hussain v Lancaster CC (1998)*; *Lippiatt v Gloucestershire CC* (1999); *Holbeck Hall Hotel Ltd v Scarborough BC* (2000).

A landowner will not be liable for a latent defect that could only be discovered by further investigation.

The interference must be in the form of indirect encroachment. This distinguishes nuisance from trespass (*St Helens Smelting Co v Tipping* (1865), smuts and smoke; *Bliss v Hall* (1838), fumes; *Halsey v Esso* (1961), fumes, smuts and noise; *Solloway v Hampshire CC* (1981), tree roots; *Pride of Derby Angling v British Celanese* (1953), industrial pollution of a river).

It must be proved that the claimant has suffered damage (compare trespass to land).

Who can sue and who can be sued?

Anyone who has the use or enjoyment of the land may bring an action. In the case of personal injuries, the claimant needs to have a proprietary interest in the land (*Hunter v Canary Wharf* (1997); *Delaware Mansions v Westminster CC* (1999); *Hussain v Lancaster CC* (1998); *Lippiatt v Gloucestershire CC* (1999)).

Defences

In addition to the usual tort defences, the defendant may plead prescription and statutory authority.

Remedies

The usual remedies are damages, injunction. The self-help remedy of abatement may also be used.

Negligence/nuisance

Note the relationship between negligence and nuisance in modern law.

The rule in *Rylands v Fletcher* (1868)

The rule in *Rylands v Fletcher* is as follows, *per* Blackburn J:

> The person who, for his own purposes, brings onto his land and collects and keeps there something likely to do mischief if it escapes must keep it in at his

peril, and if he does not do so he is *prima facie* liable for all the damage which is the natural consequence of its escape.

The House of Lords added the requirement of 'non-natural user' which has been used as control device to limit or to expand the law at various times (*Read v Lyons* (1947); *Musgrove v Pandelis* (1919); *Mason v Levy Autoparts* (1967)).

'Bringing onto land' includes digging and mining which involves accumulating waste on the land (*Pontadawe v Moore-Gwyn* (1929); *Rickards v Lothian* (1913)).

Personal injuries have been compensated under *Rylands v Fletcher* (*Hale v Jennings* (1938)). 'Pure' economic loss is probably not recoverable (*Weller v Foot and Mouth Disease Research Institute* (1966)), but may be recoverable if it is foreseeable (*Cambridge Water* case).

Defences

Liability is strict but not absolute and a number of defences limit the scope of the rule in English law: act of a stranger (*Perry v Kendricks Transport* (1956); *Rickards v Lothian* (1912); *Mehta v Union of India* (1987)); Act of God (*Nichols v Marsland* (1876); *AG v Cory Bros* (1921)); default of the claimant; consent. The general tort defences apply.

The future of *Rylands v Fletcher*

The rule has never fulfilled its potential and is unlikely to be utilised to create strict liability for many of the hazardous situations which threaten the environment in modern society. Note that the rule has been used more extensively in other jurisdictions such as India.

Liability for fire

There may be liability at common law and by statute for the spread of fire; or for causing injury or damage by fire.

The three possible common law actions are *Rylands v Fletcher* (1868); nuisance (*Goldman v Hargrave* (1967)); negligence.

There may be liability by virtue of the Prevention of Fires (Metropolis) Act 1774 although the provisions are uncertain in scope and have been interpreted restrictively. It seems that negligence of some kind is necessary.

	RYLANDS v FLETCHER	PUBLIC NUISANCE	PRIVATE NUISANCE	TRESPASS	NEGLIGENCE
Who can sue?	Anyone who can prove damage caused by 'escapee'	Any members of the public who can prove 'special damage'	Usually person with proprietary interest in land affected – especially	Person in possession	Anyone who can prove breach of duty damage
Who can be sued?	Person in control of non-natural user on land, usually landowner	The perpetrator	The creator or adoptor	Person committing act of trespass	Person causing damage
Frequency of wrongful acts?	Single act is enough	Single act is enough	Must be 'state of affairs' – some element of continuity	Single act is enough	Single act is enough
Directness?	Act may be direct or indirect	Direct or indirect act	'Indirect act only'	Direct act	Direct or indirect act
Must 'fault' be proved?	No need to prove fault	Fault must usually be proved – exception Wringe v Cohen	Must prove 'unreasonableness' – which is akin to fault. Strict liability in Cambridge Water case	Strict liability. No prove fault	Must prove fault – breach of standard of care
Is the locality relevant? Sensitivity of claimant relevant?	Not relevant / Not relevant (except thin skull rule)	Marginally relevant in some cases / Not relevant except thin skull rule)	Relevant / Relevant – unusually sensitive claimant may not succeed	Not relevant / Not relevant (except thin skull rule)	Not usually relevant but may be a consideration / Not usually relevant except in thin skull rule
Are damages for personal injuries available?	Probably – Hale v Jennings	Yes	Only to people with a proprietary interest in land affected	Yes – but no need to prove damage at all	Yes / Yes
Are damages for economic loss available?	Probably not	Possibly	Must prove economic loss arising out of damage to use/enjoyment of land	Yes – but not need to prove damage at all	Yes
Special defences?	Act of God / Act of Stranger / General Defences	General defences	Ultra-sensitive claimant Prescription. Statutory authority. General defences	Many statutory defences – eg, PACE, involuntary trespass. General defences.	General defences
Could there be a prosecution on same facts?	No, unless there is a statutory nuisance	Yes, if statutory nuisance	No	Criminal Trespass – very narrow circumstances. Public Order Act 1986	Gross negligence may result in prosecution – eg, driving and medical cases

CHAPTER 12

LIABILITY FOR ANIMALS

Civil liability for damage caused by animals has its origins in the feudal tradition, and in pre-enclosure days, when often the main form of wealth was livestock, and attitudes to straying animals were very different to those which pertain today. Indeed, it was not until after the much overdue rationalisation and reform of the law concerning animals in the Animals Act 1971, that the law recognised that the safety of drivers of vehicles on the highway should take priority over the rights of landowners to leave their property unfenced. *Searle v Wallbank* (1947), the earliest precedent ever cited in English law, was accepted as supporting that view, but is now largely overruled by s 8 of the Animals Act 1971.

Although animals are responsible for a relatively large number of injuries (estimated in 1978 by the Pearson Commission at about 50,000 per annum), very few civil actions are brought as a result, and as in the case of the torts relating to land it is important not to take a distorted view of the importance of this topic which occupies many pages of traditional textbooks but in practice rarely requires consideration.

In addition to the Animals Act 1971, the general principles of common law still apply to provide compensation for harm done by animals.

12.1   Common law relating to animals

Basic common law rules apply to the keeping of animals. For example:

- The owner of a dog which bolted across a road on a dangerous bend was liable for negligence (*Gomberg v Smith* (1962)).

- The relevance of negligence is well established, as stated by Lord Atkin:

    Quite apart from the liability imposed upon the owner of animals or the person having control of them by reason of knowledge of their propensities, there is the ordinary duty of a person to take care either that his animal or his chattel is not put to such a use as is likely to injure his neighbour.

    Negligence claims concerning animals are still important, despite the reforms in the Animals Act 1971, because liability under the Act for non-dangerous animals is dependent on actual knowledge. In addition, the abolition of the rule in *Searle v Wallbank* (1947) means that some of the relevant sections of the Act operate in negligence in relation to animals straying on to the highway.

- A farm manager was found to have been negligent in keeping a herd of frisky Charolais cows in a field which was unfenced. It was known that the cows chased dogs and, therefore, it was foreseeable that they could injure anyone walking a dog in the field (*Birch v Mills* (1995)).

- The owner of a Rottweiler was held to have been negligent when the dog bit a child in a shopping precinct. The dog was on a lead but was not muzzled, and the defendant was paying insufficient attention, as there were several ways in which he could have prevented the attack (*Mason v Weeks* (1966)).

- The owner of a dog which tripped someone up on a pavement by allowing the lead to become entangled with his legs was liable in public nuisance and negligence (*Pitcher v Martin* (1937)).

- The owner of horses which created foul stenches was liable in nuisance (*Rapier v London Tramways Co* (1893)). The test for liability in nuisance was formulated in *Peech v Best* (1931) by Lord Justice Scrutton, as that of 'extraordinary, non-natural or unreasonable action'.

- The owner of a pack of Jack Russell terriers was liable in negligence for failure to prevent them escaping and causing foreseeable harm to the claimant (*Draper v Hodder* (1972)).

- A person who teaches a dog to steal golfballs would be liable for trespass to goods (*Manton v Brocklebank* (1923)).

- Excessive noise from crowing cockerels is a nuisance (*Leeman v Montague* (1936)).

- Large numbers of pheasants congregating on the defendant's lawn and damaging the claimant's crops amount to a nuisance (*Seligman v Docker* (1949)).

- The owner of a parrot who teaches it to repeat defamatory remarks would be liable in defamation.

- The keeper of a fox in captivity who allowed it to escape could be liable under the rule in *Rylands v Fletcher* (*Brady v Warren* (1900)).

- The keeper of foxhounds may be liable for allowing them to trespass on land (*League Against Cruel Sports Ltd v Scott* (1985)).

It should be noted that local authorities have powers under s 80 of the Environmental Protection Act 1990 to seek abatement of statutory nuisances. Statutory nuisances are defined as those 'prejudicial to health, or a nuisance'. 'Prejudicial to health' means 'injurious, or likely to cause injury, to health'. In *Budd v Colchester BC* (1999), there was an enforcement action under this Act relating to a dog barking.

12.2 The Animals Act 1971

Concurrent with common law liability for animals is liability under the Animals Act 1971.

The duty owed to other people by the owner or keeper of an animal will depend upon the type of animal and the nature of the harm it causes.

The Act distinguishes between animals which are dangerous by nature because they belong to an inherently dangerous species (termed *ferae naturae* in the old common law), and animals which are not normally dangerous by nature (*mansuetae naturae*).

12.2.1 Dangerous species

Section 2(1) of the Animals Act 1971 deals with animals which are of a dangerous species. Under this section, the keeper of a dangerous animal is strictly liable for damage caused by it. A dangerous species is defined by the Animals Act 1971 as:

> ... a species which is not commonly domesticated in the British Isles and whose fully grown animals have such characteristics that they are likely, unless restrained, to cause severe damage, or that any damage they may cause is likely to be severe.

Although property damage is not expressly mentioned in the Animals Act 1971, which does specifically encompass personal injuries, it is likely that it is covered. Dangerous species include obviously dangerous animals found in other countries – such as lions wolves, bears and so on, but also wild animals commonly found in the British Isles – such as foxes.

Whether or not a particular species is dangerous is, as before the Animals Act 1971, probably a question of law, rather than one of fact. The deciding factor is the species rather than the animal itself, and it would not be possible for a defendant to argue that the particular animal was a tame member of a dangerous species.

The justification produced by the courts for this rule is that it is a matter of judicial notice. In *Tutin v Mary Chipperfield Promotions* (1980), it was held that camels were a dangerous species, even though the camel in that instance was quite docile. This contradicts the decision in *McQuaker v Goddard* (1940) that a camel is a domestic rather than a wild animal, because there is nowhere in the world a camel which is wild.

The 'keeper' is defined as:

* the owner of the animal if it is in his possession; *or*

* the head of the household if the keeper is under 16 years old; *or*

- if the animal ceases to be in the ownership or possession of any person, the 'keeper' is the person who was the keeper immediately beforehand, until the animal is taken over by a new keeper. However, a person is not deemed to be the keeper merely because he has taken care of an animal to prevent it causing harm.

It is theoretically possible for there to be more than one keeper of a particular animal at any one time.

The keeper will be liable for *any* damage which is caused by the dangerous animal. This includes damage other than that which the animal was likely to cause – for example falling off a camel (*Tutin v Mary Chipperfield Promotions Ltd* (1980)). It should be relatively easy for a potential claimant to trace the keeper, as it is necessary for keepers of dangerous animals to obtain a licence from the local authority under the Dangerous Wild Animals Act 1976. As insurance against liability for damage caused to third parties by dangerous wild animals is also compulsory under the same Act, and as the keeping of dangerous animals is comparatively unusual, it is unlikely that there will be much litigation in this area.

Note that there is provision for the licensing of activities involving certain animals under the Dangerous Wild Animals Act 1976. This Act identifies such animals and provides for liability insurance as a condition of a licence being granted. Under s 7 of the Act, a 'circus', which is defined as including 'any place where animals are kept or introduced wholly or mainly for the purpose of performing tricks or manoeuvres', is exempt from the licensing requirements.

The Dangerous Dogs Act 1991, as amended by the Dangerous Dogs (Amendment) Act 1997, defines some breeds as dangerous and creates offences such as keeping a dangerous dog in a public place without a muzzle and having a dog dangerously out of control in a public place.

12.2.2 Non-dangerous species

If damage is caused by an animal which belongs to a non-dangerous species, the keeper is liable for any damage caused by it (except as otherwise provided by the Animals Act 1971) if:

- the *damage* is of a kind which the animal, unless restrained was likely to cause, or which if caused, is *likely to be severe*;

- the *likelihood* of its being caused or of its being severe was due to characteristics of the animal which are not normally found in animals of *the same species* or not normally found except at particular times or in particular circumstances;

- those characteristics were *known to the keeper* or were at *any time known* to a person who at that time had charge of the animal as that keeper's servant or where the keeper is head of a household, were known to *another keeper* of the animal who is a member of *that household and under 16 years of age.*

The question of the causal relationship between the 'characteristics' of animals and the damage which they inflict arose in *Jaundrill v Gillett* (1996) when the Court of Appeal held that the keeper of horses which had been released onto a highway by a malicious third party was not liable to a motorist who was injured by them. It was held that there had to be a causal link between the unusual characteristics of an animal and the damage. Here, the real cause of the injury suffered in the accident was the release of the animals onto the highway, so the defendant keeper escaped what appeared to be absolute liability. In any event, serious reservations were expressed by Russell LJ as to whether horses which panic in the dark after being driven onto a highway are displaying abnormal characteristics.

An example of a 'permanent' idiosyncrasy within the first limb would be a dog with a habit of biting people carrying bags, as in *Kite v Napp* (1999). The second type of characteristics 'not normally so found except at particular times or in particular circumstances' was thought to be intended to emphasise the common law on intermittent 'viciousness'. An illustration is to be found in *Barnes v Lucille Ltd* (1906), where a bitch suddenly became fierce after producing puppies and bit the claimant. The justification for liability was stated by Darling J, who said:

> If the owner knows that at certain periods the dog is ferocious, then he has knowledge that, at those times, the dog is of such a character that he ought to take care of it.

Section 2(2) of the Animals Act 1971 has been criticised for the problems of interpretation which it poses. These difficulties are illustrated by the case of *Curtis v Betts* (1990). In this case, the claimant was unexpectedly attacked by a bull-mastiff dog which was usually docile and which he had known all his life. The Court of Appeal found in favour of the claimant because the damage was 'likely to be severe'. However, the court criticised the wording of the opening of the subsection as awkward and probably wrong, suggesting that what was probably intended by the Animals Act 1971 was that a causal link be established between the animal's characteristic and the damage.

12.2.3 Damage

It is necessary for the defendant to have known that the damage was such as the particular animal, with its special propensities, unless restrained, was likely to cause, or that any damage which that particular animal with its special propensities could cause would be severe.

This requirement is centred on the nature of the damage if the animal is not properly restrained. Obviously, there are some animals which are likely to do more damage than others, by reason of their size and qualities.

12.2.4 Characteristics of the particular animal

At first sight, it appears that this sub-section is designed to prevent an argument being advanced by the defendant that it was normal for the particular animal to behave in the way that it did because at that particular time, for example, in the mating season, many animals of the particular species behaved in the same way. However, the words 'except at particular times and in particular circumstances' have been treated, rather illogically, by the courts as referring to particular 'abnormal' tendencies. For example, the Court of Appeal held in *Cummings v Grainger* (1977) that Alsatian dogs are not normally vicious, but they may be so in special circumstances, as when posted as guard dogs. In *Curtis v Betts* (1990), the characteristic was the tendency of the dog to act aggressively when protecting its property.

In *Chauhan v Paul* (1995), a Rottweiler playfully chased a postman down a drive, causing him to fall and injure himself. The dog was of previous good character and was described as a 'big softie'. The Court of Appeal was sceptical that this was a blameworthy characteristic within s 2(2)(b) of the Act. However, in any event, there was no evidence to suggest that such behaviour was known to the keeper as stipulated by s 2(2)(c) and, therefore, there was no liability under the Act. The dog's previous good character also ruled out a successful claim under the Occupiers' Liability Act 1957.

12.2.5 The likelihood of the damage being caused or of its being severe

If the animal is of a non-dangerous species, the claimant must prove that the damage was caused by a characteristic of the particular animal which is not normally found in animals of that species, and that the defendant knew of the characteristic. In *Wallace v Newton* (1982), the claimant succeeded in obtaining damages for injuries caused by a horse which became uncontrollable when being put into a trailer for transportation. It was known that the horse was unreliable in this way, and horses are not usually unreliable.

It appears that comparisons need to be drawn between the particular animal and others of the same breed (*Hunt v Wallis* (1991)), rather than other animals of the same species, despite the fact that the word 'species' is used in the Act. This is but one example of the difficulties of interpretation with which the courts have been faced in dealing with the Animals Act 1971.

12.2.6 Characteristics known to that keeper, etc

The knowledge which is required for there to be liability is actual knowledge. It is not enough if the keeper did not actually know of the dangerous characteristic of the animal, nor if an employee who does not have charge of the animal knows about the dangerous propensity. Similarly, if a minor under 16 who is not a keeper of the animal knows of the dangerous qualities of the animal but does not tell the keeper, there will be no liability under s 2(2). Nor will there be liability under s 2(2) if the keeper did not actually know of an animal's dangerous characteristic, but ought reasonably to have known, though there may be liability in negligence. In *Draper v Hodder* (1972), the only liability was in negligence because the keeper did not know of any particular characteristic of the particular animals which are not peculiar to the Jack Russell breed as a whole, but as the harm was foreseeable, there was liability in negligence.

The determination of the animal's 'characteristics' is very difficult. In *Hunt v Wallis* (1992), it was held that assessment of characteristics should be based on the breed, rather than on 'dogs' more generally.

12.2.7 Defences

Under the Animals Act 1971, there are a number of defences to s 2.

- *Volenti* **(s 5)**

  The defendant will escape liability if the damage was due 'wholly to the fault of the person suffering it'.

  If a person is an employee of a keeper, he is not to be treated as voluntarily accepting a risk if that risk is ordinarily incidental to the employment (s 6(5)).

  A person who is injured by an animal when trespassing on the defendant's premises may be treated as *volenti*, subject to proper warnings being given of the existence of the dangerous animal (*Cummings v Grainger* (1977)).

  The question of what constitutes consent in this context was considered by the Court of Appeal in *Dhesi v Chief Constable of West Midlands Police* (2000). Here, a suspect ignored clear warnings by a police officer that he must come out of his hiding place among brambles, or a dog would be sent in. The suspect brought a claim alleging a breach of s 2(2) of the Animals Act 1971. The Court of Appeal ruled that the claimant only had himself to blame when he refused to come out and was bitten several times.

- **Contributory negligence (s 10)**

  If there is contributory negligence on the part of the claimant damages will be apportioned.

- **Trespass (s 5(3))**

  If the claimant was a trespasser on the defendant's property, the keeper will not be liable if he can prove that the animal was not kept on the premises for the protection of persons or property *or* if it was there to protect the premises or people on them, keeping it there for that purpose was not unreasonable.

  In *Cummings v Grainger* (1977), it was held that the keeping of a dog to guard a scrap-yard was not unreasonable because there was no other realistic way of protecting the premises. This decision might now be different in the light of the Guard Dogs Act 1995 which had not come into force when the events of the case occurred. Although the Guard Dogs Act 1995 does not confer a right to a civil action, it might affect civil liability indirectly by the suggestion that keeping such a dog is 'unreasonable'.

After several tragic incidents in which young children were savaged by guard dogs, Parliament passed the Guard Dogs Act 1975 which makes it a criminal offence to allow a guard dog to roam on premises without a handler.

The Animals Act 1971 does not contemplate the defences of act of God and act of a stranger which apply in other areas in which strict liability exists.

12.2.8 Damage by dogs to livestock

The keeper of a dog which injures livestock is liable for any damage so caused by s 3 of the Animals Act 1971, except where the Act provides defences. Liability is strict and it is not necessary to show that the animal was known to have a dangerous propensity to chase livestock.

There is a defence if the dog injures the animals straying onto land belonging to its owner, or on land where the dog was permitted to be by the occupier.

Fault of the claimant and contributory negligence are also defences.

There is a defence to the killing or injuring of a dog in order to protect livestock on land belonging to the defendant or his or her employer. The defence is available to any person acting on the authority of the owner of the land and livestock.

However, if a dog is injured or killed in this way, the police must be notified within 48 hours.

This defence will not be available if the person whose dog was involved in the incident would not have been liable because the livestock had strayed (see s 5(4)).

The defence will only apply if the person was properly acting in defence of livestock, which means (s 9(3)) that either:

- the dog was worrying or about to worry livestock and there are no other reasonable means of ending or preventing the worrying; or

- the dog has been worrying livestock, has not left the vicinity and is not under the control of any person, and there are no practical means of ascertaining to whom the animal belongs.

Reasonable belief that the above is true will be enough for the purposes of the defence.

12.3   Livestock

In country areas solicitors are not infrequently asked to deal with problems which arise when livestock stray onto highways and farmland.

12.3.1 Trespassing livestock

The problem of livestock straying onto other people's land was dealt with in the old common law by the very ancient action of cattle trespass. This is now covered by s 4 of the Animals Act 1971 which creates strict liability for the owner of such livestock where damage is caused by the livestock to land, or to property on land in the occupation or possession of another person; or any expenses are reasonably incurred by the other person in keeping the livestock while it cannot be restored to the person to whom it belongs, or while it is detained, or in ascertaining to whom it belongs.

12.3.2 Definition

Livestock is defined as: cattle, horses, asses, mules, hinnies, sheep, pigs, goats, poultry and deer not in the wild state (s 11).

Personal injuries are not covered by the section, the common law rule having been abolished by the Animals Act 1971 (s 4(1)(a)).

12.3.3 Defences

Defences include the following:

- **Fault of the claimant (s 5(1)) and contributory negligence (s 10)**

  There will be no defence if the animals strayed onto the claimant's land merely because there was no adequate fencing which could have prevented the animals straying onto the land; but there will be a defence if it can be shown that the straying of the livestock onto the land would not have occurred but for a breach by any other person (being a person with an interest in the land), of a duty to fence (s 5(6)). This means that although there is no general duty on landowners to fence their property to keep out straying livestock, if an obligation to fence does exist (and in some areas such duties arise customarily, and on other occasions they may arise as a result of easements or contracts), there will be a defence if the fencing was not carried out.

- **Animals straying from the highway**

  There will be a defence if animals which had previously lawfully been on the highway, stray onto the claimant's land (s 5(5)) (*Tillet v Ward* (1882)). At common law, it was considered to be a hazard of living close to a highway that animals which were being driven along it might stray onto property which adjoined the highway.

By s 5(5): 'A person is not liable under s 4 of this Act where livestock strayed from a highway and its presence there was a lawful use of the highway.'

What is lawful use of the highway will depend on the circumstances of the case. At common law, when animals were regularly driven along highways to market, there was considerable tolerance of the presence of animals on the roads. However, the more modern approach is probably that in *Matthews v Wicks* (1978), when the Court of Appeal held that it was not lawful use of a highway for the defendant to allow animals to wander there at will, so the defence under s 5(5) did not apply.

It is not clear whether there will be strict liability or liability in negligence for animals which escape first from land onto the highway and thence onto other land.

- **Animals which stray onto the highway**

  It may be possible to bring an action under s 2 of the Animals Act 1971 against the keeper of domesticated animals which escape onto a highway and cause injuries there if the animals exhibit abnormal characteristics in so doing. However, an attempt to rely on this was unsuccessful in *Jaundrill v Gillett* (1996). Here, a third party maliciously released horses onto a highway. The court held that horses which were galloping and panicking did not display abnormal characteristics. It seems that judges tend to exonerate claimants who cannot themselves be regarded as blameworthy,

  The rule at common law that landowners had no duty to keep their animals off the highway was abolished by s 8(1) of the Animals Act 1971. The ordinary principles of negligence now apply in this context.

  However, in an action for negligence to claim compensation for damage done by animals straying onto the highway from land which is unfenced, the person responsible for such animals will not be regarded as having committed a breach of duty to take care by reason only of placing the animals on the land if: the land is common land, or is in an area where fencing is not customary, or is a town or village green, and he had a right to place the animals on the land.

  Under the Registration of Commons Act 1971, everyone who had a right to graze animals on land such as common land was obliged to register that right or to lose it. It is thus easier now to prove such rights than it was before the Act.

12.4 Remoteness of damage

The Animals Act 1971 does not deal with the question of remoteness of damage, and the only means of discovering the correct approach to this matter is by examining the common law relating to animals in particular and to strict liability generally.

Most writers take the view that as many of the actions concerning damage caused by animals have several features in common with the rule in *Rylands v Fletcher* (1868), the same basic principles should apply in relation to the torts concerning animals as would apply under the rule in *Rylands v Fletcher*, which was excluded by the Privy Council from the *Wagon Mound* (1961) test for remoteness of damage. This would at any rate apply in the case of cattle trespass, now modified under the Animals Act 1971 as liability for straying livestock. Keepers of dangerous animals are liable for all the damage they cause under s 2(1), and the test seems to be one of directness rather than foreseeability once a causal link has been established.

In the case of animals of non-dangerous species, it has been seen that liability is limited to damage which is the result of unusual characteristics in the particular animal which were known to the keeper (*Granville v Sutton* (1928)). The precise damage suffered by the claimant does not, it seems, if the common law is followed, need to be foreseeable (*Behrens v Bertram Mills Circus* (1957)). There are cases which take the contrary position, however, and the law remains unclear on this point.

12.5 Damages

Damages are assessed in the usual way, and compensation may be available for psychiatric injury as well as physical harm. In *James v Oatley* (1995), the claimant who had been bitten by a dog received damages for loss of use of a limb, pain and suffering and post-traumatic stress disorder.

LIABILITY FOR ANIMALS

Common law relating to animals

This area of law is now governed by the Animals Act 1971, but there are still some relevant common law provisions which deal with certain aspects of the harm done by animals:

- nuisance for stenches created by animals (*Rapier v London Tramways* (1893));
- negligence (*Gomberg v Smith* (1962); *Draper v Hodder* (1972); *Birch v Mills* (1995); *Mason v Wells* (1990));
- public nuisance (*Pitcher v Martin* (1937); *Leeman v Montague* (1936));
- trespass to goods (*Manton v Brocklebank* (1923));
- *Rylands v Fletcher (Brady v Warren* (1900));
- trespass to land (*League against Cruel Sports v Scott* (1985));
- private nuisance of various kinds (*Seligman v Docker* (1949)).

The Animals Act 1971

The Animals Act 1971 applies concurrently with the common law.

Dangerous species

Dangerous species is defined as 'species not commonly domesticated in the British Isles, and whose fully grown animals are likely, unless restrained to cause severe damage, or any damage they may cause is likely to be severe'.

The 'keeper' is responsible, that is, the owner, or, if the owner is under 16, the head of the household, or if the animal is a stray, the person who was the keeper immediately beforehand (*Tutin v Chipperfields* (1980)).

The keeper is *strictly* liable for *any* damage the animal causes. Licences and insurance are compulsory under the Dangerous Wild Animals Act 1976.

Non-dangerous species

The keeper of a non-dangerous species is liable if:

- the damage is of a kind which the animal, unless restrained, was likely to cause, or if caused, was likely to be severe; and
- the likelihood was due to the unusual characteristics of the particular animal, not normally found in animals of the same species (*Barnes v Lucillie* (1906)); and

- the keeper or his or her employee or head of the household if the keeper is under 16 knew of those characteristics. Note that actual knowledge is required:

  Wallace v Newton (1982);

  Hunt v Wallis (1991);

  Jaundrill v Gillett (1996);

  Chauhan v Paul (1995).

There may be liability in negligence if there is no actual knowledge on the part of the person responsible but he or she ought to have known of the dangerous characteristics (*Draper v Hodder* (1972)).

Defences

Defences include *volenti*, contributory negligence and trespass (s 5(3)).

(Note the Guard Dogs Act 1975.)

- Damage by dogs to livestock: s 3 of the Animals Act 1971 (strict liability) (*Dhesi v Chief Constable of West Midlands* (2000)).

  There will be a defence if the livestock had strayed onto land belonging to the owner of the dog, or other land where the dog was permitted to go by the occupier.

- Defence to killing dogs which worry livestock.

  The police must be notified within 48 hours. The owner of the dog must have been acting in defence of livestock.

- Trespassing and straying livestock, s 4 of the Animals Act 1971 (strict liability).

  The definition of livestock: cattle, horses, asses, mules, hinnies, sheep, pigs, goats, poultry and tame deer.

  There is no strict liability for personal injuries caused by straying livestock.

Where animals stray onto the highway, defences include fault of the claimant and contributory negligence.

The person responsible for animals which stray onto a highway and do damage there may have a defence to a negligence action if the land was common land or an area where it is customary not to fence, and he or she had a right to put animals on the land.

If animals are lawfully on the highway, the owner may have a defence if they stray off the highway, onto adjoining land.

Damages

Damages may be awarded for psychological as well as physical injury caused by animals (*James v Oatley* (1995)).

CHAPTER 13

TRESPASS TO THE PERSON

13.1 Introduction

In early English law, physical interference with the person was given special protection, partly to avoid the unhappy consequences of people taking the law into their own hands by revenge attacks. Until the abolition of the old forms of action in the 19th century, *direct* attacks upon the person were protected by the action of trespass, which required no proof of damage. *Indirect* interference with the person was protected by the action on the 'case', which did require proof of damage.

Today, the basic position is that direct and intentional acts of interference are still dealt with by the tort of trespass, while indirect and unintentional acts fall under the tort of negligence. However, the situation is more complex than this suggests, and some authorities believe that, even in trespass, the claimant must now establish intention or negligence in addition to the act of interference.

In *Fowler v Lanning* (1959), Diplock J stated the position as follows:

Trespass to the person does not lie if the injury to the claimant, although the direct consequence of the act of the defendant, was caused unintentionally and without negligence on the defendant's part.

This appears to suggest that there is a form of negligent trespass, which is almost a contradiction in terms.

In *Letang v Cooper* (1965), Denning MR took the view that the deciding factor between trespass and negligence was that, if the act was intentional, it should be remedied by an action for trespass, if unintentional, by an action for negligence.

In *Wilson v Pringle* (1986), the Court of Appeal decided that the claim must be brought in negligence if the defendant acted unintentionally, even if in other respects the fact situation might have fallen within the tort of trespass.

The situation will be clarified by detailed study of the torts which fall under the general heading of 'trespass to the person'.

There are three forms of trespass to the person: assault, battery and false imprisonment. The tort in *Wilkinson v Downton* (1897) will also be dealt with in this section.

13.2 The relationship between civil law and criminal injuries compensation

Before dealing with the torts in detail, it is necessary to place them in the general context of compensation for criminal injuries, as it is not only the law of tort which compensates the victims of assaults and batteries.

As assault and battery are also criminal offences, there may be compensation forthcoming from the state under the Criminal Injuries Compensation Scheme in the same fact situations as give rise to the civil actions. Indeed, it is comparatively rare for civil claims to be brought, unless the defendant or his employer is wealthy enough to afford substantial compensation and the claimant wishes to make an example of him, as in some of the actions brought against police officers in recent years.

13.3 The Criminal Injuries Compensation Scheme

The Criminal Injuries Compensation Scheme was first introduced in 1964, and was designed to provide financial support by the state for the victims of violent crime who suffer personal injuries as a result. A statutory scheme was established in 1988 by the Criminal Justice Act, and revisions of the basic scheme took effect in 1990. The scheme is administered by the Criminal Injuries Compensation Board which is staffed by lawyers, and is responsible for the distribution of financial compensation on behalf of the government. Although there is no appeal against decisions made by the Board, its decisions are subject to judicial review (*R v Criminal Injuries Compensation Board ex p Lain* (1967)).

In order to succeed in a claim, the claimant does not need to establish that there has been a criminal conviction, though there is a discretion for the Board to refuse compensation or to make a lower award if the claimant failed to take reasonable steps to give the police details about how the injury occurred, or to cooperate in the criminal investigation. In the past, the Board took a moralistic approach to compensation in that it would reduce or withhold a payment in the light of the claimant's own 'way of life', even if it was unconnected causally with the injury. This approach received much criticism, not least because it denied a remedy when tort would not have done so, and under the new provisions in 1990, the Board can no longer take general lifestyle of victims into account, though their criminal records and conduct in relation to the particular crime are still relevant considerations. Certain injuries such as those caused by domestic violence and some of those resulting from the use of vehicles (which are covered by insurance or the Motor Insurers' Bureau) are excluded from the jurisdiction of the Board, or can only be compensated at the discretion of the Board.

In assessing damages, the Board has traditionally used the same principles as are applied by the courts when quantifying damages in tort.

There was an attempt by Michael Howard, the Home Secretary, in 1994, to change, without formal legislation, the basis of compensation under the scheme by the introduction of a tariff which would have resulted in substantially reduced compensation for many victims of crime. In an example quoted in *The Times* (16 January 1996), a nurse who was assaulted by a patient, and was reduced to using a home help and to taking anti-depressants, was awarded £126,943 but, under the proposed new scheme, she would only have received £5,000 because it would not have allowed, among other awards, compensation for loss of earnings. Under the proposed tariff, rape victims would have received the same amount as those with minor broken bones, and child abuse victims the same as people with broken noses. However, in an action for judicial review brought by the Fire Brigades Union, the House of Lords ruled that the Home Secretary had acted unlawfully in attempting to introduce the new scheme without reference to Parliament. The decision means that any tariff system has to be introduced by legislation, so under the Criminal Injuries Compensation Act 1995 a framework for implementing a new scheme was established. The scheme, which has now come into force, provides a better deal for victims than the previous Howard proposals because it does allow provision for loss of future earnings and loss of dependency and the tariff has a larger range.

The Criminal Injuries Compensation scheme has not been without its critics (see, especially, Atiyah, PS, *Accidents, Compensation and the Law*, Cane, P (ed), 1999). Some take the view that the scheme selects a group of injured people and singles them out for special treatment which is denied to other victims. However, it appears that many applicants are happy with the way in which the scheme is run, and although concern has been expressed about the delays in resolving claims, the majority of claimants appear to be satisfied with the outcome of their claims.

The case of *Hill v Chief Constable of West Yorkshire* (1989) demonstrates that the courts are influenced by the fact that a remedy may be available under the Criminal Injuries Compensation Scheme when considering whether a duty of care is owed in negligence. Fox LJ took the view that if there had been no provision for compensation under the scheme, there might have been a good reason for imposing a duty of care on the police in relation to the victims of crime.

13.4 Compensation orders

The courts have power to order people who are convicted of criminal offences to pay compensation to their victims. Such compensation is not limited to violent offenders, nor to cases involving personal injuries (see ss 35–38 of the

Powers of Criminal Courts Act 1973, as amended). There will be no compensation orders made when the crime involved a road accident, unless the offender stole the car, or for some reason compensation was not payable by the Motor Insurers' Bureau. Nor can an award, except for bereavement or funeral expenses, be made to the dependants of a deceased person. The courts must assess the compensation payable in the light of the offender's ability to pay, and in the magistrates' court, the maximum payable is £2,000.

Compensation by offenders receives the approval of most of the writers on the subject, as it is seen to benefit the offender by offering some means of rehabilitation, and the criminal justice system as a whole by encouraging more victims to report crime and cooperate with the police.

13.4.1 An important drawback

If a summary criminal prosecution is brought for *assault and battery* (that is, in the magistrates' court), no civil action can follow in respect of the same events (ss 42–45 of the Offences Against the Person Act 1861). It is therefore necessary to sue before any criminal proceedings begin, though, from the claimant's point of view, it is easier to prove a civil case once there has been a successful prosecution, as the standard of proof in civil cases is lower than that in criminal cases. Many solicitors advise their clients to let the prosecution proceed and to apply for a compensation order if a conviction is likely and the suspect has sufficient means to be able to pay compensation. At least this has the advantage of being quicker and cheaper than bringing a civil action, though the victim would need to bear in mind that the criminal standard of proof cannot always be met and that there may be various complicating factors such as plea bargaining, where the offender is charged with several offences involving other victims, which could mean that there is no conviction for the particular crime from which he suffered. One advantage of the action for trespass over negligence is that as it is actionable without proof of damage it is able to protect civil rights.

13.5   Actions against the police

Actions for trespass to the person are now frequently brought to deal with allegations of police misconduct. In these cases, the claimant may only be wanting to make a point, rather than to seek compensation, and may not have suffered any actual damage. Although actions for negligence are sometimes brought against the police, unlike in trespass, it is necessary to prove damage in order to succeed, and many negligence actions against the police fail at the duty stage (*Hill v Chief Constable of West Yorkshire* (1990)).

The Police and Criminal Evidence Act (PACE) 1984 places obligations on the police in relation to people held in custody for questioning during the investigation of crimes. Codes of Practice made under the Act set out guidelines which the police are expected to follow when dealing with suspects.

Breaches of the Act and Codes of Practice may also amount to breaches of the civil law, and could result in actions for compensation. It is significant that many of the provisions which create additional police powers are contained in PACE 1984 itself, and appear to have greater authority than the safeguards for the citizen which are to be found in the Codes of Practice.

Between 1988 and 1993, the Metropolitan Police paid almost £1.9 million in settlements and £758,000 in court damages, but disciplinary action was only taken against officers in 20% of cases in which the damages exceeded £10,000 (*Independent*, 15 April 1993).

In the case of complaints against the police, it is possible to make a complaint using the police complaints system. Set up under PACE in 1984, this system allows both informal and formal resolution procedures to be invoked. The formal procedure is supervised by the Police Complaints Authority, whose role is not to intervene but merely to supervise the conduct of complaints and to receive reports about them.

There has been general dissatisfaction expressed with the operation of the procedure, which seldom results in disciplinary action being brought against police officers, and is time-consuming and often ineffective. One particular drawback from the complainant's point of view is that an unsubstantiated complaint may result in a civil action for libel being brought against him or her, as initial complaints are not covered by the defence of absolute privilege (*Conery v Jacklin* (1985)). There may be a defence of qualified privilege but that will be lost if the person making the complaint is found to have acted with improper motive amounting to malice (*Fraser v Mirza* (1993)). Prosecutions for wasting police time are also brought on occasion (*R v Blaney* (1982)).

The procedures have been particularly criticised for lack of impartiality, because complaints against the police are investigated and overseen by police officers, and complainants who are not entitled to full and frank explanations of the findings are often denied full knowledge of the circumstances and outcome of complaints. An amended Police Complaints System has been proposed. A much more certain way of obtaining satisfaction is to sue for damages in tort.

A further disadvantage in using the system is that awards made under the Police Complaints Procedure may well not be as high as those made by juries in civil cases.

Proposals to change the police complaints system are being considered by the government, and it is hoped that the changes which will speed up procedures and abolish the right of officers not to give account of themselves to their seniors will be introduced.

There have been many successful civil actions for assault, battery and false imprisonment against the police in recent years, and as it is possible to obtain exemplary damages in these cases, some of the awards have been very high indeed, for example, in *Taylor v Metropolitan Police Commissioner* (1992), the claimant was awarded £100,000 after he had cannabis planted on him and was held against his will in a police station for several hours. He was a BBC engineer, and a lay-preacher, and had been on his way to a dominoes match at the time he was arrested. Like actions for libel and slander (which are also brought against the police when there have been false allegations against a suspect), malicious prosecution and false imprisonment must still be tried by jury, and there can be considerable sympathy excited in cases like that of Mr Taylor which result in extra compensation being awarded to express the jury's strong disapproval of the way in which the police have behaved.

In *Goswell v Comr of Police for the Metropolis* (1998), the claimant received an award of £47,600 when he was hit very hard with a truncheon and was falsely imprisoned for a short time.

In *Holden v Chief Constable of Lancashire* (1986), the Court of Appeal held that an unconstitutional act by a police officer which is arbitrary and oppressive can attract exemplary damages. The officer in this case had unlawfully arrested the claimant and held him for only 20 minutes.

The police also settle many cases out of court to avoid the adverse publicity which they attract. For example, in 1991, Lynford Christie, the athlete was awarded a 'huge sum' in an out-of-court settlement, for assault, battery, false imprisonment and libel ((1990) *Independent*, 14 March).

Some examples of the awards in such cases, some of which are brought against store-detectives for false allegations of shop-lifting, are as follows:

- *Warby and Chastell v Tesco Stores* (1989): £22,000 for libel, slander and false imprisonment;

- *White and Another v Metropolitan Police Commissioner* (1982): £51,000 for false imprisonment, assault and battery and malicious prosecution, including £40,000 exemplary damages;

- *Lawrence v Chief Constable of Dyfed and Powys* (1983): £600 for 21 hours' false imprisonment, when his initial arrest was lawful, but the length of detention was unreasonable;

- *George v Metropolitan Police Commissioner* (1984): £8,000 assault and battery, and trespass to land, including £2,000 exemplary damages;

- *White v WP Brown* (1983): a 72 year old woman was wrongly arrested by a store detective, and her handbag confiscated; £775 for trespass to goods, £520 for false imprisonment.

13.6   Assault and battery

The torts of assault and battery are usually dealt with together, because it is unusual, though possible, for them not to be committed concurrently or simultaneously.

Assault is putting a person in fear of an immediate battery, and battery is the actual application of physical force, however slight, without lawful justification.

13.6.1 Assault

Although assault seldom occurs without battery, it may be possible to sue for assault alone.

- **Putting a person in fear**

  It is possible for there to be an assault without a battery, as in *Stephens v Myers* (1830) in which the defendant made a violent gesture at the claimant by waving a clenched fist, but was prevented from reaching him by the intervention of a third party. The defendant was liable for assault.

  It is not necessary to prove that the claimant actually experienced fear. What must be proved is that it was reasonable for the claimant to expect an immediate battery.

- **Immediate battery**

  If it is clearly impossible for the defendant to carry out the threat, an action for assault will not succeed. In *Thomas v National Union of Mineworkers (South Wales Area)* (1985), there was no assault when the picketing miners made violent gestures to working miners who were safely in vehicles behind police barricades. Here, there was no danger of an immediate battery.

  The defendant may, by his own words, negate the possibility of a battery, as in *Tuberville v Savage* (1669), in which the defendant said, with his hand on his sword: 'If it were not Assize time, I would not take such language from you.' It was held that there was no assault in this case.

  Threatening words alone, unaccompanied by a threatening act, may amount to an assault, but opinion is divided on this point, with the two cases which considered the matter also taking opposite views (see Rogers, WVH (ed), *Winfield and Jolowicz on Tort*, 1998).

  An innocent act can be made into an assault by words which contain a threat (*Read v Coker* (1853)).

13.6.2 Battery

Battery is application of direct physical force to the claimant. The merest touching is probably enough to amount to a battery. Holt CJ said in the early case of *Cole v Turner* (1704): 'The least touching of another in anger is a battery.'

- **The application of force**

  It has been held that certain forms of 'social touching' which are reasonable and generally acceptable are not batteries. These would include jostling in a crowd during the January sales, touching to catch a person's attention and a hearty slap on the back by way of congratulation. A factor common to these socially acceptable batteries is that they lack the element of hostility, but bearing in mind that from the earliest times battery could be committed without the intention to injure, the real answer to the fact that such acts are not regarded as tortious, would seem to be that in such cases there is implied consent to the touching.

  Surprisingly, *Wilson v Pringle* (1986), a relatively recent decision in the long history of this tort, appears to place a new limitation on the tort of battery, by imposing the requirement of 'hostile touching'. In that case, a schoolboy was injured when a bag he was carrying over his shoulder was pulled roughly by another boy. Despite the defendant's argument that what had happened was mere horseplay, it was held that the court must decide whether the conduct was hostile.

- **Intention**

  The intention which is required in battery is not the intention to hurt the claimant, but the intention to apply physical force (see Trindade (1982)). The tort thus protects the claimant's dignity as well as bodily integrity (see *Wilson v Pringle* (1986) above).

  A surgeon who performs an operation or other medical procedure without the consent of the patient commits the tort of battery, but in such a case there may well be every intention to act in the patient's best interests as the doctor sees them, and no intention to harm the patient (*Potts v North West RHA* (1983)).

  Even if the defendant intended to injure someone other than the claimant, this could still amount to battery if as a consequence the claimant suffers some application of force. In *Livingstone v Minister of Defence* (1984), the claimant succeeded in battery when he was hit by a bullet intended by a soldier for someone else.

  Some examples of incidents which have amounted to batteries include:

  - *Nash v Sheen* (1953). The defendant, a hairdresser, gave the claimant an unwanted tone rinse, a form of hair dye, when she had requested a perm.

○ *Pursell v Horn* (1838). The defendant threw water over the claimant.

○ *Connor v Chief Constable of Cambridgeshire* (1984). A football supporter was hit by a police truncheon.

○ *Leon v Metropolitan Police Commissioner* (1986). A Rastafarian suspected of carrying drugs, was pulled off a bus by police officers and punched and kicked.

○ *Ballard, Stewart-Park and Findlay v Metropolitan Police Commissioner* (1983). Three feminists were attacked by police officers during a demonstration in Soho. One was dropped spread-eagled onto the ground after being carried away unceremoniously by officers, one was straddled by another officer when she lay on the ground, and poked in the stomach with a truncheon and hit over the eye. The third was hit in the head with a truncheon.

It is possible to bring a civil action for assault and battery in certain circumstances when the Crown Prosecution Service refuse to prosecute. For example, a woman recently succeeded in a county court action against her former employer for rape and was awarded £50,000 by jury. The Crown Prosecution Service had refused to prosecute the man because they did not consider that a prosecution would succeed on the evidence. The claimant was able to satisfy the lower standard of proof required in a civil action (*Griffiths v Williams, Truro County Court* (1996)).

- **Without lawful justification**

   Defences to assault and battery will be discussed at the end of the section on false imprisonment, as many of the defences are common to all three torts.

13.7 False imprisonment

False imprisonment consists of depriving the claimant of freedom of movement without lawful justification. There is no need to prove fault (see 13.7.4).

In *Collins v Wilcock* (1984), false imprisonment was defined as 'the unlawful imposition of restraint on another's freedom of movement'.

13.7.1 Restraint is necessary

The tort is committed if there is any act which prevents free movement. This does not necessarily mean that the claimant must be imprisoned, although some of the most serious examples of false imprisonment in recent years have involved the detention of people for questioning in respect of crimes which they did not commit, and for which there were no reasonable grounds of suspicion (*White v WP Brown* (1983)). Any restriction which prevents a person leaving a place amounts to false imprisonment. This means that simply turning a key in a lock or posting a guard outside a door is false imprisonment. An unlawful stop and search in the street would be false imprisonment if the claimant was trapped against a wall. Sitting a person between two police officers in the back of a police vehicle would also be false imprisonment if it was not part of a lawful arrest or there was no consent (see *Goswell v Comr of Police for the Metropolis* (1998)).

13.7.2 Restraint must be 'total'

The restraint imposed upon the claimant must be total restraint to amount to false imprisonment, so, if there was a reasonable escape route, there will be no false imprisonment (*Bird v Jones* (1848)). If the occupier of premises decides to place reasonable conditions on people who use the premises, this will not amount to false imprisonment. In *Robinson v Balmain Ferry Company* (1910), a ferry company put up notices that a penny had to be paid to enter or leave the wharf on one side of the river. The claimant changed his mind about taking the ferry crossing after he had paid his penny and passed through a turnstile. He refused to pay another penny to leave, and was prevented from doing so by the defendants unless he paid. It was held that this was not false imprisonment because the conditions imposed by the defendants were not unreasonable. The claimant did have a means of free exit, even if it meant taking the ferry, which he had chosen not to do.

In *Herd v Weardale Steel, Coal and Coke Co Ltd* (1915), it was held that there was no false imprisonment when a miner decided to strike when he was already in the mine, because he did not wish to carry out a task which he considered to be particularly dangerous. The defendants would not allow him to leave the mine before the end of his shift. The House of Lords held that the defence of consent was available to the employer. This decision is difficult to reconcile with other decisions and can perhaps be explained by the fact that the defendants were omitting to act rather than committing a positive act.

13.7.3 Knowledge of the restraint at the time is not necessary

The claimant does not need to know that he has been restrained in order to succeed in his action. In *Meering v Graham White Aviation Co Ltd* (1920), it was held that a person could be falsely imprisoned while unconscious. This was confirmed in *Murray v Minister of Defence* (1988).

The person who initiated the imprisonment may be liable even if the physical act of restraining the claimant was performed by someone else. This can happen sometimes when store detectives call the police and there is no justification for the original citizen's arrest.

There is no fixed period of restraint required, and even a very short period of confinement will amount to false imprisonment, though any damages payable in such a case would be nominal, unless there is an award of exemplary damages as in *Holden v Chief Constable of Lancashire* (1986).

13.7.4 Examples

Some examples of false imprisonment are as follows:

- *Lawrence v Chief Constable of Dyfed-Powys Police* (1985)

  The claimant was arrested, suspected of holiday cottage arsons, and held in isolation for 21 hours except for a single brief interview. The length of detention was held to be unreasonable, and he was awarded £600 damages.

- *Houghton v Chief Constable of Greater Manchester* (1986)

  The claimant was arrested and detained for over two and a half hours on suspicion of the offence of impersonating a police officer. A police officer had noticed him leaving a fancy dress party carrying a truncheon and dressed as a policeman. He received an award of £600 damages.

- *White v WP Brown* (1983)

  The claimant was an elderly lady who had been detained in a changing cubicle for 15 minutes by a store detective after she was thought to have stolen a birthday card. Her handbag had been taken away and searched, and eventually the police took her to the police station in the back of a police van. She received £520 damages for false imprisonment and £775 for trespass to her handbag.

- *Treadaway v Chief Constable of the West Midlands* (1994)

  The claimant alleged that while he was being interviewed by the police they had placed a bag over his head, threatening to suffocate him in order to extract a confession from him. Medical evidence confirmed his version of events. He was awarded £2,500 compensatory damages and £7,500 aggravated damages, with an additional award of £40,000 exemplary damages to reflect the serious misconduct of the police officers concerned, even though he was a convicted criminal.

- *Hsu v Comr of Police for the Metropolis* (1997)

  A hairdresser was arrested after he refused to allow police officers to enter his house without a warrant following a dispute with a tenant. He was grabbed and handcuffed and thrown into a police van where he was punched and used as a footstool. He was verbally abused at the police station with expressions such as 'I have never arrested a chink before'. When he was finally released, he was sent out into the street wearing only jeans at 11pm, and had to walk the two miles home in flip-flops. When he arrived home, he discovered that his front door had been left open and some of his property had been stolen. Doctors at Kings College Hospital confirmed that he had extensive and severe bruising to his back and kidneys and had blood in his urine, all of these injuries being consistent with his story of police misconduct. A complaint to the Police Complaints Authority was turned down, so Mr Hsu sued, and was awarded damages, reduced on appeal to £50,000.

• *Holland v Comr of Police for the Metropolis* (1993)

In an out of court settlement, Mrs Holland was paid £25,000. She had been suing the police for assault, battery, malicious prosecution and false imprisonment after police officers had refused to believe her when she explained that she was not displaying a tax disc on her car because she had recently purchased the car and had applied for the tax. She alleged that she had been pushed into a police van and taken to a police station where she had been detained for four hours. Two police officers had made statements alleging that she had pushed an officer in the chest and used abusive language to the police. These, it was alleged, were false statements. When Mrs Holland was prosecuted, she pleaded guilty to the tax disc offence and was fined £15, but her not guilty pleas to the offences of using threatening, abusive and insulting language and behaviour and failing to give her name and address were rejected. On appeal to the Crown Court, she was able to demonstrate that her mother's shop had no letter box, though the police alleged that she had forced them to speak to her through 'the letter box'. Her convictions were quashed. It took Mrs Holland four years to clear her name in this way, and the police offered no apology.

• *Tomlinson v Comr of Police for the Metropolis* (1999)

A £100,000 settlement was reached in a case in which a black estate agent claimed to have been so badly assaulted by the police that he needed several operations to save his sight.

It is now possible for the judge to give guidance to the jury in cases like these as to the range of award most appropriate in the circumstances (*Scotland v Comr of Police of the Metropolis* (1996); *Hsu v Metropolitan Police Comr* (1997)).

It should be noted that because false imprisonment is a tort of strict liability, a defendant who is unaware that he is committing the tort may be liable. In *R v Governor of Brockhill Prison ex p Evans* (2000), the House of Lords found a prison governor liable for a prisoner's detention for a longer period than had been prescribed. The governor was guilty of false imprisonment even though he had not been to blame for miscalculating a prisoner's date for release.

13.8 Defences to assault, battery and false imprisonment

There can on occasion be lawful justification for committing the torts of assault and battery and false imprisonment. General tort defences such as necessity and inevitable accident will apply, and the claimant may be found to be contributorily negligent and damages may be reduced as a result. Certain defences require special consideration.

13.8.1 Self-defence

There has been a common law right of self-defence for centuries, and this is now supplemented by a statutory right to use reasonable force to prevent a crime (s 3(1) of the Criminal Law Act 1967).

The key to a successful defence of self-defence is the element of 'reasonableness', as the defence will only operate if the force used by the defendant is proportionate to that being applied by an attacker (*Lane v Holloway* (1968)). Although it seldom operates in trespass cases, contributory negligence may sometimes apply as a defence in some situations (*Murphy v Culhane* (1977); *Revill v Newbury* (1996)).

This defence is not limited to situations when the attacker threatens personal injury. It can also be used if there is a threat to property. Occupiers may use reasonable force to eject or deter trespassers (*Bird v Holbrook* (1828)).

In *Revill v Newbury* (1996), it was held that the firing of a shot through a hole in a door in the direction of a trespasser, causing serious injury, was excessive force and the defence of self-defence could not apply.

The defence is probably limited to situations in which the defendant reasonably believes that an attack is likely.

In some cases, the Crown Prosecution Service decides to prosecute landowners who use unreasonable force. In 1985, Kenneth Noye, who has since been convicted of a road rage murder, stabbed and killed an undercover police officer in the grounds of his home. He was prosecuted, but was acquitted on the basis of self-defence. In 1993, Dean Davis, a jeweller, stabbed and killed an armed intruder who broke into his house, intending to steal. The two men faced each other in a confined space and there was a scuffle, during which the intruder let off CS gas. Dean Davis was not prosecuted because it was thought that he had acted reasonably in self-defence in a very frightening situation. In April 2000, Tony Martin, a landowner who shot and killed a burglar who was trespassing on his property was convicted of murder and sentenced to life imprisonment. His defence of self-defence failed when the jury heard evidence that he had fired an illegally held shotgun at the intruder until it was empty of bullets. He had previously boasted of his intention to shoot burglars, and had an unusually aggressive attitude towards gypsies and burglars.

13.8.2 Consent

It is unclear whether consent is a true defence or whether it is for the claimant to prove lack of consent in order to succeed in the first place as was decided in

Freeman v Home Office (1983). However, many of the books deal with consent as a defence.

If the claimant consented either expressly or impliedly to the torts of assault and battery, there will be a complete defence.

13.8.3 Sports

Those who participate in sport consent to reasonable contact within the rules of the particular game. However, there are cases in which actions for assault and battery have succeeded when the game has involved considerable hostility and deliberate punches have been thrown (*Macnamara v Duncan* (1979)). Players consent only to reasonable force in all the circumstances and not to negligence (*Condon v Basi* (1985)).

13.8.4 Brawls

Fights in the street or in pubs or clubs will usually attract the defence of consent, or indeed, maybe cases in which the claimant never succeeds in proving the elements of assault and battery because there is consent. If however, force used by one of the participants greatly exceeds that used by the claimant, the defence will not operate. In *Barnes v Nayer* (1986), the claimant's wife was killed by the defendant who had been involved in a long campaign of abuse against the whole family. It was held by the Court of Appeal that the defence could not apply in this case. Nor could the defence of *ex turpi causa* succeed in such circumstances.

13.8.5 Reasonable chastisement

It has traditionally been the case that parents have the legal right to smack their children as part of the administering of reasonable punishment. Any force used to restrain or punish a naughty child must always be reasonable or it will amount to a tort. However, there are many parents who disagree with smacking or hitting of any kind and it is no longer permitted in schools, following a series of European Court of Human Rights rulings. Corporal punishment was first banned in State schools in 1987 and has been banned in all schools since 1998.

A 48 year old Scottish teacher who pulled down his eight year old daughter's pants and spanked her at a health centre was convicted of assault and battery. He had exceeded the bounds of reasonableness.

13.8.6 Medical treatment

The patient who consents to receiving medical treatment is consenting to the torts of assault and battery and possibly false imprisonment in some cases. This is not the same as consenting to negligent treatment.

Patients who are about to undergo surgery are usually asked to sign a consent form, which is a standard form drafted with the advice of lawyers. Patients who go to the doctor or attend hospital for treatments other than surgery, for example, for treatment with medicines or various forms of therapy are taken to have given implied consent merely by consulting the doctor. There are two possible actions available to patients who claim that they have been treated without consents.

(1) If a doctor treats patients *against their will* or by giving *a different treatment* to that for which consent has been given, he or she commits the torts of assault and battery. It is only in very limited circumstances that these actions are available. Thus, if a patient refuses treatment which doctors consider necessary, it has become the practice to seek the advice of the court (*Re C (Refusal of Medical Treatment)* (1994)). In *Re MB* (1997), the Court of Appeal issued detailed guidance for doctors in cases where patients refuse essential surgery. In order for consent to be real, the patient must be broadly aware of the type of treatment and when and where it will be carried out (*Chatterton v Gerson* (1981)).

(2) If the case is one in which the patient has been made aware of the type of treatment but the doctor has failed to give sufficient detail of the risks or side effects involved, the patient would only have a remedy in negligence, which is of course, more difficult to prove than trespass to the person. This is so even if the patient makes inquiries about the risks, as in *Blythe v Bloomsbury HA* (1987). In an action for negligence brought by a patient who complains of lack of information about details of risks and side effects, the court judges the doctor by standard of the *Bolam* test. Thus, as long as the doctor gave such information as would have been given by other doctors acting in accordance with a responsible body of medical opinion, the patient is without a remedy (*Sidaway v Governors of Bethlem Royal Hospital* (1985)). However, in Australia, the High Court, the supreme legal authority there, has recently held that there was negligence in a case in which the patient was particularly worried about the possible serious consequences of her treatment, and repeatedly asked for details of all the risks, to no avail (*Rogers v Whitaker* (1992)).

There is evidence that the UK courts are moving towards a position which demands greater respect for patient autonomy (*Pearce v United Bristol Healthcare Trust* (1999), see Chapter 7).

In February 2000, Ian Brady appeared before Kay J in the High Court in Liverpool to argue for the right to die by starving himself to death (*R v Collins and Ashworth Hospital Authority ex p Brady*). His lawyers argued that it was unlawful for the hospital authorities at Ashworth to force feed him. To do so was assault and battery. They based their position on the argument that Brady's decision to starve himself to death was that of a rational, sane man, and not of a person suffering from a psychiatric disorder. They relied on arguments based on the fact that the Mental Health Act 1983 had been misapplied. They also argued that, in force feeding him, the prison authorities had breached Brady's fundamental human rights. The hearing took place *in camera*, but the judgment was given in open court.

Kay J ruled that Brady should not be allowed to starve himself to death, and that force feeding was not illegal. He based his decision on the psychiatric evidence and concluded that Brady still had symptoms of a mental illness and a psychopathic personality and needed to be hospitalised for reasons of his own health and safety and for the safety of other people. The position in English law in such cases is clear. In *B v Croydon District HA* (1994), the Court of Appeal held that the force feeding of B, who suffered from a mental illness and was detained under s 3 of the Mental Health Act 1983, was not unlawful, and that she could be given treatment which included feeding through a naso-gastric tube or intravenous feeding without consent under s 63 of the Mental Health Act 1963. It was held that the wording of that section, namely, 'any medical treatment given ... for the mental disorder from which he is suffering', included treatment given to relieve any symptoms and consequences of the mental disorder, as well as treatment intended to deal with the cause of the illness. In *Re KB (Adult) (Mental Patient: Medical Treatment)* (1994), it was held by a judge of the Family Division that a patient suffering from anorexia nervosa could lawfully be force fed, as feeding by naso-gastric tube in a case of this kind fell within the provisions of s 63 of the Mental Health Act 1983.

However, if a person is competent, any bodily interference may not take place without the consent of the individual concerned. The case law on this matter concerns refusal of caesarean section operations and other medical procedures such as blood transfusions. The cases indicate that, if a person is competent to make a decision, even if that decision is irrational in itself, there is a need for that person to give consent to any acts that would amount to assault and battery (*Re L* (1996)). In the early case of *Leigh v Gladstone* (1909), it was held that the defence of necessity would apply in a case of battery involving the prolonged force feeding of a suffragette, but the more recent decisions on refusal of consent to medical treatment by competent persons indicate an approach which places greater emphasis on personal autonomy. In *Secretary of State for the Home Department v Robb* (1994), a prisoner went on hunger strike. Although he had been diagnosed as suffering from a personality disorder, he was found on the medical evidence to be of sound mind when he was on hunger strike. As he had the capacity lawfully to refuse food and hydration, it was held that the Home Office was under no duty to prolong his life by force feeding him. Prison officials and the prison medical staff could lawfully abstain from providing him with food and hydration by artificial or natural means. A declaration to that effect was granted by Thorpe J. Authorities from other common law jurisdictions indicate that a similar approach, taking into account the need to recognise the autonomy of prisoners, is taken in some US States (see *Thor v Superior Court* (1993)).

The human rights aspects of the *Brady* case are interesting. There is a positive obligation incorporated into Art 2 of the European Convention on Human Rights, which deals with the right to life. However, this needs to be balanced against the right of an individual not to be subjected to torture or inhuman or degrading treatment. Force feeding could certainly be described as painful, and, by Brady's own account, this was particularly so in his case because no anaesthetic lubricant was used when the naso-gastric tube was inserted to begin force-feeding. However, it probably does not fall within the high level of severity of pain and suffering required to invoke the protection of the Convention. According to Keir Starmer, who cites *X v FRG* (1985):

> It would appear that the positive obligation incorporated in Art 2 can require the authorities to force feed a prisoner who is on hunger strike. Where the authorities do so, it appears that a prisoner cannot claim that the force feeding violated his rights under Art 3.

It would appear, then, that Brady would be unlikely to succeed if he does as he has threatened to do and takes the matter to the European Court of Human Rights. There can only be speculation at present as to whether application of the Convention might result in a return to the approach in *Leigh v Gladstone* (above), in which the Lord Chief Justice directed the jury that it was the duty of prison officers to maintain the life of the suffragette by force feeding her.

The claimant must establish whether negligence or trespass is the correct cause of action, and this could be important for several reasons. First, trespass is actionable without proof of damage, whereas in negligence damage must always be proved. Secondly, it is easier to prove causation in trespass than negligence. Thirdly, there is greater flexibility in the limitation period in medical negligence claims than in claims for trespass (*Stubbings v Webb* (1992) – see Chapter 20).

There are special cases which pose particular problems in relation to consent to medical treatment. The case of children under age 16 years is governed by *Gillick v West Norfolk and Wisbech HA* (1985). The child's capacity to consent depends upon whether he or she has sufficient maturity and understanding as to the nature of the treatment and what it involves. If the child lacks such understanding, the parents may be asked to provide the consent on behalf of the child, but the court has jurisdiction in some cases, to give or refuse consent for the child (*Re B (A Minor) (Wardship, Sterilisation)* (1987)). Several cases have been decided on this point in recent years and a detailed discussion of them is beyond the scope of this book.

Adults who require emergency treatment are taken to give implied consent, even if unconscious and unable to decide for themselves. It would be unlikely that such a person would receive much sympathy from a court if his life had been saved by the treatment which he later complained had been given without consent would not have been given. However, opinion is divided as to whether a doctor should do more than merely what is immediately necessary to save the patient's life, and allow him to decide for himself whether he wants further treatment when he regains consciousness. Theoretically, however, there would be no need to prove damage to succeed in an action for trespass to the person. However, note the position in the light of the Human Rights Act 1998.

A defence of necessity would also apply in cases involving incompetent patients (*F v West Berkshire HA* (1989)), and the doctor has a right to decide what treatment would, according to the *Bolam* test, be in the best interests of the patient. However, as a result of the decision in *F v West Berkshire HA*, doctors are now advised to seek a declaration that non-urgent treatment is lawful before proceeding. The position was further considered in *Re S (Sterilisation: Patient's Best Interests)* (2000) by the Court of Appeal, where the appropriate approach to be taken by a court was considered in deciding whether an incompetent patient should undergo radical and irreversible surgery on order to achieve sterilisation. This was an appeal against a decision by S, a woman with severe learning difficulties who was represented by the Official Solicitor. S, aged 28, attended a day care centre five days a week. Her mother found it increasingly difficult to cope with her. She feared that her daughter might become pregnant. Evidence was presented to the effect that she would find it impossible to cope with pregnancy. Wall J had ruled against the advice of the Official Solicitor that the court was entitled to declare that a particular course of treatment is lawful, provided that it is proper in itself and is in the interests of the patient. S lacked the mental capacity to consent to any form of medical treatment, and Wall J had granted a declaration that a sterilisation operation and/or a hysterectomy could be performed on S for therapeutic purposes.

The Court of Appeal held that the trial judge had failed to give proper weight to medical evidence concerning the considerable strides being made in the field of contraception and therapeutic treatment. Nor had he considered the view that in another five years contraception may have progressed so that something could be given to S to stop her periods altogether. He had not explained why trying out less intrusive methods of contraception and waiting for the outcome of medical advances would not be the right course. It is important that the court considered that the concept of 'best interests' was wider in scope than the medical considerations, and a judge must decide whether to accept or reject the expert medical opinion as to whether an operation is, or is not, in the best interests of a patient.

The Court of Appeal was of the view that, in cases of this kind, judges have a discretion. However, in the present case, the weight of evidence appeared to be impressive in support of the less invasive method of preventing pregnancy. The starting point of any medical decision was the principles set out in the *Bolam* test, but final decision should incorporate broader ethical, social, moral and welfare considerations. It was held that the judge had misapplied the *Bolam* test by concluding that the proposed treatment was within the range of acceptable opinion among responsible practitioners. The decision for surgery was premature and the declarations would be set aside. The appeal was allowed.

Consent will not be valid unless it is given without duress or undue pressure, misrepresentation or mistake.

Under the Mental Health Act 1983, certain forms of medical treatment for serious mental illness do not require consent by the patient but these are subject to checks and safeguards which have satisfied the concerns of many who fear that such provisions create unreasonable restrictions on the freedom of the individual. As in the case of police powers, there is constant concern that the need to protect the public should be balanced against the freedom of the individual.

The Law Commission made detailed proposals in 1995 (Law Commission Report No 123, 1995) in favour of a comprehensive statutory framework covering medical decision making for mentally incapacitated people. The report makes fascinating reading but is now unlikely to be implemented.

13.8.7 Consent to the taking of bodily samples

A number of procedures carried out at police stations to assist criminal investigations can only be undertaken with the consent of the suspect and/or the permission of a senior police officer, of at least the rank of superintendent. Intimate samples, such as swabs from bodily orifices may only be taken with the permission, in writing, of the suspect (ss 62(4) and 63(2) of PACE 1984, as amended). Non-intimate samples, such as finger-nail scrapings can only be taken after the suspect has given written permission (s 61(2)), and fingerprints can only be taken at a police station with the written consent of the suspect (s 65).

As long as the correct procedures are followed, there will be a defence to an action brought against the police for assault and battery, and the strict rules concerning written consent are important safeguards for suspects.

13.8.8 Lawful arrest, detention and stop and search

Under s 1 of PACE 1984, the police have a new power to stop and search persons whom they reasonably suspect may be carrying stolen or prohibited articles. Such a power to stop people in the street in full view of the public is regarded as a serious infringement of personal freedom and is seen by many as being unjustifiable, given that existing police powers were adequate before the Act to achieve the same objective.

An arrest may be made by warrant from a magistrate, and private citizens and police officers have powers of arrest without warrant. Under PACE 1984 and other statutes, the police have extensive powers to make arrests without warrant (see Leigh, L, *Police Powers in England and Wales*, 2nd edn, 1985).

What constitutes an arrest has been the subject of much discussion and arrest is still not easily defined (see *Murray v Minister of Defence* (1988)). However, it is clear that, if an arrest is made lawfully, there will be a defence to actions for assault, battery and false imprisonment.

While it is unclear exactly what an arrest entails, it is clear that the requirements of a lawful arrest include:

- an arrest made within the powers granted by statute and common law;

- a 'reasonable suspicion' on the part of the person making the arrest. Note this requirement is also present for stop and search;

- force which is used must be in proportion to the amount of force exerted by the suspect (s 117 of PACE 1984).

The common law and statutory powers, although complex, are not difficult to discover, and every police officer, customs officer, and indeed people like store-detectives who are likely to make arrests in their employment, will receive detailed instruction on this matter. What is much more difficult to establish is what exactly the term 'reasonable suspicion' means. The concept is not defined in PACE 1984, though the Code of Practice made under PACE does attempt to do so. A mere 'hunch' is not enough, there must be enough circumstantial evidence to lead a reasonable officer to deduce that the suspect might be guilty. What is reasonable is determined objectively (*Castorina v Chief Constable of Surrey* (1988)). The most recent Code of Practice (1991, HMSO) states:

> Whether reasonable grounds for suspicion exist will depend on the circumstances in each case, but there must be some objective basis for it ... Reasonable suspicion can never be supported on the basis of personal factors alone. For example, a person's colour, age, hairstyle or manner of dress, or the fact that he is known to have a previous conviction for possession of an unlawful article, cannot be used alone or in combination with each other as the sole basis ... Nor may it be founded on the basis of stereotyped images of certain persons or groups as more likely to be committing offences.

Despite this advice, the police do retain an enormous amount of discretion in making an arrest, and there is still evidence that officers are influenced by dress, colour, age and even accent. It would be extremely difficult to prove that an officer lacked reasonable suspicion. Following a series of proven miscarriages of justice, the Runciman Commission has reviewed the whole area of police powers and the way in which they are exercised.

An interesting statement was made by Lord Diplock who gave the only speech in *Mohammed-Holgate v Duke* (1984), in the House of Lords. Lord Diplock took the view that, as a police officer making an arrest is exercising a statutory power, and as he or she is acting as a public servant, the test to apply in deciding whether the police officer was reasonable in suspecting a particular individual is the *Wednesbury* administrative law test. He thought that the same test of *Wednesbury* unreasonableness should also be applied in civil actions for false imprisonment. The test would be: 'Was the officer so unreasonable in his suspicion that no reasonable officer would have arrived at the same conclusion in the circumstances. Did he fail to take matters into account that he should have, and/or consider irrelevant matters?' This novel approach would make it much more difficult for a claimant to succeed in a civil action than hitherto, when the ordinary tort reasonableness test has applied, as the *Wednesbury* test is notoriously difficult to satisfy, creating a difficult hurdle for those who wish to complain about the actions of civil servants. Fortunately, the *Holgate-Mohammed* test appears to have been ignored in later cases.

When an arrest is made, the arresting officer must inform the suspect in general terms and, if possible, precisely, the grounds for the arrest (s 28(3) of PACE 1984). If a person accompanies an officer to a police station merely to help with inquiries without being arrested, he must be told of his right to leave at any time (s 29 of PACE 1984).

PACE 1984 has been much criticised as giving the police too much power without providing adequate safeguards for the citizen (see Baxter, C and Koffman, L (eds), *Police the Constitution and the Community*, 1985). There is an attempt in PACE itself to ensure, among other things, that people who are held in custody receive proper supervision and that adequate records are made of their detention. They should, under normal circumstances, have access to a lawyer, and should not be detained for too long a time without charge. Confessions must not be obtained by 'oppression', and suspects must be informed of their rights. The Codes of Practice also aim to ensure that conditions in custody are comfortable. However, there are a number of exceptions to the basic safeguards in PACE 1984, depending on the seriousness of offences which do allow the police considerable discretion in the way they deal with suspects. The European Court of Human Rights has been critical of the long periods of custody before charge which are permitted in PACE 1984 (*Brogan v UK* (1989)).

People may only be kept in custody during the investigation of crimes according to the conditions and time limits laid down in PACE 1984, until such time as it is possible to charge them. If there is not enough evidence to charge the suspect when the regular custody reviews specified in PACE 1984 are made, and it is unlikely that further questioning will lead to a charge, the custody officer must order the suspect to be released. If a person is charged with an offence, he or she must be brought before a court as soon as possible and will be remanded in custody or on bail, or alternatively, may be released on police bail.

If excessive force is used in making an arrest, even if the arrest itself is lawful, in that it complies with common law or the provisions of PACE 1984, there will be grounds for an action for assault, battery and/or false imprisonment (s 3(1) of PACE 1984). Whether the force used was unreasonable is a question of fact in each case (*Farrell v Secretary of State for Defence* (1980); and *Ballard, Stewart-Park and Finlay* (1983)).

If a person is sentenced to a term of imprisonment after conviction, this will not be false imprisonment even if the initial arrest was unlawful. In *Olotu v Secretary of State for the Home Department* (1996), it was held that a prison governor was not liable when a remand prisoner remained in custody because the Crown Prosecution Service had failed to apply for an extension of a custody time limit.

13.9 Remedies

The usual remedy sought for trespass to the person is damages, and as has been seen there may be an award of aggravated or exemplary damages in an appropriate case.

The remedy of self-help may also be used. For example, a person who has been falsely imprisoned may escape, and someone who has been unlawfully arrested may resist arrest by use of reasonable force.

The ancient prerogative remedy of habeas corpus is theoretically available for false imprisonment, though this is rarely sought today. This would mean an application to the Divisional Court for an order to release the person unlawfully detained, and is only sought in emergency cases.

13.10 The tort in *Wilkinson v Downton* (1897)

A tort which it is difficult to classify is to be found in the case of *Wilkinson v Downton* which was decided before liability in negligence for nervous shock, was established; it did not fit comfortably with trespass to the person, as the damage, in this case, was indirect and there was no application of physical force, though there was an intention to commit the act.

The facts were that the defendant as part of what may have been a malicious or at best, stupid, practical joke told the claimant that her husband had been seriously hurt in an accident. She rushed to see him and suffered nervous shock, even though he was completely unharmed. The defendant was found liable in tort by Wright J who said:

> The defendant ... has wilfully done an act calculated to cause physical harm to the claimant ... and has in fact thereby caused physical harm to her. That proposition appears to me to state a good cause of action.

The legal basis for this proposition is unclear, and the case has only been followed in one other case in this country (*Janvier v Sweeney* (1919)), though there are Australian and Canadian cases. The rule has been rejected and disapproved by Lord Diplock, and is probably not part of a wider principle.

However, in situations where intentional and malicious acts are committed with the object of causing humiliation and distress, the tort in *Wilkinson v Downton* would prove a useful vehicle.

TRESPASS TO THE PERSON

Compensation for victims of crime

People who are the victims of violent crime may obtain compensation under the Criminal Injuries Compensation Scheme, administered by the CICB. There is no need for there to have been a conviction. This scheme complements the common law and damages are calculated on the same lines as tort damages.

If there is a criminal conviction, the victim may obtain a compensation order from the court at the same time, and the criminal will be ordered to pay the compensation. If the proceedings are brought in the magistrates' court, this may be the best method of obtaining compensation, though many offenders may have difficulty paying.

The alternative to the above methods of obtaining damages for physical violence is to bring a civil action for assault, battery or false imprisonment.

Note the increasing number of successful civil actions against the police.

Assault

Assault is defined as: 'Putting a person in fear of an immediate battery.'

The defendant must have had the means of carrying out the threat (*Thomas v NUM* (1985); *Tuberville v Savage* (1669)).

Battery

Battery is defined as: 'Application of direct physical force to the claimant.'

Certain forms of social touching are excluded but otherwise the least touch is enough. *Wilson v Pringle* (1986) requires 'hostile' touching.

The required intention is the intention to apply force, but not necessarily to hurt the claimant:

Nash v Sheen (1953);

Connor v Chief Constable of Cambridgeshire (1984);

Leon v Metropolitan Police Commissioner (1986).

False imprisonment

False imprisonment is defined as: 'Depriving the claimant of freedom of movement without lawful justification.'

Collins v Wilcock (1984): 'The unlawful imposition of restraint on another's freedom of movement.'

There must be no reasonable means of escape:

Bird v Jones (1848);

Robinson v Balmain Ferry Co (1910);

Herd v Weardale Steel (1915).

The claimant need not know that he or she has been imprisoned:

Meering v Graham White (1920);

Murray v Ministry of Defence (1988).

Further examples include:

Hsu v Commissioner of Police of the Metropolis (1997);

Treadaway v Chief Constable of West Midlands Police (1994).

Medical treatment

Note the distinction between battery and negligence, and the move towards greater consideration for the patient:

Pearce v United Bristol Healthcare Trust (1999);

Carver v Hammersmith (2000);

Re S (Sterilisation: Patient's Best Interests) (2000).

Defences

- Necessity (see *Brody* (1996)).
- Self-defence – *Reville v Newbury* (1996); *R v Martin* (2000).
- Consent (note, especially medical treatment).
- Statutory authority (especially PACE 1984).
- Reasonable chastisement.

Remedies

Habeas corpus for false imprisonment; damages (possibly aggravated); injunction; self-help.

The tort in *Wilkinson v Downton*

Wilkinson v Downton (1897) established that there is a tort action which protects people from deliberate acts intended to cause physical or mental harm.

Summary

Special attention has been paid in this chapter to the increasing area of litigation against the police, when it is claimed that the provisions of PACE 1984 and the Codes of Practice made under it are not followed.

There have been a number of successful actions against police officers in recent years and in some of these there have been awards of exemplary damages.

CHAPTER 14

EMPLOYERS' LIABILITY

The law imposes considerable burdens upon employers both in relation to torts committed by their employees, and in respect of duties owed by employers to their employees.

The nature of the duties of employers varies according to the circumstances and, in some instances, employers will be liable irrespective of any fault of their own, while in others it is necessary to prove fault on the part of the employer.

It is important to maintain and develop a clear picture of the framework of the common law and statutory liability of employers in order to untangle the maze of liabilities which may arise in the employment situation. In addition to the various legal remedies available to employees for injuries arising out of the course of their employment, the State provides support through the system of social security, which has particularly well developed mechanisms for dealing with illness and injury sustained at work.

14.1 Primary liability

Employers may, in certain circumstances, be liable in tort in their own right. This is termed 'primary liability'. It applies in limited circumstances even when independent contractors have been employed, and much more widely at common law to non-delegable duties.

14.1.1 Independent contractors

Employers are under a duty to ensure that the contractors whom they employ are reasonably competent to carry out the specific tasks for which they are employed. Beyond this, the employer will not normally be liable for the wrongful acts of contractors. However, once an employer discovers and condones the tort of an independent contractor, he or she may be liable for that tort. Such liability would be primary rather than vicarious.

Of course, primary liability may also arise if the contractor was acting as the agent of the employer or on his or her explicit instructions.

14.1.2 Non-delegable duties

Primary liability also extends to exceptional situations in which the duty on the employer is so onerous that it cannot be delegated to anyone else. Such duties are described as 'non-delegable' duties, and arise in circumstances when there is a duty imposed by statute or common law 'to see that care is taken', rather than the ordinary duty to take reasonable care (*The Pass of Ballater* (1942)). The circumstances in which such duties arise are listed below:

- **By statute**

  Statutes sometimes place non-delegable duties upon employers, and such duties are those statutory duties which are absolute in character. In order to ascertain the nature of the duty created, it is always necessary to look at the construction of the statute in question. It appears that duties to take care as well as duties which create strict liability can be non-delegable (*Darling v Attorney General* (1950)).

- **Common law: ultra-hazardous activities**

  Those activities which are inherently dangerous in character carry special responsibility for the person who ordered them to be undertaken. As a result, it is not possible to delegate responsibility should anything go wrong, even though the work which has been commissioned is performed by an independent contractor. Examples of such activities include: a photographer used a magnesium flash lamp close to curtains in a cinema (*Honeywill and Stein v Larkin Bros Ltd* (1934)); a contractor tried to thaw water pipes in an attic with a blow lamp (*Balfour v Barty-King* (1957)).

- **Common law: torts of strict liability**

  If the tort which is committed is one of strict liability, the employer is not able to delegate responsibility for it. For example, the duty to prevent the escape of dangerous things collected on land cannot be delegated (*Rylands v Fletcher* (1868)). The contractor who caused the escape of water which flooded into neighbouring mines was not liable to the claimant. The landowner who employed him was liable.

- **Common law: activities on or adjoining a highway**

  If work is carried out on or adjoining the highway, there is a risk that the tort of highway nuisance could be committed. The duties on the employer cannot be delegated to an independent contractor. For example, in *Holliday v National Telephone Company* (1899), a contractor employed by the defendants caused an explosion on the highway which injured a passer-by. The employer, a telephone company engaged in laying wires, was liable.

  In *Tarry v Ashton* (1876), an occupier of land adjoining a highway employed a contractor to repair a dangerous lamp overhanging the highway. The occupier was liable when the lamp was allowed to fall and injured a passer-by.

  But note that the employer is not liable if the work is carried out close to, but not adjoining the highway (*Salisbury v Woodland* (1970)). Nor does the rule that duties are non-delegable apply to the normal use of the highway, which is for passing and re-passing in vehicles or on foot.

- **Common law: activities in public places**

  The principle that activities on or adjoining highways attract non-delegable duties probably also applies to activities carried out in public places such as railway stations (*Pickard v Smith* (1861)).

- **Common law: miscellaneous cases**

  Although the duty not to commit private nuisance can usually be delegated, it is possible to find isolated examples of duties in private nuisance which are non-delegable, for example, the duty not to allow support for adjoining property to be withdrawn (*Bower v Peate* (1876)).

- **Common law: bailments**

  Duties of bailees who are paid for their trouble (bailees for reward) cannot be delegated (*Paton v British Steam Carpet Cleaning Company Ltd* (1977)) though as these duties are contractual, it is possible, though unusual, for the bailment contract to specify particularly that the duties are to be delegated.

- **General duties**

  Implied terms exist in contracts of employment to the effect that the employer will have due regard for the health and safety of all employees (*Johnstone v Bloomsbury HA* (1991)), and it is duties of this nature which cannot be delegated (*Wilsons and Clyde Coal Co Ltd v English* (1938)). Nor can the duty to provide a safe system of work be delegated (*McDermid v Nash Dredging and Reclamation Company Ltd* (1987); *Walker v Northumberland CC* (1994)). The duty of employers to provide safe equipment has been reinforced by statute, and is non-delegable. Section 1 of the Employers' Liability (Defective Equipment) Act 1969 provides that employers are liable for defects in equipment provided by them which cause personal injuries to employees, even if the fault involved acts attributable to some third party. Fault and causation must be established if the employee is to succeed, and these requirements can cause problems in themselves for injured employees. If a case is proved, however, the employer will be able to claim an indemnity from the person who is proved to be at fault.

  It should be noted that an action under the Consumer Protection Act 1987 is not precluded by the existence of the 1969 Act, and remedies under the later Act are more likely to be available to workers, since it does not require proof of fault.

14.2 Common law duties of employers to employees

Contracts of employment contain several terms which impose duties upon both employers and employees. We are not concerned here with express terms except in so far as it is relevant to explain that certain express terms cannot override some of the implied terms because the provisions of the Unfair

Contract Terms Act 1977 prevent this happening (see later, *Johnstone v Bloomsbury HA* (1991), 14.2.5).

14.2.1 Duty to employ competent staff

Employers must ensure that the staff whom they employ are competent to undertake the tasks which they are required to perform, and must train them to to use any equipment in the correct manner. This even extends to ensuring that known trouble makers and practical jokers are disciplined or dismissed. In *Hudson v Ridge Manufacturing Co Ltd* (1957), the company's notorious practical joker injured another employee in the course of one of his pranks, and the employer was liable for the injury. However, in *Smith v Crossley Bros Ltd* (1951), it was held that a single isolated prank did not attract liability for the employer.

14.2.2 Duty to provide proper plant and equipment

There is a duty at common law imposed upon all employers to ensure that any equipment provided for the use of employees is of a safe standard. This also includes a duty to ensure that the equipment is properly maintained. Although there is a duty to inspect equipment regularly to ensure that it is of a proper standard, the employer will not be liable if there was a latent defect which could not have been detected. However, employers are not liable if the employees, once properly trained, do not make adequate use of the equipment supplied. In *Parkinson v Lyle Shipping Co Ltd* (1964), an employee was injured when he tried to light a boiler. His action failed because the fault did not lie with the equipment but with himself. From the point of view of causation, if the employees would not have used safety equipment had it been supplied, the employer will not be liable for their injury merely because the equipment was not available to use. If a statute requires the supply of safety equipment, much depends upon the construction of the particular statute if a problem arises about its not being used.

The common law duty has been enacted in the Employers' Liability (Defective Equipment) Act 1969, discussed above, and injured employees will be considerably assisted by the Consumer Protection Act 1987.

14.2.3 Duty to provide a safe work place

Employers are required at common law to take reasonable steps to ensure that places of work are safe. *Jayasekera v Al-Sayeg* (1999) is an example of an extreme case in which employers not only exposed an employee to danger, but also treated her as a wage slave, and were found liable to pay a high award of damages (£77,988) when she was injured. The claimant sustained an ankle injury when she fell from a third floor window whilst trying to escape from her employment. She had come to England from Sri Lanka to work for the defendants. Every day, she was forced to work from 6 am until 2 am the following morning, cooking and doing domestic chores. She was regularly assaulted and was given only food scraps left by the defendant's children to eat. She attempted to escape after 37 days without pay.

This duty applies even though the employee may not be working at the time on the employer's own premises. In such circumstances, it may not be practical for the employer to take as much care of the employee as could be taken on 'home' premises. In *Wilson v Tyneside Window Cleaning Company* (1958), an employee was injured while cleaning windows on a client's premises. It was held that the employer had done all that was reasonable in the circumstances to ensure the safety of the employee. Employers would not normally be expected to inspect every place in which their workers are to be deployed, as in many instances enormous problems could exist for employers. Take, for example, the employers of health visitors and social workers who spend large amounts of time on the premises of patients and clients. As a matter of common sense, it would be unreasonable to expect the employer to check every possible place of work. The role of insurance may also be important in cases in which workers are engaged in tasks on the premises of people other than their employers. Such people would, in many instances (though possibly not some of the clients of social workers), carry insurance to cover occupiers' liability, and injured workers would be compensated by the insurers.

Employers are, however, expected to provide proper tools and equipment for use on other people's premises, and satisfactory instructions and training if necessary.

There has been much controversy surrounding claims for repetitive strain injury (RSI), a condition which typists and keyboard users, among others, claim to develop as a result of frequent use of such equipment. However, in *Mughal v Reuters* (1993), it was held that no damages could be awarded unless the employee could prove that a definite physical injury had been suffered. The claimant in this case was a journalist who claimed damages for personal injury as a result of using VDUs and keyboards in his employment. Although he could prove that he had suffered discomfort in his arms, there was no evidence of any definite pathological condition such as tenosynovitis, so he could not succeed in his action. It was also held that the employer had taken all reasonable care to provide a safe system of work in their office by regularly checking the equipment and providing work stations and monitoring what was found wanting. Members of staff knew that they could ask for footrests, document holders and other equipment and it would be provided. In other cases, when the employee has been able to prove that a recognised clinical condition has been suffered and that the employer took no steps to educate employees about the correct methods to use in doing the work and how to recognise warning symptoms, there have been successful actions against the employer. In *Mountenay (Hazzard) and Others v Bernard Matthews* (1993), employees were handling and preparing poultry for the market using production lines, and this work involved certain wrist and arm movements which caused recognised clinical conditions. It was held that the employer was liable because he had not ensured that the jobs were rotated to relieve the continuous use of the same muscles, nor had there been any proper education of employees about the dangers of the task. The claimant was also successful in *Mitchell v Atco* (1995) because she had suffered clinical symptoms after using heavy equipment for testing motors, and the employers had failed to introduce job rotation and had given her no advice about how to approach the work. However, in *Pickford v ICI* (1998), the House of Lords ruled that employers are not obliged to warn employees about a medical condition which has a psychological aspect, if the very warning might induce the condition.

Employers are constantly faced with new and varied problems and good systems of risk management are essential if they are to avoid legal action, bearing in mind the fact that there are also pressures on them from the Health and Safety regulations. For example, Hepatitis B, a serious blood-borne disease, can be transmitted by medical staff who are carriers. Employers of people who are classified as being at risk of contracting this illness, for example certain health care workers, police officers, social workers and prison officers, need to control the risk in order to avoid liability. This could be very expensive if testing and vaccination programmes are introduced, and difficulties can arise if employees, who fear that they may be carriers of the disease, refuse to co-operate. However, it must be remembered that employees also have duties to their employers, one of which is to obey all reasonable orders, and failure to cooperate in a risk assessment scheme could result in dismissal.

14.2.4 Duty to provide safe work systems

Not every operation which is undertaken by employees requires that a special system of work should be devised and put in place to ensure the safety of employees. This is a question of fact in each case. The duty may exist in relation to specific jobs or to the general running of the operation, and particular industries tend to have their own systems in place from which it may be difficult for individual employers to deviate except by ensuring an even safer work environment. The law does not condone dangerous practices merely because all other industries of the same kind follow them.

In *Re Herald of Free Enterprise Litigation* (1987), it was found that it was standard practice to leave the ferry door open when leaving port, but the practice was still condemned as dangerous by the tribunal. However, there is no duty on the Ministry of Defence to provide a safe system of work in battle conditions (*Mulcahy v Minister of Defence* (1996)), nor does a soldier owe a duty of care to his colleagues in battle.

Employers are expected not only to devise safe work systems where necessary, but also to ensure that their employees are trained in their use and follow them on a regular basis, even to the point of appointing supervisors to ensure that workers use necessary safety equipment (*Nolan v Dental Manufacturing Co Ltd* (1958)).

In *Alexander and Others v Midland Bank plc* (1999), the bank appealed from a decision made in favour of five of its employees who claimed that they had suffered injury as a result of high pressure work on batch processing keyboards. The claimants had been employed by Midland Bank from 1989 to 1990 at a centre which dealt with the processing of documents. In the course of their employment, they had to enter the details of cheques and other documents into a main computer – a process called 'encoding'. This process demanded great accuracy and, in seeking to increase its efficiency, the bank sought increasingly higher encoding speeds from its employees. The claimants alleged that the workstations were operated on principles which were ergonomically unsound, and that, as a result, they had suffered musculo-skeletal pains which gradually became worse. Over a period of time, breaks were cut and the pressure of the work increased.

The defendant bank denied that the pressure of work had resulted in any injury. It alleged in its defence that the injuries of which the claimants complained were psychogenic rather than physical in nature, and denied any breaches of duty, arguing that the claimants had sustained no injuries and, in the alternative, that any injuries they may have suffered were not sustained as a result of employment.

The Court of Appeal held that the judge had correctly found that he had a simple choice between two alternative explanations, as there had been no suggestion that the employees had been malingering. The claimants had to demonstrate that their injuries were more likely to have been caused by physical than psychogenic factors. The judge had to weigh the strength of the arguments about the psychogenic factors before reaching his conclusion, but it did not matter whether he did this before or after considering the claimants' case that the injuries were physical.

In *Mountenay v Bernard Matthews* (1993), it was held that employers have a duty to warn employees of risks of injury and to educate them so as to enable them to draw symptoms to the attention of doctors.

However, if, after appropriate training, an accident is the result of a one-off situation, rather than a routine work operation, an employee is expected to use common sense and take sensible precautions against being injured. In *Chalk v Devizes Reclamation Co Ltd* (1999), the claimant had been employed as a labourer at a scrap metal yard owned by the defendants. He had been trained in safe lifting techniques for routine objects, but, on one occasion, a large lump of lead had fallen off a pallet unexpectedly and the claimant had injured his back while attempting to lift it. He alleged that his injury had been caused by the employer's failure to provide a safe system of work. The Court of Appeal held that this was a one-off accident in which the claimant could have been expected to use his common sense and initiative, and that no advance advice or training could have been given in respect of this incident.

Employers must warn employees of any dangers inherent in the work which they are required to do. In *Pape v Cumbria CC* (1992), a part time cleaner contracted dermatitis because of exposure to irritant cleaning products. Although the employers had provided gloves, it was held that they should have pointed out the dangers of contracting dermatitis if gloves were not worn and that the information should have been included in a safe system of work. They must take steps to protect employees from violent clients and customers. Hospitals are undertaking risk management exercises to prevent violent injuries to accident and emergency staff, and protocols are in place to ensure that these are introduced throughout the NHS.

In *Rahman v Arearose Ltd* (1999), an employer was found liable to an employee who was assaulted and seriously injured by violent customers while working at a Burger King Restaurant in King's Cross, London. Other members of staff had also been assaulted on previous occasions, and the employer was well aware of the risks.

In *Walker v Northumberland CC* (1994), the scope of the duty to provide a safe system of work was extended to include the need to provide working conditions which do not cause undue stress to employees. The claimant was a senior social worker who had suffered a previous nervous breakdown because of the pressure of work. After a three month break, he had returned to work and discussed his problems with his superior who had reassured him that he would provide extra assistance to relieve him of some of the burden of work. However, when he did start work again, the claimant discovered that he had a huge backlog of work to complete and only very limited additional assistance. He had a second nervous breakdown six months later which resulted in his permanently stopping work. He was later dismissed on grounds of ill health and brought an action for negligence against his employer. It was held that the employers were in breach of the duty to provide a safe system of work. He eventually accepted a settlement of £175,000. This case is of great significance because it establishes beyond doubt the existence of a duty of care in English law in relation to work stress of a psychological nature. In America, this is an important basis of claims by employees and there is extensive case law on the subject but, in Commonwealth jurisdictions, it is a relatively new concept (*Gillespie v Commonwealth of Australia* (1991)). In *Petch v Comrs of Customs and Excise* (1993), the Court of Appeal had held that liability could exist in relation to work stress if the employer knows that an employee has had a previous breakdown and is susceptible, though here the case failed on causation because the employers had done their utmost to persuade the claimant not to return to work. The repercussions of the *Walker* case are likely to mean that trade unions press for greater awareness by employers of the symptoms of stress at work, and that employers will need to ensure that they have sound risk assessment policies in place in order to obtain adequate insurance cover.

In May 2000, it was reported that a record £30,000 settlement had been announced in a case involving a teacher who had suffered work stress.

It is not only the question of psychiatric problems which employees develop as a result of work pressure that has been occupying the courts. There is a developing line of case law in which employees are claiming that their employers owe them a duty of care to ensure that they do not suffer psychiatric injury in accidents in the course of their employment, even as secondary victims. The House of Lords clarified this matter in *White v Chief Constable of South Yorkshire* (1999) and, although it appears that employees who are rescuers are not in a privileged position by virtue of the employment, there does seem to be a duty to provide counselling to employees who, although not present at the scene of accidents, might suffer psychiatric illness as a result (see Chapter 4).

14.2.5 Duty to ensure health and safety

At common law, there is a term implied into all employment contracts, which no employer has power to exclude, that reasonable care will be taken by the employer to ensure the health and safety of his or her employees. This is closely related to the duty to provide a safe system of work.

After the successful claim by a police officer whose hearing had been damaged by using an ear piece for surveillance, it is likely that there will be a large number of similar claims against police forces throughout the country. The police force in the case in question had not taken sufficient care to ensure the health and safety of their employee (*Dyer v Metropolitan Police Comr* (1998)).

In *Johnstone v Bloomsbury HA* (1991), a junior hospital doctor employed by the defendants was required by his employers to work exceptionally long hours, including up to 48 hours overtime, on average, every week, and explicit provision was made for this in his contract of employment. The doctor claimed that working for such long periods (in some weeks, more than 100 hours) had made him ill, and he sued his employers for breach of the term implied into his contract of employment at common law that his employer would take reasonable steps to care for his health and safety. The Court of Appeal when asked to consider the contract of employment took the view that the employer was not entitled by an express term to exclude this implied term. By s 2(1) of the Unfair Contract Terms Act 1977, liability for death or personal injuries caused by negligence cannot be excluded by a contract term.

All three judges in the Court of Appeal agreed that there is an implied term in all contracts of employment that the employer will take reasonable care of the health and safety of employees.

The common law duties may be added to from time to time. Thus, it was suggested in *Spring v Guardian Assurance* (1995) that there is an implied duty owed by employers to write fair and careful references for employees who seek employment elsewhere.

It now seems clear that there is a duty on employers to ensure that their employees are not subjected to bullying in the workplace. In *Ratcliffe v Dyfed CC* (1998), a former deputy headmaster was awarded damages of over £100,000 in a successful claim of this kind. A factory worker who was bullied by colleagues was awarded £28,000 compensation in a recent case.

In addition to common law duties, there are also duties imposed on employers in relation to workplaces, as employers are also occupiers of premises in which work is carried out. For example, in *Silk v Comr of Police for the Metropolis* (1999), a police officer who slipped on oil in a police station car park and was injured recovered £470,933 damages from his employer.

14.3 Breach of statutory duty

Injured employees may be able to maintain an action for breach of statutory duty against an employer (see Chapter 9). This action has a number of advantages to employees, once the hurdle of establishing that a particular statute gives rise to civil liability has been surmounted. Indeed, it is well worth exploring the possibility of an action for breach of one of the many statutes and regulations which place obligations on employers in relation to their workforce and the work environment before considering whether to sue in negligence or under the contract of employment, for breach of a term. The reason for this is that the burden of proving that the statutory requirements have been met is placed upon the employer, and in some instances liability is strict. However, the law is riddled with inconsistencies, individual applications are notoriously unpredictable, and the initial hurdle of statutory interpretation is extremely difficult to deal with. The Health and Safety at Work, etc, Act 1974 contains an explicit statement that the first few sections which are general in nature do not give rise to civil liability.

14.4 New statutory duties

The EC Framework Directive on Health and Safety is being implemented by regulations, many of which state explicitly that they do give rise to civil actions. In practice, this is an important area of law in which employees injured at work are able to claim compensation more easily now than under the old UK legislation. For example, nurses who suffer back injuries are given financial support by their trade union to sue for compensation. Most of the new regulations require regular assessment of risks by employers. They cover matters such as manual handling, using VDUs and the use of personal protective equipment.

In *Fraser v Winchester HA* (1999), a claimant who had not been properly trained in the use of a camping stove succeeded in obtaining damages for breach of the Provision and Use of Work Equipment Regulations 1992.

Most of the Regulations require employers to train employees in the safe use of equipment and other safety measures, and failure to provide this type of training usually gives rise to strict liability. In practice, this makes it very much easier than ever before for employees who have been injured to obtain compensation from their employers, as long as they are also able to prove causation. For example, employers are expected to make a precise evaluation of the level of risk involved in manual handling operations and should issue precise instructions to employees if any precautions are impracticable (*Koonjul v Thamslink NHS Trust* (2000)).

14.5 An overview

The common law duties are important from the employment law perspective, but one factor which complicates this area of law is that it is interspersed with statutory provisions, breaches of which may give rise to an action for breach of statutory duty in some cases. Indeed, most actions for breach of statutory duty arise in the employment situation, as so many statutes have been enacted to provide safer work environments and to protect employees from exploitation by unscrupulous employers who are prepared to cut corners on safety in order to increase productivity. The tort of breach of statutory duty is dealt with in Chapter 9 but it must not be forgotten that conditions for employees have also improved considerably through the efforts of judges in modifying the common law rules which for many years prevented successful actions by employees against their employers. Actions for breach of statutory duty are of greater assistance to employees than ordinary negligence actions because the burden of proof is reversed once the statutory duty is established.

At one time, employees stood little chance of succeeding in suing their employers for injury even if they were prepared to risk losing their jobs by doing so. Many who were seriously injured in the days when conditions in some factories were extremely dangerous, were thrown on the mercy of relatives or the poor law. Before the advent of trade unions and employment protection legislation, there were few people with the means for, or interest in, championing the cause of workers.

Employers were protected from legal action by the doctrine of 'common employment' (not abolished by statute until 1948) which prevented an employee whose injury was caused by a fellow worker from succeeding in an action against the employer (*Priestly v Fowler* (1837)).

The defences of *volenti non fit injuria* and contributory negligence often meant that employees had little chance of success.

Judges during the 20th century slowly modified these hurdles which had been created in a different social and economic climate, by introducing the notion of the non-delegable duties of employers discussed above, and by refusing to allow the defence of common employment to apply to breach of statutory duty (*Groves v Wimborne* (1898)). The defence of *volenti non fit injuria* was also modified when the House of Lords ruled that any consent had to be given freely in *Smith v Baker & Sons* (1891). The carelessness of employees has also been treated with considerable leniency by the courts when considering the issue of contributory negligence.

There has been a form of no-fault compensation for work accidents since as long ago as 1897 when the first Workmens' Compensation Act was passed. This was extended over the years and finally became part of the welfare state legislation introduced after the First World War. Today, victims of work accidents with long term disabilities receive periodic payments under the Industrial Injuries Scheme, and there are those who would argue that such people do not deserve the preferential treatment which they undoubtedly receive when compared with the victims of other accidents, such as road accidents and medical accidents (see Atiyah, PS, *Accidents, Compensation and the Law*, Cane, P (ed), 1999). The scheme is funded by contributions made by employers and employees, and the claims are made by injured employees from the state rather than the employer. However, a report by the National Audit Office in 1994 concluded that almost half the victims of serious industrial accidents and disease do not apply for state compensation.

Employers, with the exception of very large employers who are permitted to act as their own insurers, are required to take out compulsory liability insurance cover for all their employees (Employers' Liability (Compulsory Insurance) Act 1969). This means that injured employees have better protection, through insurance, than many other accident victims.

Injured employees have the option of tort actions if the industrial injuries system is inadequate to provide the necessary compensation, and some 12% resort to these. So there is considerable support, both from the State and from the tort system, which has tended to lean in favour of injured employees, to mitigate their previous harsh treatment. This has re-inforced the conclusion that they are in a better position than other accident victims. In addition to payments made out of the industrial injuries fund, the Pearson Commission in 1978 estimated that about £70 million is paid to victims of work accidents by the tort system each year.

EMPLOYERS' LIABILITY

Primary liability

Employers are primarily liable (that is, liable in their own right) in numerous situations which involve activities carried out within the employment relationship. If the employer takes reasonable steps to ensure competence of independent contractors, he will not be liable unless the duty is 'non-delegable'.

Common law non-delegable duties

Non-delegable duties may be statutory, depending upon the construction of the statute, or they may be bound at common law. They are duties which are so important that employers are unable to shift responsibility for them onto anyone else. The following duties are non-delegable:

- **Ultra-hazardous activities**

    For example, *Honeywill and Stein v Larkin Bros* (1934).

- **Torts of strict liability**

    Rylands v Fletcher (1866).

- **Activities on or near a highway**

    For example, *Holliday v National Telephone Co* (1899).

- **Activities in a public place**

    Pickard v Smith (1861).

- **Miscellaneous cases**

    Bower v Peate (1876).

- **Bailments**

    Paton v British Steam Carpet Cleaning Co (1977).

- **Duties relating to the safety of employees**

    Johnstone v Bloomsbury Health Authorities (1991).

Employers' common law duties

Certain duties are implied into all contracts of employment. These create primary liability:

- **To employ competent staff**
  Hudson v Ridge (1957).

- **To provide proper plant and equipment**
  Parkinson v Lyle Shipping (1964).

- **To provide a safe place of work**
  Wilson v Tyneside Cleaning (1955);
  Mountenay (Hazzard) and Others v Bernard Matthews (1994);
  Mughal v Reuters (1993);
  Pickford v ICI (1998);
  Chalk v Devizes Reclamation Co (1999);
  Alexander v Midland Bank (1999).

- **To provide a safe system of work**
  Re Herald of Free Enterprise (1987);
  Walker v Northumberland CC (1994);
  Rahman v Arearose (1999).

- **To ensure the health, safety and welfare of employees**
  Johnstone v Bloomsbury (1991);
  Ratcliffe v Dyfed CC (1998).

Breach of statutory duty

Injured employees may succeed in an action for breach of statutory duty against their employers. (See Chapter 9 also.)

Note the significance of the newly implemented regulations in line with the EC Framework Directive 1989/391/EEC.

CHAPTER 15

PRODUCT LIABILITY

The 20th century has witnessed the development of a comprehensive legal framework for consumer protection. This revolution has been achieved partly through late 19th century legislation, and partly through the efforts of the judiciary, in keeping with social and economic changes in the light of mass-production of goods. After the Second World War, further comprehensive legislation was introduced as a result of the work of pressure groups representing the interests of consumers.

15.1 The position in contract

Initially, the law of contract provided the basis of consumer protection. The purchaser of defective goods could bring an action for breach of an express or implied term in the contract. The Sale of Goods Act 1893 (later updated by further statutes), provided statutory protection by implying terms into contracts for the sale of goods, the breach of which gave rise to a number of remedies depending on the gravity of the situation.

The advantage of these contractual remedies is that they are available without the need to prove fault. For example, in a contract for the sale of goods, there is an implied term that the goods will be reasonably fit for the purpose for which they are sold (s 14(3) of the Sale of Goods Act 1979). If the goods do not prove to be fit for that purpose, there is no need for the purchaser to prove that the seller was in any way to blame for that fact. Most of the terms implied into contracts for the sale of goods now also apply to contracts for the repair and exchange of goods, to hire purchase contracts, and to contracts for the supply of goods and services.

15.1.1 Disadvantages of contract

The disadvantage of the contractual remedies is that they are only available to parties to the contract. Outsiders, such as the recipient of goods as a gift, or the user of goods who was not also the purchaser, had no remedy in contract until the changes introduced by the Contracts (Rights of Third Parties) Act 1999. This Act, in certain circumstances, allows third parties to enforce or rely on contractual provisions.

15.2 Credit users

Consumers are provided with an additional remedy by the Consumer Credit Act 1974 if they purchase goods on credit. The user of a credit card can bring an action against the credit card company if he or she is dissatisfied with the goods or services paid for by credit card, providing the cash price was between £30 and £10,000 (s 75).

In the case of goods acquired on hire purchase, the acquirer, in effect, contracts with the finance company which takes the place of the seller for the purposes of the law of contract, providing the credit was no more than £25,000.

While the development of remedies in tort did provide an important supplement to contract, and no doubt the quality of manufactured products improved, it will be clear from the above discussion that there were still a number of disadvantages for consumers. Pressure for reform continued to grow, and this came to a head with the EC Directive (85/374/EEC) on product liability which Member States were required to implement into their national law. In the UK, this was achieved in the Consumer Protection Act 1987. The legislation in this country is not, however, as comprehensive as that introduced in some of the other jurisdictions, and in suitable cases, instances of 'forum-shopping' occur, whereby claimants seek to bring their actions in the States which offer the most comprehensive sets of remedies. There is an outgoing EC review of the situation in order to achieve greater uniformity throughout Member States.

15.3 The position in tort

The case of *Donoghue v Stevenson* (1932) established for the first time that, even in the absence of a contract, there may be a remedy in tort for defective goods, providing the goods also present a threat of injury to health or safety. The remedy may be sought from the manufacturer who owes a duty of care to the ultimate consumer of goods, and it must be established that the manufacturer was at fault before the remedy will be available.

Any person affected by the defect in the product could sue the manufacturer. Claimants have been drawn from a wide range of injured persons, including purchasers, members of the purchaser's family, recipients of gifts, employees of the purchaser and complete outsiders who have been affected by the defect.

The range of possible defendants has gradually been extended beyond the manufacturer of the goods to include those who assemble goods using components from elsewhere, those who repair goods and those who supply , goods, in appropriate cases.

15.3.1 Disadvantages of tort

Although this case provided a new focus for consumer protection, it was subject to some important limitations. The disadvantages of tort in protecting the consumer are:

- **Quality of goods**

  Tort is not concerned with defects in the quality of goods, as opposed to defects which give rise to dangers to health and safety of consumers. Although there was an attempt to extend liability in negligence to cover damage to the manufactured product itself, that is, defects in quality in *Junior Books v Veitchi* (1983), this type of loss (pure economic loss) is no longer recoverable since *Murphy v Brentwood DC* (1990). However, it may still be possible to recover in negligence by claiming that damaged property is separate from the product which was manufactured by the defendant, though it must clearly be separate, and not part of the final structure as in the case of a building. In effect, there will be an action if a product damages something or someone, but not if it merely damages itself.

- **Proof of fault**

  Tort requires proof of fault. It is extremely difficult to obtain evidence that manufacturers are at fault, as this would require evidence from some internal source, and detailed knowledge of the manufacturing processes used. Employees are reluctant to give evidence against their employers. To some extent, this limitation was gradually eroded by the *res ipsa loquitur* principle which was applied with increasing frequency to consumer cases in the second half of the 20th century, particularly to cases of foreign bodies in foodstuffs. (In *Donoghue v Stevenson* itself, it was never actually proved that there was a snail in the ginger beer bottle as the case was eventually settled out of court.)

  The Thalidomide cases demonstrated the difficulties of proving fault coupled with problems of proving causation which will exist under any regime, whether contract, tort or strict liability.

The negligence action will not succeed if the claimant is unable to establish that the defendant failed to exercise reasonable care. Moreover, there will be no negligence if the defendant could not have known of possible dangers because of the lack of existing scientific or technical knowledge (*Roe v Minister of Health* (1954)). However, it has been established through the cases that, if a danger becomes apparent after products have been put into the market place, a manufacturer has a duty to warn potential users and in extreme cases, to operate a system of product recall. Manufacturers insure against this possibility and most have efficient systems of product recall, many of which depend upon the completion of a 'guarantee card' by the consumer, which has little value as a guarantee because of statutory protection, but which is an essential source of information as to the distribution of products for manufacturers (and also a means of targeting future advertising).

- **Application**

  Donoghue v Stevenson applied only to products, and originally only to foodstuffs. Later, the principle was extended to any manufactured products, for example, in *Grant v Australian Knitting Mills* (1936). The claimant suffered dermatitis as a result of chemicals used in the process of manufacturing woolly underpants. He succeeded in his action against the manufacturer for negligence.

- **Examination of goods**

  Donoghue v Stevenson was limited to instances in which there was 'no reasonable possibility of intermediate examination of the goods' (*per* Lord Atkin). However, this restriction has been interpreted generously by the courts and it appears that the manufacturer will be liable if there was no reason to believe or imagine that some intermediate examination of the goods might occur. If, on the other hand, the manufacturer issues a warning about the product or suggests that it should be tested or sampled before use, he may escape liability. In effect this goes to the issue of whether or not the defendant has acted reasonably in disseminating the goods. A warning would be evidence of reasonableness on the part of the manufacturer, permitting him to escape fault. In *Kubach v Hollands* (1937), a schoolgirl was injured when a chemical exploded. The manufacturer was not liable because a warning had been issued that the chemical should be tested before use. The retailer had neither tested the chemical nor warned the school of the need to test it. Warnings may be sufficient to discharge the duty of care, but each case must be taken on its own facts, and if an intermediary is involved it may or may not be sufficient merely to warn that intermediary rather than the ultimate consumer (*Buchan v Ortho Pharmaceuticals (Canada) Ltd* (1986)). Any warnings should be distinguished from attempts to exclude liability for death or personal injuries, which are totally void since the Unfair Contract Terms Act 1977.

  One possible reason for this rule is that there is a similar limitation in contract cases.

15.4 The Consumer Protection Act 1987

The provisions of this statute provide, at first sight, a comprehensive set of remedies for consumers in the case of defective products. Not all of the measures are civil, as the criminal law may also be used to regulate unsafe products, and from a practical point of view this may ultimately prove more effective by preventing the introduction of defective goods into the market-place. A comprehensive framework for regulating product safety is now contained in the General Product Safety Regulations 1994. However, this discussion is limited to the civil law measures in Pt 1 of the Act which is dealt with in outline only.

The Consumer Protection Act 1987 places strict liability for defective products on a range of possible defendants. By s 2(1), it is provided that:

> Where any damage is caused wholly or partly by a defect in a product, every person to whom sub-s 2 applies shall be liable for the damage.

Liability cannot be limited or excluded by any contract term or otherwise (s 7).

15.4.1 Who is liable

The 'producer' of the defective article is liable under the Consumer Protection Act 1987, and the definition of producer is very wide, but does not usually mean the individual employee, rather the company or employer.

- Producers are not only those who manufacture the final product, but also the manufacturers and assemblers of component parts and the producers of raw materials (see EC Directive 1989/391/EEC).

- The term includes not only as one would expect, manufacturers, but also, in the case of substances which have been 'won' or 'abstracted' from other sources (for example, minerals), the person who undertook that process.

- The definition also includes the person who is responsible for any process, industrial or otherwise, which attributes essential characteristics to products. For example, where ingredients are mixed together by a pharmacist in a small pharmacy.

- 'Own branders', for example, large scale food and clothing retailers who employ other firms to manufacture products and then put their own brand name on the goods, are also liable as producers if they hold themselves out as such. In order to avoid strict liability as the producer, a retailer who sells own brand products would need to give an indication that the goods are made for them by another manufacturer, for example, 'specially made for Spar'.

- The importer into the EC is also treated as 'the producer' for the purposes of strict liability.

The supplier of goods direct to the customer, that is, the retailer, installer or distributor will not be primarily liable for defects under the Consumer Protection Act 1987 (though there may still be liability in contract). However, a supplier does become liable (s 2(3)), if the goods are anonymous and he or she has no record or other means of tracing his or her supplier, or if he or she refuses to identify his supplier. This means that even small corner shops must now keep detailed records of the suppliers of all their products for many years, because of the limitation periods, if they are to be sure of escaping strict liability. The injured party is required to ask the supplier for details of his suppliers within a reasonable time of the damage. The liability of direct suppliers is thus known as 'secondary liability'.

15.4.2 Joint and several liability

Liability is joint and several, which means that consumers have the option of suing all or any of the potential defendants. This overcomes many of the problems previously experienced by victims who were unable at common law to find or identify the defendant, particularly if that person or company had ceased to trade. Obvious targets for legal action under the Consumer Protection Act 1987 are the manufacturers or any person in the chain with good insurance cover, 'deep pockets' and the ability to pay substantial damages.

Any person in the chain of manufacture and distribution is potentially fully liable without proof of fault for any damage which is caused, wholly or partly, by the product.

15.4.3 Definition of a product

A 'product' is defined in s 2(1) of the Consumer Protection Act 1987 as:

> ... any goods or electricity and (subject to subsection (3)) includes a product which is comprised in another product, whether by virtue of being a component part, raw material or otherwise.

Goods are defined in s 45(1) as:

> ... substances, growing crops, and things comprised in land by virtue of being attached to it and any ship, aircraft or vehicle.

The scope of this definition is not clear, and it remains to be seen whether it will be interpreted to include such things as computer programs which have been held to be 'goods' in another context – see *St Albans City Council v International Computers* (1996).

Damage which is caused by a break in the supply rather than a defect in the generation of electricity is not covered.

Buildings as 'immovables' are not included in the definition, but building materials are, though defects in design and construction are not. Thus, if a part of a building collapsed through defects in the materials used, this could fall within the Consumer Protection Act 1987.

Primary (unprocessed) agricultural produce and game was specifically excluded from the ambit of the Consumer Protection Act 1987. If it had undergone an industrial process to give it its essential characteristics, the produce was no longer 'primary' agricultural produce. This raised difficult questions as to what constitutes the industrial processing of agricultural produce. Clearly, eggs in their unchanged state were excluded, but if they were broken and mixed with other ingredients to make mayonnaise on a large or small scale, they probably fell within the Consumer Protection Act 1987 and there would be strict liability if they proved to be infected with salmonella.

It was not clear whether freezing or canning of agricultural produce is an industrial process, nor what is meant by changing the essential characteristics of produce.

The problems raised by the possibility of contacting CJD, the human equivalent of BSE, or 'mad cow disease', from beef, illustrate the difficulties which could arise from the exclusion of primary agricultural products from the ambit of the Consumer Protection Act 1987. Questions could arise as to whether beef which is merely butchered and sold as joints would fall within the definition of 'primary agricultural products', or whether any form of cutting up of the animal would be 'processing' for the purposes of the Consumer Protection Act 1987. The making of beefburgers and the extraction of beef products to manufacture gelatine which is used in confectionery and medicines would amount to processing. As a result, the law is to be changed and primary agricultural produce now falls within the Directive (Council Directive 99/34). The UK has until 4 December 2000 to implement this provision.

15.4.4 Definition of a defect

Goods are defective if their safety is not such as 'persons generally are entitled to expect, taking into account all the circumstances'.

The burden of proof is on the claimant to demonstrate that the damage was caused by a defect in the product which made it 'unsafe'. Defects in quality alone do not attract strict liability, leaving the claimant to his or her remedies (if any) in contract.

Much will depend on the circumstances of each individual case, and the courts are entitled to take into account the following circumstances:

- the manner in which and purposes for which the product has been marketed, its get-up, the use of any mark in relation to the product and any instructions for, or warnings with respect to, doing or refraining from doing anything with or in relation to the product. See *London Rubber Co v Richardson* (2000) in which a condom had split during use. The claimant had not used additional emergency contraception by taking the 'morning after' pill;

- what might reasonably be expected to be done with or in relation to the product;

- the time when the product was supplied by its producer to another; and 'nothing in this section shall require a defect to be inferred from the fact alone that the safety of a product which is supplied after that time is greater than the safety of the product in question' (s 3(2)).

These are all important factors since, in effect, they provide defences to the producer.

15.4.5 Warnings, labelling and get-up

For example, a warning may make a potentially unsafe product safe, and misuse of product by a consumer could provide a defence (for example, apocryphal tales about disastrous results of putting poodles in microwave ovens to dry, and electric paint-strippers being used to dry hair). The question arises, however, as to what use of a product is reasonable, and manufacturers frequently include warning labels covering many possible uses of products in order to cover themselves.

In *Relph v Yamaha* (1996), a claim for personal injuries under the Act failed. The claimant had used an 'all terrain' three-wheeled vehicle contrary to the instruction manual and labelling.

When a woman who suffered from toxic shock syndrome after using a tampon brought a claim under the Act, the court held that there had been adequate warnings given in the information leaflet *Worsley v Tambrands* (2000), and her claim did not succeed under the Act.

15.4.6 Timing

The time of supply is an important factor, as a defence may apply if the product has become unsafe after it left the manufacturer and moved down the distribution chain. Much will depend on the type of product (for example, perishable goods), and the handling which it subsequently receives.

If products made and supplied after the time in question are safer than those manufactured and supplied earlier, this will not necessarily make earlier products unsafe. Manufacturers are constantly improving the design and quality of their products, partly through market competition and partly because safety measures are introduced, though not retrospectively, by legislation. However, many manufacturers, in keeping with previous common law requirements do operate efficient systems of product re-call.

As long as the claimant succeeds in establishing that the product is defective as defined above, liability will be strict, though it is questionable whether in fact liability under the Act goes much further than ordinary negligence liability, given the similarity to negligence which is detectable in the application of the tests for defectiveness (see Stapleton, J, 'Products liability reform – real or illusory?' (1986) 6 OJLS 392).

The conclusion must be that this section moves the legal goal-posts further from the notion of strict liability which the Consumer Protection Act 1987 purports to promote and closer to the ordinary law of negligence.

15.4.7 The type of damage to which strict liability applies

The Consumer Protection Act 1987 only creates strict liability in relation to unsafe products. There are certain types of damage which are specifically excluded from the ambit of the Act.

* It does not cover damage to the product itself, and in this respect provides no better remedies than the common law of tort.

   A person shall not be liable in respect of any defect in a product for the loss of or any damage to the product itself, or for the loss of or damage to the whole or any part of any product which has been supplied with the product in question comprised in it.

   This means that if a car, for example, were to catch fire because of a wiring defect, there would not be strict liability under the Act, though there could of course be an action in contract by the purchaser. If the fire injured the driver or passengers, there would be strict liability, and if the car caught fire and caused damage to other property, there would be strict liability under the Act.

   If, however, the defect was caused by new wiring, say in a radio fitted after the purchase of the vehicle, there would be liability for damage to the car because the radio was not originally 'comprised' in the car.

   These issues are raised in *Carroll v Fearon* (1998) in which the victims of a car accident caused by defective tyres succeeded in a claim against Dunlop, the tyre manufacturers, for the injuries which they suffered when tyres suffered 'blow outs' after only moderate wear.

* The Consumer Protection Act 1987 does not cover damage to business property, that is, property which is not ordinarily intended for private use, occupation or consumption and not intended by the person who suffers the loss or damage mainly for his or her own private use, occupation or consumption.

   If a word processor used for purely private purposes in a domestic dwelling were to catch fire because of a defect and the house was destroyed in the subsequent blaze, there would be strict liability under the Act, but, if the same thing happened in a commercial office building, there would be a need to prove negligence or breach of contract in order to recover damages.

* The Consumer Protection Act 1987 does not cover small property damage, that is, losses of less than £275. Contributory negligence on the part of the person injured may bring the damages below this threshold.

   Small claims for damage to property would need to be brought in the law of contract or negligence.

All personal injuries damages, however small, are covered by the Consumer Protection Act 1987.

15.4.8 Limitation of actions

The right to bring an action under the Consumer Protection Act 1987 is lost after 10 years from the date that the defendant supplied the product.

The claimant must begin proceedings within three years of becoming aware of the defect, the damage or the identity of the defendant, or if the damage is latent, the date of knowledge of the claimant, provided that it is within the 10 year limit. In the case of personal injuries, there is a discretion vested in the court to override the three year limitation period.

In all cases, the 10 year period is the absolute cut off point, and there will be no discretion whatever to override this under any circumstances, even if the claimant was under a legal disability or the defendant could not be traced before that date.

15.4.9 Defences under the Consumer Protection Act 1987 (s 4)

There are several defences listed in the Consumer Protection Act 1987:

- **The defect in the product was attributable to compliance with a statutory or EC requirement**

  It would seem that the producer must demonstrate that the defect was the inevitable result of complying with a requirement which was itself misguided, an occurrence which is likely to be extremely rare. In any case, most of the standards laid down by regulations are minimum standards and difficulties are unlikely to arise in such cases, unless the manufacturer has over-used a product, for example a chemical in a weed killer or fertiliser which later turns out to be dangerous. In such circumstances, the court would be required to consider the question of what safety standards people generally would be entitled to expect.

- **The person proceeded against did not supply the product**

  There will be a defence if the person against whom the action is brought did not supply the product but someone else did, and it will be for the defendant to prove that he or she did not do so. This will not always be as easy as it may appear, particularly in the case of clever fakes, which are becoming more common, of certain products from car components to designer jeans.

- **The product was not supplied in the course of a business, or not with a view to profit**

  The Consumer Protection Act 1987, like the Sale of Goods Act 1979, was designed to impose liability on businesses rather than private individuals.

Thus, people who sell home made products at village fairs are not caught by the Act.

- **The defect did not exist at the relevant time**

The relevant time is the time the product was supplied, or put into circulation. Certain products which are perishable and must be used within a certain time, or require regular servicing can often leave one person in the chain of distribution in a perfect condition but may have deteriorated by the time they reach the consumer, having passed through several distributors. This defence means that as long as a producer can demonstrate that at the time the goods left him they met the reasonable expectations of the consumer, he will escape strict liability. This requires proof on a balance of probabilities and producers are advised to keep detailed records of their products and to have checking systems in place with records of dates of inspection in order to be able to provide evidence if necessary of the state of goods leaving their hands.

If a product is deliberately sabotaged before it leaves a factory, the manufacturer would be strictly liable under the Consumer Protection Act 1987.

- **The development risks defence**

This defence is similar to the 'state of the art defence' in negligence (*Roe v Minister of Health* (1954)). It applies:

If the state of scientific and technical knowledge at the relevant time was not such that a producer of products of the same description as the product in question might be expected to have discovered the defect if it had existed in his products while they were under his control.

Once again, the relevant time is the time the defendant supplied the product.

As in the law of negligence, there will be a complete defence if the supplier can show that it was simply not known at the time that the product could be defective. The same defence does not apply in contract, however.

This is one of the most fiercely criticised aspects of the Consumer Protection Act 1987, and it is one which some of the other EC Member States have chosen not to adopt, as there exist sufficient loss bearing mechanisms through insurance for producers rather than consumers to be able to cope with the burden of paying for the risks which are inherent in developing new products, particularly pharmaceutical products.

It has been claimed that the Consumer Protection Act 1987 does not implement the EC Directive properly, as the defence in English law is far easier to establish than the defence recommended by the Directive which used the *general* state of scientific knowledge by which to decide liability rather than the particular state of knowledge in a certain industry.

The Consumer Protection Act 1987 states that there will be a defence if the state of scientific and technical knowledge at the relevant time was not such *that a producer of products of the same description as the product in question* might be expected to have discovered the defect if it had existed in his products while they were under his control. The Directive provides a defence if the state of scientific or technical knowledge at the time when the product was put into circulation was not such as to enable the existence of the defect to be discovered. The discrepancy between these two provisions has led to an action being brought against the UK by the EU for failure to implement the Directive properly. However, the ECJ ruled that there was no inconsistency between s 4(1)(e) and Art 7 of the Directive (*Commission v UK* (1997)).

- **The defect was in the subsequent product not the component part**

The defect was in the subsequent product not the component part and was wholly attributable to the design of the subsequent product or compliance with the instructions of the producer of the subsequent product.

This defence allows a component producer in a chain of manufacture to escape liability in appropriate circumstances, and is yet another indication that the Consumer Protection Act 1987 was not intended to create absolute liability (s 4(1)(f)).

It would not be fair for a manufacturer who had produced a perfectly safe component, or one which complied with instructions, to be saddled with liability if that part was subsequently misused.

15.5 What difference does the Consumer Protection Act 1987 really make?

Much of the previous discussion of the application and scope of the Consumer Protection Act 1987 has been concerned with the numerous exceptions and defences which are permitted to apply.

The Consumer Protection Act 1987 does not apply to all products, nor does it cover all defects, nor all kinds of damage. The limitation period under the Act is strict and, in any case, it does not apply to products supplied before 1988. There are numerous defences permitted under the Consumer Protection Act 1987 and, if any of these are applicable, the consumer or injured party will be thrown upon the mercy of the common law which, in almost every case, is less adequate; there would never have been any need for the legislation to be introduced otherwise.

One of the most serious criticisms of the Consumer Protection Act 1987 is that it permits too many of the factors which fall to be considered in the ordinary law of negligence to play a part in establishing whether the product in question is defective, almost to the extent that there is very little difference between the standard of care in negligence and that under the Consumer Protection Act 1987. The development risks defence contributes to this picture.

Even after due consideration of the question of the standard of care, it is still necessary to prove causation, that is, that the defect in the product in question caused that particular damage of which the person affected complains. This burden of factual proof is equally difficult in negligence and the Consumer Protection Act 1987 does little to help consumers. However, s 2 does provide that the producer will be liable if the damage is caused partly by the defective product and partly by some other event, which could arguably make it less difficult to pin liability on the defendant than it would in negligence.

It could be that the opportunity has been lost to develop really comprehensive remedies for those affected by defective products, with the cost of this being distributed by pricing and insurance throughout society. Numerous reasons for this lost opportunity have been suggested, including the work of pressure groups such as farmers who insisted on the exclusion of primary agricultural products from the ambit of the Act. Another possible reason is that English law is rooted in the fault system and our lawyers find it difficult to break free of a system which will not provide compensation unless there is someone to 'blame'. Even the development risks defence was introduced into the legislation because of the self-interest of the Conservative government which feared that British goods would not be competitive in Europe if price increases were required to meet the cost of insuring against liability for possible defects in newly developed products.

Ironically, there may in effect be more instances of strict liability in the common law than under the Consumer Protection Act 1987, through the *res ipsa loquitur* principle and through the imposition of stricter standards of care in practice than the abstract rules would at first suggest. For example, the settlement of most small claims by insurance companies almost without question suggests that liability is virtually strict as the issue of fault is not inquired into. Cases like *Nettleship v Weston* (1972), in which a set objective standard of care is applied, are a further indication of this trend.

Ultimately, however, the Consumer Protection Act 1987 does put manufacturers and distributors on their guard. It does give the injured party a better chance of obtaining a remedy by providing the possibility of bringing legal action against more people in the chain of manufacture and distribution of defective products. Better product recall systems have been developed in recent years and there is a greater awareness of the need to establish checking systems in the manufacturing process, and to keep accurate records of product distribution.

An EU Directive which is intended to reverse the burden of proof in the case of defective services is currently under consideration.

In 1995, the European Commission conducted a review of the implementation of the Product Liability Directive throughout all Member States. No proposals for reform were suggested as a result of this review, though various matters were highlighted, and it is interesting to observe the way in which the various Member States have approached the implementation of the Directive. France has still to introduce any legislation on the matter, claiming that its own national laws already provide better protection than that afforded by the Directive. The Directive permits Member States to chose between certain options when implementing the Directive. As a result, unprocessed agricultural products and game are excluded from the definition of a product in all Member States except Sweden and Luxembourg, and the development risks defence is permitted in all Member States except Luxembourg, Finland and Norway, though not for medicinal products in Germany and not for medicinal products, foodstuffs and food products for human consumption in Spain. These various options will interfere to some extent with the removal of trade barriers throughout the EU. There is also a financial ceiling on liability in Germany, Greece, Portugal and Spain of 17 million ECU (though with certain variations).

The Commission noted that the Directive is generally regarded as very important throughout Europe, and that its implementation makes it easier to obtain compensation for damage caused by defective products by eliminating costly arguments about liability at an early stage and encouraging and expediting settlement of claims. There is no evidence of an increase in the number of civil actions as a result of the implementation of the Directive, and only three judgments in courts of EC States could be found in 1994. However, there is evidence in the UK that consumer claims are being brought under the Directive and being settled at an early stage, which is exactly what was intended by the Directive ('Unsafe Products', Report of the National Consumer Council, November 1995). It will be many years, though, before the full impact of the Directive on certain types of claims will be appreciated, particularly those concerning pharmaceutical products and transport where there can be a long time lag between manufacture and injury. The Commission indicated in its Report that it has a policy to wait the collection of firm evidence about any benefits or difficulties associated with the Directive before deciding whether to recommend changes in the law. Nevertheless, it is still the case that the law on product liability has not been fully harmonised throughout the EU.

The question arises as to why those injured by defective products should be singled out for special treatment, as opposed to the many people who are injured in other ways or are born with inherited disabilities and illnesses. Once again, the question arises of the need for a comprehensive system of compensation for all such people, regardless of fault and irrespective of the cause of their misfortune.

PRODUCT LIABILITY

Contract

Common law, through contract and tort, provides remedies for consumers, but these areas of law have inherent disadvantages.

Liability is strict under the Sale of Goods Act 1979, and there is a remedy for defects in quality as well as for defects which render a product dangerous. However, the range of people who are entitled to compensation was limited by the doctrine of privity of contract until the extension offered by the Contracts (Rights of Third Parties) Act 1999. Only the purchaser may sue the seller. Credit users now have a remedy against the credit company under the Consumer Credit Act 1974.

Tort

Tort compensates people who are injured by defective products, and is unconcerned about privity of contract. However, tort is subject to the problems inherent in proving fault, because liability is not strict, and perhaps more importantly, the range of defects for which tort will compensate is limited by the fact that it only compensates for defects which render products dangerous to health and safety (*Donoghue v Stevenson* (1932)). Normally, the injured party will sue the manufacturer.

The Consumer Protection Act 1987

Some of the problems presented by the contract/tort dichotomy are remedied by the Consumer Protection Act 1987.

The Consumer Protection Act 1987 creates strict liability in respect of defective products and offers a range of people to sue.

The range of potential defendants

'Producers', manufacturers, assemblers, processors, own-branders, importers into the EC, suppliers to the consumer (but this last group is only secondarily liable if they are unable to identify their own supplier). Liability is joint and several.

'Product' includes any goods, including raw materials, electricity, products comprised in other products, crops, ships, aircraft, building materials, etc. Buildings and primary agricultural produce are excluded.

A product is defective if its safety 'is not such as persons generally are entitled to expect', taking all the circumstances into account. Note that defects in quality alone do not fall within the Consumer Protection Act 1987, nor does strict liability extend to any part of the product which has been supplied with the product or comprised in it. The consumer would need to rely on the remedies available at common law in respect of these defects (*Carroll v Fearon* (2000)).

Note the circumstances which will be considered by the court, for example, marketing, get-up, warnings, labelling (*London Rubber Co v Richardson* (2000); *Worsley v Tambrands* (2000)).

Note the importance of the timing of supply.

Limitation period

Note the 10 year cut off point from the date of supply.

Defences

Defences under the Consumer Protection Act 1987 include:

- compliance with statutory or EC requirements;
- defendant did not supply the product;
- supply was not in the course of a business;
- defect was not in existence at the relevant time;
- development risks defence;
- defect was in the subsequent product not the component part, and was wholly attributable to the design of the subsequent product or compliance with the instructions of the producer of the subsequent product.

Limitations on the scope of the Consumer Protection Act 1987

Note the limits on the scope of the Consumer Protection Act 1987:

- the Consumer Protection Act 1987 does not cover all products;
- it does not cover all defects nor all kinds of damage;
- there are numerous defences under the Consumer Protection Act 1987;
- too many basic negligence considerations apply in determining liability under the Consumer Protection Act 1987;
- causation will still be a problem.

CHAPTER 16

VICARIOUS LIABILITY

16.1 Vicarious liability

Employers are said to be vicariously liable for the torts of their employees which are committed during the course of employment. In effect, this means that employers will be liable to third parties with whom they have usually had no direct contact, in situations when they cannot be said to have any personal blame, merely because they have employed someone who has committed a tort.

This rule may appear to be particularly harsh, as it appears to contradict the fault principle, and it was originally based on the legal fiction that employers have 'control' over their employees and order them to do the tortious acts in question but, more recently, it has been recognised that the rule has a more pragmatic basis, which is that employers, as opposed to employees, can best afford to bear the cost of compensating injured third parties. Large companies usually insure against this type of liability, or are their own insurers. The question as to who has the benefit of insurance cover may influence the court in deciding who should be regarded as the employer – see *British Telecom v James Thomson & Sons* (1998). A distinct advantage of vicarious liability to claimants is the fact that even if the particular individual who committed the tort is unidentifiable or cannot be traced, it will usually be possible to identify the employer, and if that employer is a corporation it will be possible to bring an action even if the employee-tortfeasor has fled the jurisdiction to escape legal action. However, it should be noted that there are limits to vicarious liability. In general, it is confined to situations involving employers and employees and does not extend to husbands and wives or parents and children. Nor does vicarious liability cover 'looser' relationships. For example, in *Hussain v Lancaster CC* (1998), the Court of Appeal held that a council could not be liable for tenants' torts (see Chapter 11).

In actions against police officers for assault and battery and false imprisonment, the notion that there is someone to sue is particularly important, despite the existence of the Police Complaints System, because under the Police Complaints System a complaint will only be sustainable if the officer concerned can be identified. Civil actions against chief constables as employers are therefore often the only means of redress.

Two questions must be asked in order to establish liability.

- was the person who committed the tort an employee?;

- was the employee acting in the course of employment when the relevant tort was committed?

16.2   Employees or independent contractors?

Employers or 'masters' will only be liable for the torts of their employees or 'servants' as they are called in law. They will not usually be liable for the torts of their independent contractors (subject to some exceptions). It is therefore necessary to establish the status of the person who committed the wrongful act.

Besides tort, a number of other areas of law are concerned with the distinction between servants and independent contractors, and the matters which fall to be considered are roughly the same across all branches of law, though throughout there is little consistency of principle.

For example, in tax law, it is necessary to decide whether a person should be paying income tax under Sched D as an independent contractor, which could carry tax advantages for that individual, or whether he is an employee and should have tax deducted at source under Sched E. Similarly, the State is concerned about an individual's employment status for the purposes of national insurance contributions. In employment law, only an employee, not an independent contractor, can bring an action for unfair dismissal and is entitled to statutory employment protection.

It is difficult, despite the existence of similar tests in each area of law, to establish any true consistency of principle, as the policy issues in each branch of law are different. In tax law, it seems that the employment status of an individual will be almost what the Revenue wishes it to be for the practical purpose of facilitating the collecting of tax. The same is true of the cases on national insurance contributions. In tort, rather different considerations are at play, such as loss distribution and possibly moral issues relating to compensating the victims of accidents.

Various tests for establishing an individual's employment status have been developed through the cases, but it will always be necessary for the court to follow the well established practice of looking at all the relevant facts. The liability of employers can extend well beyond their usual place of business (see *Fraser v Winchester HA* (1999), 9.1.4).

In *Carmichael v National Power* (2000), the House of Lords held that casual staff engaged on an 'as required' basis to act as guides at a power station were not employees. They were not guaranteed that work would be available and were not obliged to take work when it was offered to them.

16.3   The nature of the employment test

What was the nature of the contract by which the employment was established? One accepted view is that people who have a 'contract of service' (an employment contract) are employees, but people who have a 'contract for services' (a service contract) are independent contractors.

A contract may specify that the person doing the work is an independent contractor, or that the contract is a contract for services, but this is not conclusive and it is open to the court to consider, as a matter of fact, the precise nature of the employment (*Ready Mixed Concrete (South East) Ltd v Minister of Pensions and National Insurance* (1968)).

16.4   The control test

How much control did the employer have over the manner in which the work was carried out? If the employer is able to tell the person engaged to do a particular job how the work should be done, the contract will usually be an ordinary employment contract and the person doing the work will be a servant rather than an independent contractor. This control test, favoured in some of the earlier cases (see Kahn-Freund, O, *Servants and Independent Contractors*, 1951), breaks down if the person doing the work is a 'trained' or 'professional' person who has worked for many years to qualify and to gain particular skills, which the employer, who could merely be an entrepreneur or perhaps a public authority, probably does not possess.

Take, for example, an oil company which employs ships' captains to navigate its ships. It is highly unlikely that senior management in the company's central office have the knowledge, skill and experience required to take a ship from the Middle East to the UK. Yet, in law, it is likely that the ship's captain is an employee if he or she is paid a regular salary by the company and contributes to the company's pension scheme.

There are many employment situations of this type; for example, doctors are employees rather than independent contractors, even though they are employed by health authorities who are controlled by managers, very few of whom have medical qualifications.

16.4.1   Professional peoples' perceptions and the control test

Professional people regard it as an unjustifiable imposition and interference with their professional discretion, for managers to try to be too directive as to the manner in which they carry out their work. In the NHS, there is a fear among clinicians that managers in the current consumer orientated climate, in which the emphasis is on containing costs, will interfere too much with the way in which medical practice is conducted, by imposing certain clinical procedures upon them. This fear was recognised by the White Paper 'Working for Patients' in 1989.

Hospitals and now health authorities are vicariously liable for the torts of the doctors, nurses, radiographers and other medical staff whom they employ (*Gold v Essex CC* (1942) and *Cassidy v Ministry of Health* (1951)). Application of the 'control' test is meaningless, and it would be much more realistic to concede that Health Authorities are vicariously liable for pragmatic reasons.

Dias and Markesinis make the point that in the past hospitals were operating on slender financial resources, and this was the reason why initially they were not vicariously liable for the torts of their employees in the early cases, such as *Hillyer v St Bartholemew's Hospital* (1909). The switch to vicarious liability came with the introduction of the NHS which placed hospitals on a safer financial footing (see Dias and Markesinis, *Tort Law*).

It is now established that health authorities are vicariously liable for the torts of their employees (*Gold v Essex* (1942); *Cassidy v Minister of Health* (1951)), and, until 1991, hospital doctors were contractually required to pay premiums to the Medical Defence Union and the Medical Protection Society, so that, in the event of a malpractice claim, the health authority could seek an indemnity from the doctor concerned. However, partly because the Medical Protection Society introduced differential premiums for doctors to meet increasingly high awards of damages against those practising in certain high risk areas of medicine, the government introduced changes in the funding of the defence of medical negligence cases in 1990 through the system of Crown Indemnity. This means that health authorities now fund and defend their own cases, and pay damages out of their budgets. Hospital doctors are no longer required to pay premiums to the defence organisations. Effectively, this means a return to the old system, and creates a problem for Health Authorities which already find it difficult to provide for all the needs of patients, let alone to pay large sums by way of damages for negligence.

The pre-NHS economic environment described by Dias and Markesinis has therefore been re-imposed, but because the vicarious liability of health authorities is well established through precedent, it would be difficult for the courts to regress to reintroducing personal liability for doctors.

16.4.2 Skilled workers' perceptions and the control test

In *Mersey Docks and Harbour Board v Coggins and Griffiths (Liverpool) Ltd* (1947), the crane driver who was hired out with his crane by his employer, the harbour authority, to another company, stevedores, was outraged at the suggestion that anyone should be able to tell him how to operate his crane, yet he was treated as servant of the harbour authority for the purposes of the law, even though the contract under which he was hired to the stevedores specified that he should be their servant.

In some circumstances, both parties in an employment situation may have their own reasons for wanting the relationship to be classified as one of independent contracting. People commissioning work may want to avoid expensive employee national insurance contributions and administrative responsibility for collecting tax from employees. They may well wish to be free from what they see as the encumbrances of employment protection legislation for employees, and the legal obligation to carry insurance cover for them. Those doing the work might prefer to have greater control over their tax and the advantage of more tax allowances by being classified as liable to Sched D income tax. In *Lane v Shire Roofing Co (Oxford) Ltd* (1995), the Court of Appeal held that there was often a real public interest in ensuring that the law discriminates properly between employees and independent contractors, especially if health and safety issues are at stake. One reason for this is that employers ought not to be able to avoid their statutory responsibility under such Acts as the Employers' Liability (Compulsory Insurance) Act 1969. The various tests for establishing the nature of the employment were referred to, including the control test, which the Court of Appeal considered important, though not always decisive, especially in cases involving skilled employees with the discretion to decide how the work is to be done. In such instances, the test should be broadened to consider whose business it was. Was the workman carrying on his own work or that of the employer? The view was that the answer to that question might involve considering where the financial risk lay and how far the worker had any opportunity to take advantage of good management in performing his tasks. Even the answer to that question might not be conclusive because ultimately this was a question of law. A distinction was drawn between the situation in employment today and that which prevailed when the *Ready Mixed Concrete* (1968) case was decided in 1968. In the 1990s, there is greater flexibility in employment, with fewer people employed, more independent contractors, and more temporary and shared employment. In the *Lane* case, it had been agreed that the defendant would be paid a lump sum for the job in question, the claimant had used his own tools but had provided no materials. He had taken his own ladder to the site and had fallen from it when he was working on a roofing job, suffering serious brain damage. The Court of Appeal, reversing the decision of the High Court, held that the worker was an employee even though he had traded on his own as a roofer/builder since 1982 and had attained self-employed tax status. The defendants were a new roofing business and they found it financially more advantageous to treat the men whom they engaged as subcontracting, self-employed workers. The outcome of this case may be surprising in the light of the pre-existing case law, and it does illustrate the importance of public policy in influencing judicial decision-making in this area of law.

The matter is clearly too complex and too dependent upon policy considerations such as loss distribution, insurance and so on, to be covered by a single simple test with prescribed rules as to how a 'servant' is to be identified. As Lord Pearce explained in *ICI v Shatwell* (1965), the doctrine of vicarious liability has grown out of rough justice and social convenience rather than from the application of clear and logical principle.

The conclusion must be that as a means of assessing contractual status for the purpose of vicarious liability the control test is artificial, out-dated and only partially helpful, and indeed this is reflected in the fact that judges now place less emphasis upon this test. Perhaps the reality is that suggested by Atiyah (*Vicarious Liability in the Law of Torts*, 1967), which is that reference to 'control' means control of when and where the work is carried out, rather than how it is performed.

16.5   The 'integral part of the business' test

A further test was proposed by Lord Denning in *Stevenson Jordan and Harrison Ltd v McDonald and Evans* (1969). The reasoning is that:

> Under a contract of service, a man is employed as part of the business; whereas under a contract for services, his work, although done for the business, is not integrated into it but is only accessory to it.

With this approach also, however, there are difficulties which were recognised in the *Ready Mixed Concrete* case. Often, people who are casual or part time employees are treated as part of a business, whereas they would not necessarily regard themselves as totally committed to it. Part time teachers and markers and examiners for public examination boards are treated as employees for the purposes of income tax, but this type of employment is often regarded by them as a supplement to their main income, and a secondary source of employment, and most would regard themselves as independent contractors.

However, the court will decide the status of each individual in the light of all the circumstances. Thus, for example, it has been held that even a controlling shareholder may be an employee (*Secretary of State for Trade and Industry v Bottrill* (1999)).

16.5.1 Who owns the tools?

If the person doing the work owns the tools which are used in that employment, he or she will usually be an independent contractor.

This is not conclusive, however.

16.5.2 Is the worker paid a wage or a lump sum for the job?

Independent contractors usually negotiate a single lump-sum price for a particular job, which may be payable in instalments (*WHPT Housing*

Association Ltd v Secretary of State for Social Services (1981)). Employees are usually paid a salary or wage at regular intervals during their employment. Again, it is possible to find exceptions to this general rule.

16.5.3 Was the worker in business on his own account?

If the person who does a particular job regards himself as running a business of his or her own, with responsibility for his or her own accounts, tax and equipment, he or she will usually be an independent contractor.

16.5.4 Who had the power to hire and fire the employee?

The person who retains the power of dismissal is usually the master for the purposes of vicarious liability.

It is clear that it is impossible to formulate a single test which covers all situations, but it may be possible to distil from the various tests principles which can be applied in particular cases. However, in practice, it is difficult to predict which tests the courts will apply and almost impossible to assess in advance the outcome of individual cases. In common with so many other areas in the law of tort, this is subject to the vagaries of policy and the prevailing economic and social attitudes and the approach of particular judges to the individual cases they are called upon to decide.

16.6 Some miscellaneous matters

There are some situations which have presented particular problems:

16.6.1 Employees on loan

If a person is the servant of one employer but is 'lent' to another for a particular job, the question may arise as to who is the employer at the time of an accident. However, a full transfer of employment can only take effect if the employee has knowledge of the change (*Bolwell v Radcliffe Homes* (1999).

In general, if an employee is 'on loan' to another employer, the first employer will be treated as the employer for the purposes of vicarious liability. In *Mersey Docks and Harbour Board v Coggins and Griffiths* (1947), a crane driver was hired out with his crane to a firm of stevedores under a contract which stated that he was to be the servant of the stevedores. His wages, however, were to be paid by his normal employer. The firm of stevedores gave instructions as to the jobs to be done on any particular day, but were in no position to instruct the driver how to operate his crane.

The House of Lords took all the facts into account, but regarded it to be of paramount importance that the original employer retained control over the manner in which the work was to be done. Accordingly, it was held that the original employer carried vicarious liability for the tort of the driver. The original employer bears the burden of proving that responsibility for the torts of the employee has shifted to the second employer, and statements in the contract of hire are not to be treated as conclusive on this matter.

In *Chief Constable of Lincolnshire v Stubbs* (1999), an employment law case, it was held that police officers seconded to another force remained, for all purposes, employees of their home force.

16.6.2 Cars on loan

There are some cases in which cars have been driven by someone other than the owner for a purpose in which the owner has an interest. The question then arises as to whether the owner of the vehicle could be vicariously liable for the negligence of the driver. In *Britt v Galmoye* (1928), the driver of a car was allowed, for his own convenience, to borrow a vehicle from its owner. The owner was not vicariously liable for his negligent driving. By contrast, in *Ormrod v Crossville Motor Services Ltd* (1953), the owner of a car asked someone to drive the vehicle to Monte Carlo, where he planned to join him for a holiday. As there was a joint purpose here, the owner was vicariously liable when the driver had an accident.

In *Morgans v Launchbury* (1973), Denning MR attempted to extend this principle to a situation in which a wife had lent the family car, registered in her name, to her husband to go on a drinking spree with some friends. He had promised his wife that if he became too drunk to drive, he would ask one of his friends to take the wheel. Unfortunately, the friend who did the driving was also drunk, and there was a very serious accident as a result of his negligent driving. As he was uninsured, it became important, for the purposes of obtaining compensation, to fix liability. Lord Denning, using the notion of the 'matrimonial car', was determined to establish that the wife was vicariously liable. However, the House of Lords held that the mere fact that she had given permission for her husband or his friend to use the car, while she had no other interest in the venture, was no reason why she should be vicariously liable, as there was no such rule in English law, and if the law was to be changed, it was for Parliament, and not for Lord Denning, to do so.

It seems that, in such cases, there must be an interest in the venture which is common to both the owner and the driver of a vehicle, before there will be vicarious liability. This is straying rather a long way from the notion of 'employment', but the courts do appear to be prepared to take those steps.

16.7 The course of employment

A master will only be liable for torts which the employee commits in the course of employment. Although this is a question of fact in each case, there is little consistency in the decisions, and once again the only sensible conclusion must be that the judges are influenced by considerations of policy which fall outside the facts and are seldom discussed. It is therefore extremely difficult to state the law simply.

There are two lines of cases, those cases in which acts of employees are held to be within the scope of employment, and those which fall outside it. Examining each line of cases in an attempt to elicit general principles is futile, but it appears that an employer will usually be liable for wrongful acts which are actually authorised by him, and for acts which are wrongful ways of doing something authorised by the employer, even if the acts themselves were expressly forbidden by the employer.

16.7.1 Authorised acts

If an employer expressly authorises an unlawful act, he or she will be primarily liable. The position is more difficult in cases in which the employer is said to have authorised a wrongful act by implication. This 'implied authority' approach seems to have lost currency, but it was accepted in the early years of this century (see *Poland v Parr & Sons* (1927)), and it was even then probably little more than a means of justifying the outcome which the courts desired.

16.7.2 Wrongful modes of doing authorised acts

In the following cases, it was held that the employer *was* vicariously liable for the torts of the employee:

- *Limpus v London General Omnibus Company* (1862)

  Bus drivers were in the habit of racing, a practice which was strictly forbidden by the companies. In the course of a race, the claimant was injured. The employer was vicariously liable because this was merely an unauthorised way of performing the job of driving, which the driver was employed to do.

- *Rose v Plenty* (1976)

  A milkman had been forbidden by his employer to allow young boys to ride on the milk floats and assist in delivering milk. A 13 year old boy was injured partly as a result of the driver's negligence and partly through his own carelessness, and the employer was vicariously liable. The Court of Appeal held that the milkman was carrying out, albeit in a prohibited manner, the task which he had been employed to do, so the employer was liable. Lord Denning's suggested justification for the decision was that the boy had been furthering the interests of the employer.

- *Century Insurance Co Ltd v Northern Ireland Transport Board* (1942)

  The employee threw down a lighted match while petrol was being transferred from the lorry which he was employed to drive into a large petrol tank at a garage. It was held that the employer was vicariously liable for this negligent act because at the time the employee was engaged upon his duties.

- *Bayley v Manchester, Sheffield and Lincolnshire Railway Co* (1873)

  One of the company's porters, who was charged with the job of ensuring that passengers were on the correct coaches, pulled the claimant from a train, injuring him. The company was liable.

In the following cases, it was held that the employer was *not* vicariously liable:

- *Beard v London General Omnibus Company* (1900)

  A bus conductor decided to try driving the bus. The employer was not vicariously liable for his negligence, as he was doing something outside the scope of what he was employed to do.

- *Hilton v Thomas Burton (Rhodes) Ltd* (1961)

  A group of workmen decided to take an unauthorised tea break and on the return journey the driver negligently crashed their employer's van, killing the claimant's husband. They were on 'a frolic of their own'. The employer was not liable.

Although it is difficult to extract a general principle from the cases, it appears that, if the person who is injured was performing some act which contributed to, or provided some benefit to the business of the employer, there will be vicarious liability (*Rose v Plenty*). If the employer derives no benefit from the forbidden act (*Twine v Beans Express*), there may be no vicarious liability.

Employers will not usually be liable for deliberate criminal acts of employees which also give rise to civil liability. However, if the criminal act is part and parcel of the employment, the employer may be liable. If the employment involved the employee being entrusted with particular goods, then any theft or mishandling of the goods by the employee will give rise to vicarious liability. In *Morris v Martin & Sons* (1966), an employer was liable when an employee who worked at his dry-cleaning business stole a fur coat. This was a bailment situation, however, in which particularly onerous duties are placed upon those who are entrusted with goods. Such duties cannot be delegated, and the decision of the Court of Appeal is not surprising.

In *Barwick v Joint Stock Bank* (1867), it was held that an employer could be vicariously liable for the frauds of an employee, and in *Lloyd v Grace Smith & Co* (1912), an employer, a solicitor, was vicariously liable for the mortgage fraud committed by an employee, even though the employer did not stand to derive any benefit from the crime. The employee did, however, have ostensible authority from the employer to carry out the act involved (arranging a mortgage), and the employer had placed him in that position of authority.

However, employers are not usually liable for assaults committed by their employees, see *Keppel Bus Co Ltd v Ahmad* (1974), in which a bus conductor hit a difficult passenger with his ticket machine. In the New Zealand case of *Petterson v Royal Oak Hotel Ltd* (1948), a nightclub bouncer committed assaults in the process of protecting his employer's property, and the employer was held vicariously liable. He was perceived to be furthering the interests of the employer, in much the same way as the boy in *Rose v Plenty*.

In *Generale Bank Nederland v Export Credits Guarantee Department* (1999), it was decided by the House of Lords that an employer was *not* vicariously liable when, in the course of employment, an employee had committed acts which were not in themselves tortious but had been carried out to assist fraudulent acts committed by an outsider. In this case, the employee had knowledge of the scheme to defaud the bank.

The position in relation to crime *per se* is that employers will not normally be prosecuted for the crimes of their employees, unless the employee was instructed to commit the crime in question, or committed it under duress. However, tort actions may arise out of the same fact situations as certain crimes (for example, assault and battery), and it is these torts for which the employer may be vicariously liable.

16.8   The *Lister v Romford Ice* principle

There is a term implied at common law into contracts of employment that an employee will exercise all reasonable care and skill during the course of employment. An employee who is negligent is in breach of such a term and theoretically, the employer who has been held vicariously liable for the tort could seek an indemnity from the employee to make good the loss. In *Lister v Romford Ice and Cold Storage Co Ltd* (1957), a father was injured by his son, who was employed by the respondents. The employers were vicariously liable for the son's negligence and met the father's claim. Exercising their right of subrogation under the contract of insurance, the employers sued the son. The House of Lords held that the son was liable to indemnify the employer and consequently the insurers.

This situation can clearly cause problems for relations between employers and employees, and as a consequence of the difficulties which have been predicted, insurers have entered into a gentleman's agreement not to enforce their rights in such circumstances in the future if there is no wilful misconduct or collusion between the employer and employee.

VICARIOUS LIABILITY

Vicarious liability for torts of employees or servants

The law places heavy responsibilities on employers who may be vicariously liable or primarily liable.

The employer is to be liable only if the person who committed the tort was an employee, not an independent contractor and the employee must have been acting in the course of employment at the time.

Employees or servants

Note the tests which have been employed to establish whether the person who committed the tort was an employee or an independent contractor: the nature of the contract; the control test; the 'integral part of the business' test; who owns the tools?; a wage or a lump sum?; who could hire and fire (*Lane v Shire Roofing (Oxford) Ltd* (1995); *Secretary of State for Trade and Industry v Bottrill* (1999))?

Special cases include: employees on loan (*Mersey Docks and Harbour Board v Coggins and Griffiths* (1947)); cars on loan (*Ormrod v Crossville* (1953); *Britt v Galmoye* (1928); *Morgans v Launchbury* (1973); *Chief Constable of Lincolnshire v Stubbs* (1999); *Carmichael v National Power* (2000)).

Acting in the course of employment

The employer will be liable for authorised acts and for wrongful ways of performing them. Note the inconsistency in the cases:

Limpus v London General Omnibus Co (1862);

Rose v Plenty (1976);

Century Insurance v NI Transport (1942);

Bayley v MSL Railway Co (1873).

The employer was not liable in the following cases: *Beard v LGO Co* (1900); *Hilton v Thomas Burton* (1961); *Twine v Beans Express* (1946).

In some cases, employers may even be liable in tort for the consequences of crimes committed by employees:

Barwick v Joint Stock Bank (1867);

Morris v Martin (1966);

Lloyd v Grace Smith (1912);

Keppel v Ahmad (1974);

Generale Bank Nederland v Export Credit Guarantee Department (1999).

CHAPTER 17

TRESPASS TO GOODS

From the earliest days of the common law, a number of torts were developed specifically to protect interests in goods, in a similar way to those torts which developed to protect interests in land. However, by the 1970s, it had become clear that the torts relating to chattels were badly in need of reform and, in 1977, the Torts (Interference with Goods) Act was passed in an attempt to clarify the law. Although this statute did introduce radical changes, it was not sufficiently comprehensive to remove all of the difficulties and there are some areas of ambiguity. Many of the common law rules still apply, and the Torts (Interference with Goods) Act 1977 must be read in the light of these.

17.1 The common law

At common law, the most important torts which could be used to protect or recover chattels were trespass to goods and conversion. Another tort developed later to protect goods by means of an action on the case for damage to reversionary interests in goods. In order to understand the changes which were introduced in the legislation, it is also necessary to consider the common law rules.

17.1.1 Trespass to goods

Trespass to goods can be defined as 'direct, immediate interference with personal property belonging to another person'.

This tort essentially provides protection for the person entitled to immediate possession of the chattels in question, and in that, and other ways, it resembles trespass to land.

In common with other forms of trespass, the act in question had to be direct (as in trespass to land). For example, in *Fouldes v Willoughby* (1841), it was said to be trespass to goods to scratch the panel of a coach.

Any form of deliberate destruction of the goods could amount to trespass, but even using goods without permission could constitute trespass, and it is no defence for the defendant to claim honest but mistaken belief that the goods belonged to him (*Kirk v Gregory* (1876)).

Acts of trespass to goods, like trespass to land, are actionable *per se* (that is, without proof of damage) but, since the decision in *Letang v Cooper* (1965), it may be the case that trespass to goods will follow trespass to the person and require the act to be deliberate, though the extension has never been made judicially.

This tort survives today after the Torts (Interference with Goods) Act 1977 and the Act specifically states that the defence of contributory negligence will not be available in answer to this tort (s 11(1)).

17.1.2 Conversion

The tort of conversion consists of dealing with goods in a manner inconsistent with the rights of the true owner, so denying the right of the owner to the goods, or asserting a right which is inconsistent with the owner's right.

The claimant must prove that he had possession of the goods or the right to immediate possession of them at the time of the wrongful act.

It is necessary to prove that the defendant had the intention to deal with the goods, though there is no need to prove the intention to deny the owner his or her right or title to the goods. Thus, the only relevant intention is that of committing the act of interference. Indeed, the tort may be committed even in circumstances when the defendant had no knowledge that the goods belonged to the claimant, for example when goods are purchased in good faith from a thief. The tort features prominently in considering the issue of title to goods when there is a question of mistaken identity in contract (*Lewis v Averay* (1972)).

Examples of conversion are:

- Contradicting the title of the true owner.

- Detaining goods which belong to the claimant without permission when there has been a demand for the goods which has been refused. It has been suggested that if cars are wheel-clamped or towed away from land on which they are parked without the permission of the occupier, there could be an action for conversion available to the car owner. However, it was held in *Arthur v Anker* (1996) that, as long as certain reasonable steps were taken by the clamper, no tort would be committed. These steps included the placing of a notice to warn trespassing motorists of the possibility of being wheel-clamped, the provision of information as to how to communicate with the clamper and the imposition of a reasonable release fee.

- Destruction of goods belonging to the claimant, or intentionally risking the confiscation or destruction of goods. In *Moorgate Mercantile Co v Finch* (1962), the defendant had used a car belonging to a finance company for smuggling drugs. When the car was confiscated by the Customs and Excise authorities, the defendant was guilty of conversion.

- Selling goods without the claimant's permission.

- If goods are taken or damaged by police officers in the course of a search, there will be a successful action for conversion if the police acted beyond their common law or statutory powers in so doing. People whose property has been confiscated by the police have a right to bring an action in a magistrates' court under the Police (Property) Act 1892 for its recovery. However, if a recipient of goods merely keeps them for someone whom he or she honestly believes to be entitled to them, there is no conversion (see Blackburn J in *Hollins v Fowler* (1875)).

- Receiving goods which have been obtained by fraud, and selling them in good faith to someone else (*Hollins v Fowler* (1875)).

The Torts (Interference with Goods) Act 1977 provides that the receipt of goods under a pledge which is unauthorised is also conversion (s 11(2)).

A change brought about by the Torts (Interference with Goods) Act 1977 is that, if the defendant merely makes a verbal statement denying the claimant's title to goods, there is no conversion (s 11(3)).

Contributory negligence is not a defence to conversion (s 11(1) of the Torts (Interference with Goods) Act 1977).

Many of the cases concerning title to goods which are studied in the law of contract are conversion cases.

17.1.3 Action for damage to reversionary interests in goods

In circumstances when the defendant unlawfully interfered with goods at a time when the claimant did not have possession or an immediate right to possession of them, there could be no action available under the three existing common law torts. In the mid-19th century, the courts developed the action on the case for interference with the reversionary interests of the claimant. This has a parallel with the development of the action on the case relating to land in similar circumstances, when there was a less direct relationship between the parties and the property concerned.

17.1.4 The Torts (Interference with Goods) Act 1977

This statute, acknowledging the overlaps and ambiguities of the common law, attempted to tidy up the rules in this area. Among the reforms introduced were these:

- the right to sue for negligent loss by a bailee of goods entrusted to him was transferred to the tort of conversion by s 2(2);

- a general concept of tortious liability was introduced for wrongful interference with goods, with corresponding remedies which the court is given the power to order;

- contributory negligence was extinguished as a defence to conversion and intentional trespass, except in relation to banks;

- new rules were introduced whereby goods which had not been claimed could be disposed of;

- people who had improved goods while they were in possession of them were provided with the means of claiming an allowance for their efforts;

- provision was made to deal with actions between co-owners, a problem area at common law;

- reversal of the old rule that defendants were not allowed to plead that a third party had a better title to the goods than the claimant.

17.1.5 Remedies for conversion

Damages obtainable for conversion allow recovery of the market value of the goods and special damages. This extinguishes the claimant's title. Alternatively, the true owner of the goods can have them restored plus special damages.

Many of the common law actions still survive.

Statutory reforms were introduced by the Torts (Interference with Goods) Act 1977.

TRESPASS TO GOODS

Trespass to goods

Trespass to goods can be defined as 'direct, immediate interference with personal property belonging to another person'. Note the similarities with other forms of trespass:

>   *Fouldes v Willoughby* (1841);
>
>   *Kirk v Gregory* (1876).

Conversion

Conversion can be defined as 'dealing with goods in a manner inconsistent with the rights of the true owner'.

The claimant must prove that he or she had possession or the right to immediate possession at the time the wrongful act was committed.

Note the significance of this tort for the law of contract:

>   *Lewis v Averay* (1972);
>
>   *Moorgate Mercantile Co v Finch* (1962).

Action for damage to reversionary interests in goods

A 'new' action developed in the mid-19th century, alongside a similar development relating to land. This permitted a claimant to sue for interference with goods even though he did not have possession of them, or a right to immediate possession, at the time of the interference.

Torts (Interference with Goods) Act 1977

The 1977 Act tidied up the law and *inter alia*:

*   abolished the old action of detinue;

*   provided new remedies;

*   abolished the defence of contributory negligence in conversion and intentional trespass;

*   introduced new rules for the disposal of unclaimed goods;

- provided an allowance for people who had improved goods which turned out to belong to another person.

Remedies

Damages include restoration of the goods or damages. Special damages are available in both cases.

CHAPTER 18

DEFAMATION AND OTHER TORTS AFFECTING THE REPUTATION

There are some torts which have been developed to compensate for damaged reputations, just as others have emerged which compensate for bodily injury. In addition to compensation, equally important is the need for injunctions to prevent threatened damage to the reputation. The relevant torts are libel, slander, injurious falsehood, malicious prosecution.

18.1 Freedom of speech, the media and the law

Although not exclusively concerned with the activities of the media, the majority of defamation actions do concern statements made by the press. Freedom of communication is jealously guarded by the media, and as there is no written constitution in the UK, it is the judges who have undertaken the role of guardians of this freedom, although they have no overriding obligation to protect freedom of speech. Rather, the role of judges is to undertake an exercise which aims to achieve a fair balance between the right to free expression and the need to protect the reputation of the individual. Freedom of speech, in the absence of a written constitution, exists only so far as it has not been removed or eroded by common law or statute, including the Human Rights Act 1998, and the balance between the various conflicting interests changes from one time to another according to the political climate. The role of the law of defamation is to ensure that freedom of speech does not outweigh the interests of the individual, although it is arguable that the damages which are awarded in defamation cases distort the extent of the protection which the individual should reasonably expect. There are also some who would argue that the conflicting interests involved cannot be balanced, and that the role of the courts should not be regarded as a balancing exercise, as the interests are not of equal weight.

How much the defamation action actually protects all individuals is debatable, as in general it is only the rich who can afford the luxury of suing for defamation. There is no legal aid available for these actions, and the costs involved can be extremely high, partly because juries are required to hear them, and partly because the lawyers who deal with such cases regard them as particularly complex and difficult and justifying high fees. In *Taylforth v Metropolitan Police Comr and The Sun Newspaper* (1994), Gillian Taylforth was left with a bill for costs of around £500,000 after an 11 day hearing. In 1993, a libel action brought by Anita Roddick of the Body Shop cost £1 million for the claimant alone. In *Joyce v Sengupta* (1992), the claimant circumvented the rule about legal aid by bringing her action for malicious falsehood instead of defamation, with the approval of the Court of Appeal.

In *Spring v Guardian Assurance plc* (1994), an ex-employee of the defendant brought an action for *negligence* because he had been unable to obtain employment after the defendants had written a damaging reference for him. Not only did this circumvent the legal aid problem, but it also prevented the defendant relying on the defence of qualified privilege which would have been available to an action for libel.

The Third Royal Commission on the Press defined press freedom as:

> That degree of freedom from restraint which is essential to enable proprietors, editors and journalists to advance the public interest by publishing facts and opinions without which a democratic electorate cannot make responsible judgments.

Press freedom is protected by the defences to the defamation action, many of which influence editors and their legal advisors in arriving at the decision of whether or not to publish dubious material. Often, as far as the media and its legal advisors are concerned, the real question is how far they will be able to exploit the notion of press freedom in order to sell copy, without the fear of a libel action. Newspapers are commercial concerns and depend for their existence on the number of copies they are able to sell. Publication of potentially defamatory material is a calculable risk, given that juries are unpredictable and defences such as justification and fair comment may operate to the advantage of the press. Moreover, although libel damages generally are not tax-deductible expenditure (*Fairie v Hall* (1947)), as when a solicitor writes a defamatory letter, there are authorities which suggest that for newspapers libel damages are tax-deductible (see the Australian case of *Herald Weekly Times Ltd v FTC* (1932)). Against the advantages of increased sales, editors must set the disadvantages of high awards of damages, including exemplary damages in cases where it is obvious that a libel has been published for reasons of sensationalism with a view to making a handsome profit (*Broome v Cassell* (1964)).

It should not be forgotten that journalists, like members of the public, also have the opportunity to sue for libel. In 1995, an investigative journalist received £31,500 plus costs of £55,000 when he was libelled by Michael Heseltine. Taxpayers met this bill under Treasury guidance which allows public resources to be used to deal with matters arising in the course of official duties of ministers and civil servants.

The European Convention on Human Rights, which was ratified by Britain in 1951, attaches special importance to freedom of expression. Article 10(1) states:

> Everyone has the right to freedom of expression. This right shall include freedom to hold opinions and to receive and impart information and ideas without interference by public authority and regardless of frontiers.

The Article does recognise certain exceptions to this freedom which initially appear to curtail it greatly (Art 10(2)):

The exercise of these freedoms, since it carries with it duties and responsibilities, may be subject to formalities, conditions, restrictions or penalties as are prescribed by law and are necessary in a democratic society, in the interests of national security, territorial integrity or public safety, for the prevention of disorder or crime, for the protection of health or morals, for the protection of the reputation or rights of others, for preventing the disclosure of information received in confidence or for maintaining the authority and impartiality of the judiciary.

In practice, despite these exceptions, the European Court of Human Rights has tended to lean in favour of the media in its interpretation of Art 10, and the Article does require much clearer statements of the legal limits to freedom of speech than are available in English law. (See Robertson, M, *Media Law*, 1985, and Burnet, D, *Ethical Issues in Journalism*, Belsey, A (ed), 1992.)

Article 10 has now been incorporated into English law by the Human Rights Act 1998, but it was referred to in the case of *Derbyshire CC v Times Newspapers* in the Court of Appeal (1992), where it was accepted that it had affected the right of a governmental body to sue for libel. In the House of Lords [1993] AC 534, it did not appear to be necessary to invoke Article 10, and the decision was reached by reference to common law alone.

In the cases of *Rantzen v Mirror Group Newspapers* (1993) and *John v MGN Ltd* (1996), the Court of Appeal referred to Art 10 in an effort to understand the correct approach to reviewing the jury's award of damages. Their Lordships recognised that Article 10 must be regarded as underlying common law principles relating to freedom of expression.

In July 1995, the European Court of Human Rights was critical of the approach taken by the English courts when it reviewed the award of damages which a jury had made to Lord Aldington in 1989. The English jury had found that Lord Aldington had been libelled by Count Nikolai Tolstoy in a pamphlet written about his alleged wartime involvement in the deaths of 70,000 Cossacks and Yugoslavs. Count Nikolai Tolstoy had been forced into bankruptcy by the huge award of damages fixed by the jury at £1.5 million and by the costs involved in the action. The European Court in Strasbourg ruled that the award of damages was excessive and that it amounted to a violation of the Count's right to freedom of expression, as 'taken in conjunction with the state of the national law at the time' it was 'not necessary in a democratic society'. The court accepted that there is no upper or lower limit on the award of damages in English law which a jury can make and that the role of the judge in giving guidance is limited. Perhaps because of the firm line taken in this case by the European Court of Human Rights, there is the definite possibility of some modifications to the law through the recent case of *John v MGN* (1996) and the Defamation Act 1996. These changes are discussed later in this chapter.

18.2   Libel and slander

Defamation consists of the torts of libel and slander. There are distinctions between libel and slander which are attributable to their origins and development, and have little real justification in modern law. The differences between libel and slander have been abolished in some commonwealth jurisdictions and in 1975 the Faulks Committee recommended that they should be abolished in English law, but the distinction remains, despite the Defamation Act 1996.

18.2.1   Distinction

The basic differences between the two torts are as follows:

- **Libel is a defamatory statement in some permanent form, for example, writing, recorded film or speech**

  Some examples of libel are: *Monson v Tussaud's Ltd* (1894) (the placing of a wax image of the claimant in the chamber of horrors at Madam Tussaud's waxwork exhibition amounted to libel); *Youssoupoff v MGM Pictures Ltd* (1934) (the claimant was portrayed in a film as having been seduced by Rasputin. This was a permanent form of defamation and therefore amounted to libel).

  By s 16 of the Defamation Act 1952, and ss 166 and 201 of the Broadcasting Act 1990, defamatory statements in radio and television broadcasts are libel.

  Under s 4 of the Theatres Act 1968, defamatory statements made in public performances of plays are libel.

  A purely transitory defamatory statement is slander. Examples are gestures and words which are spoken but not recorded.

  There is some doubt as to whether defamatory words recorded on disc, tape or CD are libel or slander. Street considered that libel required a visual communication, whereas the editor of *Salmond and Heuston* thinks any permanent recording would be libel (*Salmond on Tort*).

- **Libel is actionable *per se* (without proof of special damage which is calculable as a specific sum of money), slander is not**

  To succeed in an action for slander, damage must be proved except in four instances, which are as follows:

  (a) Where there is an allegation that the claimant has committed an imprisonable offence. The offence must be one which carries a sentence of imprisonment at first instance, rather than one which merely carries a possible prison sentence or a fine.

  (b) Where there is an imputation that the claimant is suffering from a socially undesirable disease, such as smallpox, or perhaps more relevant today, venereal disease or AIDS. There has been a suggestion that the list of diseases in this category is now fixed.

(c) Where there is an imputation that a woman has committed adultery or otherwise behaved in an 'unchaste' fashion (Slander of Women Act 1891). It has been held that an allegation of lesbianism is included in the term 'unchastity' (*Kerr v Kennedy* (1942)).

(d) Where there is an imputation that the claimant is unfit to carry on his trade, profession or calling. The statement must disparage the claimant in the way in which he or she exercises his or her profession or job. In *Hopwood v Muirson* (1945), it was held that an allegation that a headmaster had committed adultery was not actionable *per se*, but it would have been had the adultery been alleged with a pupil or a teacher at his school. This common law position has been altered by s 2 of the Defamation Act 1952 which merely requires that the claimant could possibly have been injured in relation to his or her trade or calling by the statement.

- **Libel may be a crime as well as a tort, whereas slander is only a tort**

It was thought that criminal libel had become virtually obsolete, but the mere threat of proceedings by Sir James Goldsmith in 1977 succeeded in forcing *Private Eye* to withdraw copies of its magazine from bookshops (*Goldsmith v Pressdram* (1977)). Criminal libel is very similar to civil libel but it does not require the person defamed to be alive, nor is it necessary to publish the statement to a third party. Both of these elements are required for a successful action for civil libel. In criminal libel, it appears that the requirement that there should be a threatened breach of the peace no longer applies (*R v Wicks* (1936)). This has never been a requirement of civil libel. In other respects, the two types of libel are the same.

18.3 Who can sue for defamation?

Only living persons can sue for defamation. It is permissible to speak ill of the dead, at least in law. Even if an action has been initiated, if the claimant dies immediately before the trial, the action is said to die with him. This is important from the point of view of defendants who might be tempted to spin out the pre-trial periods for as long as possible waiting for a sick or elderly claimant to die, as has happened in some cases. Measures taken recently to speed up litigation should remedy this situation, but it must be remembered that, in any case, the defendants will have to pay their own costs if the claimant does die before the trial commences.

Any person who can prove that the defamatory words refer to him can sue for defamation. However, there is some doubt as to the position of corporate bodies. It appears that trading corporations do have a right to sue for defamation (*Upjohn v BBC and Others* (1994) in which the makers of the drug 'halcion' sued over allegations that they had concealed dangerous side effects for 20 years and *South Hetton Coal Company v North Eastern News Association Ltd* (1894)). However, in *Derbyshire CC v Times Newspapers Ltd* (1992), the House of Lords held that local authorities do not have a right at common law to maintain an action for defamation. The decision was explained by Lord Keith in these terms:

> It is of the highest public importance that a democratically elected governmental body, or indeed any governmental body, should be open to uninhibited public criticism. The threat of a civil action for defamation must inevitably have an inhibiting effect on freedom of speech.

The Court of Appeal had held that to allow a local authority to sue for libel would greatly inhibit freedom of speech and would be contrary to Art 10 of the European Convention on Human Rights.

Individual officers of a local authority would be able to sue in their own right for libel, and local authorities are at present able to bring an action for criminal libel.

18.4 A working definition of defamation

Whether a statement amounts to libel or slander it must satisfy the general requirements of the law to be actionable. A useful starting point is a definition of defamation which is as follows:

> Defamation consists of publishing a defamatory statement which refers to an identifiable claimant, without lawful justification.

This definition will be examined in detail to identify and explain the various elements of the tort.

18.4.1 Publication

The statement must be published to a person other than the claimant alone. It is not actionable in civil law merely to make a defamatory statement to the claimant alone out of ear-shot of a third person, nor to write a letter to the claimant containing defamatory material. If the claimant decides to show a potentially defamatory letter to someone else, there is a defence of *volenti* as the claimant, not the defendant, has published the statement.

In *Hinderer v Cole* (1977), the claimant was sent a letter by his brother-in-law which was addressed to 'Mr Stonehouse Hinderer'. It contained a vicious personal attack on his character, describing him as 'sick, mean, twisted, vicious, cheap, ugly, filthy, bitter, nasty, hateful, vulgar, loathsome, gnarled, warped, lazy and evil'. The defamatory words in the letter were shown by the claimant to other people, but the defendant had only sent them to him. There was therefore no publication by the defendant to a third party, and those words could not form the basis of a libel action. However, the claimant did obtain damages of £75 because the word 'Stonehouse' was held to be defamatory, as it implied that the claimant was like John Stonehouse, an MP who had recently disappeared by faking his death from drowning to escape paying his debts.

Every fresh publication of the statement will give rise to a fresh cause of action, so that each repetition will be important. This is evidenced by the recent libel allegations against *Scalliwag* and the *New Statesman* by John Major and Clare Latimer. The avowed purpose of the *New Statesman* article was to quash defamatory rumours about Mr Major, but that involved repetition of them, even though the article was critical of the rumours. Potentially, for example, in the case of a libel in a newspaper, the journalist, the sub-editor, the editor, the publisher, the distributor and newsagent could be sued (subject to the defence of innocent dissemination, discussed later). However, the claimant will be advised to sue those who can best afford to pay. Newspapers and broadcasting companies will usually be vicariously liable for the statements of their employees, and there can be difficult situations in relation to phone-in programmes, which explains why they are usually subject to a five second time-lag.

18.4.2 Examples of publication

The following situations *will* amount to publication:

- words written on a postcard or open message;

- defamatory statements placed in an envelope and addressed to the wrong person (*Hebditch v MacIlwaine* (1894));

- speaking in a loud voice about the claimant so that people nearby can overhear (*White v JF Stone (Lighting and Radio Ltd)* (1939));

- sending a letter to the claimant in circumstances when it is likely to be opened by a third party (*Pullman v Hill* (1891) – a secretary/clerk opened a letter) (*Theaker v Richardson* (1962) – a husband opened a letter addressed to his wife);

- allowing unauthorised defamatory statements to remain on one's premises (*Byrne v Deane* (1937)). In *Cunningham v Essex County Council* (2000), it was held that the casual onward transmission of a draft letter in preparation for a reference, alleging criminal proceedings against the claimant, could not attract a defence of qualified privilege. This was an actionable publication for the purposes of a libel claim;

- making a statement which carries the natural consequence of being repeated by someone else (*Slipper v BBC* (1991)). In this unusual decision, the defendant was liable not only for the original statement in a television broadcast, but for later newspaper reviews which repeated the 'sting' of the statement;

- making the statement to the claimant's spouse;

- a publication on the internet (*Godfrey v Demon Internet Ltd* (2000)).

18.4.3 Statements which were not 'published'

The following situations *will not* amount to publication:

- placing defamatory material in an unsealed letter (*Huth v Huth* (1915));

- making defamatory statements which are later repeated by someone else (*Ward v Weeks* (1930)). This usually breaks the chain of causation and the original maker of the statement will not be liable for repetitions, though there have been exceptions to this (see *Slipper v BBC* (1991));

- making the statement to one's own spouse (*Wennhak v Morgan* (1888));

- there is some doubt as to whether communications in inter-departmental memos sent or circulated within an organisation would be 'published'. Opinion on this was divided in *Riddick v Thames Board Mills Ltd* (1977). In any case, in such situations, there could well be a defence of qualified privilege.

18.4.4 A defamatory statement

As a basic definition of a defamatory statement, that which was formulated by Lord Atkin in *Sim v Stretch* (1936), is a good starting point:

> A statement which tends to lower the claimant in the estimation of right thinking members of society generally, and in particular to cause him to be regarded with feelings of hatred, contempt, ridicule, fear and disesteem.

Although simple vulgar abuse is not defamatory, other statements which are intended only as humour or satire could be actionable. Indeed, political opinion frequently finds expression in satire which has the effect of ridiculing prominent people. However, satirists can often escape liability for defamation by using the defence of 'fair comment on a matter of public interest'.

Statements which reflect on a person's moral character or professional competence clearly will be defamatory. What is defamatory in one age will not necessarily be so in another. The following are examples of defamatory statements:

- *Cosmos v BBC* (1976)

   The BBC broadcast a programme giving details about holidays, and the dangers of choosing holidays from glossy brochures. When showing a film of a Cosmos holiday camp in Majorca, they used the music which accompanied a popular series entitled 'Escape from Colditz' about a notorious prisoner-of-war camp. Cosmos succeeded in obtaining damages from the BBC.

- *Savalas v Associated Newspapers* (1976)

  Actor Telly Savalas, who played Kojak in the long running television series of the same name, was awarded £34,000 for being described as 'a big amiable beast of a man who cannot cope with superstardom'.

- *Cornwell v Daily Mail* (1989)

  Actress Charlotte Cornwell successfully sued for a statement made by a columnist that she had 'a big bum' and 'the kind of stage presence that blocks lavatories'.

- *Stark v Mail on Sunday* (1988)

  Actress Koo Stark successfully sued the *Mail on Sunday* for an article headed 'Koo dated Andy after she wed', alleging that she still had a 'lingering love' for Prince Andrew after she had married the Green Shield Stamp heir Timothy Jeffries.

- *Keays v New Woman* (1989)

  Sarah Keays brought a successful libel action against *New Woman* for an article which included her name with those of 'two other kiss and tell bimbos', alleging that she was obsessed with obtaining revenge against MP Cecil Parkinson who was her former employer and the father of her child.

- *Proetta v Sunday Times* (1991)

  Carmen Proetta, incensed that the newspaper had accused her of lying and described her as 'the Tart of Gib', successfully sued for libel.

- *Liberace v Daily Mirror* (1959)

  Musician Liberace was described as 'the summit of sex, the pinnacle of the masculine, feminine and neuter ... This deadly, winking, sniggering, snuggling, chromium-plated, scent-impregnated, ice-flavoured heap of mother love'. Liberace was famous before and since for his flamboyant stage act, but he toned-down his performances for a time, appearing in a sober suit, and successfully sued for defamation.

- *Roach v Newsgroup Newspapers Ltd* (1992)

  It was held to be defamatory to describe the well known actor who played the part of Ken Barlow in Coronation Street as 'boring'.

- *Grappelli v Derek Block Holdings Ltd* (1981)

  There was no libel in this case, as the words used were likely to excite sympathy rather than disrespect. The musician Stephan Grappelli was described by the defendants as seriously ill and unlikely ever to tour again.

- *Percy v Mirror Group Newspapers* (1996)

  A jury awarded Mr Percy £625,000 after the *Daily Mirror* had described him as 'Dr Dolittle', alleging that he had not attended a patient with head injuries but had instead arranged for a bed for the patient in another hospital 200 miles away, where the patient died.

18.4.5 Who decides?

It is important to separate the functions of the judge and jury in these cases. Under the previous practice, the judge explained to the jury the legal meaning of defamation, but if he considered that no reasonable man would actually conclude that the words in question were defamatory, the case was withdrawn from the jury and failed at that point. If, however, the judge thought that the words were capable of being defamatory in the eyes of a reasonable man, he would put the words to the jury and ask them to decide whether the words were defamatory (see *Capital and Counties Bank v Henty* (1882), and *Lewis v Daily Telegraph* (1964)). By s 7 of the Defamation Act 1996, the court shall not be asked to rule whether a statement is 'arguably' capable of bearing a particular meaning. This rule was introduced to enable the court to fix in advance the ground rules on possible meanings. Either party may now apply for an order to determine before the trial whether the words in question are *actually* capable of bearing a particular meaning.

In *Mapp v Newsgroup Newspapers Ltd* (1997), the Court of Appeal held that the judge should evaluate the words and delimit the range of possible meanings in the light of the authorities. Such an application should not be treated as an application to strike out part of the pleadings. If it appears that none of the words complained of are capable of having a defamatory meaning the judge may dismiss the claim or make any other appropriate order.

The role of the jury is to establish the standard of 'right-thinking members of society'. The meaning of this phrase was tested in the case of *Byrne v Deane* (1937), in which the claimant had informed the police that there were illegal gambling machines on the club premises, and, sometime later, a notice appeared on the club notice board in these words: 'But he who gave the game away, may he byrne in hell and rue the day.'

The claimant claimed that he had been libelled, but the Court of Appeal held that he had not, because right-thinking people would approve of his informing the police of illegal goings-on. See, also, *Prinsloo v SA Associated Newspapers Ltd* (1959) in which it was held that an allegation that a student had been spying for the police could not be defamatory.

Sometimes, the words 'reasonable people', 'ordinary people' and 'sensible people' are used to describe the relevant standard in defamation cases.

18.4.6 Innuendo

The jury must also consider certain statements which are not defamatory on the face of them but which contain an innuendo which has a defamatory meaning. The hidden meaning must be one that could be understood from the words themselves by people who knew the claimant (*Lewis v Daily Telegraph* (1964)) and this special esoteric hidden meaning must be pleaded by bringing additional information before the court to explain the meaning.

In *Allsop v Church of England Newspaper Ltd* (1972), it was held that, if the words of which the claimant complains (in this case, the claimant was said to be 'pre-occupied with the bent') are capable of any meaning or implication outside the dictionary meaning, details of all such meanings should be explained in the pleadings to give the defendant the opportunity to know what case has to be answered. In this case, the court had considerable difficulty with the word 'bent', referring to the *Oxford English Dictionary* for assistance.

The following are examples of innuendo:

- *Tolley v JS Fry & Sons Ltd* (1931)

  The claimant was an amateur golfer who was shown in a drawing on an advertising poster with a bar of Fry's chocolate and a speech bubble praising the chocolate. He successfully claimed that there was an innuendo that he had prostituted his amateur status by accepting money for the advertisement.

- *Cassidy v Daily Mirror* (1929)

  The claimant was the wife of a man who had been pictured with a young woman at a race meeting and described as engaged to her. The newspaper reporter had been given that information by Mr Cassidy and had no reason to doubt his word, but the claimant succeeded in proving an innuendo because the implication was that she would be regarded as a mistress not a wife.

- *Plumb v Jeyes Sanitary Compounds* (1937)

  The claimant, a retired policeman, had been photographed on traffic duty some eight years previously. His photograph appeared in a newspaper with the words 'Phew, I'm dying to get my feet into a Jeyes Fluid foot bath'. His successful action was based on the fact that the innuendo was that his feet were so disgusting that no ordinary soap and water could ever drown the smell!

18.4.7 Referring to the claimant

The claimant must be able to demonstrate that the defamatory words referred to him or her. This does not mean that his or her name has to appear, merely that anyone who knew the claimant would know that the words referred to him or her. Indeed, the satirical magazine *Private Eye* regularly refers to people by odd names, but they are still identifiable. For example, Sir James Goldsmith, a regular target of the magazine, was referred to as 'Goldenballs'. A similar approach is taken sometimes in the satirical radio programme 'Week Ending', and the television programme 'Spitting Image'.

If a class of people is defamed, there will only be an action available to individual members of that class if they are identifiable as individuals. It would not be defamatory to describe all jurors as incompetent, but it would be defamatory to describe all 12 members of a particular jury as incompetent. In one case the *Spectator* paid damages to the group of journalists who covered trials in the Old Bailey for describing them as 'beer sodden hacks'.

In *Knupffer v London Express Newspaper Ltd* (1944), the House of Lords held that where a class of people is defamed no individual can succeed in defamation proceedings unless he or she can prove that the statement was capable of referring to him or her and that it was in fact actually understood to refer to him or her.

There have occasionally been cases in which writers of fiction have innocently chosen a name for a character, which is also by chance the name of a living person. That person has then claimed that he or she could be taken to be the character in the book and if the character is depicted in an unfavourable light a successful libel action has followed. A similar situation could exist if someone claims that a character in a book is intended to be based upon him or her. These situations are now covered by the difficult defence of 'unintentional defamation' and will be dealt with later.

18.4.8 Malice

In many areas of the law of tort, the presence or absence of malice is irrelevant, or if it is relevant, it may only go to enhancing the amount of damages payable. However, in defamation actions it may be especially important to consider whether the statement was published maliciously, not only to allow the claimant to recover a higher award of damages, but because it is a necessary element in the law itself.

It is important to appreciate the meaning of the term 'malice' as it is used in the law of defamation, as it is often alleged in the pleadings, virtually as a formality, that the publication was made 'maliciously'. This means that the publication was made spitefully, or with ill will or recklessness as to whether it was true or false. The bad feeling must have led to the words being published and must, in particular, have been directed towards the claimant.

The presence of malice will destroy defences of justification in relation to 'spent' convictions, unintentional defamation, fair comment on a matter of public interest and qualified privilege.

18.5 'Without lawful justification' – defences

There are a number of important and extremely complex defences to defamation, and the complexity reflects the difficulty in satisfying the desire to balance the need for freedom of speech against the need to protect the reputation of the individual. The media are constantly reminded of this balancing exercise by the high awards of damages made against them in well publicised cases brought by leading politicians, actors and public figures. The threat of legal proceedings is often enough to deter publication of salacious material which would greatly increase the circulation of newspapers, but sometimes the decision is to publish, and in such cases the press often claim that it was their 'duty' to make the revelations, even at the risk of having to pay exemplary damages. Robert Maxwell was notorious in Fleet Street for the use of 'gagging' libel writs, and countless libel actions died with him.

The defences will be considered in detail, and careful note should be made of the particular circumstances in which each may apply. In some cases more than one defence may be applicable.

18.5.1 Innocent dissemination

The defence of innocent dissemination is designed to protect booksellers and distributors of materials which may contain libellous statements. This defence was explained in *Vizetelly v Mudie's Select Library Ltd* (1900), in which publishers had requested the defendants, a circulating library, to return certain books which were likely to contain libels. They did not do so and were liable for defamation. It was held that the defence could apply to libraries, booksellers and other 'mechanical' publishers of libels, provided that:

- the publication is innocent, in the sense that they did not know that it contained a libel; and

- there were no circumstances which ought to have made them aware that the publication could have contained a libel; and

- there was no negligence on their part in not knowing of the libel.

The position of those who sell or distribute certain satirical magazines is difficult. Indeed, *Private Eye*, which has been sued many times for libel, even has a 'libel fund' to which readers are invited to contribute. It could be argued that extreme caution should be taken by its sellers and distributors. In *Goldsmith v Sperrings Ltd* (1977), Sir James Goldsmith, in an alleged mission to close down *Private Eye*, brought a series of libel actions, some criminal and some civil, including some against booksellers, in respect of statements which he considered to be libellous in *Private Eye*. Many settled on the understanding that they would cease to sell *Private Eye*. Section 1 of the Defamation Act 1996 modernises this defence to reflect technological advances.

By s 1 of the Defamation Act 1996, the defence of innocent dissemination was made available to internet service providers (ISPs). However, certain problems are becoming apparent in relation to internet libel, and an application is being made to the European Court of Human Rights concerning the liability of ISPs for libels published inadvertently by them.

18.5.2 *Volenti*

It has already been explained that consent of the claimant to the publication of a statement, by showing other people defamatory material which the defendant meant for his or her eyes alone, will create a situation in which technically there has been no publication by the defendant (*Hinderer v Cole* (1977)).

However, if the claimant in some way invited the recording, and later publishing of the material, this will also amount to *volenti*.

In *Moore v News of the World* (1972), singer Dorothy Squires, in an attempt to launch a musical come back, gave a detailed account to the *News of the World* reporter of her life with her former husband Roger Moore. The piece was written in the first person as though she actually made the statements, but she said that it was complete fiction, and sued for libel because she claimed that the article portrayed her as the sort of person who was prepared to discuss her private life in intimate detail for the entire world to read. She succeeded in her action, but had she been willing to give an account of herself in that way, the newspaper would have had a defence of *volenti*.

18.5.3 Accord and satisfaction

Accord and satisfaction is a contract to settle the case, whereby the claimant agrees to give up the action in return for a cash settlement and/or an apology. There are number of factors which lead to the settlement of libel actions, not the least being the anxiety of escalating costs, and the fear that if the case is unsuccessful the claimant may have to pay the costs of the defence in addition to his own costs.

18.5.4 Apology and payment into court

The defence of apology and payment into court under s 2 of the Libel Act 1843 is only available to newspapers and periodicals, but it is seldom used because of its practical disadvantages. The following steps must be followed:

- the defendant must prove that the statement was made with no malice and no gross negligence;

- the defendant must prove that at the earliest opportunity, he published a full apology, or if the periodical appears at intervals of more than one week, has offered to publish an apology in another newspaper of the claimant's choice;

- a sum of money has been paid into court by way of amends.

18.5.5 Apology and mitigation

Although an apology will not be a defence to a defamation action, it may operate as a mitigating factor in the assessment of damages if the case is continued and the claimant succeeds in the action. The defendant must have made the apology as soon as possible.

18.6 Justification or truth

It would seem logical that only false statements can be the subject of defamation proceedings, so if the statement made about the claimant is true, there can be no action for defamation. Although this is the principle which underpins the defence of justification, the defence is by no means as simple as might be expected, for three main reasons.

Sometimes, people bring defamation actions simply to clear themselves of damaging allegations. As the case of *Aitken v Al Fayed* (2000) demonstrates, this can be a risky enterprise and can result in financial ruin if the defence can convince the jury of the truth of the statements.

In *Irving v Penguin Books* (2000), the judge delivered a devastating condemnation of the claimant when he failed to establish that the defendants had published false information about the existence of the Holocaust. The claimant's reputation here was damaged further by his efforts to vindicate himself and he faces a bill of £2.5 million in legal costs.

18.6.1 Burden of proof

The burden of proof is on the defendant to prove that the statement made is true, rather than on the claimant to prove that it was false. As Dias and Markesinis point out in *Tort Law*, 2nd edn:

> A ludicrous side effect of this is that a claimant may leave court with substantial compensation, but with his name not necessarily cleared. For this award does not necessarily imply that what the defendant said of him was false, but only that he failed to prove that it was true.

The rule also makes matters exceptionally difficult for the defendant, who will need to satisfy the jury that on a balance of probabilities, his or her version of events is true. Unless affidavits were taken from witnesses as the story was investigated, a procedure which is frequently carried out by the press in cases of doubt, witnesses may have disappeared and be difficult to trace, or their evidence may be discredited for a variety of reasons.

Thus, in the case of *Archer v the Star* (1987), in which a Conservative politician was alleged to have visited a prostitute, much of the defence case turned on evidence given by the woman concerned, who was never treated as a credible witness, while the claimant relied on evidence from his wife, a woman of high professional and social standing, described by the judge to the jury as 'elegant' and 'fragrant'. The result was that the defence, given the general background and reputation of their main witness, never really stood a chance and, for the claimant, the memory of the allegations lingers on.

18.6.2 Selective defamation

Section 5 of the Defamation Act 1952 deals with the defence of justification in the following terms:

> In an action for libel or slander in respect of words containing two or more distinct charges against the claimant, a defence of justification shall not fail by reason only that the truth of every charge is not proved if the words not proved to be true do not materially injure the claimant's reputation, having regard to the truth of the remaining charges.

For example, if the defendant called the claimant 'a liar, a thief and tone deaf', and the defence could prove the first two statements but not the third, the defence of justification would succeed, unless the claimant was a professional singer.

The defence would appear at first sight to be of great assistance to defendants. However, the almost incredible decision of the House of Lords in *Plato Films v Speidel* (1961) appears to encourage the practice of 'selective defamation' by permitting the claimant to chose which allegations upon which to sue, so leaving the defendant without recourse to s 5. In that case, the defendant made a film about the claimant's activities during the Second World War, when he had been supreme commander of the Axis Land Forces in Europe. Much of the film concerned the war crimes and atrocities allegedly committed by the claimant, but he chose only to base his action on allegations that he had been involved in the murder of the King of Yugoslavia and that he had betrayed Rommel. The House of Lords held that evidence of the wider context of the film, including specific facts about the war crimes and atrocities, of which apparently the defendants had proof, could not be introduced either as part of their defence or in mitigation of damages. They were, however, entitled to show that the claimant had a bad reputation in general, in order to mitigate the damages payable. The reasoning seems to be that to permit the introduction of specific details of numerous events in the claimant's life would turn the trial into a series of detailed allegations and counter-allegations which would place an unfair burden on the claimant and lead to protracted litigation. Nevertheless, the approach is now unfair to defendants and has attracted much criticism from the Press Council. The Faulks Committee recommended that the law should be changed to allow the defendant to rely on all the allegations in the publication as part of the defence. They also recommended that any matter, general or particular, which is available at the date of trial about the claimant's character, and which relates to the defamation, should be admissible as part of a plea in mitigation, provided adequate notice of the allegations is given to the claimant. Currently, the case of *Scott v Sampson* (1882) prevents specific acts of the claimant being referred to in mitigation.

The s 5 defence should be read in the light of the related issues which were raised in the case of *Charleston v Mirror Group Newspapers Ltd* (1996) which did not concern the defence under s 5 of the Defamation Act 1952, but which gave rise to consideration as to whether the claimant is entitled to sue on specific defamatory matters in a publication when the rest of the publication clearly negates the apparent libel. In that case, the claimants were actors who appeared in the Australian soap opera 'Neighbours' which is popular in the UK. They played the characters of Madge and Harold. A Sunday newspaper published photographs of two people apparently engaged in an act of sexual intercourse, the woman dressed in tight leather gear with her breasts bare. The headline read 'Strewth! What's Harold up to with our Madge?'. Smaller print below read 'Porn shocker for Neighbours Stars'. The rest of the article made it very clear throughout that the photographs were produced by the makers of a pornographic computer game, and that the faces had been superimposed on the bodies without the knowledge or permission of the stars. The House of Lords held that the headlines and photographs could not be read in isolation from the rest of the text which was not defamatory when read as a whole, because it was not permitted for the claimants to sever part of a publication from the rest of other parts of the article in order to negate the defamatory sections. Nor could the claimant rely on the fact that the defamatory meaning was conveyed to the very limited category of readers who only read the headlines. However, making it clear that their Lordships were not pronouncing on questions of journalistic ethics, Lord Bridge commented:

> Whether the text of a newspaper article will, in any particular case be sufficient to neutralise the defamatory implication of a prominent headline will sometimes be a nicely balanced question for the jury to decide, and will depend not only on the nature of the libel but also on the manner in which the whole of the relevant material is set out and presented.

It appears that two different situations may arise, in one of which the claimant can choose certain false allegations on which to base the action knowing that the defence of justification will not succeed (*Plato Films* (1961)), and another in which the libellous material is clearly cancelled out by the rest of the publication (*Charleston* (1996)). In the first of these situations, the claimant may well succeed because the defence of justification cannot be relied upon because of the way in which the courts have interpreted s 5 of the Defamation Act 1952.

In the second situation, because the defence under s 5 is not relevant, the claimant is without a remedy.

18.6.3 Rehabilitation of Offenders Act 1974

The defence is complicated by the Rehabilitation of Offenders Act 1974 which provides that certain criminal convictions, depending upon their seriousness, are to become 'spent' after certain periods of time have elapsed, and treated as if they had never happened. Very serious sentences such as life imprisonment for murder will never become 'spent', while an absolute discharge is 'spent' after six months.

Section 8 provides that in defamation actions which are based on allegations that the claimant has committed offences which would otherwise be 'spent', justification can be used as a defence except where the publication was made with malice. The meaning of 'malice' in this context has not yet been settled by judicial interpretation.

18.6.4 Tracing sources

If the defendant is merely repeating a defamatory statement which he or she has heard from another source, it is not enough merely to prove that it came from that source. The truth of the statement must also be proved. This can often be extremely difficult if the original maker of the statement did not swear an affidavit and can now no longer be found, particularly if the person who is being sued is a better bet as far as the claimant is concerned because he has more money than the person who first uttered the defamatory statement.

Moreover, if the original statement contained an innuendo, the truth of that must also be proved.

18.6.5 Pleadings

A defendant must remember to make it clear in the pleadings which statements he intends to prove true in order to establish the defence of justification.

18.7 Unintentional defamation

Section 4 of the Defamation Act 1952 provides the defence of 'unintentional defamation' to cover situations in which the defendant was unaware that certain statements could be defamatory, and for which at common law he or she was liable for defamation.

For example, in *C Hulton & Co v Jones* (1910), the claimant, who was called Artemus Jones, was a barrister. He succeeded in a defamation action against the defendants who had published a story about a fictitious character called Artemus Jones, a church warden in Peckham, who was portrayed as having a mistress in Dieppe. It contained this statement:

> Whist! There is Artemus Jones with a woman who is not his wife, who must be, you know, the other thing ... Really, is it not surprising the way our fellow-countrymen behave when they come abroad? Who would suppose by his goings on, that he was a church warden in Peckham?

The claimant called several witnesses who swore that they thought the article referred to Artemus Jones, the barrister, even though he had never lived in Peckham and had never been a church warden.

In *Newstead v London Express Newspaper Ltd* (1940), the defendants were liable for libel when they published a news item which stated that Harold Newstead, a 30 year old Camberwell man, had been convicted of bigamy. They were referring to another man of the same name who also lived in Camberwell, but as it was held that an 'ordinary man' would have concluded that the words referred to the claimant, his claim was successful.

A slightly different situation also gave rise to liability at common law. This is illustrated by the case of *Cassidy v Daily Mirror* (1929) in which an unfortunate reporter, who had no reason to doubt Colonel Cassidy's word, merely repeated his statement that the woman who accompanied him was his fiancée. His repetition of the defamatory statement was entirely unintentional, but this was no defence at common law.

Although s 4 was intended to remedy such situations as these, in fact, it complicates matters further.

A defence is provided as long as the words were published 'innocently', which is defined in the Defamation Act 1952, and the defendant can prove that he made an offer of amends. The constituents of the defence are as follows:

(a) The statement must have been made innocently, that is:

- the publisher must not have intended the words to apply to the claimant, and must not have known of any circumstances by which they might be understood to refer to the claimant (as in *Hulton v Jones* (1910)); or

- the words were not defamatory on the face of them and the publisher did not know of any circumstances by virtue of which they might be understood to be defamatory of the claimant (as in *Cassidy v Daily Mirror* (1929)).

And, in either case, the publisher (or his servant or agent) must have exercised all reasonable care in relation to the publication.

(b) If the defendant is prepared to claim that the words were published innocently, and that is no mean feat, he or she may make an offer of amends which includes a payment into court and an offer to publish a suitable correction and apology. This must be accompanied by an affidavit which clearly sets out why the publication was innocent.

(c) If the offer of amends is accepted there is a bar to further action for defamation.

(d) If the offer of amends is rejected there will be a defence if the defendant can prove:

- that the publication was innocent, and there was no negligence. The defendant is limited to evidence which was stated in the affidavit;

- that the offer of amends was made as soon as possible after the complaint;

- that if he was not the author of the statement, the person who was the author made it without malice.

The one case of any importance that has been decided on in this section illustrates how difficult it is to use the defence. In *Ross v Hopkinson* (1956), a little known actress whose name was used for a character in a novel, and portrayed in a defamatory light, succeeded in her action for defamation despite the defence, because the author had not checked whether a woman of the same name existed, and she was acting in the West End at the time.

The defence has been much criticised and the Faulks Committee drew attention to its many shortcomings. It is time consuming and expensive to swear affidavits, and if the publisher omits any evidence from the affidavit it cannot later be referred to, yet he is required to make the offer of amends as soon as possible! It is virtually impossible for a publisher to prove that certain authors acted without malice, especially if they are no longer available for comment. The Faulks Committee recommended a complete overhaul of the defence.

One of the aims of the Defamation Act 1996 was to modernise the defence of unintentional defamation and produce a more straightforward and usable defence (ss 2–4). There is now a presumption of innocent publication which can be rebutted under this Act.

In order to encourage libel cases to settle before trial, under new rules that came into effect in February 2000 under the Defamation Act 1996, newspapers are able to avoid expensive litigation by making an offer of amends that includes an agreement to make a correction and apology and to pay appropriate damages and costs. The court can fix the sums to be paid in the event of the parties not reaching an agreement. If the offer is rejected, that factor may be used as a defence to any subsequent trial and as a means of persuading the court to make a lower award.

Judges are able to dispose of cases quickly without a jury if there is no prospect of the parties arriving at an agreement or if there is no realistic defence. They can award damages of up to £10,000 and order the defendant to publish a summary of the judgment. Judges have the power to force claimants to accept this new procedure in certain cases, but not in complex libel proceedings. Although the new procedure was intended to make defamation actions accessible to ordinary people, there are few defamation cases which are simple enough to qualify for the fast track.

18.8   Absolute privilege

There are certain occasions on which the law regards freedom of speech as essential, and provides a defence of absolute privilege which can never be defeated, no matter how untrue or malicious the statements may be. All communications in the situations listed below are protected from defamation proceedings, and are described as 'absolutely privileged'.

Absolute privilege applies to:

- Statements made in either House of Parliament. MPs frequently say very rude things about one another and about people in the public eye. They are permitted to say whatever they like in Parliament, but are frequently challenged to repeat the statements outside the House, as a means of testing whether they would be prepared to make such remarks unprotected by the defence of absolute privilege.

  However, although it was stated in the Bill of Rights 1688 that the freedom of speech and debates or proceedings in Parliament ought not to be impeached in any court, this privilege may be waived under s 13 of the Defamation Act 1996. This matter and other issues of constitutional importance concerning the relationship between the Courts and Parliament were discussed at length by the House of Lords in *Hamilton v Al Fayed* (2000). The House of Lords held that the waiving of the parliamentary privilege has the effect of allowing challenges, in the course of defamation proceedings, to evidence given before parliamentary committees, without it being treated as an infringement of the autonomy of Parliament.

- Parliamentary papers of an official nature, that is papers, reports and proceedings which Parliament orders to be published, s 1 of the Parliamentary Papers Act 1840. Extracts from parliamentary papers are covered by qualified privilege by s 3 of the same Act.

- Statements made in the course of judicial proceedings or quasi-judicial proceedings. This covers statements made by judges, witnesses, jurors and advocates in any superior or inferior court, providing the statements relate to the proceedings.

- Fair, accurate and contemporaneous reports of public judicial proceedings before any court in the UK (s 3 of the Law of Libel Amendment Act 1888). The same privilege was extended to radio and television broadcasts of judicial proceedings in similar circumstances by the s 9(2) of the

Defamation Act 1952. However, the Law of Libel Amendment Act 1888 does not state whether the privilege is absolute or qualified, and Parliament did not clarify the matter when it had the opportunity to do so in enacting the extension to broadcasts of judicial proceedings in 1952. The assumption in the leading textbooks is that the privilege is absolute, and the only two reported cases on the matter take it as read that the privilege is absolute. Now that courts are permitted to refer to *Hansard* (*Pepper v Hart* (1992)), it will be possible, should the matter be raised judicially in the future, for the matter to be clarified by reference to *Hansard* of 6 June 1888, in which the intention that the defence of absolute privilege should apply was expressed. The Faulks Committee recommended that this point should be clarified by statute.

Note, also, that there are certain restrictions placed upon the reporting of some court proceedings by other statutes, for example, the Contempt of Court Act 1981.

This defence is of particular importance to the press, and particular attention should be paid to the terms 'fair' and 'accurate' in relation to court reporting. Reports must state both sides of cases, and it is not acceptable, for example, only to report an outline of the prosecution case and not to include a summary of the defence in a report of a criminal trial. This should be done even if several days pass, other more important news supervenes and space is short. Accuracy is also of the utmost importance as even a slight inaccuracy will destroy the absolute nature of the privilege. Names and addresses of parties and witnesses must be correct, and the facts must be correctly reported.

- Communications between lawyers and their clients. Such communications are regarded as of vital importance to those people who need to give confidential information in the process of seeking legal advice. They, therefore, attract the defence of absolute privilege.

- Statements made by officers of state to one another in the course of their official duty (*Chatterton v Secretary of State for India* (1895)).

18.9 Qualified privilege

Qualified privilege operates only to protect statements which are made *without malice*. The defence applies both at common law and by statute.

In each case, the judge must decide whether the situation is one in which privilege may apply and whether the information was related to the privileged occasion. If so, the jury must then decide whether the defendant acted in good faith or whether there was malice which defeats the privilege.

Qualified privilege has the potential for being very broad in its scope, and in some ways it provides a more useful defence than absolute privilege, which is limited to very specific circumstances. In *Watts v Times Newspapers* (1997), Hirst LJ remarked that 'the categories of qualified privilege are never closed'.

'Malice' in the context of qualified privilege could amount to attempting to use the privileged occasion as an excuse to make defamatory statements (see Faulks Committee), or it could mean recklessness as to whether the statements made were true or not. If, as in *Horrocks v Lowe* (1975), the defendant honestly believed that the statements were true when he made them, there will be no malice. In that case, the defendant, enraged by the actions of a councillor from the opposition party over the compulsory purchase of a piece of land, made the following statement:

> I don't know how to describe his attitude, whether it was brinkmanship, megalomania or childish petulance ... I suggest that he has misled the committee, the leader of his party and his political and club colleagues, some of whom are his business associates.

It was held that, even though the defendant was guilty of gross and unreasoning prejudice, he believed that everything he said was true and justifiable, and therefore the defence of qualified privilege could apply.

18.9.1 Statements made in pursuance of a legal, moral or social duty

Qualified privilege will attach to statements made in pursuance of a duty only if the party making the statement had an interest in communicating it and the recipient had an interest in receiving it. For example, in *Watt v Longsden* (1930), the claimant was the overseas manager of a company of which the defendant was a director. When the defendant received a letter about the claimant which claimed, among other things, that he 'lived exclusively to satisfy his own lusts and passions', he showed the letter to the chairman of the company and also to the claimant's wife, who started divorce proceedings. It was held that the communication to the company chairman was privileged, as there was a duty to inform him, and he had an interest in receiving the information, but that the communication to the claimant's wife was not privileged as no-one should interfere between man and wife, and there was no legal, moral or social duty to make the contents of the letter known to her.

In *Stuart v Bell* (1891), the test for the existence of a duty was suggested to be this: 'Would the great mass of right-thinking men in the position of the defendant have considered it their duty under the circumstances to make the communication?'

In *Spring v Guardian Assurance plc* (1994), it was held that the person who gives a reference owes a duty of care in *negligence* to the person about whom the reference is written. The difficulties arising from this case are discussed in Chapter 5. The remedy available in defamation may well be defeated through the defence of qualified privilege unless there is malice.

It may be that communications between lower ranking public officials do not, like those between their superiors, attract the defence of absolute privilege, but only carry a defence of qualified privilege (see *Merricks v Nott-Bower* (1965)).

In *Reynolds v Times Newspapers Ltd and Others* (1998), the Court of Appeal gave careful consideration to the application of qualified privilege in relation to newspaper publications and, after reviewing the Porter Committee Report of 1948 and the Faulks Committee Report of 1975, laid down a series of tests. In order to maintain a proper balance between freedom of speech and the right of individuals in public life to protect their reputations, the Court of Appeal held that the defence of qualified privilege was available to newspapers, as long as the following tests were satisfied:

- the newspaper must have had a legal, moral or social duty to the general public to publish the material in question;

- the general public must have had a corresponding interest in receiving the information; and

- the nature, status and source of the material and the circumstances of its publication must have been such as to justify the protection of such privilege in the absence of malice.

When this case proceeded to the House of Lords, the last of these three criteria was rejected. It was made clear that, if the statement or communication goes beyond the class of persons with a reciprocal interest or duty to receive it, the communication to the wider class of people is in excess of the privilege and the defence cannot be relied upon in respect of this further communication. The appellants had attempted to argue that there was scope for the common law, through incremental development, to create a new category of qualified privilege arising from political information – that is, 'information, arguments and opinions concerning government and political matters that affect the people of the UK'. They had argued that, with the exception of malicious publications, political information should be privileged, regardless of its source or status and the circumstances of the publication. The House of Lords rejected that contention on the grounds that it would put the judge in the position of an editor, rendering the outcome of cases unpredictable and giving the court an undesirable role as a censoring body. In the view of the House of Lords, that would not provide sufficient protection to the reputations of individuals, but the defence of fair comment on a matter of public interest does allow the court to give appropriate weight to the importance to the media of freedom of expression.

Despite the reservations expressed above, Lord Nicholls, expressing the majority view, laid down 10 criteria for the operation of the defence of qualified privilege. These are thought to have widened the scope of qualified privilege, making it difficult to predict the outcome of cases involving media publications. He suggested that those 10 matters were illustrative only and were not to be regarded as exhaustive, and the decision as to whether common law qualified privilege applied was always a matter for the judge. They are:

(1)   the seriousness of the allegation;

(2)   the nature of the information;

(3)   the source of the information;

(4)   the steps taken to verify the information;

(5)   the status of the information;

(6)   the urgency of the matter;

(7)   whether the claimant was invited to comment;

(8)   whether the article contained the gist of the claimant's story;

(9)   the tone of the article.

(10) the circumstances, including the timing of the publication.

The House of Lords made its ruling in the light of European human rights law and was satisfied that the decision was not inconsistent with the case of *Lingens v Austria* (1986). The decision was hailed as a victory for press freedom, but, on close examination, much of the ruling is unclear and there is still confusion as to what constitutes malice.

18.9.2 Statements made in protection of an interest

If a statement was made to protect an interest, it will attract a defence of qualified privilege. The relevant interests may be public interests or the defendant's own interests in property or even in his reputation. The following are some examples of successful application of the defence:

○   *Bryanston Finance v De Vries* (1975): the defendant was permitted by the operation of the defence to make statements in the protection of business interests, by dictating a memo to a secretary.

○   *Osborn v Thomas Butler* (1930): the defendant relied on the defence after making potentially defamatory statements in protection of his own character.

○   *Knight v Gibbs* (1834): the defendant was a landlord who was able to rely on the defence after making statements about the character of lodgers to a tenant. There was a common interest involved here.

○   *Beech v Freeson* (1972): a complaint by the Law Society to an MP about the behaviour of a solicitor was protected by qualified privilege.

18.10 Statutory qualified privilege

18.10.1 Fair and accurate reports of parliamentary proceedings

Such reports fell within the scope of the defence of qualified privilege even at common law, and also now under s 3 of the Parliamentary Papers Act 1840, extracts from reports and papers published by order of Parliament carry a defence of qualified privilege. Broadcasts of extracts from parliamentary papers are protected by Sched 20, para 1 of the Broadcasting Act 1990.

18.10.2 Fair and accurate reports of public judicial proceedings in the UK

The defence of qualified privilege will apply in circumstances when absolute privilege may not be available as, for example, when the report is not published contemporaneously with the proceedings, or the court is acting outside its jurisdiction or the report does not appear in a newspaper. This privilege has been extended by the Defamation Act 1996 to cover all court and other public proceedings and official publications worldwide.

18.10.3 Statements privileged by s 7 of the Defamation Act 1952

Section 7 of the Defamation Act 1952 applies to statements made in newspapers and radio and television broadcasts. The statements fall into two categories, those which are privileged without any explanation or contradiction, and those which are privileged subject to explanation or contradiction.

Some of the statements which fall into these two categories are listed below, but the lists are not exhaustive and the Defamation Acts of 1952 and 1996 should be consulted for further details.

- **Statements privileged without explanation: Pt I of the Schedule**

   These are listed in the Schedule to the Defamation Act 1952 and include (in summary) fair and accurate reports of the following: proceedings of the Parliaments of HM Dominions; proceedings of international organisations of which the UK is a member; proceedings of International Courts; proceedings of Courts Martial; copies of extracts from public registers (for example, of births).

- **Statements privileged subject to explanation: Pt II of the Schedule**

   The defence will not apply if the claimant has requested the defendant to publish a letter by way of explanation or contradiction of the statement and he or she has refused to do so. This is the only approximation to a 'right of reply' existing in English law.

Statements in this category include the following: fair and accurate reports of the decisions of trade, professional and industrial associations; associations to promote art, science, religion; associations for promoting the interests of any game, sport or past time to which the public are invited; public meetings.

Also included are fair and accurate reports of: meetings of local authorities which the press are permitted to attend; proceedings before tribunals of inquiry and commissions etc; meetings of public companies; official notices issued by public figures such as chief constables and government officials.

18.11 Fair comment on a matter of public interest

The defence of fair comment probably originated in the 18th century, and is frequently relied upon by the press, as it is designed to protect statements of opinion on matters of public concern. There are many examples of seemingly outrageous libels contained in satirical and other controversial publications and broadcasts, which pass unchallenged by defamation actions, presumably because of legal advice that the defence of fair comment would apply.

The defence has been criticised for the many technical difficulties which it presents, and for the fact that it suffers from a misleading misnomer, in that it applies even in the absence of 'fairness'.

The main elements of the defence will be considered in detail.

18.12 'Fair' comment

The defence is called 'fair' comment, but unfair and exaggerated expressions of opinion are also protected by it. The Faulks Committee suggested that a more accurate name for the defence would simply be 'comment'.

The cases suggest that the test is subjective to the defendant and is not based upon what a reasonable man would consider 'fair', but on whether the defendant honestly held the view which was expressed. In *Merrivale v Carson* (1887), Lord Esher stated the test in these terms: 'Would any fair man, however prejudiced he may be, however exaggerated or obstinate his views, have said that?' This test, which appears to be almost a contradiction in terms, does attempt to import a certain element of objectivity but, in *Slim v Daily Telegraph* (1968), the suggested test was whether the *defendant* was: 'An honest man expressing his genuine opinion.'

However, in *Telnikoff v Matusevitch* (1991), it was the view of the Court of Appeal that the defendant does not need to prove that he or she held an honest belief as long as the opinion is considered fair by application of an objective test. It is for the claimant to prove malice if he or she claims that the defendant has not acted in good faith.

Like qualified privilege, the defence of fair comment will be defeated by malice, though in this context 'malice' is difficult to define and to prove, as some of the statements which have been protected by the defence appear on the face of them to be laced with malice. It is the element of malice which will make the comment unfair and therefore defeat the defence. If the defendant suggests that the claimant is guilty of a bad motive in the sense of corruption or dishonesty, the defence appears to be narrower and imputations which are 'honest' comment will not be protected unless it is put to the jury to decide whether the defendant had an honest belief and that the belief was in fact a correct one (see *Dakhyl v Labouchère* (1908), in which a doctor was described as a 'quack').

An example of malice defeating the defence is found in *Thomas v Bradbury Agnew* (1906). A review of a book written by the claimant was more an attack on the writer personally than a genuine review of the material in the book. Moreover, during the trial, the defendant made it clear that he disliked the claimant personally, so the claimant succeeded in proving express malice. It is precisely this element of independently actuated spite which is necessary for the defence to be defeated.

In *GKR Karate UK Ltd v Yorkshire Post Newspapers* (2000), the Court of Appeal ruled that it was reasonable, in order to save time, for a judge to order that qualified privilege and malice be tried as separate preliminary issues before the main hearing.

There is a problem for newspapers which publish letters criticising works of art and popular television or radio broadcasts, as it is not always possible to trace authors. It was held in *Lyon v Daily Telegraph* (1943) that a newspaper will not necessarily be liable if it cannot prove that a statement which it published on its letters page was not the writer's honest opinion.

18.12.1 Comments

Only 'comments', that is, expressions of opinion, are protected, and any facts stated must be set out accurately, as the defence does not protect statements of opinion which are based on incorrect facts. For this reason, the defence of justification is usually pleaded in conjunction with fair comment. Clearly, opinion must be based on something, and that 'something' must be factually correct. Writers do not need to set out all the facts on which they rely in arriving at their opinions. In writing a review of a play or book, the reviewer need only make passing reference to the particular aspects upon which the opinion is based. One of the leading cases is *Kemsley v Foot* (1952), which concerned an attack by Michael Foot on an article in the *Evening Standard* which he described as 'one of the foulest pieces of journalism perpetrated in this country in many a long year'. This comment was protected by the defence. However, the article appeared under the headline 'Lower than Kemsley'.

Kemsley was a newspaper proprietor who had no connection with the *Evening Standard*, and the comment would, the House of Lords held, be taken to refer to the quality of the Kemsley press, rather than to the character of its proprietor. As there was sufficient reference, though only a passing reference, to the Kemsley press, a fact upon which the comment was based, the defence could apply in this context too.

If a libellous comment is made with no reference to fact, the defence can fail. For example, to say 'X is a megalomaniac', without stating why and giving no indication as to how that opinion has been arrived at, would probably not derive any protection from the defence of fair comment.

By s 6 of the Defamation Act 1952, the defence of fair comment, like that of justification, will not fail merely because 'the truth of every allegation of fact is not proved if the expression of opinion is fair comment having regard to such of the facts alleged or referred to in the words complained of as are proved'. The difficulties of this in relation to justification, which have already been explained, will also apply to fair comment.

18.12.2 On a matter of public interest

The defence only applies to comments made on matters of public interest. Such matters include comments on works of literature, music, art, plays, radio and television programmes. Public figures such as politicians, actors, clergymen and members of the royal family and indeed anyone who comes into the public eye are considered to be interesting to the public and will attract comment which is covered by the defence. Since it is often the press who place unsuspecting people in the public eye by focussing attention on them, it hardly seems fair that the press can then claim to be making fair comment on such people.

18.13 Remedies for defamation

The remedies for defamation are damages which may include exemplary damages and injunctions.

18.13.1 Injunctions

The person who fears an imminent threat to their reputation may obtain an injunction to prevent the publication of the defamatory material. Initially, an interim injunction will be obtained, and this often happens immediately prior to the publication or broadcast of potentially defamatory statements, but later a permanent injunction may be granted. The media often regard injunctions as procedures for gagging free speech. However, all the drawbacks associated with the discretionary nature of the remedy will apply.

18.13.2 Damages

Damages in libel actions are extremely difficult to predict. Juries have a tendency to regard defamation actions as David and Goliath situations, in which the little person is pitted against the might of the media. Yet, often, the ordinary person of moderate means is denied the possibility of bringing a libel action by the Legal Aid Rules, and as in the cases of Robert Maxwell and Sir James Goldsmith it could well be a case of Goliath against Goliath.

As no legal aid is available in defamation cases, individuals may find themselves without legal assistance for defending actions brought against them by multinational companies, for example, *Macdonalds v Steel and Morris* (1997). However, the development of conditional fee agreements is making defamation actions available to a greater number of private individuals. The suggestion has been made that judges who wish to bring libel claims will be able to recover their costs from the public purse.

18.13.3 Nominal damage

In some cases, only nominal damages will be awarded if the jury consider that the case is proved but that the claimant has suffered very little damage.

18.13.4 Contemptuous damages

If the jury is of the opinion that the conduct of the claimant was reprehensible, even though technically a case of defamation is proved, contemptuous damages may be awarded. In *Dering v Uris* (1964), the jury awarded a halfpenny damages to the claimant, who was clearly guilty of serious war crimes, but had succeeded in proving that certain statements made about him were false and defamatory. There was a very small award in *Plato Films v Speidel* (1961) for the same reason.

In personal injuries cases, it is a judge who decides on the size of the award, and this decision will be based upon rigorous academic and practical education and training followed by many years of experience as a practising lawyer. Judges are familiar with the usual awards that are made for particular injuries and have access to the standard texts and precedents to help them to arrive at the final figure.

In defamation cases, however, it must be the jury who decide on the sum to be awarded by way of compensation, and the judge can do little more than attempt to give some guidance as to the rough outline of the award. In some cases, judges and counsel speak in terms of 'coins rather than notes', or 'the cost of a good foreign holiday', or 'the price of a modest three bedroomed house in the home-counties', exhorting juries to avoid 'a mickey mouse award' and so on.

18.13.5 Exemplary damages

A complicating factor in defamation cases is the fact that exemplary damages may be awarded, particularly if it emerges that the defendant published the statement in a calculated attempt to increase sales or circulation. The award of damages will then be inflated in an attempt to express disapproval of the unscrupulous conduct of the defendant. In *Cassell & Co v Broome* (1972), the House of Lords upheld what was then an extremely high award of damages against the defendants because they had been reckless about the statements made and hoped that their sensational nature would increase sales.

Claimants have to contend with certain procedural difficulties when deciding whether to accept an offer to settle. In *Roach v Newsgroup Newspapers Ltd* (1992), the claimant, who played the part of Ken Barlow in Coronation Street sued the defendant publishers for an article which described him as 'boring'. He obtained an injunction to prevent repetition of the statement, and eventually, an award of £55,000 damages, the same sum as had been paid into court by way of an offer to settle before the start of the trial. The Court of Appeal held that the claimant had to pay his own costs and those of the defendant from the date of paying in. The total sum involved would almost certainly have exceeded the award of damages.

A major criticism of the awards for defamation is that they appear to be disproportionately high in comparison with awards for personal injuries. Does an injured reputation deserve a higher award than brain damage and its attendant pain, suffering and humiliation? Many people believe that it does not, and given that the only people who can afford to bring defamation actions are those who are already wealthy there is a certain irony in the size of some of the awards. Lord Aldington was awarded £1,500,000 in a libel action! The Lord Chancellor's Working Party on Defamation (December 1992) expressed concern about this matter:

> Putting it bluntly, there is a need to discourage that small minority of claimants who wish to proceed to trial for purely financial motives, rather than being motivated by the desire for vindication.

Some examples of recent awards for defamation are as follows:

Clive Jenkins v Paul Foot (1977)	£	1,000
Horobin v Daily Telegraph (1979)	£	4,000
Dorothy Squires v News of the World (1981)	£	30,000
Bremner v Sunday People (1982)	£	100,000
Goldsmith v Ingrams (1983)	£	85,000
Barbara Cartland v BBC (1983)	£	50,000
Maxwell v Ingrams (1986)	£	500,000
Jeffrey Archer v Star (1987)	£	500,000

Koo Stark v Mail on Sunday (1988)	£ 300,000
Keays v New Woman (1989)	£ 105,000
Sutcliffe v Private Eye (1989)	£ 60,000
Proetta v Sunday Times (1991)	£ 150,000
Jason Donovan v Face (1992)	£ 100,000
Lord Aldington v Tolstoy and Watts (1989)	£ 1,500,000
Percy v Daily Mirror (1996)	£ 625,000
Souness v Mirror Newspapers (1995)	£ 750,000
Garfoor v Walker (2000)	£ 400,000

Until very recently, the problem has been that the Court of Appeal has been unable to reduce high awards of damages made by juries in libel cases unless they were completely 'divorced from reality' or had been misdirected by the judge.

Excessively high awards by juries in defamation cases are no longer commonplace and the judges are now permitted to draw the attention of juries to awards made to other claimants, such as those who are seriously injured in accidents. In *Hamilton v Al Fayed* (2000), Morland J warned the jury against making a very high award of damages and specifically mentioned the sort of awards made to people suffering from grievous physical injuries.

18.14 A new approach relying on Art 10 of the European Convention on Human Rights

However, a new approach was sanctioned in *Rantzen v Mirror Group Newspapers* (1993), by the Court of Appeal by reference to a new Act, the Courts and Legal Services Act 1990, to reduce an award of damages made to Esther Rantzen. Section 8 of the Courts and Legal Services Act 1990 permits the Court of Appeal to substitute a fresh award of damages if it considers the original jury award to be 'excessive or inadequate'. The court accepted the argument that the term 'excessive' must be interpreted in the light of Art 10 of the European Convention on Human Rights, which must be regarded as 'underlying' common law principles where freedom of expression is concerned (*per* Lord Goff in the *Spycatcher* case). Article 10 provides that freedom of expression can only be limited by such restrictions or penalties as are 'necessary' in a democratic society. The test for the Court of Appeal should be 'Could a reasonable jury have thought that this award was necessary to compensate the claimant and re-establish his reputation' (*per* Neill LJ). However, the Court of Appeal did not consider it appropriate to use previously decided cases on personal injuries as a guide to awards for libel damages. Nor should previous awards in defamation cases be referred to.

Rather, a new body of law should be built up under s 8 of the Courts and Legal Services Act 1990 to give guidance as to the amount of damages which should properly be awarded for defamation. Meanwhile, juries should be invited to assess libel damages in the light of their 'purchasing power', and should be asked to consider the award of such sums as are proportionate to the damage suffered, and necessary to re-establish the claimant's reputation. In this particular case, the award to Esther Rantzen was reduced from £250,000 and substituted by an award of £110,000. She had succeeded in proving that she had been libelled in articles which had accused her of protecting a teacher who had sexually abused children.

There is little indication from the case as to how the sum of £110,000 was arrived at, and it was not clear how this case would impose any certainty on future awards (see Milmo (1993)).

The position was clarified by the case of *John v MGN Ltd* (1996). The case was brought by the singer Elton John about an article which had been published about him in a national newspaper. His photograph had appeared on the front page with the words 'World exclusive', and 'Elton's diet of death'. The article had alleged that Elton John had been observed chewing food and spitting it out at a party in Los Angeles, and continued with a description of the eating disorder known as *bulimia nervosa*. The claimant sought exemplary damages on the grounds that the defendants had been reckless in not checking whether he had attended the party in question, and the judge at first instance had found sufficient evidence of recklessness to justify referring the jury to the matter of exemplary damages. The jury found that the statement was defamatory and awarded damages consisting of £75,000 compensatory damages and £275,000 exemplary damages. The defendants appealed on the grounds that the damages were excessive and the judge had misdirected the jury on the correct approach to assessing exemplary damages. The Court of Appeal reviewed the principles of law relating to damages in defamation cases and held that in making the assessment of compensatory damages a judge can in future refer the jury to conventional scales of damages in personal injury cases by way of comparison, as well as to previous awards made or approved by the Court of Appeal in libel cases, and that there was no reason why the judge or counsel should not give some idea of what level of award they considered to be suitable. As far as references to other libel awards were concerned, the court agreed with the *Rantzen* decision not to remind juries of the awards made by juries in previous libel cases, as these would not have been subject to specific judicial guidelines. However, again in accordance with the *Rantzen* case, the court took the view that previous Court of Appeal awards could be referred to, and that eventually a framework of guidance could be built up. Reference to awards in personal injury cases would be permitted because it is rightly offensive to public opinion that a claimant in a defamation case could receive larger damages than a personal injuries claimant who had been seriously injured or permanently crippled. There was no reason why counsel and judges should not indicate to the jury what the appropriate level of the award should be.

Admitting that these were changes of practice, the Court of Appeal considered that they would support the constitutional role of the jury by rendering their decision making more acceptable to public opinion. The sums of £25,000 compensatory damages and £50,000 exemplary damages were substituted. It was further held that exemplary damages would only be appropriate if the jury were satisfied that the publisher had no genuine belief in the truth of the statement, and suspecting that it was untrue took no steps to check. Even then, it would only be when the sum of compensatory damages was insufficient to punish the defendant and to deter others that exemplary damages would be appropriate. Referring to Art 10 of the European Convention on Human Rights, Bingham MR said:

> The European Convention is not a free standing source of law in the United Kingdom. But there is ... no conflict or discrepancy between Art 10 and the common law. We regard Art 10 as reinforcing and buttressing the conclusions we have reached.

18.15 Proposals to reform the law of defamation

There have been many criticisms of the law of defamation and over recent years several proposals for reform have been suggested, only some of which have been implemented in the Defamation Act 1996.

18.15.1 The Faulks Committee's proposals

In 1975, the Faulks Committee (Cmnd 5909) undertook a major review of the law of defamation and made a number of proposals for reform, almost all of which have yet to be implemented.

Their main recommendations are summarised below:

- the law of libel should govern both libel and slander and the distinction between the two torts should be abolished;

- defamation should be defined in a statute as: 'The publication to a third party of matter which in all the circumstances would be likely to affect a person adversely in the estimation of reasonable people generally';

- the defence of justification should be modified and re-named simply 'truth'. Defendants should be able to rely on the entire publication in seeking to use the defence, even though the claimant is only suing on part of the publication;

- the defence of fair comment should be modified and should be re-named 'comment'. There should be no distinction between cases involving imputations of bad motive and other cases in which fair comment is relied upon as a defence. The term 'malice' should not be used in deciding whether the defence should not succeed. Instead, it should be stated that the defence should fail if the statements do not reflect the maker's genuine opinion;

- 'malice' should no longer be used in qualified privilege to defeat the defence. Instead, the defence should fail if the defendant was taking unfair advantage of the privileged occasion. Qualified privilege should be available to cover press conferences;

- live broadcasts of parliamentary proceedings should attract the defence of absolute privilege;

- the defence of unintentional defamation should be modified to simplify the procedural requirements and to abolish the rule that the publisher of statements must prove that their author acted without malice;

- punitive and exemplary damages should not be awarded for defamation;

- the personal representatives of a deceased claimant should be able to continue defamation actions for the benefit of the estate to recover general and special damages;

- close relatives should have a right to sue for a declaration that certain material published about a deceased person was untrue. An injunction, but not damages, should be available in such cases;

- an action for defamation should survive against the estate of a deceased person;

- the limitation period for defamation actions should be three years, not six years as at present, from the date of publication;

- legal aid should be available for defamation actions. Because of the unavailability of legal aid, the Broadcasting Complaints Commission claims that it is being used as a 'poor man's libel court' at present;

- jury trials in defamation cases should be at the discretion of the judge, and if used, the jury should not assess the award of damages except to give an indication as to whether the damages should be nominal, contemptuous, moderate or substantial.

18.15.2 The Lord Chancellor's proposals

The Lord Chancellor (December 1992) proposed to reform the law of defamation, and in particular the following reforms have been suggested:

- abolition of the rule in *Scott v Sampson* (1882) which prevents a defendant, when attempting to mitigate damages, from relying on evidence of specific acts of the claimant which could be regarded as discredited;

- introduction of a new procedure to allow claimants to claim damages only up to a fixed 'ceiling';

- a new 'offer of amends' procedure under which damages will be fixed by the defence.

18.15.3 The Defamation Act 1996

The Defamation Act 1996 implements some of the proposed reforms. The Act provides a new fast track procedure for libel cases involving up to £10,000, with judges assessing the damages in these cases and dismissing claims which are weak before the costs escalate. The aim is to dispose of small libel cases quickly and cheaply. It also introduced a new 'offer of amends' defence for newspapers where the libel was unintentional and the newspaper is willing to publish a suitable correction and apology, with damages assessed by a judge. There is a facility for some cases to be heard by a judge alone. The Act also envisages that the smaller libel cases may eventually be heard in the county court. The limitation period for defamation and malicious falsehood action has been reduced from three years to one, with a discretion for the court to allow later action to proceed if reasonable.

However, the Defamation Act 1996 has been criticised because it will do little to afford the realistic possibility of libel actions to less well off claimants and because it might even result in lower awards with little reduction in costs. It has also been suggested that the Defamation Act 1996 is too heavily weighted in favour of the media. If the parties cannot agree on the wording of the apology it would be up to the judge to adjudicate, and this is seen as an unwarranted interference with press freedom. A recent example of the advantages held by the media is the calculated risk taken by the *Daily Mail* in publishing a story accusing five men of the murder of Stephen Lawrence with the words 'sue us if we are wrong'. To date, none of the men has brought a claim.

The UK libel laws are likely to be challenged in the European Court of Human Rights, after the Court of Appeal upheld the allegations of libel in a case brought by McDonalds, the fast food company, against Dave Morris and Helen Steel. The original trial lasted for 314 days and arose out of criticisms which the two environmental campaigners had made of McDonalds in a leaflet which they had drafted and distributed. The award of damages made by the trial judge was reduced by £20,000 to £40,000 by the Court of Appeal, but the case highlighted the inequities of the UK libel laws and emphasised the fact that it is very difficult for the courts to uphold the concept of freedom of speech. Despite the fact that some of the serious allegations made by the defendants against McDonalds were found to be true, and the comments of the defendants were part of an important public debate about health, the defendants, who could not afford lawyers, were subjected to the ordeal of a long trial, while the claimant company had the best legal advice and representation at its disposal.

18.16 Malicious falsehood

Malicious or injurious falsehood consists of publication of disparaging remarks about a person's goods and/or services.

The claimant must prove that there has been publication, that there was malice on the part of the defendant and that he has suffered actual loss as a result. In *Allason v Campbell* (1996), an action for malicious falsehood failed because the claimant did not show a monetary loss.

Unlike defamation, it is possible to sue the estate of a deceased person for malicious falsehood.

A further distinction between defamation and malicious falsehood is that legal aid is available only for the latter.

While actions for malicious falsehood are rare in comparison with those for defamation, in a recent case, the claimant did base a claim in malicious falsehood in order to circumvent the rule that no legal aid will be available for libel. The case afforded the Court of Appeal the opportunity to review this tort. In *Joyce v Sengupta* (1992), the claimant sued for malicious falsehood when the defendants had published false statements accusing her of stealing intimate letters from the Princess Royal and giving them to a national newspaper. She was able to obtain legal aid to pursue her claim, but at first instance the judge agreed to strike out her claim because it should have been based on libel, not malicious falsehood, and was therefore an abuse of process.

On appeal, the Court of Appeal held that a claimant must be permitted to take full advantage of all the remedies which the law affords. Despite the fact that any damages payable in malicious falsehood would be small in comparison to defamation damages, the Legal Aid Board was the correct forum to decide whether or not to grant legal aid, and it was not for the court to decide on the merits of the award of legal aid, but for claimants to take up such a point with the Legal Aid Board when legal aid is being decided upon. The Court of Appeal pointed out that the claimant did have an arguable case, in that there could have been malice on the part of the defendants, and the claimant could well have suffered a financial loss in that she would find it difficult to obtain future employment which placed her in a position of trust and confidence. Once a financial loss has been established it is also possible to obtain damages for injured feelings and distress in cases of malicious falsehood. The five men accused of murder by the *Daily Mail* in February 1997 can only succeed in malicious falsehood which does qualify for legal aid if they can prove that the article was published maliciously, with knowledge that it was untrue. Aggravated damages may be awarded for malicious falsehood (*Kodoparast v Shad* (1999)).

18.17   Malicious prosecution

The tort of malicious prosecution provides redress for those who are prosecuted without cause and with malice. It is, however, notoriously difficult to prove because of the onerous requirements on the claimant. Indeed, the tort has been described as 'riddled with protections for the prosecutor'. (See Harrison, J, *Police Misconduct, Legal Remedies*, 1987.) A research study for the Royal Commission on Criminal Procedure in 1980 presented the view that the tort is 'no obstacle to the dishonest prosecutor and no real protection to the innocent who are prosecuted'. Indeed, it is usually preferable for the claimant and his lawyers to explore other remedies before delving into the difficulties of an action for malicious prosecution, and, if there is an action brought, it is usually one of several, including possibly trespass to the person, libel and slander.

In order to succeed, the claimant must prove that there was a prosecution without reasonable and probable cause, initiated by malice, and the case was resolved in the claimant's favour. It is necessary to prove that damage was suffered as a result of the prosecution.

The elements of the tort will be considered in detail.

18.17.1   A prosecution

There must have been a prosecution initiated by the defendant. The person to be sued is the person who was 'actively instrumental in putting the law in force' (*Danby v Beardsley* (1840)). This will usually be a police officer, but sometimes store detectives are sued for malicious prosecution, as in *Warby and Chastell v Tesco Stores* (1987). Any person who is prepared to sign a charge sheet and appear as a witness will be liable for action for malicious prosecution if the other elements of the tort are proved.

The House of Lords held in *Martin v Watson* (1996) that what is required here is for the defendant to have been actively instrumental in the instigation of proceedings, and that merely giving information to a police officer, who then goes on to make an independent judgement on the matter, will not be sufficient to form the basis of an action for malicious prosecution. In this case, the defendant was a person with a long history of ill feeling against the claimant, and she had gone out of her way to deceive the police, intending them to take action and to prosecute the claimant. This did amount to her having been sufficiently instrumental in the prosecution to provide the basis for a successful civil claim.

Since the introduction of the Crown Prosecution Service (CPS), it is a moot point as to whether a Crown Prosecutor would be open to an action for malicious prosecution. This is doubtful, as Crown Prosecutors do not initiate prosecutions by charging people. Their function is to review cases which are sent to them by the police and to decide whether to continue with the prosecution process. Occasionally, however, a prosecution may be initiated by the Director of Public Prosecutions, the head of the CPS. Whatever the role of the CPS, prosecutors are Crown servants and as such their decisions would be challengeable by judicial review rather than by a civil action. The test which would then be applicable to establish liability would be the administrative law test laid down in the case of *Associated Provincial Picture Houses v Wednesbury Corpn* (1948).

In *Gregory v Portsmouth CC* (2000), the House of Lords held that the malicious institution of disciplinary proceedings would not give rise to a claim for malicious prosecution. Other remedies, such as defamation, malicious falsehood, conspiracy and/or misfeasance in Public Office might be available.

18.17.2   Without reasonable and probable cause

Here, the claimant is required to prove a negative, a most difficult task at the best of times, but even more so when the defendant and his colleagues are probably in possession of all the evidence. It is difficult to ascertain exactly what is meant by 'reasonable and probable cause' from the cases, as the judges do not agree on what approach should be taken. If an objective test is applied, it is rather easier to establish liability than when a subjective test is applied. The objective approach would be to ask whether a reasonable person in possession of all the facts, would conclude that there was sufficient evidence to cause the police to think that the accused was probably guilty and should face trial. The subjective approach would be to ask whether the police actually believed in the particular case that the accused was probably guilty and should face trial.

18.17.3   Initiated by malice

Here, 'malice' means motivation by some desire other than that of bringing the accused to justice (*Stevens v Midland Counties Railway* (1854)). If there are mixed motives for the prosecution, the claim will succeed if the malicious motive was dominant. The presence of malice is a question for the jury to decide, but it is difficult to prove unless a witness, possibly another police officer, is prepared to give evidence against colleagues. In *Taylor v Metropolitan Police Commissioner* (1990), the police officer who had planted cannabis on the claimant in a deliberate attempt to frame him had been involved in a similar case the previous week, and Mr Taylor's action for malicious prosecution was successful. However, it is possible for the police to act with reasonable and probable cause even if they also act with malice. In such a case an action for malicious prosecution would fail. See, also, *Martin v Watson* (1996) (above, 18.17.1).

18.17.4 The case must be resolved in the claimant's favour

If the claimant is acquitted, or the proceedings are dropped or discontinued, or the claimant is convicted but the conviction is quashed on appeal, there will be a good basis for an action for malicious prosecution.

18.17.5 Damage

In order to succeed, the claimant must prove that he or she has suffered loss of reputation, loss of life or limb or liberty, or financial loss. Once damage under one of these heads is established, other damage which flows from it, such as distress, may also be compensated.

18.18 Malicious abuse of process

This unusual tort is an action brought against a person who has begun a process against the claimant, falling short of prosecution, for example, requesting the issue of warrants for search or arrest of the claimant. It is necessary to prove lack of reasonable and probable cause and malice, but it is not necessary to establish any particular head of damage.

Some decisions suggest that if a claimant starts a civil action for the purpose of a collateral attack on a decision against him or her in criminal proceedings this may amount to abuse of process (*Hunter v Chief Constable of West Midlands* (1981); *Walpole v Partridge and Wilson* (1994)).

18.19 A wider protection for privacy?

The tort of breach of confidence protects certain categories of confidential information, but there are numerous exceptions. It has been suggested that there is a developing area of law concerned with protecting the reputation (through the defamation action) and confidentiality, as well as other aspects of personal privacy. With the enactment of the Human Rights Act 1998, future years could see the further development of the common law in this respect.

DEFAMATION AND OTHER TORTS AFFECTING THE REPUTATION

Note the climate in which the torts which protect the reputation have evolved. In particular, note the modern climate, in which there is a constant tension between the need for freedom of the press and the need to protect the reputation and privacy of the individual (European Convention on Human Rights, Art 10(1); *Derbyshire CC v Times Newspapers* (1992); *Rantzen v Mirror Group Newspapers* (1993); *John v MGN Ltd* (1996)).

Libel and slander

Note the distinction.

Who can sue?

Only living persons may sue for defamation. These include private individuals, trading corporations and trade unions, but not local authorities (*Derbyshire CC v Times Newspapers* (1993)).

Definition

'Publication of a defamatory statement which refers to the claimant, without lawful justification.'

Publication

The statement must be made to someone other than the claimant or the defendant's spouse. *Volenti* and qualified privilege may prevent publication (*Hinderer v Cole* (1977); *Huth v Huth* (1916); *Slipper v BBC* (1991); *Riddick v Thames Board Mills* (1977)).

Defamatory statement

Definition of defamatory statement: 'A statement which tends to lower the person in the estimation of right-thinking members of society generally, and in particular to cause him to be regarded with feelings of hatred, contempt, fear, ridicule or disesteem.'

Examples include: *Cosmos v BBC* (1976); *Savalas v Associated Newspapers* (1976); *Cornwell v Daily Mail* (1989); *Stark v Mail on Sunday* (1988); *Keays v New Woman* (1989); *Proetta v Sunday Times* (1991); *Liberace v Daily Mirror* (1959); *Roach v Newsgroup* (1992).

'Right-thinking' members of society

A statement which would attract the approval of right-thinking people cannot be defamatory (*Byrne v Deane* (1937)).

Innuendo

Even statements which appear to be innocent may be defamatory if innuendo is proved (*Allsop v C of E Newspapers* (1972); *Tolley v Fry* (1931); *Cassidy v Daily Mirror* (1929); *Plumb v Jeyes Sanitary Compounds* (1937)).

Reference to the claimant

The claimant must be pointed to personally by the statement (*Knupffer v London Express* (1944)).

Defences

Defences include:

- Innocent dissemination (*Vizetelly v Mudie's Select Library* (1900); *Goldsmith v Sperrings* (1977)).

- *Volenti* (*Moore v News of the World* (1972); *Hinderer v Cole* (1972)).

- Accord and satisfaction.

- Apology and payment into court.

- Justification (note the criticisms of s 5 of the Defamation Act 1952) (*Plato Films v Speidel* (1961); s 8 of the Rehabilitation of Offenders Act 1974). But distinguish *Charleston v Mirror Group Newspapers* (1996).

- Unintentional defamation (note the criticisms of the complexities of s 4 of the Defamation Act 1952 – Faulks Committee – it is time consuming, complex and expensive to use): *Hulton v Jones* (1910); *Newstead v London Express* (1940); *Cassidy v Daily Mirror* (1929). See, also, ss 2–4 of the Defamation Act 1996.

- Absolute privilege: *Hamilton v Al Fayed* (1999).

- Qualified privilege (note the relevance of 'malice' (*Horrocks v Lowe* (1975)). The defence only protects statements made without malice, but malice is notoriously difficult to prove): *Reynolds v Times Newspapers* (2000).

- Fair comment on a matter of public interest (note the criticisms: the defence in fact protects 'unfair' comments in certain circumstances and is regarded as complex and unwieldy. Note, also, the relevance of malice which will defeat the defence) (*Merrivale v Carson* (1887); *Telnikoff v Matusevitch* (1991); *Thomas v Bradbury Agnew* (1906)).

Remedies

Injunctions, both interlocutory and permanent, are important. Damages in defamation cases have attracted much criticism. The jury has been blamed for many of the excessively high awards (*Cassell v Broome* (1972)). The Court of Appeal has now approved a new practice for awarding exemplary damages (*John v MGN Ltd* (1996)).

Reform of the law of defamation

The Faulks Committee 1975 and Lord Chancellor's proposals 1992 made important proposals for reform. The Defamation Act 1996 implements some of these. The enactment of the Human Rights Act 1998 is likely to lead to further development.

Malicious falsehood

Publication of disparaging remarks about a person's goods and/or services is malicious falsehood. The claimant must prove malice and actual loss. Legal aid is available (*Joyce v Sengupta* (1992)). The estate of a deceased person may be sued. The action will fail if no financial loss is proved (*Allason v Campbell* (1996)).

Malicious prosecution

The claimant must prove that the defendant initiated the failed prosecution without reasonable and probable cause. Malice must be proved. Damage to the claimant in the form of loss of reputation, life, limb or liberty, or financial loss: *Martin v Watson* (1996). This action does not apply to maliciously brought disciplinary proceedings; *Gregory v Portsmouth CC* (2000) – malicious institution of disciplinary proceedings could not form the basis of a claim for malicious prosecution.

Malicious abuse of process

Similar to malicious prosecution and available for processes which fall short of prosecution but which are malicious and unjustified. No particular head of damage need be proved (*Hunter v Chief Constable of West Midlands* (1981); *Walpole v Partridge and Wilson* (1994)).

CHAPTER 19

REMEDIES IN TORT

Claimants in tort actions may be seeking monetary compensation (damages), or perhaps an injunction to prevent further repetition of the wrongful acts by the defendant. Occasionally, both remedies are sought.

19.1 Damages

In the vast majority of tort actions, the claimant is seeking compensation for personal injuries or damage to property which arise out of accidents. Very few cases ever actually reach the courts, the majority being settled out of court. However, such awards as are made by the courts form the basis of out of court settlements.

It is therefore very important for all lawyers practising in the field of personal injuries to be aware of the current figures which the courts are awarding for particular types of injuries. These figures are published regularly in *Kemp and Kemp* and in *Current Law*. The *New Law Journal* also carries details of recent awards and the Judicial Studies Board publishes regular updates of the broad bands of damages awards. Lawyers also need to be aware of the principles which underpin the awards of damages.

The Law Commission is in the process of reviewing many aspects of the law relating to damages and practical matters concerning the way in which compensation is paid. Some of its recommendations are implemented by the Damages Bill 1996. The most recent reports were produced in November 1999 (Law Com No 262). They make several recommendations and are accompanied by a draft Bill aimed at modernising the law.

19.1.1 How accurate is tort compensation?

Assessment of damages involves a prediction of what would have happened to the claimant if the accident had not occurred. The object of tort damages is to put the claimant in the position he would have been in if the accident had never happened, and this, of course, is impossible to achieve. While it is possible to calculate almost exactly the award of special damages, that is, actual financial losses to the date of trial (for example, lost earnings, the cost of private medical care and so on), it is impossible ever to predict exactly what the claimant has lost for the future, or to translate intangible losses such as pain and suffering into money, and it is in this area, the assessment of general damages, that most of the problems arise, and most of the injustice or unfairness is seen to exist. The judge must take into account the claimant's current medical condition and the prognosis for the future. This is a difficult exercise, and medical witnesses are called at great expense to try to help in the calculation. Fees quoted in 1993 in the *British Medical Journal* for the cost of medical witnesses range from £90 to £160 an hour. Although it is now also possible for provisional awards of damages to be made in some cases in which the medical prognosis is uncertain, even this procedure has drawbacks, and is not available in every case.

The question of assessing future economic losses is no simpler. In fact, as Lord Scarman said of this in the case of *Lim Poh Choo v Camden and Islington AHA* (1980): '... there is really one certainty: the future will prove the award to be either too high or too low.'

Although the courts aim for full compensation, in many cases this can lead to over-compensation, particularly if the injury is only small and could be covered entirely by social security benefit. This highlights yet another problem with our system which is that there are no consistent rules governing the interrelationship between tort compensation and State compensation. However, a study for the Law Commission by Professor Hazel Genn in 1995 suggests that many accident victims may be under-compensated.

19.1.2 How fair is tort compensation?

It will be seen from a study of the cases that awards of damages to rich people for loss of future earnings are considerably higher than awards of damages to poor people, even though the injuries may be identical. Some people regard this as unfair because it means that the rich person is taking out of the system relatively more than he or she is putting in in insurance and other payments (see Atiyah, P, *Accidents, Compensation and the Law*, Cane, P (ed), 1999). Moreover, the rich may be awarded a higher sum for loss of amenity than the poor since they are able to enjoy a better lifestyle and recreational activities.

Another reason why calculation of tort damages is regarded as unfair is that some 'heads of damage' have been developed in relation to general damages, which only certain people can claim. For example, in the case of bereavement damages, introduced under the Administration of Justice Act 1982, only parents of people under 18, and husbands and wives may be awarded damages for bereavement. Yet, who is to say that parents of people over 18 and cohabitees suffer less than these categories of people? The sum is fixed at £7,500, an arbitrary figure fixed by the Lord Chancellor. To take an example of the operation of the law: in the Hillsborough Football Stadium disaster, parents whose children died there under the age of 18 were awarded damages for bereavement; those whose children were over 18 received nothing. It is difficult to see why those who lost loved ones in this way should be treated differently.

A further criticism of our tort system is that it singles out people with disabilities which have been caused through the *fault* of others, and places them in a better position than those who are unable to prove fault. For example, if a person is born with an illness which cannot be attributed to anything other than a genetic cause, that person will no doubt suffer as much as a person who is injured through the negligence of the doctor who delivered him. Yet, providing fault can be proved, the person damaged at birth will be compensated and receive possibly a very large award, whereas the person with a genetic or inherited disorder will simply be dependent on state benefits. As Atiyah points out, we do not know what the current sense of justice expects.

Studies (for example, the Pearson Commission in 1978) have been undertaken into the question of whether people injured through fault should expect more by way of compensation than those who are injured or become ill through some natural cause, and these have concluded that it is morally impossible to justify compensating one category rather than the other, except on the grounds of punishing the wrongdoer and general deterrence, which are not the primary objects of the law of tort.

A further problem which contributes to the unfairness of the present system is the fact that liability insurance underpins the law of tort. This means that insurance companies are able to influence the way in which the law has developed. For example, the lump sum payment which has for many years been criticised by commentators (see Pearson Report) is often impracticable from the victim's point of view and a series of periodic payments would be much better. The claimant who receives a large lump sum could spend it all on a trip around the world and come back merely to rely on state benefit, yet damages are assessed by the court on the assumption that claimants will invest an award to beat, or at the very least keep pace with inflation. The Damages Act 1996 requires the courts, when deciding on the return to be expected from a lump sum, to take account of such a rate of return as may be prescribed by the Lord Chancellor. The real advantage of periodic payments is that they can be varied depending upon the victim's condition at any given time. The plain fact is however that insurance companies do not like their files being kept open in order to pay periodic payments. Administratively, it is much more convenient, once the case is finished, to pay a lump sum and close the file. Lawyers also like to be paid in one lump sum once the case is settled (but see the Damages Act 1996).

The new system of structured settlements, which will be discussed later, has provided a means of paying claimants their damages over a period of time, but this is only available in a limited number of cases.

Claimants are almost always at a disadvantage because the forensic process requires the claimant to prove the case by amassing sufficient evidence against the defendant and establishing fault. This is a lengthy process, and witnesses are not always ready to come forward, particularly in the case of work accidents and medical accidents. Defendants, on the other hand, are usually insured, or are large concerns such as health authorities or local authorities which are self-insurers, or they would not be worth suing. As such, they are in the business of fighting claims on a regular basis, and have developed tactics with which claimants, however well advised by good lawyers, may not be able to cope, from a psychological point of view. Many claimants are worn down by the negotiating process which precedes settlement or trial. If they are not supported by a trade union or by legal aid, or some other financial assistance, or in the chance event of being injured in a mass accident, by the report of a public inquiry, many claimants will discontinue their claims or settle for less than they deserve. The whole process of making a claim is a major event in the life of an individual, whereas, to an insurer it is merely part of an elaborate 'game'.

19.1.3 How efficient is tort compensation?

Assuming that an efficient system of compensation should compensate all deserving victims quickly and cost effectively, tort fails on almost all possible counts.

There are many delays involved especially if the medical prognosis is uncertain. For example, a musician who had been severely burned in the King's Cross fire fought for eight years for his damages and was disappointed with the final sum.

Many accident victims fail even to initiate legal actions because they are unable to obtain the necessary evidence to prove fault on the part of the defendant, or because they lack sufficient financial resources and are ineligible for legal aid, or simply because they are unaware of the possibility of making a claim.

Compared with other systems of support which are available for the victims of injury or sickness, such as the social security system, tort is inefficient because it often takes several years before settlements or court awards are made, during which time the claimant may well have to endure pain, sickness, poverty, hardship, and the fear of impending litigation.

Even when tort does pay its accident victims, they are usually paid in the form of a lump sum, with all its attendant disadvantages already discussed.

Tort is also inefficient from a financial perspective when compared with other systems of compensation. The administrative costs of tort amount to approximately 85% of the sums which it pays to victims (approximately 45% of the total compensation and administration costs), while Social Security runs at 11% of the sums which it pays out (figures based on the Pearson Commission Report 1978).

Nor can tort, like Social Security, claim to be an egalitarian system, as for reasons already discussed, it does not compensate all victims equally.

A Law Commission Report, *How Much is Enough?* (Number 225, 1995) which is the result of an empirical study headed by Professor Hazel Genn, of the experiences of accident victims several years after receiving their awards of damages, makes gloomy reading. It is the report of detailed structured interviews with 761 accident victims who received compensation between 1987 and 1991, and it investigates the long term effects of accidents on work, family and social life and the extent to which the victims recover from their injuries after they receive compensation. The report finds that one-third of cases over £100,000 were still not settled six years after the accident, and that claimants who are originally satisfied with their compensation award become increasingly more dissatisfied with the passage of time. Many had originally thought that their award would be adequate to cover all their future needs, but found years later that it was inadequate to cover the long-term effects of their disability, including their medical and general care. Four out of five of those interviewed were still experiencing pain, and a high proportion had either given up work because of their injuries or had been unable to return to work as they had hoped. Few had received adequate financial advice as to how they should invest their award, and the majority were very concerned that they should make good use of their capital, so dispelling the myth that many successful claimants are profligate. In fact, the report concluded that only a small percentage of the accident victims were able to maintain a lifestyle similar to that before their accidents.

This report is the best evidence to date that in many instances the tort system probably fails even those whom it compensates. The Law Commission is continuing its major review of the tort compensation system.

Lord Woolf, after a thorough review of the present system for compensation, has made proposals for procedural reforms, which have now been implemented in the Civil Procedure Rules 1998 (see Chapter 21), which it is hoped will remove some of the obstacles which prevent claimants obtaining compensation within a reasonable time.

Already the introduction of conditional fees has opened up the possibility of litigation to people who, because they do not qualify for legal aid, might not otherwise have been able to afford it. There have been criticisms of this new system, but although imperfect, it is the best compromise which is likely to be achieved in the near future. Suggestions for introducing 'no-fault' compensation have been made from time to time, but at present this is not on the political agenda, as a comprehensive no-fault system would prove far too expensive, and a limited no-fault scheme for particular categories of accident victims, such as those injured in medical mishaps, would be unfair to other categories of victims.

19.2 Types of damages

It is possible to classify the various kinds of damage which are payable.

19.2.1 Nominal damages

Nominal damages are awarded if the action is proved but the claimant has suffered no loss. The claimant in such a case would receive a very small sum of money and this would in fact merely demonstrate to the world that the claimant has won the case.

19.2.2 Compensatory damages

Most damages are intended to be compensatory, that is to compensate the claimant for loss which has been suffered. If the damages can be calculated exactly, they are described as special damages. Other types of damages which are not capable of financial assessment in any accurate way are called general damages. General damages include pain and suffering, loss of amenity, etc.

The aim of compensatory damages is to put the claimant in the position he or she would have been in had the tort never been committed.

19.2.3 Contemptuous damages

Contemptuous damages are usually awarded in libel actions in which the claimant has technically proved the case but the court wishes to express its disapproval that the action was ever brought in the first place. The sum awarded will usually be the smallest coin of the realm.

19.2.4 Aggravated damages

Aggravated damages may be awarded if the court wishes to express disapproval of the defendant's behaviour, as a result of which the claimant has suffered more than would normally be expected in the situation.

19.2.5 Punitive or exemplary damages

Punitive damages may be distinguished from aggravated damages in that here the intention of the court is to punish the wrongdoer by an additional award on top of the award of compensatory damages, and perhaps to deter others who might be tempted to act in the same way as the defendant. In the leading case of *Rookes v Barnard* (1964), it was stated that damages of this type would only be awarded in specific cases and then only very exceptionally. Three classes of cases were considered. First, where servants of the government behave in an oppressive, arbitrary or unconstitutional way. Cases concerning police misconduct and racial discrimination fall into this category, for example, *Holden v The Chief Constable of Lancashire* (1986).

In the case of *Broome v Cassell & Co Ltd* (1972), the House of Lords explained that the term 'servants of the government' could be interpreted to include people who were not actually servants of the Crown, for example local government officers and police officers. The category does not extend to private individuals or corporations (*Gibbons v South West Water Services Ltd* (1992)).

The second category includes cases where the conduct of the defendant was calculated to profit from the tort in the sense that any compensation payable would be less than any profit which might be made. Some of the damages awarded in libel cases are examples of this.

Guidance on these damages was set out by the House of Lords in *John v MGN Ltd* (1996), and this is outlined in Chapter 17.

The third category of cases is where some statutes have expressly permitted payment of exemplary damages, for example, s 17(3) of the Copyright Act 1956.

These three categories of exemplary damages are strict and the only one which might allow for expansion in the future is the second category, in which the defendant's conduct was calculated to make a profit for himself. It is only rarely that exemplary or punitive damages are awarded, probably because to award such damages would be to usurp the function of the criminal law and to stray from the boundaries of tort itself. Nevertheless, it is possible to find high awards of exemplary damages in cases involving misconduct by police officers (see Chapter 13 on Trespass to the Person), for example, *George v The Metropolitan Commissioner of Police* (1984), where the claimant was the mother of a young man whom the police needed to question. Some officers forced their way into her house and ransacked it for a full half hour. They hit and kicked the claimant and then invented a false allegation to deceive the court. She was awarded £6,000 for trespass and assault and £2,000 exemplary damages.

In *Scotland v Comr of Police for the Metropolis* (1996), the Court of Appeal held that if a judge provided guidance to a jury on the range of appropriate compensation in a claim for personal injuries for malicious prosecution and/or false imprisonment, it was essential that the jury understood that it was only guidance. This was analogous to the new practice approved by the House of Lords in defamation cases in *John v MGN* (see 18.14 above) which is discussed at length in Chapter 18.

In *Hsu v Metropolitan Police Commissioner* (1997), the Court of Appeal issued detailed guidelines as to the directions to be given to juries in assessing damages in claims against the police, indicating that aggravated damages could only be awarded where they were claimed by the claimant and there were aggravating features in the defendant's conduct which justified the award. An award of £220,000 was reduced to £35,000.

The case of *Goswell v Commissioner of Police of the Metropolis* (1996) illustrates the fact that very high awards may be made by juries in cases involving the 'arbitrary and oppressive' abuse of power by the police. The claimant had been hit by a police officer with a truncheon and needed five stitches. He was awarded £120,000 for the injury, £12,000 for false imprisonment and £170,000 exemplary damages, the total award being £302,000. This was reduced on appeal to £47,600, following the guidance in *Hsu v Commissioner of Police for the Metropolis* (1994).

In *Treadaway v Chief Constable of West Midlands* (1994), in which it was found that the police had tortured the claimant to obtain a confession from him by suffocating him with bags over his head, compensatory damages of £2,500 were awarded, together with aggravated damages of £7,500 and exemplary damages of £40,000.

In the rare tort cases when juries are used, s 8 of the Courts and Legal Services Act 1990 lowers the threshold for intervention by the Court of Appeal in the award made by the jury (*Clark v Chief Constable of Cleveland* (1999). This applies both where the damages are excessive and where they are inadequate. In *Thompson v Comr for Police for the Metropolis* (1998), guidelines were established in the form of starting figures and maximum figures for awards.

19.3 Calculation of special damages

For the purpose of calculating the award, damages are divided into two kinds. These are special damages and general damages.

Special damages are quantifiable pecuniary losses up to the date of trial. These are assessed separately from other awards since they can be pleaded, because the exact amount to be claimed is known at the time of the trial. The amount is certain and probably relatively easy to calculate. Nevertheless, basic principles of assessment apply to these in the same way as the future losses.

From 1 October 1997, any State benefit received by the claimant over £2,500 for a period of five years will be deducted only from special damages (Social Security (Recovery of Benefits) Act 1997).

Benefits which are not recoverable are: child benefit; family credit; earnings top-up; guardians allowance; one parent family benefit; housing benefit; maternity allowance; Industrial Diseases (Old Cases) Act 1975 benefits; statutory maternity pay; retirement pensions; retirement allowance; social find payments; war pensions; and widows' benefits.

The rules which determine which of the many recoverable benefits are recovered from which particular head of compensation are complex, and, in January 1999, the Compensation Recovery Unit issued guidance to assist on this matter. These issues are of great importance on a day to day basis to lawyers in personal injuries practice, but are beyond the scope of this text. Details can be obtained from the Compensation Recovery Unit.

19.3.1 Reasonable expenses to the date of the trial

Only such expenses as are considered reasonable by the court are recoverable, and this is a question of fact. There are many cases in which the parties are in dispute about the minute details of a claim, and long and detailed schedules of damages are drawn up by both sides. This aspect of our adversarial system can be exceptionally difficult for accident victims to cope with, and, although it is desirable to prevent fraudulent claims, there are some matters which should be dealt with in a particularly sensitive fashion. An example of a case which caused considerable embarrassment to a claimant is that of Margaret Westmoquette, outlined in an article in *The Times* on 22 July 1998, in which Bill Braithwaite QC explained that the claimant had suffered terrible injuries in a car accident in which her husband was killed. She had lost both legs and one arm and had been very badly burned. Defence counsel argued that her part of claim should be calculated on the basis that she would not be needing to buy tights, as she no longer had legs.

In the case of *Cunningham v Harrison* (1973), the claimant claimed that he needed a housekeeper and two nurses to live in his home and look after him. He claimed that the total cost at 1973 rates was £6,000 per annum. The court refused to allow this amount on the grounds that it was unreasonably large.

Medical expenses can also be claimed under this head if they are calculable to the date of the trial. Under s 2(4) of the Law Reform (Personal Injuries) Act 1948, the rule is that in an action for damages of personal injuries there shall be disregarded, in determining the reasonableness of the expenses, the possibility of avoiding those expenses by taking advantage of NHS facilities. Medical expenses cover any services or treatment or medical appliances or the unpaid services of relatives or friends.

In *Fish v Wilcox and Gwent HA* (1993), the 40 year old appellant gave birth to a child in 1985 who suffered from spina bifida. She had previously suffered a miscarriage and the foetus had been found on that occasion to be anencaphalic and suffering from a condition called exomphalus, but the appellant had never been informed of the abnormalities in that foetus. She became pregnant again and gave birth to a normal child in 1979 but, when she was pregnant with the child who had spina bifida, she had not been given any tests or scans which might have enabled her to decide on a termination of that pregnancy. There was no dispute about liability. It was accepted that the defendant should have informed her of the abnormalities of the 1977 foetus and given her the opportunity to have her pregnancy terminated later, after appropriate scans and tests. The appellant had since developed multiple sclerosis and her marriage had dissolved. She had given up her job to care for the child, who needed constant attention but, because of her own medical condition, she would be unable to nurse her unassisted after another six months, it was estimated, from the date of the trial. The only legal issue in this case was as to the amount of damages recoverable in negligence. The appellant claimed that she should have been awarded a sum for lost earnings, in addition to the sum for the cost of nursing care which they had provided for the child. The Court of Appeal upheld the decision of the judge at first instance and held that, under the rule of *Housecraft v Burnett* (1986), she could not claim damages twice. She would only be entitled either to the cost of her lost earnings after giving up work or to the cost of nursing care, but not to both. As Lord Stuart Smith explained the situation: 'She cannot do two jobs at once and she is not entitled to be paid for doing two jobs at once.'

In relation to private medical care and treatment, s 5 of the Administration of Justice Act 1982 discriminates between claimants who receive private medical care and those who receive NHS care. The Act states:

> Any saving to an injured party which is attributable to his maintenance wholly or partly at public expense in a hospital, nursing home or other institution shall be set off against any income lost by him as a result of his injuries.

At present, the courts do not treat as unreasonable a claimant who opts not to make use of NHS facilities (*Harris v Brights Asphalt Contractors* (1983)). Moreover, the cost of paying relatives who give up employment in order to care for their injured loved ones can also be claimed (*Donelly v Joyce* (1973)). This is in line with the underlying principle that the law of tort compensates accident victims for expenses which are reasonably incurred, so that they may be restored to the pre-accident position, insofar as money can achieve this. Also in accordance with this is the rule that, if a tort victim receives NHS care, any saving made because he or she has been kept at public expense in an NHS institution must be set off against any income lost through injury (s 5 of the Administration of Justice Act 1982). Although these principles do have internal logic and consistency, nevertheless, in this respect, the law appears to discriminate between people who choose NHS treatment and those who decide to use private sector care. Although the law may indeed be in need of some short term amendment in this area, perhaps the long term solution lies in more radical changes than merely tinkering with the provisions of statutes.

The Road Traffic (NHS Charges) Act 1999, which amends the Road Traffic Act 1988, enables NHS hospitals to recover the costs of treating accident victims on the NHS from defendants' insurers. Under the Act, the Secretary of State is responsible for collecting the charges and there is a centralised national administrative agency. The body which undertakes the collection is the Compensation Recovery Unit, which is part of the Benefits Agency. The charges are made on the basis of a simple tariff which mirrors the real cost of treatment.

19.3.2 Expenses to cover special facilities

Expenses to cover the cost of special living accommodation or other capital assets can also be claimed as part of the award of special damages. The measure of damages in this case will be the sum spent to obtain the special facility and its running costs, but not the capital cost of any facility, such as a car, which the claimant would have had anyway. Therefore, in the case of a car, the cost of its special adaptation to suit certain disabilities would be claimed but not the full cost of the vehicle itself.

In the case of *Povey v The Governors of Rydal School* (1970), the claimant received an award of £8,400 to cover the cost of the renewal of a special hydraulic lift to take a wheelchair in and out of a car.

A large amount of money can be spent to adapt a house for people with particular disabilities, for example light switches may need to be moved lower down the wall for people in wheelchairs, special lifts may need to be installed to allow people to negotiate stairs, special equipment may be needed in bathrooms and so on. All this can be claimed as part of special damages to the date of trial.

This usually consists of the net loss from the date of the accident to the date of the trial with salary updated covering promotions, increments and so on, but of course the situation is more complicated if the claimant was previously self-employed and has lost commission. A claimant receiving sick pay equivalent to normal pay has suffered no loss, and as tort damages are intended to compensate for losses there will be no recovery (*Turner v The Minister of Defence* (1969)). If an employer lends money to the claimant until the trial which covers the difference between wages and sick pay, this can be claimed.

If the claimant was covered by first party insurance, any payment by the insurance company will not be deducted.

The Court of Appeal held in *Hardwick v Hudson and Another* (1999) that, if the claimant's wife gives her unpaid services to her husband's business because he is unable to run it as a result of his injury, no award will be made to compensate for her time and effort. Contrast this principle with that relating to the awards payable for voluntary nursing and personal care given to injured claimants (see below, 19.5.8)

19.4   Calculation of general damages

Although some solicitors refer to all financial losses as 'specials', in fact, the correct classification of future financial losses is under the heading 'general damages'. The term 'general damages' covers all losses which are not capable of exact quantification.

19.5   Pecuniary losses

General damages can be subdivided into pecuniary and non-pecuniary damages.

19.5.1 Loss of future earnings and initial care

The court needs to arrive at a sum which is the present value of a future loss, and the way in which the courts approach this problem is to employ the notions of multiplicand and multiplier.

The multiplicand is an annual sum to represent the claimant's net annual lost earnings at the date of the trial. This essentially is a question of fact.

The multiplier, on the other hand, is a notional figure which represents a number of years by which the multiplicand must be multiplied in order to calculate the future losses. It is impossible to predict an exact figure.

A number of possibilities are taken into account when arriving at the notional figure given to the multiplier, for example the likelihood that a young woman might give up work to care for her children should she get married.

Essentially, the multiplier is extremely arbitrary, it can never be precise and is calculated by looking at previous comparable cases. Even in the case of young accident victims who would have had a lifetime of earning before them, it is unusual to see a multiplier of higher than 19. The prospect of introducing higher multipliers has been discussed and rejected in several cases. For example, in *McIlgrew v Devon CC* (1995), the Court of Appeal reduced a multiplier of 22 to 18 in a case involving a seriously injured claimant. Sir John May said:

> Unless there is some really radical change in the economic situation or in the rates of interest commonly obtainable, I think that the maximum award on the conventional basis should still not exceed its present maximum of 18 years' purchase.

The multiplier never represents the actual number of potential years of earning left to the claimant because it is intended to take into account the uncertainty of prediction. For example, the possibility that a claimant may have lost his job at some future point, or perhaps, looking at family history, the claimant would have a heart attack in 20 years' time and have to give up work. If the wage earner had been claiming benefit and 'moonlighting', he or his dependants will not be able to claim for loss of the illegally acquired income on grounds of public policy (*Hunter v Butler* (1996)).

The expectation is that the claimant will invest any money which he or she receives in a lump sum and use the income, and possibly some of the capital, to cover living expenses during the years when he or she would have been earning, so that, by the time of retirement, the whole of the sum awarded would be exhausted. Multipliers assume that the capital sum which will be invested will yield 4.5% after tax and inflation are taken into account. The real rate of return at any given time may be substantially higher than that, however. Interest rates often change many times in any given year and there are occasions when investors make losses, and other occasions when they can make substantial gains. So, the figure of 4.5% is purely notional. The real problem is that the claimant's investments are expected to keep pace with inflation, because rates of inflation also vary from time to time.

The rationale for this approach was stated in *Cookson v Knowles* (1979) by Lord Diplock, who explained that:

> Inflation is taken care of in a rough and ready way by the higher rates of interest obtainable as one of the consequences of it, and no other practical means of calculation has been suggested that is capable of dealing with so conjectural a factor with greater precision.

However, the possibility of a practical solution was provided by the introduction of Index Linked Government Securities (ILGS) in 1981 which make it possible to predict almost exactly the loss of income for which the claimant is to be compensated. ILGS carry no risks when compared with even the most careful investment policies. Thus, if the loss is £10,000 per annum, for example, the claimant can be awarded compensation which, if invested in ILGS, will provide that sum. The Law Commission in its Report No 224 favoured moving away from the present arbitrary system towards a system in which the rate of return would be based on ILGS net return.

The House of Lords has ruled in favour of claimants in three cases concerning the rate at which the courts should assume lump awards should be invested when calculating damages. In *Page v Sheerness Steel, Wells v Wells* and *Thomas v Brighton HA* (1998), it was decided that lump sum payments of compensation should be based on a rate of return of 2.5–3% to allow for the fact that claimants are entitled to invest their awards in safe, index linked government securities. Before this decision, damages were lower because claimants were expected to take greater risks by investing in equities, and the courts based the calculation on a rate of return of 4.5%. In arriving at their conclusions, their Lordships referred to the views of textbook writers and to Law Commission Report No 224 (1994), which was based on comprehensive research. It is widely expected that, following these decisions, new record awards of damages will be seen; the insurance industry is bracing itself for a difficult time ahead.

Although the NHS has been promised a large increase in funding, this decision of the House of Lords will mean that much of the extra allocation of cash could be swallowed up in higher damages paid to claimants who bring successful medical negligence claims. This would make conditional fee agreements more attractive in cases where there are large claims for future care. Some commentators suggest that there may be pressure on the Lord Chancellor set the discount rate at a higher level than the 3% prescribed by the House of Lords. He has the power to set the discount rate on multipliers under s 1 of the Damages Act 1996.

Yet another recent report of a 'record' settlement in a cerebral palsy case is *Mansell v Dyfed-Powys HA* (1998). The claimant was 11 years old at the time of the settlement, which was approved by a High Court judge in Manchester. The incident which led to the claimant's injuries had occurred at or around the time of his delivery, when he was starved of oxygen during two failed attempts to deliver him using obstetrics forceps. He was born by emergency caesarean section but was severely brain damaged and now requires constant 24 hour care. Although his life expectancy is normal, the claimant has problems communicating and is unable to use his arms and legs. It is necessary to turn him up to 50 times every night and he cannot wash or dress without assistance. His IQ is within the normal range, but the long term prognosis is that his physical condition will never improve. A global award of £3,281,199.10 was made, and the cost of future care for the claimant was estimated at around £100,000 per annum.

This case is the first of several which demonstrate that the House of Lords' decision is likely to have a significant impact on the levels of awards, particularly in cases where the damages would be high in any event. It had been predicted that awards of damages could be as much as 40% higher, following the House of Lords ruling. However, this is merely one factor which will lead to spiralling awards of damages. Solicitors and counsel are more meticulous than ever before in the compilation of schedules of damages. Details of the sums of money which will be necessary to provide adequately for the claimant's future care are painstakingly collected in consultation with numerous experts who assess in detail what equipment, nursing, medical and other care the claimant is likely to need. Another factor adding to the expense is the development in technologies which are leading to the provision of ever more sophisticated and expensive equipment to enable injured claimants to have better quality of life, and to communicate their needs to their carers.

Although there was criticism by the claimant's solicitor in the *Mansell* case of the very long time lapse between admission of liability and final settlement of *quantum*, the claimant must surely have benefited by the fact that this settlement was made after the House of Lords' decision. There were 14 experts instructed in order to determine the extent of the care which the claimant would require, and the case illustrates the fact that this exercise is becoming very much more precise. If interim payments can be arranged, it is greatly to a claimant's advantage to take whatever time is necessary to ensure that the prognosis and final calculation of the sums required for future care are as detailed and accurate as possible.

The family of Joshua Yedid, a New York banker, received an award in the region of £4 million. Negligence was alleged to have occurred when Mr Yedid, who was on a business trip in London when he was taken ill, was admitted to Westminster Hospital for emergency surgery. Doctors failed to intubate the 60 year old patient during exploratory surgery in 1986, after he had been admitted with gastric bleeding. He was severely brain damaged but survived in a persistent vegetative state until his death in 1991, but there was a dispute about the cause of death, as the man finally died after a heart attack which the defendants claimed he might have suffered in any event. However, Gage J concluded that the most likely cause of death was the persistent vegetative state caused by the negligence of the defendants.

The exceptionally high level of this award can be explained by the fact that the deceased was an extremely high earner before he became ill, and his wife and two children had a substantial claim under the Fatal Accidents Act 1976 for loss of dependency. Although his wife has since remarried, the marriage prospects and even actual remarriage of widows is not relevant and must not be considered when damages are calculated. £3 million has already been awarded under the Fatal Accidents Act, but it is expected that damages will be further increased by the cost of the long period of medical care which the patient received before his death.

Of course, all this presupposes that the claimant will invest the money responsibly and not simply spend it on having a good time. Courts refuse to consider expert actuarial evidence and the likely future rates of inflation and will not take inflation into account at all in relation to the future (*Cookson v Knowles* (1979)). Logically, this means that claimants are under-compensated because of inflation which seldom runs at 0%. It would seem sensible to use actuarial evidence in order to work out more exactly what the claimant should be awarded. However, the courts have all shown a distrust of this type of evidence, even though they have in some cases treated it as admissible.

In *Barry v Aberlex Construction (Midlands) Ltd* (2000), Latham J made reference to the fact that the Lord Chancellor has not acted to set a new discount rate under s 1(1) of the Damages Act 1996. Accordingly, he made an award of damages in a personal injury claim on the basis that it was appropriate to reduce the discount rate applicable in calculating multipliers to 2%.

According to the judge, this case raised the issue of principle as to whether market conditions currently prevailing justified a reduction from 3% to 2%. He considered that there had been a significant change in market conditions, of the kind envisaged by the majority of the House of Lords in *Wells v Wells* (1998) to justify a change in rate which applied to calculating multipliers for future losses, such as future care required by claimants. When *Wells v Wells* was decided, the average gross redemption yields from index linked government securities, in which it was established that multipliers should be based, suggested a figure of 3%, based on the previous three years. The decision in *Wells v Wells* indicated, according to Latham J, that it would be in order for courts, in the future, if the Lord Chancellor took no action, to consider the appropriateness of the discount rate at regular intervals. Courts might consider that it would be appropriate to vary the 3% set in *Wells v Wells*, if there had been a 'marked' or 'very considerable change in economic circumstances'. He thought a whole percentage point change was sufficiently significant to justify the change, on the basis that the Lord Chancellor would be likely to decide that the rate should be amended in the light of the changed conditions since *Wells v Wells*. He suggested a test, which was to ask whether the Lord Chancellor, following the principle adopted in *Wells v Wells*, could sensibly reach any conclusion other than that 3% was no longer an appropriate rate.

The Scottish courts have not followed the example set in *Barry v Aberlex* and have ruled that economic circumstances have not changed sufficiently to justify a departure from the 3% rate (*Macie-Lillie v Lanarkshire Health Board* (2000).

19.5.2 Actuarial evidence

Lord Oliver in the case of *Auty, Mills, Rogers and Popow v NCB* (1985) said:

> As a method of providing a reliable guide to individuals' behaviour patterns or to future economic and political trends, the predictions of an actuary can be only a little more accurate and certainly less entertaining than those of an astrologer.

Thus, actuarial evidence when admitted is used simply as a means of checking the calculations which have been made according to the multiplier/multiplicand method. The Law Commission, in their report on personal injuries litigation (Law Commission Report No 56) concluded that the multiplier is the best and most satisfactory method of assessing loss of future earnings and expenses, and that the usefulness of actuarial evidence is limited.

However, the Law Commission has expressed approval of the use of actuarial evidence in court, and under the Civil Evidence Act 1995 actuarial evidence is now permitted. Recommendations were made in its Report in November 1999 to investigate further the use of actuarial evidence.

Nevertheless, even actuaries would not be able to make accurate predictions about inflation in the future, and it seems that the arguments put forward in *Lim v Camden and Islington HA* (1980) by Lord Scarman do make sense. He said:

> Victims of tort who receive a lump sum award are entitled to no better protection against inflation than others who have to rely on capital for their future support. To attempt such protection would be to put them into a privileged position at the expense of the tortfeasor, and so impose upon him an excessive burden which might go far beyond compensation for loss.

In the case of *Cookson v Knowles* (1979), it was recognised that in exceptional cases allowances may be made for inflation. However, the courts have wisely refrained from making predictions about future rates of inflation, as rates have varied considerably over the last two decades. Therefore, no addition is made to the lump sum award to allow for inflation, and the assumption is made that the claimant will invest the sum and be able to expect a return of about 4.5% in interest. It is assumed that interest rates will automatically rise to take account of inflation leaving a sum for the claimant to live on. Nevertheless, there have been times when once invested, inflation reduced the value of money faster than interest rates could restore it.

19.5.3 Income tax

When calculating loss of future earnings, the court considers the net annual earnings of the claimant after tax which would have been deducted. This rule was established by the House of Lords in the case of *British Transport Commission v Gourley* (1956). This, like future inflation, presents a problem as it is impossible to predict future rates of income tax and the calculation must be made according to current rates. Such a calculation will mean that the claimant may be over-compensated or under-compensated and, worse, the rule means that the claimant may have to pay double the tax on the money, because after it has been invested it will, of course, be subject to taxation. This was pointed out by Lord Oliver in the case of *Hodgson v Trapp* (1988). (See, also, the Law Commission Consultation Paper on Interim Damages, Provisional Damages and Structured Settlements (No 224, 1994) for further discussion of this matter.)

It should be noted that even if the case does not involve compensation for personal injuries, the income tax position should be taken into account when the award is assessed. In *Deeny v Gooda Walker Ltd (No 2)* (1996), the House of Lords held that damages awarded to the Lloyd's names against their managing agents for negligently conducting their underwriting business, were taxable in the hands of the claimants. The receipt of damages by the names constituted a receipt of the names' underwriting business and was taxable in their hands.

It is the insurance company which gains as a result of this rule, not the defendant, since the tax which has been deducted is never claimed back by the state.

Social security contributions are also deducted in the calculation of future loss of earnings in the same way as income tax, and like income tax deductions these can never be accurately calculated.

Although loss of pension rights as a result of occupational and other pensions not being paid (as the taxpayer will no longer be earning) are compensatable, these are calculated as a separate head of damages.

Furthermore, in calculating loss of future earnings, the courts will take into account any possible promotions and salary increases from which the claimant may have benefited during his career.

If the multiplier is likely to be on the low side, the claimant may benefit from the settlement being delayed, and during that time special damages would be allowed to accumulate and would, in fact, reflect the actual loss suffered while reliance on general damage would be left.

19.5.4 The lost years

At one time, the prevailing rule was that established in the case of *Oliver v Ashman* (1962). The Court of Appeal had held in that case that if the claimant's life expectancy was reduced, then damages for future loss of earnings would not be available during the years of life which were lost to him. He would, in effect, only be able to obtain damages for the years that were left.

This rule was regarded as unfair and the House of Lords took the opportunity to change it in the case of *Pickett v British Rail Engineering Ltd* (1980), so that claimants who are still alive at the time of trial may now recover damages from lost earnings even for the years which are lost to them, although there is a deduction for living and other expenses during that period.

The present position, then, is that dependants of claimants who are still living at the time of the trial will not lose out on the money which they would have inherited as long as they are favoured in the claimant's will, or can take on intestacy.

Relatives of deceased claimants can, of course, claim in their own right for loss of the breadwinner under the Fatal Accidents Act 1976, and this claim subsumes the lost years of the deceased.

The right to claim for the lost years does not survive for the benefit of the claimant's estate under the Law Reform Act 1934 if the claimant has died by the time the trial is held. This is to avoid double compensation.

19.5.5 Loss of future earnings and very young claimants

Calculation of the awards of loss of future earnings for very young people who have not yet started to earn is, of course, extremely difficult and the awards in these cases are usually very low (*Gammel v Wilson* (1982)). Exceptionally, there may be an award if a child, for example, showed great promise perhaps as a pianist.

19.5.6 Deductions

As the victims of accidents often receive financial support from several sources in addition to tort, for example, income support, sick pay, private insurance and, in some cases, from charities, there may be certain deductions made from the damages to account for these. These are listed below.

- **Private insurance payouts**

  These are not deducted from damages. The reasoning behind this appears to be that the claimant's foresight and prudent planning before the accident should not benefit the defendant by reducing any damages which he or she may have to pay (*Bradburn v Great Western Railway* (1874)).

- **Payments by charities**

  Often, when there is a major disaster such as the Hillsborough Stadium accident in which many people were killed or injured in a crush at a football ground, or the Marchioness disaster, when a pleasure boat collided with another vessel in the Thames, and several people were killed and injured, charitable funds are established, on a wave of public sympathy, to collect money to assist potential claimants. Other long established charities such as the RNIB also give payments to accident victims who may have been involved in individual incidents rather than mass accidents. Any payments made from such charitable sources are not deducted from damages.

  For these and other reasons, victims of mass accidents are frequently in a stronger position to obtain compensation than individual accident victims, not least because the task of collecting and evaluating evidence is often undertaken by a public inquiry.

- **Occupational disability pensions**

  In the case of *Parry v Cleaver* (1970), it was held that a policeman who received an occupational disability pension should not have that deducted from the lost future earnings award. Both he and his employer had contributed to the pension during the term of his employment and Lord Reid thought that there was no real difference between this and any other form of insurance. However, the policeman had taken up a less demanding clerical job elsewhere and it was held that wages from this alternative employment should be set off against loss of future earnings for police work which he was no longer able to do.

  In *Smoker v London Fire and Civil Defence Authority* (1991), the House of Lords confirmed *Parry v Cleaver* and held that the rule applied whether or not the pension was contributory.

- **Occupational sick pay**

  Sick pay will be deducted from the award of damages if it is paid as part of the claimant's contract of employment. Such pay is regarded as a partial substitute for earnings and therefore not like a pension which would be payable after the employment ceased (*Hussain v New Taplow Paper Mills Ltd* (1988)). However, if payments of sick pay by the employer are purely gratuitous, they will not be deducted as they are akin to charitable payments unless the employer is also the defendant in the case.

- **Redundancy payments**

  Sometimes, the claimant will be made redundant because, as a result of the injuries sustained, he or she will be more likely to be selected for redundancy in a proper scheme which prioritises all long-term sick employees for redundancy. Any redundancy payment would then be deducted from damages (*Colledge v Bass, Mitchells and Butlers Ltd* (1988)).

However, if the employee would have been made redundant anyway under the scheme which the employer operated regardless of the injury, there will be no deduction of redundancy payments.

- **Social Security benefits**

The Social Security Act 1989 which has been amended by the Social Security (Recovery of Benefits) Act 1997 (see 19.3) changed the previous position for claiming back benefits paid out by social security.

Since s 22 of the Social Security Act 1989 came into force, there is a system for recouping Social Security benefits from tortfeasors, by the Compensation Recovery Unit (CRU). This applies to any payments of compensation made after 3 September 1990 in respect of accidents occurring after the 1 January 1989 or, in the case of diseases, where the first claim for benefit was made after that date.

The relevant period prescribed is five years from the date of the accident, injury or first claim for the disease, although a payment in final discharge of the claim before the end of the five years also ends the relevant period. After the relevant period, the provisions for recouping the payments do not apply.

The relevant benefits are set out in the legislation.

The value of certain specified benefits received by the claimant in the relevant period is deducted from damages before they are paid. The sum is paid directly to the Secretary of State. Under the 1997 Act, no deductions may be made from awards of general damages, and only specified benefits may be deducted from sums awarded for loss of earnings, cost of care and loss of mobility. Even if the amount of recoverable benefits is greater than the amount that can be deducted from the damages, the defendant or his insurer, must pay the full amount of these benefits to the Secretary of State (see 19.3).

There have been many criticisms of the law in this area, not least because in some cases claimants may receive double compensation with the result that the compensation payable does not reflect actual losses of the claimant.

The law has also been criticised for creating difficulties from a practical point of view for companies, employers and other compensators who are required to reimburse the Department of Social Security when making compensation payments.

In *Wiseley v John Fulton (Plumbers) Ltd* (2000), the House of Lords held that a claimant in a personal injuries case was entitled to recover interest on all his damages for past loss of earnings, where he had received social security benefits which would be repayable to the Secretary of State for Social Security by the tortfeasor.

19.5.7 Deductions from the multiplier

Deductions may also be made by adjusting the multiplier downwards to allow for certain future contingencies. In an attempt to assess the appropriate sum which should be awarded for loss of future earnings, the courts gaze into a imaginary crystal ball, and try to make the award in the light of what might have been the claimant's future.

Points are subtracted to take account of possible early retirement through illness, based on family history or the claimant's own medical history. A previous back problem revealed in the claimant's medical notes (which are now available to courts in their entirety) might reduce an award. The possibility of the claimant's having given up work for several years to deal with child rearing is also a relevant factor.

For example, in the case of *Moriarty v McCarthy* (1978), a young woman was seriously injured in a car accident. She was disfigured by scars, and suffered back pain and certain loss of bladder control. Points were deducted from the multiplier to allow for the years when the court considered that she would have given up work to get married and bring up her family. The assumption of the court in that case was that all women marry, and that all married women do have children and that they do give up work in order to look after them for some time. It is doubtful, however, whether this assumption accords with reality and it is unfair to penalise young women in this way. The unfairness was compounded in *Moriarty v McCarthy* by the fact that the courts awarded exactly the same sum as was deducted by the alteration of the multiplier, as compensation for loss of marriage prospects through disfigurement and loss of sexual function. This humiliating procedure for claimants could be avoided by simply making the full award for loss of earnings in the same way as an award would be made to a young man in similar circumstances.

Some courts now adopt a more realistic and up-to-date approach to this problem, as in the 1985 case of *Hughes v McKeown* in which Leonard J decided that there should be no deduction from the multiplier in the case of a woman who might at some future date give up work to look after her children. The reasoning was that she would be working in her home, contributing to the general household, and her husband would be taking advantage of the work she was doing in child-rearing and household chores. In these cases, loss of marriage prospect should be compensated in terms of the loss of companionship and emotional support she might have received from a husband rather than by reference to any financial support a woman might have from being married. However, although the Court of Appeal appears to have endorsed this approach in *Housecroft v Burnett* (1986), in that case, it was considered that a small discount should be made from the multiplier if an award is made for loss of marriage prospect, and this is more in line with the older cases.

19.5.8 Other future losses

There are many ways in which future financial losses could be incurred. It is important for the claimant to take account of all of these when calculating damages.

However, the courts will not make an award if the proposed project is to be contrary to public policy, or is unrealistic and unlikely ever to be achieved. In *Briody v St Helen's and Knowsley HA* (2000), the claimant, who had been left infertile as a result of clinical negligence, claimed compensation to cover the cost of funding surrogacy treatment, in addition to claiming under more usual heads of damages. The claim for surrogacy costs raised a novel issue, as it had never been claimed as a head of damages in the past, though the courts are not precluded from recognising new heads of damages if necessary. The claimant submitted that the defendants had deprived her of her childbearing capacity, and, so far as possible, compensatory damages should put the victim in the position she would have been in had it not been for the negligence. The defendants, she argued, should pay for her attempts to have a surrogate child. The surrogacy costs would have included treatment in California, and the judge took into account evidence from a range of sources, including evidence of infertility experts. She considered the current guidelines of the Human Fertility and Embryology Authority, and the most recent view of the British Medical Association and a series of Family Division cases, and referred to the 1985 Act.

She took the view that it was in order to consider whether the damages sought would be likely to be successfully applied to achieve the desired objective, and concluded that, on the facts, there were very poor prospects of success for a surrogacy arrangement. Indeed, the chances of success were so low that it would be unreasonable to require the defendants to fund the treatment. It was not the business of the law of tort to provide a legal remedy which is doomed to almost inevitable failure and is outside the law. As a matter of public policy, the claimant was attempting to obtain damages to acquire a baby by a method that did not comply with the present law. Although a court could retrospectively approve an adoption in the interests of a surrogate child, it was an entirely different matter to award damages to enable an unenforceable and unlawful contract for surrogacy to be entered into. The claimant did succeed in obtaining some compensation to cover the psychological distress she had suffered as a result of her infertility.

- **Future care**

  The claimant is entitled to an award of damages to cover the cost of future care. In some cases, notably those involving serious brain damage or paralysis, when the claimant needs constant attention, this sum will form the highest component of the award, and it is these cases which are most likely to involve structured settlements. Competent and experienced solicitors acting for claimants are able to produce detailed lists of claimants' future needs in terms of care, and 'care specialists' are able to assist in the compilation of 'check lists' for future care. Teams of experts are often enlisted to assess the nursing requirements, technological aids, speech therapy, occupational therapy, and so on which will be required by the claimant in the future. Architects, nurses, physiotherapists, neurosurgeons, gardeners, house decorators and other experts may need to be consulted before a really comprehensive list of requirements can be completed.

- **Future medical fees and nursing care**

Prospective private medical fees will form part of the award, and the court will not treat it as unreasonable that the claimant did not make use of NHS facilities (s 2(4) of the Law Reform (Personal Injuries) Act 1948, and *Harris v Brights Asphalt Contractors* (1983)). However, by s 5 of the Administration of Justice Act 1982, any saving to the claimant through being kept in an NHS hospital at public expense must be off set against income lost through the injury.

Nursing fees for the future can be claimed, and the cost of paying a reasonable sum to a husband, wife or other person who gives up work to give full time care to the claimant can also be claimed, though this claim is that of the claimant, not of the third party in his or her own right (*Donnelly v Joyce* (1974)).

Third parties are theoretically encouraged by the law to be charitable by providing their services to injured relatives and friends. The House of Lords considered this principle in *Hunt v Severs* (1994), a case in which the voluntary carer was also the defendant. The claimant had been seriously injured in a motorbike accident caused by his negligence, and after she was discharged from hospital she married him and he continued to care for her on a voluntary basis. The Court of Appeal had made an award totalling £77,000 to the claimant which included sums representing the value of services rendered to her by the defendant in the past and for the future. What this meant in fact was that a tortfeasor who gave services voluntarily to the claimant could have the cost of such services included in the damages awarded against him (and paid by his insurance company). He was thus providing services to the claimant and also paying for them. The House of Lords reversed the decision of the Court of Appeal, deciding that, if a voluntary carer is also the defendant, there is no basis for an award of damages to cover the care so provided. It was accepted, however, that as a general principle a claimant is entitled to recover the reasonable value of services rendered by a relative or friend who provides nursing or domestic care of a kind required by the claimant's injuries. The only issue in this case was what the position is in law if the carer is also the defendant.

The Law Commission has recommended reform of the rule in its 1999 Report.

- **Future financial management**

  The claimant is able to claim a sum for future management of his financial affairs, and for negotiating with the Court of Protection (*Hodgson v Trapp* (1989)).

- **Cost of bringing up children**

  There was a series of cases in which the courts had awarded damages to cover the cost of bringing up children born after unsuccessful sterilisation operations. The courts recognised the problems and attempted to grapple with the difficulties since claims of this kind were first made in the UK in the early 1980s, but not until November 1999 has the issue been considered by the House of Lords. In the Scottish case of *McFarlane v Tayside Health Board* (1999), the difficult issues involved in these cases were carefully analysed, and the House of Lords has concluded that parents of a healthy child born after a failed sterilisation were not entitled to damages in respect of the cost of caring for and bringing up the child. This case concerned a married couple, the claimants, who had been assured by doctors employed by the Health Board that the husband was no longer fertile after undergoing a vasectomy operation. Some time later, the wife became pregnant and gave birth to a healthy daughter in May 1992. Mr and Mrs McFarlane claimed general damages of £10,000 for the pain and distress suffered by Mrs McFarlane during the pregnancy and birth, and also a sum of £100,000 to cover the cost already incurred and likely to be incurred in the future in bringing up the child. Both parents stated that they loved and cared for the child and had accepted her as part of their family, even though, for economic reasons, they had not wanted another child.

  In the course of their deliberations, the House of Lords reviewed the earlier cases dealing with the question of damages for failed sterilisation in the UK and in other jurisdictions. It was recognised by all but Lord Millet that the claim by the mother for the pain and inconvenience of childbearing should be compensated. Although different approaches were taken by all five judges to the question of compensation for the cost of rearing the child, they were unanimous in their view that these expenses should not be recoverable. Lord Slynn treated the claim as one which fell into the broad category of economic loss. It should be handled with caution, in the light of the reluctance of the courts to create liability for pure economic loss in the absence of a closer link between the act and the damage than were foreseeable. His Lordship concluded that it would not be fair, just and reasonable to impose a duty on the doctor or his employer in the circumstances of this case (*Caparo Industries v Dickman* (1990)).

  Lord Steyn did not consider the question of duty of care in depth. He concentrated on the question of distributive justice, taking the view that law and morality are inextricably woven and, although there might be some objections to the fact that the House of Lords acts, on occasion, as a court of morals, the court must apply positive justice. He approached the matter from the perspective of the 'notional commuter on the Underground' and concluded that such a person would not be in favour of awarding compensation to the parents equivalent to the cost of bringing up the child to his or her 18th birthday. Continuing in this pragmatic vein, he said:

> The realisation that compensation for financial loss in respect of the upbringing of a child would necessarily have to discriminate between rich and poor would surely appear unseemly. It would also worry them that parents may be put in a position of arguing in court that the unwanted child, which they accepted and care for, is more trouble than it is worth.

His Lordship was anxious not to perpetuate the practice of masking the true reasons for the decision with formalistic propositions by denying a remedy on the grounds that there was no foreseeable loss or no causative link between the act of negligence and the damage. He said:

> Judges ought to strive to give the real reasons for their decision. It is my firm conviction that where judges have denied a remedy for the cost of bringing up an unwanted child, the real reasons have been grounds of distributive justice ... Judges' sense of the moral answer to a question, or the justice of the case, has been one of the great shaping forces of the common law.

Lord Hope tried to strike a balance between the intangible benefits which parents receive in terms of love and affection and, in later life, support from their children, against the cost of rearing them. He took the view that it would not fair, just or reasonable to leave these intangible benefits out of the account. As it is impossible to calculate the cost of those benefits in money terms and set them off accurately against the cost of bringing up the child, he argued that:

> ... the logical conclusion, as a matter of law, was that the costs to the parents of meeting their obligations to the child during her childhood were not recoverable as damages.

Lord Clyde considered the matter from the starting point that any damages awarded should put the injured party in the same position as he or she would have been in if he or she had not sustained the wrong. In this instance, without surrendering the child, the parents could not possible be put into the same position as they would have been in had the negligent act never been committed. To relieve the parents of their financial obligations or caring for the child did not seem reasonable in his view, because it would be going beyond what should constitute a reasonable restitution.

Lord Millett emphasised that the admissibility of any head of damages is a matter of law, and if the law took the approach that an event was beneficial, claimants could not could not make it a matter for compensation, merely by saying that they had not wanted that event to happen. In his view:

Claimants are not normally allowed, by a process of subjective devaluation, to make a detriment out of a benefit ... The law must take the birth of a normal healthy baby to be a blessing, not a detriment.

The final ruling by the House of Lords coincides with that in the earliest case on this point to be decided by a court in the UK – *Udale v Bloomsbury HA* (1999). The judge in that case made the poetical observation that, although this world be a vale of tears, the birth of a child is 'a blessing and an occasion for rejoicing'. However, two years later, the case of *Emeh v Kensington and Chelsea HA* (1985) established that claims for the cost of bringing up a child can succeed. Many couples who have been able to establish negligence in failed sterilisation cases have since received the benefit of large settlements or court awards.

The definitive ruling in the *McFarlane* case is to be welcomed, not least because the law in this area is now certain, at least if the child is born healthy. In recent years, however, many of these claims have failed at the causation stage. It has been very difficult to prove that the parents had not been warned of the possibility of natural reversal of the sterilisation surgery. Even if they have *not* been warned, it has been argued successfully by defendants that the failure to warn would have made no difference.

It is right that the woman who has to carry the child, suffer the discomfort of pregnancy with its attendant difficulties such as morning sickness and undergo the pain of labour and delivery should receive an award of compensation. Only Lord Millett, who regarded pregnancy and birth as natural processes and part of the price paid for parenthood, did not approve that aspect of the claim in this case. The sum awarded to Mrs McFarlane of £10,000 is substantially higher than that suggested by the Judicial Studies Board guidelines of £3,000 to £4,000, and it is unknown whether Mrs McFarlane had a particularly difficult pregnancy and delivery.

In *Rand v East Dorset HA* (2000), it was held that, where a disabled child was born as a result of negligent advice provided about the condition of the foetus, the parents could receive an award to compensate them for bringing up a child that was disabled. They could not, however, recover the full cost of bringing up the child. Damages were assessed by calculating the difference between the cost of bringing up a normal child and a child that is disabled.

Mr and Mrs Rand had a claim based upon the extended principle in *Hedley Byrne & Co Ltd v Heller & Partners Ltd* (1963) for the financial consequences flowing from the admitted negligence of the defendant, but this was limited to the consequences flowing from the child's disability. The claim for the cost of maintenance and the cost of care for the child was a claim for pure economic loss, as was the claim for loss of profits of the residential care home that Mr and Mrs Rand ran. Following the judgment in *McFarlane*, Mr and Mrs Rand could only recover damages in respect of such economic loss as was proved to have arisen from the child's disability, and not from the fact of her birth. The claim for economic loss did not terminate, as a matter of law, upon the child's reaching her 18th birthday.

- **Compensation for handicap on the labour market**

  The court will consider whether the claimant has suffered a handicap on the labour market and make an award accordingly (see *Smith v Manchester Corp* (1974)), but the sum awarded will be speculative, as it is seldom possible to arrive at an accurate figure on the basis of what a person's earning capacity might have been had the accident never happened.

  In *Doyle v Wallace* (1998), the Court of Appeal held that damages were recoverable for loss of earnings from a job for which the claimant might have become qualified, had it not been for her accident. Here, the relationship between causation and *quantum* becomes unclear (see Chapter 8) and the correct approach to arriving at a figure is for the court to evaluate the chance and apply a percentage amount as a means of quantification. In this case, the judge had taken the view that the claimant had a 50/50 chance of obtaining a teaching qualification and finding a job. This rather difficult area of law was clarified in *Allied Maples Group Ltd v Simmons and Simmons* (1995) and *Stovold v Barlows* (1995), in which the distinction between what matters fell within the concept of 'loss of a chance' and what was required to be proved on a balance of probabilities was explained.

  The claimant in *Anderson v Davis* (1993) was estimated to have had a two-thirds chance of obtaining promotion to the post of principal lecturer, and the final award was calculated on the basis of two-thirds of his lost earnings.

19.6 Non-pecuniary losses

Losses which are intangible are extremely difficult to quantify, and over the years the courts have developed the practice of classifying general damages under various 'heads of damage'. The list of heads of damage is not exhaustive, and the court may add to it from time to time. The main heads of damages are considered below. Lawyers frequently refer to figures published regularly by the Judicial Studies Board based on recent cases to give them a broad idea of the financial brackets for general damages. More detailed information is obtainable from *Kemp and Kemp*, an encyclopaedia of damages cases.

- The Court of Appeal has taken the opportunity to comment upon the status of the Judicial Studies Board Guidelines in *Reed v Sunderland HA* (1998). Sir

Christopher Staughton stated that, although the very title 'guidelines' might suggest that the guidance issued by the Judicial Studies Board might have some legal authority, in fact, they did not. He explained that the law relating to *quantum* lay in statutes and decided cases, and the Judicial Studies Board did not have legislative power. Damages awarded to the claimant for negligent diagnosis of a medical condition were reduced from £365,493 to £246,407.40 by a unanimous decision of the Court of Appeal.

19.6.1 Pain and suffering

Pain and suffering are subjective, and are impossible to measure in terms of money. However, an award will be made to cover nervous shock, psychiatric symptoms and physical pain and suffering.

It is believed that people who are unconscious do not suffer any pain and therefore no award will be made under this head in cases where the claimant is in a coma, as in *Wise v Kaye* (1962), in which the claimant was unconscious from the moment of the accident. In such cases, however, there is a very high award for loss of amenity.

In the 'failed' vasectomy cases, there is an award to the mother for the discomfort of pregnancy and the pain and anxiety of child birth, though against this it is necessary to set the pain that would have been experienced had her pregnancy been terminated! (*Allen v Bloomsbury HA* (1993).)

Since the Administration of Justice Act 1982, there is no separate head of damages for loss of expectation of life. Instead, that is now absorbed into the general head of 'pain and suffering' caused by the knowledge that one's life has been shortened by the accident.

19.6.2 Loss of amenity

The claimant is entitled to damages for the inability to enjoy life in various ways, in particular, impairment of the senses. This will include, for example, inability to run or to walk, or to play football, to play the piano, to play with one's children, inability to enjoy sexual functions or marriage. Claimants who are in a persistent vegetative state or in a coma will receive a very high award for loss of amenity. In *Wise v Kaye* (see 19.6.1 above), the claimant was unconscious and had been so for more than three years at the time of the trial; she did not know what she had lost and was not, apparently, suffering any pain. The Court of Appeal awarded her £15,000 for loss of amenity, which at that time was an exceptionally large sum.

In *West and Son Ltd v Shephard* (1964), the claimant was a woman aged 41 years when she suffered a severe head injury. Although she could not speak, there was evidence from her eye movements that she understood her predicament. She received a high award for loss of amenity. The object of awarding her damages was to try to place her in the position she would have been in if she had never been injured. It is impossible in cases such as this to know how much, if anything, a person is suffering. Awarding a large sum for loss of amenity avoids such speculation.

A number of serious fears have been expressed about the making of high awards for loss of amenity in cases such as this. Relatives of patients with a condition known as PVS (persistent vegetative state) have much to gain if the claimant is kept alive until the trial or settlement, as high awards for loss of amenity and future care will be made. If patients in this state are allowed to die very soon after the accident, the only available claim would be under the Fatal Accidents Act 1976 to dependent relatives for loss of a breadwinner. Once the trial is over, if the life support machine is switched off and the accident victim dies, the relatives stand to gain under the will or intestacy of the deceased far more than would have been available to them under the Fatal Accidents Act 1976, particularly if the deceased was young and no claim would have been available at all for loss of dependency. While there is no suggestion of any impropriety in any known case, the danger remains, and the situation is now further complicated by the decision in *Bland v Airedale Trust* (1993), in which the House of Lords sanctioned the withdrawal of artificial feeding from a young PVS patient. Although this matter was not specifically considered by the Law Commission in its report on structured settlements, this is yet another important reason why their use should be encouraged.

19.6.3 Levels of general damages

Recent Court of Appeal decisions will have some impact on the size of future awards of general damages. In a series of appeals, *Heil v Rankin; Rees v Mabco (102) Ltd; Schofield v Saunders and Taylor Ltd; Ramsay v Rivers; Kent v Griffiths; Warren v Northern General Hospital NHS Trust; Annable v Southern Derbyshire HA; Connolly v Tasker* (2000), the Court of Appeal gave full consideration to the question of whether it would be appropriate to change the level awards for general damages. Guidelines were established on the level of damages for pain, suffering and loss of amenity in personal injury and clinical negligence claims worth over £10,000. The awards would be tapered, the rate of increase growing with the size of the award, up to a maximum increase of one-third on awards at the highest level. The modest increase was required to bring some awards up to the appropriate standard, which was a sum which was fair, reasonable and just.

In these eight appeals, which turned solely on *quantum*, the five member Court of Appeal issued a single judgment made in the light of the Law Commission's Report No 257 (1999). This Report contained a recommendation that the level of damages for non-pecuniary loss for personal injuries should be increased. The Law Commission had recommended that, in respect of injuries for which the then current award for non-pecuniary loss for the injury alone would be more than £3,000, damages for non-pecuniary loss should be increased by a factor of at least 1.5, but not more than a factor of 2. It had also recommended a tapering of increased awards in the range £2,001 to £3,000 of less than a factor of 1.5. The Law Commission had recommended that legislation be avoided if possible, and had expressed the view that the Court of Appeal and House of Lords should lay down guidelines to deal with this matter in a series of cases.

The Court of Appeal took the view that it was well equipped to make decisions on the matters discussed in the Law Commission Report. There was no need to depart from basic principles used in the assessment of damages in reaching its conclusion, but it acknowledged that any process of attempting to convert pain suffering and loss of amenity into financial damages was artificial and difficult. In the view of the court, changing the current levels of damages, if they are no longer reflecting what should be the correct level of awards, was part of the courts' duty. This was a duty that was not to be shirked.

On the issue of damages for pain, suffering and loss of amenity, it was held that consideration of the evidence had led to conclusions which would not radically alter the present approach to the assessment of damages. The Court of Appeal thought that it would be inappropriate to increase the levels of awards to the substantial extent recommended by the Commission. However, a modest increase was necessary to bring some awards up to the standard, on which both sides were agreed, to a sum which was fair, reasonable and just. It was in the case of the most catastrophic injuries that the awards were most in need of adjustment. The scale of adjustment required reduced as the level of existing awards decreased. At the highest level, there was a need for awards to be increased by in the region of one-third. At the other end of the scale, there was no need for an increase in awards which were at present below £10,000. Between those awards at the highest level, which required an adjustment upwards of one-third, and those awards where no adjustment was required, the extent of the adjustment should taper. The means of tapering downwards was illustrated by the decisions in the individual appeals.

19.6.4 Damages for the injury itself

Some injuries are virtually impossible to assess in money terms and figures are almost plucked from the air. For example, in *Thurman v Wiltshire HA* (1996), an award of £50,000 was made to a woman who had lost a foetus and became permanently infertile as a result of medical negligence. Injuries are itemised and particular sums are awarded for these on the basis of precedents. These cases may be consulted in *Current Law* or *Kemp and Kemp*, and awards increase with the passing years. For example, a broken arm will be worth a certain amount, loss of an eye a certain figure, a scar would be worth a certain sum and so on.

19.6.5 Damages for bereavement

Until s 3 of the Administration of Justice Act 1982, there was no award of damages for bereavement. However, under that Act, which substituted a new s 1A to the Fatal Accidents Act 1976, it is possible for parents who lose an unmarried child under the age of 18, and any person who loses a spouse, to claim damages for bereavement. The sum currently available is £7,500 and this, if the parents of a deceased child are separated, is divided equally between them.

The action does not survive for the benefit of a deceased relative's estate.

Atiyah regards this sort of compensation as 'solace' and not as deserving of an award, as it is impossible to assess, and is yet another factor which puts those who can prove fault and who are therefore entitled to tort damages, in a much more advantageous position than the victims of mere misfortune.

What appears to perpetrate further injustice is the fact that the statute discriminates between different types of claimant. A wife, for example, who may be heartily glad to be rid of a drunken husband would be entitled to the same amount of money as a wife who was devastated by the loss of her husband, but a cohabitee would not be entitled to an award of bereavement damages at all. No one can measure the grief which such people feel, and it is almost insulting to place a financial sum on it.

In *Doleman v Deakin* (1990), an unmarried youth, aged 17 years, was severely injured by a negligent driver as he walked across a pedestrian crossing. He died 25 days after his 18th birthday, though tragically, for all practical purposes, he might as well have died immediately, as he never regained consciousness after the accident. The Court of Appeal held that the parents' claim for bereavement was unsuccessful because the cause of action accrues at the date of death, and not at the date of the accident.

19.6.6 Interference with consortium

Although the head of damages known as 'loss of consortium' under which a husband could previously claim for the loss of his wife's services and society, was abolished by the Administration of Justice Act 1982. In *Hodgson v Trapp* (1989), the husband of a severely injured woman succeeded in obtaining an award of £20,000 for impairment of the relationship which he had previously enjoyed with his wife. She had been a very active woman, a freelance artist and teacher, and partner in her husband's business, as well as a good mother to their children. Through the defendant's negligence, she had suffered brain damage in an accident at the age of 33 years. After the accident, she was unable to walk, to bath or dress herself, or to go to the lavatory unaided. Her speech was slow and child like and her sight was poor. She was no longer good company for her husband, and was constantly frustrated by her condition.

19.7 Damages payable on death

Death may affect a cause of action which already exists, or it may create a new cause of action for the dependant relatives or other dependants of the deceased.

19.7.1 Survival of existing causes of action

Although at common law the position was that the cause of action died if the claimant or defendant died, since 1846, there has been incremental statutory reform of the common law rules, which has kept pace with the changes in society which followed the introduction of fast-moving vehicles.

The only tort action which still dies with the claimant or defendant is defamation. When Robert Maxwell died, it was said that over 100 defamation actions died with him.

In 1846, the Fatal Accidents Act gave the dependant spouse and children of an accident victim separate actions in their own right to sue his killer for lost dependency.

As there would be no damages forthcoming to the dependants if the perpetrator of the accident also died, it was necessary to make provision for the right of action to continue against the estate of a deceased tortfeasor. By the Law Reform (Miscellaneous Provisions) Act 1934, the insurer of the tortfeasor remains liable to the dependants of the accident victim.

By the same Act, the estate of a deceased accident victim is entitled to carry on an existing action after his death.

Section 4(1) provides that where damage has been suffered as a result of the act or omission of the deceased which would have given rise to an action had he lived (for example, where a driver causes an accident in which he is killed but others survive), it is deemed that the cause of action existed before his death.

Any damages recoverable are calculated without reference to other benefits which the estate may receive on the death of the claimant (s 1(2)(c)). Such benefits might include the proceeds of an insurance policy. Similarly, losses to the estate must not enter into the equation. Funeral expenses of a reasonable amount may also be recovered by the estate.

The basis of the calculations under the Law Reform (Miscellaneous Provisions) Act 1934 is the same as if the claimant were still alive (except of course the claim for funeral expenses). Special damages and general damages are recoverable, including damages for pain and suffering and loss of amenity (see above).

In *Hicks v Chief Constable of South Yorkshire* (1992), the House of Lords considered whether damages would be payable under the Act for pain and suffering in the last few minutes before death, a claim which is recognised in

America where it is termed 'pre-death trauma'. The Appeal was brought by the Administrators of the estates of two sisters who were killed in the Hillsborough football stadium disaster. The defendant had admitted liability and the only issue was as to whether the terror, pain and suffering which the girls experienced immediately before they died could be the subject of an award. Medical evidence was that the girls had died of traumatic asphyxia, and that, after a short period of pain and suffering, they would have lost consciousness, and death would have followed in a matter of minutes. Fear of impending death is taken into account in assessing claims for pain and suffering, and is treated as suffering which occurs with the knowledge that one's life has been shortened by the accident (s 1(1)(b) of the Administration of Justice Act 1982).

The House of Lords upheld the decision of the Court of Appeal which had been based on the finding of fact that there was no established psychiatric injury because death followed the accident so quickly, so the claim failed. In the words of Lord Parker:

> The last few moments of mental agony and pain were in reality part of the death itself, for which no action lies under the 1934 Act.

In that case, the most to which the parents would have been entitled was a reasonable sum for funeral expenses and an bereavement award of £7,500 for the death of the one sister who was under the age of 18 years. Of course, as Lord Bridge acknowledged, there could be no money compensation which would be adequate for the deaths in the case of two young girls 'at the very threshold of life'.

Under the Law Reform (Miscellaneous Provisions) Act 1934, there can be no award of loss of future earnings for the 'lost years' (s 4(3) of the Administration of Justice Act 1982), as this would have meant double recovery for relatives who might also have a claim for loss of dependency under the Fatal Accidents Act 1976.

However, under the Law Reform (Miscellaneous Provisions) Act 1934, there will still be a claim for loss of amenity during the interval of time between the accident and the death providing, as was held in *Hicks* (see above), this is long enough. As Lord Parker explained in the *Hicks* case:

> There is, of course, no doubt at all that where a person is by negligence caused injuries which result in pain, suffering or loss of amenity he has a cause of action in respect thereof. If he dies later, that cause of action survives for the benefit of his estate.

Exemplary damages do not survive for the benefit of the deceased's estate (s 4(2)(a) of the Fatal Accidents Act 1976).

19.7.2 Death as a cause of action: loss of dependency

Dependants of a deceased person have a claim in their own right against the tortfeasor providing the deceased could have maintained an action against him (s 1 of the Fatal Accidents Act 1976).

Only if the deceased would have had an action will the dependants be entitled to sue. This means not only that the dependants will have no action if the deceased would have been barred from making a claim by the Limitation Acts, or for some other reason, but also that any defences which would have applied if the deceased had himself lived to bring the action will also affect the claims of the dependants. In some cases, it may even be the dependant who contributed to the death of the deceased, and if this is so there will be a suitable apportionment of the damages. If the deceased had been contributorily negligent, there will be a reduction from the award of damages made to the dependants (s 5 of the Administration of Justice Act 1982).

For example, in *Barrett v Minister of Defence* (1995), the widow of an airman who died during a heavy drinking session while in the care of the defendants had a reduction made in her award because her husband was found to be 25% contributorily negligent.

Under s 4 of the Administration of Justice Act 1982, the right to sue for any years lost to the deceased does not survive the death of the claimant.

19.7.3 Who are the dependants?

The categories of people who are entitled to claim for loss of dependency have been increased over the years, the latest expansion being made by the Administration of Justice Act 1982.

Dependants who are entitled to claim under the Fatal Accidents Act 1976 now include: spouse, former spouse; cohabitees who were living with the deceased immediately before his death and have lived with as husband or wife of the deceased for two continuous years before the death; parents or other ascendants; people treated by the deceased as parents; children or other descendants of the deceased; people who are children of a person to whom the deceased was married, and who were treated by the deceased as 'children of the family' immediately before his death; brothers, sisters, aunts and uncles of the deceased and their issue. Relations by marriage are treated as blood relations, and relations of the half-blood are treated as whole-blood relations. Children born outside marriage are treated as though they were born within marriage.

As far as the Criminal Injuries Compensation Scheme is concerned, it has been proposed by the Government that compensation rights be extended to homosexual partners. This has not been officially suggested yet for tort damages.

It is, of course, usually the spouse, partner and children of the deceased who claim for loss of dependency. If the victim was young, it is unusual for the parents to claim. One such claim was made by the parents of a promising young ballet dancer, aged 19, who had died in the *Marchioness* riverboat disaster. They were able to prove that the family shared everything, that the parents had invested heavily in their daughter's career and had been promised a share in her success later in life.

Although the action is usually brought on behalf of the dependant person by the personal representatives of the deceased, if the action is not begun within six months of the death, any dependant may bring the action on behalf of all the dependants.

Damages under the Fatal Accidents Act 1976 are only available to those people in the categories specified in the Act if they can prove that they were, or would at some stage become dependant on the deceased person. Essentially, the action is for loss of a breadwinner, and for the income and financial support which would have been provided over the years but which has been lost because of the act of the tortfeasor. The calculation therefore resembles the calculations discussed above in the case of claimants who survive accidents and who claim damages for loss of future earnings. The multiplier/multiplicand method is utilised as previously described, and the object of the compensation is to provide the dependants with a lump sum which may be invested to yield income for the future, to cover the years during which the person would have been dependant upon the deceased.

In *Cookson v Knowles* (1977), the House of Lords ruled that damages for loss of dependency should be divided into two parts to cover losses up to the date of the trial, and future losses, in a similar approach to that taken in the case of living claimants who are accident victims.

All that need be proved is a reasonable expectation of future dependency in cases in which the claimant has not been dependent upon the deceased before death. For example, there are some parents of older children about to finish training or education who expect to be able to depend upon their children financially when they start to earn (*Kandalla v British European Airways Corporation* (1981)).

19.7.4 Adjusting the multiplier

The multiplier will be adjusted to take account of the dependant's future, so that, for example the assumption is that children will cease to be dependent on their parents once they leave full time education.

19.7.5 Financial dependency

In the case of a dependant spouse, the likelihood of a divorce had the deceased lived will be taken into account. In *Martin v Owen* (1992), the Court of Appeal reduced the claimant's multiplier from 15 to 11 to take account of the fact that her marriage to the deceased had only lasted for one year, and that she had later committed adultery twice.

Although the possibility of divorce may be considered, with all the distasteful prying into the marriage between the claimant and deceased spouse which that entails, the courts are not permitted to inquire as to the re-marriage prospects of widows who claim under the Fatal Accidents Act 1976. This change in the law was introduced in 1971 after a vigorous campaign by the women's movement following a series of cases in which widows were subjected to embarrassing cross-examination about their personal lives.

One inevitable result of this rule is that those widows who remarry are over-compensated, and there are even instances in which widows have already remarried wealthy men before the case comes to trial. (See Atiyah, where the rule is described as 'one of the most irrational pieces of law reform ever passed by Parliament'.) Irrational though it may seem today, the change in the law was not surprising given the zeal of the women's movement against the cattle market approach and the offensive questions put to young widows in some of the cases. Nevertheless, the law has not created a situation of true equality between the sexes, as widowers' remarriage prospects may be considered (though none of the cases reveal the distasteful approach found in the widows' cases), and the remarriage prospects of a widow may be considered in relation to claims by her children for loss of dependency.

Cohabitees tend to be awarded lower sums for loss of dependency than widows and widowers (s 3(4) of the Fatal Accidents Act 1976).

19.7.6 Non-financial dependency

Even non-financial dependency may be claimed under the Fatal Accidents Act 1976, as in the case of domestic services which will no longer be available (*Spittle v Bunney* (1988)). The award is assessed on the basis of the diminishing cost of hiring a nanny until a child has grown up. If another relative, say the father, gives up work to care for children, a reasonable sum may be claimed on the same basis (*Hayden v Hayden* (1992)).

It has become the practice since *Spittle v Bunney* (1988) to assess the award for the loss of a mother as a carer in terms of a judge directing himself as if he were a jury, and mere mathematical calculations based on the cost of hiring a nanny are rejected on this basis, so that the award is frequently lower than it would have been if calculated mathematically, as this permits a qualitative assessment to be made (see *Stanley v Saddique* (1991) discussed below).

In *Watson v Wilmott* (1991), the claimant's parents were killed in a car accident. The mother was killed and the father, who had minor physical injuries suffered a serious psychiatric condition and committed suicide. The claimant was adopted by an uncle and aunt and the defendant contended that as an adopted child of new parents who now had the legal responsibility of maintaining him he had no right to a claim under the Fatal Accidents Act 1976 for loss of dependency. It was held that the position of the child with his new parents should be compared with his position had his natural parents lived, and that the measure of damages should be the difference between the two positions if the present position was worse than the previous one. Damages were therefore assessed on the difference between his dependency on his natural father and that on his adopted father. However, as the adopted mother had substituted her care for that of the natural mother no damages were payable in respect of that.

By comparison, in *Stanley v Saddique* (1991), a child whose mother had not been married to his father was cared for by his father's new wife after the death of his mother, which had been caused by the defendant's negligence. The substitute mother provided a better quality of care than that which the child had enjoyed with his own mother. However, the Court of Appeal held that the fact that the child now enjoyed a better standard of care should be disregarded in the light of s 4 of the Fatal Accidents Act 1976 which states that any benefits which accrue to the claimant must be disregarded when the courts assess damages for loss of dependency. However, the claimant's damages for lost dependency were reduced because his natural mother would probably not have given him good quality care.

In *Hayden v Hayden* (1992), the 'judge as jury' approach was approved by the Court of Appeal, when a qualitative rather than a quantitative assessment was again made. It was considered that the father, in giving up his employment to care for the children, had provided at least as good a service as the mother, so that calculating the cost of providing services as that of a notional nanny would not have been appropriate. The full cost of a nanny would have been £48,000 here, but the award amounted only to £20,000.

This approach appears to be unfair financially and unduly hard in emotional terms on the carers, who as family members will already be grieving the loss of the relative for whom they are substituting care. It is also likely to prolong litigation by requiring evidence as to the care previously provided by the lost relative and of the substituted care, in order to allow the judge to make a qualitative assessment.

Any benefits which will or may accrue to the claimant from the estate of the deceased will be disregarded when the court is assessing the award (s 4 of the Fatal Accidents Act 1976). This may lead to over-compensation in some cases, but the tendency over the past century has been to reduce the instances in which deductions will be made from the awards payable to dependants.

Such benefits may include substantial gains under life insurance policies or pensions payable on the death of the deceased to dependants. In *Wood v Bentall Simplex* (1992), the deceased, a farmer, had been asphyxiated when he went to the assistance of a farm labourer who had become trapped in a slurry storage system. In assessing damages payable to the widow and children under the Fatal Accidents Act 1976 as amended 1982, it was was held to be irrelevant that a loss might be established from one source which could be made good from another by using a benefit from the deceased's estate.

Damages for bereavement may be claimed under s 1A of the Fatal Accidents Act 1976. The sum to be awarded may be increased by statutory instrument at the instigation of the Lord Chancellor when he sees fit to do so.

19.7.7 The Law Commission Reports

The Law Commission produced two Reports in 1999, entitled *Damages For Personal Injury: Medical, Nursing And Other Expenses; Collateral Benefits* (No 262) and *Claims for Wrongful Death* (No 263).

These Reports made a number of recommendations aimed at modernising the existing legislation to bring this area of the law into line with the values of modern society, and to render the law fairer and more certain. They were critical of the law that arbitrarily excludes certain people who are financially dependent on the deceased from entitlement to compensation for financial loss. The Law Commission recommended reforming the position by adding a generally worded class of claimant to the present fixed list.

The Reports considered it unjustified that the award of bereavement damages is available only to the deceased's spouse and parents, and recommended extending the list to include the deceased's children, siblings and long term partner. There was also a proposal that the amount of bereavement damages should be raised to £10,000 (with an overall maximum award for any one death of £30,000) and that it should subsequently be adjusted to keep pace with changing economic conditions through index linking.

In order to avoid over-compensation, the Law Commission recommended reform of the law that requires all benefits accruing to a dependant as a result of the death to be ignored, and suggested that the Ogden Working Party – an expert body of lawyers and actuaries – should consider and explain more fully how actuarial tables now being generally used in the assessment of damages should be applied or amended to produce accurate assessments of damages in wrongful death cases.

19.8 Interest on damages

The rules for accumulation of interest on damages are arbitrary and impossible to make sense of by rational discussion. In any event, the rate of interest is very low and varies from one form of damages to another. Special damages (pecuniary losses to the date of trial) carry interest from the date of the accident at half the special investment account rate for money paid into court. Future losses, both pecuniary and non-pecuniary, accumulate no interest. Non-pecuniary loss in personal injury cases before the trial carries interest at 2% from the time the writ is served, and non-pecuniary loss in non-personal injury cases before the trial accumulates no interest.

19.9 New methods of paying damages in personal injury cases

For many years, the lump sum method by which tort damages are usually paid has been regarded as unsatisfactory, particularly in cases in which the claimant is seriously injured and unlikely ever to be able to cope with full-time employment, and in cases in which the medical prognosis is uncertain. (See Pearson Commission Report 1978.) However, the rule at common law that damages are payable once only still applies, and a number of reasons for its persistence have been suggested, which go beyond the notion that the rule continues to dominate the payment of damages in common law systems because it is the 'product of history and inertia' (Bale, *Issues in Tort Law*, Steel (ed)).

The Law Commission Consultation Paper (No 125) *Structured Settlements, Interim and Provisional Damages* (1992), suggested four reasons for the continued predominance of lump sum payments of damages:

- historical reasons based on the fact that damages were originally determined by juries;
- the importance which common law attaches to finality in litigation;
- the practical impossibility in the past of achieving a system of periodic payments;
- the relatively low awards of damages in previous years before technology permitted sophisticated methods of loss assessment.

The Consultation Paper recognised that lump sum awards are not without advantages, notably the certainty which allows claimants freedom to choose what they wish to do with their compensation and to devote their energies to recovery and rehabilitation, and the lack of a need to monitor patients with its attendant expense.

However, the disadvantages attached to lump sum payments were discussed at length and focus on the fact that such payments can never be an accurate reflection of what has been lost because they are based on a series of predictions and rely on the crude formulae of multiplier and multiplicand. Moreover, although the risk of the claimant's dissipating the award is unknown as there is no recent reliable research on the matter, it is still a possibility which cannot be ignored, though in recent cases the increasing occurrence of a head of damages for 'professional fees' to cover investment and handling of the award may be an indication that claimants are being encouraged by their lawyers to invest their compensation wisely.

The Damages Act 1996 confirms the power of the courts to make consent orders under which damages take the form of periodical payments.

Over the years, a variety of methods have been developed by which lump sum payments may be avoided. They are as follows: split trials and interim damages; provisional damages; structured settlements.

19.9.1 Split trials and interim damages

The split trials and interim damages method means that liability can be settled at an early stage and the issue of *quantum* settled later when the prognosis for the patient has become more certain. Although it is by no means certain that this method will make the medical prognosis any clearer, as many conditions can take years to develop and the patient may suffer 'compensation neurosis', a recognised phenomenon which delays improvement in the claimant's medical condition until after the trial, split trials are permitted by the Civil Procedure Rules.

Once liability has been established, the claimant will be able to receive a sum to cover special damages which have already been incurred to assist him or her financially until *quantum* is finalised. By CPR 25.1, the court can make an order for interim damages if the claimant shows 'need'. Although the Rules do not require a claimant to show need before an interim payment can be ordered, it has become the practice that this is in fact done on the basis of the submission of medical evidence, and the Law Commission in its consultation paper recommended the continuation of this requirement in the interests of defendants.

Some solicitors do favour this method, particularly in cases where it is clear that the claimant is enduring financial hardship, but, in practice, it is not a popular option because, particularly in smaller cases, the new regime for recouping Social Security payments may eat up the interim payments, and because it involves solicitors in swearing lengthy affidavits in support of special damages already incurred.

Another criticism of split trials is that they delay the hearing of cases, and a major criticism of the tort system has been its delays.

19.9.2 Provisional damages

Introduced by s 6 of the Administration of Justice Act 1982, which inserts a new s 32A into the Supreme Court Act 1981, provisional payments of damages, which can be adjusted at a later date, may be made in cases where the medical prognosis is uncertain and where there is a chance that a serious disease, or serious deterioration in the claimant's physical or mental condition will occur at a later date.

The claimant must specify what the 'feared event' is likely to be in considerable detail. An example might be the possibility of epilepsy developing some years after a head injury.

The judge must specify the period within which the claimant must apply for a further award, but the claimant can apply for an extension of that period within the specified time. Indeed, there is no limit to the number of applications for an extension and this means that the period of time involved could well be indefinite.

The case law is still developing on the question as to whether there is a 'chance' of 'serious deterioration' in the claimant's condition and as to the meaning of these terms.

In *Willson v Ministry of Defence* (1991), the claimant, who had an ankle injury, was concerned about the possibility of arthritis developing at some future date and requested an order for provisional damages. However, despite the fact this would appear at first sight to have been a suitable case for provisional damages, he was refused an order on the grounds that arthritis is simply a progression of the particular disease and this is not the same as a 'chance event'.

The Damages Act 1996 makes provision for the situation where death supervenes after damages have been awarded during the lifetime of an accident victim on the basis that if the disease or injury deteriorates in the future, he might be entitled to a further award of compensation. In such cases, where the claimant dies, the lifetime award to the victim will not prevent dependants from claiming under the Fatal Accidents Act 1976, though their award would not include damages in respect of losses already covered by the lifetime award.

19.9.3 Structured settlements

Structured settlements are not the result of legislation but of practical moves by lawyers and insurers in consultation with the Inland Revenue, to circumvent the lump sum payment and improve the lot of claimants.

Basically, structured settlements involve the substitution of pensions for lump sum payments, and because of tax concessions by the Inland Revenue, the result is lower payments by insurers and higher incomes for claimants. The recipient of the damages receives his money free of tax under this scheme, whereas the claimant who receives a lump sum award must pay tax on any income once it is invested. After initially working out the sum which would have been received in conventional lump sum form, part is paid to the claimant immediately to cover special damage incurred to the date of the settlement, and the rest is utilised by the insurer to purchase an annuity for the benefit of the claimant. The amounts payable may be structured over a period of time to take care of various contingencies. However, structured settlements must be agreed by the parties and will only be used in cases involving substantial sums of money, as they involve heavy administrative burdens. They are particularly appropriate in cases which involve serious personal injury and where the claimant's life expectancy is uncertain. They are also useful where a vulnerable claimant needs to be protected from the influence of others or is unable to manage investment of a lump sum award. Claimants who pay tax at higher rates or have substantial capital will also benefit.

Apart from the tax advantages, a major benefit is that the income can be protected from inflation.

Further advantages of structured settlements identified by the Law Commission are that they encourage early settlement, so saving time and costs and they provide certainty for claimants at an early stage, combined with flexibility of operation.

However, there are some disadvantages in structured settlements which the Law Commission identifies. These include the fact that once decided upon, a structured settlement cannot be changed: '... the pressure to get it right at an early stage is extreme.' There is still a pressing need to make predictions and there is a risk that monies provided will be insufficient to meet the claimant's needs. Moreover, some individuals may be persuaded into a structured settlement which they do not want.

Even investigating the likely costs of setting up a structured settlement can prove to be an expensive exercise, and, in *Conneely (A Minor) v Redbridge and Waltham Forest NHS Trust* (1999), it was held that, in approving a structured settlement in a medical negligence case, it is possible for the judge to order that the costs of such an investigation be limited to a reasonable set figure. Here, the defendant sought an order to limit the costs which the claimant could incur, to be borne by the defendant (under standard NHS practice) in investigating whether or not a structured settlement should be arranged. The defendant's argument was that it was normal practice to cap the allowable expenditure for the investigation at £5,000. However, it was argued for the claimant that there should be no cap on allowable expenditure, as the claimant had moved to Eire.

The settlement was approved, but subject to the defendants' undertaking to pay the claimant's costs of investigating a structured settlement being limited to the sum of £5,000. There was to be a reconsideration of this limit, up to a maximum of £7,000 if the sum of £5,000 was reasonably shown by the claimant to have been insufficient.

Structured settlements were first developed in the US and Canada in the 1980s, and have now increased in popularity in the UK since the concession by the Inland Revenue in 1978 made them possible. The first structured settlement which was judicially approved in England was in the case of *Kelly v Dawes* (1990), and they are considered so important that they were the subject of a major consultation by the Law Commission. The Damages Act 1996 aims to provide statutory support for structured settlements.

19.10   Property damage

The award of damages relating to property is calculated in a similar way to that relating to personal injuries. However, property damage is easier to quantify than personal injuries.

The heads of damage, the first three of which are set out in *Liesbosch v SS Edison* (1933), are:

- the market value of the property. The damages are based on the loss of the property and its value at the time of loss, rather than the cost of replacing it. However, the cost of the loss may sometimes be the same as the cost of replacement;

- cost of transporting replacement property to the place in question, if relevant;

- loss of profit which is reasonably foreseeable;

- loss of use until the time the property is replaced;

- reduction in value if the property is damaged rather than destroyed. This usually amounts to the cost of repairs calculated at the time of damage or when damage ought reasonably to have been discovered.

19.11   Economic loss

The assessment of damages for economic loss which is unconnected with personal injuries is a complex process, but it does not pose the same difficulties as the assessment of intangible and unpredictable losses in personal injuries cases. However, the basic principle is that the claimant must be restored to the position he would have been in if the tort had never been committed.

Swingcastle Ltd v Alastair Gibson (1991) illustrates some of the difficulties. The House of Lords held that, in a case involving a negligent house survey which had resulted in a loan being made by the claimant's finance company to the mortgagors, where the loan would not have been made at all had the survey not been negligent, the measure of damages should be the difference between the amount lent and the amount which would have been lent if the survey had been competently carried out. In this case the sum lent was £10,000 and the sum which would have been lent was £0. If interest was to be payable on the sum which had been lost, it was up to the claimants to adduce evidence as to what use they would have put the money by way of investment, loans, etc, during the time it was out of their hands. This is in keeping with the principle that tort damages are intended to put the claimant in the position he or she would have been in had the wrong never been committed.

19.12 Injunctions

In some cases, the claimant requires a remedy which will do more than simply prove financial compensation. There may also be circumstances in which there is a need to prevent repetition of the wrongful acts.

The appropriate remedy in such cases is the equitable remedy of an injunction.

For example, in libel cases, the claimant often seeks an injunction to prevent publication of defamatory material. In trespass and nuisance cases, the claimant will require an injunction to prevent the defendant persisting in the wrongful conduct, such as swinging of a crane over property.

Injunctions may be mandatory or prohibitory. A mandatory injunction is an order of the court instructing the defendant to undo some wrongful act, for example, to dismantle a building which obstructs a right to light, for example, *Kelsen v Imperial Tobacco Co* (1975). A prohibitory injunction is an order of the court instructing the defendant not to do a wrongful act, such as the commission of a trespass.

If an injunction is required as a matter of urgency, for example, to prevent an imminent television broadcast which could contain defamatory statements, the claimant may apply to the court for an interim or interlocutory injunction as a temporary measure until the full hearing can be arranged, after which a perpetual (permanent) injunction may be obtained if the case is proved. Guidelines for the granting of interlocutory injunctions were laid down by the House of Lords in *American Cyanamid Co v Ethicon* (1975). One important consideration is the balance of convenience between the parties; but the judge must first be satisfied that there is a serious question to be tried.

Injunctions are equitable remedies and are therefore discretionary in nature, which means that in certain cases, even though the claimant succeeds in proving the case, the court may refuse the order and grant damages in lieu of an injunction. Special problems arise when injunctions are sought to restrain nuisances.

Despite the discretionary nature of injunctions, it appears that some of the underlying principles are rigid and courts are reluctant to take into account the merits of the defendant's conduct. In *Kennaway v Thompson* (1981), the Court of Appeal granted an injunction to prevent a nuisance caused to the claimant by power boat racing, despite agreements that the activity had certain social merits and the defendants would have preferred to pay damages in lieu (cf *Miller v Jackson* (1977)). In *Shelfer v City of London Electric Lighting Company* (1895), the judge granted an injunction to prevent vibrations even though the consequence was that a large area of London was deprived of electricity. There are various reasons for refusal of equitable remedies which it is beyond the scope of this work to examine in detail. The main reasons for not awarding an injunction are delay by the claimant (laches), some impropriety on the part of the claimant, and impracticality, such as circumstances which require constant supervision of the order.

The courts also have power to award an injunction in addition to damages in an appropriate case.

19.13   Other remedies in tort

There are certain remedies which are peculiar to particular torts. These are dealt with in the course of discussion of those specific actions.

REMEDIES IN TORT

Damages

Many criticisms have been made of the way in which the law of tort approaches the problems which are inherent in making money awards for injuries and illnesses. The system is considered to be inaccurate, unfair, and inefficient.

Types of damages

It is possible to clarify the various kinds of damage which are payable: nominal; compensatory; contemptuous; aggravated; punitive or exemplary (*Rookes v Barnard* (1964); *Broome v Cassell* (1972); *John v MGN Ltd* (1996)).

Personal injuries

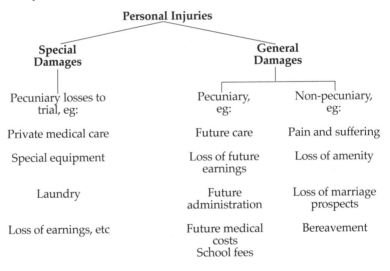

Pecuniary losses

Note the problems with the 'lost years'. The old rule that a claimant whose life-expectancy had been reduced could not claim damages for the years which had been lost to him seemed unfair, although it was logically correct. This was changed by the House of Lords in *Picket v British Railways Board* (1978).

Loss of future earnings

Calculation of loss of future earnings is based on the use of the multiplier and multiplicand system. Note, also, 'handicap on the labour market', 'loss of a chance': *Doyle v Wallace* (1998).

Deductions

Certain deductions are made, for example, income tax (*BTC v Gourley* (1956)).

As the victims of accidents often receive financial support from several sources in addition to tort, for example, income support, sick pay, private insurance and, in some cases, from charities, there are certain deductions made from the damages to account for these. Note, also, the effect of the Road Traffic (NHS Charges) Act 1999; Social Security (Recovery of Benefits) Act 1997.

Future care

Note the high levels of awards in these cases. The claimant is able to claim for the cost of 'future care'. This includes: medical expenses; nursing fees; travel and holidays; laundry; school fees; note changes concerning costs of bringing up a child: *McFarlane v Tayside Health Board* (1999); *Rand v E Dorset HA* (2000).

Note *Wells v Wells* (1998); *Barry v Aberlex* (2000).

Non-pecuniary losses

Intangible losses are very difficult to quantify. These include: pain and suffering (*Wise v Kaye* (1962)); loss of amenity (*West v Shephard* (1964)); the injury itself; bereavement (Administration of Justice Act 1982, *Doleman v Deakin* (1990), note cut off point).

There is no award for pre-death trauma (*Hicks v Chief Constable of South Yorkshire Police* (1992)).

Note, also, the loss of marriage prospect.

Heil v Rankin (2000) is an important case concerning levels of general damages.

Effect of death

Note the function of the Fatal Accidents Act 1976, as amended by the Administration of Justice Act 1982, and the Law Reform (Miscellaneous Provisions) Act 1934. Any damages recoverable are calculated without reference to other benefits which the estate may receive on the death of the claimant. Special and general damages are recoverable including damages for pain and suffering and loss of amenity.

Note the long list of dependants who can now claim under the Fatal Accidents Act 1976 and the position of widows and widowers.

Even non-financial dependency may be claimed (*Spittle v Bunney* (1988); *Watson v Wilmott* (1991); *Stanley v Saddique* (1991)).

Criticisms of lump sum payments

Lump sum payments have a number of disadvantages, but are favoured by lawyers and insurance companies for administrative reasons.

Alternative methods of paying damages

Alternative methods of paying damages include: split trials and interim damages; provisional damages; structured settlements.

(Note Civil Procedure Rules 1999.)

Damages for economic loss and property damage

Damages for economic loss and property damage attract less criticism because they are more easily calculated than those relating to personal injuries: Law Commission Report No 127.

(*Note Rand v E Dorset HA* (2000).)

Injunctions

The most important equitable remedy in tort is the injunction. However, as it is an equitable remedy, it is discretionary and may not be easy to obtain, but note the special difficulties in nuisance cases (*Kennaway v Thompson* (1981); *Shelfer v City of London Electric Lighting Co* (1895)).

Criteria: *American Cyanamid Co v Ethicon* (1975):

- a serious issue to be tried;

- balance of convenience between the parties.

CHAPTER 20

DEFENCES

There are a number of defences which apply specifically to particular torts. These are discussed in detail in the sections which are concerned with those torts, for example the tort of nuisance, and the rule in *Rylands v Fletcher*.

There are other defences, however, which apply throughout the whole of the law of tort and this chapter deals with these general defences.

20.1 Contributory negligence

The defence of contributory negligence operates to apportion the damages, so reducing the damages payable to claimants if it can be proved that they contributed in some way to the damage suffered by failing to take sufficient care for their own safety. This defence does not only apply to the tort of negligence.

The defence is governed by statute, the Law Reform (Contributory Negligence) Act 1945, and is relatively new in the history of the common law, having been adapted from a maritime law practice.

20.1.1 Development of the law

Originally, if a claimant was to blame in some way for the harm which he or she suffered, there would be a complete defence available, and no damages would be payable (*Butterfield v Forrester* (1908)). However, it became clear that this rule was too harsh, and new principles developed by which the courts were able to circumvent the rule.

By using the rules of causation, a claimant could succeed in a claim despite his or her own act, if placed in a dilemma by the defendant. In *Jones v Boyce* (1816) the claimant was a passenger in a coach which went out of control through the defendant's negligence. Fearing that he would be seriously injured if he stayed in the coach until it crashed, he decided to jump out, and in so doing he broke a leg. It was held that he was not contributorily negligent because he had acted reasonably in making the decision to jump out. The chain of causation was not broken by the claimant's own act.

However, since the introduction of the new law on contributory negligence with the Law Reform (Contributory Negligence) Act 1945, the courts are willing, in some circumstances, to find that the claimant was partly to blame for the damage suffered, and to apportion the loss. This is what happened in *Sayers v Harlow BC*, and in the Canadian case of *Holomis v Dubuc*

(1975), where a passenger was travelling in a sea plane which hit a submerged object in a lake, and as water was pouring into the passenger area, he decided to jump out without a life-jacket and try to swim to safety. Unfortunately, he was drowned, but, if he had stayed in the plane, he would have been safe. The court held that the damages payable were to be reduced by 50% because of the man's contributory negligence.

The reason for the change in attitude by the courts is probably that it is now possible to apportion the damage, whereas, before the Law Reform (Contributory Negligence) Act 1945, the claimant would have received no award at all if there was a finding of contributory negligence.

20.1.2 The last opportunity rule

Even before 1945, by inventing a new principle called the 'last opportunity rule', the courts made it possible for claimants who would otherwise have received no compensation to receive an award. The rule operated in such a way as to make the person who had the last opportunity of avoiding an accident bear the entire loss. In *Davies v Mann* (1842), the owner of a donkey had left the animal tethered in the street in full view, but just as it was getting dark the defendant ran into the animal with his wagon. As the person who had the last opportunity of avoiding the accident, the defendant was liable to the claimant.

With the passage of time, it became difficult to establish who exactly had the last opportunity of avoiding accidents, particularly with the advent of fast-moving vehicles. The injustice of the all or nothing approach to contributory acts appeared even more glaring in a system which has as its underlying basis the fundamental principle that the injured person should be compensated, rather than that the person causing the injury should be punished. Accordingly, the principle of apportionment which had been introduced into English maritime law in 1911 under the Brussels Convention, was enacted in tort in the Law Reform (Contributory Negligence) Act 1945.

20.1.3 The Law Reform (Contributory Negligence) Act 1945

Under the Act:

> Where any person suffers damage partly as a result of his own fault, and partly as a result of the fault of any other person or persons, a claim in respect of that damage shall not be defeated by reason of the fault of the person suffering the damage, but the damages recoverable in respect thereof shall be reduced to such extent as the court thinks just and equitable having regard to the claimant's share in the responsibility for the damage ...

The full amount of compensation which would have been payable, had it not been for the claimant's contributory negligence, is first calculated. The court will try to establish the percentage of the damage for which the claimant was responsible, and the award will be reduced accordingly. In order to raise a defence of contributory negligence, it must always be mentioned in the pleadings (*Fookes v Slaytor* (1978)).

The apportionment for contributory negligence will operate not only to the disadvantage of the living claimant, but also, if the deceased was contributorily negligent, to the disadvantage of the relatives of a deceased accident victim who make claims under the Fatal Accident Acts for loss of a breadwinner.

20.1.4 The standard of care in contributory negligence

There is no need for the defendant to establish that the claimant owed a duty of care. It need only be established that the claimant failed to take proper care for his or her own safety in all the circumstances. This is bound to involve a more subjective approach than that taken by the courts when dealing with the tort of negligence. The defendant must prove, first, that the claimant did not take ordinary care for himself and, second, that this was a contributory cause of the damage suffered. For example, in *Brennan v Airtours plc* (1999), the claimant was found to be 50% to blame for injuries which he incurred while fooling around after drinking heavily at a party organised by the defendant. He had ignored the defendant's warnings.

Moreover, the court is able to decide what is 'just and equitable' in each case, and this may also be why there is a more subjective approach to the conduct of the claimant in contributory negligence than in negligence itself. This is particularly noticeable in the case of children (see *Gough v Thorne* (1966)).

Accident figures suggest that the worst injuries are suffered by elderly people and children. It appears that children find it difficult to judge the speed and distance of approaching vehicles, and that age is an important factor in the ability to take care of oneself. The use of the subjective approach means that children and elderly people are not unduly penalised.

Through a strange twist of logic, the seat-belt cases demonstrate that the courts are trying to impose standards of care upon claimants. Despite the more subjective approach which the courts are usually willing to adopt in contributory negligence cases, there seems to be a more objective attitude to the problem in cases in which the claimant has taken a chance with his or her safety by not wearing a seat-belt.

20.1.5 Causation in contributory negligence

It is always necessary to establish that the claimant's conduct contributed to the damage which he or she suffered before a reduction will be made for contributory negligence.

For example, in *Woods v Davidson* (1930), the claimant, who was drunk, was run over by the defendant. Since he would have been run over by the defendant even if he was sober, there was no contributory negligence.

Problems of causation can arise in cases where there is more than one defendant.

In *Fitzgerald and Lane v Patel* (1989), the claimant stepped into the road without looking and was hit by the defendant who was driving negligently. As a result of the impact, the claimant was pushed out into the road and was struck by the second defendant's car. The judge at first instance held that the claimant should receive two-thirds of the total award because all three parties were equally to blame for the damage. However, the House of Lords decided that once liability has been established the court must assess whether the claimant has contributed to the injury which he or she suffered, and if this is the case, what proportion of the damage could be attributed to the claimant's own carelessness. Apportionment of liability between the claimant and defendant must be kept separate from the apportionment of responsibility for the accident itself as between co-defendants. The claimant should be no better off because he has been injured by two people. In the event, the claimant received only 50% of the possible damages.

Sometimes, arguments have been advanced that not wearing a seat-belt can on some occasions save a driver or passenger from serious injury. People even claim that they make a conscious decision not to wear a seat-belt for that very reason. However, research into numerous accidents over many years suggests that in most instances, the wearing of seat-belts saves people from serious injury. This was the message which Lord Denning was attempting to communicate to the public when the Court of Appeal decided *Froom v Butcher* (1976). In fact, that case made little difference to public awareness of the need to use seat-belts, although even one or two of the tabloid newspapers carried accounts of the decision. In 1972, only 20% to 25% of people wore seat-belts, despite a nationwide intensive advertising campaign featuring Jimmy Saville advising us to 'clunk, click every trip'. The greatest impact on the wearing of seat-belts has been made by the introduction of a criminal statute in 1979, which required all front seat passengers to wear seat-belts in cars in which they were fitted. This has now been extended to all passengers, and new cars are routinely fitted with seat-belts. The penalty for not wearing a seat-belt is a fine, and a heavier fine for parents who do not ensure that their children wear seat-belts. The result is that now at least 90% of car-users wear seat-belts. This demonstrates that the criminal law is a far more effective deterrent than the law of tort.

The seat-belt cases involve consideration of causation in relation to the damage suffered by the claimant. In the seat-belt cases, the claimant's failure to wear a seat-belt does not cause the accident itself but may contribute to his injuries.

In *Froom v Butcher* (1976), the claimant was driving carefully, within the speed limit, on the correct side of the road. The defendant was travelling too fast on the wrong side of the road, and his negligence resulted in a serious collision with the claimant's vehicle. The claimant was not wearing a seat-belt at the time, and the injuries which he suffered were serious. He would not have suffered such serious injury had he been wearing a seat-belt. Lord Denning made a clear distinction between the cause of the accident, the defendant's negligent driving, and the cause of the injuries, the claimant's carelessness for his own safety in not wearing a seat-belt. He identified three situations in which causation would be relevant to the award of damages available:

- if the wearing of a seat-belt would have made no difference to the injuries suffered, there will be no reduction for contributory negligence;

- if wearing a seat-belt would have reduced the injuries suffered, there will be a 15% reduction;

- if wearing a seat-belt would have prevented the injuries altogether, there will be a 25% reduction in the award.

However, the Court of Appeal would allow some exceptions for people who could not be blamed for failing to wear a seat-belt, such as very fat people or pregnant women.

In *Biesheuvel v Birrell* (1998), it was held that the same principles apply to the wearing of rear seat belts. In *Condon v Condon* (1978), in which the claimant claimed to suffer from a seat-belt phobia, there was no reduction from the final award of damages.

20.1.6 Drunk drivers

The courts tend to deal with passengers who accept lifts from drunk drivers by finding them contributorily negligent in appropriate cases. In *Owens v Brimmel* (1977), the claimant and defendant went on a pub-crawl together, and the defendant volunteered to drive. They each consumed about nine pints of beer, and on the journey home at the end of the heavy evening's drinking, the car left the road and collided with a lamp post. The car was a write-off, but the claimant was thrown partly clear of the wreckage, probably saving his life. However, he did suffer extensive injuries, including brain-damage, loss of an eye, fractured facial bones and a fractured bone in the leg. The defendant failed to establish exactly how the injuries occurred, or indeed that wearing a seat-belt would have reduced the extent and degree of injury, so in relation to not wearing a seat-belt the defence of contributory negligence failed. The question of accepting lifts with drunk drivers had not previously arisen in English law since *Dann v Hamilton* (1939), discussed below (see 20.2.1 below). The judge considered the commonwealth cases on the subject. It was decided that in accepting a lift with someone who was drunk, the claimant was contributorily negligent, even if he was himself too drunk at the time to know how drunk the driver was. This was because the two had set out together on a pub-crawl, and the claimant must have been aware of the possible consequences. There was a 20% reduction from the award. Watkins J said:

> Thus, it appears to me that there is widespread and weighty authority for the proposition that a passenger may be guilty of contributory negligence if he rides with the driver of a car whom he knows has consumed alcohol in such a quantity as is likely to impair to a dangerous degree that driver's capacity to drive properly and safely. So may a passenger be guilty of contributory negligence if he, knowing that he is going to be driven in a car by his companion later, accompanies him on a bout of drinking which has the effect of robbing the passenger of clear thought and perception and diminishes the driver's capacity to drive properly and carefully.

Accepting lifts with drunken drivers. Cases on this topic suggest that the courts are becoming less lenient towards those who are given lifts by people who are drunk, but the burden of proof is still on the defence to prove that the claimant knew that the driver was unfit to drive.

Limbrick v French (1993)

The defence of contributory negligence failed, because although the claimant knew that the defendant was drunk, it was not possible to prove that she knew he was unfit to drive.

Stinton v Stinton (1993)

The claimant and defendant set out together on a pub-crawl. At the time of the accident, the claimant was so drunk that he was unconscious, and argued that he was not a direct participant, but this was not accepted by the judge who decided that short of actual participation this was a case of the maximum possible blameworthiness. The damages were reduced by one-third.

Donelan v Donelan (1993)

Both claimant and defendant had been drinking very heavily when the claimant asked the defendant to drive his car. He knew that she was an inexperienced driver and had never handled a large powerful car. The judge decided that the claimant was the dominant party in the venture and reduced his damages by 75%.

In *O'Connell v Jackson* (1972), the claimant's damages were reduced because he did not wear a crash helmet when riding a motorbike, as a result of which his injuries were far worse than they would have been had he worn a helmet.

20.1.7 Who benefits from the rule?

The defence of contributory negligence merely allows the defendant to escape having to pay the full award which would otherwise have been available to the claimant. In the line of cases involving the negligent over-valuation of property, which has emerged as a result of the fluctuations on the property market, the House of Lords has ruled that, where the basic loss exceeds the amount of the over-valuation, the deduction for contributory negligence (if any) must be made before the calculation is made (that is, the calculation established in *South Australian Asset Management Corpn v York Montague Ltd* (1997), where it was decided that, if the basic loss suffered by the claimant exceeds the extent of the over-valuation, that figure is the limit of the allowable loss).

This rule was laid down in *Platform Homes Ltd v Oyston Shipways Ltd* (1999), in which Oyston Shipways had been found negligent in their over-valuation by £500,000 of a property which the claimants had accepted security for a loan. Their basic loss was calculated as £611,748, but they were found to have been 20% contributorily negligent.

Contributory negligence can never completely exonerate a defendant from all liability, and must be distinguished from the defence of '*volenti non fit injuria*', which does operate as a complete defence, and will be dealt with later. If *volenti* applies, the claimant can be said to have been willing to run the risk of being injured, and is therefore unable to complain about the defendant's conduct at a later date. This is illustrated by the case of *Morris v Murray* (1990) (see 20.2.1 below).

20.2   Consent (*volenti non fit injuria*)

The defence of consent or *volenti non fit injuria*, which is frequently referred to as *volenti* is used in circumstances when the claimant has consented to take the risk involved, and is therefore not permitted to complain of the consequent damage.

The difficulty of distinguishing between *volenti* and contributory negligence and the preference of the judges for the latter has already been explained. Judges, unwilling to deny claimants a remedy altogether, frequently opt for a finding of contributory negligence as a compromise.

However, there are some circumstances in which the defence of *volenti* does succeed. People who agree to medical treatment, to being searched by police officers, to allowing others to walk across their land, are all consenting to various torts being committed, and will not be able to complain later.

For there to be operative consent on the part of the claimant, there must be proper understanding of risks involved. In *Stermer v Lawson* (1977), a Canadian case, the claimant was permitted by the defendant to use his motorbike, but was not given proper instruction on how to use it. He was held not to have been *volens* when he was injured because he could not handle the machine properly. See, also, *Ratcliffe McConnell* (1999).

So far as negligence is concerned, merely because a person knows that a risk exists does not necessarily mean that the person has agreed to accept the consequences of that risk. Moreover, consent under protest does not operate to deny the claimant a remedy. In *Smith v Baker & Sons* (1891), the claimant was working in a quarry, and from time to time a crane swung large loads of rock over his head without warning. Unhappy about this, the claimant complained several times to his employer, but this made little difference, and he had no choice but to continue working in this situation if he wanted to keep his job. Eventually, a rock fell and injured him and the House of Lords held that he was not *volens*.

20.2.1 Dangerous jobs

In very few cases will an employee be held to be *volens*, so great is the employer's duty as to care and safety of employees. One unusual case is *Gledhill v Liverpool Abattoir Co Ltd* (1957), in which the claimant, who worked in a slaughter house, was injured when a pig, which had been slaughtered and hung up by its legs, fell on top of him. This was a danger of which employees at the slaughter house were all aware, and it was held that the claimant was *volens*.

It is now more likely, since the Law Reform (Contributory Negligence) Act 1945, that there will be a finding of contributory negligence than of *volenti* in employment cases.

Moreover, the employer's duty of care in relation to the health and safety of employees cannot be excluded by a term of the employment contract (*Johnstone v Bloomsbury HA* (1991)).

It might seem obvious that anyone who is foolish enough to accept a lift with a drunken driver is agreeing to run the risk of being injured and that the defence of *volenti* should operate to the full advantage of the defendant. In the case of *Dann v Hamilton* (1939), this matter was considered, and the judge decided that it should not so operate unless it was a clear and glaring example of a passenger consenting to run a very great risk. In this case, the defendant had driven the claimant and her mother to London to see the lights. They all visited several pubs, and it was clear that the defendant was drunk. One of the passengers got out of the car, but the claimant decided to accept the risks involved and stayed put. Soon afterwards, the claimant was injured, but the judge decided that she had not been contributory negligent. (Note, however, that this was before the passing of the Law Reform (Contributory Negligence) Act 1945.)

Since s 149 of the Road Traffic Act 1988, defendants are prevented from relying on the defence of *volenti* in circumstances when insurance is compulsory (as it is in the case of car owners' liability for injury to their passengers). It cannot therefore now arise that *volenti* could be pleaded as a defence in a road accident case, though it may be relevant in the case of other vehicles, such as aircraft (*Morris v Murray* (1990)).

In *Pitts v Hunt* (1990), in which the claimant and defendant were engaged on a joint illegal enterprise, and in which the claimant was aiding and abetting the criminal behaviour of the defendant, there was scope for another defence to operate, that of *ex turpi causa*, which allowed the defendant to escape liability altogether.

The defence of *volenti* is now seldom relied upon, partly because of the Road Traffic Act provisions, and partly because contributory negligence is likely to be favoured by the courts who may be anxious to find a source of compensation for the claimant, but have the option to inflict a small 'punishment' for carelessness. If the defendant is insured, this is often a better option than that of denying the claimant a remedy altogether, except in the most extreme cases.

In fact, contributory negligence operates for the benefit of insurers who pay the damages in car accident cases and work accident cases, and indirectly it benefits all premium-payers by keeping down the cost of insurance. A finding of contributory negligence shifts the loss away from the insurer and can work to the grave disadvantage of the claimant, or the relatives of a deceased claimant. The Pearson Commission considered the effect of abolishing the defence altogether. In Scandinavia, the abolition of the contributory negligence defence has increased the cost of motor insurance premiums by at least 7.5%.

20.2.2 Dangerous sports

Participants in dangerous sports are taken to have agreed to submit to acts of trespass which occur within the rules of the particular sport, but not acts of violence which occur outside those rules. In *Simms v Leigh Rugby Football Club* (1969), the claimant was tackled and thrown against a wall, and the defendants were not liable because it was held that the leg was probably broken in the course of the tackle, which was within the normal rules of the game. Had it been broken when the claimant was thrown against the wall, he would not have been *volens*.

An action for negligence was successful in the case of *Smoldon v Whitworth and Nolan* (1997) when a young rugby player who had broken his neck when a scrummage collapsed contended that the referee was in breach of his duty of care to the players in not controlling the game adequately. The judge made it clear that although the claimant had accepted a degree of risk by playing rugby, he deserved protection from the referee.

Those attending sporting events as spectators may be consenting to run the risk of injuries caused by negligence. In *Woolridge v Sumner* (1963), Lord Diplock took the view that spectators take a risk of injury being caused to them by participants, though in that case the claimant, a photographer, was held to have consented when he entered the track during heavy hunter trials, hardly the usual behaviour of a spectator. If the event is run on business lines, liability for death or personal injuries caused by negligence or breach or the occupier's duty to visitors cannot be excluded (Unfair Contract Terms Act 1977).

20.2.3 Drunk drivers

The defence of *volenti* cannot apply in cases in which the claimant has accepted a lift in a car with a drunk driver, because of the operation of s 149 of the Road Traffic Act 1988 (see earlier in this chapter on contributory negligence (see 20.1.6). However, the defence did operate to deny the claimant a remedy when he went on a joyride with the defendant in a stolen aircraft in *Morris v Murray* (1990). Both men were involved together in a heavy drinking session, and the finding of *volenti* was based on the fact that the claimant must have known that his companion, who was killed when the plane crashed, was in no fit state to pilot it.

20.2.4 Rescuers

A rescuer will seldom be found to have consented to run the risk of injury, provided that the rescue was necessary to save life, limb or property. The tendency of the courts in previous years to lean in favour of rescuers in the cases involving nervous shock has already been described, and this is yet another example of the special attitude which judges have towards rescuers.

The rationale for the lenient attitude of the courts is that a person who creates a situation of danger must foresee that a rescuer is likely to come to the assistance of the victims. It is also foreseeable that the rescuer may suffer physical injury or psychiatric harm (*Chadwick v British Railways Board* (1967)). However, the matter is more likely to be a question of policy, in that although there is no positive duty to effect a rescue, the person who puts at risk his own safety to save another should be afforded a remedy if harmed. The loss should, morally, and perhaps also, from a practical perspective, if the defendant is insured, lie with the person who creates a danger.

This principle applies even if the rescuer is a professional member of the rescue services. In *Salmon v Seafarers Restaurant* (1983), the claimant was a fireman who was injured attempting to extinguish a fire in a fish and chip shop. The fire had been caused by the negligence of the owner in failing to turn off the heat under large vats of fat used for frying the fish and chips. In *Ogwo v Taylor* (1987) and *Hale v London Underground* (1992), the successful claimants were also firemen.

It is important that the rescue is necessary or the claimant may be *volens*. In *Haynes v Harwood* (1935), the claimant was a policeman who was injured when he stopped a horse from bolting down a street where some children were at play. He was not *volens* but, in *Cutler v United Dairies* (1933), the claimant entered a field to try to calm frisky horses, and he did not succeed in a claim for compensation. He was *volens* because he had intervened in a situation which was non-urgent in that there was no risk to people or property.

20.3   Consent in the medical context

In recent years, the issue of consent has become increasingly important in the context of medical treatment, and many of the cases turn upon the question of whether the patient consented to run the risk of suffering side-effects associated with certain treatments.

There are two separate lines of cases: those which turn on consent to trespass to the person and those which turn on negligence.

20.3.1 Trespass to the person

The patient who consents to medical treatment is in fact consenting to the torts of assault, battery and possibly false imprisonment. Any touching or treating or giving of an anaesthetic without such consent is unlawful and actionable. To treat a person against his or her will is regarded as a serious threat to personal liberty, and will only be approved in the most extreme circumstances, subject to numerous checks and safeguards. Compulsory medical treatment under the Mental Health Act 1983 falls into this category.

There is a considerable body of case law building up on the subject. For example, in *Potts v North West RHA* (1983), the claimant was injected with 'depoprovera', a long lasting and slow acting contraceptive drug, without her prior consent at the same time as she was given a rubella vaccination, shortly after the birth of a baby. She was awarded £3,000 damages for assault and battery because she had never been given the opportunity to accept or refuse the treatment. The judge said: 'To deprive her of the right to choose is to deprive her of the basic human right to do with her body as she wishes.'

A spate of recent cases concerning the treatment of Jehovah's Witnesses and others who, because of religious convictions, refuse blood transfusions, indicate that the courts are becoming increasingly drawn into the picture by doctors and social workers who are concerned for the welfare of patients, and who, because they are trained to save lives, find it difficult not to treat them even in the face of refusals. The approval of the courts after long hours of deliberation is an important protection for the doctors concerned. In the case of babies and people under the age of 16 years, the courts appear to take the view that treatment should be given even if the parents refuse consent (*Re J (A Minor) (Wardship: Medical Treatment)* (1990)), unless the proposed treatment would inflict greater suffering and prolong a life of agony (*Re W* (1981)). The courts have inherent wardship jurisdiction, and jurisdiction under s 100 of the Children Act 1989, to decide what is in the best interests of the child concerned.

The cases on enforced caesarean sections raise some important ethical issues and pose difficult dilemmas for doctors and judges. In this line of cases, doctors have sought declarations from the High Court as to the legality of treatment against the will of women who refuse to have caesarean sections. In most of the cases the treatment is urgently required and judges are called upon in emergency situations, sometimes during the night, to sanction treatment which would otherwise amount to a battery. After a series of cases in which the courts have found the means of circumventing the basic rule that an adult patient who is of sound mind has the absolute right to refuse treatment even if the refusal appears irrational, the Court of Appeal laid down guidelines to be applied in such situations in *Re MB* (1997). It was emphasised that, even if the mother and baby are both in danger of dying if the surgery is not carried out, the wishes of the mother should be respected as long as she is capable in law of giving or refusing consent to treatment. Lady Justice Butler Sloss said:

> The law is, in our judgment, clear that a competent woman who has the capacity to decide may, for religious reasons, other reasons or for no reasons at all, choose not to have medical intervention, even though the consequence may be the death or serious handicap of the child she bears or her own death.

There is to be a presumption that a woman is competent and the test for establishing incompetence which the Court of Appeal laid is whether there is some impairment or mental dysfunctioning rendering a woman unable to make treatment decisions.

In none of the cases so far brought before the English courts has a woman been found to be competent to refuse a caesarean section. It remains to be seen whether the guidelines will make any difference in the future.

In the case of people over 16 with a mental disability, the consent of the court to any form of surgery is not absolutely required, but it is advisable to apply to the High Court for approval (*F v West Berkshire HA* (1989)). See *Re S (Sterilisation)* (2000) for clarification by the Court of Appeal of what is meant by 'best interests' (and see Chapter 13).

In the case of consent to treatment by people under 16, the doctors are guided by the directions of the House of Lords in *Gillick v West Norfolk and Wisbech HA* (1985), a case concerning consent by a young woman under 16 to contraceptive treatment. People over that age can consent to medical treatment in their own right (s 8(1) of the Family Law Reform Act 1969), but those under the age of 16 will only be able to give valid consent to treatment if they have sufficient maturity and understanding to realise what is involved. It is up to the doctor to assess this.

Numerous problems arise in relation to refusal of treatment. For example, in *Re M (A Minor) (Medical Treatment)* (1999), a 15 year old patient, identified only as M, who had been perfectly fit and well until about three months previously, had developed heart failure and had only one week, or thereabouts, to live. Her parents had already consented for her to undergo a heart transplant operation, but, on learning that her only chance of survival was the operation to which they had agreed, M refused her consent. The High Court judge who was to hear the case, Johnson J, insisted that M should speak to a solicitor to explain her views. M said that she would prefer to die than to have the operation and take medication for the rest of her life, saying that the idea of being different from other people and living with someone else's heart made her feel very depressed. The official solicitor, on learning of her views, believed that M was too overwhelmed at the discovery of her fatal illness and the seriousness of her situation to make an informed decision. He recommended that the surgery should take place, and the judge accepted this recommendation on the basis that the surgeons should act in accordance with their clinical judgement. He sanctioned the surgery.

The present state of UK law on consent to treatment and refusal of treatment by minors is illogical. Although a person under the age of 16 can consent to medical treatment, as long as the criteria established in the *Gillick* (1986) case are satisfied, he or she is unable to refuse to undergo treatment for which parental consent has been given, as the parents have the right to overrule the refusal of a *Gillick* competent child *(Re R (A Minor) (Wardship) (Medical Treatment* (1991)). In cases in which sensitive issues are raised and the parents and child are in dispute, such as M's case, a declaration is usually sought from the Family Division, despite clear authority that the parents can overrule the consent of the child. The Official Solicitor is involved as a matter of course in complex cases, and the court has power to overrule parental consent to any treatment which it considers is not in the best interests of the child. In *Re M,* the judge explained the jurisdiction of the court to deal with this matter, referring to the case of *Re W (A Minor) (Medical Treatment: Court's Discretion)* (1992), and in particular to the words of Lord Donaldson MR, who said:

> There is ample authority for the proposition that the inherent powers of the court under its *parens patriae* jurisdiction are theoretically limitless, and that they certainly extend beyond the powers of a natural parent. There can, therefore, be no doubt that it has the power to override the refusal of a minor, whether over the age of 16 or under that age but *Gillick* competent ... Nevertheless, such a refusal is a very important consideration in making clinical judgements and for parents in deciding whether themselves to give consent. Its importance increases with the age and maturity of the minor.

In M's case, the court took the view, with some caution, that it would be appropriate for the treatment to be given against M's wishes.

The general principle, which was established by the Court of Appeal in *Re W* and *Re R* (above), has been the subject of considerable criticism. It is inconsistent with the views expressed by the House of Lords in the leading case on consent and minors, *Gillick v West Norfolk and Wisbech AHA* (1986). As Balcombe LJ pointed out in *Re W*, 'in logic there is no difference between an ability to consent to treatment and an ability to refuse treatment'.

Detailed discussion of the important legal and ethical issues in these cases is beyond the scope of this book but, for further reading, see Brazier, M, *Medicine, Patients and the Law*, 1993 and Grubb, A, *Principles of Medical Law*, 1999.

20.3.2 Negligence

Patients consenting to treatment do not consent to negligent treatment, merely to the torts of assault and battery. The question of a negligence action arises, however, when a patient claims that he or she would not have consented to the particular treatment if information about possible risks and side-effects had been given. The distinction between the two types of case is illustrated by the following case. In *Wells v Surrey AHA* (1978), the claimant was in extreme pain after a long and difficult labour. She was seen by a consultant who recommended a caesarian section, and for the first time mentioned the possibility of a sterilisation. She signed a consent form agreeing to both a caesarian section and a sterilisation. She already had two children, but she was a devout Roman Catholic, and she later claimed that under normal conditions, had she not been in such a state of pain and exhaustion, she would never have agreed to the sterilisation, because it was against her religious convictions. She sued for trespass to the person on the grounds that the consent which she had given was not true consent. She also claimed damages for negligence because she had not been properly counselled before the operation. The judge found, on the facts that she had given her consent, so the action for trespass failed, but that there had been negligence on the part of the doctor in not providing her with proper advice about the operation to sterilise her, which was not always reversible.

20.3.3 Informed consent

In English law, patients are not entitled to the fullest possible information about the treatment they receive. Instead, it is up to the doctor to decide how much information to give, and the test to be applied in deciding whether a doctor has acted reasonably in the amount of information given is that in *Bolam v Friern HMC* (1957). If a doctor is able to demonstrate that he or she acted in accordance with a responsible body of medical opinion, he or she will not be negligent. *Bolitho* has now been extended to cases of this kind (see *Pearce v United Bristol Healthcare Trust* (1999), discussed in detail in Chapter 13).

In *Sidaway v Governors of Bethlem Royal Hospital* (1985), already discussed in connection with the standard of care in negligence (7.2.14), the House of Lords gave long and detailed consideration as to how much a doctor is required to explain to a patient about the possible side effects and risks involved in a particular treatment before the patient agrees for the procedure to begin. In that case, the risks inherent in surgery of long term damage to the nerves in the claimant's arm were put at 1%, and the House of Lords did not consider that it was necessary for the claimant to have been informed of so small a risk. The House of Lords decided that the *Bolam* test should apply in these circumstances, and that the doctor should assess how much information it is necessary to give a patient in the circumstances of each individual case. As long as the advice the doctor gives conforms with the advice which would be given by a responsible body of medical practitioners in the same field, there will be no negligence.

This case demonstrates that it is difficult for a patient to succeed in an action for negligence based on consent given through lack of information. However, a recent Australian case departs from this principle. In *Rogers v Whitaker* (1992), a woman who had repeatedly asked an eye surgeon about the risks involved in a particular operation, and who was not informed of a one in 14,000 risk of total blindness, succeeded in an action for negligence. The High Court of Australia, the highest legal authority there, held that *Bolam* only applies in connection with treatment and diagnosis, not to the decision to inform of inherent risks. There is some evidence that the UK courts may now be moving closer to the position in *Rogers v Whittaker* (1992) (see 7.2.14), *Pearce v United Bristol Healthcare Trust* (1999) and *Carver v Hammersmith* (2000).

20.4 Exclusion clauses and consent

Certain statutes, such as the Occupiers' Liability Acts 1957 and 1984 provide that the defence of *volenti* may apply in appropriate circumstances. However, the scope of this defence has been greatly limited by the Unfair Contract Terms Act 1977 which outlaws clauses excluding or limiting liability for negligence or breach of an occupiers' duty of care resulting in death or personal injuries, and those excluding or limiting liability for other types of harm unless it is reasonable in all the circumstances to do so. These provisions apply only in a business context, however, and it is still possible to exclude or limit liability in other situations.

The legislation which prevents the use of exclusion clauses is the result of changing attitudes of the courts and later of Parliament towards the issue of consent. It became clear during the course of the 20th century that on many occasions when people appear to consent they do not in fact do so freely. This picture first emerged in relation to contractual situations in which it was acknowledged that consumers and employees have little or no control over the terms of the agreements into which they enter. The courts developed the role, by convoluted means, frequently twisting and turning in order to circumvent unfair contractual provisions of protecting consumers. This approach spilled over into the law of tort and is part of a wider movement towards greater emphasis on affording protection to the weaker party in many situations.

20.5 Illegality: *ex turpi causa non oritur actio*

If the claim of the claimant is tainted in some way by illegal acts on his or her part, the defence of illegality based on the ancient principle of *ex turpi causa non oritur actio* may apply. Underlying this defence are notions of 'public policy' and, in more recent cases, illegality is sometimes treated as a reason for denying the existence of a duty of care rather than as a defence, so this area of law is rather vague and unpredictable. There is no definite test to determine whether the defence applies. Several tests have been suggested for illegality, including one of 'offence to the public conscience', though this was discredited as too dependent on emotional factors in *Pitts v Hunt* (1991).

Causation is an important factor as the defence is only likely to succeed if the illegal act or acts are related to the damage which is complained of. It is therefore important to establish first whether there is a link between the illegal act and the tort.

Even if there is a relationship between an illegal act and the tort in question the defence of illegality may not operate, as it would be regarded as unfair to deny a remedy to a claimant merely because he or she was guilty of some minor criminal offence. Many a successful claimant who has been injured in a car accident was speeding at the time of a collision (though of course damages may be reduced for contributory negligence in such circumstances, so satisfying the requirements of 'justice'). However, it is possible to find extreme circumstances in which the defence has been successful, for example, *Pitts v Hunt* (1991), in which the claimant, a passenger on a motorbike, had encouraged the driver to ride dangerously. In *Ashton v Turner* (1981), the defence denied a claim to a person injured in a car accident who was escaping after committing a crime. Nevertheless, there are some cases in which there is no definite link between a criminal act and the claim in tort.

A recent case in which the defence of illegality was rejected demonstrates the uncertain nature of this defence in circumstances even when a claimant has been convicted of connected criminal offences. In *Revill v Newbury* (1996), the Court of Appeal confirmed an award of damages to the claimant despite the fact that he sustained the injuries of which he complained in the course of breaking into the defendant's property. The defendant raised the obvious defence of illegality, to the actions for assault, breach of the Occupiers' Liability Act 1984 and negligence which were brought against him. The leading cases were reviewed and this case was distinguished from *Pitts v Hunt* (1991) in which the parties were engaged together on a criminal enterprise and the defence applied. Here, the claimant was acting alone in his criminal endeavours, so the defence was considered less appropriate. This did not, according to the Court of Appeal, mean that the defence can never apply in this type of case, because the underlying principle was that the public interest demanded that a wrongdoer should not be allowed to profit from his wrongs, but, in this particular case, it would, if applied, have meant that the claimant, although a criminal and a trespasser would be left without any remedy for his injuries. It was one matter to prevent a person from reaping the profits of illegal activity and quite another to render that person an outlaw. As Lord Justice Evans explained, relying on the Law Commission Report, *Liability for Damage or Injury to Trespassers* (Cmnd 6428), the law recognised that trespassers do have some limited rights. There was of course a large element of contributory negligence on the part of the claimant in *Revill v Newbury* (1995).

The popular press were fiercely critical of the decision in this case, and in the name of the 'public conscience' fought hard for the right of landowners and property owners to defend their property with vigour. Although the position in the law of contract was distinguished in this case from that in tort, similar public policy issues influence the outcome of cases in both branches of the law. In this instance, the relevant factors included the need to find a balance in the protection of property against criminal acts.

In practice, the defence of illegality is seldom encountered. The absence of a consistent approach to the problem by the courts and the fact that it probably has virtually no deterrent effect on criminal behaviour have led to many criticisms, and the issue is referred to most frequently in the press in relation to trespassers who are injured in the course of illegally entering property, with intent to steal (see Chapter 10). However, the defence was raised (successfully) in *Clunis v Camden and Islington HA* (1997) (see Chapter 6).

In that case, the Court of Appeal held that the defence could apply where, on grounds of public policy, the claimant should be prevented from relying on his or her own criminal act as a means of bringing a claim in negligence, unless it could be proved that the defendant's mental responsibility was so impaired that he or she was incapable of understanding the nature and quality of his or her act, or that what he or she was doing was wrong.

In a claim for damages for trespass to the person, it was held that the defence of *ex turpi causa* could succeed if the defendant's acts were linked inextricably with the unlawful conduct of the claimant. In *Cross v Kirby* (2000), the claimant and his partner, Mrs Davies, were trying to sabotage a hunt on the defendant's land. She bit the defendant when he was escorting her off his land. Seeing this, the claimant intervened and attacked the defendant. At the same time, Mrs Davies fetched an iron bar and the claimant took a baseball bat, threatened to kill the defendant and jabbed him in the chest with it. As the defendant tried to walk away, the claimant followed, striking him again. The defendant, after a struggle, took the bat away from the claimant and hit him on the head, fracturing his skull. The defences of self defence and *ex turpi causa* were raised. The trial judge found that the force used by the defendant had been disproportionate to that used against him. However, the Court of Appeal disagreed and ruled that the defence could be sustained in the circumstances of the case, as the defendant had himself been under attack from the same weapon.

The cases on *ex turpi causa* were reviewed by the Court of Appeal, starting with *Holman v Johnson* (1775), in which the defence was thought to have originated. There, Lord Mansfield had stated that the question was whether the claimant was precluded from recovering because of his illegal conduct. In the present case, the Court of Appeal held that the claimant's injury had indeed arisen from his own criminal conduct, and, because of *ex turpi causa*, the claim should not succeed.

20.6   Inevitable accident

The defendant may escape liability by establishing that the cause of the claimant's injury was an accident rather than any wilful or negligent act on his part.

An inevitable accident is one which no human foresight could have prevented, an accident which could not have been prevented by the exercise of reasonable care on the part of the defendant.

In actions for negligence, the consideration that an event is a pure accident will be part of the general consideration as to whether reasonable care had been taken by the defendant. In a road accident, for example, the driver who is taking all possible care in a sudden snow-storm, but whose vehicle goes into an uncontrollable skid, would be excused negligence because the claimant would not be able to establish that there had been a want of reasonable care on his part in all the circumstances.

Inevitable accident, on the other hand, is a defence in which the burden of proof is on the defendant to show that what happened was an unforeseeable accident.

In *Stanley v Powell* (1891), a case of trespass to the person, the defendant successfully pleaded inevitable accident when he accidentally shot the claimant. A pellet from his gun, when he was shooting pheasants, ricocheted off a tree at an unusual angle, and injured the claimant. In *Evans v NCB* (1951), it was stated that the defence could also be applied successfully in trespass to goods.

However, it has now been established that in trespass to the person there must be proof of intention or negligence on the part of the defendant, and it is therefore arguable that any question of inevitable accident would not be treated as a separate defence but merely as part of the issue of whether the defendant has achieved the requisite standard of care in all the circumstances.

Inevitable accident is therefore a very limited defence, as it cannot apply as such in negligence, nor does it apply in torts of strict liability when the defendant is liable regardless of whether the event was an accident (though there may be a closely related defence of 'act of God' or 'act of a stranger').

20.7 Mistake

There is no specific defence of mistake in the law of tort. If a person uses goods belonging to another person in the mistaken belief that they are his own, or trespasses on the land of another person, mistakenly believing that he is still within his own boundaries, there will be no defence to an action for trespass (*Basely v Clarkson* (1681)).

If liability depends on the defendant's motive, the fact that the defendant was mistaken may be a relevant consideration in deciding the issue of 'honest belief'. Thus, in the tort of deceit, the burden of proving lack of honest belief is on the claimant. If he cannot do so because the defendant was genuinely mistaken, the action will fail.

In negligent misstatement, a mistake will not necessarily excuse the defendant as the question to be considered is what a reasonable man would have believed in all the circumstances.

20.8 Necessity

The defence of necessity may excuse the defendant if he or she made a choice between two undesirable courses of action and was forced to take the measures which he or she eventually decided upon to prevent even greater damage. In effect, the court is being asked to agree or to disagree with the defendant's decision on the basis of the facts which were available to the defendant at the time.

In the case of actions for trespass to the person, this can be a crucial issue in determining liability, particularly if the claimant is refusing life saving medical treatment, and recent cases demonstrate that courts are becoming much more concerned about the claimant's freedom to make choices, even if the decision is to refuse treatment. This represents a change of approach from that taken in the case of force-feeding suffragettes (*Leigh v Gladstone* (1909)), and the entire area of law is shot through with issues of policy, depending on the political, moral and philosophical issues of the day. Inevitably, in the case of very young children, the courts are anxious to provide the best possible hope of life even if the child or minor is refusing treatment on religious grounds (*Re J* (1992)).

In *F v West Berkshire HA* (1989), it was held that, if medical treatment is given in an emergency, it will be a defence to plead necessity in the best interests of the patient.

If the defence is to apply, it must be proved that the defendant acted as a reasonable man would have done (the *Bolam* test applying in medical cases) to avert the greater evil (*Cope v Sharpe* (1912)).

It is unusual for the defence of necessity to be pleaded successfully. It does not apply to negligence.

20.9   Self-defence and defence of property

The use of reasonable force in an attempt to protect persons or land may operate as defence to the torts of assault, battery and false imprisonment. What force is reasonable depends on all the circumstances of each case. For example, it might be reasonable to lock an armed intruder in a room while waiting for the police to arrive, but unreasonable to shoot and kill him. The defence of self-defence is frequently pleaded alongside that of *ex turpi causa* (see above, 20.5).

20.10   Limitation of actions

Although, in equity, the claimant who delays for too long before bringing an action may, in the exercise of the court's discretion, be denied a remedy under the equitable doctrine of laches, at common law, there was no limit to the time in which a claimant was able to bring an action. The only limitation periods have been created by statute, the most recent of which is the Limitation Act 1980, a consolidating Act. For detailed analysis of this complex subject, see James, R, *Limitation of Action*, 1993.

It would be unfair to defendants if claimants could bring legal action against them at an indefinite future time, and the imposition of time limits helps to sting claimants into action, an important consideration, given the difficulty which many witnesses have of recalling events several years after they occurred.

One important distinction between contract and tort is that, put simply, in contract, time begins to run from the moment of breach, whereas, in tort, time begins to run from the moment of the damage.

20.10.1 Limitation period in tort

By s 2 of the Limitation Act 1980, an action in tort must be brought within six years from the date on which the action accrued.

In the case of torts which are actionable without proof of damage, the limitation period starts to run from the date of the defendant's wrongful act, though the court has a discretion to allow actions outside that period in exceptional circumstances.

20.10.2 Limitation period in defamation

In the case of defamation, there is a one year limitation period, but the court has a discretion to extend this in some circumstances.

20.10.3 Limitation period in personal injuries cases

In actions for personal injuries, the limitation period is three years from the date on which the cause of action accrued, or the date of knowledge, whichever is the later, although the court does have a wide discretion to allow action outside the limitation period in these cases. Guidelines for the exercise of this discretion are to be found in s 33 of the Limitation Act 1980.

In the case of death, the personal representatives or dependants of a deceased person, where death occurs within the three years from the accrual of the cause of action, have a fresh limitation period which runs from the date of death or from the date of knowledge of the death, under s 11(5) of the Limitation Act 1980.

It is not always immediately apparent whether the damage involves personal injuries. For example, in *Pattison v Hobbs* (1985), the claimant had a baby following a vasectomy which had been negligently performed on her partner. The claim was not for the pain of childbirth but was limited to the cost of bringing up the child and to the mother's lost income. This was held by the Court of Appeal to fall within the six year limitation period rather then the narrower three year limitation period which applies in personal injuries cases. However, in *Walkin v South Manchester HA* (1995), it was held that, if the claim is for an unsuccessful female sterilisation, the limitation period is three years.

20.10.4 Latent damage

If the action arises out of latent damage (that is, damage which has been lying 'dormant' perhaps for many years), the date on which the cause of action accrues is governed by the Latent Damage Act 1986. Under this Act, there is a six year limitation period from the date on which the cause of action accrued, or a period of three years from the 'starting date', whichever is the later. The starting date is the same as the 'date of knowledge'. There is a further bar on actions under the 'longstop' provisions which prevent actions being brought more than 15 years after the date of the negligent act. There are many instances in which damage can be latent, especially in relation to faults in buildings which occur through negligent construction (for example, *Pirelli General Cable Works v Oscar Faber & Partners* (1983)).

20.10.5 Consumer Protection Act 1987

Under the Consumer Protection Act 1987, the limitation period is three years from the date on which the damage was suffered, or from the date on which the necessary knowledge was acquired, if later. The longest period within which action can be brought is 10 years from the date on which the defendant supplied the product to another person (that is, put the product into the market-place).

If there has been fraud or concealment by the defendant, under s 32(1) of the Limitation Act 1980, the limitation period does not begin to run until the claimant has, or with reasonable diligence ought to have discovered the fraud or concealment.

20.10.6 Persons under a disability

Claimants under a disability, that is minors and people of unsound mind, have a right to bring an action when that disability ceases. Time starts to run from the date on which the disability ceases or the person who would have brought an action dies, whichever is the earlier. In the case of people under the age of 18, time starts to run when they reach full age. This has important implications for medical records which need to be kept safely for many years in case a person decides to bring an action after reaching the age of 18 in respect of an injury which was caused years earlier.

20.11 Accrual of the cause of action

The legal clock begins to tick, and the counting begins, from the time when the cause of action is said to 'accrue'. This is the usual date when 'time starts to run', the earliest time when an action could be brought (*Reeves v Butcher* (1891)). For example, in the case of personal injuries, time starts to run, that is, the three years is counted, from the date on which the cause of action accrues or from the date of knowledge, whichever is the later. The date of knowledge, by s 14(1) of the Limitation Act 1980, is the date on which:

- the claimant first had knowledge of the fact that the injury was significant; and

- that it was attributable in whole or in part to the act or omission which is alleged to constitute negligence, nuisance or breach of duty; and

- the identity of the defendant was known; and

- if it is alleged that the breach of duty was that of a person other than the defendant, the identity of that person was known as well as additional facts which support the bringing of the action against the defendant (for example, as in cases of vicarious liability).

An injury is significant for the purposes of the Limitation Act 1980 if the claimant would reasonably have considered it sufficiently serious to justify his or her instituting proceedings for damages against a defendant who did not dispute liability and was able to satisfy a judgment.

'Knowledge' includes knowledge which the claimant might reasonably have been expected to acquire from facts observable or ascertainable to him or her or from facts ascertainable to him or her only with the help of advice from experts, medical or otherwise (s 14(3)).

In *Broadly v Guy Clapham and Co* (1994), it was held that the claimant had 'constructive knowledge' that a surgical operation had caused her some form of injury, which meant time began to run as soon as she had this knowledge. The Court of Appeal considered that she did not need to have knowledge which was detailed enough to draft a statement of claim for time to start running. In *Dobbie v Medway HA* (1994), actual rather than constructive knowledge was involved. Here, the claimant had a breast removed unnecessarily when she underwent surgery to have a lump removed. The surgeon had assumed that the tumour was malignant, and immediately after the operation led her to believe that the removal of her breast was usual and correct and that she should count herself fortunate. Some time later, she discovered that the lump in her breast should have been removed for microscopic examination before the breast was removed. The Court of Appeal upheld the first instance decision that the claimant had the necessary knowledge under s 14(1) for time to start running within three years of the operation and that it would not be equitable to allow her claim to proceed out of time. Sir Thomas Bingham explained:

> She knew of this injury within hours, days or months of the operation and she at all times reasonably considered it to be significant ... She knew from the beginning that this personal injury was ... the clear result of an act or omission of the health authority. What she did not appreciate until later was that the health authority's act or omission was arguably negligent or blameworthy.

In medical negligence cases, the date of knowledge is based on a subjective test, depending on the knowledge which the claimant possessed rather than on an objective test based on a reasonable layperson's knowledge without confirmation of expert advice. In *Sprague v North Essex District HA* (1997), the claimant was claiming damages for medical negligence arising from the misdiagnosis of a psychiatric condition which resulted in her being detained for much longer than was necessary. The writ was issued 12 years after the claimant had been released from hospital but it was argued on the claimant's behalf that she did not have 'knowledge' for the purposes of the Limitation

Act 1980 until less than three years before the writ was issued because she did not have expert medical confirmation of what she suspected. However, as it was clear that she had strongly suspected a causal connection between the damage which she had suffered and the misdiagnosis when she first sought legal advice in 1986, her claim was held to be statute barred. The Court of Appeal did, however, point out that a person who has some idea (though not a clear idea) that his or her condition is capable of being attributed to a certain negligent act or omission but realises that the suspicion needs to be confirmed by a medical expert, does not have sufficient knowledge under s 14(1) of the Limitation Act 1980 (*Nash v Eli Lilly* (1993)).

20.11.1 Claims outside the limitation period

The power of the court to allow a claim outside the limitation period for personal injuries is an important one. This can happen, provided the court takes all the circumstances into account and has particular regard to:

- the length of time and reasons for any delay on the part of the claimant;

- the effect of this delay upon the evidence;

- the conduct of the defendant after the cause of action arose, including his or her response to the claimant's reasonable request for information;

- the duration of any disability of the claimant arising after the accrual of the cause of action;

- the extent to which the claimant acted promptly and reasonably once he or she knew that he or she might have an action;

- the steps, if any, taken by the claimant to obtain medical, legal or other expert advice and the nature of any such advice as he or she may have been given.

In *Stubbings v Webb* (1992), the House of Lords upheld the Court of Appeal decision and ruled that if the claim is for deliberately inflicted harm, in this case alleged indecent assault and rape of the claimant when she was a child, the limitation period is fixed at six years from the time the cause of action accrues, and there is no possibility of exercising a discretion, as s 2 of the Limitation Act 1980 applies. The discretion to extend the time limit only applies in cases of *accidentally* inflicted personal injuries. This case has been strongly criticised because it means that many people who were sexually abused as children, and who only become aware of the psychiatric harm caused by that abuse many years after they reach full age, have no redress. The decision also means that claimants in medical cases who claim that they had not consented to treatment and wish to sue for assault may be seriously disadvantaged. The same is true of claimants suing police officers for assault, battery and false imprisonment. There is pressure to reform the law in this area, as claimants can receive very high awards of damages for child abuse, and it is both illogical and unfair that they should be denied a remedy because of this anomaly in the limitation rules (two women who had been abused as children by the notorious Frank Beck in a children's home and who brought their action *within* the limitation period received £145,000 and £80,000 respectively).

The Law Commission has undertaken a comprehensive review of law of limitations and has made a series of proposals for reform, some of which are regarded as very controversial. This is currently under consultation (Law Commission Consultation Paper 151).

DEFENCES

Contributory negligence

Note the harshness of the rules before 1945, and the various attempts to circumvent them.

The Law Reform (Contributory Negligence) Act 1945 allows for apportionment if the claimant has failed to take sufficient care for his or her own safety.

The standard of care in contributory negligence is more subjective than that in ordinary negligence, being determined with closer reference to the age, mental and physical condition of the claimant, but note the objective standard in the seat-belt cases:

Gough v Thorne (1963);

Froom v Butcher (1972);

Condon v Condon (1978).

Causation in contributory negligence

The defendant must prove that the claimant's lack of care contributed to the damage:

Woods v Davidson (1930);

Fitzgerald and Lane v Patel (1989);

Froom v Butcher (1972);

Owens v Brimmel (1977);

O'Connell v Jackson (1972);

Brennan v Airtours plc (1999).

Note the relationship between contributory negligence and *volenti*. Since the introduction of contributory negligence, the defence of *volenti* is less often relied upon:

Morris v Murray (1990);

Pitts v Hunt (1990).

Note the implications for the insurance industry and the possible effect of abolishing contributory negligence in motor accident cases.

Volenti non fit injuria (consent)

There must be proper understanding of the risks:

Stermer v Lawson (1977);

Ratcliffe v McConnell (1999).

Note consent in the medical context (below).

Dangerous jobs

Employees will seldom be found to have consented:

Smith v Baker (1891);

Gledhill v Liverpool Abattoir (1957);

Johnstone v Bloomsbury HA (1991).

Dangerous sports

Participants in sports agree to run the risks of injury within the rules of the game:

Simms v Leigh Rugby Football Club (1969);

Woolridge v Sumner (1963);

Smoldon v Nolan (1996).

Accepting lifts with drunk drivers

Volenti cannot apply in drunk driving cases (s 149 of the Road Traffic Act 1988).

The defence may apply in the case of aircraft:

Morris v Murray (1991).

Rescuers

Rescuers will almost never be denied a remedy by the defence of *volenti*:

Chadwick v British Railways Board (1968);

Salmon v Seafarers Restaurant (1983);

Ogwo v Taylor (1987);

Hale v London Underground (1992).

Rescue must be necessary:

Haynes v Harwood (1935);

Cutler v United Dairies (1933).

Medical context

Note the different roles of trespass to the person and negligence in these cases:

Potts v NW RHA (1983);

Sidaway v Governors of Bethlem Royal Hospital (1985).

People under 16

Special care must be taken in the case of those under 16 who cannot always give consent themselves:

Re J (A Minor) (1990);

Gillick v West Norfolk and Wisbech HA (1985);

Re M (A Minor) (1999).

Negligence

A doctor who does not explain major side-effects and problems with treatment could be found negligent but everything depends on the circumstances of the case and the *Bolam* test:

Wells v Surrey HA (1978);

Sidaway v Governors of Bethlem Royal Hospital (1985);

Rogers v Whittaker (1992).

This case in Australia departed from English law and endorsed the doctrine of informed consent:

Pearce v United Bristol Healthcare Trust (1999);

Carver v Hammersmith (2000).

Exclusion clauses

The Unfair Contract Terms Act 1977 outlaws certain clauses which would otherwise deny the claimant a remedy. The Act limits the scope of the defence of *volenti* by clauses which exclude or limit liability or render void death or personal injury on business premises or in the course of a business.

Other clauses in a business context will only be valid if considered reasonable in all the circumstances.

Illegality (*ex turpi causa*)

The absence of consistent principles in the application of the defence of illegality has led to many criticisms of its operation. However, the defence is probably based on notions of 'morality' and 'conscience', similar to those found in the law of contract. The claimant may be denied a remedy if his or her acts are criminal in nature, and can be related to the tort for which compensation is being claimed:

Ashton v Turner (1981);

Burns v Edmaan (1970);

Pitts v Hunt (1990);

Revill v Newbury (1995);

Cross v Kirby (2000);

Clunis v Camden and Islington AHA (1997).

Inevitable accident

An accident which no human foresight could have anticipated will be a complete defence. The burden of proof is on the defendant:

Stanley v Powell (1891);

Evans v NCB (1951).

Mistake

If the defendant was mistaken, there is a possibility that he or she may escape liability, but the defence is of little significance in modern law. There are some specific torts to which mistake may operate as a defence, for example, deceit.

Probably of most significance in the tort of trespass to the person, and particularly in medical cases, is *F v West Berkshire HA* (1989).

The *Bolam* test determines the standard. This defence applies if it can be proved that the claimant consented to run the risk of harm.

Self-defence

Reasonable force can be used to protect persons or property.

Limitation of actions

The Limitation Act 1980 deals with the limitation periods.

Note the distinction between contract and tort.

Tort actions must be brought within six years of the date of accrual of the cause of action.

In personal injuries actions, the limitation period is three years, though the courts have a discretion to extend the time, but not in actions for trespass to the person (*Stubbings v Webb* (1993)). In defamation cases, there is now a one year limitation period (Defamation Act 1996).

Under the Consumer Protection Act 1987, there is a long stop of 10 years from the date on which the defendant put the product into the market place.

Note the problems of latent damage.

Note the way in which the accrual of the cause of action is determined.

Note the Law Commission's Report and recommendations.

CHAPTER 21

CRITICISMS OF TORT – REFORMS

Before reading this chapter, re-read the example drawn from a commonplace road traffic accident at the end of Chapter 1. That situation identifies some of the aspects of the law of tort which have attracted criticism. Some difficulties arise as a result of the rules of tort law, while others can be attributed to the operation of the legal system and are more general in nature. There follows a very brief outline of some of the criticisms of tort and its operation in the legal system.

21.1 Some criticisms of the rules of tort

21.1.1 Fault

There have been numerous criticisms of the fact that in order to succeed in obtaining compensation it is necessary for the claimant to establish fault on the part of the defendant. Perhaps the only real justification for this is the imposition of some kind of punishment on the defendant and the possible general deterrent effect that the fault system generates. Yet, if the defendant is not personally required to pay the damages, and if people generally are aware of this, these arguments lose much of their value.

The fault principle is unfair on claimants because it is not always possible to obtain the necessary evidence against the defendant, particularly in medical negligence cases, and those involving employers liability. Victims of mass-accidents, after which public inquiries are held to amass the evidence, are at a distinct advantage over the victims of isolated accidents who may not have the means, financial or otherwise, of establishing the truth and acting upon it.

Tort is unfair on defendants because the law does not distinguish between different degrees of culpability, and in some instances judges are prepared to find that there has been negligence even when it cannot be said that the defendant was in any way to blame, as in *Nettleship v Weston* (1971).

Tort is unfair on society as a whole because the fault principle distinguishes between different types of injury and illness, compensating in tort only those who are able to establish blame in the legal sense, and leaving uncompensated the victims of pure accidents and chance illnesses or genetic disease.

As there is no truly objective approach to the problem of establishing fault, the system is open to arbitrary and inconsistent decisions.

21.1.2 Uncertainty

There is too much uncertainty in the law of tort because of the operation of judicial policy. This aspect of the law of tort has been discussed in detail in Chapter 3, and the specific areas of the law which give rise to difficulty because of policy considerations have been highlighted as they have arisen throughout the book. Although it is possible for the law of tort to be adapted by judges to meet changing social needs and circumstances, this can also mean that it is difficult too for lawyers predict the outcome of individual cases in order to advise their clients. This leads to undue emphasis being placed upon certain areas of law which in practice seldom concern the average lawyer.

21.1.3 Failure to meet its objectives

The rules of tort do not enable it to achieve its objectives. Although the main aim of tort is compensation, in many instances, tort is an inefficient compensator. It is frequently difficult to prove fault in those torts which require it, and causation also presents difficulties in practice. Some accident victims whom many would consider to be morally entitled to compensation are unable to obtain any. Many people who suffer injuries at the hands of others receive no compensation at all and those who are compensated are often under-compensated because of the rules by which damages are calculated, and because of lump sum payments.

The notion of tort as a deterrent is espoused by some of the writers but most recognise that the law of tort has little deterrent effect. The main deterrent value of tort lies in its ability to grant injunctions to restrain wrongful acts. However, as negligence is the tort which is most frequently relied upon in practice, the role of the injunction is relatively small in comparison with the number of negligence actions for which, of course, injunctions are inappropriate remedies. Tort is of little deterrent value when compared with criminal law and even when it does act as a deterrent as in the medical negligence cases, this can be counter-productive. In that instance, tort has led to the practice of defensive medicine. This means that some medical procedures are carried out with the purpose of enabling doctors to avoid litigation rather than in the interests of patients.

The rules of tort and the legal system itself do not always enable the claimant to achieve revenge or vindication by allowing the claimant his or her 'day in court'. As the outcome of so many cases is uncertain, the vast majority of claims are settled out of court or dropped at a fairly early stage. In libel cases, people are afforded the opportunity to have a public airing of their grievances but as there is no legal aid for these proceedings only the very rich can take advantage of this.

21.1.4 Inefficiency

Almost every stage in tort litigation involves some form of lottery. In personal injury cases, this is a very serious matter because people who are sick and suffering are forced to take crucial decisions at a time when they are probably least able to do so. The social security system provides a far more efficient and humane means of support.

21.2 Criticisms of the legal system

The *Woolf Report* (1996) sums up the problems in the civil justice system as arising from delay, expense and complexity.

* *Delays*. Cases take a very long time to achieve settlement or to come before the courts. Delays are especially frustrating for claimants, particularly those who have suffered personal injuries. Sometimes, there are very good reasons for the delays. For example, compensation cannot be properly assessed without waiting for expert medical reports on prognosis. Nevertheless there are many people who have criticised the legal system for permitting long delays, often to the benefit of the defendant who can gain by delaying for as long as possible. Most defendants are insurance companies and they have legal departments or employ lawyers who are accustomed to defending legal claims and who are unconcerned on a personal level about the outcomes of cases. For most claimants in tort actions, there is considerable personal strain and fear of litigation which is frequently exacerbated by delays.

* *Administrative costs*. The administration of the tort system is very expensive. The Pearson Commission pointed out in 1978 that the costs of administering the Social Security system are only a fraction of the costs of administering the tort system despite the fact that far more is paid out in total by Social Security which deals with many more individual cases.

* *The adversarial system*. Tort cases are decided on an adversarial basis, with lawyers regarding cases as battles to be fought and won. This makes the legal process stressful and distressing for claimants, especially those who eventually reach the trial stage.

Despite all these criticisms, the number of claims is increasing and there is a higher level of claims consciousness among people in general today than ever before. In particular, claims for medical negligence are rapidly increasing.

21.3 The value of tort

Although it is customary to criticise tort and the catalogue of instances outlined above gives the impression that there is much to criticise, the law of tort does have considerable value and it has survived for many centuries to protect interests of many kinds from unlawful infringements. Property rights and personal freedoms are among the many interests protected by the law of tort and more general duties in the law of negligence protect from a wide variety of wrongs.

Over the centuries, tort has proved to be infinitely flexible, and even the ancient rules are capable of being adapted to meet modern problems. The tort of negligence which has emerged relatively recently as a tort in its own right has been developed through case law to cover many important situations in life. By far the most tort actions arise out of road traffic accidents – a situation which would have been unimaginable in the middle ages.

Tort encourages careful conduct and, in modern times, formal risk management. This prevents injury to individuals and their property, reduces the spread of disease and the manufacture of dangerous products. Although this is also the function of other areas of law, in particular, regulatory law, tort still plays a part because civil actions in tort can arise from breaches of regulatory law. We have seen this in relation to employers' liability for breaches of statutory duty.

Tort also has a symbolic moral value in that it places emphasis on fault and encourages wrongdoers to compensate their victims. It has a moral ideological dimension which is of value to people seeking vindication. Even if that aspect is eclipsed by the use of insurance and methods of loss distribution which move the emphasis away from the wrongdoer, the focus in legal actions is nevertheless on the wrongful act and loss distribution is a consequentialist factor.

21.4   Reform of tort

Although there have been many suggestions for reforming the law of tort, and some improvements have been made over the years by the introduction of strict liability for defective products under the Consumer Protection Act 1987, and for vaccine damage under the Vaccine Damage Payments Act 1979, these statutes do have their drawbacks, as has been seen. Procedures to speed up litigation and to arrange for ways of paying damages at an earlier stage than was possible previously have also been introduced. However, there has been no major reform of the law of tort. The most radical suggestion was that of the Pearson Commission in 1978 for a no-fault system for compensating the victims of road accidents. Although this had several flaws, it did provide the opportunity to introduce the means of compensating more people. Other suggestions have been for a no-fault system for medical mishaps, and, separately, for an arbitration system to deal with medical negligence claims.

Three major recent developments are expected to have a significant impact on the law of tort. These are the introduction of new procedural rules in 1999, the withdrawal of legal aid for most civil claims and the enactment of the Human Rights Act 1998.

21.4.1 The Civil Procedure Rules 1998

From 26 April 1999, new procedural rules apply in the conduct of civil cases, and simpler more accessible legal terminology will be used, together with interim arrangements for dealing with cases already in the pipeline. The changes introduced by the new Rules are radical, and will by now be familiar, to lawyers handling clinical negligence and general personal injury cases. There is no space here to deal with all the changes in depth, but there follows a broad overview which will give some insight into the new system and into the philosophy which underpins the structure.

The reforms are the result of recommendations made by Lord Woolf, who had identified numerous problems in the old system which led to high costs, delays, inequalities in access to justice, uncertainties, poor organisation and many injustices. The overriding objective of the new system is to produce just outcomes of civil cases, and the primary purpose of the new procedures is, therefore, to ensure that, so far as possible, justice is done. Rule 1.1(1) states:

> These Rules are a new procedural code with the overriding objective of enabling the court to deal with cases justly.

By r 1.3, 'the parties are required to help the court to further the overriding objective'.

The Rules are to be interpreted purposively rather than literally, in order to achieve the overriding objective, and, although they are only procedural rules rather than rules of substantive law, the new Code will inevitably have some impact on the advice which lawyers give about how cases should be handled.

Under the Rules, the judges, rather than the parties, will control the progress of cases, and in so doing judges must follow and ensure that the parties also follow, so far as is practicable, the following five basic principles:

(a) ensure that the parties are on an equal footing;

(b) save expense;

(c) deal with cases in ways which are proportionate to the amount of money involved, the importance of the case, the complexity of the issues and the financial positions of the parties (the principle of proportionality);

(d) ensure that matters are dealt with fairly and expeditiously;

(e) allot to each case an appropriate share of the resources of the court, while taking into account the need to allot resources to other cases.

In order to ensure that contested cases are dealt with quickly and efficiently, there are three separate 'tracks' or types of proceedings. The small claims track is intended for cases worth under £5,000, except personal injuries claims, where the limit is £1,000. The fast track is intended for cases between £5,000 and £15,000 (or between £1,000 and £15,000 in personal injuries claims). The multi-track is for more complex cases and includes all claims which are not normally within the small claims or fast tracks, and other cases which would have been in the fast track but for the fact that the trial will probably last for longer than one day.

Once the case has been allocated to a particular track, the court, guided by the Rules and their overriding objectives, will take control over the steps which need to be followed in order to deal with matters efficiently. However, an important aspect of the reforms is the use of pre-action protocols, which are also intended to regulate the relationship between the parties. The two most relevant in personal injuries cases are the Protocol for the Resolution of Clinical Negligence Disputes and the Protocol for Personal Injuries Claims. These documents will demand greater openness between the parties, early disclosure of documents, and even meetings between the parties and their experts to identify and narrow down the issues which are in dispute.

These protocols contain details of what should be contained in the letter of claim and response, as well as time limits for achieving the various steps, and recommends that alternatives to litigation, such as mediation and the NHS complaints system (in clinical negligence cases) be explored by the parties.

Take the Clinical Negligence Protocol as an example. This governs the conduct of claims involving clinical negligence (note that the word 'clinical' is preferred to 'medical') and was drafted by the Clinical Disputes Forum, which is a multi-disciplinary body which has existed since 1997. The protocol encourages openness when it is apparent that there has been a mishap of some kind in the treatment of a patient. It provides general guidance on how this new culture of co-operation may be achieved, and recommends a timed sequence of measures for all those involved in a clinical negligence case to follow. Its aims are to resolve disputes in ways which are appropriate to both parties, reduce delays and costs and reduce the need for litigation.

Patients and their advisers are directed to express any concerns as soon as possible, to consider the full range of options available to them, and to inform the healthcare provider as soon as they are satisfied that the matter has been concluded.

It is hoped that the Civil Procedure Rules, which have been embraced whole-heartedly by the judiciary, but which some lawyers have been reluctant to accept, will mean that claimants are treated on an equal basis with defendants. The heavy penalties which are likely to be imposed on lawyers who delay inadvertently fail to meet deadlines will make civil practice very challenging. Strict rules about disclosure of documents and punitive interest (up to 10% above base rate) for defendants who refuse offers which are matched if the case goes to trial will mean that, in many cases, settlements can be arrived at much earlier than previously and court hearings will be a last resort. As the matters in issue between the parties will need to be identified early in the process, and as fewer expert witnesses will be used, the entire process should be less expensive and much faster.

21.4.2 Funding of claims

In order for access to justice to be available to all, the problems involved in funding claims must be addressed. Legal aid has been withdrawn in personal injuries claims (Access to Justice Act 1999) and replaced by the conditional fee (no-win, no-fee) system, under which the client only pays the solicitor if the case is won, when a success fee will be charged. Conditional fees usually apply only to the client's own solicitors' fees, and sometimes apply to counsel's fees, but costs will still be payable for the opponent's costs, experts' reports, court fees and all disbursements if the case is not won. People wishing to bring claims will need to insure against the cost of losing and having to pay the costs of the opposing party. As the cost of premiums for clinical negligence claims is still very high, it has been agreed by the Lord Chancellor that legal aid will remain for the time being for these cases, but this is only a temporary reprieve. However, only solicitors who are officially recognised clinical negligence specialists will be able to take on legally aided cases of this kind.

The conditional fee system has a number of potential disadvantages. It could have the effect of deterring lawyers from taking on cases in which success is rather uncertain, especially those in which it will be necessary for then to invest large amounts of time, and poorer clients will be reluctant to bring claims.

21.4.3 Reform of tort law through the Human Rights Act 1998

The Human Rights Act 1998 is widely regarded as one of the most important and far reaching pieces of legislation introduced in the UK for many years. The Act, which relies on the main provisions of the European Convention on Human Rights, gives recognition to certain fundamental human rights (the rights set out in Arts 2–12 and 14 of the Convention, Arts 1–3 of the First Protocol and Arts 1 and 2 of the Sixth Protocol). The Act will operate as described in Chapter 1.

21.5 The value of tort

Tort is a developing subject and the reforms outlined above will serve to ensure that it continues to adapt to changing social economic and political conditions in the 21st century. The latest series of reforms should speed up this process.

Although it is customary to criticise tort, and the catalogue of instances outlined above gives the impression that there is much to criticise, the law of tort does have considerable value and it has survived for many centuries to protect interests of many kinds from unlawful infringements. Property rights and personal freedoms are among the many interests protected by the law of tort and more general duties in the law of negligence protect people from a wide variety of wrongs.

Over the centuries, tort has proved to be infinitely flexible and even the ancient rules are capable of being adapted to meet modern problems. The tort of negligence, which has emerged relatively recently as a tort in its own right, has been developed through case law to cover many important situations in life. By far the greatest number of tort actions arise out of road traffic accidents – a situation which would have been unimaginable in the Middle Ages.

Tort encourages careful conduct and, in modern times, formal risk management. This prevents injury to individuals and their property and reduces the spread of disease and the manufacture of dangerous products. Although this is also the function of other areas of law, in particular regulatory law, tort still plays a part because civil actions in tort can arise from breaches of statutory duty.

Tort also has a symbolic moral value, in that it places emphasis on fault and encourages wrongdoers to compensate their victims. It has a moral, ideological dimension which is of value to people seeking vindication. Even if that aspect is eclipsed by the use of insurance and methods of loss distribution which move the emphasis away from the wrongdoer, the focus in legal actions is nevertheless on the wrongful act and loss distribution is a consequential factor.

CRITICISMS OF TORT

Criticisms of tort are linked with criticisms of the legal system:

- fault as a basis of liability creates problems of proof and results in injustice;

- tort does not achieve its objectives;

- the tort system is a lottery;

- delays;

- expense;

- administrative costs;

- the adversarial system.

The value of tort:

- tort has stood the test of time;

- tort is flexible;

- tort encourages careful conduct and risk management;

- tort distributes losses;

- tort has a symbolic moral value.

Reform of tort

There have been some improvements over the past 50 years.

- The Woolf Report 1996 made radical proposals for reform of the Civil Justice System. Many of these have now been implemented in the Civil Procedure Rules 1998, which came into operation in April 1999. The Rules are likely to have an important impact on decisions about whether to fight or settle claims, and should help to redress the balance in favour of claimants.

- The Human Rights Act 1998 will undoubtedly bring about changes to tort law. More radical proposals for reform such as the implementation of a 'no fault' system are regularly mooted.

FURTHER READING

Background reading

Atiyah, PS, *The Damages Lottery*, 1997, Oxford: Hart

Birks, P, *Wrongs and Remedies in the Twenty-First Century*, 1996, Oxford: Clarendon

Cane, P, *The Anatomy of Tort Law*, 1997, Oxford: Hart

Cane, P, *Tort Law and Economic Interests*, 2nd edn, 1996, Oxford: Clarendon

Conaghan, J and Mansell, W, *The Wrongs of Tort*, 1993, London: Pluto

England, I, *The Philosophy of Tort Law*, 1993, Aldershot: Dartmouth

Genn, H, *Hard Bargaining: Out of Court Settlements in Personal Injury Actions*, 1987, Oxford: Clarendon

Harlow, C, *Understanding Tort Law*, 1987, London: Fontana

Harris, D, *Remedies in Contract and Tort*, 1988, London: Weidenfeld & Nicolson

Ison, TG, *The Forensic Lottery*, 1967, London: Staples

Landes, WM and Posner, RA, *The Economic Structure of Tort Law*, 1987, Cambridge: Harvard UP

Lees, D, Dennis, S and Shaw, S, *Impairment, Disability and Handicap: A Multi-Disciplinary View*, 1974, London: Heinemann

Markesinis, B, *Tort Damages in English and German Law: A Comparison*, 1985, Siena: Facolta di Giurisprudenza

McLean, S (ed), *Compensation for Damages: an International Perspective*, 1993, Aldershot: Dartmouth

Nolan, V, *Understanding Enterprise Liability: Rethinking Tort Reform for the Twenty-First Century*, 1995, Philadelphia: Temple UP

Owen, DG, *Philosophical Foundations of Tort Law*, 1995, Oxford: Clarendon

Prime, T, *Contract and Tort Statutes*, 1993, London: Butterworths

Spry, I, *Principles of Equitable Remedies*, 4th edn, 1990, London: Sweet & Maxwell

Weinrib, EJ (ed), *Tort Law*, 1991, Aldershot: Dartmouth

Williams, G and Hepple, BA, *Foundations of Tort*, 1984, London: Butterworths

General

Atiyah, PS, *Accidents, Compensation and the Law*, Cane, P (ed), 1993, Weidenfeld & Nicolson, Chapter 23

Fleming, SG, *An Introduction to the Law of Torts*, 1997, Oxford: Clarendon

The Woolf Report, *Access to Justice*, 1996, London: HMSO

Remedies

Birts, PW, *Remedies for Trespass*, 1990, London: Longman

Chase, G, *Taxation Treatment of Compensation and Damages*, 1994, London: Butterworths

Chery, JF, *Guidelines for the Assessment of Damages in Personal Injury Cases for the Judicial Studies Board*, 1996, London: Blackstone

Goldstein, I and De Haas, M, *Structured Settlements: A Practical Guide*, 1993, London: Butterworths

Grant, D and Mason, S, *Disasters, Debacles, Disappointment and Damages*, Newcastle: Newcastle University Travel Law Centre

Holding, F and Kaye, P, *Damages for Personal Injuries: Recent Developments and Future Trends*, 1993, London: Chancery Law

Kemp and Kemp, *Quantum of Damages*, 1982, London: Sweet & Maxwell

Kemp, D, *Damages for Personal Injuries and Death*, 1995, London: FT Law & Tax

Law Commission, *Report on Liability for Damage or Injury to Trespassers*, Law Com 75, 1976, London: HMSO

Law Commission, *Aggravated, Exemplary and Restitutionary Damages*, 1993, London: HMSO

Law Commission, *Structured Settlements and Interim and Provisional Damages*, Law Com 224, 1994, London: HMSO

Law Commission, *Personal Injury Compensation: How Much is Enough?*, Law Com 225, 1994, London: HMSO

Law Commission, *Common and Public Law: Liability for Psychiatric Illness*, Law Com 137, 1995, London: HMSO

Law Commission, *Damages for Personal Injury: Non-Pecuniary Loss*, Law Com 140, 1995, London: HMSO

Law Commission, *Damages for Personal Injury: Medical, Nursing and Other Expenses*, Law Com 144, 1996, London: HMSO

Mann, R and Harvard, D, *No Fault Compensation in Medicine*, 1989, London: Royal Society of Medicine, BMA

Miers, D, *State Compensation for Criminal Injuries*, 1997, London: Blackstone

Munkman, J, *Damages for Personal Injuries and Death*, 1996, London: Butterworths

Napier, M and Wheat, K, *Recovering Damages for Psychiatric Injury*, 1995, London: Blackstone

Lewis, R, *Structured Settlements: The Law and Practice*, 1993, London: Sweet & Maxwell

Sugarman, S, *Doing Away with Personal Injury Law: New Compensation Mechanisms*, 1989, New York: Quarum

Negligence

Atiyah, PS, *Accidents, Compensation and the Law*, Cane, P (ed), 1993, Weidenfeld & Nicolson, Chapters 2, 3 and 4

Bernstein, B, *Economic Loss*, 1993, London: Longman

Bingham, L, *Motor Claims Cases*, 1994, London: Butterworths

Brazier, M, *Medicine, Patients and the Law*, 2nd edn, 1992, Penguin

Buckley, RA, *The Modern Law of Negligence*, 1993, London: Butterworths

Burns, P and Lyons, S, '*Danglowe v Stevenson* and the modern law of negligence', in the *Proceedings of Paisley Conference 1991*, 1991, Vancover: Continuing Legal Education Society

Channing, J and Ridley, J, *Safety at Work*, 4th edn, 1994, London: Butterworths

Charlesworth, J and Percy, RA, *Charlesworth and Percy on Negligence*, 1997, London: Sweet & Maxwell

Dingwall, R, Fenn, P and Quam, L, *Medical Negligence: Review and Bibliography*, 1991, Oxford: Centre for Socio-Legal Studies

Dugdale, M, Stanton, K, *Professional Negligence*, 1995, London: Sweet & Maxwell

Ferguson, P, *Drug Injuries and the Pursuit of Compensation*, 1996, London: Sweet & Maxwell

Fleming, JG, 'Requiem for *Anns*' (1990) 106 LQR 525

Gild, S, *Counting the Cost of Medical Negligence: Brain Damaged Children and the Tort System*, 1990, London: Brunel University Department of Law

Harpwood, V, *Legal Issues in Obstetrics*, 1996, Aldershot: Dartmouth

Harpwood, V, 'NHS reform and the standard of care in negligence' (1994) 1(3) Medical Law International 240, pp 240–89

Harpwood, V, *Medical Negligence and Clinical Risk: Trends and Developments*, 1998, London: Monitor

Hart, HLA and Honoré, T, *Causation and Remoteness of Damage*, 2nd edn, 1985, Oxford: Clarendon

Harworth, D, Kenning, PH and Phillip, H, *Tort Liability of an Industrialist*, 1985, London: Sweet & Maxwell

Jackson, R and Powell, J, *Professional Negligence*, 1994, London: Sweet & Maxwell

Jaffey, A, *The Duty of Care*, 1992, Aldershot: Dartmouth

Jones, MA, *Medical Negligence*, 2nd edn, 1996, London: Sweet & Maxwell

Lawson, FH, 'Duty of care: a comparative study' (1947) 22 Tulane LR 111

Leigh, S, Hatton, AJ, *Managing Medical Negligence Actions*, 1996, London: FT Law & Tax

Markesinis, BS, 'An expanding tort law – the price of a rigid contract law' (1987) 103 LQR 354

Markesinis, BS, 'An economic and comparative analysis of the tort of negligence from *Anns to Murphy*' (1992) 55 MLR 619

McLean, S, *Law Reform and Medical Injury Litigation*, 1995, Aldershot: Dartmouth

Mesher, J, 'Occupiers, trespassers and the Unfair Contract Terms Act 1977' (1979) Conv (NS) 58, pp 58–65

Millner, M, *Negligence in Modern Law*, 1967, London: Butterworths

Mullany, N and Handford, P, *Tort Liability for Psychiatric Damage*, 1993, Sydney: LBC

Munkman, J, *Employers' Liability*, 1990, London: Butterworths

Minnis, E and Nobes, C, *Accountant's Liability in the 1980s: An International View*, 1985, Croom: Helm

Nelson-Jones, R and Burton, F, *Medical Negligence Case Law*, 1995, London: Butterworths

Phillips, A, *Medical Negligence Law: Seeking a Balance*, 1997, Aldershot: Dartmouth

Powell-Smith, V, *Problems in Construction Claims*, 1990, Oxford

Powers, MJ and Harris, N (eds), *Clinical Negligence*, 3rd edn, 2000, London: Butterworths

Stauton, K, *Breach of Statutory Duty in Tort*, 1986, London: Sweet & Maxwell

Stapleton, J, 'The gist of negligence' (1988) 104 LQR 213

Wikeley, N, *Compensation for Industrial Disease*, 1993, Aldershot: Dartmouth

Nuisance and trespass/ liability for animals

Adams, M and McManus, F, *Noise and Noise Law*, 1994, London: Wiley

Brooman, S and Legge, D, *Law Relating to Animals*, 1997, London: Cavendish Publishing

Buckley, RA, *The Law of Nuisance*, 1981, London: Butterworths

Gearty, C, 'The place of private nuisance in a modern law of torts' [1989] CLJ 214

Heuston, RFV, 'Judges and judgments' (1986) 20 British Columbia UL Rev 83

Law Commission, *Civil Liability for Animals*, Law Com 13, 1967, London: HMSO

Law Commission, *Civil Liability for Dangerous Things and Activities*, Law Com 32, 1970, London: HMSO

North, P, *The Modern Law of Animals*, 1972, London: Butterworths

Penn, C, *Noise Control: The Law and its Enforcement*, 1995, Crayford: Shaw

Pugh, C, Day, M, *Pollution and Personal Injury: Toxic Torts*, 1995, London: Cameron

Spencer, J, 'Public nuisance – a critical examination' [1989] CLJ 55

Sandys-Winsch, G, *Animal Law*, 1984, London: Shaw

Defamation

Barendt, EM, *Libel Law and the Media: The Chilling Effect*, 1997, Oxford: Clarendon

BBC Video (journalist training video), *Putting Off the Writs: A BBC Guide to Libel*, London: BBC

Braithwaite, N, *The International Libel Handbook: A Practical Guide for Journalists*, 1995, Oxford: Butterworth-Heinemann

Carter Ruck, P, *Carter Ruck on Libel and Slander*, 5th edn, 1997, London: Butterworths

Crane, T, *Law and the Media – An Everyday Guide for Professionals*, 1995, Oxford: Focal

Faulks, N (Sir), *Report of the Committee on Defamation*, Cmnd 5909, 1975, London: HMSO

Graham, T, *Contaminated Land*, 1995, Bristol: Jordans

Ingrams, R, *Goldenballs*, 1980, Sevenoaks: Coronet

Law Commission, *Report on Criminal Libel*, Law Com 49, 1985, London: HMSO

Neill, B (Sir), *Report on Practice and Procedure in Defamation*, 1991, London: Lord Chancellor's Department

Vidal, J, *McLibel*, 1997, Basingstoke: Macmillan

Yeager, P, *The Limits of Law: Public Regulation of Private Pollution*, 1991, Cambridge: CUP

Consumer law and product liability

Consumer Safety Unit, *The Home Accident Surveillance System: Data*, 1981, London: Consumer Safety Unit

Hodges, JS, *Product Liability, European Laws and Practice*, 1993, London: Sweet & Maxwell

Stapleton, J, *Product Liability*, 1994, London: Butterworths

INDEX